THE ATLANTIC CAMPAIGN

THE ATLANTIC CAMPAIGN

World War II's Great Struggle at Sea

Dan van der Vat

with research by
Christine van der Vat

1817

An Edward Burlingame Book

HARPER & ROW, PUBLISHERS, New York
Cambridge, Philadelphia, San Francisco
London, Mexico City, São Paulo, Singapore, Sydney

The Atlantic Campaign was published simultaneously in Great Britain by Hodder & Stoughton Ltd.

FIRST U.S. EDITION

Library of Congress Cataloging-in-Publication Data

Van der Vat, Dan.
  The Atlantic campaign.

  Includes index.
  "An Edward Burlingame book."
  1. World War, 1939-1945—Campaigns—Atlantic Ocean.
2. World War, 1939-1945—Naval operations.   I. Title.
D770.V28 1988   940.54′5   88-45067
ISBN: 0-06-015967-7

88 89 90 91 92 HC 10 9 8 7 6 5 4 3 2 1

For Karen and Sara, our children

CONTENTS

PREFACE

THE general reader, for whom this book is intended, will want to know why it has been written at this juncture when so many other works on what is usually called "the Battle of the Atlantic" already exist. In fact the number of books in English and covering the entire campaign is very small, as an examination of the Note on Sources at the end of this volume will show. Only one general work drawing on primary as well as secondary sources has appeared since it was revealed in 1974 that the British had broken the German "Enigma" machine-cipher: the 1977 account by Terry Hughes and John Costello. I am also aware of only one comparable work in German (by Günter Böddeker, 1981). The British and American official histories of the Second World War at sea by Captain S. W. Roskill, RN, and Rear-Admiral Samuel Eliot Morison, USNR, make no mention of Enigma and are in any case panoramic (yet enormously detailed) accounts of the worldwide naval operations of the two countries. For the rest, the lengthy "Atlantic" shelf is filled to overflowing with books about one aspect or another of what is probably the most heavily documented campaign in history. There are also books dealing with related themes such as intelligence and the war in the air which touch upon the central struggle of 1939 45: the Atlantic Campaign. To all these forerunners I should like to express my gratitude; it has been a long trail, but it was well blazed and I should have got lost without them.

When the Enigma secret was revealed, the entirely understandable reaction was that the history of the "Battle of the Atlantic" in particular and the war in general would have to be rewritten. This is true in the sense that new light has been thrown on a number of events and decisions. It is also clear that many lives (and many ships with their valuable human and material cargoes) were saved and that the war against Nazi Germany was shortened by this "Ultra" intelligence. After studying all the other aspects of the campaign, however, the present author has come to the conclusion that the dramatic nature of the revelation, especially in Great Britain, where official secrecy and the complementary obsession with espionage are exaggerated to the point of morbidity, has unduly inflated its importance. The absence of any reference to Ultra in the official naval history has since been more than compensated for by the appearance of Professor Hinsley's official history of British Intelligence in the war. But the attentive reader of Roskill will find, on page 208 of his second volume at a point where he describes the no less remarkable German penetration of British ciphers, the following sentence: "The reader should not, of course, assume that we British were meanwhile idle in achieving the opposite purpose." Roskill was not given to overstatement, but some might say that this is one of the great understatements of contemporary history. Yet the meaning is surely clear: the British, like the Germans, penetrated the enemy's ciphers. They were not attempting it but "achieving" it – and Captain Roskill said so in 1956!

Scepticism about the "war-winning" importance of Ultra is reinforced by the knowledge that the British were reading the German naval cipher for almost the whole of the First World War. The scale of the effort in the Second was however such that it may have led some to conclude that, if it was such an enormous effort, it must have been important. And so it was. But not so almightily crucial that Ultra's absence from the Atlantic campaign for most of 1942 and several interruptions and delays at key moments crippled the Allied war-effort. It would have been virtually useless anyway in the period of greatest losses of shipping, the first half of 1942, because the reason for those was the American refusal to put vessels in escorted convoys along their coast like those crossing the Atlantic. The finest intelligence is of little use when the will or the means to exploit it is absent. The reader will be taken more deeply into these matters in the ensuing narrative, but the point can be made here, a good decade after the Ultra secret came out, that intelligence was only one factor (and not the most important) among many behind the hard-won Allied victory over the German submarines. There was no single "magic ingredient" in this most important triumph of the war. Even airpower, the key to it, could hardly have won the struggle alone.

If the value of intelligence to the Allies (but not to the Germans) has been overstated, the worth of the Canadian contribution to the campaign has generally been rather more seriously understated. This applies not only to previous American and British accounts but also even to Canadian, until Dr Marc Milner published his definitive book in 1985. If the present volume makes any additional contribution to redressing the balance, its author will be only too pleased.

A third aspect in which this book differs from those which have gone before is in the attention paid to the largely forgotten fact that the First World War came at least as close to being lost by the Allies as the Second for exactly the same reason: massive destruction of shipping by German submarines. The only major factor contributing to victory in the "second round" that was missing in the first was radar. It is true that aircraft could not "kill" a submarine in 1914–18 – but they were on hand by the end to play a vital role, as was intelligence. The reason for giving a full summary of the neglected first round is that it throws light on many of the successes – and mistakes – of the second.

Finally, rather more space than usual is devoted here to events between the wars. These also help to clarify why and how the Atlantic Campaign of 1939–45 developed as it did. One hitherto particularly neglected strand in the record is the fascinating tale of how the Germans based their Second World War submarine fleet on the boats they built in the First: Dönitz's "grey wolves" were their direct descendants, designed and even built in secret by men who uninterruptedly kept Germany ahead in submarine technology for more than thirty years. Unfolding this story has a double advantage. It earns its place with the intrigue, the dummy companies, skulduggery and embezzlement that went into the clandestine programme; and it helps to explain why the Germans were such lethally proficient submariners at the outset, when they had so few boats available.*

Many people and institutions provided valuable help during the gestation period of this fourth venture into the naval history of the twentieth century, and I should like to offer my most grateful thanks to all of them. Some were doing their jobs in meeting my requests for information from archives or finding rare books, but they all seemed ready to go beyond mere duty in doing so. Others – friends, colleagues, experts in the relevant fields – provided good advice, sounding-boards for ideas and stimulating conversation, trustingly lent irreplaceable books and papers, gave introductions or otherwise offered guidance and comfort on a very long voyage.

Pride of place goes to my wife, whose name appears by right on the title-page. With her academic training and knowledge of German she plunged into uncharted waters for a whole year, keeping the research going while I was otherwise engaged.

The archivists who provided their invaluable guidance are named in the Note on Sources. I should also like to thank the staff of the Twickenham branch of the Borough Library of Richmond upon Thames, as well as the following individuals.

In Great Britain: Felicity Bryan of Curtis Brown, my literary agent; John Dekker; Peter Hennessy; Richard Hough; Lieutenant-Commander Peter Kemp, RN (retd.); Richard Norton-Taylor; Peter Padfield; Peter Preston, Editor of *The Guardian*, and his Deputy, Peter Cole; Ion Trewin, Editorial Director of Hodder and Stoughton, and his Assistant, Christine Medcalf.

---

* This is the only footnote that will be found in this volume. As stated at the beginning of this Preface, the book is intended for the general reader. In other contexts the author is also a general reader, and as such is powerfully prejudiced against texts bespattered with numbers, whether they refer to footnotes or entries at the back, which usually contain such illuminating references as "ibid." or "op. cit." These are of use to few and a nuisance to most readers as well as the writer. All the sources consulted are listed at the end of the book. There is no fiction or "faction" in these pages and I take full responsibility for everything that is not a direct quotation from a stated source (and for the accuracy of all quotations).

In Canada: Professor Bev Carson (Commander, RCNVR); Ann Greer-Wootten; Professor Wilfred Innerd and Dr Jane Innerd.

In West Germany: Yorck von Reuter and family; Professor Dr Jürgen Rohwer, of the Bibliothek für Zeitgeschichte, Stuttgart.

In the United States: Edward L. Burlingame, Vice-President of Harper and Row; Brian and Virginia Crowe; Jim Morrell; Jon Snow; Michael White; Sir Oliver Wright, former British Ambassador in Washington.

If anyone has been inadvertently omitted, I apologise. Any error in what follows is exclusively my responsibility.

Acknowledgment is due to the following for permission to quote from copyright material.

The Bodley Head, for *U333*, by Peter Cremer; Curtis Brown, for *The Secret Capture*, by Stephen Roskill; Hamish Hamilton Ltd, for *Very Special Intelligence*, by Patrick Beesly; Peter Hennessy, for the paper listed under his name in the Note on Sources; the Controller of HM Stationery Office, for *The War at Sea*, by Stephen Roskill, and for *British Intelligence in the Second World War*, by F. H. Hinsley; Dr Marc Milner, for *North Atlantic Run* and the two papers listed; Permissions, for *Alan Turing: the Enigma*, by Andrew Hodges; Michael Joseph Ltd, for *Convoy*, by John Winton; William Kimber & Co Ltd, for *U-boat 977*, by Heinz Schaeffer; Oxford University Press, for *History of the US Naval Operations in World War II*, by Samuel Eliot Morison; Bernard & Graefe Verlag, Koblenz, for *Memoirs*, by Karl Dönitz. The Note on Sources at the end of this book gives the full references to these works.

The author sought permission to cite some forty words from Churchill's *History of the Second World War*. Cassell PLC, uniquely in my experience, asked a fee of £25. On this tariff, quoting a total of 2,000 words from copyright material would cost £1,250. The quotation, an embellishment rather than a revelation, has therefore been omitted.

ILLUSTRATIONS

ILLUSTRATION ACKNOWLEDGMENTS

1. BBC Hulton Picture Library
2. Popperfoto
3. The Keystone Collection
4. The Imperial War Museum
5. Robert Hunt Library
6. Dan van der Vat/The Imperial War Museum
7. King's College, Cambridge
8. Bruce Robertson
9. Syndication International
10. UPI/Bettmann Newsphotos
11. Chaz Bowyer
12. US Naval Institute Photo Collection

MAPS

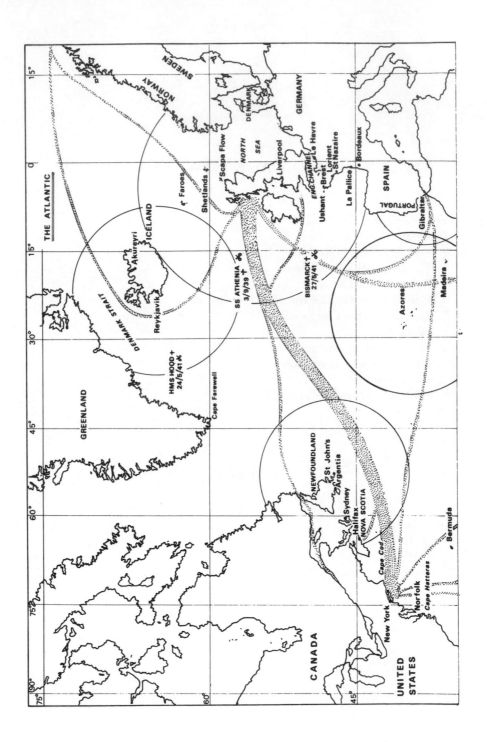

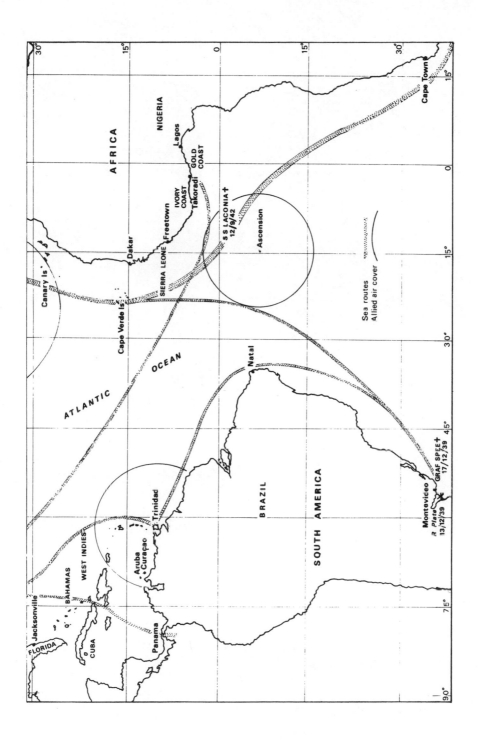

AFRICA

NIGERIA

Lagos

GOLD
COAST

IVORY
COAST

Takoradi

Freetown

SIERRA LEONE

S S LACONIA †
12/9/42

Ascension

Dakar

Canary Is.

Cape Verde Is.

ATLANTIC

OCEAN

Natal

Sea routes
Allied air cover

BRAZIL

SOUTH AMERICA

Montevideo

GRAF SPEE †
17/12/39

R Plate
13/12/39

Trinidad

Aruba
Curaçao

WEST INDIES

BAHAMAS

Jacksonville

FLORIDA

CUBA

Panama

Cape Town

30°   15°   0°   15°   30°   15°

30°

15°

0°

15°

45°

75°

90°

INTRODUCTION

3 SEPTEMBER 1939

Churchill returns to the Admiralty – Germany unready – the first shot sinks the Athenia *– replay of the "Lusitania factor" – Britain adopts convoy*

WINSTON IS BACK! The Royal Navy's worldwide network of wireless transmitters sent this brash and electrifying message to each other and to all His Majesty's ships on the evening of Sunday, 3 September 1939. The news that Winston Leonard Spencer Churchill had been appointed First Lord of the Admiralty, the political head of the Navy, was received with joy by the Fleet. It helped to relieve the tension caused by the awesome signal transmitted at 11 a.m. the same day – TOTAL GERMANY. At that moment the British Government's two-hour ultimatum to Germany to withdraw its troops from Poland ran out, and the Prime Minister, Neville Chamberlain, announced on the BBC Home Service that the British Empire was at war with Germany for the second time in a quarter of a century. One of Chamberlain's first acts after the chilling broadcast was to send for Churchill to offer him a seat in the War Cabinet.

For the 64-year-old *enfant terrible* of the Conservative Party the offer opened the way to a double return. Having spent the past several years in the political wilderness issuing dire warnings on the revival of German militarism under Adolf Hitler, Churchill simply could not be left out of the Government once the warnings proved justified. If parliamentary opinion was still divided about the claim to office of this controversial and pugnacious figure, public opinion demanded his promotion. Many inside and outside Westminster thought he should, and soon would, replace the discredited Chamberlain in Number 10 Downing Street.

But it was with decidedly mixed feelings that Churchill went to the Admiralty to relieve the nonentity, Lord Stanhope, as First Lord. That he should be given this of all posts was piquant and ironic, and was rendered even more so by the Navy's delight which had already set the wires and the airwaves humming. This was the second time he had been given the Admiralty. At the end of his first term, which lasted from October 1911 to May 1915, his most glorious protégé, Admiral David Beatty, wrote: "The Navy

breathes freer now it is rid of the succubus Winston." Another admiral wrote
to King George V: "He was, we all consider, a danger to the Empire."

He had been made to resign because of the lacklustre performance of
the Navy in the opening months of the First World War, culminating in its
failure to force the Dardanelles. That, and the ensuing tragedy of the Gallipoli
invasion which haunted Churchill for the rest of his days, would not have
been necessary had the Navy seized its chance to prevent the Germans
sending their naval Mediterranean Division of just two ships to Constantinople. This enabled them to force Turkey into the war on their side and to
cut Russia's shipping lifeline between the Mediterranean and the Black Sea.
The British admirals responsible for this and many other failures had been
appointed, from a remarkably indifferent lot, by Churchill, who thus with
some justice became an early victim of rising bewilderment and anger over
"bungling in high places," a theme which endured in Britain for the rest of
the war.

But now he was back in his old office, demanding that all the furniture
and fittings of his earlier term be found and restored, and the Navy and the
nation were well pleased. Far more important than the dimly recalled,
dubious record of the First Lord in the previous war was the political need
of the hour. Appeasement of Hitler, forever identified with Chamberlain,
had failed. The nation had changed its mood from years of hoping to
avoid another war (and being prepared to pay almost any price, including
humiliations, for such deliverance) to one of making a stand against Adolf
Hitler. The man who had stood out against appeasement when it was in
vogue had to be given a direct role in the prosecution of the war when
appeasement was finally discredited. He was charged with political control
of the country's most powerful and important service, the only arm strong
enough to face the enemy with confidence and to protect a nation with a
small army and a partly modernised, under-equipped air force. Only the
Navy, on which British power had rested for centuries, was in a position at
the opening of hostilities to confront an enemy, whom Churchill demeaned
with relish and deliberate mispronunciation as the "Nahzies," on better than
equal terms. The Navy's first move was its traditional one in a war with a
European power: the imposition of a blockade.

OPEN HOSTILITIES WITH ENGLAND AT ONCE was the signal sent to all units
of the *Kriegsmarine*, the German Navy, at lunchtime on September 3.
Hitler's navy was not ready, a fact which had nothing to do with the quality
of its equipment, most of which was excellent, or the condition of its men,
which was fine, but resulted from a fundamental miscalculation by the
Führer himself. He had ordered Grand Admiral Erich Raeder, the naval
Commander-in-Chief, to be ready for war with Britain in 1944 at the earliest.
Having got away with the reoccupation of the Rhineland, the absorption of
Austria into the Reich by means of the *Anschluss*, the dismemberment of

Czechoslovakia and its subsequent occupation, Hitler believed that his move against Poland on September 1 would provoke Britain and France no more than his previous territorial moves, despite their guarantees to the Polish Government. When the British ultimatum telegram was brought to him in his grand office in the Chancellery in Berlin, the dictator was stunned. His political strategy of making gains by instinctive opportunism, bluff and aggressive rhetoric had failed for the first time since he came to power in January 1933.

Strategically, therefore, the German navy seemed to its commanders to be hopelessly ill-equipped for a war with Britain. Tactically, however, they had done what they could in the last days of peace to deploy their forces for that eventuality. Captain Karl Dönitz, *Führer der Unterseeboote* (Submarine Leader), returned early from long leave to the naval base at Kiel on August 16. At his disposal was a total of fifty-seven submarines, of which eighteen were ordered to take up predetermined stations in the eastern Atlantic from the west of Scotland to the Strait of Gibraltar. All thirty remaining operational submarines were in the North Sea and the Baltic, leaving nine which were refitting, on trials or in use for training – and none at all in reserve. Also in the last days of August, just two of Germany's eight operational major surface warships, the "pocket battleships" *Deutschland* and *Admiral Graf Spee*, were in the Atlantic with their supply vessels. All units at sea were ordered not to attack French vessels (in case France could be detached from Britain) and to observe Prize Law in operations against merchant shipping. This required submarines to throw away their advantages of stealth and surprise by following the rules laid down in the Hague Convention on sea warfare. They were to behave like commerce-raiding cruisers, operating on the surface to stop and search ships; if these were found to be candidates for justified sinking because they were British or carrying goods for Britain (contraband), any passengers and the crew were to be given time to board lifeboats and every reasonable step taken to ensure they reached land in safety. Only troopships, armed merchantmen, vessels under naval or air escort and ships showing resistance or endangering the submarine (such as by sending a wireless alert) could be sunk without warning. This code, set out in the German Prize Rules, had been accepted by the Reich after the Anglo-German naval conversations of 1935 even though it effectively neutralised the submarine. Raeder was all for declaring the waters round Britain a blockade-zone for unrestricted submarine warfare on the First World War pattern, but Hitler's hopes of an early settlement with Britain and France and his determination not to antagonise neutral nations, particularly the United States, ruled this out for the time being. In any case, the Germans (correctly) anticipated that the British would start arming merchant ships (it being well known that many had strengthened decks for the purpose), which would make them subject to sinking without warning. So when the German submarine commanders opened their sealed operational orders at sea in response to

Dönitz's signal of September 3, they found a clear instruction to observe Prize Rules.

At that time the submarine *U30*, commanded by Lieutenant Fritz-Julius Lemp, was in its allotted position some 250 miles north-west of Ireland, patrolling slowly on the surface. Just after 7.30 p.m. as the light was beginning to fade, a lookout in the conning-tower sighted a large merchant ship sailing westward on a zig-zag course. Lemp, a career officer aged twenty-six, decided without further ado or examination of what was unmistakably a passenger-liner to submerge for an attack. The *U30* dived, levelled off at periscope-depth and took position bow-on to where her captain estimated the ship would be in a few minutes, with her port side passing to his north.

Aboard the SS *Athenia*, excited young children were being put to bed for their second night at sea. The ship had left Glasgow on September 2 and called at Liverpool and Belfast for more passengers. Captain James Cook of the Donaldson Line had told the passengers at midday of the terrible, but by then entirely predictable, news of Britain's declaration of war, picked up by the ship's specially alerted wireless operators. Most of those aboard, including more than 300 Americans, were there precisely because of the threat of war. The ship, of 13,581 tons, lacked the glamour of the great modern transatlantic liners and had become something of a workhorse in her 16-year career, but the 1,103 passengers were relieved to be on their way to Montreal with her crew of 305. Captain Cook had tried to calm the fears aroused by the news of war by expressing confidence that his ship was fully protected by international law from submarine attack.

Of the salvo of torpedoes fired at almost point-blank range by the *U30*, one struck the ship squarely on the port side, a little aft of amidships, throwing up a huge fountain of water. The bulkhead between the boiler-room and the engine-room was blown away and an oil-tank was shattered, though miraculously without an explosion. The stairs from the third-class and tourist dining-saloons to the upper decks were also destroyed, making it impossible for people in those areas to escape. The ship rapidly developed a list of thirty degrees to port, making it difficult to launch the lifeboats on the starboard side, but she then settled in the water to remain afloat for several hours, enabling all boats to be lowered. Remarkably there was no panic aboard the *Athenia* as she went into her protracted death-throes, and passengers and crew abandoned her in orderly and calm fashion; 118 people, including twenty-eight Americans, were killed.

At 8.59 p.m. Malin Head radio station at the north-west corner of Ireland picked up her distress call: "SSS [the signal for a submarine attack] *Athenia* GFDM [her call-sign] torpedoed position 56°44′ [north latitude] 14°05′ [west longitude]." Soon a small armada of ships, naval and mercantile, were on their way to help.

Long before any relief could arrive, Captain Lemp brought his boat to the surface only half a mile away from the crippled liner to assess the damage he had caused. The submarine fired two shells from the single gun sited before the conning-tower, apparently trying to bring down the ship's wireless aerials. According to Malin Head, the Germans had tried to jam the *Athenia's* repeated distress calls but with little success. Unarmed, the liner sounded eight short and one long blasts on her foghorn and the submarine vanished, without trying to do any more damage – or offer any help.

The first to come to the rescue was the Norwegian cargo-ship *Knut Nelson*. Tragically, she unwittingly caused the last deaths from among the complement of the *Athenia* when one of the liner's lifeboats drifted round her stern into her wake as the Norwegian was manoeuvring. The boat was sucked under and broken up by the propeller. The Swedish steam yacht *Southern Cross*, the American tanker *City of Flint* and the Royal Navy destroyers *Escort*, *Electra* and *Fame* soon joined the rescue operation. HMS *Fame* conducted an anti-submarine sweep round the area in case the enemy boat was still in the vicinity. The other two destroyers picked up about 500 survivors between them, the *Knut Nelson* saved 430, including ten injured, and the Swedish yacht about fifty.

The propaganda significance of the attack was seen at once by all concerned as soon as they heard about it. Commander P. N. Walter of the *Fame* reported later that he had been detached from the Eighth Flotilla not only for the obvious humanitarian reason but also "in view of the probable political importance of the sinking"; and by the time the *Knut Nelson* brought her survivors to Galway on the west coast of Eire, the American naval attaché from London, Captain Kirk, and his assistant, Commander Hitchcock, had already flown in to conduct an investigation on behalf of the United States Government. In London, Churchill was still at the Admiralty, arranging his office and sending people in all directions to bring him documents and to look for the furniture he wanted reinstalled, when the news of the sinking received from Malin Head was brought to him shortly after 10.30 p.m. on the 3rd. The *Athenia* was still afloat (she sank at daybreak on the 4th) as the first moves were made to capitalise on her destruction.

The Admiralty lost no time in telling the news agencies that the liner had been torpedoed. The time-difference enabled the American press to report the attack in the same breath as it announced that Britain and France had declared war. The Germans were at a disadvantage. According to the War Diary of Dönitz's submarine command, the first report of the sinking, as intercepted by the German naval radio monitoring service, reached his headquarters only at 10.35 a.m. on the 4th. There was nothing from Lemp, who was under orders to maintain radio silence. When the news was brought to Hitler, he was sufficiently alarmed to order an urgent signal to all warships: "Passenger-ships until further notice shall not be attacked even if escorted." To underline the importance of the message, it was prefixed with the words: "By order of the Führer," and was sent just before midnight on the 4th. The first German announcement about the sinking came in a radio broadcast on the afternoon of the 4th, when a text prepared by the Ministry of Propaganda led by Dr Josef Goebbels claimed that the *Athenia* must have been sunk in error by a British warship or a British mine.

This disingenuous suggestion was mild compared with what followed in the succeeding days and weeks. Much was made of the providential presence of several British destroyers in the area to support a claim that Churchill had arranged the sinking himself to influence neutral opinion. So intense was the German propaganda offensive that it took a whole year before the American Government accepted the British version of the event. When the *U30* returned home on September 27, Lemp confirmed that he had sunk the *Athenia*. On Raeder's orders, he and his crew were sworn to silence, the boat's log was altered to remove any reference to the sinking and in the submarine command War Diary the *U30* was credited only with sinking two British cargo ships totalling 9,699 tons. The real reason for all the energy devoted by the Germans to obfuscation, denial and distortion was revealed by Goebbels himself on September 22, when he personally accused Churchill on German radio of having the ship blown up and ordering the three destroyers to finish her off. This was all part of Churchill's "devilish game" of making sure that the war began with "a new *Lusitania*."

The torpedoing without warning of the *Athenia* had at once reminded many people on both sides of the Atlantic of one of the most notorious incidents in the First World War at sea. The SS *Lusitania*, 30,000 tons, was the contemporary queen of the transatlantic route between Liverpool and New York. This pride of the Cunard Line was sunk at 2.15 p.m. on 7 May 1915 by a single torpedo from *U20* (*Kapitänleutnant* Schweiger). Among the 1,198 people killed in one of the greatest of maritime disasters were 128 American citizens, and the fury of the American Government and people knew no bounds. The fact that 173 tons of munitions had very foolishly been loaded into her cargo holds in New York (something which could not have been known to Captain Schweiger when he fired) made no difference to the adverse American and other neutral reaction and the consequent damage to the German cause. The sinking of the world's most illustrious passenger-liner off Queenstown (now Cobh), Ireland, on the last leg of her homeward voyage was held to be a barbarous act incompatible with Germany's claim to be regarded as a civilised nation. Kaiser Wilhelm II reacted in much the same way as Hitler was to do twenty-four years later: he banned attacks on liners proceeding in a non-offensive manner, although he did not call off Germany's first unrestricted submarine campaign until October, more than six months after it had started. The United States did not enter the war until 6 April 1917, eleven months later; but it was the Germans' unrestricted use of submarines in general and the sinking of the *Lusitania* in particular that propelled a reluctant President Woodrow Wilson and Congress into declaring war on Germany, the event which ensured her defeat.

This lesson of history alone was enough to make the sinking of the completely innocent *Athenia* a crucial event at the beginning of the new conflict with Germany: Hitler was as anxious as the Kaiser not to provoke the United States, which was as reluctant in 1939 as it had been in 1914 to become involved in European conflict. But the first shot of the new war at sea had an even more important direct effect on the British conduct of naval operations from the opening day of hostilities. It led the Admiralty to conclude that the Germans would begin unrestricted submarine warfare immediately, and it put an end to any doubts about the urgency of introducing a comprehensive system of convoy for merchant shipping. Even though the assumption about German intentions was premature (the last few restrictions on submarines were lifted only in August 1940), the impetus given to the convoy strategy was of crucial importance.

Despite the long history of successful use of convoy by the British and other navies since time immemorial, despite even the very recent lessons of the First World War, there were still naval officers who had their doubts about its usefulness. This minority never quite lost its voice, and its view was to be heard again at the very peak of the coming struggle over the Anglo-American transatlantic trade route which was the main artery of the Allied war effort. Those opposed to convoys based their case partly on the unquestionably lengthy delays to shipping it caused but mainly on its seemingly inglorious, defensive nature (a feeling shared by Churchill). They overlooked the fact that a ship delayed by waiting for a convoy and sailing slowly between congested ports stood a distinctly better chance of survival than the perennially favourite target of submariners – ships sailing alone. Only the fastest of vessels could get away with that. They also did not see that convoys forced submarines to risk a fight with the naval escort in order to be able to attack merchantmen, thereby giving the defenders their best chance of engaging the enemy. Those sceptical of convoy went along with it but they also opened a second front by diverting vitally important escort-strength into "hunting groups" long before the Navy was strong enough to spare them. These groups chased rumours all over the ocean to minimal effect instead of staying with the shipping which was the submarines' principal objective. In consequence the British came close to losing the Atlantic Campaign, the most important struggle in both world wars and of the twentieth century, before it had properly begun. The importance of this dilution of the convoy principle will be shown in due course. But it is already clear, thanks to the echo of the *Lusitania* provided by the sinking of the *Athenia* and the Admiralty's immediate reaction, that an examination of the submarine campaign in the First World War is necessary for a proper understanding of its successor in the Second.

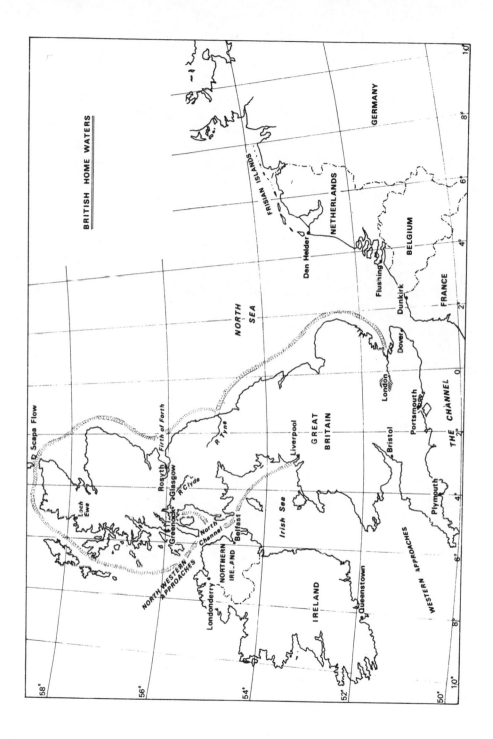

BRITISH HOME WATERS

Scapa Flow
Loch Ewe
Rosyth
Firth of Forth
Glasgow
Greenock
R Clyde
R Tyne
North Channel
Belfast
Liverpool
NORTHERN IRELAND
Londonderry
NORTH WESTERN APPROACHES
IRELAND
Queenstown
Irish Sea
GREAT BRITAIN
Bristol
London
Dover
WESTERN APPROACHES
Plymouth
Portsmouth
THE CHANNEL

NORTH SEA
FRISIAN ISLANDS
Den Helder
NETHERLANDS
Flushing
Dunkirk
BELGIUM
GERMANY
FRANCE

58°
56°
54°
52°
50°

10°
8°
6°
4°
2°
0
2°
4°
6°
8°
10°

PART I

THE FIRST BOUT AND
THE INTERVAL

1

THE FIRST ROUND, 1914–1918

*The blackest month ever – Germany embraces the submarine –
Britain panics – the submarine as retaliation for the British
blockade – British Intelligence – sinkings mount – Germany vacil-
lates – unrestricted warfare – the greatest "ace" – the crisis –
convoy – aircraft – the lessons*

DURING the worst month in the history of sea transport throughout the ages,
881,000 tons of merchant shipping and their cargoes were sent to the bottom.
The overwhelming majority of this unparalleled destruction was caused by
submarine attack, and two-thirds of the losses were British. This blackest
month in Britain's long record of reliance on seaborne trade and on naval
power to protect it occurred, not in the crisis early in 1943 of what Churchill
christened "the Battle of the Atlantic," but in April 1917. It helped to reduce
Britain's reserves of essential supplies to just six weeks (a crisis unmatched
at any time in the Second World War), and threatened her with imminent
defeat before the Americans could come to her aid in the war they had just
joined.

The early German submarines, the first ever to be deployed in war, were
fragile, precarious and unreliable. Grand-Admiral Alfred von Tirpitz, architect of the Imperial Navy which fought in the First World War, was a late
convert to their potential. In 1901, when France, Britain and other naval
powers were beginning to take a serious interest in them, he said: "Germany
has no need for submarines." The first *Unterseeboot* (undersea or submarine
boat), *U1*, was completed only at the end of 1906. It was not until 1908,
when the tiny craft with its single torpedo tube in the bow successfully
completed a 600-mile cruise in home waters, that the Germans woke up to
its potential.

By 1909 they had produced a pair of boats with four tubes and a gun
each, and capable of twelve knots on the surface. In 1913 the *U19* had an
endurance of 5,000 miles at eight knots without refuelling, notably more
efficient diesel engines, the world's best periscope (thanks to the German
lead in optics) and a powerful wireless transmitter. German submarines had

become as superior, boat for boat, as their conventional men-of-war ship for ship – and in an even shorter time. The British, though they had developed their own submarines, looked down on them as an ignoble, underhand weapon rather like the mine. Churchill in his first term as First Lord dismissed the possibility of a submarine campaign against trade: "I do not believe this would ever be done by a civilised power." The opposite view was taken by Admiral Lord "Jacky" Fisher, First Sea Lord (operational head of the Navy) until his retirement in 1910 and creator of the "all-big-gun" capital-ship squadrons which reaffirmed British naval supremacy in time for the First World War. A man of remarkable prescience who was to be reinstated soon after the war began, Fisher was out of office when he might have turned his fertile mind to countering the new weapon.

The Admiralty took the view that the submarine, capable of only a few knots when submerged, was subject to the same Prize Rules as the surface commerce-raider. These rules went back to the sixteenth century but had been rewritten and enshrined in international law. Under them a ship might be stopped and searched if it belonged to, or was carrying goods for, the enemy, whereupon it was open to being taken as a prize. If no prize crew could be provided, it could be sunk – provided passengers and crew were not harmed. Since all this seemed beyond the capabilities of the puny submarines of the time, hardly designed with Prize Rules in mind, the British took German self-restraint for granted and dismissed the submarine as a threat to trade. They saw it as an adjunct to the surface-fleet for reconnaissance and on the outbreak of war they had seventy-four boats. Of the twenty-eight in German service, twenty were operational.

Most of these were deployed in a defensive screen, on the surface and stationary, in the Heligoland Bight by August 1, when Germany declared war on Russia. The latter's partners declared war on Germany on August 4 when the Kaiser did not respond to a request to respect Belgian neutrality. Two days later, ten German submarines left Heligoland on the first offensive mission of its kind in history (the Greeks had sent two submarines to patrol off the Dardanelles in the Balkan Wars of 1912 against Turkey, but they achieved nothing). Spread out over some forty miles, the Germans had as their target nothing less than the British Grand Fleet at its wartime anchorage in Scapa Flow, among the Orkney Islands off the north of Scotland. The concept was boldness itself, but the execution soon went awry. As the submarines converged on the Orkneys on August 8, one blew up on a mine. The *U15* managed to fire torpedoes at three British capital ships but missed them. Forced to the surface by mechanical trouble on August 9, she was sighted, rammed and sunk by the light cruiser *Birmingham* (Captain Arthur Duff, RN), with the loss of all hands. The remaining eight returned undamaged but empty-handed. The submarine had been blooded – in its own blood. But the German boats were the first both to launch an attack on an enemy and to suffer losses in combat. The episode ended ingloriously for them – but they continued in the ensuing weeks to send out their submarines in ones and twos to look for enemy warships to attack in the North Sea. It was not until the war was a month old, in the first week of September, that the submarine claimed its first victim. Lieutenant Otto Hersing in the *U21*, one of the first to be fitted with diesel engines, attacked HMS *Pathfinder*, a light cruiser leading a destroyer-flotilla of the Grand Fleet. The unlucky warship of 2,940 tons took a direct hit on one of her magazines, which exploded. She broke up and sank in four minutes with the loss of 259 men. To her belongs the sad distinction of being the first ship to be sunk by a submarine.

It may have taken the new naval weapon a month to draw enemy blood, but its psychological effect was well in evidence from the moment of the discovery of the first abortive mission against Scapa Flow. From then on submarine sightings, nearly all of them imaginary, in the British Fleet rapidly mounted as the entire Royal Navy succumbed to the new ailment of "periscopitis." The anxiety and confusion this created began to make the British realise that they had severely underestimated the submarine's potential. How much had still to be learned was made clear on September 22 off the Dutch coast. Three old armoured cruisers, the *Aboukir*, *Cressy* and *Hogue*, manned mostly by reservists, were patrolling there against German light forces in case they tried raiding the Channel. Many naval leaders from Churchill down had already expressed concern for the trio's vulnerability to a swift attack by modern enemy surface-ships. But on the morning of September 22, the *Aboukir*, sailing at a leisurely ten knots and not zig-zagging, was rocked by an explosion and sank twenty-five minutes later, just before 7 a.m. The *Hogue* promptly went to her rescue, firing in all directions at "periscopes"; she too was struck twice, taking only ten minutes to sink. The *Cressy*, the last of the three 10,000-ton cruisers, stopped to lower her boats and pick up survivors from the other two. At 7.17 a lookout shouted warnings of a periscope and then a torpedo-track. The *Cressy* in turn was hit twice, turned turtle and sank, with no boats left for her own crew. A total of 1,460 men lost their lives in a completely unnecessary disaster.

Its cause was Lieutenant Otto Weddigen, commanding the *U9*, which was powered by paraffin-engines and already obsolete. There was jubilation in Germany over this spectacular victory against the world's most powerful navy – never mind that the victims were elderly vessels which would have been better used as blockships or scrapped. At the Admiralty there was consternation, shared by Admiral Sir John Jellicoe, the C-in-C of the Grand Fleet. Those few minutes of horror in the North Sea proved that the loss of the *Pathfinder* had been no fluke; the submarine might not be a gentleman's weapon but it had to be taken rather more seriously than anyone on the humiliated British side had so far done.

The next lesson came on October 20, off southern Norway, when the *U17*, also paraffin-powered, sent the SS *Glitra*, a British cargo-ship of just

866 tons, to the bottom – the first merchantman to be sunk by submarine. Prize Rules were punctiliously observed. The *U17* (*Kapitänleutnant* Feldkircher) stopped the ship by firing a shot across her bows, sent a boarding-party to confirm she was British, politely ushered the crew into their own lifeboats and prudently saved ammunition by opening the seacocks in the bottom of her hull. This first use of the submarine against commerce prompted thoughts in Germany of possible countermeasures against the tight British surface blockade, which was being ruthlessly applied by the Royal Navy amid much interference with neutral shipping. What the Germans did not know was that the submarine had already imposed a major psychological defeat on the British by forcing the Grand Fleet out of the North Sea. Understandably nervous of the submarine threat, Jellicoe felt he could not afford the risk of anchoring in Scapa Flow, which lacked defences. First he took to spending the night at sea ringed by a protective screen of destroyers; then he moved from the North Sea to the Atlantic coast of Scotland, and after that Lough Swilly on the north coast of Ireland was used as the Grand Fleet's refuge while Scapa Flow was fortified. This did nothing to assuage the British public's thirst for good news from the Navy, the nation's bulwark and expression of her power. It looked to Jellicoe for another Trafalgar, preferably before Christmas, by which time everybody "knew" the war would be over. Jellicoe, a worrier who could not delegate, made the preservation of his ships his first priority and fretted increasingly about the hitherto underestimated threats posed by the mine, the torpedo – and the German submarine.

At this early stage the majority of German submarines were still powered by noisy, two-stroke paraffin-engines which tended to emit dense white smoke by daylight and showers of sparks and even flame by night. The boats numbered *U5* to *U18* were all of this type, displacing about 500 tons on the surface and equipped with four torpedo tubes, six torpedoes, six mines and one light gun. From *U19* they were powered by diesel-engines, which were quieter, much less temperamental, did not visibly betray themselves and used less volatile fuel. It took the invention of the nuclear reactor to supersede the diesel-submarine, which even now is very much in use three-quarters of a century later. The early submarines proved capable of upwards of twelve knots on the surface and around nine on battery power submerged. The Imperial Navy's building programme before the war envisaged a strength of seventy-two submarines, but when the war began, design difficulties and construction delays left Germany with forty-five boats in service or under construction. Another seventeen were ordered on mobilisation, and five under construction for Austria, Germany's ally, were taken over by agreement in November 1914. In October, fifteen coastal submarines of the *UB* type, displacing only about 125 tons, were ordered, to take advantage of Germany's early occupation of the Belgian ports. The first was completed in an astonishing seventy-five days and delivered in three sections by rail and canal to Bruges. Fifteen more of the *UC* class, based on the *UB* but adapted for minelaying, were ordered in November. The Germans may have been slow and cautious in taking up the idea of the submarine, but these early wartime decisions showed serious intent to exploit its possibilities.

After the Grand Fleet had expended large quantities of coal, oil and ammunition on shelling a seal at Scapa and the battlecruisers under Admiral Beatty had made a similar mistake over a destroyer's bow-wave at his base in the Cromarty Firth, damaging a couple of houses in the village of Jemimaville with errant shells, the loss of the *Pathfinder* could be seen to have made the Navy very nervous. The evacuation of the Flow was rather more serious, and thoughtful naval officers could not understand why the Germans failed to take advantage of British disarray. In the first five months of the war submarines accounted for just seven secondary warships and ten merchantmen with a total tonnage of about 20,000, mostly sunk under Prize Rules. The great battlefleets of the two North Sea enemies had been dismayingly inactive, the Germans being no keener to risk their capital ships in a major action than the British. Such surface activity as there was, apart from the British raid on Heligoland at the end of August, took place in distant waters and virtually came to an end when the German cruisers overseas were accounted for by early December. The first British defeat at sea in a century at the Battle of Coronel, a profound shock to the nation and a terrible blow to its naval pride, was avenged at the Battle of the Falkland Islands five weeks later, on December 8. The value of the Royal Navy's distant blockade of Germany was not generally understood, especially as its chief instrument, the Grand Fleet, was completely on the defensive against an invisible enemy to which it had no answer. Yet its most serious loss, the sinking of the brand-new "super-Dreadnought" battleship *Audacious* off Northern Ireland on October 27, had been caused by a German mine.

The implications of the British blockade were understood all too well in Germany, where it was felt, with some justice, that the Royal Navy was going beyond international law in applying it to neutral shipping. Both sides had illegally confiscated merchant ships caught in the wrong ports at the outbreak of war and both had made preparations for the arming of merchant vessels. No agreement had been reached before the war on restricting the use of mines, a cheap defensive and offensive weapon in which the Germans were markedly superior. These erosions of the idealistic, late nineteenth-century spirit of humanitarian self-restraint in war and the unexpected effectiveness of the first submarines led to demands in Germany for a counter-blockade of Britain by submarines, taking advantage of their greatest asset, surprise. Junior German staff officers had calculated in prewar papers that Germany would be able with about 200 submarines to wage a new and deadlier version of cruiser-warfare, the *guerre de course*, against commerce. The strategy, of catching enemy merchantmen unawares and inadequately protected, was traditional; the difference lay in the tactical advantage of submersibility, giving the marauder overwhelming superiority over his victim once found. Slower than any modern conventional warship, the submarine could exploit its one asset only by attack without warning, which was a fundamental breach of international law. The loss of its overseas cruisers, the light losses inflicted on the enemy by its fast merchant-auxiliary raiders (though not without daring) and the inability of the High Seas Fleet to influence events led the German High Command to press for unrestricted submarine warfare. The Chancellor, Theobald von Bethmann-Hollweg, resisted the pressure, already strong in the latter part of 1914, on political grounds: it would alienate neutral, particularly American, opinion. But on 4 February 1915, with the approval of the Kaiser, the German High Command declared the waters round the British Isles to be a war-zone, in which Allied ships could be sunk without warning. Neutrals were pointedly reminded of the high risk they ran by sailing their ships in the area. The British had won the clash at the Dogger Bank on January 24 between the battlecruisers (capital ships with higher speed but less armour than battleships), a useful if also misleading tactical victory; German submarines had sunk six merchant ships in one day on January 30. The evidence seemed to point to keeping the big ships at home and letting the submarines have their head.

The submarine force available was still only about twenty operational boats, as at the very beginning of the war. Seven had been lost to accidents, mines and ramming and a few others were out of action because of damage or breakdown. Only one in three of those operational could be on offensive patrol at any one time (the rest being on the way out, on the way home or in port). About half were small coastal craft not suitable for the deeper and rougher waters south and west of Britain. But production of new and better boats was accelerating.

In January 1915 they sank 47,900 tons of merchant shipping. With the gloves off in February they accounted for 65,000 tons. In the first half of May they destroyed 120,000 tons of shipping, and then there was a lull which led Churchill, just before his dismissal from the Admiralty, rashly to claim that the submarine threat had failed. The Germans lost three more boats during this period: one was the *U12* under the newly promoted Commander Weddigen who had sunk the three old cruisers off the Dutch coast. His boat was rammed and sunk by HMS *Dreadnought*, the first modern battleship, near Scapa Flow on March 18. Not one submarine had been sunk by gunfire. The Allies had lost thirty-nine merchant ships. The captain of an American oil tanker was killed in April in an attack which failed to sink his ship but which aroused American opinion. So did the sinking of the British ship *Harpalyce* on her way to the United States to collect food for the starving in Belgium: she flew a white flag and the purpose of her mission was painted in huge letters on her sides. American disapproval of the British blockade of Germany, which had interfered with US trade, was overborne by a tidal wave of anger on May 7, when *Kapitänleutnant* Walter Schweiger in the *U20* sank the *Lusitania*.

On the morning she left New York (May 1) advertisements signed "Imperial German Embassy" appeared in the New York press, warning that British ships were "liable to destruction" in the waters round the British Isles: "Travellers sailing in the war-zone . . . do so at their own risk." The warning appeared immediately under the Cunard Line's customary sailing notice, which also gave May 29 for her next departure from New York to Liverpool. The atmosphere as the great liner of 30,000 tons prepared to sail was therefore decidedly tense. Journalists and cameramen thronged the quay; some of them did nothing for passengers' nerves by announcing they were there to record the *Lusitania's* "last voyage."

Her master, Captain William Turner, nicknamed "Bowler Bill," was almost alone in dismissing the fears aroused by the warning, inserted on the initiative of German-American community leaders in New York who feared the consequences to themselves of rising anti-German sentiment caused by the submarine campaign. Captain Turner, a vastly experienced seaman of fifty-eight with a peremptory manner and no liking at all for passengers, whom he was wont to compare with monkeys, did his best to calm the palpable anxiety on board: "There is always a danger," he told the customers, "but the best guarantees of your safety are the *Lusitania* herself and the fact that wherever there is danger your safety is in the hands of the Royal Navy." The ship's top speed was twenty-six knots, she had a double bottom and watertight compartments and she had, like the *Titanic*, been described as unsinkable. She sailed at noon, two hours late, with 1,257 passengers in all, 197 of them Americans. The most famous US citizen aboard was Alfred G. Vanderbilt, aged thirty-seven, multi-millionaire scion of the railway and shipping dynasty and a renowned amateur horseman.

A small library has been written about the loss of the great ship and still not all of the mysteries relating to her last voyage have been cleared up. For example, shortly after she sailed, three German stowaways were found hiding in a steward's pantry. They were detained for questioning in Liverpool, but never got there. If they were German agents, one can only conclude that they were either foolhardy, under strict orders or not newspaper readers. The greatest controversy surrounds the contents of her cargo-holds. The cargo manifest, not a secret document, showed that the *Lusitania* was carrying rifle ammunition, shrapnel shells and fuses for explosives. Much persuasive evidence has been unearthed indicating that this was by no means the whole story, and that the munitions may have sealed the ship's fate by sympathetic explosion when she was hit. Even the exigencies of a war on land like the unprecedented slogging match on the Western Front do not explain the rashness of loading any ammunition aboard a passenger-liner, for obvious and elementary reasons of safety. The well-advertised, unrestricted submarine campaign was after all already three months old. There were also rumours that she was carrying gold bullion, about the last item that needed to be risked on a voyage to Britain when so much war matériel was being bought in America.

At 9 a.m. on May 5 British Naval Intelligence was told of the presence of a German submarine a few miles north-west of the Fastnet Rock off the south-western tip of Ireland. The information came from the Admiralty's Room 40, the scene of a brilliant and sustained cipher-breaking operation made possible by the Russian gift to the British of the German naval cipher-book from the cruiser *Magdeburg*, sunk in the Baltic in October 1914. A wireless signal from the *U20* to Germany had been intercepted and passed to Room 40 for decryption. On May 5 and 6, the *U20* sank three ships in the area, and on the evening of the 6th, remarkably tardily in the circumstances, Admiral Sir Charles Coke at the nearby naval base at Queenstown was moved to warn shipping: "Submarines active off south coast of Ireland." This was handed to Captain Turner at 7.50 p.m. as he was about to join the fare-paying monkeys for the gala dinner and concert marking the last evening at sea. It was only when a repeat of the warning was passed to him at table at 8.30 that he doubled the watch, ordered the lifeboats swung out on their davits ready for launching, had as many watertight doors as possible closed, darkened ship and reduced speed so that he would pass Fastnet by night rather than by daylight. "On entering the war-zone tomorrow we shall be securely in the care of the Royal Navy," he told those honoured by a place at his table. The ship sailed on through intermittent fog.

At mid-morning on the 7th, the Admiralty broadcast another warning to all ships: "Submarines active in southern part of Irish Channel. Last heard of twenty miles south of Coningsbeg Light. Make certain *Lusitania* gets this." Captain Turner reacted by altering course twenty degrees to the north from his easterly line, bringing his ship closer to land. The morning fog had long since dispersed, the sun was high in a clear sky and the sea calm.

By this time, well pleased with his haul of three sinkings, Schweiger had decided to run for home. He had just spent an hour submerged and spotted nothing further through his periscope. He was down to his last three torpedoes and his diesel fuel gave him little margin for more hunting. But at 1 p.m., sitting on the conning-tower of his surfaced boat, the captain himself saw smoke ahead and soon identified its source as a large, four-funnelled liner, making towards land off the Old Head of Kinsale, just twenty-five miles from Queenstown harbour. The *U20* dived and strained at her maximum underwater speed of nine knots to reach a point ahead of the target. At 1.40 p.m. Captain Turner ordered a sharp turn to starboard, back to his easterly course, so that a precise navigational fix could be obtained by using the Head as a reference. This put the *Lusitania* across the bow of the *U20* at a range of less than half a mile. It was 2.10 p.m. and the proud mistress of the Atlantic had eighteen minutes to live.

When *U20's* single torpedo struck the starboard side of the ship at an angle of ninety degrees and ten feet below the waterline amidships, two lookouts had seen it coming and alerted the bridge in the minute or so it took to strike home. Captain Turner had time to see it also, but not to do anything about it. It was a perfect shot. Watching through his periscope, Schweiger dictated what he saw for the boat's war-diary and log. Noting that there were two explosions after his single torpedo had struck, he said:

> The superstructure above the point of impact and the bridge are torn apart, fire is breaking out and smoke is enveloping the high bridge. The ship stops at once and heels over to starboard very fast, sinking by the bow at the same time.

As the debris was still falling from the 150-foot column thrown up by the blasts, the liner's radio-operator was tapping out:

SOS COME AT ONCE. Big list. Ten miles south Old Head Kinsale. SOS . . .

The torpedo had torn a hole just abaft of the bridge, causing empty coal-bunkers there to flood instantaneously and accounting for the list, initially of fifteen degrees. But the fact that her bow was awash within moments can only be explained by a consequential explosion hundreds of feet away from the point of impact. This may have come from methane-gas and coaldust in a forward bunker; or it might have been munitions. Dives on the wreck have revealed extensive damage forward, far more serious than amidships. Nor did the great ship stop; her momentum once her stem was awash actually drove her down by the bow, even though the engine-room was already flooded. She listed further over to starboard as she went under.

Terrible scenes ensued on the dying liner as Captain Turner gave the orders to launch lifeboats and abandon ship. Her continuing movement made lowering the boats hazardous anyway; her list made it impossible to lower those on the port side, while those on the other swung out too far for many passengers to be able to reach them without falling into the sea. As boatloads of screaming passengers slid and scraped down the port side, some boats turning over, others disintegrating under the strain, Captain Turner's efforts to regain control of his ship failed. She was now inexorably bound for the bottom under her own momentum. When he stopped the destructive launching of the lifeboats for a few moments, an American passenger drew a pistol and ordered a seaman to cut his boat loose. The boat slithered down the port side over a carpet of writhing bodies, crushing many of them and adding at least thirty to the number of dead.

The living and the dead floated in the swell with wreckage raining down and the four tall scarlet funnels with their black collars looming over them.

Mr Vanderbilt, who could not swim, devoted his last moments to saving as many children as he could. Finally the bow of the ship hit bottom, the hull rose to an impossible angle until the stern sank slowly back into the water, and the *Lusitania* disappeared with an unearthly, keening moan as the air was forced from her hulk. Captain Turner stayed on the bridge until the rising water forced him to climb out and his stricken ship was taken from under him. He was rescued, clutching a piece of flotsam, by the fleet of boats which came from Queenstown. Of the 1,198 who were lost, 785 were passengers and 413 crew, ninety-four were children including thirty-five babies and toddlers, and 128 were Americans. The era of total war, in which civilians, infants and other innocent bystanders could find themselves in the front line, had arrived at sea aboard His Imperial German Majesty's submarine *U20*. Schweiger left the scene for home at 2.25 p.m., three minutes before his victim sank. He was killed in 1917 when his latest boat, the *U88*, hit a mine.

President Wilson broke down when told of the sinking – and sent a protest note to the Kaiser. Contrary to British expectations and hopes, America stayed out of the war and its leaders and people were angrily dismissed as cowards. The German press hailed the exploit and the authorities justified it by pointing to the warning advertisements and the munitions aboard, which Schweiger blamed for the second explosion. He was even praised for not firing a second torpedo when he saw all the people in the water. Sinkings tailed off sharply for the rest of May, giving misplaced comfort to the Admiralty as it sought desperately for an effective counter to the submarine. Hundreds of trawlers and other small craft, many of them slower even than submerged submarines, were requisitioned for coastal patrol, much use was made of nets and sweeps with explosive tips (the idea being that they would explode on contact with a submarine) and of decoy tactics. A British submarine linked to a trawler by telephone was able to sink a German boat lured to the scene by the helpless-looking target. This ploy worked just once. The Q-ship – a vessel with hidden weapons and deployed as bait – accounted for half a dozen German submarines before the ruse was known to all captains. It probably proved counter-productive in the end by encouraging the German tendency to sink without warning when in doubt, which was still not universal. The Royal Navy, extreme manifestation as it was of the British class system at its worst, had failed on grounds of snobbery and the wrong kind of education to take an interest in science and technology. Fisher, who had given the Navy its great new ships and its submarines, was of humble origin and more open to ideas. When he resigned as First Sea Lord in spring 1915 after a row with Churchill, just before the First Lord himself departed, Churchill's successor at the Admiralty, Arthur Balfour, created the naval Board of Inventions and Research and put Fisher in charge. The Board itself was short-lived, but it opened the way to harnessing scientists to the war-effort, a factor which was to be of enormous importance in the

Second World War. In summer 1915 the BIR set up an anti-submarine committee, whose most dynamic member was the New Zealander Ernest Rutherford, the Cambridge atomic scientist. His major contribution was in the detection of submarines by listening device, still the main means of finding them today. Having determined that this was the key, Rutherford went to see Commander C. P. Ryan, who, unregarded by his superiors, was already at work on the principle at a practical level. He had started to develop the hydrophone or underwater ear, based on the technology of the telephone, at Granton on the Firth of Forth. Ryan was allowed to spend the sum of £1 on each experiment; Rutherford strongly recommended an end to this extraordinary stinginess and that Ryan should be given his head. Rutherford also took an interest in detection by reflected sound: instead of just passively listening, the submarine-hunter could transmit an ultrasonic beam which would be returned to him when it struck an underwater object. With his report to the BIR late in 1915 Rutherford opened the way to countering the invisibility of the submarine. He also did vital work in direction-finding by sound. The other half of the anti-submarine equation – having located a submarine, how to destroy it – was the underwater bomb, or depth-charge, on which promising experiments had begun in the first half of 1915.

After the deceptive lull late in May 1915, in which both sides seemed to take a brief breather, the submarine campaign began again. A double crisis came in August, political for Germany but for Britain a matter of life and death. In the course of the month, 185,800 tons of shipping were lost, 165,000 tons to submarine attack. For the first time the monthly total of merchant ships lost to enemy action exceeded Britain's capacity to build replacements. A declining ability to bring home the munitions and raw materials essential for the prosecution of the war and to feed the people spelt defeat. So much for the "failure" of the submarine campaign. But luck and German ineptitude came to the aid of the British in the nick of time. The U24 torpedoed the British liner *Arabic* near the Irish coast. Although there were only three Americans among the dead, the sinking compounded the "*Lusitania* factor" and the United States protested strongly enough to give the Germans pause. At the end of the month, submarines were ordered not to attack any passenger-ship except under prize regulations. Since increasing numbers of Allied ships carried guns, the risk of intercepting any large ship that might be carrying any passengers at all was now too great for submarine commanders.

Unbeknown to the anxious British, the unrestricted campaign had split the German leadership, with the Chancellery and the Foreign Ministry demanding a halt for fear that the Americans with their limitless resources would be precipitated into the war, and the Kaiser, the military High Command (which also controlled the Navy) and the naval leadership wanting to press it home. Admiral Henning von Holtzendorff, the naval Chief of Staff, promised to force Britain to surrender in six months if his submarines were given a free hand. He was probably right. But the boats were withdrawn from British waters in the middle of September and diverted to the Mediterranean, where rich pickings (and almost no Americans) were to be found. Britain was thus given a chance to get her second wind, although the continuing losses of shipping in the Mediterranean could hardly be shrugged off. The haemorrhage had ceased but the bleeding went on. Some submarines remained in British waters to lay mines. By the end of 1915, 855,000 tons of Allied shipping, 748,000 tons of it British, had been sunk, against a loss of just twenty submarines. Meanwhile sixty-one new boats had been built, giving the Germans a net total of fifty-eight operational submarines at the turn of the year. They had won the first round of total war at sea, even though the British blockade was unaffected. German protests about this were however drowned in neutral anger about the nature of untrammelled submarine warfare, skilfully stoked up by British propaganda. The "Hun" (a term for Germans first used by the Kaiser) now had a reputation for committing atrocities, born of early outrages in Belgium and nurtured by the submarine campaign. One of the great ironies of the First World War is that Germany, having attracted such opprobrium, did not live up to her ruthless reputation by resolving to be hanged for a sheep rather than a lamb. The temporary change of heart, which bears all the hallmarks of the Kaiser's vacillating character, cost Germany the war. Nevertheless the German submarines returned to British waters to hunt merchant ships in February 1916. Commanders were ordered to leave passenger-ships strictly alone, to attack without warning only armed merchant-ships outside the declared war-zone and to confine unrestricted attacks to non-passenger ships inside the zone. As the German admirals had predicted, it was only a matter of time before a commander made a mistake, while others hesitated for fear of error. The blunder came on March 24, when *UB29* (Lieutenant Pustkuchen), a small boat from the Flanders Flotilla, attacked the cross-Channel passenger ferry *Sussex*, 1,350 tons, with 380 passengers aboard. One torpedo hit the steamer in the bow in mid-Channel, leaving a gaping hole; but she stayed afloat, although about eighty were killed or injured. Twenty-five of the dead were American. Pustkuchen claimed that he had seen people moving about on the deck and thought the *Sussex* was a troopship. The weather at the time was excellent. The survivors were picked up by a British destroyer and a French trawler and the ferry was beached. Two hours later the *Salybia*, a cargo-ship bound for the Thames from the West Indies, was torpedoed in the same area; so when Count Bernstorff, the German Ambassador, claimed in Washington that the *Sussex* had struck a mine he was not believed. The American Government was slow to react to his disclaimer; but when it did, on April 20, it included a threat for the first time:

Unless the Imperial Government should now immediately declare and effect an abandonment of its present methods of submarine warfare against passenger and freight-carrying vessels, the Government of the United States can have no choice but to sever diplomatic relations . . .

The Germans replied:

The German Government cannot but reiterate its regret that sentiments of humanity, which the Government of the United States extends with such fervour to the unhappy victims of submarine warfare, have not been extended with the same feeling to the many millions of women and children, who, according to the avowed intention of the British Government, are to be starved, and who by suffering are to force the victorious armies of the Central Powers into an ignominious capitulation.

Unfortunately blockades are invisible in their workings while torpedoes are not. The propaganda defeat of Germany because of her submarine offensive was brought about by the modern mass media of press and cinema-newsreel. Artists' impressions, photographs and even the occasional moving picture of ships in agony on the high seas touched millions where stories of hungry but still living Germans could not (British civilians were also subjected to strict rationing). Once again Chancellor von Bethmann-Hollweg overcame Admiral von Holtzendorff and on April 24 the submarines were ordered to revert to Prize Rules. On May 4 the German Government sent a Note acceding to the American ultimatum of April 20. Diplomatic relations remained in place, but anti-German feeling in America mounted (and so did anti-Americanism in Germany, where Washington was widely accused of hypocrisy).

Despite all the uproar about attack without warning, the Germans used their guns rather than scarce and costly torpedoes to sink the majority of their victims. Submarines were fast enough to catch most merchant ships of the day, and the usual method of attack in 1916 was by shelling from the surface, which remained true even as the number of merchant ships equipped with defensive guns passed the 1,000 mark in April 1916. But an armed merchantman proved more than three times as likely to survive an attack than an unarmed one, and there is no way of measuring how often a submarine was deterred by the sight of a gun on deck through the periscope. With so many targets to choose from, commanders instinctively went for the easiest.

The German return to Prize Law under American pressure came too late for the 131 ships totalling 442,000 tons lost to submarine attack by May in 1916. By then Britain alone had lost more than one million tons of shipping at a cost to Germany of just thirty-two submarines and their crews of up to thirty-five men each. Also lost, and often overlooked in the maze of statistics, were valuable cargoes of food and war matériel and such exports as Britain could produce to help pay for them. Far away from the terrible clash in the Flanders mud, a war to the death was going ahead at sea, with each side trying to strangle the entire economy of the other. Meanwhile the Admiralty in London, despite the gradual introduction of the depth-charge in penny-packets, usually two to a ship, had no tactical answer to the submarine. The infant Naval Staff, introduced by Churchill as one of his best ideas in 1912, was not yet up to its job and the great majority of indifferent admirals and excellent ship's captains in the Royal Navy instinctively believed that the submarine could be checked only by the offensive approach. They therefore committed their ships to hunting the Germans along the shipping lanes, a pastime akin to looking for a needle in a haystack when the needle can be freely moved about if the seeker gets near. The ships devoted to the offensive searches and the patrolling of routes had no reliable means of detecting submarines other than the eyeball (early hydrophones worked best when several ships were on hand, preferably motionless in calm weather), and no reliable means of killing them once found. The Navy demanded destroyers and more destroyers for hunting and patrol. Huge minefields and net barriers were laid.

The same men who floundered helplessly for an answer to the submarine thought it natural to provide strong escort for the ships which took the troops to France, and to use destroyers to protect capital ships (and light cruisers to protect the destroyers). In the new lull of summer 1916 the Admiralty's attention was drawn to the importance and vulnerability of the trade between Britain and the neutral Netherlands. In June the British Government persuaded the Dutch to increase desperately needed food exports to Britain, to the corresponding detriment of their German neighbours. In the same month the British steamer *Brussels* was captured by German destroyers from Flanders. Her master, Captain Fryatt, was shot after a travesty of a court martial because in March 1915 he had run his unarmed ship straight at a submarine about to attack, forcing it to dive. In July another ship on the important Holland–England route was captured. It was then decided to substitute for distant destroyer-cover by the Harwich Force a system of sailing the ships in groups closely escorted by destroyers or sloops. All these escorting measures were taken with surface-raiders in mind (from April 1917 the groups even had air-cover). But the principle of herding ships together for protection by armed escort was as old as the distinction between the merchantman and the man-of-war; even when trading ships had carried their own guns they came together to look after themselves. The word for this application of the herd instinct to the protection of trade is convoy. In 1653, in the first Anglo-Dutch War, the Dutch sailed a convoy of 450 merchantmen escorted by eighty-eight men-of-war; in 1794, during the Napoleonic Wars, the British assembled a convoy for the western trade of no fewer than 600 ships, escorted by thirty-four men-of-war. The very thought of the immense effort involved in assembling such a collection of ships in the days of sail, to say nothing of keeping them together on the move, is daunting in the extreme: obviously those in charge thought it worthwhile. This makes it all the stranger that men who looked back on the time of Nelson as the Royal Navy's greatest glory, and longed to emulate Trafalgar in a fleet action with the Germans, shut their eyes to the fact that the highly successful Admiralty of the day saw nothing wrong in convoys. On the contrary, they had been akin to a law of nature at sea in wartime since the thirteenth century. Convoys maximised the value of warships by grouping them together (concentration of force) in defence of the enemy's objective, commerce. To bring him to action you either awaited his attack on your convoy or you sought out his. The art of admiralty had always been focused on attacking or defending *ships*, not routes or areas of water. The hardest naval lesson of the First World War was to be that all the bewildering series of technological changes from steam to submarines, aeroplanes and radio did not invalidate this principle.

The long-awaited clash between the battlefleets came at the end of May 1916. The appointment of Admiral Reinhard Scheer as C-in-C of the High Seas Fleet led to a more aggressive policy, and Room 40 soon got wind of a new readiness to take risks. So when the Germans finally came out in strength in the hope of luring part of the British Fleet to destruction, the entire Grand Fleet was also at sea with Beatty and the battlecruisers coming up in support. In the resulting Battle of Jutland on May 31 and June 1, the Germans suffered fewer losses than the British; but this first fleet-action in the North Sea was also the last. The Germans may have lost fewer ships but many were so badly damaged that they were out of action for months in some cases, whereas Jellicoe reported the slightly reduced Grand Fleet ready for sea again in a matter of days. The British were bitterly disappointed that they had lost the chance of another Trafalgar in the fog of war which enveloped this still controversial battle. The fact that the Germans never seriously risked the bulk of their fleet again was a strategic victory for the Royal Navy of unparalleled importance for the outcome of the war as a whole.

Merchant-shipping losses declined in June 1916 to 37,000 tons, the lowest total since August 1915. But in the year so far, almost half a million tons had been lost, 150 percent more than the British shipbuilders were able to construct in the first half of 1916. The increasing shortfall in the carrying capacity of the reduced British Merchant Navy was filled by neutrals willing to risk the high level of losses for the sake of the high rewards on offer. And while the Admiralty in London was all too ready to be lulled into a false sense of security by the summer easing of the submarine campaign, the German war leaders once again, after Jutland, became all the more keen to make maximum use of the one naval weapon which promised to turn the war in their favour. Even with the submarines limited to minelaying in British waters and to such sinkings as they could achieve among the armed merchantmen in the Mediterranean, the Germans were winning the economic war of attrition at sea.

In October 1916 Scheer won consent to ordering the submarines to resume sinkings in British waters under Prize Rules while maintaining unrestricted sinkings in the Mediterranean. As more and more boats came into German service (58 operational at the beginning of 1916, 140 at the end) while German submarine losses were only two or three per month, British shipping losses in the last four months of 1916 totalled 484,000 tons, bringing the figure for the year to about one million. The French coal-trade was badly hit. So was neutral shipping (102,500 tons sunk in the period), which posed a threat to the strategically vital supply of Swedish iron ore from Narvik in Norway, essential to British war production. Total British losses to submarines in October alone amounted to 176,000 tons, the worst month of the war so far. In a particularly disquieting development, the *U53* sank three British and two neutral ships in a single day in October – just outside the territorial waters of the United States off Rhode Island, with US Navy vessels in sight but unable to intervene.

The apotheosis of the submarine as a weapon against trade was achieved in the Mediterranean by the *U35*, under Commander Lothar von Arnauld de la Perière, arguably the greatest "ace" of either war. In four weeks of July and August 1916 he sank fifty-four ships of 91,150 tons with 900 shells and only four torpedoes. By the time Perière left the *U35* near the end of the war, they had together sunk 195 vessels – three warships, five troopships and 187 merchantmen (one-third of them sailing ships) – totalling almost 500,000 tons. And the aristocratic captain reached this astounding total under Prize Rules, which meant nobody was hurt on an unarmed vessel. Chivalry was not entirely extinguished, even in the German submarine service. His boat was 212 feet long, displaced 685 tons surfaced (878 submerged), had a maximum speed of 16.7 knots (9.7 submerged), a crew of thirty-five, four torpedo tubes (two at the bow, two at the stern) with six torpedoes, and mounted one gun. The most remarkable fact about the *U35* is how closely she resembled the type VII boat that was to be the backbone of the German submarine fleet in the Second World War (except that the *U35* was *faster* underwater by two knots, if of shorter range). German submarine design had matured remarkably quickly.

Only after the disastrous autumn of 1916 did the British Admiralty and Government finally realise that the submarine campaign was the chief menace at sea. Neutral shipowners could not be appeased only by a generous, government-backed marine insurance-scheme. Junior staff officers had been sending calls for convoy into the void from summer. On October 29 Jellicoe sent a memorandum on the "submarine menace" to the First Lord, Arthur Balfour, in which, among many other things, he said:

> *The destroyer*, although very effective in confined waters and when present in large numbers, is ineffective for offence in open waters . . . [but] *is, of course, very efficient defensively as a screen* to individual ships, or *to a large number of ships*. [Author's italics]

Curiously enough this irrefutable argument for convoy was not advanced as such, even though it was staring the admiral in the face in his own hand-writing. It was part of a case for a complete but general rethinking of the anti-submarine strategy, which Jellicoe regarded as so inadequate that the country might be forced to sue for peace in six months (shades of von Holtzendorff); or, in plain English, Britain faced defeat. Any doubt about how seriously he regarded the crisis is dispelled by the memorandum's concluding proposal: that a whole squadron of Grand Fleet battleships should be stood down for the sake of releasing its destroyer flotilla to the anti-submarine campaign! Jellicoe was invited to London from Scapa for a meeting of the War Cabinet on November 2, chaired by the Prime Minister, Henry Asquith. David Lloyd George, the Minister of Munitions in the National Government, raised the issue of convoys, supported by the Con-servative leader, Andrew Bonar Law. The idea was rejected by the others present, including all three admirals. There was no mention of convoy at a meeting the next day at the Admiralty, attended by Jellicoe, when the creation of an anti-submarine department was inconclusively discussed. The First Sea Lord, Admiral Sir Henry Jackson, wanted Jellicoe to leave the Grand Fleet and lead such a department, but did not raise the idea for fear of causing offence. The paralysis and depression at the Admiralty were however about to be subjected to severe shock-treatment. It was not before time: by December 1916 Britain had lost 738 ships of more than 2,300,000 tons, one-fifth of the world's largest merchant fleet, most of it to submarines, with mines and surface raiders accounting for the rest.

Arthur Balfour for one had been impressed by Jellicoe's paper unconsciously crying out but not explicitly appealing for convoys, and decided to make him First Sea Lord, with Beatty replacing him in command of the Grand Fleet. Jellicoe took over from Jackson on December 5, and brought with him Rear-Admiral Alexander Duff as Director of the new Anti-Submarine Division. The submarine was to be the top priority of the new Board of Admiralty, now leavened by officers who had seen service at sea in the present war. The new men had hardly found their way to their offices, however, before the Government itself fell. Asquith was driven out by public disquiet over the lack of progress in the war, the setbacks on land and at sea, and anger about the way the war was being run – "bungling in high places" did not exclude Downing Street itself. The obvious man to take over the leadership of the National Government was Lloyd George, with his seemingly inexhaustible supply of energy and his long experience of government. Though a Liberal, he had the crucial backing of important Conservatives such as Bonar Law and Sir Edward Carson, and on December 11 the small Welshman with the walrus-moustache and white hair, the passionate nature and the brilliant oratory, became Prime Minister. Balfour was given the more appropriate post of Foreign Secretary and Carson replaced him – for just eight months – at the Admiralty, where he proved to be a remarkably poor political chief. As the leading lawyer of his day who had served five months as Attorney-General early in the war, he was an impressive personality with a sharp mind, but no talent for administration. On arrival at the Admiralty he told the staff he was "very much at sea" in naval affairs and did not wish to interfere with the professionals in technical matters. The admirals thought this an excellent arrangement, but it was precisely the opposite of what was needed. It was a bizarre position for one of the keenest critics of weak government under Asquith to adopt on his first day in a key department. It became an important factor in his downfall.

The new admirals threw everything they could think of into the anti-submarine effort. There were to be more and stronger ship-patrols, and also air-patrols by more aircraft and airships of longer range, equipped with bombs. There were to be more and better depth-charges and hydrophones and more British submarines to hunt Germans, more protected "safe" channels and sea-areas guarded by warships, more Q-ships. But the Independently Routed Ship (IRS) sailed on down the protected lanes to her doom. To the despair of some middle-ranking staff officers and commanders at sea, there were to be no convoys. Some of them had friends in high or influential places outside the Admiralty and risked taking their cause elsewhere.

In October 1916 German submarines in all operational areas sank a total of 337,000 tons of shipping of all flags. From November to January 1917 inclusive, they accounted for another 961,000 tons. During this period the Germans were still pulling their punches in the waters round Britain for fear of American intervention in the war, but the recurrent dispute about unrestricted submarine warfare was raging again in the German High Command. Chancellor von Bethmann-Hollweg offered peace-talks in a Reichstag speech of 12 December 1916, but was rebuffed by Lloyd George in the Commons on the 19th and by an Allied Note on the 30th. President Wilson was not prepared to intercede. At a conference in the Kaiser's headquarters on 9 January 1917, the Chancellor was persuaded to agree to a declaration of unrestricted submarine warfare in a much larger war-zone with effect from February 1. Admiral Scheer and his *Führer der Unterseeboote* (High Seas Fleet submarine chief), junior Captain (soon to be Commodore) Hermann Bauer, believed they could reduce the quantity of shipping available to the British by about forty percent in six months. The High Seas Fleet was to be used to back up the new, all-out offensive as far as practicable, a complete reversal of roles between the little submarines and the capital ships they had originally been built to serve. A wide area round Britain and off the French coast, the whole of the Mediterranean and, a little later, the waters off Northern Norway (whence came Britain's iron ore), were to be open to attack without warning on all shipping. The announcement was duly made on February 1, and neutrals were given time to get home, while their countries were given designated immune channels for their own trade. The only obvious step the Germans did not take with their convoluted system of military, naval and Imperial command was to put all their submarines under one head. Bauer commanded the German-based flotillas of the High Seas Fleet, but separate commands ran those based in Flanders, on the Baltic, in the Mediterranean and in Turkish waters.

Nonetheless, freed of all restraint except what they chose, like Perière, to exercise themselves, the submarine commanders sank thirty-five ships in the first week of February (520,000 tons for the entire month, or sixty percent more than in January). That first appalling week shocked the Admiralty yet seemed to mesmerise it. It took an army officer, Lieutenant-Colonel Sir Maurice Hankey, Secretary to the Cabinet, to precipitate action. He drew up a brilliant, deceptively mild memorandum advocating the immediate introduction of convoy which he presented to Lloyd George, who summoned Carson, Jellicoe and Duff to Number Ten to read it. The admirals were unmoved; Carson, as was his wont, deferred to them but agreed to the calling of a conference with merchant skippers to sound out their views. When Jellicoe chaired this meeting on February 23, the masters were against convoy too, mainly because of the extra time and effort involved. Meanwhile, on French prompting, a limited convoy system had already been introduced on February 7, because the colliers taking British coal to France were not getting through in anything like adequate numbers. This was due not so much to submarine attacks as to the fear of them, which held up the coal-boats in port for long periods (an interesting reflection on the argument of the opponents of convoy that it would lead to unacceptable delays). The coal convoys were delicately named "controlled sailings." Beatty, cooped up in Scapa Flow with the Grand Fleet, now proclaimed himself a convert to the convoy principle, and became increasingly fretful about Admiralty tardiness in seeing the light. The Fleet's ideas on the issue were to bear fruit in a few weeks.

The Germans, who had begun 1917 with 138 boats, 105 of them operational, sank another 564,000 tons in March, a total of more than one million tons in less than nine weeks.

Back at the Admiralty, Commander R. G. H. Henderson, the officer responsible for the French coal convoys-by-any-other-name, had an idea. He was naturally interested in statistics on arrivals and departures from British ports, but found to his astonishment that there were none. He then began to wonder where the Admiralty in Churchill's time had got its proud claim that there were 5,000 shipping movements per week (arrivals plus departures). Henderson applied to the Ministry of Shipping, which was able to organise a complex but highly revealing count in a few days. Two and a half years into the most all-embracing war in history it was discovered that the magic 5,000 was wildly misleading. It had been used as a means of dismissing the importance of the loss of the odd few dozen ships as insignificant *and* of demonstrating the sheer impossibility of organising convoys for so much traffic. Yet if a dredger sailed from Yarmouth to Felixstowe, it was counted once. If it sailed back the next day it was counted again. If it then went to Harwich, it was counted a third time. If it made the reverse journey inside the same week, it would be counted six times. After checking the new figures forwards, backwards and sideways, the Shipping Ministry concluded that the true total of movements by *ocean-going* vessels, real ships of over 1,600 tons, averaged twenty arrivals and twenty departures a day. The Admiralty's 5,000, airily conjured up at the beginning of the war, had shrivelled to less than 300.

The crisis of the war at sea came as these figures began fundamentally to transform perception of its nature, the two events being intimately connected. The Germans achieved the all-time record of 881,000 tons sunk in April 1917, 564,000 of them, or more than 300 ships, British. That left Britain with some five million tons of ocean-going shipping, or about 3,200 vessels. With losses running at a good ten per day, this pointed inexorably to a loss rate of ten percent per *month*, a level of destruction which neutral shipping and new construction could not hope to make up. Of the stock of ships, 1,900 were at this stage engaged on war work, leaving only 1,300 for food. On this basis the German calculation of six months to bring Britain to her knees seems pessimistic. But on April 6 the desperate position of the Allies was transformed. The United States at last declared war, provoked by the "Zimmermann Telegram" (the State Secretary in the German Foreign Office cabled Count Bernstorff, the Ambassador in Washington, about seeking an alliance with Mexico: it was intercepted and decoded by Room 40) – and by the unrelenting submarine campaign.

On Beatty's insistence, convoy was introduced in April on the vital Scandinavian route, where shipping losses were running at an incredible twenty-five percent. From April 21 losses quickly declined to one quarter of one percent, or one hundredth of the previous total.

Angered by the Admiralty's "amazing miscalculation," Lloyd George decided to take direct action. "The blunder on which [Admiralty] policy was based was an arithmetical mix-up which would not have been perpetrated by an ordinary clerk in a shipping office," he wrote later. Jellicoe brought another long memorandum to Cabinet on April 23, stating that "the situation calls for immediate action" but still not mentioning convoy. Lloyd George therefore raised it, citing Beatty and the American Admiral William Sims as being in favour of convoy. Jellicoe said the matter was "under consideration." At another Cabinet meeting on the 25th, Lloyd George announced, after consulting Carson, that he proposed to visit the Admiralty and take action on convoys. He told the Board that he wanted to investigate all methods of anti-submarine warfare because it was clear there was not enough co-ordination of effort, and that he would summon any officer he saw fit to give information. Coming from the Prime Minister, this was an ultimatum to introduce convoy or resign. On the 26th, Admiral Duff concluded that "the time has arrived when we must be ready to introduce a comprehensive scheme of convoy at any moment" and sent a note to Jellicoe, who approved on the 27th. When Lloyd George arrived as threatened on the 30th, he found there was no battle left to fight.

Although many grievous losses at sea were still to follow, the decision was the salvation of the United Kingdom and the Allied war effort. An enormous amount of work had to be done before a comprehensive convoy system covering all the major trade routes was in place. Not the least of the difficulties was the reluctance of the United States Navy to follow the newly converted British down the convoy route. It was extremely fortunate for the Allies that Rear-Admiral Sims, sent to command USN forces in Europe, was both one of the ablest of American admirals and a firm believer in convoy. But the convoying of ships on the all-important transatlantic route was introduced very slowly, with the first "experimental" convoy sailing eastward from Hampton Roads only on May 24. Two ships could not keep up and were sent back to Halifax, Nova Scotia; one of them was torpedoed. The other ten were shepherded over by a single cruiser without further incident, to be met by eight destroyers from Devonport for protection in British waters. To the subsequent amazement of the Admiralty, ships and escorts perfected the technique of zig-zagging as one while keeping station, something most naval officers had thought beyond the wit of merchant captains. The masters had to suppress their normal instinct for giving any other ship a wide berth and learn the new disciplines of steady speed and sailing with ships about 1,200 yards away on either side (and as near as 600 yards ahead and astern). Their compensation for this was that the strain of keeping a constant lookout for submarines passed to the escorts; all the masters had to do was to keep a careful eye on the convoy Commodore and his signal halyard. This meant that they and their watch-officers and crew all got more sleep than they had had in years. Other experiments with convoy on the Gibraltar route also went well.

The losses of shipping duly fell in May, but only by a good quarter overall, to the still stupendous total of 600,000 tons; they rose again in June to 685,000 tons. In July, with the Admiralty and the Department of the Navy in Washington dragging their feet about implementing convoy universally, the sinkings went down again to 550,000 tons. The majority of ships were still sailing independently, and the submarines had plenty of targets. At first inward-bound ships were far more likely to be organised into convoys than outward-bound. It comes as no surprise to discover that the bulk of the losses occurred among the independently routed, outward-bound vessels – even the Admiralty noticed the difference. By the end of June a Convoy Section was set up under the Admiralty's Trade Division, headed by Fleet-Paymaster H. W. E. Manisty as "Organising Manager, Convoys." In September the Section was subordinated to the Director of Mercantile Movements, Captain F. A. Whitehead, the first bearer of this title since the eighteenth century, whose appointment signalled the reversion of the Admiralty to its ancient and proper role as guardian of all shipping in war. The Convoy Section worked hand-in-glove with its namesake at the Ministry of Shipping, headed by Mr Norman Leslie. A chart-room was set up showing the position of each convoy at sea and its past and future course.

By this time the future Grand-Admiral Karl Dönitz was a submariner himself. He describes graphically in his memoirs the effect on his service of the introduction of convoys:

> The oceans at once became bare and empty; for long periods at a time the U-boats, operating individually, would see nothing at all; and then, suddenly, up would loom a huge concourse of ships, thirty or fifty or more of them, surrounded by an escort of warships of all types . . . The lone U-boat might well sink one or two of the ships, or even several, but that was but a poor percentage of the whole. The convoy would steam on . . . bringing a rich cargo of foodstuffs and raw materials safely to port.

The sudden rarity of attacking opportunities caused by convoy made submarine crews work until they dropped with exhaustion to make the most of them, often at high risk, said Dönitz. One effect of convoying was to force submarines to put out many more wireless signals to base and to each other, which significantly increased British chances of interception. These frequent position-reports enabled Room 40, working closely with the convoy chart-room, to give tips for diverting convoys away from known submarine positions. How many ships this saved cannot be guessed, there being no reliable means of computing the effect of preventive measures; that diversion saved large numbers, however, is beyond doubt. Prevention may be better than cure, but it is even less appealing to the "offensive" spirit than the "defensive" tactic of convoy. Once the paranoically secretive Director of Naval Intelligence, Rear-Admiral Sir Reginald Hall, let Room 40 take a hand in the anti-submarine measures, it helped the chart-room to plot the Germans and the convoys together on a chart measuring nine feet by six.

With the reluctant admirals making much more fuss about the odd ships lost in convoy than they had ever done about the monthly national catastrophe before convoys were in widespread use, a disaster which occurred in October 1917 led to many cries of, "I told you so." By then the Scandinavian convoys had reduced losses on the route to an insignificant level, to the justifiable satisfaction of Beatty at Scapa Flow. In the second week of October, Room 40 got wind of a flurry of naval movement in the German North Sea ports and, as was its wont, told Beatty what it thought he ought to know, which was rather less than he actually needed (the same treatment was meted out to Jellicoe during Jutland). But Beatty sent forty-two ships – thirty cruisers and twelve destroyers – to sea well south of the convoy routes in case of a move by the High Seas Fleet. The Germans sent out two, the light cruisers

Bremse and *Brummer*. Room 40 knew, but assuming they were to lay mines did not tell Beatty, whose ships continued to patrol with no idea of what they were looking for.

Meanwhile a convoy of twelve ships from Bergen in Norway, escorted by the destroyers *Mary Rose* and *Strongbow*, was on the short run to Lerwick in the Shetland Islands on the same morning, the 17th. When they were just sixty-five miles from safety, the German cruisers appeared at high speed. They were initially mistaken for British until they opened fire at optimum range on the *Strongbow* (Lieutenant-Commander Edward Brooke), which had no time to fire back before being crippled by the Germans' greatly superior guns. Pausing only to fire two torpedoes, which missed, the forty-five survivors of the hail of gunfire took to the boats, which were also fired on, and were later picked up, the badly wounded Brooke among them, by a trawler. *Mary Rose* (Lieutenant-Commander Charles Fox) came rushing back from her position seven miles ahead of the convoy in the belief that the *Strongbow* had opened fire on one of the many German submarines that were wont to pass through the area. The German cruisers were engaged in shooting up the convoy when the destroyer opened fire from 3,000 yards. Fox tried to draw the Germans away from the merchantmen but all he drew was a few minutes of their concentrated fire until the forward magazine of his ship was hit and the *Mary Rose* blew up, with the loss of her captain and all but ten of her crew. In another forty-five minutes the Germans sank nine of the twelve ships in the convoy, now completely unprotected, and left for home at 8.20 a.m. The tonnage lost amounted to 10,248, equivalent to about one-third of an average day's loss in April 1917.

What became known to the British as the "*Mary Rose* convoy" (Fox had been senior officer) was a useful coup for Admiral Scheer, who had been considering an attack on the Scandinavian route, within easy reach of the German North Sea ports, for some time. The neutral press attacked British carelessness as strongly as German brutality and the Admiralty ordered an inquiry. But all the disaster had shown was that convoy was not a panacea, especially not against a much superior force of surface-warships. New thought was given to escort-tactics in such circumstances. It would have made no difference if the destroyers had used their superior speed to stay clear of the enemy while calling for support (provided they had been more alert in the first place), and less damage would have been done to their charges if they had been ordered to scatter. The controversy died down in Britain by the end of October, despite the fact that 460,000 tons of shipping were lost during the month, compared with 345,000 in September (mainly due to the even greater tardiness in the introduction of convoys to the Mediterranean).

The Germans continued to send out surface-raiders from time to time against the Scandinavian convoys, completely destroying one with its escort in the middle of December. The Grand Fleet gave heavier and heavier support until Scheer saw a chance of achieving the old German ambition of destroying a substantial element of it by sending a superior force against it. The last sortie of the High Seas Fleet, complete with battlecruisers, three squadrons of battleships and escorting light forces, set out to attack a large convoy on 23 April 1918, in the hope of also catching a British squadron or perhaps the battlecruisers. Scheer imposed wireless silence to conceal his preparations but got his timing wrong. By the time the Grand Fleet left its new base in the Firth of Forth in the afternoon, a broken-down battlecruiser and the absence of a convoy to attack had already led the Germans to turn back.

One of the legacies of Lloyd George's descent on the Admiralty a year earlier had been the establishment of a much-needed Department of Statistics in May 1917. The same officers whose social élitism led them to disdain convoys as "infra dig" sneered at this plebeian innovation – especially when the first Director of Statistics turned out to be a railway administrator from the Army, Lieutenant-Colonel George Beharrell. Despite the ignominious "5,000 ships" fiasco, the sneers continued well beyond September 1917, by which time Beharrell and his men had assembled enough figures to put the value of convoys beyond dispute for anyone with an open mind. Although a full ocean-convoy system was not in place until November, the rate of loss among convoyed ships for 1917 was about 1.2 percent of all sailings, compared with the twenty-five percent of the worst days of April – and the fifteen percent sustained over the year by independently routed ships. Beharrell's General Review of January 1917 showed that convoys in home waters had reduced losses there by ninety percent, and that submarine attacks had declined in monthly frequency by thirty-five percent between February 1, the opening of the unrestricted campaign, and the end of the year.

By that time an important milestone had been reached: the rate of destruction of submarines in the last quarter drew level with the rate of construction in Germany, thanks largely to anti-submarine minelaying and "kills" by escorts and patrols. But it was not until June 1918 that the shipbuilding rate at last overtook mercantile losses at sea for the first time since the unrestricted campaign began. We may take this as the true moment of victory, but the threat from the submarine was never extinguished: Allied losses still averaged more that 140,000 tons per month in the last six months of the war, even though air escort was routine by this time; and the submarine destruction-rate never overwhelmed the rate of new building. There have been narrower strategic victories – but surely not many. The balance of the First World War at sea was that the British blockade of Germany exceeded the effect of the submarine counter-attack by a small but decisive margin.

A number of questions remain to be answered. If, for example, convoy was the solution to the submarine problem, why did shipping losses persist at a disturbing rate until the very end of the war? The answer is that the system was introduced gradually, first for inward-bound ships on some routes, then for outward-bound, then on more routes, until in the closing months ninety percent of all sailings were in convoy (and the bulk of the losses were among those which were not). Only in the last five months of hostilities did a full-scale coastal convoy-system complement the ocean convoy-network. This glaring gap was closed in response to the German shift away from the protected shipping on the open sea to the still largely unprotected (and much more dense) traffic along the coast.

Why all those admirals could not see the advantages of convoy and had to be dragged kicking and screaming, not into the twentieth century but back to the eighteenth, is a much more complex mystery. Undoubtedly the invention of ships that did not depend on the vagaries of the wind for their motive power had something to do with it. Sailing a ship from A to B had become a highly predictable business and therefore somehow "safer" because so much more orderly. The open sea was also so vast that an independently routed ship and one of a small number of submarines or surface-raiders seemed mathematically unlikely to cross paths except at certain high-density areas for shipping, which could surely be adequately protected by the 5,000 vessels, large and small, eventually allocated to patrol. The fact that the most consistently and heavily convoyed ships of all, the prized capital ships of the Grand Fleet with their destroyer screens and cruisers to protect the destroyers, would never go out unescorted, and that troopships were also heavily covered, escaped the notice of most of Their Lordships of the Board of Admiralty. Their adherence to the spirit of Nelson was highly selective. They remembered the zest in attack of the greatest English admiral and his contemporaries and overlooked his readiness to break the rules of conducting naval engagements when he saw advantage in it. They also overlooked the fact that many great past naval battles had arisen from the escort of convoys, and that merchant ships were actually forbidden by law by the end of the Napoleonic Wars to sail except in convoy during wartime. Further, between the selectively remembered days of greatest naval glory and the First World War there had been the Industrial Revolution. This took Britain to the apogee of her power in the world but never cured upper-class disdain for "trade," those engaged in it – and by extension, perhaps, in naval circles where only officers of good family won acceptance, the merchant ships which carried it. Those who made fortunes in industry became country gentlemen and sent their sons to Eton. There and at other exclusive schools they were taught to play fair. Britain then tried to apply its concept of fair play by international convention to warfare itself – Clausewitz rewritten by the Marquis of Queensberry. It was not understood that the underdog (as Germany was at sea) might take the view that a "fair" fight as defined by a superior opponent was indistinguishable from suicide, a fact known to any schoolboy subjected to bullying.

The disdain of mercantile convoy defended by His Majesty's men of war seems redolent of development arrested at the stage of adolescence. Was not the job of the Royal Navy to seek out and destroy the enemy, rather than skulking about the ocean like a shepherd with his bleating flock? The admirals of 1914 were under the impossible stress of opposed pressures as well as being products of their time and their society. They believed that the best form of defence was attack; yet in their book the loss of a warship was the ultimate sin, which meant no risks, massive escort for ships of the line and no dangerous individual initiatives. One of the miracles of the First World War at sea was the high morale of the lower decks, which survived so many setbacks and disappointments, making it possible to launch the heroic failure of the Zeebrugge Raid against the Flanders submarine bases as late as April 1918.

Being an armchair admiral, an occupation open to anyone with a little time and access to a few books, is infinitely easier than the real thing. Hindsight is the greatest advantage of the chairbound variety but can so easily become a source of delusions, not least of grandeur. One of the main criticisms of many admirals in both world wars has been that they did not grasp the fact that convoys were not defensive but rather the opposite: that the best form of attack is defence. If the naval enemy's objective is seaborne trade, as has historically been the case in wars with Britain, then the best chance of a crack at the enemy is to put your warships between him and his target. Convoys with escort fulfil the important military principles of concentration and economy of force. If you cannot catch the submarine by looking for it all over the ocean, force it to come to you and fight on your terms. But there are grounds for believing that describing convoy as the best, indeed the only viable, *offensive* strategy in seaborne trade-warfare is itself a play on words designed to appease those who still (as they do) doubt its value. There should be no need for shame or apology in saying that convoy is in essence a method of *defence* of trade which happily offers the best chance of *counter*-attacking the forces trying to disrupt it. The primary purpose of convoy is the safe and timely arrival of shipping; destroying (as distinct from evading or frustrating) those who would interfere is secondary, a luxury for those with warships to spare.

Before we move on from the largely forgotten menace posed to Britain's survival by the first German submarine campaign, not forgetting the lessons it offered (to those willing to learn) for the second, a word needs to be said about the contribution of the other new weapon of the period, the aircraft. Of ships in convoy which also had air-cover, increasingly common in the last year of the war, only *five* were lost to submarine attack. These early aeroplanes and airships had no weapon with which they could sink or even seriously damage a submarine. With his prescient bent, Fisher not only foresaw the threat of the submarine but also the value of aircraft in countering it. In the First World War their value lay exclusively in submarine-spotting, which nevertheless rapidly became a serious deterrent to the Germans. As their numbers increased so did the numbers of submarines sunk, until the Germans were forced to hunt in areas out of range of the primitive machines of the day. Unfortunately these crucial facts were not appreciated at the time, especially after the formation in April 1918 of the Royal Air Force with its flying monopoly.

The scale of the airborne effort against the German submarine was, however, to become enormous. Originally the non-rigid airship bore the brunt as the earliest military aircraft lacked performance and endurance. The "submarine-scout" airships which needed reasonable weather conditions but could go much further out to sea than aircraft, totalled twenty-nine by the end of 1915 and sixty a year later, with twenty-seven more on order. At the end of 1916, with the creation of the Anti-Submarine Division at the Admiralty, the air-effort was reorganised and partly integrated with the anti-submarine campaign as a whole, and a rapid expansion in aircraft-construction was ordered. The focal points of the escalating struggle were now the Western Approaches to southern England, the Irish Sea and the Channel, where the ships converged from all over the world. Seaplane-bases were set up in South Wales, Cornwall and the Scilly Isles. In the black month of April 1917 land-based aircraft were brought in for the first time, as not enough seaplanes were available for the increasing number of patrols. The next step was the provision of air-cover for specific convoys on the Dutch and French shipping routes. Flying-boats searched the route to Holland before ships sailed, and then provided close escort to the convoy. Not a single ship was lost on this route after the introduction of convoys, although the Dutch coast lay between the Germans' home bases and their submarine nests in Flanders. By the end of 1917 just one had been lost to the entire submarine effort from all the ships sailed in convoys with air-escort. As the New Year came, 291 seaplanes, twenty-three aeroplanes and about 100 airships were reserved exclusively for anti-submarine work. At the end of the war in November, there were 285 seaplanes, 272 aeroplanes and 100 airships, a total of 657.

The Germans responded to the growing use of aircraft by installing "altiscopes" – upward-looking periscopes to search the sky before surfacing – and changed their tactics. For a while they moved away from the profitable (because busiest) coastal waters to the outer Western Approaches, which could be reached by only a few aircraft. They also gave up surface attacks by day, especially on convoys. When the submarines moved out towards the leaner (but safer) pickings of the Atlantic proper, the Royal Navy wanted to use adapted bombers of the longest range then available. The brand-new Royal Air Force however succeeded in keeping all such aircraft for long-range bombing. They were used against the submarine bases in Flanders with increasing frequency and weight of attack throughout the war. German operations were not affected and not one submarine was sunk or even significantly damaged. But the Naval Staff concluded that whereas patrols by aircraft over the open sea were a failure, their use to escort convoys in the First World War had been "very successful as an anti-submarine measure."

The first Atlantic Campaign only just failed to bring Britain to her knees: 4,837 ships of 11,135,000 tons had been sent to the bottom, a monumental total which deserved a better monument in lessons learned and applied than it was to get before the second campaign. The Merchant Navy lost 15,313 men, or about five and a half percent of its strength, mainly to the submarine offensive, and the Royal Navy lost 22,811, or four percent, about one-third of them in the defence of trade against the submarine. According to the Naval Staff History of the Second World War, "no comprehensive British history of the U-boat and anti-submarine operations in 1914–18 was written after the First World War," although a few specialised papers were written and some lectures given to officers. Otherwise there was only Commander Rollo Appleyard, RNVR, a civil engineer on the Admiralty staff, who started work in 1917 on the first analysis ever made of why convoys are effective and how to defend them with surface escorts. *The Elements of Convoy Defence in Submarine Warfare* proved, among other lessons which had to be painfully relearned after 1939, that bigger convoys were safer than small ones. Unfortunately the monograph proved impenetrable for all but the most numerate and persistent of naval officers. John Winton, the leading historian and advocate of convoys, describes it as "like an account of the Trojan War written by Euclid." It was also a naval "Confidential Book" with restricted circulation. Appleyard's painstaking findings should have been subsumed into a tactical manual and made compulsory reading for every officer in the relevant branches of the Navy. It was scrapped altogether in 1939, just when it might have come into its own.

Without excessive hindsight we may now list a number of points arising from the first submarine campaign which are of direct relevance to our main concern, the second. These are the lessons which were paid for in blood and unprecedented destruction during the First World War at sea.

The potential of the submarine was seriously underestimated by both sides before the war, leaving the Germans with far fewer boats than their advocates felt to be necessary, yet catching the British almost completely unprepared. Not only did the British wilfully refuse to recognise the ancient principle of convoy until the last moment; the Americans, when they began to make a significant contribution at sea, at first refused to learn the lesson so painfully and belatedly absorbed by the British. The weakness of the Naval Staff, founded only in 1912, led to disdain for, and neglect of, such useful if unglamorous tools as statistical analysis. Thus the British failed to note such matters as where ships were when they sank a submarine (escorting a convoy or, much less likely, on area patrol). Nobody noticed that the number of ships lost related directly to the number of submarines at sea, a factor which was much more important in the crisis of 1917 than the actual resumption of unrestricted submarine warfare in February of that year. Convoys were resisted because it was said they caused enormous delays to shipping, but the work involved in separately dispatching independently routed ships was far greater and the hold-ups cumulatively much worse. After the introduction of convoys, it was not noted that as the number of ships sailed in them rose, the number of ships sunk fell. Not enough attention was paid to the elementary principle that submarine commanders invariably went for the easiest target available to them.

On the German side, vacillation was an outstanding factor in the ultimate, though very narrow, failure to press home the advantage gained by unrestricted submarine warfare. The Kaiser was not the man to miss an opportunity for changing his mind when one presented itself; and the factions for and against total war at sea took turns in holding the upper hand. This and the diversion of submarine effort from British waters to the Mediterranean in September 1915 gave the Allies respite from time to time just when they needed it. In the end the Germans took all the opprobrium attached to unrestricted warfare without finding the last ounce of resolution to persist with their ruthless strategy undeterred: there was no thought in Berlin that one might as well finish the job. This was in part a major victory for British propaganda. The submarine campaign also went full circle: the boats started and finished in British coastal waters, because that was where the greatest number of ships was to be found. In between, each successive area chosen as focus for the onslaught on commerce was favoured because it was the place where defensive measures were weakest at the time, or where conditions were safest.

During the First World War nearly all the main principles of anti-submarine warfare were discovered. They are: underwater detection by sound, the depth-charge, location of enemy boats by their own radio-signals (active detection by radar was to follow in the 1930s), and of course the use of aircraft. To these must be added the value of intelligence, important in every aspect of warfare. The Admiralty's Room 40 did priceless work by correlating data about ships and submarines on a single plot and even towards the end diverting convoys on the basis of interception of submarine wireless transmissions. Although the *Magdeburg's* code book was an invaluable stroke of luck, it was not even necessary to understand an enciphered transmission in order to exploit it by using the signal itself to pinpoint the sender's position.

The Germans built 344 submarines during the war to add to the mere twenty-eight with which they began it. At the end a further 226 were under construction with 212 more planned. They commissioned ten new boats in 1914 after the war began, fifty-two in 1915, 108 in 1916, ninety-four in 1917 and eighty in the last ten months of the war in 1918. Only in the last six months did the number sunk per month exceed the rate of replacement, a development which more or less coincided with the moment when the Allies were able to outbuild shipping losses. The figures vary from source to source, but about 178 submarines were lost with upwards of 6,000 men, and a similar number of boats surrendered at the end. A handful were scuttled. In terms of manpower and results, the losses to Germany in the submarine campaign of the "war to end all wars," the greatest conflict in history, had been tiny; in terms of money and material, the submarine fleet was a first-class investment, especially when compared with the incalculable cost of the losses in ships, goods and war-matériel suffered mainly by the British. It beggared the British Empire and very nearly bankrupted it, and made inevitable the transfer of power across the Atlantic to the United States, including the seapower which had for so long been the foundation of Britain's standing in the world. This is a staggering achievement for a weapon which had only been a gleam in the eye of a handful of inventors a few short years before the war broke out. Small wonder that the British and their allies required a defeated Germany neither to build nor to operate submarines in its drastically limited postwar navy.

2

DISARMAMENT FAILS, 1919–1933

Versailles – revolution in Germany – Soviet ambivalence – Western equivocation – the German Navy adjusts – the great submarine fraud – the German Navy revives – the British Navy declines – the American Navy awakes – naval arms "limitation" – Asdic – naval aviation – 1933 as a turning-point

THE Treaty of Versailles, which at the end of June 1919 formalised the Armistice of 11 November 1918, placed strict limits on the size and composition of the German armed forces, including a total ban on submarines and aircraft. The bulk of the High Seas Fleet, interned in Scapa Flow under the Armistice, was declared forfeit but evaded this fate by scuttling itself in the greatest maritime act of material self-destruction on record. Of the seventy-four ships interned, fifty-two actually went to the bottom on 21 June 1919, to the undeclared relief of the British. They privately saw the underused warships as a threat to the Royal Navy's supremacy, which they were now concerned to preserve against American competition, no matter how the German fleet might have been divided among the victorious powers. Publicly however the Allies expressed outrage and demanded reparations for the loss of the unwanted fleet so conveniently disposed of by its owners just before the Treaty was signed. They scoured the prostrate Reich for such items as floating docks and all manner of harbour equipment and took it away. Versailles limited the army of what had so recently been the world's greatest military power to 100,000 men; the navy, which had been second only to the British, was limited to 15,000 regular ratings with 1,500 officers. It was to have no more than six armoured ships of a maximum displacement of 10,000 tons each, six cruisers of 6,000, twelve destroyers of 800 and twelve torpedo-boats of no more than 200 tons each. As we shall see, these restrictions were to become a challenge to the considerable ingenuity of German ship-designers, builders and suppliers, to say nothing of the naval officers who soon began to look for ways of getting round and undermining Versailles, long before Adolf Hitler became a name to conjure with.

Politically, the Reich was rocked by the leftist revolutionary wave which had arisen in the last months of the war and led the Germans to sue for peace. In the Imperial Navy it took the form of a generalised mutiny; in the Army, rebellion by units up to divisional level led General Erich Ludendorff and his colleagues to advise the Kaiser's last Government under Chancellor Max Prince of Baden to seek the Armistice. The social unrest in Germany itself, caused by severe food shortages and civilian demoralisation after more than four years of war (largely the result of the British blockade), enabled arch-conservatives such as Ludendorff to make the specious and highly dangerous claim that the Army had been "stabbed in the back." The Kaiser fled to the Netherlands two days before the Armistice as Germany teetered on the verge of following the example of the Bolshevik Soviets two years earlier. Since it was the Social Democrats (SPD) who eventually took over the reins of government after the war, the officer-corps found it easy to blame the "Sozis" for Germany's defeat, conveniently obscuring the fact that the Army on the Western Front had itself cracked and made a continuation of the war impossible. The evil myth of the stab in the back, widely believed and soon to be masterfully exploited by Hitler, combined with the extremely harsh provisions of Versailles to form the political acid which began eroding the foundations of the first German republic (named after Weimar where its constituent assembly met) from the outset. Other elements were soon added to the corrosive brew.

The formation of the German Communist Party mainly from the SPD Left gave the Russians a fifth column which they manipulated so ineptly that it played into Nazi hands – for a time it allied with them against the SPD, identified by both as the main enemy. A united German Left would have been the only force apart from the Army strong enough to defeat Nazism. Soviet dogmatism and dislike of the "bourgeois" SPD and Stalin's interference in German politics aided Hitler's rise to power, with all that this was to entail for the Soviet Union itself.

At the same time Stalin helped resurgent German militarism to train secretly with tanks and aircraft inside the Soviet Union, a massive breach of Versailles. This was revealed to a generally indifferent world in 1926 by *The Manchester Guardian*, which also reported co-operation in arms development. This extraordinary, not to say insane, dual policy towards Germany culminated in the Nazi–Soviet Pact of August 1939, enabling Hitler and Stalin to carve up Poland and the Baltic states and leaving the Germans free to concentrate in the West when war broke out with Britain and France. The Russians hated Germany for imposing the Treaty of Brest-Litovsk on Lenin in 1917 as well as for intervening in the Civil War after the Revolution. Some apologists see in Stalin's policy towards Germany a long-term grand strategy for the eventual demolition of the only nation in Europe capable of standing up to Soviet power, especially if it could find allies in the West. While it is true that the invasion of Russia in summer 1941 sealed Hitler's military fate, the loss of twenty million Russians in the ensuing war does seem a price out of all proportion, even for someone with Stalin's notorious indifference to mass-killings. We may note that Brest-Litovsk was as harsh as Versailles and thus the best moral argument against those many Germans who complained so loud and long about the latter.

We may also note that the bizarre contradiction in Soviet policy between political subversion and military aid was matched by the less spectacular, if no less erratic, conduct towards Germany of the victorious Allies. French vengefulness was a principal motive for the imposition of an enormous war-reparations burden on Germany which crippled its economy and led to the unique "Great Inflation" of 1923. Soon afterwards the Americans took the lead in easing the reparations problem, although the worldwide slump which followed upon the Wall Street Crash of 1929 was to ensure that postwar economic woes affected Germany more than any other country in the capitalist world, providing political ammunition for the Nazis. Just as the Kaiser always demanded "a place in the sun" for Germany (what that meant was never fully defined), Hitler wanted *Lebensraum*. From 1933, under the Nazis, Germany once again became the cuckoo in the European nest, always demanding. Yet the wartime Allies, this time led by the British, opted out of resisting Hitler's territorial demands (which could have been nipped in the bud by a firm response to his precarious adventure of reoccupying the Rhineland). They opted instead for Appeasement, nowadays a dirty word but undoubtedly a highly popular policy in Britain at the time; and the French seemed, if anything, even more prepared to pursue peace at very nearly any price, while the Americans became strongly isolationist. The only way in which the "German Question" of the period between the wars could have been answered so as to reduce postwar tension in Europe would have been for the Allies to follow the retreating Germans over their border in 1918 to occupy Berlin and the whole country, as they finally did in 1945 with the Russians to the fore. We may conclude this brief, introductory overview of Germany's history between the wars with the crucial observation that almost every German politician and party, Left as much as Right, opposed Versailles, the unravelling of which led to the Second World War. There was to be much vicious political in-fighting, on and off the streets, in Germany during the period, conducted by private armies of Right and Left; but if there was any element of consensus in the war among the parties, it was hatred of Versailles. As we now go back to consider the clandestine growth of Germany's second navy, we should not lose sight of this underlying truth.

In November 1918 the German Navy effectively disappeared from the seas. Many of the men it was permitted to retain went into two Marine brigades, often after service in the *Freikorps* (volunteer units of ex-soldiers formed to fight the revolutionaries and soon notorious for their brutality). The brigades, led by Wilfried von Loewenfeld and Hermann Ehrhardt, naval officers and former *Freikorps* leaders, served as infantry and were hostile to the Republic.

The Ehrhardt Brigade marched on Berlin in support of the abortive "Kapp Putsch" and occupied the capital. This attempted coup in March 1920 was prompted by a Government order to disband the Berlin garrison commanded by General von Lüttwitz, of which Ehrhardt's formation was part. The plot was foiled by a general strike lasting five days, and both the SPD Government and the command of the *Reichswehr* (state defence force, including both army and navy) were reshuffled. This victory for republicanism over reaction was frittered away by the indecisiveness of Chancellor Hermann Müller's administration, which enabled the military to consolidate its position in the state amid outbreaks of serious disorder in many parts of the country, notably the Ruhr and Bavaria. Within the *Reichswehr*, therefore, dominated by General Hans von Seeckt as head of the Army Command, the officer-corps was full of anti-democratic reactionaries. This applied at least as much to the underoccupied Navy as to the Army.

From 1920 the Navy, despite a very high turnover of manpower at all levels caused by lack of opportunity in a drastically reduced and under-employed service, began to turn its attention away from politics towards its proper business of manning ships. Some of the elderly, usually prewar, ships still in German hands were recommissioned and in 1921 the first postwar order for a new ship, a 6,000-ton cruiser, was placed. She was commissioned in January 1925 as the *Emden*, a name associated with both the zenith and the nadir of the Imperial Navy's surface role in the First World War (the first *Emden* had a brilliant career raiding commerce in the Indian Ocean; from the second was issued the order to scuttle the High Seas Fleet at Scapa Flow). By the time she was launched, the cut-down Navy had more or less settled down to its reduced role, recovered from its wartime failures and the ensuing mutiny which had aroused popular distrust of Germany's junior service – and could look forward to a steady though modest flow of new ships.

The High Seas Fleet which had cost so much and achieved so little – the apple of the Kaiser's eye which helped to topple him with its mutiny – was a main cause of the Navy's low esteem in the immediate aftermath of Germany's defeat. The Army, as we have seen, managed to evade this kind of opprobrium. Even the Kapp Putsch was blamed on the Navy rather than the Army, thanks to Ehrhardt's prominent role. But there was one important area in which the Navy had more than justified itself – in its successes against enemy trade. Ironically these were achieved by forces regarded as mere adjuncts to the glorious but ultimately useless battlefleet. Admiral Graf Spee's cruiser-squadron in the Pacific had inflicted the first defeat in more than a century on the Royal Navy at the Battle of Coronel in 1914 (even if he was destroyed by a superior avenging force off the Falklands shortly afterwards), and the revered *Emden* had also been under his flag. Merchant ships converted to auxiliary cruisers had scored brief but spectacular runs of success in the Atlantic. But it was the German submarine which turned out to be the most formidable and successful weapon deployed by the Kaiser. It was narrowly frustrated in the end; but Germany finished the war with by far the most profound experience and expertise in this new and terrible form of warfare. The submarine may have begun as a little-regarded addition to the battlefleet; but its part in the war marked a return to first principles in naval warfare, though in a new and deadly guise: that the main purpose of navies is bound up with seaborne trade, to defend or to attack it. The German Navy was not about to throw away its enormous lead in submarine warfare, whatever Versailles might say. The result was a remarkable conspiracy by naval officers and shipbuilders to stay ahead of the game. It began before the ink was dry on the hated Treaty and continued for sixteen years until Hitler abrogated Versailles, when the Germans stunned the world by commissioning a flotilla of twelve boats just four months after the Anglo-German Naval Agreement allowed them to have submarines again.

A total of 176 submarines was delivered to Britain in 1918 and eventually distributed among the British, Americans, French, Italians and Japanese, all of whose postwar building programmes were considerably influenced by the booty. A few others unable to make the surrender voyage and all those under construction were broken up in Germany under the eyes of the Allied Control Commission. As soon as that was complete the U-boat Inspectorate and the U-boat Office were disbanded; but in 1920 a new U-boat Section was set up within an Inspectorate of Torpedoes and Mines at Kiel, ostensibly to collate documents for the archives and for the official history, as well as to study anti-submarine technique. This too was wound up in 1922. But the new Navy kept in touch with former submariners – and the yards with their skilled workers. The shipbuilders moreover had not been required to surrender their plans and drawings. The builders, with the willing co-operation of the Naval Directorate, discreetly began to offer designs and advice to foreign countries. The first customer was Japan, which bought plans for two types of large submarine in 1920 and built them under German expert supervision. A "retired" wartime submarine commander was duly supplied for the trials when the time came. In 1921 Argentina called in German advisers to help create a new submarine service of ten boats. Early in 1922 the Italians and the Swedes took German advice in the construction of their latest submarines. Business was beginning to look positively brisk, and the Navy asked three of the main German wartime submarine builders (two of them owned by the steel and arms conglomerate Krupp of Essen) to form a consortium for the Argentine project and similar ventures. The idea was to provide a complete service from drawing-board to sea-trials. It would have the double advantage of bringing in revenue, as well as keeping German skills abreast of developments and continuously occupied. Such a company formed specifically to build submarines, even if exclusively abroad, was bound to conflict with the anti-submarine provisions of Versailles. The yards had legitimate work of many kinds in general shipbuilding, but a consortium solely devoted to submarine construction could hardly be set up in Germany.

So in July 1922 the German specialists went to the Netherlands and founded a company called *NV Ingenieurskantoor voor Scheepsbouw* (Engineer-office for Shipbuilding Ltd or Inc), or IvS. This innocuously named establishment had as its technical director Dr Hans Techel, a leading figure in German submarine construction, and its commercial director was Commander (retired) Ulrich Blum, late of the Imperial Navy's submarine service. The supervisory board was manned by directors from the three yards, each of which provided a modest 4,000 guilders as start-up capital. The neutral Dutch were hesitant about permitting the formal company registration of IvS, so at first it operated surreptitiously from an office in Kiel, until it was able to move to The Hague in summer 1925 – where it stayed until the German surrender in May 1945. The bright hopes which had prompted the foundation of IvS soon dwindled. Having sifted through the drawings, plans and other papers left over from the war, the company based its first tenders for overseas contracts on tried and tested designs; but the Argentines changed their minds and the Italian project fell through.

But all was not lost. A certain *Kapitänleutnant* Wilhelm Canaris, veteran of the Spee squadron, secret service work in Spain and the Mediterranean campaign in which he had commanded a submarine, and of the Kapp Putsch, was detached from his staff job in the Baltic Fleet office and sent to Spain to seek contracts. IvS wanted a share in the Spanish submarine-building programme involving forty boats. The future chief of Hitler's military intelligence service made much progress, but fierce foreign competition, Spanish wariness of the Krupp connection and political problems led Spain too to cancel its entire plan.

All these frustrations convinced IvS that it could not compete without proper financial backing in quantities only governments could find in those hard times – the struggling shipyards could not do it and the Navy was constrained by Versailles (officially it had no connection with IvS). The solution was to mount a clandestine operation with close resemblances to the most elaborate commercial frauds. A slush-fund was created from the secret budget of the Navy's Sea Transport Section under Captain Walter Lohmann, who then set up a dummy company called Mentor Bilanz as a link between the Navy and IvS to handle finance, and another called Tebeg to deal with the technical side. Both were run by "retired" naval officers, and in addition to helping with competition for foreign orders they were secretly to choose designs and prepare plans for the creation of a new *German* submarine arm. The two fake companies were conveniently sited in the same Berlin building as the Sea Transport Section, which was either brazen or careless or possibly both. At the same time Canaris successfully suggested the formation of a new and secret submarine department in the naval command, disguised as the *Anti*-submarine Defence Section under Captain

Arno Spindler. All this was done during 1925 when IvS was at last able to open its head office in The Hague.

Two years later the Lohmann network began to crumble. The secret involved too many people for it to last, the press got wind of financial irregularities and questions began to be asked in the Reichstag about misuse of Government funds. The key issue was inept speculation with public funds to try to increase an overstrained secret military budget, which brought down Gessler, the Minister of Defence. The brunt fell upon Lohmann himself, diverting attention from the real purpose of his fraudulent machinations. The Lohmann Scandal was about money, not submarines, and as the devious captain bowed out, his department, Tebeg and Mentor Bilanz were all wound up by spring 1928. But the subterranean submarine-work carried on regardless after streamlining and simplification. A new dummy company called Igewit GmbH (an acronym for Engineer-office for Economics and Technology Ltd or Inc.) was set up and a new name given to Lohmann's old department within the naval administration. Between them they took over the work of Lohmann's section and the two earlier "front" companies in the submarine field. Most of their staffs carried on as before, and when Spindler left the "anti-submarine" section in 1929, Lieutenant (retired, of course) Hans Schottky, already effective head of the post-Lohmann section in the naval administration and thereby of Igewit, also succeeded him in running the submarine department in the naval command. All this made him, surely, one of history's most important ex-lieutenants.

Meanwhile IvS, secure in the backing of the secret network inside Germany, achieved a breakthrough by winning a contract to build two submarines for Turkey in 1926. The boats were constructed under the supervision of German experts and "retired" submariners at the Fijenoord yard in Rotterdam. A wholly German crew tested the boats exhaustively in 1927 and delivered them to Turkey in spring 1928, where they set up a submarine training-establishment. The Germans also won a contract to build three submarines in and for Finland from 1926 to 1930. Over the same period experimental boats were built with the help of German funds in Spain, Estonia and Finland again. All this work provided invaluable opportunities for designers, builders and naval men to keep Germany in the forefront of submarine development.

The boats built for foreign customers were linear descendants, with considerable improvements, of the three most successful types of German submarines of the First World War – one coastal, one ocean-going and one minelaying. From 1926, and on instructions from the Navy, IvS added to its work abroad the task of designing boats of these three types for Germany itself. This was not a plot to defy Versailles so much as a contingency-plan in case of another European war, in which event the Germans would be obliged, the Navy felt, to build submarines in self-defence and for maritime counter-attack. The first "mobilisation plan" of 1926 envisaged the construction of thirty-six coastal, forty-two ocean-going and six minelaying boats with all the latest modifications. In 1928 the plan was changed to thirty-six each of the first two types and twelve minelayers of a new and larger design. The scheme was adapted and adjusted as technological developments and practical experience gained abroad suggested from time to time.

All in all, therefore, it should now be clear that the defeat of 1918 did not even interrupt German interest in the submarine or work on its further development. Even as the First World War flotillas were being surrendered, shared out or broken up, the great store of accumulated knowledge was being put to work to lay the foundations of the submarine fleet that would fight in the next war, whenever it came – and it was the same men, whether civilians or naval officers, who did it. Just as the Second World War arose out of the First, so the better-known "Battle of the Atlantic" grew out of its underestimated, under-reported but no less serious predecessor – and the boats which fought in both, like their crews, were as closely and directly related as parent and child. The most striking human embodiment of this continuity was Karl Dönitz, submarine commander at the end of the First World War, chief of the submarine service between the wars and throughout the Second, then commander-in-chief of the Navy and finally, for a few days, head of state in succession to Hitler.

The victors of 1918 knew from their diplomats and spies that the Germans were deeply involved in building submarines abroad and therefore that they must be fully abreast of contemporary technology. They also knew, because the fact was in the public domain, that the German armed forces had secret funds and must therefore have had secret projects. They knew of the Soviet military connection. In short, they were fully aware that Germany was doing all it could abroad to keep up with developments in types of weaponry denied to it at home by Versailles, a treaty which nearly all Germans regarded as fundamentally unfair. But the undeniable difficulties of keeping a major nation all but disarmed led the western powers gradually to surrender the will to enforce the spirit, and often enough the letter, of Versailles.

The Navy's domestic submarine plans were supposed to be secret; those in the know treated the subject as taboo if they were German and swept it under the carpet if they were former enemies. The first crisis about the Navy's place in the state had arisen directly from its central role in the Kapp Putsch of 1920. The second arose from two controversies which more or less coincided: the Lohmann affair and the almighty political row which broke out over *Panzerschiff* (armoured ship) *A*. After recommissioning a few elderly ships and ordering the *Emden* in 1921, the Navy had been modestly adding new ships to its strength whenever funds permitted and without notable opposition: one torpedo-boat in 1924, five more plus a cruiser in 1925, six and two respectively in 1926, nothing in 1927. But the estimates for 1928, presented in 1927, included the first of three *Panzerschiffe*. These were of an entirely new type, designed to conform with the Versailles upper tonnage-limit of 10,000 while at the same time making the most of it – the "pocket-battleship" concept. They were to have six 28-centimetre (11-inch) guns, three to a turret fore and aft, medium armour and high speed. In fact there were only three British capital ships – the three battlecruisers – which could both outrun and outgun them. The specifications made it clear to naval strategists that the ships were intended primarily as commerce-raiders. Why, they wondered, should Germany's Navy want such vessels? Inside Germany the pocket-battleship became a great bone of contention between the Left, which wanted to contain the military, and the Right, which resented the country's political-pygmy status. In the outside world it became the symbol of the German will to rearm, with all that this implied, less than ten years after the worst war in history. The political row in Berlin was won by the Right: the keel of the *Deutschland* was laid in 1928 and a cruiser was ordered as well. Two more pocket battleships were ordered in 1931 and 1932 – the *Admiral Scheer* and the *Admiral Graf Spee*. All three displaced rather more than the 10,000 tons allowed by Versailles. No other new warships were ordered between 1928 and 1933 (one cruiser), for financial reasons. The pocket-battleship was a triumph of the German shipbuilder's art, a demonstration of how to get a quart into a pint-pot.

The other major development in the German Navy in 1928 was the appointment of Vice-Admiral Erich Raeder, head of the Baltic Naval Station, as Chief of the Naval Command (*Marineleitung*) in the rank of Admiral. His title sounds odd, but Versailles forbade Germany to have a general or a naval staff, barring the use of such terms as "commander-in-chief"; the ban was pointless as it took only a modicum of linguistic flexibility and informality about titles to get round it (we have already seen what power could be exercised by an ex-lieutenant). Each service had a fully-fledged command structure of the kind which had long since made the Germans a byword for organisational ability and thoroughness.

Raeder was born the son of a teacher near Hamburg in 1876 and joined the Imperial Navy at the age of 18, becoming an officer three years later. During the First World War he served in the High Seas Fleet, commanding a cruiser for a while, and on the staff. He was chief of staff to Admiral Hipper, the brilliant commander of the German battlecruisers at Jutland in 1916; by the end of the war he was in the Admiralty in Berlin. Having served on the staff of Grand-Admiral Tirpitz, the founder of the Imperial Navy, Raeder had the most grandiose conceptions of the role of the Navy and powerful conservative-nationalist leanings, which led him actively to support the Kapp Putsch. After that he was shunted into the Naval Archive, where he wrote the two volumes of the German official history of the war at sea dealing with the overseas cruisers. He returned to staff work, including officer training, until he was given his Baltic post in 1925. Although Raeder never served in submarines, and although the German submarine campaign of the Second World War is forever linked with the name of Dönitz, it was Raeder who urged unrestricted submarine warfare against Britain from the beginning – and who commanded the German Navy through the period of its greatest successes in the Atlantic campaign. As the undemocratic chief of the Navy in the new German democracy, Raeder's autocratic leadership put an end to public discussion within the Navy about the role of the service in national affairs. But the tighter discipline he imposed did not relieve the Navy from involvement in political controversy nationally, of which the *Panzerschiff* issue (1928–32) was only a part. Under him, the Navy of the Weimar Republic ceased to confront the state without giving up any of its ambitions to rebuild its strength. It learned to dissimulate and to live with the delays to its expansion programme imposed by the Reichstag until parliamentary government was superseded by the use of the presidential emergency decree from 1930, leading to the appointment of Hitler as Chancellor in January 1933. But it was in November 1932 that General Kurt von Schleicher, Minister of Defence, decided upon a reconstruction of the Reichswehr. This included providing the Navy with a new, though small, battlefleet and sixteen submarines by 1938. A week later, on November 22, the Navy began to set up an "experimental motorboat" branch to develop the new submarine arm. Key decisions followed in December as the shell of Weimar, eaten away from within, began to crack. Two IvS designs, proven abroad, for boats of 750 and 250 tons were chosen. The way was left open for the development of a new 500-ton class. Kiel, Germany's principal Baltic port and naval base, was chosen as the site for a new submarine depot. The detachment of 100 officers and men to found the new branch was authorised. Thus the basis of Hitler's submarine fleet was laid before he came to power, and the Nazi Navy as a whole simply grew out of the plans conceived and nurtured under the Weimar Republic.

The British Navy's greatest loss in the First World War was its own air arm. About 2,500 aircraft and 55,000 men were transferred to the new Royal Air Force with effect from 1 April 1918. The United States Navy, which had succeeded the German as the great rival of the Royal Navy, did not make this fundamental error. It also had newer and therefore generally superior capital ships, having expanded later than the British. The crippling cost of the war condemned the Royal Navy to a long period of make-do-and-mend. Its first loss in peacetime therefore was the greatest of all, and everlasting: the end of British maritime supremacy. Economics forced the adoption of a "one-power standard," keeping the Navy equal to any other in the world; but parity with the US Navy, which is what this meant, was always something of a chimera and open to differing interpretations. By the end of 1920 both navies were seriously considering new building programmes. The British were constrained by finance and also by fear of becoming involved in a construction race with the American Navy which they could not hope to win, even though they had only one really modern capital ship compared with the sixteen approved or already under construction for the US Navy. But in Washington too there was a powerful lobby opposed to massive naval expenditure; and within the Navy opinion was beginning to shift in the direction of aircraft-carriers, already identified by such sages as Admiral William Sims as the capital ships of the future.

While the Americans were considering and then rejecting a separate air force (set up only after the Second World War) the British air-marshals set about establishing and defending a monopoly over all military flying. The RAF set up a Coastal Area Command, as it was originally called, to co-operate with, but not to serve under, the Navy. Its chief, Air Vice-Marshal A. V. Vyvyan, regarded anti-submarine air-patrols and air-escorts for convoys as a waste of resources that would be better used bombing enemy submarine bases. His memorandum to the Admiralty on the subject was written on the first anniversary of the Armistice and opened a controversy which lasted into the Second World War, with appalling consequences. These could not easily be foreseen in 1919; but the failure to learn the lessons of the war just ended looks inexcusable, as does the inter-service rivalry which the creation of the RAF provoked. Sir Hugh Trenchard, "Father of the RAF" and its first Chief of Air Staff, also sired the strategic bombing theory, which was bound to divert resources away from the vital task of supporting the Navy, at about the same time. The position now was that in naval aviation matters the Navy proposed but the RAF disposed. Admiral A. E. M. Chatfield, the member of the Board of Admiralty in charge of aviation, fought for control of naval aviation in 1921, but could not prevail against the megalomania of Trenchard, who seriously suggested at the same time that the new and voracious Air Ministry should take responsibility for the entire defence of Britain!

Financial difficulties made the British interested in international naval restraint. Indeed Versailles, which imposed disarmament on Germany, was supposed to lead to general disarmament: there was, for example, serious debate about banning submarines during the peace conference, but it was the French who prevented such a move. Yet it was the Americans, in the person of Charles Evans Hughes, the Secretary of State, who invited the leading naval powers to what we would now call an arms-limitation conference in Washington. Delegates from Britain, France, Italy and Japan joined the Americans in November 1921 and heard Hughes as chairman propose the abandonment of all capital shipbuilding programmes, the adoption of existing strength as the standard for future relative strengths among the Five, the scrapping of certain older warships and the use of capital-ship tonnage as the yardstick of naval strength with a pro rata allowance of smaller vessels. Hughes went so far as to offer to scrap fifteen old battleships and fifteen then under construction, even though two had already been launched and some others were nearly complete. The total of 850,000 tons this represented was greater than the tonnage scuttled by the Germans at Scapa in 1919. He proposed a 5:5:3 ratio for Britain, the USA and Japan (which had already embarked by 1927 on a vast naval building programme including twenty-seven capital ships) and a ten-year holiday from naval construction. The visiting delegates were stunned. The British First Sea Lord, Admiral Beatty, was generally in favour and proposed the total abolition of submarines; his main objection was the tonnage-criterion, which he wanted replaced by numbers of ships. The first Washington Treaty was concluded on 13 December 1921 and the conference eventually produced a total of nine treaties and twelve resolutions by spring 1922. The haggling and horse-trading diminished Hughes's grand design considerably. The British, for instance, were allowed to build two new capital ships (ordered in 1922), while the Americans kept the two they had already launched (and scrapped two more old ships). There were no restraints at all on numbers of smaller warships (cruisers, destroyers, submarines), but cruisers were limited to 10,000 tons and 8-inch guns (although larger guns could be fitted provided they were of a new and untried design, a provision which enabled the Germans to claim that their pocket-battleships conformed both to Versailles and to Washington, to which they had not been invited). The "restrictions" on cruisers proved to be a challenge to all concerned to build *up* to the limits and led to a boom in construction, especially by Britain, which thus built too many cruisers and too few destroyers.

Capital ships were limited to 35,000 tons, ratios were agreed among the five powers and so was the ten-year holiday in capital shipbuilding. Any participant was permitted to build two aircraft-carriers of up to 33,000 tons (the Americans were alone in immediately ordering two). All extant carriers were classified as experimental and open to replacement at any time. The British contented themselves with converting two rather smaller ships into carriers, while the Americans built theirs on the hulls of two large, modern battle-cruisers. The overall limits on carrier-tonnage were set at 135,000 for the British and Americans, 81,000 for the Japanese and 60,000 for France and Italy. The Washington package, to last until 1936, also allowed the preparation of merchant ships for arming with guns of up to 6-inch calibre in the event of war. The British call for a total ban on submarines was rejected and while limits were imposed on their use (Prize Rules), none at all were placed on numbers. In June 1922, therefore, the Treaties of Washington Bill which would formally terminate British supremacy on the sea was introduced at Westminster. Anglo-American rivalry in capital ships was for the time being at an end, but competition in the building of the smaller ships was intensified. Both navies took full advantage of the Washington provision allowing the addition of up to 3,000 tons of displacement per capital ship in the form of more protection. All such ships were fitted with "bulges" (British) or "blisters" (American), an outer skin underwater to absorb blast from torpedoes and mines. New ships were built with internal double hulls for the same purpose.

*   *   *

The embattled Board of Admiralty in London received a most important consolation prize amid all its worries about aviation, the state of the Fleet and the shortage of funds in this early postwar period. The work of the Allied Submarine Detection Investigation Committee (ASDIC), inspired by Ernest Rutherford and equally by his French colleague, Paul Langevin, bore fruit in summer 1920, when the first active submarine detectors were fitted experimentally. A year later, after many trials at sea, the admirals firmly believed that the device, with its characteristic pinging transmissions and henceforward known as Asdic, was the answer to the submarine. The admirals were little short of euphoric. It was indeed one of a handful of British technical breakthroughs which were to be of crucial importance in 1939, and it brought the further benefit of the foundation of a small but permanent anti-submarine branch at the Admiralty. But it also led to dangerous complacency about submarines, including almost total neglect of anti-submarine tactics. The blessing of Asdic was real; it was also decidedly mixed. The Americans soon developed their own version, called Sonar.

The Washington Treaties enabled the British to make a virtue of necessity. The naval estimates of March 1922 scrapped twelve capital ships and kept only fifteen, cancelled four battlecruisers approved in 1921 and also cut the number of destroyers, scrapped twenty-seven submarines, closed down two naval commands, and cut manpower in the Navy by 20,000 and in the naval dockyards by 10,000. The starts of the two "Washington" battleships were put off until 1923. What alarmed the Admiralty most however was a separate proposal from the Geddes Committee, which had been looking for economies, to slash the air squadrons earmarked for work with the Navy from seven to two. The issue wound its way through several committees and three different governments (the Liberal Lloyd George was displaced by the Conservative Bonar Law in October 1922; Ramsay MacDonald became the first Labour premier in January 1924). The outcome was a qualified victory for the Navy, enshrined in an agreement between Trenchard of the RAF and Admiral Sir Roger Keyes for the Admiralty. The Fleet Air Arm was to remain part of the RAF, but the Admiralty would determine performance and numbers of aircraft. The Air Ministry would be responsible for specifications and construction. The RAF would train crews for tasks chosen by the Navy, which was henceforward allowed to provide up to seventy percent of Air Arm officers who would be temporarily attached to the RAF. This curious compromise to appease the vanity of one man (Trenchard) was agreed in 1924, just in time for crewing up the two aircraft-carrier conversions. Even then the wrangling did not stop: prolonged demarcation disputes bedevilled, and in the Navy's view impaired, the fitting-out and equipping of the carriers. Meanwhile the Americans forged ahead, coordinating design, production, training and research so well that by the mid-twenties they had built the foundations on which the Navy and the aircraft industry were able to expand at phenomenal speed in wartime. The key factor was not money but enthusiasm for naval aviation throughout a Navy which had full control of it, a service which was at all times to be "a navy second to none." The phrase is much more positive than the defensive "one-power standard" of the British and reflects the difference between the two countries, their political and naval leaderships – and their naval air services – between the wars.

The disgraceful tug-of-war between Admiralty and Air Ministry continued throughout the 1920s over the size and control of the Fleet Air Arm. The Navy clearly recognised the importance of aircraft-carriers, but not to the extent that the admirals put them before capital ships. Despite the disappointment of Jutland, they still thought in terms of another Trafalgar, to be decided by the big guns. They fell behind the Americans in the air, even though the US Army and Navy had their own demarcation-disputes about the roles of their respective air forces. But these had no effect where it mattered: in the Fleet, which managed to make itself expert in the use of carrier-aircraft. Only the smaller but rapidly expanding Japanese Navy was keener on naval aviation. The British were less adventurous in the air and put too much faith in the new generation of anti-aircraft guns – in which, however, they invested too little.

Too many Royal Navy officers defied the hard-won experience of the First World War by indulging in a renewed and prolonged bout of scepticism about convoys, difficult though this is to believe today. The pocket-battleships led them to practise defence against surface-raiders, but not a single exercise in protecting a merchant convoy against submarine attack was held between the end of the First and the beginning of the Second World War. Asdic, it was felt, had made this unnecessary. In 1928 Winston Churchill, in charge of Britain's overstretched finances as Chancellor of the Exchequer, came up with his "Ten-Year Rule" whereby it was to be assumed for defence purposes that in any given year there would be no war for a decade, unless the forces or the Foreign Office could produce an argument for abandoning the rule. The Committee of Imperial Defence readily adopted this dubious principle.

The following year, in May, Ramsay MacDonald returned to office even though Labour lacked an overall majority, and stopped all work on warships ordered in 1928 while he strove to organise a follow-up naval conference of the Washington Treaty powers. In September he visited President Herbert Hoover and in October all five powers had agreed to come to London in January 1930. The result was a series of additions to the Washington limitations, reducing permitted British cruiser strength from seventy to fifty by the end of 1936 and limiting total American cruiser tonnage to 323,000. This at least put an end to a prolonged, post-Washington dispute between the Americans and the British about cruisers which had come to a head at the Geneva Peace Conference of 1927. Both countries put more emphasis on building smaller, 6-inch cruisers so as to be able to go to the limit on numbers without exceeding the tonnage-ceiling.

The next relevant international conference was much more general and was held under the auspices of the League of Nations. The long-awaited General Disarmament Conference began in February 1932 amid enormous difficulties. The Germans demanded the removal of the ball-and-chain of Versailles, which angered the French. In an attempt to break the multiple deadlock, the British suggested the scrapping of all airpower. The talks in Geneva were adjourned in July without substantial agreement, and in September the Germans withdrew temporarily because their demand for equal rights had not been accepted. The conference dragged on until it was adjourned *sine die* in June 1934; by then the Germans had withdrawn altogether and also left the League of Nations, of which the USA was never a member.

Meanwhile the unfortunate Fleet Air Arm was still a political football. The Government cancelled the aircraft-carrier included in the 1929 programme, but the Air Arm was already short of aircraft for the five carriers in service and for the aircraft-launching steam catapults which had begun to be fitted to capital ships and cruisers once again, as they had been in 1914–18. The best news for British naval aviation in this period was the appointment of the first Flag Officer, Aircraft Carriers, Admiral R. G. H. Henderson, in March 1931. He proved a formidable defender of the Fleet Air Arm, whose control was the main concern of Admiral Chatfield when he took over as First Sea Lord in January 1933. The American Navy was still chasing numerical parity in ships with the British, but they kept and increased their lead in carrier-aviation.

It was not only the appointment on January 30 of Adolf Hitler as Chancellor by the senile President, Field Marshal Paul von Hindenburg, apotheosis of Prussian militarism, which made 1933 the pivotal year between the wars. In the United States, Franklin D. Roosevelt was waiting to take over the Presidency in March after his election victory in November 1932. Japan, the fastest-growing naval power, also left the League of Nations over its invasion of Manchuria in 1931. The Disarmament Conference was irretrievably bogged down. The World Economic Conference in London completely failed to deal with the Depression. The Soviet Union and the United States established diplomatic relations for the first time since the Russian Revolution. Disarmament having failed, rearmament began in earnest on all sides.

3

REARMAMENT PROCEEDS, 1933–1939

*Hitler – secret submarine school – illegal rearmament – Versailles
breached – naval agreements – Karl Dönitz – the Z-plan – Britain
rearms – and America – Isolationism – FDR – convoy plans –
British Intelligence – and German – intelligent British – Admiral
Pound – escorts – the road to war*

As leader of the largest party in a democratically elected Reichstag, Adolf
Hitler was constitutionally entitled to Hindenburg's reluctant invitation to
head a government (the present German usage of *Machtergreifung* – seizure
of power – to describe the Nazi accession is misleading). His first concern
was to eliminate the constraints imposed on him by his Nationalist Party
coalition partners. Command of the domestic political scene was his absolute
priority, and foreign affairs, finance and military matters were very much
secondary. The Reichstag fire conveniently enabled Hitler to persuade
Hindenburg to sign a decree suspending civil liberties on February 28; the
"Enabling Act" of March 23 transferred legislative power from the Reichstag
to the Cabinet. But the Nazis had risen to power on the backs of the
"respectable" Right and the military. Once in the Chancellery, Hitler had
every reason to believe he would be able to see off the conventional politicians
and indeed the groundwork for this was laid at a Cabinet meeting on January
30, the day of his appointment. The military would need more subtle handling
as their support was central to his strategy.

His first move was to appoint General Werner von Blomberg Minister
of Defence. His second was to address the most senior generals and admirals,
including Raeder, for two hours at the home of General Kurt von Hammerstein, chief of the Army Command (*Heeresleitung*) since 1930, on February 2. Hitler made two main points. He assured his audience that there was
no danger of a civil war (the military had watched the mushroom growth of
the SA or *Sturmabteilung*, the Nazi Party's private army including many
war-veterans, with alarm). Then he held out the prospect best calculated
to win over any military élite: fast, and vast, rearmament. These promises
and the appointment of Blomberg were more than enough to buy time
and toleration from the services, although they were only the first steps

in a process of completely subordinating them to the Nazi state by forms of ruthlessness and duplicity never envisaged in the Prussian officer's code.

On the very day of the discreet meeting at Hammerstein's home, Blomberg gave his consent to a naval request for a submarine school at Kiel to train the crews for the first two boats, whose construction was planned to start in autumn 1933. It was given the cover-name of *U-bootabwehrschule* (school for defence against submarines) and was under the nominal control of the Torpedo Inspectorate, which had also been working hard on new torpedo designs. The first eighty pupils assembled on October 1, the day on which the building of the first two small submarines was due to begin. Ironically, however, Hitler, the great rearmer, stepped in and for the first time since the war the Navy's painstaking campaign to rebuild itself was interrupted (the political rows in the last years of Weimar, notably over the pocket-battleships, had only slowed things down). Just one cruiser was ordered in 1933; but detailed planning both for a new submarine arm and for new capital ships in defiance of Versailles continued undisturbed. The students of the first submarine course received unexpectedly thorough theoretical training. The reason for the interruption lay in Hitler's foreign policy. His plans for the eastward expansion of Germany, as advertised in *Mein Kampf* (always an under-read publication), obviously ran counter to the traditional British policy of a balance of power on the European Continent, which, after the general catastrophe of the First World War, meant striving for a general settlement by exclusively peaceful means. Hitler was determined to rearm, but felt naval expansion could proceed only if the British were persuaded to tolerate it. How seriously, or for how long, he hoped for an Anglo-German alliance is a moot point; but he was anxious to send a signal that a resurgent Germany did not want to compete with the British Empire. He had, apparently, learned the historical lesson of the naval arms race begun by the Kaiser at the turn of the century, a principal cause of the 1914–18 war.

So on 17 May 1933 he made one of the most dazzling speeches in a long career of using rhetoric as a political weapon by telling people what they wanted to hear. He pegged his first major foreign-policy address, made to the now impotent Reichstag, to President Roosevelt's Note of the previous day to world governments powerfully urging general disarmament. Hitler disingenuously offered to renounce the weapons which Germany did not have yet, if other nations destroyed what they did have. Germany, after all, had no aggressive designs on its neighbours and was prepared to sign pacts to prove it. The West was bowled over with delight and chose to ignore the warning contained in the renewed demand for equal rights for Germany, short of which it would leave the League of Nations and the immobilised disarmament conference. There was much sympathy for equal treatment, especially in Britain, where the sentiment that Versailles had been "unfair" grew steadily from 1920 to Munich in 1938. It became clear only in October 1933 that the real message of the so joyously welcomed speech was equal rights (*Gleichberechtigung*) – or else. It was then that Hitler withdrew Germany from both League and conference on learning that the other powers required eight years to disarm to the German level. He called a referendum on the issue, dissolved the Reichstag and gave secret orders for military and naval resistance to invasion: his withdrawal meant rearmament in defiance of Versailles and he took warnings of an invasion in such an event seriously. It was a typically Hitlerian gamble, too, because the forces stood no chance of being able to resist a real attack. Illegal rearmament, if not a *casus belli*, was a case for sanctions including military measures. But Hitler, the master of opportunism, based his gamble on the general dread of another war in Europe. The trick was to work time and again until September 1939.

At the end of 1933 the secret submarine-building plans were dusted off, revised and rescheduled. A clandestine flow of components began to cross the Dutch border from the Ruhr to IvS, which shipped them round the coast to Kiel, all under the noses of the Netherlands Customs. The devious route reduced the chance of detection to a minimum: on the overland section of the route the parts would appear destined for the Dutch coast, and their delivery by sea to Kiel was much more secure than it would have been from inland. It took until August 1934 to assemble the parts for the first six 250-ton boats in Kiel; work also began on building up a modest stock of torpedoes, some propelled conventionally by compressed air, others by electricity, a new and much less detectable type. Parts for six more small boats and two 800-tonners had also been ordered.

The naval rearmament plan for 1933–8 which Hitler inherited was drawn up with the Versailles limits in mind. In discussions between Hitler and Raeder during 1934, particularly on June 27, this five-year programme was sharply inflated. *Panzerschiffe D* and *E*, conceived as improved pocket-battleships, were to become full-blown battlecruisers of three times the tonnage (the *Scharnhorst* and the *Gneisenau*). The sixth postwar cruiser and nine destroyers were also ordered in 1934, making it the most important year for naval building in Germany since before the war. The size of the big ships was to remain as closely guarded a secret as the clandestine submarine programme, pending the conclusion of a naval accord with Britain. This did not stop Raeder and Hitler from agreeing that eventually there would have to be a reckoning with the British, which meant that *Panzerschiffe F* and *G* would need to be super-battleships of over 45,000 tons (the *Bismarck* and the *Tirpitz*), and from *H* onwards they would need to progress in stages to monsters of 100,000 tons! At this point these extrapolations lay in the mental outfield between reverie and raving, but in 1934 the amended expansion programme envisaged a battlefleet of four capital ships, two aircraft carriers and eight cruisers, plus destroyers and forty-six submarines. Only one carrier, the *Graf Zeppelin*, was ever built; even though it was launched in December 1938, it was never completed.

Naval building may have been interrupted for diplomatic reasons (the 1934 programme did not get going until 1935), but elsewhere rearmament was proceeding at top speed. The Army had been given a secret deadline of 1 October 1934 to treble its manpower to 300,000. Hermann Göring as Minister of (civil) Aviation secretly began building up the Luftwaffe, ordering military aircraft and using the pilots trained in Russia to pass on their skills to volunteers in the deceptively named League for Air Sport. In the German industrial heartland of the Ruhr, Krupp had never complied with the postwar ban on its involvement in arms manufacture and now stepped up its production of guns and armour-plate. IG Farben, the chemical conglomerate organised as a trust, got contracts to make synthetic motor-fuel and rubber from coal. The new Reich Defence Council drew up plans for involving a quarter of a million German factories in arms production. Much of this – so vast it could hardly stay hidden for long – was known to the other signatories of Versailles. It upset them, but not sufficiently to provoke an attempt to enforce the Treaty. Instead the British and the French in February 1935 made Hitler an offer of equal rights in armaments and a general European settlement. The latter would extend to eastern Europe the acceptance of borders and international arbitration of disputes agreed between Germany and the western European powers in the Locarno Treaty of 1925. Hitler did not want an "eastern Locarno" as it would inhibit his *Lebensraum* plans, but responded evasively rather than negatively and immediately set about driving a wedge between France, which had sought mutual assistance pacts with Czechoslovakia, Poland and the USSR, and Britain, which had not.

The British defence White Paper of 1 March 1935, urging judicious rearmament in response to rearmament in Germany and elsewhere, led Hitler to postpone a meeting in Berlin with Sir John Simon, the Foreign Secretary, arranged for March 6, by succumbing to a diplomatic illness. At the same moment the French extended military service from eighteen to twenty-four months to compensate for the trough in the birthrate during the First World War. On these specious excuses, Hitler let Göring announce the existence of the Luftwaffe to a British journalist, and a week later himself announced the return of conscription in Germany and a plan for a standing army of 500,000 men – thirty-six divisions or twelve corps. Versailles was dead and millions of ordinary Germans, pro- and anti-Nazi alike, boisterously celebrated the fact. So did the generals, although they had not been consulted about a plan which could easily stretch the Army's absorption capacity to breaking point. Once again the other powers limited themselves to protest: Britain, France and Mussolini's Fascist Italy met at Stresa on April 11 to condemn Germany and support Locarno and Austrian independence. The League of Nations set up a committee to look for ways of limiting the German resurgence. France concluded a mutual assistance pact with Russia. The British politely asked whether Sir John Simon would still be welcome in Berlin for the postponed talks, and were told he would. It was time for Hitler to make another of his supremely cynical speeches about Germany's peaceful intentions to the Reichstag. Once again he pulled out all the stops; once again most of the rest of the world heard only what it wanted to hear and was duly delighted. After the Saar plebiscite, which had overwhelmingly restored that coal-rich province to German rule from French postwar tutelage, Germany had no claims on France and renounced any idea of regaining Alsace-Lorraine (recovered by the French in 1918). Germany had a non-aggression pact with Poland and had no intention of absorbing Austria. Locarno stood, and might be supplemented with an agreement on airpower. For Britain there was a special offer in this speech of 21 May 1935: Hitler was willing to limit the new German Navy to thirty-five percent of the strength of the Royal Navy (which would also leave it fifteen percent smaller than the French Navy). Germany, he said, wanted no repetition of the Kaiser's naval arms-race which had led to the only Anglo-German war, and recognised Britain's special claim to naval power to protect its empire.

All this was sweet music to the ears of the British Government. No discordant note was heard even when the Germans told London the thirty-five percent "offer" was not negotiable. Nobody in the Cabinet seemed, or wanted, to realise that for the Germans to "limit" themselves to about a third of British naval strength would require them to build ships at a speed and on a scale that would overstretch the relevant industries for a decade. This was self-aggrandisement thinly and crudely dressed up as self-restraint, and with barely credible naïvety the British rushed to accept the offer, formally put to them in London in June. They told neither the other Stresa conference powers nor the League before the partly secret Anglo-German Naval Agreement was made. It was the first deliberate breach of Versailles by one of the victors of 1918, and it allowed Germany to have five battleships, twenty-one cruisers and sixty-four destroyers. Submarine strength was to be forty-five percent of the British – but was to be allowed to rise to 100 percent if the Germans in special circumstances felt the need! Thus the basis was laid, not only for the ultra-modern German Navy with which Britain had to contend for the first two and a half years of the Second World War, but also for the submarine-building capacity which was once again to come so close to defeating her. The fact that the Luftwaffe had apparently sprung fully armed from the brow of Göring was something for which the world had been prepared by a series of leaks. The completion of the first submarines only four months after the Agreement astonished everybody, even though the British had been officially informed by the German delegates that some "experimental" construction was going on. In fact the German Navy had already decided upon and begun work on the three main types of submarine they would deploy from 1939. These were the coastal type II of 250 tons, the medium, ocean-going type VII of 625 tons and upwards and the long-range type IX of 1,030 tons and more; all three were derived from First World War designs.

As the Washington Naval Treaty of 1922 was due to expire in 1936, the British invited the relevant powers to a conference at the end of 1935 with a view to extending or replacing it. Germany was not invited because France felt that such a step would formalise the burial of Versailles. The London conference became bogged down within a few days of opening in November; in January the Japanese walked out. Once again a British proposal for the abolition of submarines was vetoed by the French. In March 1936 the British, Americans and French concluded the London Naval Treaty, to come into effect in summer 1937. It brought further improvements in Anglo-American relations, provided for naval rearmament by both powers if world events made this appear necessary, and incorporated a few tinkerings with the permitted tonnages of various categories of ship. Another apparent benefit was a special protocol, open to signature by all naval powers, banning unrestricted submarine warfare. By the outbreak of war some forty nations had subscribed to it – including Germany, which had given a similar assurance in concluding the Anglo-German Agreement in 1935. The British, with their world-lead in submarine-detection, found this most comforting. They still believed Hitler was a man of his word. The dictator himself was overjoyed with the Agreement and the ease with which he had got everything he wanted, as he confided to Raeder immediately afterwards. To get it he had lied about the tonnages of the four capital ships on which work was now in hand – *Scharnhorst, Gneisenau, Bismarck* and *Tirpitz*. He believed that his strategy for German expansion – keeping the British sweet while he redrew the map of central and eastern Europe – was off to a very good start.

Construction of the first submarine flotilla of the new Navy had begun inside the purpose-built concealment-sheds in Kiel on 1 February 1935. The time had now come to find someone to take command. The man chosen was the captain of the cruiser *Emden*, then on a world tour to "show the flag." His name appeared in the unpublished list of officer appointments for autumn, circulated in the first week of June (the secrecy of such lists since the end of 1932 was to conceal the scale and nature of the expansion of the *Wehrmacht*, as the German Armed Forces had been called since 1934). *Fregattenkapitän* (junior captain) Karl Dönitz was then forty-three years old, an officer of wide experience in the service – surface-ships, submarines, light forces, staff-posts – with a string of exceptionally warm commendations from successive superiors in his personal file.

Dönitz was born at Grünau, near Berlin, on 16 September 1891. His father was a prosperous engineer. He joined the rapidly expanding Imperial Navy as a cadet in 1910 and became an officer in 1913. When war broke out he was signals officer aboard the light cruiser *Breslau* which, with the battlecruiser *Goeben*, formed the Mediterranean Division under Admiral Wilhelm Souchon. The two ships ran the gauntlet of the French and British navies on the outbreak of hostilities in August 1914 to enter the Dardanelles and help bring Turkey into the war on Germany's side. After that they fought a successful "private war" with the Russians in the Black Sea. Dönitz was awarded the Iron Cross, first class. He was posted to the submarine service at the end of 1916, joining *U39* under the command of the "ace" *Kapitänleutnant* Walter Forstmann in the Mediterranean in January 1917. Dönitz had married Ingeborg Weber, a military nurse and daughter of a German general, whom he met in Constantinople, in May 1916. He joined the service just in time for the lifting of all restrictions from submarine warfare on 1 February 1917, and after learning the job from a master was appointed captain of *UC25* at the beginning of 1918. For his work in the combined minelayer and torpedo-attack boat he was awarded the Knight's Cross of the Order of Hohenzollern on the personal instruction of the Kaiser. His superiors in their reports on the hard-working lieutenant noted his fine military bearing, energy, good manners, diligence, enthusiasm, popularity and tact with officers and men, thoroughness and skill.

For the last few months of the war Dönitz was in command of *UB68*, a medium-sized *UBIII* type (ancestor of the type VII), with a scratch crew of undertrained recruits. By this time the German submarines in the Mediterranean had taken to working in pairs, or sometimes in larger formations, because of the numbers of aircraft on patrol over the major sea-lanes in the closing stages of the war. Dönitz therefore was not the first to use the "pack" tactic that was to prove so devastating in the later conflict, as one might gather from his memoirs; but he fully recognised the possibilities of such deployments against convoys. In the early hours of 4 October 1918 the *UB68*, having sunk a British steamer and pursuing the rest of its convoy, dived for another attack – and went out of control, probably as a result of inexperienced handling by an untried crew. The over-correction of a potentially fatal plunge towards the bottom caused the boat to pop out of the water in the middle of the convoy, where she came under fire. Unable to dive again because all the compressed air had been used up, Dönitz gave the order to scuttle and abandon. Four men were lost; the rest were taken prisoner. Deeply depressed by the failure, Dönitz struck his captors and later interrogators in Malta as highly temperamental, sulky and angry by turns and obsessed by the loss of his boat. Bitter and defiant in subsequent imprisonment in England, Dönitz tried to get himself repatriated by feigning insanity (which may not have been very difficult and might indeed have been dangerous for someone of his mentality). He was sent to a mental hospital in Manchester and got back to Germany relatively early in July 1919. He was at once invited to join the new postwar Navy, eventually being given command of a torpedo-boat.

He survived the purge of the naval officer-corps which followed the

Kapp Putsch (Dönitz did not betray the fledgling republic) and the ensuing personal crisis about whether to stay in the Navy. His father-in-law, General Weber, head of the Reichswehr's northern area Army command, persuaded him to stay on, and in January 1921 he was promoted *Kapitänleutnant*, still with the torpedo-boats. Two years later he joined the staff of the Torpedo Inspectorate in Kiel, moving to more general staff duties in Berlin late in 1924. After the upheaval caused by the Lohmann scandal Dönitz was posted to the Baltic command, serving on a cruiser before being given command of a half-flotilla of four torpedo-boats. The flow of good reports continued, reflecting his total dedication to his work, which was rewarded by promotion to *Korvettenkapitän* (commander) in 1928. Two years later came another staff job at the North Sea station in Wilhelmshaven. The chief of staff there was Captain Canaris, whose assessment of Dönitz after a year of observation was much more penetrating – and less flattering – than the eulogies which had gone before. The future *Abwehr* (military intelligence) chief thought his subordinate immature, insecure, poor at delegating, very ambitious, inclined to interfere in others' fields of responsibility, over-conscientious, excitable and restless to the point that he suffered from stomach complaints. All this was in addition to the usual remarks about his competence, reliability and capacity to express himself orally and in writing. Some of this must have been communicated to Dönitz, for one year later Canaris described him as having calmed down considerably. One is tempted to guess that he did so in obedience to a direct order. But his general reputation in the service must have been of the highest, since he was awarded a presidential travel grant in 1933, open to just one officer per year. He went to the Far East for six months, returned to his old post, was promoted once more and took command of the *Emden*, a plum job, in autumn 1934. On the eve of the ship's world cruise Dönitz was introduced by Raeder to Hitler. There is no evidence that anyone felt the earth move on that formal occasion. Such was the man, model officer in the Prussian tradition, who at the end of September 1935 reviewed the three small submarines then assigned to the First Flotilla at Kiel. On 1 October 1935 he was promoted full captain (*Kapitän-zur-See*); one year later he was appointed *Führer der U-boote* (chief of submarines). By then the first type VIIs were being worked up in the Second Flotilla.

Hitler, the frustrated architect, had a penchant for drawing grandiose designs for public buildings which led to work on a master-plan for the reconstruction of Berlin by the real architect and Führer-favourite, Albert Speer. The Nazi leader was no less interested in battleships and filled sketchbooks with drawings of marine leviathans which he would proudly display to Admiral Raeder. From the ensuing conversations, and from Hitler's growing conviction that there would have to be a reckoning with Britain, once Europe had been sorted out, so that Greater Germany could spread its power across the world, there grew the naval Z-plan. Drawn up early in 1938, it provided for a great new German battlefleet of ships so powerful that even the Royal Navy would be swept from the sea. This fleet would take a decade or so to complete, but he assured Raeder time and again that there would be no war with Britain before 1944, by which time there would be enough Z-plan ships available to keep the British in check at sea because they had so many other commitments round the world. This was a rehash of the fatally flawed naval strategy developed by Grand-Admiral Tirpitz and the Kaiser before the First World War, which was one of the main causes of that conflict. It took no account of the fact that although the British were still pursuing a policy of peace at virtually any price, they had already begun serious naval rearmament in 1936 – in response to the thirty-five percent fleet conceded to the Reich in the Anglo-German Agreement. It also took no account of the colossal pressures on the German economy from the current general rearmament, exacerbated by all-out competition between the services, which had already made the 1935 naval building programme very hard to adhere to. Dönitz believed 300 submarines would be essential for a war against Britain, and the Z-plan provided for them – by the late 1940s. The result of the plan, even though it was never put into effect, was to ensure that Germany had far too few submarines for an early victory against Britain when war actually came. The German Navy was as unready in 1939 as it had been in 1914.

Before considering British rearmament we may note two other points about Hitler's navy. It was the only national institution that did not need *Gleichschaltung* (the Nazi word for forcing into line). Its leaders represented an unbroken link with the Prussian past. This was a great irony for a service whose mutiny in 1918 had done so much to bring down the Second Reich. But the Navy's role in the Kapp Putsch less than two years later showed prompt reconversion to the right-wing tendencies which were to be so cunningly exploited by Hitler. Leftists tried to infiltrate the Navy in the 1920s (Dönitz was responsible as a staff officer for repelling or expelling them) but the Kaiser's officers who still headed the Navy were not about to let those who had humiliated them in 1918 do it again. Naval leaders in the Nazi state found it as easy to trim their outlook to Nazi requirements as to trim their ships.

The other point concerns naval aviation. Not only did the German Navy never commission a carrier; it was also denied a true air-arm. For this Göring was responsible. The Reichsmarschall, an air-ace in the First World War, was an incompetent strategist and the most voracious empire-builder among the Nazi leaders. He insisted, like air-commanders elsewhere, that everything which flew was his. Even Raeder could make no impression, even in wartime, when there were to be many rows about it. And Hitler might fancy himself as a master of ship-design but he understood nothing of naval strategy.

In Britain, by contrast, it took the Royal Navy twenty years of lost opportunity and administrative warfare with the RAF to regain control of naval aviation

– but it did win an important if qualified victory just in time for the coming war.

Naval rearmament began in 1934 with the authorisation of an aircraft-carrier, four cruisers, nine destroyers, six sloops and three submarines, the biggest naval building programme since two battleships and a minelayer had been ordered in 1922.

In the United States Roosevelt's New Deal, incorporating a vast pro-gramme of "public works" in the widest sense, opened the way to something much more formidable, a foretaste of what US industry could do. In line with an eight-year plan put forward by Admiral Pratt, Chief of Naval Operations, in 1933 and the Vinson-Trammell Act of 1934 to bring the Navy up to its full permitted strength, seven battleships, a carrier, seven cruisers, eighty-nine destroyers and thirty-seven submarines were ordered in 1934. The British responded in 1936 with two and in 1937 with three battleships, two carriers and seven cruisers in each of those years, plus a total of thirty-four destroyers, twelve sloops (significantly described as "escort-vessels") and fifteen submar-ines. In 1938 the Americans under the second Trammell Act ordered three more battleships, two carriers, eight cruisers, eighteen destroyers and ten submarines, while the British chose a carrier, seven cruisers, three submar-ines and three minelayers. The last prewar estimates in Britain in 1939 provided for one more carrier, two cruisers, a minelayer, sixteen destroyers – and seventy-eight escort-vessels (the Americans ordered just one submar-ine). It will be seen from this that the concept of the fleet action was at least as strongly and stubbornly alive in the British and American navies as in the German: even the Americans with all their new expertise in naval airpower thought the line of battle made up of "all-big-gun" ships was the decisive element in seapower. But it will also be seen that the recognition of the importance of convoy-escorts put in a powerful final spurt, especially in Britain, in the nick of time.

The Royal Navy turned a corner in its debilitating struggle with the RAF in 1934, when Air Ministry objections to that year's carrier, on the grounds that its aircraft would reduce home-defence strength, were over-ruled. But the main role of naval aircraft was seen as protecting the battlefleet while the big guns fought it out. At the same time the main threat to trade was seen in the mid-1930s as coming from surface-raiders, to be countered principally by cruisers. Fortunately from 1933 all destroyers had Asdic; less happily, very little practice was acquired with it. The destroyer was still regarded as an adjunct to the battlefleet. But a plethora of committees in London looked at every aspect of defence and rearmament in this period, including trade-protection. This prolonged the debate on many important issues, including the wrangling between Navy and RAF, but it also paved the way for some important decisions. The Air Ministry abandoned its opposition to convoy (which had been based on the claim that it offered easier targets) and thus its plans to reduce Coastal Command, while the

Chiefs of Staff decided that 339 shore-based aircraft were needed for the defence of trade, about half for convoy escort (although this was far more than was available or even planned). The Navy clung, even as it expanded, to its trust in the Anglo-German Agreement as firmly as to its belief in Asdic, despite the fact that the device was useless for detecting submarines on the surface. Until the Munich crisis in September 1938, faith in Hitler's word survived even the delivery by a spy to Naval Intelligence of the German design for new, larger submarines in 1937.

In July of that year, after two inquiries, the Cabinet of Prime Minister Stanley Baldwin accepted two key proposals on naval aviation. The Fleet Air Arm was to be handed over completely to the Navy while Coastal Command remained under the RAF. It was still a compromise because the Admiralty had wanted to take over both; the way was left open for more disputes about allocations of aircraft between the planned "strategic bombing" offensive and naval co-operation. No doubt Admiral Chatfield's threat to resign as First Sea Lord helped to resolve the inter-departmental clash which had begun before the end of the First World War. The handover of the Fleet Air Arm to the Navy was formally completed on 24 May 1939, after the establishment of a new Air Division at the Admiralty under a fifth Sea Lord. The genuine (as distinct from bureaucratic) difficulties involved in the transfer made it clear that the Navy would have been biting off more than it could chew had it taken over Coastal Command as well. As it was, the Fleet Air Arm was 100 pilots short when the war began; but the RAF too was short of fliers and fighters. What the row about airpower cost the British Navy is illustrated by the fact that its American contemporary had 2,000 aircraft in service while the Fleet Air Arm could barely muster 400. Some of this was a matter of money; most of it was two decades of entrenched obduracy at the Air Ministry.

Although the US Navy, unrestrained by defunct naval treaties and positively encouraged by the general mood of expansion under the New Deal, was growing truly formidable in the late 1930s, domestic politics were being played to an entirely different rhythm. Isolationism was to become as dirty a word in the United States as appeasement did in Britain; but not yet, and not as quickly. The dispute between those who believed in American expansion after the conquest of the continent was complete – "Manifest Destiny" – and those who did not first arose in the dying years of the nineteenth century. Neither the Spanish–American War of 1898 nor the First World War resolved the matter; on the contrary, it is still alive a century later. It goes to the root of the origin of the United States, created by people who had in many cases come to get away from the endless international entanglements of the Old World.

The issue came to a head in 1933 just as Hitler was consolidating his hold on power in Germany. France defaulted for the third time on debts incurred in the First World War; at the same time Britain offered $460 million in final settlement of similar debts of $8,000 million. The Senate passed the Johnson Act on 14 January 1934, banning loans to countries in default on earlier debts. The Bill was proposed by Senator Hiram Johnson, a Republican from California, and Roosevelt signed it into law on April 13. It failed in its primary aim of forcing the debtors to pay up; its main effect was to make it extremely difficult for Britain to obtain munitions once the war started.

The isolationists were opposed to American intervention in European wars, to alliances that might lead to war and to membership of the League of Nations, which Washington never joined. Even in the First World War the United States had not been an ally but an "associated power" on the Anglo-French side. They were neither pacifists nor conservatives, nor Axis sympathisers (though there were elements of all three). They did not want to turn their backs on the world in other fields but wanted total American sovereignty with freedom of action abroad: for them America's proper concern in defence under the "Monroe Doctrine" was the western hemisphere. Thus they opposed naval expansion from the very beginning. They believed the United States could most effectively lead the world by example, in building up democracy and prosperity at home, rather than exposing both to risk by foreign entanglements. Roosevelt was not among their number but, consummate politician that he was, he saw no choice but to let himself be carried along by this clear majority opinion. It was at its strongest in the Midwest, attracted more Republicans than Democrats, more rural people than urban, more women than men. It was particularly strong among Roman Catholics and Lutherans, but not for religious reasons: these churches were largely made up of Irishmen and Italians, and of Germans respectively. It was more a sentiment than a movement, but Roosevelt needed the support of its political proponents to get his New Deal working, and it reached its peak during his first term (1933–7). When he ran again in 1938 his foreign policy was not an issue and most isolationists supported him.

After the Johnson Act, the Senate rejected the idea of the World Court in 1935, when Congress also passed the first of a series of Neutrality Acts which seriously inhibited the President in his efforts to help the British until Pearl Harbor. It was only then that the long dispute, which had its political origin in the widespread suspicion that America's entry into the earlier war had been based on deceit, came to an end. The four Acts signed into law by November 1939 imposed an arms-embargo on belligerents and prevented them getting loans or credits; restricted the use of American shipping to carry munitions and withdrew protection from US citizens travelling in belligerents' ships; forbade the arming of American ships trading with belligerents; gave the President discretion to impose "cash and carry only" conditions on purchases of any goods by states at war and to deny their ships use of American ports. The 1939 Neutrality Act, passed as the war began, repealed the arms-embargo but made "cash and carry" mandatory. This was modified two weeks later by another law authorising the arming of merchant ships and letting them carry goods to belligerents' ports. The President was also empowered to declare combat and neutral zones at sea. It was only after summer 1940 that his acute political nose detected a shift in public opinion, away from neutrality and towards hostility to the Axis and support for the isolated British, following the fall of France and the Battle of Britain. Even after his unprecedented third victory in November 1940 Roosevelt felt it necessary to tread carefully in giving the British "all aid short of war." Once the war began no aid proposal he put to Congress was defeated; but he ruthlessly deployed the power of the state in a dirty political war on the waning isolationists well before Pearl Harbor. He used smear-tactics to label them Nazi sympathisers, unleashed the FBI on them, had their telephones tapped and their most powerful lobby, the "America First" Committee investigated. Meanwhile he gave as much encouragement as he could to the "Committee to Defend America by Aiding the Allies," founded by William Allen White, a Kansas newspaper publisher.

Franklin Delano Roosevelt learned deviousness at his mother's knee. In American terms his background was as aristrocratic as Churchill's was in British. On his father's side he was descended from an old line of Dutch settlers and on his mother's from similarly venerable Huguenot stock (Delano derives from de la Noye). Both families were highly influential in New York State from the beginnings of European settlement there. An only child born in 1882 to suffocatingly indulgent parents, the young Roosevelt enjoyed all the privileges of "old money" – private tuition, school at Groton, Connecticut, Harvard University and travel to Europe from an early age, where he learned German and French in his boyhood.

The dominant figure in his youth and for a long time thereafter was his formidable mother, Sara. Soon finding out that he could never overcome her wishes by confrontation but having inherited all her willpower, he learned to get his way by other means, not excluding dissimulation, evasiveness and out-and-out lying, which he did easily. As a young man he cut a magnificent and charming figure. Over six feet tall, he soon discovered and profited from his devastating attraction to women. His physical grace and natural athleticism concealed an unusual proneness to all manner of infections, which may help to explain why he was savagely cut down by poliomyelitis (then known as infantile paralysis) at the age of thirty-nine, in summer 1921.

This cataclysmic turning-point in his life may also have had less direct causes. By then a promising political career had already gone spectacularly off the rails in a welter of scandal. Accustomed to getting everything he wanted, Roosevelt progressed smoothly from law-practice to a seat in the New York state senate and from there, in 1913, to Assistant Secretary of the Navy under President Woodrow Wilson. He proved thoroughly competent for most of his term but was consistently disloyal to his boss, Josephus Daniels, who as Navy Secretary was the only administrative superior in Roosevelt's entire political career. By this time Churchill was First Lord of the Admiralty: the two men appear to have met for the first time at a dinner in London in 1918, when Churchill was Minister of Munitions, a brief encounter the latter forgot but Roosevelt did not.

He left the Navy Department in August 1920 to seek nomination for US Vice-President on the Democratic ticket headed by James M. Cox, Governor of Ohio. A forlorn hope in a Republican year, the move brought recognition and confirmation of Roosevelt's status as a coming man and did him no harm. Once he had thrown in his lot in 1918 with the immensely powerful and corrupt Tammany Hall political machine based on New York City (he began by opposing it, but being unable to beat the system he blithely threw principle overboard and joined it), his future in the party was assured.

But in 1921 he was brought low by a delayed-action scandal which went back to his days at the Navy Department. He had launched an undercover investigation of rampant homosexual assaults on young recruits at the Newport, Rhode Island, Naval Training Station. To obtain evidence, the investigators made such untrammelled use of entrapment that they soon became morally indistinguishable from the men they were supposed to bring to justice. Roosevelt, directly responsible for the inquiry, denied all knowledge of the methods used but was roundly condemned by a Senate committee in summer 1921. It was by far the greatest and the only notable setback in a glittering career, the first time he had fallen from grace and a terrible blow to someone unused to failure. It was in this psychologically diminished condition that he contracted the virus which paralysed him from the waist down.

Having avoided hardship for so long, he was forced by his illness to make up for earlier good fortune in full measure. By weakening him physically the mysterious affliction may have made a real man of him. At any rate he fought for years to recover before accepting that the damage was permanent. Meanwhile he learned to sympathise with others who lacked luck – without losing any of the unscrupulous opportunism and ambition of earlier years. Returning to politics after a few years of indifferent legal work and rather more successful dabbling in business, he used his physical disability for dramatic effect at political rallies, where his gift for rhetoric proved undiminished. He was elected Governor of New York in 1928, and dramatically won the Democratic nomination for President in 1932. On 4 March 1933 he moved into the White House as thirty-second President of the United States with his long-suffering wife, Eleanor, a generation after his distant cousin Theodore (Teddy) had done so as a Republican. His guiding political principle was to gain and hold the middle ground, and he was the first political leader to use modern mass-communications like radio to give the impression that he was taking an entire nation into his confidence, as in his famous "fireside chats." On this extraordinary man – political manipulator without equal, pragmatic visionary and hyperactive cripple – the survival of the United Kingdom was soon to depend, regardless of whether the United States took up arms or not.

But it was Britain which was to bear the brunt of the naval resistance to Nazism. The rise of Hitler prompted the first moves towards rearming the Royal Navy. This change of policy was reinforced rather than undermined by the Anglo-German Naval Agreement – once London realised that its initial relief was misplaced, because the pact was not a self-denying ordinance but a licence for the Germans to expand their small navy to the limits laid down. Another powerful impetus to rearm came in September 1938, when the international tension preceding the Munich Agreement of the 30th aroused fears of war and the Navy was mobilised as a precaution. All this revealed weaknesses in naval equipment and organisation which some commanders and Whitehall administrators were alert enough to recognise – and tough-minded enough to pursue through a labyrinth of committees, inter-departmental rivalries, financial constraints and changes of government.

The Admiralty Trade Division, responsible for supervising seaborne commerce in the First World War, had shrivelled to a single officer with a desk in a corner of the Plans Division. But in 1936 Captain F. R. Garside was appointed to revive it. In March 1937 the Admiralty set up a Shipping Defence Advisory Committee to consult shipowners about wartime arrangements. At the same time liaison-officers were appointed to train the Merchant Navy in ship-defence. Thus by the outbreak of war more than 10,000 merchant officers had been trained, 2,000 of them in gunnery, and 1,500 seamen had been taught to operate guns. Nearly 1,000 ships had been "stiffened" to take guns on their decks. Also in this period of reawakened concern about the safety of shipping in wartime, Paymaster Rear-Admiral Sir Eldon Manisty, the man who organised the convoys from 1917, was sent on a tour, twenty years later, to organise the collation and distribution of intelligence on shipping movements by naval officers throughout the Empire and Dominions and by consular officers elsewhere round the world. This led to the creation of the Naval Control Service (supplemented by Consular Shipping Advisers) early in 1939, a network of serving or retired naval officers who fed the Admiralty with daily reports of shipping movements: altogether an excellent piece of foresight. Not all the hard-won lessons of the First World War had been forgotten.

In addition to these foundations of a wartime convoy organisation, the Royal Navy also had sufficient wit to remember the remarkable achievements of Room 40 under the Directorate of Naval Intelligence in 1914–18, first as a decrypting centre and later as a rudimentary intelligence evaluation service, despite the abidingly ludicrous British obsession with secrecy for its own sake which prevented its contributions from being used properly. This too dwindled away in peacetime as the Admiralty's Naval Intelligence Division itself became a backwater. There were enough Room 40 veterans and enthusiasts in the Navy in the late 1930s, however, to remember the value of intelligence. A few Room 40 people set up the Government Code and Cipher School (GC & CS) after the war, a small body which eventually came under the control of the Foreign Office but managed to keep some vital skills alive at its headquarters, first in Victoria, London, and then at Bletchley Park, outside Bletchley in the north-west of Buckinghamshire. Meanwhile Admiral Sir William James, Deputy Chief of Naval Staff, was seriously alarmed by the desuetude of NID during the Abyssinian crisis of 1936: he had been head of Room 40 in the latter part of the First World War. So deep was the torpor of Naval Intelligence that its knowledge was out of date, it was compartmentalised and uncoordinated and tended to store its information in Dickensian ledgers. There was no proper provision for the dissemination of such material as it had; and thirty years after the use of wireless had become general among navies, Britain possessed just five direction-finding listening posts round the world – two in Britain, one in Malta and two in Asia. The GC & CS, headed by Commander Alistair Denniston, formerly of Room 40, and its handful of brilliant 1914–18 veterans, most notably Alfred Dilwyn ("Dilly") Knox, kept in training but were in tenuous contact with the intelligence sections of the Navy and the other services. It was on the instigation of Admiral James that Rear-Admiral Troup, the Director of Naval Intelligence, appointed Paymaster Lieutenant-Commander Norman Denning in June 1937 to head a new Operational Intelligence Centre (OIC), which was to act as a clearing-house for naval intelligence from all sources. Denning, who started with just one clerical assistant, proved to be the perfect man for the job, a natural intelligence officer of unsurpassed ability. Almost his first action was to spend a month at the GC & CS, which he saw at once was likely to be a crucial source for the fledgling OIC. The "School" already had a separate Naval Section.

The Spanish Civil War, which was so ruthlessly exploited as a training school by the German and Italian air and ground forces, also gave the OIC a chance to cut its teeth by keeping track of ship-movements in and around Spanish waters. Denning was able to establish the usefulness and importance of having one agency – his own – to collect all available information from all sources in its raw state and then decide what gleanings from it should be sent to naval commands and ships at sea. He also set up a wall-chart showing the latest ship-positions, a pilot-scheme for the Submarine Tracking Room which was to play such an extraordinary role in the coming worldwide conflict. Denning campaigned successfully for more direction-finding posts and "Y-stations" which eavesdropped on foreign radio transmissions and even recruited a handful of key personnel to help him in the event of war. One such was Lieutenant-Commander Peter Kemp, recently invalided out of the Navy after losing a leg, who was to take charge of the direction-finding operation throughout the war (and to become a distinguished naval historian, official and unofficial, after it). Most of this invaluable groundwork was done by Denning and his single assistant before the value of their work was appreciated and a few more staff were added to the OIC. The Centre was put on a war-footing at the time of Munich and housed in a new complex under the Admiralty alongside a new Operations War-Room, the Trade Plot (which charted the whereabouts of the merchant fleet) and the War Registry, which handled communications with shipping. A secure teleprinter and telephone network was set up to link OIC with RAF and naval commands and GC & CS. The result of all this was the creation of a flexible, swift and efficient mechanism for the collection and distribution of information that was to be at least as valuable for the prosecution of the war as its most important and spectacular source of intelligence – the penetration of the German cipher system and the "Enigma" machine around which it was built, of which more later. Suffice it to say here that the GC & CS was already at work on this when the war began, thanks to pioneering efforts by Polish mathematicians and cooperation with French Military Intelligence.

This was more than merely fortunate, as the German Navy's *Beobach-tungsdienst* (*B-dienst*, or observation service) was just as busy in the last months of peace keeping a watch on the naval movements of likely enemies and their signals traffic. A special section, *xB-dienst*, had already made much progress in penetrating British naval ciphers, which were hand operated and not mechanised. The head of the English section chiefly responsible for this coup was Wilhelm Tranow. Before he became chief of the Abwehr (Wehrmacht intelligence service) in 1935, Captain (later Admiral) Canaris had already revived the *Etappendienst*. This "staging service" for the German surface fleet was originally set up before the First World War to make up for Germany's lack of shore bases. It consisted of a network of naval officers and agents in ports around the globe whose job was to provide intelligence, funds and supplies and to run support-ships strategically situated to help commerce-raiders and blockade-runners. It naturally kept a close eye on the movements of merchantmen.

The British were well prepared to avoid one catastrophic error of the First World War – allowing exceptionally gifted men to be swallowed up in the fighting forces. In 1936 the Ministry of Labour began to compile a list of intellectuals in the universities, the professions, the City of London and industry, who were to be earmarked for cerebral roles in a future war. The process was greatly accelerated during the Munich crisis, so that by the end of 1938 a central register of the exceptionally gifted had been created by Miss Beryl Power, a rarity indeed as a female senior civil servant who had been a suffragette. By the outbreak of war her office in an inconspicuous converted shop in West London had 80,000 people on file. It was here that the names of likely recruits for the GC & CS and other "backroom" organisations so vital in wartime were kept, so that they could be mobilised overnight, as began to happen in the last days of peace. The creation of this reservoir of talent helped to offset British technological backwardness and may well have been the most imaginative harnessing of ability in the history of British public administration, of which naval intelligence was a particular beneficiary.

The Navy was not quite so fortunate in the man who was chosen shortly before the war to lead it as First Sea Lord. Admiral Sir Dudley Pound, until then C-in-C in the Mediterranean, was appointed in June 1939, with the rank of Admiral of the Fleet, at the age of sixty-two. He suffered from osteo-arthritis in his left hip, which shortened his left thigh-bone, made him limp and prevented him from sleeping properly. This physical handicap would probably have put a premature end to the career of someone less exalted, and with reason; it may well also have accounted for certain personality traits which can fairly be described as liabilities. He lacked humour and the ability to delegate and had no interests outside his work. He was seen by some as possessing Olympian calm and by others as a seething pressure-cooker barely under control. Some of his contemporary critics thought he was too ready to come to terms with the other services in the endless wrangles over limited resources. He drove his subordinates hard and repeatedly interfered in operations at sea to override the decisions of commanders on the spot. He was also a poor communicator who often left key colleagues in the dark about decisions and plans. But his long experience – he was a captain at Jutland in 1916 – and a first-class brain enabled him to cope with the searing experience of working closely with Churchill. His defenders say that his moral courage in restraining some of the wilder naval schemes devised by a Prime Minister (and former First Lord) always on the lookout for chances to hit back at the enemy was a major contribution to the war-effort. There is much in Pound's character that is reminiscent of Jellicoe, his predecessor as First Sea Lord in the latter part of the First World War. His deference to more assertive characters among political and military leaders and his inability to trust the judgement of subordinates contributed to some of the Navy's worst wartime setbacks. At the same time, left in peace to conduct a purely naval operation from the Admiralty, Pound showed sound personal judgement and readiness to shoulder responsibility for fateful decisions which were correct at least as often as they proved wrong.

As we have seen, the British began to wake up to the need for more escort vessels in 1936 and 1937, when Admiral Manisty was at work on laying the foundations of a convoy system. In the naval estimates for that year was an allocation for six sloops described specifically as "escort-vessels." The Munich naval mobilisation aroused unprecedented concern over the uncomfortably obvious shortage of escorts, and the last peacetime estimates of early 1939 provided for no less than seventy-eight such ships.

The Royal Navy had a tried and tested escort vessel of around 1,300 tons displacement (variable according to class) with a pedigree going back to the First World War, when it was first used for the purpose. This was the sloop, originally built as a fleet minesweeper but soon and easily adapted for escort and patrol work. The earliest were given the names of flowers and four survived to serve in the Second World War. The escort-sloop with its shallow draught, turbine engines and speed of twenty knots was, appropriately equipped, a match for contemporary submarines on the high seas. Minesweepers and patrol-sloops, intended for coastal work, were similar but smaller and usually slower, especially in heavy weather. These types continued to be built throughout the war, but of the seventy-eight escorts ordered before the outbreak of hostilities only two were sloops – because Britain's capacity to make the high-precision blades needed for turbine engines was already stretched to the limit by competing rearmament demands inside and outside the Navy. Twenty "fast escort-vessels" – small destroyers of 900 tons and twenty-six knots under another name to deceive Parliament, which the Admiralty thought might balk at an order for twenty extra destroyers – were included in the same estimates alongside sixteen conventional destroyers. Once war came the "fast escort-vessels" could safely be renamed "escort-destroyers" of the "Hunt" class; many more were to follow.

The turbine-blade shortage (destroyers needed them too) obliged the Admiralty to cast about for a vessel which could serve as an escort, be powered by the simpler reciprocating engine and be built by mercantile shipyards to ease the strain on naval construction facilities. The winning design came from Smith's Dock of Middlesbrough – an adaptation of their successful whalecatcher *Southern Pride*. This 925-ton ship was sturdy and simple with excellent seagoing qualities. Its tendency to roll exuberantly was discounted because the new type – known for naval purposes as a corvette – was envisaged as a coastal escort. Unfortunately these corvettes, all named after flowers like the earliest sloops, were soon forced into a role for which they had not been designed – ocean-escort work. Their top speed of sixteen knots was slower than that of a surfaced submarine, and their pronounced rolling made them most uncomfortable. But the first fifty-six "Flower"-class corvettes, reinforced by others built in Canada and later types adapted for oceangoing, were to play a disproportionate role in the coming battle over the convoys. The stand-in became a star; the battle was not lost for the want of a turbine-blade.

Even so, at the beginning of the war the Royal Navy had just 220 vessels equipped with Asdic – 165 destroyers, thirty-five smaller escorts and twenty trawlers. These had many duties, leaving few ships for covering convoys against the fifty-seven submarines available to the Germans. Of those, thirty

Below: Coastal and ocean-going boats meet at sea, 1917.

Left: Captured German submarine in British hands, 1917.

Below: Hitler, on a rare peacetime visit to the Navy, inspects the pocket-battleship *Deutschland*.

Above: Survivors of the *Athenia* land at Galway.

Below: The *Graf Spee* sinking.

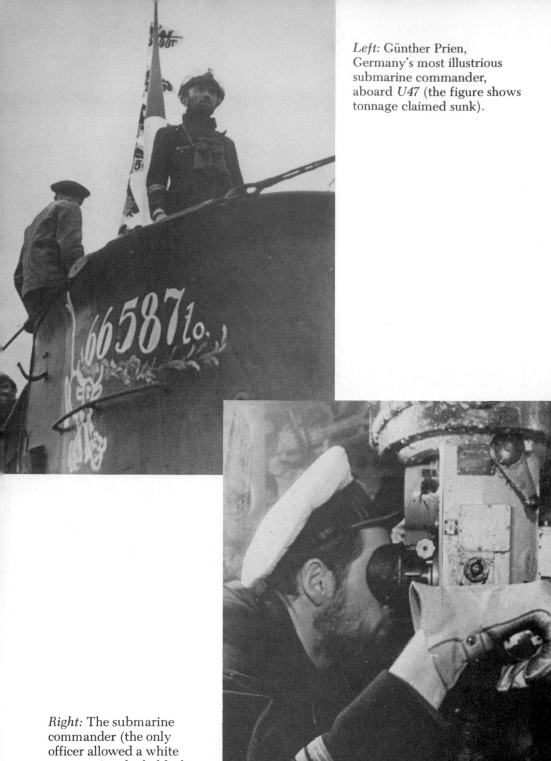

Left: Günther Prien, Germany's most illustrious submarine commander, aboard *U47* (the figure shows tonnage claimed sunk).

Right: The submarine commander (the only officer allowed a white cap-cover), who holds the customary rank of *Kapitänleutnant*, surveys his handiwork.

Above: Convoy proceeding south along England's east coast.

Left: A convoy conference.

Left: Grand-Admiral Erich Raeder.

Below: Grand-Admiral Karl Dönitz, commander of the German submarine fleet, inspecting a returned submarine crew.

Above: The *Altmark* in Jøssingfjord.

Right: British seamen released from the *Altmark.*

Below: The raider *Atlantis* in one of her many disguises.

Above: Admiral Pound (centre) and Admiral Noble (left).

Left: Admiral Tovey, C-in-C Home Fleet (right) meets Commodore Dowding of PQ17.

were of the smaller, coastal type and twenty-seven ocean-going. The German surface-fleet – two battlecruisers, three pocket-battleships, six cruisers and supporting craft – was of course heavily outnumbered by the British (twelve battleships, three battlecruisers, sixty-two cruisers, seven aircraft- and two seaplane-carriers). But the Royal Navy had to protect a worldwide Empire and trade, whereas the havoc that could be wrought by a single German capital ship against a convoy meant that the greater part of the British fleet had to be deployed in scattered groups to cover the handful of big ships available to Raeder. Before the war began the British therefore regarded the surface-ships as the main threat to commerce and planned to deploy accordingly.

Hitler meanwhile seemed to be unstoppable. On 7 March 1936 he had marched unopposed into the demilitarised Rhineland, a breathtaking bluff with just one division. After that he started building the "West Wall" or "Siegfried Line" on the German side of the Rhine. In 1937 he concluded the Rome–Berlin Axis with Mussolini. In Britain the arch-appeaser Neville Chamberlain succeeded Baldwin as Prime Minister while the British armed forces began major rearmament (a confusing pair of signals). Hitler annexed an enthusiastic Austria in 1938, when he also took personal command of the Wehrmacht. In September appeasement reached its high-water mark with the Munich Agreement, which gave Germany the Sudetenland (and with it Czechoslovakia's fortified defence-line), and at once began to ebb: the British Navy was mobilised amid general fears of war and Anthony Eden, Foreign Secretary, and Duff Cooper, Minister for War, resigned from the British Cabinet over Munich. Britain and France then guaranteed Poland against aggression, which did not deter Hitler from occupying the rest of Czechoslovakia early in 1939 and then taking Memel in the Baltic from Lithuania. The Nazi-Soviet non-aggression pact was signed on August 23. On 1 September 1939 Hitler invaded Poland, and Britain and France went to war for a country they could not save. The Second World War had begun.

At the end of June 1939, Karl Dönitz, the commander of submarines, wrote to his commander-in-chief, Erich Raeder, about his own and his officers' anxiety over the possibility of war against Britain when the German Navy was so unprepared. On July 27 Raeder came to the submarine base at Swinemünde on the Baltic to address the officers. Having consulted the Führer on the matter of war with England, he said, he was in a position to put their minds at rest. Under no circumstances would such an event be allowed to come about, for "that would mean *finis Germaniae*." So it did; but the end of Germany was a long time coming.

PART II

THE MAIN EVENT

4

SEPTEMBER 1939 TO JUNE 1940

*Convoys start – German Navy unready – British Navy old – air –
mines –* Royal Oak *–* Graf Spee *– Norway – Prime Minister
Churchill – Iceland – Blitzkrieg – Enigma – Alan Turing – the
B-dienst – torpedo crisis – Asdic – air – disguised ships – French
bases – "Operation Catapult" – convoy system – USA neutral –
Roosevelt and Churchill – Germany rampant – losses at sea*

THE British Admiralty did not after all ignore the greatest naval lesson of the
First World War, the need for mercantile convoys. The first was formed in
anticipation of war with Italy as well as Germany, which would make the
Mediterranean unsafe; it sailed from Gibraltar for Cape Town on 2 September
1939. Churchill, back as First Lord, and his admirals however ignored a key
corollary of convoy-doctrine: that when escorts were scarce, their place was
with the merchantmen, the prime targets of submarines. They thus suffered
the same delusion which seduced him and the previous generation of admirals
in 1914–18 – that the way to tackle submarines was to form hunting groups
to seek them all over the ocean, "like cavalry divisions" as Churchill was
wont to say. Since British ocean-going, anti-submarine vessels outnumbered
German submarines by more than three to one this may have appeared
perfectly logical. But such a view took no account of the submarine's main
asset of invisibility or of the magnitude of the escorts' task (and of the ocean
itself). Britain needed to import 55,000,000 tonnes of goods by sea in 1939,
including all its oil, most of its raw materials and half its food. The merchant
fleet included some 3,000 ocean-going and 1,000 larger coastal ships totalling
21,000,000 gross register-tons. Some 2,500 vessels were at sea worldwide at
any time. One shepherd for every forty sheep was a rather more relevant
ratio than the misleading 3:1 "advantage" of the shepherds over the unseen
and unpredictable seawolves.

But the Admiralty's main concern at the outset was with the apparently
more immediate threat posed by the German surface-raiders, particularly
the three purpose-built pocket-battleships (*Deutschland, Scheer* and *Graf
Spee*) with their enormous endurance of 21,500 miles and their superiority
in firepower or speed (or both) over any British ships except the three

battlecruisers (*Hood, Repulse* and *Renown*). The British were forced to divide their forces by deploying capital ships and groups of cruisers round the Atlantic so as to be able to bring superior force to bear on any individual German raider wherever it might appear. The Germans had a much smaller fleet in 1939 than in 1914, but by using it to threaten the transatlantic trade route, all-important to Britain, as they had not done in the earlier conflict, Admiral Raeder was able both to tie down and to disperse the much larger enemy battlefleet. This was a big return on a small investment, compounded by the British belief that these ships were the main threat. The *Graf Spee* had passed undetected into the Atlantic on August 21 and the *Deutschland* three days later.

As early as August 15 Naval Operations in Berlin told Commodore Dönitz's Submarine Command in Kiel that there would be a "submarine officers' reunion" on Saturday, August 19. This was the coded signal to send all available boats to their war-stations round Britain. The smaller, coastal types were to cover the North Sea while the ocean-going submarines went to positions north and south of Ireland. By the end of the month thirty-nine boats were in place. The other eighteen were either on station in the Baltic or unavailable for other reasons – under repair or in use for training. Dönitz regarded his forces as ridiculously inadequate and on the outbreak of war won Raeder's wholehearted support for his demand that submarine construction be given priority. Hitler agreed in principle but his hopes of an early, negotiated settlement with the British and French and the clamorous, competing demands on war industries from the Army and Göring's Luftwaffe led to delays in fulfilment which amounted to a priceless reprieve for British maritime resources.

But the Z-plan for the vast expansion of the surface-fleet was dropped at once: only those capital ships under construction – the super-battleships *Bismarck* and *Tirpitz* and, for the time being, the sole aircraft-carrier *Graf Zeppelin*, as well as four heavy cruisers – were to be completed. When the war began, therefore, the most formidable ships in the German Navy were the pair of battlecruisers (as the British classified them; the Germans called them battleships) *Scharnhorst* and *Gneisenau*, faster than any extant British or French capital ship. These, the pocket-battleship *Scheer*, the heavy cruiser *Hipper*, the light cruiser *Leipzig*, supporting destroyers and small craft and the First Submarine Flotilla of nine boats were under the command of the C-in-C West, responsible for the North Sea and adjacent areas. The Naval High Command, based at the *Tirpitzufer* in Berlin, kept direct operational control of the two other pocket battleships and three submarine flotillas (ocean-going).

The Royal Navy, vastly superior in numbers in all categories of warship except for parity in submarines (not regarded as important), had an ageing fleet weak in air-support, anti-aircraft guns, cruisers, escorts and anti-submarine weapons and experience. The much-vaunted Asdic had yet to be

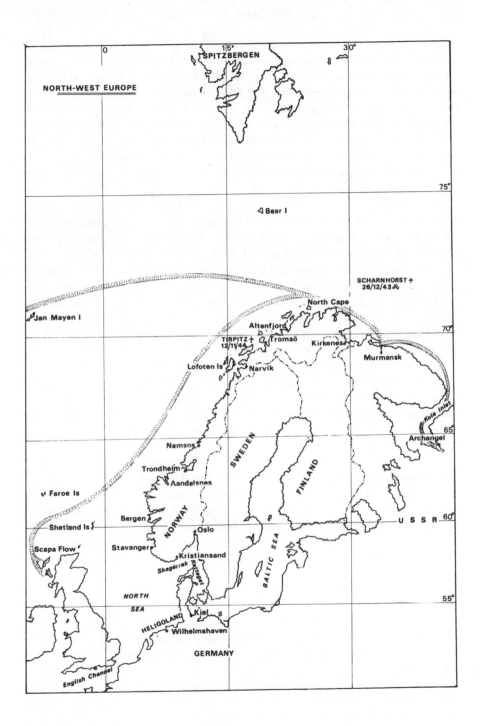

NORTH-WEST EUROPE

SPITZBERGEN

Bear I

SCHARNHORST +
26/12/43

Jan Mayen I

North Cape

Altenfjord

TIRPITZ +
12/11/44

Tromsö

Kirkenes

Murmansk

Lofoten Is

Narvik

Kola Inlet

Archangel

Namsos

SWEDEN

FINLAND

Trondheim

Aandalsnes

U S S R

Faroe Is

Bergen

NORWAY

Oslo

BALTIC SEA

Shetland Is

Stavanger

Kristiansand

Skagerrak

Kattegat

Scapa Flow

NORTH
SEA

Kiel

HELIGOLAND

Wilhelmshaven

GERMANY

English Channel

put to a real test. With this force the Admiralty, the only government department which was also an operations centre, had to cover home waters, the Mediterranean against Italy and the Far East against Japan, which was expected to start hostilities later. The Far East was therefore left with a token naval presence, to be reinforced if the need arose. Some support was provided by the Dominion navies while the French covered the western Mediterranean and sent its *Force de Raid* of two battlecruisers, an aircraft-carrier, three cruisers and ten destroyers to the North Atlantic.

The British Home Fleet was the dominant formation, with its main base at the great anchorage of Scapa Flow in the Orkney Islands off the north coast of Scotland, as in the First World War. It consisted of five battleships, two battlecruisers, one aircraft-carrier, twelve cruisers and supporting vessels (seventeen destroyers, seven fleet-minesweepers). A second aircraft-carrier was based at Rosyth in the Firth of Forth, a submarine flotilla of ten at Dundee and another of six at Blyth in Northumberland. There were six shore-based naval home commands centred upon Portsmouth (for the south of England), Dover (the Channel), the Nore (Thames Estuary and eastern England), Rosyth (east and west Scotland), Orkneys and Shetland (north of Scotland), and Western Approaches (south-west England and the Irish Sea). Of these, the last was to be the nerve-centre for the coming struggle over the convoys, and at the outset it was given more destroyers – thirty-two – than any other command. Various naval forces were distributed among the ports and harbours within these command areas for a range of tactical tasks; a strong strategic force of two battleships, two carriers, three cruisers and nine destroyers (the Channel Force) was based at Portland, in the central section of the English south coast.

The overseas commands included the Mediterranean (the largest, based on Alexandria in Egypt, with three battleships, a carrier and seven cruisers); North Atlantic (Gibraltar); South Atlantic (Freetown, Sierra Leone) including the South American Division of four cruisers; America and West Indies (four cruisers); China; and the East Indies. Also available were the six cruisers of the Australian Navy, two more from New Zealand, and six destroyers of the Royal Canadian Navy. Britain also had one further battleship in dock and five new ones building. Six aircraft-carriers were also on the stocks, and on the declaration of war orders were placed for six cruisers, fifty-eight destroyers and sixty more corvettes. With these forces the Royal Navy was required to protect British trade, blockade the enemy (his trade as well as his warships), cover troop-movements, guard against invasion and control the movement of all merchant-shipping, which was begun by the Admiralty on August 26.

The Fleet Air Arm, as it was still unofficially called after its transfer to the Navy by the RAF from 1937 to 1939, had 232 first-line aircraft, almost all obsolescent, and 191 in use for training, on six carriers and at four naval air-stations. RAF Coastal Command consisted on paper of seventeen squadrons, some of which could not be fully mobilised at the outset because of a shortage of men, in three groups. Their duties were to protect convoys and to carry out reconnaissance and patrols over northern waters. The Command was poorly equipped. Its mainstay, the Anson aircraft, had to turn round sixty miles short of Norway for lack of fuel capacity, so that the rest of that patrol-line had to be covered by a chain of submarines. Although it had been firmly agreed at the end of 1937 that the Command could not be diverted from its maritime duties to other RAF roles, it lacked effective striking power and was regarded as the Cinderella of the Air Force. This meant that Bomber Command had to be called in when air-attacks on major naval targets were necessary; but its crews were not trained for operations at sea. The RAF's biggest bomb in 1939 weighed 500 pounds; and the naval depth-charge had not yet been adapted for use by aircraft. Coastal Command had no fighters at all, and although Fighter Command was to protect ports and naval bases as part of the Air Defence of Great Britain scheme, no air-cover was initially provided for the heavy convoy-traffic sailing up and down the exposed east coast of Britain. This gaping hole in the defence of shipping was recognised in summer 1939, when orders were given for the formation of four Trade Protection Squadrons under Fighter Command. These were not properly in place until some time into 1940, by which time terrible and unnecessary losses of shipping had occurred within a few miles of the coast.

The Luftwaffe certainly played its part in the onslaught on Britain's trade, but almost always on its own account. Raeder fought with Göring on the issue from 1935 until February 1939, when they signed an agreement which gave operational control to the Navy of all air units assigned to work with it. It was child's play for Göring to undermine the pact. All he needed to do was to starve the naval squadrons of aircraft while building up separate units under his own control for work at sea. A long-range reconnaissance wing of thirty Focke-Wulf 200 *Kondor* aircraft was earmarked for detachment to the Navy from Bomber Group 40 before war broke out, but the aircraft were not ready until summer 1940. Before then Navy Group West and Navy Group North each had a coastal reconnaissance squadron of medium-range aircraft, which were soon to be whittled away by Göring. Thus the German Navy was even worse off than the British in air-support. Both nations badly underestimated the possibilities of naval airpower, a strategic error not made by the Japanese or the Americans, whose interest in the Pacific – much bigger than the Atlantic – led to early recognition of the potential of carriers.

The Luftwaffe made its first negative intervention in naval affairs within weeks of the opening of hostilities. One of the first and most important initial duties of the German Navy was to lay defensive minefields off its own coast and offensive ones off Britain, by every available means. The Germans had secretly developed a highly effective magnetic mine, but stocks were very limited. The overriding priority was to lay them as quickly as possible for maximum effect before the British managed to recover some and penetrate their secrets as a basis for counter-measures. The Navy sowed them by submarine and fast surface-ships, mainly destroyers, and they soon became a devastating threat to British ships. But Göring refused to lend the Navy his highly trained bomber-crews and their aircraft to complete the task. The Navy was driven to use its few seaplanes with crews inexpert in these matters. Late in November 1939 one of these obligingly dropped two magnetic mines in the soft mudflats of Shoeburyness on the east coast of England, conveniently close to a naval workshop. Technicians bravely waded out to them and began the delicate but successful work of dismantling one. Then it was only a matter of time until they were effectively countered – but not before some spectacular casualties were added to the losses already caused by mines.

One of the first British moves was to lay a thick barrage of mines across the Straits of Dover to close the Channel to all German vessels. One submarine is known to have slipped through before the work was complete. But in October 1939 two were destroyed and one more ran aground and was abandoned. The Germans sensibly gave up any attempt to use the direct route to the Western Approaches; they were forced to use the long way round Scotland and Ireland until the fall of France. The British however lost more than a quarter of a million tons of shipping to mines by the end of 1939. It is not hard to imagine what would have happened had the Germans possessed more than the mere 1,500 magnetic mines with which they started the war (compared with 22,000 contact mines). The British submarine *Salmon* (Lieutenant-Commander E. O. B. Bickford) managed to cripple two precious German light cruisers, *Leipzig* and *Nürnberg*, while they were covering a minelaying expedition by destroyers off the Tyne in December.

As we have seen, the first German submarine success on the opening day of the war with Britain and France – the sinking of the *Athenia* – proved to be an "own goal" in propaganda terms. Eleven days later the Royal Navy experienced a heart-stopping near-miss when the *U39* (*Kapitänleutnant* Gerhard Glattes) fired a salvo of torpedoes at the carrier *Ark Royal*. This major target was on detachment from the Home Fleet as the core of a hunting group looking for submarines with an escort of destroyers west of the Hebrides, the chain of islands off the north-west of Scotland. The destroyers sank the *U39* – the first lost in action – and captured the crew. The relief at the Admiralty over the narrow escape of Britain's most modern aircraft-carrier was to be short-lived. On September 17, *Kapitänleutnant* Otto Schuhart was taking the *U29* home after sinking three British merchantmen, all tankers. He was on the lookout for a convoy reported by another boat, in case he could add to the useful tally of his first war-cruise, when he sighted a very large and ungainly ship, standing tall in the water, through his periscope. After some hesitation she was identified as HMS *Courageous*, 22,500 tons, the oldest aircraft-carrier in the British Navy. She too was leading a hunting group on a fishing expedition for submarines off the west of Ireland – and two of her four destroyer-escorts had gone away to help a merchant ship in trouble after an attack. Schuhart tried for two hours to get his boat into a favourable attacking position, which was very difficult because of her low submerged speed. But Captain W. T. Makeig-Jones suddenly altered course to enable some of his twenty-four Swordfish aircraft to land into the wind on the flight-deck. The manoeuvre put the old converted battlecruiser across the bow of U29, which fired three torpedoes at a range of 2,500 metres. Two struck home and the carrier sank in fifteen minutes with the loss of about half her crew – 519 men including the captain. The destroyers hunted the attacker for four hours but Schuhart got away to become the German Navy's first war-hero – a well-deserved honour. Hitler took the trouble to travel to Wilhelmshaven, the main German North Sea naval base, for the triumphal return of U29 and to congratulate and decorate the crew. The unqualified coup of sinking a big ship and getting home unscathed worked wonders for the morale of the submarine arm – and by the same token caused alarm at the Admiralty and among the British public with its high regard for the Navy. It led war-leaders on both sides to take the submarine more seriously, and the Admiralty to withdraw the other carriers from hunting-group duties. This reaction did not deprive the convoys of much needed air-cover so much (the carriers were not engaged in escorting but in looking for submarines independently) as it distracted the admirals from considering how airpower might be better used for the protection of trade.

Submarine sinkings of merchant ships, especially those sailing alone, continued as Dönitz reflected on a plan for a stroke at the very heart of the enemy navy, a scheme which had been vainly attempted twice by German boats in the First World War. He wanted to send a boat into Scapa Flow for a torpedo attack on the Home Fleet's battleships – a most daunting challenge for which a very special commander was needed. Dönitz knew all his captains personally: it was his custom, whenever possible, throughout his time as submarine commander to interview them on their return from operational missions. His choice fell without undue difficulty on *Kapitänleutnant* Günther Prien, captain of U47 and as such the first to sink a British merchant-man (the *Bosnia* on September 5, north of Spain).

Günther Prien, destined to become the most famous submarine captain in history for an extraordinary exploit, was born in Leipzig, Saxony, in 1909, to middle-class parents. His father died early and his mother, ruined like so many others by the great inflation of 1923, scratched a living selling lace and her own drawings. The young Prien kept a picture of the great Portuguese navigator, Vasco da Gama, over his bed and left school at fourteen to go to sea as a cabin-boy. He rose to be an officer in the merchant marine but was sacked in the Depression. Disillusioned and embittered by being consigned to the scrapheap in his early twenties, he drifted for a while and joined the

Nazi Party in 1932. At the beginning of the following year he went to Stralsund on the Baltic and joined the Navy as an ordinary seaman. Soon spotted as officer-material, he became a cadet, transferred to the infant submarine arm and got his commission, rising to command in 1938. As a captain he was a martinet: after one peacetime cruise his boat returned to port with a third of the crew on minor disciplinary charges. When war broke out he was already in the Atlantic; recalled to re-equip his boat, the *U47*, he sank three small British steamers on his way home.

In his autobiography, *Mein Weg nach Scapa Flow* ("My Way to Scapa Flow"), Prien recounts the first sinking by submarine of a cargo-ship in the Second World War, showing how chivalry was very much alive on both sides in the early days of the conflict. After telling how he set the *Bosnia* on fire by shelling when she refused to stop and tried to raise the alarm with her wireless, Prien describes the scenes as the steamer burned, the crew abandoned her and the *U47* stayed behind to do what she could for her victim. Approaching the second lifeboat, he wrote, in his not altogether deathless prose:

> "Where is the Captain?" I shout over the water. An officer stands up in the boat and points over to the *Bosnia*. "On board," he replies. I look at the ship. Wreathed in smoke and flames, a floating volcano, it [still] glides through the water. "What's he doing there, then?" – "He's burning the papers." For a moment I reflect on the situation. The man there, alone on the burning ship, hundreds of miles from land, with no lifeboat, is standing there in smoke and fire destroying his ship's papers so that they do not fall into the hands of the enemy. All respect!

Later, the submariners fish an unconscious man from the water.

> I go down from the tower and have a look at the man . . . He lies there like a dead man. He is a small, thin fellow, still pretty young, but worn down like an old horse. Traces of black coaldust on his face and his clothes – apparently a stoker on the *Bosnia* . . . He is pitifully thin. His ribs stand out clearly like the bars of a cage. Dittmer has taken him by the arms and is giving him artificial respiration. Next to me is standing the First [Officer] of the *Bosnia*, he is also looking down at the senseless man, and suddenly he says: "The Germans are really a great-hearted people, Sir." I look at him standing there, fat, well-nourished and probably highly delighted with his grovelling slyness. And all at once I cannot contain myself and I say, crudely, "It would have been nicer if you'd given the poor creature something better to feed on . . ."

Prien made sure all the survivors got aboard a freighter from Norway (still neutral), come to investigate the blaze, which could be seen for miles. Eventually he saw a man jump overboard from the burning wreck. "It must be the captain. Apparently he has finished with his papers. 'You must rescue that man there as well,' I said. The Norwegian nodded and sent his boat over." Only then did Prien fire a torpedo to sink the all too visible evidence of his attack, carried out with punctilious attention to Prize Rules as laid down in submarine standing orders at that time.

Back in Wilhelmshaven waiting for his next mission, Prien, who had recently married, was able to spend some time with his wife. Looking in at the officers' mess on Sunday, October 1, he was summoned to Dönitz's office. Like most people in such circumstances, he wondered what he might have done wrong. He found the submarine chief bent over a large map of the Orkney Islands. Dönitz revealed his plan and made no bones about the hazards of the mission. "What do you think of that, Prien?" Dönitz asked:

> I want no answer now. Think the thing over in peace. Take all the papers with you and work your way through everything thoroughly. I expect your decision by noon on Tuesday . . . I hope you understand me properly, Prien. You are completely free in your decision. If you come to the conviction that the mission cannot be carried out, report it to me. No black mark will fall on you then, Prien. To us you'll always be the same old [Prien].

U47 set sail on October 8, only her captain aware of her destination. The crew became a little restless when the boat took pains to avoid potential targets. The timing of the operation was crucial and carefully worked out for the night of October 13, when there would be no moon and the tides would be right for passing in and out of the chosen channel into the great anchorage by night. In those days, before Italian prisoners of war closed the stable door by building the remarkable Churchill Causeway linking the five islands and islets down the eastern side of the Flow, there were seven channels – four to the east, two to the north-west (all narrow) and one to the south (the Sound of Hoxa). Dönitz had chosen the northernmost entrance on the eastern side, between the principal island of Mainland and the islet of Lamb Holm. The channel (now closed) was called Kirk Sound. All the entrances were guarded by a combination of blockships (many sunk during the First World War), nets, booms, cables and guard-boats. Despite prewar warnings to the Admiralty, the defences of Britain's most important naval base were still not complete in the sixth week of hostilities. Kirk Sound was only half-blocked with cables and wires. The fifty-foot gap had been spotted in photographs taken by German aerial reconnaissance (the aircraft flew over again on October 12).

Having crossed the North Sea with the utmost caution, Prien took his boat within sight of the Orkneys, whereupon he revealed to his men what their target was and withdrew to the open sea. U47 spent the daylight hours of October 13 on the seabed, surfacing at 7 p.m. There was no moon – but that wondrous phenomenon of those latitudes, *aurora borealis* or the Northern Lights, appeared to be doing everything possible to protect the British fleet's anchorage. Fortunate for the Royal Navy also was the fact that the bulk of the Home Fleet had not yet returned from vainly chasing a strong German surface-force led by the battlecruiser *Gneisenau*, which had made a probing sortie into the North Sea. The main force of Admiral Sir Charles Forbes, the C-in-C, was at Loch Ewe, on the western coast of the north of Scotland, leaving only two large ships in the Flow: the old seaplane-carrier *Pegasus*, which was in use as an aircraft-ferry, and the no less elderly but refitted battleship *Royal Oak*, 29,150 tons, with a main armament of eight 15-inch guns.

Prien decided to ignore the natural illuminations and fought his boat against the tide through Kirk Sound and into the Flow. Once in the anchorage, the two big ships were visible some five miles to the north, at anchor in the shelter of the small Scapa Bay. He came in on the surface, which speaks volumes for the nerve of the entire crew, because he needed the power of his diesels to cope with the adverse current and to be able to use maximum speed in the attack.

> At such moments [wrote Prien] feeling turns off. One thinks with the boat, one is the brain of this steel animal which is creeping up on the great, overpowering [ship]. In such instants one must think in iron and steel – or go under. Ever nearer. Now one can clearly make out the couplings of the gun-turrets, from which the barrels point threateningly. The ship lies there with lights turned off, like a sleeping giant . . .
>
> Then there occurs something that nobody [could] imagine, which nobody who had seen it would ever forget again in his life. Over there a curtain of water rises. It is as if the sea is suddenly standing up. Dull thumps sound rapidly in succession, like an artillery barrage in a battle, and grow together into a single, earsplitting crash – bursts of flame spring up, blue, yellow, red. The sky vanishes behind this hellish firework [display]. Black shadows fly like giant birds through the flames, falling with a splash into the water. Fountains metres high spring up where they fall. They are huge fragments from the masts, the bridge, the funnels. We must have made a direct hit on a magazine and this time the death-dealing ammunition tore up the body of its own ship . . .
>
> I call below: "She's finished!"
>
> Seconds of silence. And then a yelling, a single, animal cry in which the frightful tension of the past twenty-four hours released itself. A cry as if the boat, this great steel beast, were itself screaming. "Silence!" I roared – and the boat was still.

Amid the ensuing pandemonium in the Flow, with small boats rushing about, destroyers searching, survivors (a handful) being picked up, Prien, still on the surface, passed out of Scapa the same way as he had come in, tossed in the current which was now running in the opposite direction and against which he barely made headway. In the midst of this struggle a destroyer approached and turned her searchlight on the *U47*. Then she flashed a signal – and turned away to join her sister-ships in unloading depth-charges all over the Flow. The Germans had hit the battleship with four out of seven torpedoes fired. One of the *U47's* four forward tubes jammed. The first salvo of three scored one hit on the bow, which did so little damage that Captain W. G. Benn, RN, thought there must have been a spontaneous explosion in the paint-store, or perhaps a bomb from the air. A small hole was found in the starboard bow, below the water-line, and those on watch had seen a pillar of water go up. One torpedo fired from the *U47's* stern tube missed.

It took Prien, who thought the first hit had been on another battleship, the *Repulse* (which was at Loch Ewe), about a quarter of an hour to reload his three functioning forward tubes and adjust his aim for a second salvo, which scored three hits amidships and set off sympathetic explosions among the ship's heavy ammunition. Captain Benn was one of the lucky few blown overboard. As the Board of Enquiry found ten days later, he "remained in the ship until the last possible moment, until in fact the ship left him." Rear-Admiral H. E. C. Blagrove, the divisional flag officer, was less fortunate. Refusing a lifebuoy, he stayed aboard to help some of the injured into the water and went down with the ship. So did 785 others. The attack took place just after 1 a.m. on the 14th. The *U47* got back to Wilhelmshaven and a delirious welcome unscathed on the morning of the 17th.

On October 15 an old steamer arrived in the wreckage-strewn Flow. She had come to be sunk as a blockship in Kirk Sound – in response to a decision by the Admiralty taken on 10 July 1939 to close the gap. Had Prien waited for the Northern Lights to go away, as he had thought of doing, Britain might have been spared the shock and humiliation of losing a battleship inside the principal base of the Royal Navy. Winston Churchill was however generous enough to describe Prien's brilliant attack as "a magnificent feat of arms." The 31-year-old ace of aces was given a tumultuous reception in port and later in Berlin, where Hitler personally invested him with the Knight's Cross of the Iron Cross, the decoration which became traditional for outstanding submarine captains. Dönitz, who had conceived the operation and planned it meticulously, was at once promoted to Rear-Admiral.

Nor were these the only consequences. German propaganda was naturally cock-a-hoop. The Luftwaffe came over within days to bomb Scapa Flow and units of the Home Fleet in the Firth of Forth. The battered Admiralty, under attack in the press, was forced to add to its own humiliation by ordering the Home Fleet to scatter to anchorages on the west coast of Scotland, abandoning Scapa Flow until its defences were tightened. Dönitz had thought of this also, sending out his submarines to lay mines off alternative anchorages in Scotland in the latter half of October. The shining new cruiser *Belfast* broke her back on a mine laid by *U31* off the Firth of Forth on November 21; seventeen days earlier HMS *Nelson*, the battleship and flagship of the Home Fleet, had been severely damaged by a mine laid by *U33* off Loch Ewe. Both ships were out of action for many months. It was not until March

1940 that the Royal Navy returned to Scapa Flow. Only after the war did it become known that on October 30, *U56* got the *Nelson*, the *Rodney* (another battleship) and HMS *Hood*, the great battlecruiser which was the pride of the Royal Navy – "the Mighty *'Ood*" – in her sights. *Kapitänleutnant* Wilhelm Zahn fired a salvo of three torpedoes from his tiny type II coastal boat and hit the *Nelson* twice. The missiles did not explode. The Home Fleet sailed serenely onward along the east coast of Scotland, completely unaware of the catastrophe it had so narrowly avoided.

Just as at the beginning of the First World War, when Churchill was also in charge at the Admiralty, the British public was longing to hear news of a thoroughgoing naval victory. A nation brought up on tales of Nelson's brilliant victories over Napoleon's navy still had high expectations of the service on which it principally depended for its preservation in war. As in the earlier conflict, it had to endure a series of naval disasters before the first half of the first December of the war brought news of a palpable triumph, and from the same area – the south-west Atlantic.

Before that, however, the Home Fleet received a message for which it had been longing, on November 23. It came from the armed merchant cruiser (converted liner) *Rawalpindi*, which reported sighting a German battlecruiser. If she was right, this was the first known sortie of the powerful twins, *Scharnhorst* and *Gneisenau*. Captain E. C. Kennedy, RN, later, wrongly as it happens, amended his message, having decided he had spotted the pocket-battleship *Deutschland*. But Admiral Forbes ordered his force to sea from Loch Ewe. The *Rawalpindi*, part of the Northern Patrol on the lookout for the enemy's big ships between Scotland and Scandinavia, had sighted the *Scharnhorst*. The Germans had come out to test the British blockade and cause general disruption to shipping and naval movements. Between Iceland and the Faroe Islands the *Scharnhorst* sighted and opened fire on the *Rawalpindi* with her nine 11-inch guns. The cruiser gallantly responded with her old 6-inchers, scoring just one hit before being totally destroyed in fourteen minutes of German gunnery. The *Scharnhorst* picked up twenty-one survivors. As Admiral Forbes was mustering seven capital ships and all available cruisers and destroyers to chase the Germans, the next ship in the Northern Patrol line, the cruiser *Newcastle*, sighted the Germans and set about keeping in touch with them. But, lacking radar, an aid only beginning to be installed in a few ships at the time, she lost them in bad weather. The ensuing search for the German battlecruisers, at that time the two most powerful enemy ships, came to nothing. The unfortunate *Rawalpindi*'s legacy was three weeks of confusion at the Admiralty, which thought the *Deutschland* was at large again in the north Atlantic, as she had been from August 24 to November 8, whereas she was in port, unbeknown to British naval intelligence. Her sister-ship, the *Graf Spee*, was however still causing trouble at the other end of the ocean.

Under Captain Hans Langsdorff the ship was sent into the Atlantic on 21 August 1939 to cruise south of the Equator and await further orders. She displaced 12,000 tons, 2,000 more than the Versailles Treaty limit to which she was supposed to have been built, and 16,000 tons with her full wartime load of fuel, ammunition and stores. She had two triple turrets of 11-inch guns, eight 5.9-inch and six 4.1-inch guns, eight torpedo-tubes and the armour-plating of a heavy cruiser. She carried two small float-planes for reconnaissance and a catapult to launch them. Her maximum speed was twenty-eight knots and she cruised at twenty; she could carry her crew of 1,150 men up to 21,500 miles without refuelling. As Germany had no overseas bases, she relied on the support of the tanker *Altmark* for replacement supplies. Her task was to disrupt and destroy enemy commerce but to avoid action with even the weakest warships unless essential for the achievement of her main purpose. She and the *Deutschland*, assigned to the area north of the equator, were held back until September 26, when Hitler gave up hope of a quick peace with Britain and France.

The presence of the *Graf Spee* in the south Atlantic was revealed on October 1, when the crew of the British-owned SS *Clement*, her first victim sunk on September 30 off the Brazilian coast, was brought ashore by another ship. The British seamen had been gulled by the Germans into believing they had been cast adrift by the third pocket-battleship, the *Scheer*, which was not involved in such operations. But the Admiralty now knew there was one major raider at large to the south. It was only on October 21, when some rescued Norwegian seamen reached the Orkney Islands, that the presence of another raider in the northern half of the ocean was revealed. The next day the American SS *City of Flint* sailed into the north Russian port of Murmansk with a German prize crew from the *Deutschland* aboard. To American outrage she had been seized for carrying contraband in the shape of supplies for Britain, which entitled the Germans to act under Prize Rules. On October 5 the Admiralty and the French Navy assembled eight groups of major warships – five British, two French and one joint – to look for the German raiders. The Atlantic was divided into seven zones of operation while the eighth group covered the Indian Ocean, an enormously disruptive redistribution of Anglo-French naval strength which weakened their forces worldwide, as Admiral Raeder planned it should. Battleships and aircraft-carriers had to be diverted to cover convoy traffic, which entailed taking destroyers away from escort duties to protect the big ships. Merchant masters were instructed to get off a radio message beginning with the letters RRR (for raider) as soon as they sighted one, which laid their ships open to instant destruction by the Germans, even under Prize Rules.

The *Graf Spee* seized six merchantmen between September 30 and October 22 and then seemed to vanish. The *Altmark*, which frequently borrowed the identity of neutral ships as a disguise, was sighted but not recognised by an aircraft from the *Ark Royal* west of the equatorial Cape

Verde Islands (a favoured German refuelling area throughout the Atlantic campaign) on October 9. Langsdorff had in fact been diverted into the Indian Ocean for about a month, sinking just one small tanker, and was back in the south Atlantic before the end of November. He refuelled from the *Altmark* once again off Tristan da Cunha on November 27, undetected by Forces H and K, hunting to the east, Forces M and N, patrolling the gap between Brazil and West Africa, and Force G – the South American Division of the Royal Navy with four cruisers – to the west, along the east coast of South America. Between them they were able to exact some revenge for the *Graf Spee's* depredations by seizing half a dozen German merchant ships. But it was only on December 2 that a fresh clue to the raider's whereabouts was given by an "RRR" message from the British SS *Doric Star*, from a position which indicated that Langsdorff had gone back to the northernmost part of his operational area, north of Brazil. Admiral Sir G. H. d'Oyly Lyon, C-in-C South Atlantic, promptly organised a general sweep northwards by his groups of ships. Force G, led by Commodore Henry Harwood, guessed however that the *Graf Spee* would now come south, drawn by the rich pickings likely to be found off southern Brazil and the River Plate estuary between Uruguay and Argentina. He therefore decided to place three of his four ships – the 8-inch cruiser *Exeter*, the New Zealand Navy's *Achilles* and the *Ajax* (both 6-inch cruisers) together about 150 miles off the estuary, where they assembled on December 12. The *Graf Spee* meanwhile had sunk another ship on the 3rd and her tenth on the 7th, taking her tally over 50,000 tons.

Just after 6 a.m. on Wednesday, December 13, the *Ajax*, which flew Harwood's pennant, sighted smoke to the north-west. The commodore sent *Exeter*, his best-armed ship, to investigate. At a quarter past the hour, back came the restrained message: "I think it is a pocket-battleship." Harwood immediately went into the attack, sending the *Exeter* to open fire from the south and the other two cruisers from the east. This gave the British, who were heavily out-gunned, the double advantage of dividing the enemy's attention and enabling the cruisers to report the fall of each other's shot. They opened fire at their maximum range and at first the *Graf Spee* turned one turret on the *Exeter* and the other on her two allies. Then Langsdorff, identifying the *Exeter's* larger guns as the main threat to him, concentrated all six of his 11-inch guns on her, with immediate effect. Captain F. S. Bell soon lost the use of one of his three 8-inch turrets and then his main steering. Switching to the emergency steering, Bell advanced his ship at her maximum speed of thirty-two knots and tried a torpedo attack, taking terrible punishment in the process. With only one main turret (two guns) still in action, the *Exeter*, 8,250 tons, was forced to withdraw, still firing but with a bad list to starboard.

Ajax (Captain C. H. L. Woodhouse) and *Achilles* (Captain W. E. Parry), each of about 7,000 tons, meanwhile exchanged salvoes with the *Graf Spee's* secondary armament of 5.9-inch guns – sixteen 6-inch guns against eight.

The *Achilles* was lightly damaged by one, and the *Ajax* more seriously by two, 11-inch shells when Langsdorff briefly turned one of his main turrets on them. Harwood therefore put up a smokescreen and withdrew after an hour and a half. *Achilles* had lost her radio gunnery-control system and *Ajax* two of her four turrets. The *Graf Spee*, hit twenty times and having lost thirty-six men but with all her weaponry intact, turned west towards the River Plate followed by the two cruisers, with which she exchanged the occasional salvo. The *Exeter* was limping southwards to the Falkland Islands for repairs; from there Harwood's fourth cruiser, the *Cumberland* with eight 8-inch guns, was racing north to replace her. Seventy-one men had been killed, sixty-four on the *Exeter*. Their enemy, with a six-foot hole in her side and a badly damaged superstructure, sailed into the harbour of Montevideo, capital of neutral Uruguay.

Under international law, Langsdorff was entitled to stay there for twenty-four hours to make emergency repairs. He knew the wolves would be gathering over the horizon (the British began to send all available ships as soon as Harwood reported the engagement had begun, including a battleship and an aircraft-carrier as well as several cruisers). Ironically, therefore, it suited both sides to have the *Graf Spee* stay on in Montevideo as long as possible. The German Embassy got a seventy-two-hour extension, and the British helped by sending their merchant ships in the harbour out to sea at daily intervals – which meant the Germans had to give each one twenty-four hours to get clear before their warship could leave. The BBC broadcast tall stories about the Royal Navy build-up going on at sea. Langsdorff soon realised that his position was desperate and on December 16 he cabled Admiral Raeder for orders.

The only plan he could offer was to fight his way across the broad estuary to Buenos Aires in Argentina, where pro-German sentiment was strong and thoroughly benevolent neutrality could be expected. He was certain that an attempt to break out into the open sea was foredoomed to failure and requested a decision on going into internment or, as a last resort, scuttling. Raeder went to see Hitler, who was most irritated by a drama which had captured the attention of the world through press and radio. The Führer forbade internment and agreed to a scuttle if necessary – provided it was fully effective.

Twenty-four hours after receiving this reply, Captain Langsdorff set sail in the early evening of the 17th. His ship, still scorched and blackened by shell-blasts, had her battle colours up, and in her wake was the German steamer, SS *Tacoma*. As they slid slowly into the powerful stream of the River Plate, *Ajax*, *Achilles* and *Cumberland*, waiting in international waters a little downstream, went to action stations, swinging their guns and waiting for the Germans to cross the invisible line. Thousands of people stood on the riverbank in silence to watch the second round of the battle. No other British ship was in sight. But just as the sun began to go down behind the

Graf Spee, she stopped on the three-mile boundary and members of her crew were seen transferring to the *Tacoma*. The breathless hush was torn minutes later by the first of a series of shattering internal explosions aboard the pocket-battleship, rising to a monstrous crescendo as the scuttling charges set off her ammunition. She settled on an even keel on the riverbed, and flames flickered from her superstructure all night. The *Tacoma* took the entire crew and the captain to Argentina. There, on December 20, Hans Langsdorff, whose attacks on British shipping cost not a single life, put the ensign of the Kaiser's navy under which he had fought at Jutland round his shoulders and shot himself with his own pistol. He left as his last testament a letter with the German ambassador in Montevideo in which he wrote: "I am fully content to pay with my life for any possible discredit on the honour of the flag." There was, of course, none, even though he should not have put in to port.

Hitler's reaction was sour and laconic: "He should have sunk the *Exeter*." The response in Britain to the loss of the *Graf Spee*, named after the admiral who had destroyed a British squadron in the same region twenty-five years earlier, was one of near-hysterical rapture. Never mind that it was not the Royal Navy's shells but Langsdorff's explosives which had sent her to the bottom: the Navy had found him, attacked him and trapped him, forcing him to take the road to self-destruction. Just as the annihilation of Graf Spee's squadron by an avenging British force at the Falklands had brought the first good news from the Navy in the First World War, so the elimination of his monument in the same waters provided the first such uplift in the Second. The American Government, having persuaded the states of the Americas to declare the western edge of the Atlantic a neutrality zone, lodged an official protest in London and Berlin against the blatant intrusion by warships of both sides. Unofficially the Americans, who had been following the unfolding drama by radio almost as it happened, were generally full of praise for the "little" cruisers' undoubted gallantry, which was Hitler's first palpable setback in the military sphere. Harwood was at once knighted and promoted rear-admiral.

There was to be a postscript to the *Graf Spee* drama which was no less dashing and also bore momentous strategic implications. It came nine weeks later but belongs here. The episode concerns the *Graf Spee's* support-ship, the *Altmark*. Her master, Captain Dahl of the Merchant Marine, parted company with the *Graf Spee* east of the Brazilian "bulge" on December 6. On board were 299 British seamen from the *Graf Spee's* victims, confined in grossly uncomfortable conditions in the holds. The *Altmark*, having heard of the River Plate events, lurked in the empty wastes of the south Atlantic, well away from the shipping lanes, until Dahl could be sure that the enemy naval forces had dispersed. On 24 January 1940 he began the long and daunting run home, right the way up the Atlantic, between Greenland and Iceland and over to the north Norwegian coast without being spotted (a remarkable exploit in itself, given that he crossed the convoy routes). By the time he got there, his ship, a large one in its day of 12,000 tons with capacity for 14,000 tonnes of oil, had a grey hull and white upperworks and was pretending to be Norwegian. She carried two concealed 4.1-inch guns and a pair of light repeating cannon under cover on her bridge. Her master, a member of the naval reserve and a prisoner of war in the earlier conflict, loathed the British and took out his feelings on his captives, who were living in conditions approximating to a floating concentration camp. A naval detachment from the *Graf Spee* under a lieutenant was aboard to keep order.

None of this was known to the British, who simply regarded the *Altmark* as an item of unfinished business to be disposed of if and when possible. Dahl managed to creep all the way down the long Norwegian coast, usually inside territorial waters between the mainland and the string of offshore islands, almost invisible in the short hours of daylight and the bleak northern winter. Neutral Norwegian patrol boats stopped but did not search her on two occasions, contenting themselves with the master's assurances that all was in order and mindful of the acute sensitivity of German–Norwegian relations. Late on February 15 Admiral Forbes of the Home Fleet received intelligence from Norway that the wanted tanker had passed Bergen southbound at noon. Happily the light cruiser *Arethusa* and five destroyers of the Fourth Flotilla, led by Captain Philip Vian in HMS *Cossack*, had left Rosyth on the 14th to hunt German ore-carriers. These ships brought the strategically vital Swedish iron ore from the Norwegian port of Narvik during the winter, when the direct route from Sweden across the Baltic was icebound.

Forbes alerted Vian, who was working his way round the southern Norwegian coast from Kristiansand westward. At lunchtime on the 16th, a Coastal Command patrol sighted the *Altmark*. An hour or so later the *Arethusa* spotted her (by the red line of protective paint just showing above her waterline), some thirty miles south of Stavanger. She was inside territorial waters and was accompanied by two Norwegian patrol vessels. Two British destroyers tried to put men aboard but were frustrated by the Norwegians, who let the *Altmark* enter the Jøssingfjord, an inlet in the coastal cliffs. Vian took the *Cossack* in after her. The Norwegian torpedo-boat *Kjell* interposed herself and Vian was told that the tanker had been boarded off Bergen, found to be unarmed and allowed to continue her voyage in territorial waters. Nothing was known of British prisoners aboard.

Vian withdrew into international waters and asked the Admiralty direct for instructions. Churchill himself, as First Lord, consulted the Foreign Office and ordered Vian to offer to accompany the Norwegians with the *Altmark* back to Bergen -- and if refused, to board the German regardless. The Admiralty was gambling that the *Altmark* must have something to hide: the impending violation of Norwegian neutrality was otherwise completely indefensible, as well as illegal under any conditions. Vian re-entered the

Jøssingfjord, and when the *Kjell* refused to co-operate, put a strong boarding-party on the *Altmark* amid exchanges of small-arms fire between the British and German sailors, under the searchlight of the *Cossack*. It was all over by midnight. The British crammed their overjoyed seamen aboard and stripped the *Altmark* of her remaining array of machine-guns (the mountings of the heavier guns were found empty). Forbes, angry that the Admiralty had gone over his head in sending orders direct to Vian, sailed out his battleships to cover the *Cossack's* jubilant return to Rosyth on the 17th. The affair was a minor incident in itself, but it gave an excuse for another general celebration, stoked up by newspaper headlines of the "Hell-Ship Horror" variety.

The *Altmark* affair also focused the minds of the British and German staffs on the strategic importance of Norway, not only because of its significance to both sides as a source or supply-route for raw materials like iron ore but also because of its long Atlantic coastline from the North Cape to the entrance of the Baltic at the Skagerrak. Churchill was profoundly frustrated by the immunity of the German ships carrying the Swedish ore down the Inner Leads, the waterway between the Norwegian islands and the mainland. He had often proposed sowing mines there since the beginning of the war but was opposed by the Foreign Office because of Norway's neutrality (and the effect on neutral American opinion of ignoring it). The Germans hoped for a political coup by the notorious Norwegian Nazi leader, Quisling, to secure Norway for them. Meanwhile the Wehrmacht drew up Operation *Weserü-bung* for a pre-emptive invasion if the British and French showed signs of intending a military occupation. Raeder, aware of the risk to his limited forces implicit in an invasion, was behind the Quisling coup plan. When it failed to materialise, Hitler signed an order for the invasion of Denmark and Norway on March 1, to be carried out early in April, before the already planned *Blitzkrieg* against the Low Countries and France.

On the British side, the insecurity of the homeless Home Fleet was eased by a cautious return to Scapa Flow. The defences had been significantly strengthened by the stationing of three squadrons of Hurricane fighters at Wick on the Scottish mainland, only a few minutes' flying time from the Orkneys; a sevenfold increase in the number of heavy anti-aircraft guns covering the base; and much work on the fixed defences round the anchorage itself. Although some work remained to be done, the return of the Fleet was heralded at the beginning of March by the arrival in the Flow of two make-believe battleships. This pair of sheep in wolf's clothing had been knocked together in Belfast by attaching false superstructures and dummy guns to the hulls of two old merchant ships. They had then been solemnly escorted by destroyers to the Firth of Forth for the benefit of the Luftwaffe – an early example of the elaborate deceptions used by both sides to cause confusion. The dummies were soon followed by five examples of the real thing. The Luftwaffe attacked in the middle of the month, damaging a cruiser before the fifteen bombers were driven off by the new defenders. The Home Fleet put to sea in the third week of the month, partly because bright moonlight was expected but also to support probing operations by cruisers and destroyers around southern Norway. It was also to cover an enterprise given the codename "Operation Wilfred" by Winston Churchill.

This was the much-discussed and oft-postponed mining of the Norwegian Inner Leads against the iron-ore traffic to Germany. The constant brake on British action, the *Altmark* incident notwithstanding, was Norwegian neutrality. The general naval blockade had only disrupted the flow because searches for contraband could not be carried out in neutral waters. The operation envisaged one diversionary and two serious minelaying sorties aimed at shipping coming from the ports of Narvik and Trondheim, at points where it was obliged by the convolutions of the coastline to pass briefly into the open sea. The British Admiralty's thinking had progressed far enough to envisage the possibility of a strong German reaction to such a move, and "Plan R4" was drawn up for a pre-emptive occupation of the four main western Norwegian ports – Narvik, Trondheim, Bergen and Stavanger – should the Germans show signs of moving against them in retaliation. The minelaying itself was to be covered by the battlecruiser *Renown* and supporting vessels. Troops, transports and escorts for a move against Narvik and Trondheim were assembled in the Clyde, in the south-west of Scotland; at Rosyth in the Firth of Forth to the east, four cruisers embarked army units to be landed at Bergen and Stavanger.

Lest it be thought that the impending clash over ore-supplies seems far removed from the struggle over the Anglo-American transatlantic trade route, the merest glance at a map of the North Atlantic reveals the strategic importance of the long Norwegian coastline. In German hands, the ports would give their submarines direct access to an ocean which could otherwise be threatened only from Germany's own very short North Sea coast. Both sides were concerned in their diametrically opposed ways with the iron ore, but the British (and the French, who provided naval and military support) clearly did not take the Germans under Hitler seriously enough; otherwise they would surely have sent the bulk of the Home Fleet to sea as insurance against any eventuality. The Admiralty knew that minelaying would provoke the Germans and proved their foresight by preparing an invasion – but this was only to go ahead under R4 if the Germans, who were rather closer to Norway, threatened to occupy it. The British were thus prepared to make the opening move by the pinprick of minelaying, and then to leave the initiative to the aroused enemy.

The "Wilfred" ships began to leave on April 5 to carry out their tasks on the 8th. On the 6th, the destroyers HMS *Glowworm* (Lieutenant-Commander G. B. Roope), one of four escorting the *Renown*, got lost in bad weather while searching for a man overboard. Two days later, still alone, she crossed the path of the German heavy cruiser *Hipper* and her powerful escort west of Trondheim. The single, ingloriously named British destroyer of 1,345 tons took on the *Hipper* (14,050 tons) by the simple expedient of ramming at full speed, tearing a 120-foot gash in the cruiser's side, before she was blown out of the water. When the facts of this extraordinary encounter became known, Roope was posthumously awarded the Victoria Cross, the highest award for gallantry in the King's gift, for eventually confining the *Hipper* to port for several months.

The *Hipper* group was not the only strong German force at sea. From April 4 British Naval Intelligence had been receiving information of possible German moves against Norway. Ironically, however, the Admiralty had its eyes on its proper strategic priority, the threat to transatlantic shipping, which was feared at that time to be directly menaced by a breakout of the *Scharnhorst* and *Gneisenau*. But by concentrating on the lifeline itself, the British failed to see the imminent new threat to it posed by the rapidly materialising German designs on Norway. Still the Home Fleet stayed in port, as reports came in of German naval groups moving north, and then of a fruitless Bomber Command attack at sea on a force of three heavy ships and ten destroyers, on April 7. When Admiral Forbes decided that evening to take the fleet to sea, he sailed north – indicating that the north Atlantic rather than Norway was his concern. The Admiralty had begun to take the reports of German moves against Norway seriously – but let him go. On the 8th, London ordered the First Cruiser Squadron at Rosyth to leave its troops behind and join the fleet – without telling Forbes until it had been done. Then the cruiser and six destroyers in the Clyde, which were to escort the troop-transports waiting there, were ordered to Scapa Flow to back up the Home Fleet. The First Sea Lord, Admiral Pound, thereby made the execution of Plan R4 impossible. Also on the 8th, the Admiralty pulled the minelayers back from the approaches to Narvik, leaving it uncovered, while Forbes sent ships to look for the *Glowworm*, whose last signals he had heard. The minelaying destroyers were told by London to join the *Renown* – which had been ordered by Forbes to cover the area they abandoned.

The unfortunate Home Fleet commander was further confused by an aircraft report that a strong enemy force was heading west – out to sea – well to his north. In fact this was the damaged but still battleworthy *Hipper* and her escort, steaming up and down while awaiting the moment to enter Trondheim. Forbes sent his other battlecruiser, the *Repulse*, to join her sister-ship *Renown* (Vice-Admiral W. J. Whitworth commanding the Battle-cruiser Squadron) off the Vestfjord leading to Narvik, while he turned south with his two battleships (*Rodney* and *Valiant*) and supporting forces.

The Germans had chosen April 9 as the date for their invasion of Denmark and Norway. The contrast between their plans and those of the British underlines the profound difference in attitude between the two sides at this stage of the war. For the British it was still the "Phoney War" in which not very much seemed to be happening. The British Expeditionary

Force had crossed to France, as in 1914, but had not been otherwise inconvenienced. Ships were being lost at sea to mines, bombers, surface-raiders and submarines; but the only military confrontation of note had been the separate war between Finland and the Soviet Union, which had invaded at the end of November 1939 and, at enormous cost, forced a capitulation on the Finns on March 12. The Russians had also invaded Poland – the other state that broke away in the 1917 Revolution – on September 17, in connivance with Hitler, who had concluded a new treaty of friendship with Stalin on September 29 under which they took roughly half of Poland each. While Hitler was entirely content with the neutrality of Norway, Denmark and Sweden, he was not prepared to let the British interfere with the benefits he derived from it. His plan to deny Norway to the British was unfettered by doubt, scruple or half-measures. He could use the Luftwaffe to offset enemy naval superiority and his own absolute power to overrule Admiral Raeder's objection to the deployment of every single usable ship, including most of the submarines.

Six naval groups were assigned to seize Narvik, Trondheim, Bergen, Kristiansand and Oslo, the capital. Other naval forces were simultaneously to land troops at key points in Denmark, including Copenhagen. On the 8th, the Polish submarine *Orzel*, operating with the British, sank a German transport and Norwegian vessels picked some of the troops out of the water. They told their rescuers they had been on their way to Bergen to "protect" it against attack by the British and French. Oslo was told but failed to alert its forces; the Germans feared that the whole enterprise had been compromised; the British, informed in their turn, did not grasp the significance of the presence of a shipload of German troops in such waters. The last warning had sounded.

On the day, Trondheim and Bergen were taken by the Germans without difficulty. At Bergen, the Norwegian Coastal Artillery, the only part of the kingdom's armed forces which was able to respond at once, damaged two light cruisers, *Bremse* and *Königsberg*, leaving the latter dead in the water. Royal Navy aircraft flew over on the 10th and sank her by bombing. Even if she was by then a sitting target with no power or steering, the *Königsberg* went down in history as the first major warship ever to be sunk by aircraft. It could be done. Kristiansand fell after a few hours of fighting ashore. At Oslo the inevitable was staved off for twelve hours. The German Naval Group Five entered the Oslofjord at midnight on the 8th-9th, led by the brand-new heavy cruiser *Blücher*, sister-ship of the *Hipper*. Four hours into the narrow waterway, the cruiser reached the most constricted point, still some eighteen miles south of the city. With true German thoroughness, she carried not only troops but also an embryo occupation-government complete with officials, filing cabinets, stationery and spare uniforms. At that moment, 4.20 a.m., the redoubtable Coastal Artillery blasted her at optimum range from both sides of the channel. Two hours later, helped on her way to the bottom

by salvoes of torpedoes from the shore, the *Blücher* sank with severe losses.
The pocket-battleship *Lützow* (formerly the *Deutschland*, a name reserved
by Hitler in November for something grander) took over command and led
a withdrawal, landing troops ten miles down the fjord while the Luftwaffe
mounted heavy air-attacks and delivered airborne units to capture the capital.
But by then the Royal Family, the Government and the gold reserves had
been evacuated to the north.

Narvik was taken by the ten destroyers of Group One, which crippled
two Norwegian coastal defence vessels and landed troops according to time-
table. Out to sea, however, the *Renown* and her destroyers sighted the
Scharnhorst and *Gneisenau* going north and opened fire on them. The
German battlecruisers had been ordered north to divert the British Fleet
during the Norwegian invasion and were commanded by Vice-Admiral
Günther Lütjens in the *Gneisenau*; they had arrived with the Narvik destroyers. Shortly afterwards, a ten-minute exchange of fire took place in
appalling weather. The *Renown*, her destroyers unable to keep up in the
conditions, fought the pair alone, took two superficial hits from the eighteen
11-inch guns of the faster and more heavily armoured Germans, and scored
three hits with her six 15-inch guns on the *Gneisenau*. One knocked out the
flagship's gunnery-control system, and another one of her turrets. Admiral
Whitworth finally lost touch in the foul weather, long before any reinforcement could have reached him.

With the Germans ashore in Norway, the British now looked for ways
of dislodging them before they could establish themselves. More naval
reinforcements were sent north, including the battleship *Warspite* and the
carrier *Furious* (which had been allowed to sail without her fighter-squadron
just as the Germans began to seize Norwegian airfields), from the Clyde.
Forbes wanted to attack Bergen but was told to concern himself with Narvik
and Trondheim while reinforcing cruisers took on the former task. The
Admiralty then cancelled the attack on Bergen, apparently regarding the
southern port as too difficult for the four cruisers and seven destroyers
available. Coastal Command wanted to attack Stavanger airfield, already
seized by the Luftwaffe, but was told this would contravene the British
regulations then in force on the bombing of towns, which were to be left
alone if there was any risk of civilian casualties. This helped the Germans to
acquire local air superiority which they immediately turned against the ships
of Admiral Forbes in the southern coastal area.

At Narvik, Captain B. A. W. Warburton-Lee took five destroyers of his
Second Flotilla, with the *Renown* until detached, up the Vestfjord to attack
the ten large destroyers of the German Group One. Bombarded by a stream
of direct orders from the Admiralty over the heads of Admirals Forbes and
Whitworth, he nevertheless managed to find the time to inflict disproportionate damage on an unexpectedly superior enemy in adverse conditions.
Starting with the advantage of surprise, he sank the command ship *Wilhelm*

Heidkamp and one other, and damaged three more, with just three "H"-class destroyers of 1,340 tons apiece. All five joined up to sink five merchant ships. But the five other German destroyers, which had been dispersed, now arrived to counter-attack, sinking two of the British including HMS *Hardy* with Warburton-Lee aboard. The surviving three got away, one badly damaged, and sank an ammunition-ship on the way to the exit of the Vestfjord. Warburton-Lee was awarded a posthumous VC.

Unable to trouble him any longer with its long-distance interference, the Admiralty switched its attentions to Admiral Whitworth, still off Narvik with the *Renown*. On his own initiative he sent his four remaining destroyers and the light cruiser *Penelope* to the aid of Warburton-Lee, but too late. Whitworth now received orders to prevent reinforcements reaching the enemy, to block the escape of their remaining Narvik destroyers and to attack them. The last of these instructions were sent direct to the *Penelope* and his destroyers. He ventured to protest, but the second attack on Narvik was planned for the 12th. The *Penelope* ran aground on the 11th. The attack was called off. London however had firmly decided that Narvik was the first priority and told Forbes that troops would be landed. Forbes was off Trondheim with his main force, preparing to send the torpedo-bombers from the carrier *Furious* into the attack. But the *Hipper* and one of her four destroyers managed to slip out on the night of the 10th and escape homeward, leaving only three German destroyers. The bombers did them no harm and Forbes took his ships to Narvik. The Germans meanwhile were using the short route to Oslo to establish control of Norway with six army divisions. Lütjens serenely brought the battlecruisers back from the far north, linked up with the returning *Hipper* on the morning of the 11th off south-west Norway and made for home, unaware that ninety-two RAF bombers had failed to find them even after reconnaissance aircraft had spotted them. The unrelenting bad weather helped the Germans, but it was not the only factor. Of the returning German naval forces, the light cruiser *Karlsruhe* had to be sunk after being crippled by the submarine HMS *Truant*, and the *Lützow* (ex-*Deutschland*) was put out of action for a year by a torpedo from the submarine *Spearfish*.

On the 12th, Forbes arrived off Narvik, but the aircraft from the *Furious* could inflict no damage on the Germans in atrocious flying conditions. The Admiralty now told him to eliminate the German force at Narvik by sea, so Forbes sent the *Warspite* and nine destroyers up the Vestfjord under Whitworth's flag. The battleship's spotter-plane sighted and sank *U64* as it reconnoitred ahead of the assault group, and warned of one German destroyer lying in ambush. This was sunk as the force approached Narvik, where seven more large German destroyers were sent to the bottom in a fierce action, in which just two British destroyers were seriously damaged. Whitworth was now urged by the Admiralty to put a landing-party ashore to capture the port while it was defenceless from sea and air, but he prudently decided that a few Royal Marines and a force of sailors would not be enough to dispose of 2,000 first-class, well dug-in German troops. He called for a proper military force from Britain. By the 12th of April the first phase of the Norwegian campaign was over, leaving the Germans with a precarious toehold in the north but a well-established beachhead in the south which was being powerfully expanded and reinforced by the hour with troops, aircraft and supplies. A very considerable Anglo-French effort would now be required to reverse the position.

Much attention has been given here to this event for three reasons. Firstly, the opening phase proved decisive; the Germans were not to be dislodged from Norway until May 1945. Second, it marked the end of the Phoney War; the first sustained, multiple engagement involving all three armed services on each side laid bare important weaknesses to those who wished to see. Last, it offered Admiral Raeder a long Atlantic coastline with a profusion of natural lairs for submarines and warships which could be supported by internal lines of communication (and there would also be plenty of steel for, *inter alia*, submarine construction). It proved to be an irretrievable failure of British seapower and a unique success for German combined operations. The seizure of Denmark and Norway was a classic Hitlerian gamble in which he once again successfully staked his own ruthlessness against the irresolution of his enemies.

The first British troop convoy for Norway left the Clyde on April 11 – one day after the Admiralty had added another complication to the ad hoc command structure it was inventing in its uncertainty as it went along: the appointment as Flag Officer, Narvik (in German hands at the time) of Admiral of the Fleet the Earl of Cork and Orrery, a man who outranked almost every officer in the Royal Navy, living or dead, including the First Sea Lord. On April 13, the first British landing on Norwegian soil took place at Namsos, north of Trondheim, when 350 sailors and marines were put ashore to deny it to the Germans. Later, troops were to use it as a base for "Operation Maurice," an attack on Trondheim from the north by British and French units. The Germans immediately started bombing it. Another little landing was made at Aandalsnes, south of Trondheim, where the same thing happened. The British had no fighters and exposed priceless anti-aircraft cruisers to heavy bombing because no AA-guns were available to be put ashore. No sooner had a total of 12,000 men been landed in central Norway than the Cabinet in London decided (on the 28th) to withdraw them. The carrier *Glorious* brought obsolescent Gladiator fighters to the area to operate from a frozen lake, but these were soon obliterated by German bombing. The Germans reinforced Trondheim by land and air because they saw it as the key to the control of all northern Norway. The Admiralty ordered Forbes to assault it with the Home Fleet on the 14th, and again on the 15th (he was in Scapa at the time and resisted strongly, because of German airpower, the idea of an opposed landing without air support). He said he would take the troops in warships but not in transports and demanded a week's intense and careful preparation. "Operation Hammer" was cancelled on the 19th; no doubt the Home Fleet C-in-C's successful resistance was encouraged by an order to be sparing with AA ammunition, which was running out. At any rate, Forbes saved the Fleet. The abject flounderings of the Chiefs of Staff went on, now focused on Narvik as the key to the stable-door which had been slammed in their faces by Hitler. Forbes was told on the 28th to evacuate the troops from Aandalsnes and Namsos in the ensuing few days. On the next day the cruiser *Glasgow* collected the Royal Family, Government and gold of Norway from a blazing Molde, near Aandalsnes. The troops were, against all the odds, successfully re-embarked and brought home under constant air attack, at a cost of one British and one French destroyer and generalised damage. It was a brilliant evacuation, the first of a series.

The commander of the land forces to attack Narvik was a mere major-general by the name of P. J. Mackesy, who only met the peppery and three times more exalted Lord Cork for the first time in the Lofoten Islands off Narvik on April 15, when troop convoy NP1 arrived. They immediately fell out. Cork wanted to attack at once; Mackesy pointed out that the transports had been incorrectly loaded, so that immediately needed equipment was underneath less urgently needed supplies in the holds. Cork was appointed supreme commander on the 20th, but it still took until 28 May 1940 to capture Narvik with the assistance of General Sir Claude Auchinleck – four days after the British and French decided to abandon Norway altogether. Once again, in the opening days of June, very nearly all the 30,000 men of the abysmal Narvik enterprise were brought back safely – British, French and Poles. Norway was written off because rather more serious disasters threatened further south. But before turning to them we should take a brief look at German naval operations during the evacuation.

Considering the high risks to which such a large proportion of the Royal Navy's strength was exposed during the prolonged Norwegian fiasco, British losses were remarkably light, whereas the damage done to the small German fleet was considerable. With reason, Hitler regarded his naval losses as a very fair price for Norway, the retention of which was to remain a priority throughout the war. The British also had a stroke of luck on April 15 as troop convoy NP1 was arriving. Two of its escorting destroyers found and sank *U49*, and from the wreck was recovered information about Dönitz's submarine contribution to covering the invasion of Norway, in which twenty-eight boats were involved. The main benefit of this was probably psychological; the most important reason for the ineffectual submarine effort was an internal crisis to which we shall return.

Vice-Admiral Wilhelm Marschall, the German Fleet Commander, decided to send a strong force to the relief of Narvik when British interest settled upon the area. The plan to attack Harstad in the Lofoten Islands, the main local enemy base, went ahead on June 4 in complete ignorance of the

British withdrawal from Narvik. *Scharnhorst, Gneisenau*, the temporarily patched-up *Hipper* and four destroyers sailed from Kiel, and it was only when they were at sea that they discovered the high level of British naval activity connected with the evacuation. After sinking a tanker, an empty troopship and a trawler off central Norway on the 8th, Marschall ignored orders to press on to Harstad because he had concluded that the British were withdrawing. Sending the rest of his ships to Trondheim to refuel, he took the two battlecruisers on a sweep – and soon sighted the carrier *Glorious* (Captain G. D'Oyly-Hughes), escorted by just two destroyers, on the afternoon of the 8th. They were passing central Norway on their way home, and the carrier had the last RAF fighters from the Narvik expedition aboard after a hair-raising recovery operation in which the pilots had been obliged to make their first-ever landings on a flight-deck. She also had her own aircraft, which meant that she was extremely short of space. D'Oyly-Hughes, given the importance of his ship's contents – trained pilots and crew, much-needed fighters – and the weakness of his escort, seems to have been inexcusably careless. He made no use of his own aircraft to look out for enemy ships, and when attacked made no attempt to strike back with them. The destroyers did their brave best by laying smokescreens and by suicidal torpedo attacks, but the *Ardent* (Lieutenant-Commander J. F. Barker) was soon sunk. The *Glorious* caught fire, heeled over to starboard and sank after those who could do so had abandoned ship. The *Acasta* (Commander C. E. Glasfurd) charged the *Scharnhorst* and hit her squarely in the stern section with a torpedo before going down. The loss of the sister-ship of HMS *Courageous* with her priceless cargo and her escorts was the worst in the entire, sorry saga of the Norwegian campaign. It was also another setback to the cause of intelligent use of airpower at sea, of which, as we have seen, the British had little enough to spare. The *Scharnhorst* was sufficiently damaged for Marschall to retire to Trondheim, which ensured the safe passage of Lord Cork's lightly escorted, main evacuation convoy through the same area.

There is a striking similarity between the opening phase of the Second World War at sea and that of the First. It goes rather deeper than the extraordinary coincidence of the first good news for the British in each conflict coming from the south Atlantic in the first December of the war and being bound up with the name Graf Spee. The Royal Navy, Britain's senior service and principal prop of her power, had the same political chief in the person of Winston Churchill as First Lord of the Admiralty on both occasions, and on each his tenure ended in the first May of hostilities. The poor performance of the Navy in both periods cannot be laid exclusively at his door because it derived from deep-seated flaws in British society and the "Establishment" of which Churchill was at least as much a victim as a beneficiary.

These weaknesses are beyond the scope of this book, but the evidence of events described so far shows false economy, poor leadership, underestimation of the Germans and a blinkered approach to the proper exploitation of human intellect. Insofar as such failings affected the Navy, as they clearly did, its political leader cannot escape some of the blame. This applied to Churchill rather more strongly in the First World War, as he had been at the Admiralty for three years before it began, than in the Second, when he took over only on the outbreak. But his "Ten-Year Rule" fiscal device, whereby it was determined, year on year, that there would be no war for a decade, had as much to do with the weakening of Britain's defences between the wars as any other factor – just as his warnings from the political wilderness in the 1930s against the dictators had much to do with the awakening of his compatriots to their plight. In many respects, Norway was a re-run of the Dardanelles inasmuch as it was a Churchillian stroke at the enemy's flank with British seapower, which collapsed under the weight of its own muddle.

In 1915, Churchill was made the scapegoat and fell from power. In 1940, Neville Chamberlain, the Prime Minister himself, was the victim. On May 9 he won a Pyrrhic victory at the end of a House of Commons debate on a motion of no confidence in his government, when his majority was reduced by 150. It was the final account, not just for Norway and the general irresolution of the conduct of the war so far, but also for the appeasement which both failed to prevent war and left Britain perilously weak when it came. On Friday, May 10, Chamberlain went to King George VI at Buckingham Palace and tendered his resignation. Shortly afterwards, Churchill was summoned to the Palace to kiss hands on his appointment as Prime Minister. The Admiralty's loss of a relentlessly demanding, impetuous and tempestuous chief who could not leave even the competent to get on with a job was the nation's gain: the overriding Churchillian qualities of defiance, will to resist, irrepressible energy and enthusiasm, confidence and the ability to inspire were recognised as essential. As a national rather than a departmental leader, his taste for the broad view came into its own – and there was a much broader range of talent to support and restrain him.

The German invasion of Denmark and Norway led the British to occupy the Danish Faroe Islands (between the Shetland Isles and Iceland) on April 13, and in response to the new Atlantic threat posed by the German capture of the Norwegian coast, a new boldness (or desperation) was shown with the seizure of neutral Iceland four days before Churchill came to power. Possession of this large, bleak island with its geographical dominance of the north Atlantic was to prove of great value indeed as the submarines moved further into the ocean in search of targets. But one obvious extension of British defences to the west which Churchill had pressed for as soon as he returned to the Cabinet as First Lord was to be denied. In 1938, as a goodwill gesture to Ireland (granted independence from Britain in 1921 except for six north-eastern counties which remained part of the United Kingdom), the two naval bases of Lough Swilly on the north coast and Bear Haven on the south coast of the Free State, originally retained by the Royal Navy, were handed over. Their possession would have extended the range of British cover for shipping 200 miles westward in both the North-Western and the Western Approaches. But Eamon de Valera, the Irish Taoiseach (prime minister), refused all pleas to return them for the duration of the war, even rejecting an offer of negotiated reunification of all Ireland after the war in return. Ireland stayed resolutely neutral; the British made do with their Ulster enclave.

On the very day of Churchill's promotion the Germans attacked the Netherlands, Belgium, Luxemburg and France with 134 divisions. In just six weeks of Blitzkrieg Hitler was to achieve in the west what the Kaiser's armies had failed to do in fifty-one months: the elimination of France from the war. The German Navy was scarcely involved in this dazzling land campaign. A handful of Dutch warships got away, but British attempts to wreck Dutch and Belgian ports failed. "Operation Dynamo," whereby a third of a million British and French troops were rescued from Dunkirk, became the greatest evacuation of them all. Another 200,000 troops were brought back from ports further south in "Operation Aerial." The main naval burden of British attempts to limit the colossal damage done to their cause by Hitler's triumph in the West fell on the destroyers, already diminished by Norway and now severely reduced in these dashing salvage operations. They left the Royal Navy with forty-three battleworthy destroyers and fifty-one under repair in home waters. With the coast of Europe from the North Cape to the Pyrenees under German control, Britain now faced the double threat of invasion and of rapid intensification of the enemy submarine campaign against the transatlantic trade route, which had become more important than ever.

On the evening of 16 August 1939, Colonel Gustave Bertrand, head of the cryptanalysis section of French Military Intelligence, stepped down from a first-class carriage of the boat-train from Dover at Victoria station in London. Among his baggage was an official courier's bag containing a heavy oblong object. Waiting to meet him was Colonel Stewart Menzies, obviously come from a formal dinner as he was wearing evening dress (complete with the little red rosette of the *Légion d'honneur* in his buttonhole as a gesture to his visitor). Menzies was acting head, very recently appointed, of the Secret Intelligence Service or MI6. The Frenchman handed the heavy bag to the Scot. Inside was a version, made by Polish intelligence officers and technicians, of the German "Enigma" coding machine.

This electro-mechanical device was originally developed by the Germans in the 1920s as a machine for the encipherment of commercial messages. It consisted of a typewriter-keyboard connected to a panel of electric lights laid out in the same pattern, one for each letter of the alphabet. When the operator pressed a key, one of the lights would come on. Which one depended on the workings of an electrical maze between the keyboard and the panel. The core of the machine was a steel cylinder into which three wheels were inserted. Their order was interchangeable, and the three in use could be chosen from a set of up to eight eventually supplied with the machine. Each wheel had twenty-six settings, one for each letter, and on either side a similar number of brass contacts. Those on one side were connected to those on the other, one to one, by internal wires in an illogical pattern unique to each wheel. Every time any key was pressed, the right-hand wheel rotated one notch; after twenty-six such movements, the middle wheel rotated one notch; and after twenty-six times twenty-six movements by the right-hand wheel, the left-hand one would rotate by one notch, on the same principle as an adding machine but with twenty-six possible positions for each wheel instead of ten. Between the keyboard and the wheels was a further complication in the form of a "plugboard," like a miniature telephone switchboard with twenty-six sockets. Up to ten pairs of these holes were linked at random by wires with a plug at each end. The plugboard was situated under the keyboard. Between the wheels and the panel of lights was a "reflector" which contained one more illogical pattern of wires but did not rotate. On such a machine, therefore, the letter on the key being pressed went through five conversions – plugboard, three wheels, reflector – before it lit up on the panel.

The operator enciphered a message by punching the letters on the keyboard and writing down the letters shown on the panel in the same order. The only way the message could be read was by putting the enciphered version through an identical machine – provided that the recipient's plugboard was set in the same way as the sender's and that the former started the process of decipherment with his wheels in the same settings as the latter's had when he began enciphering. As a further refinement, movable rings were fitted to the wheels so that the settings themselves were encoded; and eventually the German Navy alone added a fourth wheel. The machine was named after Elgar's *Enigma Variations* and in its most sophisticated versions provided some 150,000,000,000,000,000,000 possible substitutions for each letter! The beauty of the machine was that neither its existence nor its technology, which was nineteenth-century, had to be secret but only the way in which it was set from day to day. The early German patents were on file in London, and the British and the Americans developed comparable machines between the wars which were used by the RAF, the British Army and the American forces, though not by the Royal Navy.

Colonel Bertrand's gift was presented on behalf of Polish Intelligence, which had been working on methods of deciphering Enigma traffic since the Germans began to use the machine for military purposes in 1928. In 1932 the French obtained from a spy in Germany the first of a series of documents related to the use of the machine. By using these and their own mathematical brilliance, the Poles were able to work out the internal wiring of the three wheels the Germans were then using. By 1939 the Poles had built fifteen machines with precisely the same characteristics and were in a position to give their two guarantor-powers, Britain and France, one each. Having solved the wiring problem in 1933, the Poles moved on to the greater difficulty of the variable settings. They knew that everybody on a given Enigma network had to have his plugboard similarly set, his wheels in the same order, the ring set in the same place on each wheel and the three wheels in the same starting position each day, according to secret written orders distributed in advance. The German cipher-clerk's first task was to choose his own setting for each wheel, which had therefore to be given (twice for clarity's sake) to the recipient at the beginning of each message. To do this he put the wheels in the listed starting position and punched his chosen setting twice, giving six letters. Then he reset the wheels to his chosen setting and got on with enciphering the message. It may be seen from this that for the first six letters of every message on the network, no matter how differently they read, every machine must be identically set. Once the Poles discovered this Achilles' heel – that the first six letters enciphered the same three letters twice over from the same setting in every message – they were able to begin penetrating the system by analysing the opening groups.

Such was the elementary beginning of the enormous effort to break into the Enigma traffic which the British undertook throughout the war. The Poles were the first to realise that it took a machine to overcome another machine. In order to penetrate Enigma's output they needed machines with the same wiring to go through the possible settings. They invented such a device and called it the *"bomba"* (bomb – because it ticked as it worked). Since three Enigma wheels could be put in six different orders, they needed six *"bombas"* – but at the end of 1938 the Germans provided two extra wheels for the Enigma, which could now use any three from five in any order – sixty, rather than six, possibilities for the wheels alone.

This was the end of the line for the Poles, who in July 1939 turned to the British and the French. Delegations from the Government Code and Cipher School, which had done a little work on Enigma, and French Intelligence, which had been working with the Poles, went to Warsaw. It was then that the Poles promised each ally an imitation Enigma and details of the *"bomba."* The British agreed to concentrate on new methods of discovering the daily settings used by the Germans. The question was how.

One of the very first wartime recruits to the GC & CS at Bletchley Park was Alan Mathison Turing, then twenty-seven years old, the son of an official in the Indian Civil Service and an intellectual Anglo-Irish mother. When he died in the most tragic circumstances imaginable in 1954, his former housemaster at Sherborne School in Dorset wrote in the obituary which appeared in the school magazine: "During the war he was engaged in breaking down enemy codes

. . . His work was hush-hush, not to be divulged even to his mother." This may be the only occasion on record when a humble school magazine published what any journalist or contemporary historian would recognise as a scoop. But it was to be another twenty years before Alan Turing's unique contribution to the defeat of Nazism was revealed to a wider public than the pupils and old boys of Sherborne – and a further eight before a biographer did him justice. Andrew Hodges sums up Turing's towering role by saying that the British "built a colossal machine around his brain."

Turing had gone into Beryl Power's file of intellectuals of potential value in wartime in 1938. Despite his youth, he was already an archetypal "mad professor" figure, eccentric, untidy in dress, absent-minded and given to wild cackles of laughter at imperceptible jokes. Soon after his arrival at Bletchley Park on September 4, the second day of the war, he acquired the nickname of "the Prof." It was not until well into his schooldays that he showed the soaring mathematical brilliance first recognised at Sherborne as genius. Shy, sensitive and solitary, he could also be blunt to the point of rudeness, had no fear of authority and possessed a self-deprecating sense of humour. He was an exceptionally enduring long-distance runner and rowed at university – Cambridge, where he won an open scholarship in mathematics to King's College, of which he became a Fellow after his doctorate. In his two years of post-graduate work at Princeton he sat at the feet of Albert Einstein. As a mathematician Turing had done much outstanding work on large numbers and their computation, an interest which was later to lead him to develop "the turing machine" (the small "t" is a great honour in higher mathematical circles) – a logical as distinct from mechanical construct for handling very large numbers.

Of the many anecdotes about him, let one suffice: while he was out running near Bletchley Park a policeman stopped him and asked why he was *wearing* the gasmask every Briton had to carry throughout the war. He patiently explained that he had discovered it filtered pollen from the air and he was a hay-fever sufferer. The added strain on his lungs caused by the difficulty of breathing normally in a mask while exerting himself did not strike him as a worse danger by far.

His first assignment at the GC & CS was to build a British *"bomba"* (now restyled *"bombe"* as in *bombe surprise*). The first was delivered in May 1940 and was much more powerful than the Polish device, as well as being designed on different principles. Using the latest contemporary data-processing equipment, the *"bombe"* automatically searched through the Enigma material fed into it for repetitions or clues to patterns among the letters. When it found one, the machine stopped and its operator, who had no idea what she was looking after, reported by telephone. At work the *"bombe"* sounded like a high-speed knitting-machine.

Meanwhile, in the opening months of the war, the attack on Enigma continued "by hand" with inspired guesswork by "Dilly" Knox and others.

At the end of 1939 a two-month-old German army message was finally unravelled – the first. In the opening days of 1940 another message was read on the day it had been sent. In March a series of Luftwaffe messages was broken – but turned out to be innocent test-transmissions such as nursery rhymes. Altogether in the first quarter of 1940 Bletchley Park solved about fifty Enigma settings with varying periods of delay. On February 12 the well-named minesweeper *Gleaner* sank *U33* as the boat was laying mines in the Clyde. Three Enigma wheels were recovered from the survivors. On April 26 the German patrol boat *VP2623* was captured near Narvik, yielding enough Enigma papers to enable Bletchley Park to read six days' naval messages from April by the end of May – the first penetration of naval material. It was the papers relating to the use of Enigma rather than the machine itself (we would now say the software rather than the hardware) that the GC & CS needed most, especially the advance lists of ring-settings for the wheels. The Germans printed all such matter on soluble paper.

On May 1 the Germans dropped the daily pre-settings for the wheels (but not for the rings relative to the wheels). Now the cipher-clerk chose his own initial wheel-setting at random. He sent this once, and then picked for the message a second setting which he sent twice, increasing the "indicator" at the top of the message from six to nine letters. This caused a drought at Bletchley Park – until May 22, when a connection was made between a message sent under the old system and the identical signal sent under the new, a bad security lapse by the Germans.

Throughout this early period of groping, very little naval Enigma traffic was cracked, and very little information of operational use at sea was obtained. But once a daily setting was broken, a mass of material became available within hours, and much of the army and air force output was of operational significance. As yet, however, no machinery had been set up for the efficient distribution of the knowledge gained. But the Royal Navy's Operational Intelligence Centre (OIC) warned senior commanders in January 1940 that they could look forward to high-quality signals intelligence, which would be sent in Flag Officers' cipher. The source was not even hinted at. All such messages would be prefixed with the codeword "Hydro" (changed to "Ultra" in June 1941).

Before we turn to the German intelligence effort, it should be borne in mind that many other intelligence-gathering methods were in use on the British side as Bletchley Park got to grips with Enigma. Sources included spies, informers, photographic reconnaissance by air, analysis of radio traffic and direction-finding, sea and air patrols and prisoners of war. Nor should the Enigma machine be confused with a teleprinter: it was a battery-powered encipherment machine in a hardwood box, for use before transmission or after receipt of a message. It was both completely portable and entirely reliable, and very easy to use.

*   *   *

The *Beobachtungsdienst* (German Naval Intelligence) was responsible for gathering information on enemy navies and analysing it. By far its most important source of material was British naval radio traffic. Aided by the inherent conservatism of the British Admiralty, the *B-dienst* was able by the beginning of the war to read all the British naval ciphers (which, as we have seen, were not mechanised) in regular use except those of the highest grades. The Germans had been able to gain experience in eavesdropping on the Royal Navy during the Abyssinian crisis in 1936 by studying its wireless output in the Mediterranean from listening posts in Italy. They were able to keep up to date by doing the same when the British patrolled the Spanish coast during the Civil War of 1936–9. The *B-dienst* thus gathered its own information, deciphered it and collated it for circulation to the High Command and operational units; it intercepted enemy radio-messages, operated direction-finding stations for the location of ships and in 1939 employed 700 people on cryptanalysis, the breaking of ciphers, a service within the service which became known internally as the *xB-dienst*.

The fundamental difference between the German and Allied cryptanalysis-efforts was not one of size (although Bletchley Park alone was to employ more than 10,000 people at its peak) but of organisation. The British had just one service devoted to enemy ciphers – Bletchley Park – and all three armed forces worked in and with it, as did co-opted civilians like Turing and any relevant authority, such as the Post Office. The Germans had seven authorities involved in cryptanalysis: the Foreign Office, Wehrmacht High Command, the three services, a separate Research Bureau (under Göring of course) which studied foreign diplomatic communications, and the *Reichssicherheitshauptamt* (RSHA) which controlled all Germany's police forces. Such an arrangement could only lead to duplication, dilution of talent and the inter-departmental disputes which were such a feature of the Hitler regime. But one would expect a regime bent on aggression, which always has the initiative until effectively confronted, to pay much less attention to reading the enemy's mind than the potential victims, desperately anxious to know when and where the next blow would fall. For the British, and in due time the Americans, penetrating enemy ciphers had a very high priority from the outset, especially in the Atlantic where the submarines kept the initiative for so long.

Nevertheless the *B-dienst* began with an advantage which it was able to retain until well into the war. Able to read many of the enemy's signals from the beginning, it would intercept messages to and from warships, merchant ships and convoys and pass details to the submarine command so that boats could be diverted to areas offering targets. Naturally the British tried to keep such traffic to a minimum by issuing instructions to shipping in writing or by teleprinter or telephone in port and imposing wireless silence at sea, whenever possible; but the inevitable changes in arrangements – dates, times, rendezvous, escorts, ships in company, stragglers, breakdowns and enemy attacks – gave the Germans more than enough to work on. All such information went on the great plot on a green baize table kept at Dönitz's headquarters – a chart which also showed, from penetrated signals, where the British thought the German submarines were, as well as their actual positions and enemy shipping information. Thus the airwaves were as important to the submarine arm as a source of information about the enemy as they were to the control of its own operations. Dönitz's command kept in touch across a wide range of radio frequencies, from the Very Low Frequency (VLF) long-wave channels on which a submarine could receive (but not transmit) signals up to sixty-five feet below the surface, to VHF (Very High Frequency); half a dozen channels, varied according to season and time of day, were always open. Once the Germans had control of the Dutch, Belgian and French coasts they were able to set up a chain of new radio stations for the submarine service. As for the security of Enigma, the Navy was more careful than any other German user of the device, as we have already begun to see. The *B-dienst* took it for granted that the enemy would get hold of a machine (if he did not have one already), and even that he would be able to read its output for a short time if he got hold of the current software. In such an event, captured submarine commanders were under standing orders to report that it had been compromised (by including in a letter home from a prisoner-of-war camp, for example, a special codeword). The way in which the software was to be used once the warning came in was changed by a prearranged, coded radio message to all boats at sea.

Like its British antagonists, who were rather luckier overall, the *B-dienst* occasionally profited from the fortunes of war. One such occasion was unique: the German capture, in the Skagerrak area on 5 May 1940, of the large British minelaying submarine, HMS *Seal*. The boat was herself damaged at the stern by a mine (probably German). Her captain, Lieutenant-Commander R. Lonsdale, RN, without scuttling charges, with wounded men aboard and unable to manoeuvre, saw no alternative to surrendering as a Luftwaffe seaplane closed in for the kill. When Lonsdale ran up the white flag, Lieutenant Günther Mehrens touched down alongside to take the unfortunate commander into captivity while a German vessel towed the *Seal* into harbour. (We may note here that on returning to Britain from prisoner-of-war camp after the war, Lonsdale was court-martialled for needlessly surrendering his boat. He was honourably acquitted and went on to become a priest in the Church of England.)

German intelligence experts swarmed over his 1,520-ton boat. It became clear to them from the radio log and messages that the British were locating German submarines by radio direction-finding. Dönitz's War Diary records that a comparison between actual positions and those reported to *Seal* revealed that the "fixes" thus obtained by the enemy at this stage were poorer the further they lay from the British coasts. The unparalleled opportunity to search through the boat's signals and communications material was of great interest and value to the *B-dienst*. But the *Seal* also helped the German submarine service out of a profound crisis that had arisen elsewhere.

The German submarines, despite their early individual successes in a shooting gallery full of Aunt Sallies, had gone to war with an unreliable main armament. The British were worried enough about their losses to submarines; if they had known what they were spared by one enemy torpedo-malfunction after another their anxiety would have been rather more severe. It will be recalled that *U56* hit the battleship *Nelson* with two out of three torpedoes of a salvo on 30 October 1939 but neither went off, and that *U39* had been caught and sunk when her torpedoes completely missed the carrier *Ark Royal* at optimum range six weeks earlier. It was also noted that the German submarines were largely withdrawn from the campaign against trade to support the invasion of Norway, during which they failed to shine. The explanation for this poor performance was not only the British capture of a chart showing their dispositions (offset by information on British submarine plans found in the *Seal*) but also the great German torpedo crisis.

As early as January 1940 Dönitz calculated that a third of a million tons of enemy shipping that might have been sunk had escaped because of torpedo failures; he was aware of serious weaknesses in German torpedoes by November 1939. Two types were in use in the opening phases of the war: the G7a, powered by an internal combustion engine which burned a mixture of petrol and compressed air and therefore left a trail of bubbles, and the G7e, propelled by a battery-powered electric motor which left no trail in the water. Every torpedo had two "pistols" (detonation devices): one set off the warhead when the missile's nose hit a target, the other fired when a target's magnetic field was close enough to move a delicate magnetic switch inside the torpedo. The submarine captain decided which pistol to use before firing. In general, the contact pistol concentrated the force of the explosion on a small area of the target's hull while the magnetic one set it off from a short distance below the hull, which would be enough to break the back of a merchantman.

The crisis came to a head during the Norwegian campaign. On 13 April 1940, during the British destroyer attack on Narvik, the *U48* got the battleship *Warspite* in her sights from close range and fired a salvo to no effect. Two days later in the same area, Prien in the *U47* (some of whose torpedoes had failed in Scapa Flow) saw "a wall of ships" through his periscope, fired four torpedoes and got no result. He surfaced to fire another four, of which only one exploded – against a deep-lying rock in the distance. As he withdrew, he sighted the *Warspite* and fired two more torpedoes: one detonated too soon, the other too late, and Prien was hunted for hours by destroyers dropping depth-charges. All this was too much for "the Bull of Scapa Flow" (*U47* sported a bull on her conning-tower), especially as some staff-officers at submarine headquarters blamed boat-commanders for being too nervous or inexperienced to get firing procedures right. In a report to Dönitz, Prien wrote angrily: "I cannot be expected again to fight with a wooden gun." In his War Diary Dönitz noted: "The boats are thus practically without a weapon." The complaints of Germany's most illustrious submarine commander could hardly be ignored, backed as they were by so many reports from others. Admiral Raeder himself set up a committee of inquiry while the Norwegian campaign was still going on.

The problem proved to be multifarious. The magnetic pistol was hypersensitive, reacting to natural magnetism in the earth beneath the sea, especially in coastal waters near an area full of iron ore, and even to the North Pole. The contact pistol worked against a sheer surface, like the side of a ship, but not against a curved one, where it could glance off without detonation. More generally, German torpedoes had never been tested in wartime conditions, when they were carried about for weeks on end through varying temperatures and depths in all kinds of weather. The Navy itself had designed, built and tested the weapons without reference to outside ideas, and the only result of misgivings about torpedo performance expressed during the Spanish Civil War was the creation of a second naval torpedo-testing department to compete with the existing one, which was responsible for the faults in the G7 types. The ensuing court martial of Vice-Admiral Wehr and two junior officers of the original Torpedo Trial Establishment also found that the G7's tendency to run too deep was known before the war but not corrected because it was thought that the magnetic pistol would compensate. The contact pistol, being essentially so simple, was just assumed to be in order without serious testing. Eventually, the three culprits were gaoled for six months each – and allowed to return to armaments work afterwards, a mild punishment indeed in Hitler's Germany which suggests that they were only scapegoats. Dönitz, desperately concerned for the morale of his crews, reached for the first readily available expedient: the sturdier, simpler and more effective contact pistol of the British 21-inch torpedo, as found aboard HMS *Seal*. He stole the design as a stopgap, but it was to be another two years before the Germans had a fully reliable torpedo and the last major flaw had been identified and corrected.

On the British side there was no such dramatic single technical setback. Instead wartime conditions brought out a long series of design faults, inadequacies in weaponry and other shortcomings. The most important anti-submarine weapon, the Asdic underwater detector, soon proved to have serious limitations in use. The device transmitted a radio beam in a chosen direction; when the beam struck something with its famous "ping" it was reflected back to a receiver. The time between transmission and receipt gave the distance of the located object. One of the troubles was that this object was as likely to be a wreck, a shoal of fish or even the bottom of the sea as it was to be a submarine. Only long practice gave the operator the sixth sense enabling him to tell a ping from a submarine apart from all the others. Another fundamental drawback of Asdic was that it could not locate a submarine on the surface. A ship using its Asdic also had to slow down quite considerably to reduce the noise of its passage through the water so that the operator could study the pinging properly. Nor was Asdic a reliable indicator of the hunted submarine's depth in the water; and its inability to find anything at very close range meant that the attacking ship was "blind" at the moment it dropped its depth-charges. If the submarine was very deep, this blind period could be as long as two minutes – plenty of time to alter course even at the slow speeds available to a submerged submarine.

The Germans soon discovered that lying on the bottom or going down as deep as their hulls could tolerate offered hope of escape. Nonetheless they treated the new listening device with respect even after they developed evasion tactics. Submariners were obliged to wear soft-soled footwear and to observe exaggerated silence-routines when their boat was being hunted. This indicates that they believed the device was a highly sensitive hydrophone (a passive listening instrument carried by all ships, including submarines, which worked like an ear-trumpet) somehow capable of hearing a pin drop at a great distance. Asdic, however, did not listen to the submarine but to the echo of its own radio-beam as it bounced back from the hull. The Germans' overreaction was very similar to the widespread belief that a bomber-pilot could use a cigarette-end burning 20,000 feet below to light his path to a strategic target. Asdic's blind spots and the fact that until well into the war anti-submarine ships had to drop their depth-charges over the stern (which meant they had to get ahead of the evading submarine's estimated position before attacking) made killing submarines much harder than the Admiralty had thought before the war. The unreliability of Asdic for establishing the depth of a submarine meant that depth-charges had to be dropped in a pattern adjusted to explode at various depths. They were detonated by water-pressure, and it was a simple matter to predetermine at what depths they would explode by adjusting the pressure-sensitive device attached to the detonator. It was only in April 1940 that the Admiralty ordered Asdic sweeps to be made round the clock instead of just during daylight. Until then the prewar belief that submarines would attack only by day and submerged had prevailed, but the Germans soon turned to surface attacks by night – as Dönitz himself had warned they would in his book, *Die U-bootswaffe*, published a few months before the war, and as German submarines had already done towards the end of the First World War. Like the German torpedoes, Asdic had been shown to be deficient during the Spanish Civil War; like the Germans, the British chose to gloss over the weaknesses.

Nevertheless, Asdic could, in the right conditions, find submarines underwater, even if the Germans seemed to be right in their early conclusion that the feared British detection device was by itself no answer. Much practice and refinement, and supplementation by other instruments, proved necessary before anti-submarine ships were up to the job.

The greatest British invention of all in this context was the Radio Direction-Finder (RDF), a deliberately misleading name for what the Americans, and soon the entire world, renamed "radar" (from RAdio Detection And Ranging). This used high-powered radio-pulses which revealed the presence of objects by bouncing off them and returning to the operator, who studied them as displayed on a screen. The Germans had radar too, but they used it at sea for its ranging capability initially – as an aid to accurate gunnery, although they noticed it discovered targets as well as revealing how far away they were. The British used it as a detection device, in the beginning most notably in static defence against aircraft, but also aboard a handful of large ships in 1939. The spread of radar to escorts and aircraft required much work on miniaturisation and technical refinement; the necessity of war soon began to force rapid improvement.

The dim perception on the British side of the value of airpower at sea was not improved by the absence of an effective airborne anti-ship (or anti-submarine) weapon. The RAF's anti-ship bomb proved useless: it had never been properly tested before the war. Even a direct hit (a matter of pure luck without an effective sighting device) usually had no effect because the bomb often did not go off when dropped from a low height; and when it did go off, it proved capable of destroying the attacking aircraft with its blast. But in April 1940 the Air Ministry decided, independently of the Navy, not to proceed with the development of the air-dropped depth-charge. Fortunately Air Marshal Sir F. W. Bowhill, the C-in-C of RAF Coastal Command, forced through the continuation of trials so that a few began to be issued from summer 1940. It was to be another year before the weapon was in general use. The substitution of a depth-activated weapon for the impact-activated aerial bomb solved the problem of how an aircraft was to kill a submarine (the aerial torpedo, in use since the First World War, was useless against a submersible enemy until an acoustic type was invented).

If the Air Ministry was completely wrong about the air depth-charge, it was absolutely right in its prewar assessment that anti-aircraft (AA) guns alone would not be enough to protect ships against air-attack, especially the backward British models. The naval "pom-pom" gun was not enough by itself, and only a few of 1,500 Swiss Oerlikon anti-aircraft machine-guns with exploding shells ordered just before the war arrived in Britain before the fall of France cut off further supplies. The Oerlikon, and the Swedish Bofors rapid-fire anti-aircraft cannon, had to be made under licence in Britain and the United States. For heavy anti-aircraft defence, the eventual invention of the High Angle/Low Angle multipurpose gun relieved the navy of having to choose between a high-angle weapon against air-attack and a low-angle one against submarines and small vessels. Yet a combination of AA-cruisers and fighter-cover from shore proved highly successful in protecting the twenty-five convoys that sailed in each direction between Britain and Norway before the latter was occupied. In fact, of the 1,337 ship-sailings involved, only two ships were lost (both stragglers from convoys) to submarines – and one to the frequent air-attacks. German air-attacks on less well-protected British ships elsewhere were more effective, in large measure because the Luftwaffe had perfected the technique of dive-bombing in Spain.

One further weapon was deployed during this opening period of the war at sea by both sides, but for diametrically opposed purposes: the disguised armed merchantman. The ruse was adopted by the British in the First World War as a trap for submarines in the days when Prize Rules and surface attacks by submarines on merchant ships by day still obtained. The Q-ship looked like any other merchantman but was armed with depth-charges, torpedoes and 4-inch guns concealed in false upperworks. The British used them as decoys, sending out a total of eight into the north and south Atlantic between December 1939 and March 1940. But a stratagem which had only encouraged the German submariners of the First World War to attack without warning when in doubt proved completely useless and even more counterproductive in the later conflict. The decoys never sighted a single submarine, whereas two were sunk in submerged attacks in the Western Approaches; and all of them caused disproportionate disruption in the conventional fleet because of the elaborate security surrounding their movements. After an inquiry in summer 1940 the idea was abandoned.

The Germans had used adapted merchantmen in the First World War, initially as minelayers and then as auxiliary cruisers (*Hilfskreuzer*). When their conventional warships and then the auxiliary cruisers had been swept from all the world's oceans except the North Sea, they turned to the disguised raider, with which they scored some spectacular successes even as late as the beginning of 1918. Inspired by this example and mindful of the tiny conventional raiding-forces at his disposal, Raeder planned before the war to arm twenty-five suitable merchantmen with a main armament of 5.9-inch guns plus torpedoes, AA- and machine-guns. In the end only ten were completed, of which the first six sailed in spring 1940, starting with the *Atlantis* on March 31. She proved to be the most successful, sinking nearly 150,000 tons of shipping (three times as much as the *Graf Spee* and seven times the haul of the *Deutschland*) before she was sunk by HMS *Devonshire* twenty months later. These highly dangerous and effective raiders spread beyond the north and south Atlantic to all the oceans of the world, a constant menace to Allied trade and a cause of unending disruption to the Allied navies. Their deployment added another burden to those borne by the Admiralty in the naval crisis which followed Norway and the fall of France. Before the submarines temporarily withdrew from the campaign against trade from March to May 1940 in support of the German attacks on northern and western Europe, most of the restrictions on their use had been removed.

Only concern for American feeling was likely to restrain them when they returned to the assault.

When the occupying Germans carved up France between themselves and Marshal Pétain's collaborative Vichy regime, they took care to seize the entire Atlantic coastline down to the border with Spain (which was ruled by pro-German Fascists). This transformed the strategic situation in the Atlantic by giving Dönitz bases 400 miles further west than he had possessed before, favourably positioned south of blockading Britain. The Luftwaffe also benefited. But if the British were unable to do much about this new German proximity, the concomitant threat of invasion across the Channel and the loss of their one major ally, France, they could at least strike a blow in defence of their naval strength, already dangerously overstretched. As the French military position crumbled in June, A. V. Alexander, Churchill's successor as First Lord of the Admiralty, and Admiral Sir Dudley Pound, the First Sea Lord, flew to Bordeaux, to which the French Government had withdrawn from threatened Paris, for a meeting with Admiral Jean Darlan, the French naval C-in-C. They pleaded with him to order the French Fleet to sail out of reach of the Germans to British, French West Indian or neutral American ports, but the most he would do was to assure the British that the Germans (and the Italians, who had declared war on France and Britain on June 10) would not be allowed to make use of the considerable French Navy. This comforted the British no more than the pious promises of Hitler and Mussolini not to use French warships against Britain if France surrendered. The meeting took place on June 17, the very day when Marshal Pétain's new government asked for an armistice and when Churchill broadcast his offer of union with France (the armistice was signed on June 21).

The British acted with a new-found resolve born of the utterly desperate situation in which they stood after the collapse of France. They ordered Vice-Admiral Sir James Somerville to take command of the newly created Force H, a "detached squadron" from the Home Fleet which was intended to replace the French. By the end of June Force H consisted of the battle-cruiser *Hood* (flagship), the carrier *Ark Royal*, the battleships *Valiant* and *Resolution*, the cruiser *Arethusa* and four destroyers. It was based at Gibraltar, alongside but independent of the locally based flotilla of the Flag Officer, North Atlantic. Of the French naval forces, two old battleships, two large and two small destroyers, seven submarines and a handful of smaller vessels came over to Britain; in the eastern Mediterranean, Admiral Sir Andrew Cunningham, the C-in-C Mediterranean, persuaded the French East Mediterranean Squadron of four cruisers to join him at Alexandria in Egypt. Of the rest, the incomplete battleship *Jean Bart* went to Casablanca in Morocco, where she could not be finished, and the battleship *Richelieu* was at Dakar in French West Africa; six cruisers were in Algiers and four in Toulon. The core of the fleet – two modern battlecruisers, the *Dunkerque* and *Strasbourg*, two older battleships, a seaplane-carrier and six large destroyers were in the Algerian port of Mers-el-Kebir, and the adjacent harbour of Oran held seven more destroyers and four submarines.

On July 3 Somerville gave Admiral Gensoul, the commander of these forces, an ultimatum: to join the British, to go into British internment, to sail to the West Indies, to scuttle within six hours – or to face attack by Force H. Gensoul decided to call Somerville's bluff – only to find that the British were in deadly earnest. The *Strasbourg* and five destroyers got away to Toulon; the rest were sunk or crippled. This tragedy upset the Royal Navy almost as much as the French, but "Operation Catapult" won a surprising amount of approval in the United States, which had been shocked by German disregard of Norwegian and Dutch neutrality and alarmed by Nazi domination of the entire eastern Atlantic coastline. Many Americans were relieved that the British had shown such determination to stay on top at sea, and Roosevelt frankly told the new Vichy Government that he would have done the same in similar circumstances. On July 7, a Force H detachment damaged, but did not destroy, the *Richelieu* in Dakar. But the grim and ruthless British action effectively removed the French Fleet from the board for the rest of the war. It is difficult to imagine a Cabinet in London still led by Neville Chamberlain taking such a harsh, but in the circumstances necessary, decision; but on June 4, Churchill set a new tone in an immortal speech to the House of Commons:

> We shall defend our island, whatever the cost may be, we shall fight on the beaches, we shall fight on the landing grounds, we shall fight in the fields and in the streets, we shall fight in the hills; we shall never surrender . . .

And on July 14, in a world broadcast, he said:

> During the last fortnight the British Navy . . . has had imposed upon it the sad duty of putting effectually out of action for the duration of the war the capital ships of the French Navy . . . The transference of these ships to Hitler would have endangered the security of both Great Britain and the United States. We therefore had no choice . . .

Amid many distractions, hesitations and difficulties the Royal Navy had recognised in September 1939 that its main task was the protection of the seaborne trade on which Britain's life in the most literal sense depended. Whatever its reservations and despite its understandable but misconceived desire to seek out the enemy instead of letting him risk action with well-defended targets, the Admiralty had decided to rely upon convoy.

The first systematic convoy-service was established along the east coast of Britain between the rivers Thames and Forth on September 6. These convoys were, ship for ship, as important as the transatlantic ones which began the next day: as had been discovered in the First World War, there was little point in escorting an ocean convoy to British waters only to let its ships disperse and come under attack from submarines and aircraft in an undefended condition. The coastal convoys were an integral part of the defence of the transatlantic lifeline; they were made up of the selfsame ships. Outward-bound transatlantic convoys assembled off Southend in the Thames estuary and sailed round the south coast of England, collecting ships from Southampton, Plymouth and Falmouth and forming up off Land's End. These convoys were numbered in order with the prefix OA; OB convoys started from Liverpool and sailed down the Irish Sea, collecting more ships from the Bristol Channel. From OA and OB convoys, ships bound for Gibraltar and the Mediterranean broke away to form OG convoys off the Scilly Isles. The westbound convoys were given an ocean escort, typically two destroyers in the early days, to longitude 12°30' west, from which they sailed another day in company without escorts before making their own way to their various destinations in North America. The escorts would then wait for an incoming convoy and escort it in the opposite direction. The first inward-bound convoy sailed from Sierra Leone in West Africa on September 14, and the first from Kingston, Jamaica, the next day. On the 16th, the first convoy sailed from the Canadian port of Halifax, Nova Scotia: HX1 was the first of a long series bringing ships from the North American ports on the main transatlantic route along which the essential supplies (wheat from Canada, munitions and industrial goods from the United States) travelled. Convoy HXF1 – a fast one – sailed from Halifax on the 19th, and HG1 sailed for Britain from Gibraltar on the 26th. The Norwegian convoys were running from early November, bringing iron ore from Narvik (the British also imported Swedish ore, but unlike the Germans had other sources).

Ships which could not maintain a steady speed of nine knots, and those capable of sustained sailing at fifteen knots or more, were excluded from the convoy system and travelled as independently routed ships. These limits, especially the lower, condemned hundreds of vessels to death for the sake of a false economy in time. As First Lord of the Admiralty, Churchill in the early days of the war grew anxious about the delays caused by the system. Convoys could sail only at the speed of the slowest ship, much time was lost in assembling ships and waiting for latecomers, and the ports were subjected to severe congestion as groups of ships arrived together. But "better late than never" was a principle which should have become clearer sooner. Very fast ships, such as modern liners, could easily outrun the submarines of the time, even if pursued on the surface, and could reasonably be allowed to sail alone. Ships which could not sustain more than eighteen knots were at some risk; but the very slow ones were extremely vulnerable and should not have been allowed out alone. They suffered terrible losses. But by the end of 1939, as the convoy system with its interlocking sailing times gradually got into its stride, 5,756 ships had been sailed in convoy – and only four were lost to submarine attack.

To reduce the demand on shipping, the British Government set out to cut imports by about twenty percent, to around forty-five million tons. This was achieved by doing without unnecessary items and also by rationing. Petroleum products were rationed from the very beginning, and on September 29 the entire British population of forty-five million were registered for identity-cards and ration-books. But general rationing was introduced only gradually – until severe shortages of such items as certain cereals made it unavoidable by summer 1940. Once in its stride, the British rationing system became a model. Throughout the war bread was never rationed, and a reasonably balanced, if often meagre and dull, diet was provided. It was never necessary to resort to the inevitable black market to survive.

To bring the imports which Britain needed to live and to carry on the fight, there were 2,000 fewer ships under the Red Ensign of the British Merchant Navy than there had been in the First World War, but the average tonnage of each ship was more than double, about 5,250 tons compared with 2,300. If each ship could carry twice the load, each loss to a mine, torpedo, bomb or shell was twice as serious. About a quarter of the essential supplies had to be carried in neutral ships. The Merchant Navy, which bore the brunt of the convoy struggle, started the war with almost 160,000 men, including about 4,500 masters, 13,000 officers and 20,000 engineers. Service in the Merchant Navy exempted seamen from conscription to the armed forces, and the informality and unquestionable importance of the work seemed to offset the discomfort and danger of wartime sailing for many thousands of volunteers. When sailing in convoy, they came under the overall command of a convoy commodore, who was usually a retired senior Royal Navy officer of fairly advanced years. The commodore's job was to manoeuvre the convoy and keep it in order – no easy task in the rough seas of the Atlantic, with frequent bad weather, breakdowns, the problems of keeping station and signalling when the use of wireless was banned all adding to the threat posed by an unseen and unpredictable enemy. But it was the Senior Officer, Escort, who was responsible for the safe and timely arrival of the convoy. This Royal Navy officer, often as junior as a lieutenant-commander, had to deal typically with a sixty-year-old retired rear-admiral as convoy commodore, and in the early days there were jurisdictional disputes until it was made clear that the SOE had tactical command. The Admiralty determined the overall course and timing of each convoy through its Naval Control Service and could order precautionary diversions en route; the SOE defended it; the commodore sailed it.

In these early days a typical convoy on the Atlantic routes might consist of thirty-six ships sailing in nine parallel rows of four each, with the commodore in the leading ship of the middle row and an escort to the fore on either side. The advantage derived from the fact that Admiralty foresight had drawn up the convoy system before the war began was to some degree offset by the plethora of regulations to which prudence and time gave birth, to the irritation of masters and commodores and the mutual misunderstanding of Merchant and Royal navies.

Sensibly enough, procedures were laid down for use of wireless, signalling, what to do in the event of damage or the loss of a man overboard or of air, surface or submarine attack and in fog. But the masters soon began to complain about the weakness and, in their view, premature departure of the escorts, the avalanche of signals, the mass of footling information sent by radio which had to be painstakingly decoded regardless of its degree of importance, and the number of people who seemed to know convoy sailing-dates. Admirals with direct responsibility for covering convoys and convoy commodores tended to add to the mound of rules (the proliferation of paperwork may help to explain why it took the captain of the *Bosnia* so long to destroy his papers to prevent Prien seeing them!). The Navy for its part complained of poor station-keeping by many merchantmen, bad manoeuvring, sloppy radio and signals discipline, disregard of orders and failure to follow blackout rules. The two services had to learn to work together and to understand each other's related but different problems. The convoy conference which took place in the port of departure, involving commodore, masters and Naval Control Service, just before sailing soon proved a valuable institution.

Another prewar measure by the Admiralty Trade Division was the establishment in June 1939 of the Defensively Equipped Merchant Ship (DEMS) organisation. Old naval guns and related equipment were collected and stored in the main ports. The plan was to arm 5,500 vessels of all sizes, and by the end of 1940, 3,400 ships had been given some kind of armament, most often one or more low-angle guns. These were manned at first by Royal Navy or Royal Marine reservists or by trained Merchant Navy men. DEMS weaponry eventually absorbed 24,000 Royal Navy men and 150,000 merchant seamen, and even the Army was called in to help protect shipping: soldiers would be put aboard an inward-bound ship with their own machine-guns to defend it against air-attack, and once in port would take their weapons to an outward-bound vessel which they would protect similarly until taken off by the escort. From this ad hoc arrangement grew the Maritime Regiment, Royal Artillery, which at its wartime peak counted 14,000 men. Quite often the value of ancient weapons on merchant ships was purely psychological, a useful antidote to feelings of helplessness among seamen; the universal arming of merchant ships gave the Germans another excuse for moving towards unrestricted submarine warfare. The arming of merchant ships also proved positively dangerous to their own side's aircraft until merchant seamen and the RAF developed efficient communications.

This was one of many dangers for the coastal convoys, which were forced by the protective minefields just offshore to sail in single or even double file in lines up to twenty miles long, with little room for the surface escorts to move up and down and with aircraft suddenly appearing overhead. The

Luftwaffe found rich pickings at either end of the coastal route, where ships accumulated as they waited to enter the narrow lane between coast and mines. So did the submarines.

One other British experiment with the protection of early convoys – setting a thief to catch a thief – proved unhelpful. Enlisting submarines as escorts only inhibited or confused surface-warships on the lookout for Germans. The most readily available reinforcement for convoy-protection was the Armed Merchant Cruiser (AMC), a converted fast merchantman which could be equipped with enough guns (6-inch and others) to deal with a surfaced submarine but precious little else; the fate of the *Rawalpindi* exposed the weakness of such vessels but it was to be another year before a better role was found for them, as troopships.

From the moment war broke out, Britain and France, and now Britain alone, looked to the United States for help and assumed it would be forthcoming. The inhibitions imposed on President Roosevelt, who fortunately believed from the outset that it was in America's interest to support Britain and France, by the Johnson and Neutrality Acts were described in the previous chapter. The fierce debate of autumn 1939 which ended with Congress modifying this body of law sufficiently to end the arms-embargo and permit supplies on a cash-and-carry basis showed that isolationism was still a power in the land even if the supreme political strategist in the White House now had the upper hand. But British gold and dollar reserves amounted in 1939 to little more than £1,000 million, and exports were being slashed by war priorities imposed on home industries. The Germans correctly read the situation in Washington in 1939 as being that the United States would stay out of the war but would find ways of sending munitions and other items. The US Army, after all, was at this period barely capable of putting five divisions in the field and the Army Air Force was weak; only the US Navy had strategic significance, but it was far from being up to the job of a "two-ocean Navy," capable of covering the western Atlantic while guarding the Pacific against the rising Japanese sun. American industry was struggling to meet the substantial orders for aircraft and other items placed by the British and French at the beginning of the war.

Secret, exploratory staff talks between the American and British military in May 1939 had determined that the US Navy would have to cover the west and south Atlantic in the event of war. The creation of the Neutrality Zone in these areas by the twenty-one American republics on Washington's urging, and the establishment of a new US Navy Atlantic Squadron (five battleships, nine cruisers and supporting ships) to enforce it was soon to prove a boon to the hard-pressed Royal Navy. But one of the most important events of all in the early days of the war was Roosevelt's personal letter to Churchill of 11 September 1939, in which the President offered the First Lord a private line of communication. Roosevelt's motive was scepticism about Prime Minister

Chamberlain's will to fight and a desire to be in touch with the one Cabinet member in London who embodied total resistance to Nazism. Underlying that was the conviction that a British settlement with Hitler would be tantamount to a surrender that would open the way to Nazi domination of the Atlantic with the aid of Germany's many powerful friends in South America. Thus began one of the most extraordinary and important dialogues between political leaders in all history, which was pursued by letter, cable, telephone and personal contact until Roosevelt's death on the eve of victory.

The period from the opening of hostilities to the isolation of Britain in Europe ended with Germany in a position so dominant that the only recourse for the British if they were to carry on the fight was the transatlantic lifeline from North America. What this could mean was shown in the last of these first nine months, when Dönitz, released from his unrewarding minor role in the Norwegian and western offensives and having eased the torpedo crisis, relaunched the submarine attack on Britain's trade. The new underwater onslaught accounted for very nearly half of the 585,000 tons of British, Allied and neutral shipping sunk by enemy action round the world in June 1940 – a monthly total twice as high as the next worst, which was May, the only month of the war in which aircraft surpassed submarines in sinking merchant ships during the special circumstances of the Norwegian and western operations by the Wehrmacht: aircraft sank three tons for every one sunk by submarine.

During this period, the total loss of shipping available to the British in home waters and the Atlantic resulting from enemy action was 2,250,000 tons, of which forty-eight percent went to submarines, twenty-six to mines, thirteen to aircraft, six to surface raiders and the rest to other or unknown causes. The monthly loss of available tonnage to all causes and worldwide touched 280,000 tons and represented a net loss of nearly five percent of the total stock in the period – when new building capacity was only about 88,000 tons a month.

The Germans began the period with fifty-seven operational submarines and ended it with fifty-one. Twenty-four boats were lost, one by accident, two each to British submarines, air-attacks and unknown causes and three each to mines and hunting patrols. One was sunk by a passing destroyer and another by a combination of air and surface-escorts. The remaining nine were destroyed by ships escorting convoys. The submarines sank a total of 215 merchantmen and two major warships; but of the victims 195 were sailing independently while only twenty-two were under escort. Since a total of eleven submarines were sunk in and around convoys, the German success-rate against them – two ships sunk for every boat lost – was in fact a dismal failure, masked by a rate of sinking independents that was almost eight times higher at fifteen ships sunk for each boat lost.

Throughout this period the Germans had an average of just six boats at sea at a time, the rest being on their way out or back, in port or on other duties. The average life of a submarine at sea on operations was barely three months, and the yards were providing replacements at a rate some ten percent below the loss rate. Dönitz had too few boats for pack tactics (he had tried them) and had found that sending flotilla commanders to sea to direct combined attacks was useless compared with operational control by radio from his headquarters. But the construction-rate was picking up and he had every reason to believe that with more boats and new tactics – and so many independent ships at sea, which had surprised him – the next phase would bring even richer pickings.

On other fronts, the German invasion of Poland on 1 September 1939, which began the war, culminated in the fall of Warsaw on the 27th. The Soviet Union invaded Poland on the 17th and signed a Boundary and Friendship Treaty with Germany, complete with secret clauses, on the 29th; it divided Poland between her two mighty neighbours and traditional enemies. Most of the other principal geopolitical events during this period, apart from those in the West described in this chapter, were also initiated by Moscow. The Russians negotiated an end to their border-conflict with the Japanese in the Far East (the Japanese, having invaded Manchuria in 1931, finally set up a puppet government in China, based in Nanking, on 30 March 1940). The Winter War with Finland which began on 30 November 1939 proved very difficult for the Red Army, which took until 12 March 1940 to force the Finns to surrender. The Soviet Union incorporated Finnish Karelia. In mid-June 1940 it occupied the Baltic states of Latvia, Lithuania and Estonia (with the blessing of Hitler and his treaty); at the end of the month the Russians took the regions of Bukovina and Bessarabia from Rumania. With that Stalin recovered almost all the territory Russia had lost as a result of the 1917 Revolution except for half of Finland and half of Poland, which remained under Nazi control until the latter days of the war.

5

JUNE 1940 TO MARCH 1941

Dönitz in Brittany – Britain at bay – disguised raiders – Mediter-ranean closed – Canada helps – "No surrender" – US aid – "destroyers for bases" – secrets for sale – Lend–Lease – Anglo-American rapprochement – the Happy Time of the German aces – Battle of Britain – wolf-packs – escort-groups – Western Ap-proaches – the Gap – surface actions – Luftwaffe – loss of three aces – Intelligence – life in the submarine arm – radar, HF/DF – tactics – Kondors – "clear the ports" – losses at sea

THE German Navy, still nursing its many wounds from the Norwegian campaign, stood on the sidelines as the Army raced to the North Sea and Channel coasts and then swept southward along the French Atlantic littoral. But the naval staff had not been idle. The fundamental strategic advantage to be derived in the maritime struggle against the sole undefeated enemy, Britain, by possession of the French ports was not only fully understood but also well provided for in advance. So on 23 June 1940, just two days after the armistice with France, a great convoy of trucks left Wilhelmshaven and the other north German naval bases, loaded with torpedoes, mines, spare parts and submarine equipment. This *Torpedozug* (torpedo train), as Dönitz called it in his War Diary, was bound for Paris, where he temporarily set up his headquarters, for onward movement to the coast as soon as the French naval bases could be made ready to receive it and the accompanying mainten-ance personnel.

This excellent example of staff work ensured that the first Atlantic submarine base was open for business at Lorient on July 6; the first boat to put in was Lemp's *U30* on the 7th. Minesweepers and small craft were already in place, for escort and port work. Shortly afterwards Dönitz and his small command staff moved from Paris to a commandeered villa at Kernevel near Lorient, from which they directed their now immensely enhanced campaign for the next three years. The submarines were some 450 miles closer, in sailing terms, to the enemy's vital sealanes, which meant they could extend the range of operations of the ocean-going boats and also send the smaller, coastal types to operate all round the British Isles, conveniently within range of their limited fuel supplies. The torpedo "jinx" had been subdued, if not completely overcome, by Commander Victor Oehrn in the *U37*, who returned to Wilhelmshaven on 9 June 1940 after sinking ten ships with the remarkable combined tonnage of 41,200 and damaging one more, of 9,500 tons, all in less than five weeks. Operating in the Western Approaches and off the coast of southern England, he was able to stop and search several of his victims and use gunfire or scuttling charges to sink them. He had no success with the modified magnetic pistols now fitted to the German torpedoes – but he scored four hits fair and square with the copied British contact pistol they now carried. Word went swiftly round the boats and morale was restored. The submarines were able to achieve their highest monthly score of the war in June, even before the French bases became available: almost 250,000 tons of shipping destroyed.

This was not only the result of restored confidence on the German side. The British now faced a terrible dilemma because the Wehrmacht was in total command of the eastern side of the Channel, which had ceased to be "English" for the first time since Napoleon's day. Mammoth guns were already fighting lumbering artillery duels across the Dover Straits, and the Germans were also using theirs to fire on shipping. The Luftwaffe was able to attack ships in strength off the southern and eastern English coasts with short-range aircraft. E-boats, fast light craft superior to anything built by the British in this category, were able to make hit-and-run raids from Dutch ports into the North Sea. Opportunities for minelaying were multiplied. The British were forced into a hugely disruptive reorganisation of coastal shipping which involved shifting much of the burden from east to west-coast ports, re-routeing ocean convoys away from the Western to the North-Western Approaches (from the south to the north of Ireland) and restricting the use of the most exposed waters to essential local traffic. Previously only German traffic could not risk passing the Channel; now the Straits were available to neither side. But for the British all these new disadvantages were dominated by the threat of imminent invasion. The stark choice they faced lay between redisposing naval and air strength against such an attack and ensuring the survival of the people by protecting the shipping that brought the vital supplies. Even the Royal Navy could not hope to do both, especially after all its recent destroyer losses; and Churchill's Cabinet and the Chiefs of Staff were unanimous in giving priority to preventing or resisting a German invasion.

The German surface-fleet was rapidly reviving and the Luftwaffe had huge numbers of bombers, dive-bombers and fighters well placed to use apparent air superiority to offset naval inferiority. It was clear to both sides that there would shortly be a struggle for domination of the airspace over the likely invasion routes. RAF Fighter Command with its uniquely developed radar-support on the ground was inferior neither in quality nor in quantity to Göring's available fighter forces, but it was dangerously short of reserves in both aircraft and pilots and it faced a potentially overwhelming multiplicity of targets as well as enemies which could dissipate its strength. Certainly there was nothing to spare for coastal convoy escort.

As the Home Fleet under Admiral Forbes once again abandoned Scapa Flow in favour of the Firth of Forth, so as to be in a better position to rush south against an invasion fleet, both it and the Western Approaches Command were stripped of destroyers. Against Forbes's advice, cruisers were dispersed round the endangered coastline as another measure to counter the feared assault on south-east England.

A hugely confident Adolf Hitler asked for reports on readiness for an invasion of England on 2 July 1940. Two weeks later he issued his Directive number sixteen "on preparations for a landing operation against England" – Operation Sealion, in which the Luftwaffe was ordered to destroy British air-defences, the Navy to assemble an invasion fleet and the Army to provide an army group for the task. The next Directive, on August 1, ordered intensified air-attacks against the RAF, its bases, the aircraft industry in Britain and related targets from August 5; on the same day he set the invasion-date as September 15. The Navy, strongly represented by Raeder, succeeded in overcoming the Army's simplistic and over-confident plan for an assault on a broad front. There were to be only four landing-points, on the Kent and Sussex coasts. Troops, ships, barges and other craft were assembled in ports from Delfzijl in the Netherlands to Le Havre in Normandy, where they were bombarded from time to time by British ships and aircraft. On August 17 Hitler declared a total blockade in all the waters round Britain, in which all ships, including neutrals, were subject to attack without warning. The restricted area coincided almost exactly with the zone barred to United States shipping by American neutrality law, which eliminated the danger of sinking US vessels. Hitler and Raeder were as anxious as ever to avoid unnecessary provocation of Washington in a presidential election year.

As the air forces braced themselves for the coming clash, the navies studied the geography of the Atlantic Ocean, in particular the islands which might confer an advantage on one side or the other as the maritime struggle moved westward. As we have seen, the British Royal Marines landed in Iceland early in May, after Norway, and were reinforced later in the month by Army infantry. Hvalfjord, north of Reykjavik, was chosen as a naval base. British Marines and troops also took firm control of the Faroe Islands. In June the Iceland garrison was further reinforced by Canadian troops direct from Halifax. An Admiralty request in June for the stationing of reconnaissance aircraft in Iceland by RAF Coastal Command was not met, because of the shortage of aircraft: only a handful of elderly planes of limited range were based there for the time being. Bomber Command still enjoyed absolute priority in supplies of longer-range aircraft because the bombing of Germany or German-controlled territory was for a long time virtually the only way in which the British were able to take the offensive. What was lamentably misunderstood by the Air Ministry until rather later in the war was the great difference just a small number of adapted bombers – one or two squadrons out of hundreds – might make to the elemental fight for survival represented by the struggle over the transatlantic trade routes.

Other islands considered by both sides were the Spanish Canaries and the Portuguese Cape Verde and Azores groups. Portugal, Britain's oldest ally, was neutral; so was Spain, wisely kept out of the war despite the pressures on Franco from his fellow-Fascists, Hitler and Mussolini, who had done so much to help him overthrow the Spanish Republic. In the end each side decided not to move against these islands unless the other did, or seemed about to do so. Their capture would have been simple enough, but keeping them against counter-invasion would have been more trouble than they were worth. It was only much later in the Atlantic campaign that the Azores came to play an important role; in the meantime, each side made free use of the remote waters round these islands according to need. It also suited both belligerents to maintain the status quo in the Iberian Peninsula rather than to disturb it by seizing the possessions of the two neutrals which shared it.

The waters in the Azores region were particularly favoured by the German surface-raiders and disguised merchant cruisers, which often went there to rendezvous with their supply-ships. The disguised raiders which, as noted above, began to slip out in March 1940, started to make their elusive presence felt on the world's oceans in June. In each of the previous two months they sank just one ship, but in June they accounted for four, totalling nearly 30,000 tons. Hard information about this new threat to Britain's worldwide trade came on July 18, when survivors from two British merchant-men came ashore on a small West Indian island and told their story. By that time the whole of the first wave of six such raiders was at sea, having set sail between March 31 and July 9 at a rate of one per month except for June, when two left. Earmarked before the war for their long endurance, each had six modern 15-centimetre (5.9-inch) guns and four torpedo-tubes (one had six). They averaged between seven and eight thousand tons, slightly larger than the normal run of merchant ships of the time, and most of them had a maximum speed of eighteen knots, also higher than usual but not extraordinary. A typical raider of this kind might have been a fruit-boat in peacetime (one captive had the wit to demand a banana when brought aboard a raider) and they all carried a supply of mines when they set out. Variously romanticised in German propaganda as "ghost-ships" or "ships without a harbour," they relied on the *Etappendienst* network of supply-ships or on their own captures for fuel and stores; in the Pacific they were able to make use of remote Japanese island possessions, even before Japan entered the war in December 1941.

They had enormous supplies of paint with which they frequently changed their identities, and carried dummy funnels, telescopic masts and bits and pieces of fake superstructure which could be added or taken away to change the outline in keeping with the selected disguise. The armaments were hidden in the upperworks; the sudden transformation, as the flaps were hydraulically raised or lowered and guns worthy of a cruiser appeared, shocked those unfortunate enough to be tricked by them. They even carried one or two small seaplanes for scouting purposes and altogether amounted to a devastating weapon against the overstretched navy of the world's leading mercantile trading power.

By the end of 1941 seven of these ships had destroyed almost 600,000 tons of shipping, including one cruiser and three armed merchant cruisers. They relied on surprise and were particularly careful to monitor a victim's radio. If they picked up an attempt to get off the standard "QQQ" signal indicating a disguised raider, they would waste no time in unmasking their guns and blasting the captive's superstructure. Otherwise a party from the crew of about 350 men would board, check the cargo, take the victim's seamen prisoner and dispose of the vessel by explosive charges or gunfire (unless it was a tanker or other immediately usable prize) before moving well away from the scene. British anxiety about these dangerous ships was reflected in hostile propaganda about underhand methods of waging war, but in general the raiders, though obliged to be ruthless, were not wilfully brutal. One captain, Hellmuth von Ruckteschell, who commanded first the *Widder* and later the *Michel*, was convicted as a war criminal by a British military court in Hamburg in 1947; his seven-year sentence reflected the quality of the evidence (it was comparatively light). He had escaped prosecution for alleged war-crimes as a submarine commander in the First World War.

An example of the disruption the disguised raiders caused, in addition to material damage, is provided by the reaction of the British naval C-in-C, West Indies and America, to the story told by the two survivors. Admiral Sir Charles Kennedy-Purvis diverted all convoys in his area to sail as close as possible to the US coast to take advantage of the American neutrality zone, and ordered his handful of mostly elderly cruisers to patrol the seaways among the West Indian islands. He also took the eminently sensible step, which could usefully have been imitated elsewhere on a permanent basis, of banning all sailings by independently routed ships. As the raiders were given licence to roam all the oceans they are peripheral to the story of the Atlantic struggle except in one important respect: the considerable extra strain they imposed on the Royal Navy's resources for that crucial conflict, just as so many other new factors came into play against the British at sea. The sometimes remarkable adventures of the raiders – the *Komet* went to the Pacific from Bergen in Norway via the mostly frozen waters north of Russia with Soviet assistance, a two-month epic which was more than enough to ensure total surprise – will therefore be referred to only when they impinge directly on the Atlantic theatre. The Italians were soon discouraged from joining in this form of warfare. Their sole armed merchant raider, the *Ramb I*, was caught and sunk in the Indian Ocean in February 1941 by a British cruiser (*Leander*), just one week after setting out from the Horn of Africa and without having caused any damage.

British intelligence about the German raiders remained vague. Many losses caused by them were attributed to submarines, mines or accidents. Their disguises added to the confusion, but when a ship was discerned to exist as a distinct entity, it was given a letter ("Raider A" and so on) and an attempt was made to track its movements on the Admiralty's plot. The British gave the ships letters in the order in which they discovered their existence, not the order in which they sailed (which was unknown to London). Thus the first, *Atlantis*, was labelled Raider C by the Royal Navy (and referred to in German coded messages as *Schiff* – ship – 16!).

The first suspicion that a new element was in play came as early as May 1940, when it was discovered that German mines had been laid off Cape Agulhas in South Africa, the southernmost extremity of the African continent. This was thousands of miles beyond the range of any contemporary submarine (unless it had been refuelled at sea, a practice the Germans had not yet made routine); no conventional surface-raider was known to be in the area at the time.

There was a powerful new reason for sowing mines so far afield on the Cape route. Italy's entry into the war on 10 June 1940 had effectively closed the Mediterranean to British merchant ships, which were thus denied the use of the Suez Canal on their way to India, the Far East and Australasia. Vessels bound for such destinations therefore had 10,000 miles added to the round trip, an extra six weeks at sea. Taking the traffic on these routes into account, this meant that the equivalent of 150 ships were lost to the already dwindling stock available to the British. Under siege by sea and air, its army saved by a brilliant though desperate evacuation but without the precious equipment abandoned in France, Britain was in even greater danger than it had been in the time of Napoleon, the last enemy to contemplate invasion. Hitler's intention to invade seemed real, and was taken as such in London. German planning was so far advanced for the planned occupation that a house on the brow of Richmond Hill, with a splendid view over the River Thames west of London, had been earmarked for use as a guest-house for the Führer.

There was only one direction in which to look for aid: westward to North America. The phrase is chosen with care, for it was not only to the might of the nascent superpower of the United States that Churchill looked but also to the Dominion of Canada, which was the first nation to provide significant overseas aid in this principal strategic contest of the war.

If there is an injustice or omission in the historiography of the great maritime conflict as published in Britain or the United States, it is the consistent neglect of the Canadian contribution. There are a number of reasons for this, including the fact that the Royal Canadian Navy fought under British and then American command until it was granted a naval C-in-C of its own for the first time ever – after the crisis of the campaign had passed. Where the hard work of the RCN was not simply subsumed into the record of the British Navy, it tended to be discounted as ineffectual, even incompetent, which is to ignore or demean the colossal effort which went into it. There is also the fact that Canada is a small nation living in an area larger than the United States but with only one tenth of its mighty neighbour's population. Before we turn to the first substantial aid provided by the United States – which was given after much hedging and hesitation – we should try to do some justice to the Canadian effort, which not only began rather earlier but also did not come at the high price the Americans sometimes attached to helping Britain to protect them from Nazi world domination.

Canada declared war on Germany one week after Britain, on 10 September 1939. As in the First World War, its first practical move was to send an army division to Britain (later to be expanded to a corps). Apart from its young men, Canada had many other valuable items to offer: food, in the form of grain from the prairies; ports on the western Atlantic seaboard; a refuge for evacuees (and the British Fleet, Royal Family, Government and movable assets if necessary); training, docking, arming and repair facilities; a staging-post for the supply of US industrial goods and munitions; trained pilots; and a small but readily expansible industrial and shipbuilding base. What it did not have in September 1939 was a navy of significance. How this deficiency was made good is one of the most remarkable (and neglected) stories of high-speed mobilisation in military history – complete with its sometimes tragic consequences.

In 1939 the Canadian Navy, founded in 1910, boasted six destroyers and eleven other seagoing vessels (minesweepers and patrol boats), plus a small miscellany of the minor craft to be found in all navies. These were riches indeed compared with the strength of the RCN in the First World War (in which it played no significant part, unlike the Canadian Army). In 1914 it had two old cruisers, one on each coast; by 1918 it had attained a strength of 9,000 men who patrolled the long east coast in small ships. In 1922 it had shrunk to one destroyer and a pair of trawlers per coast, and had become the butt of dismissive jokes about Canada's "two-ocean navy." Although two new destroyers were added in 1931, the RCN came within a hair's breadth of being abolished altogether to save the Army and Royal Canadian Air Force budgets in the Great Depression, which hit Canada as hard as any country. No less a person than the contemporary Chief of Staff of the armed forces proposed scrapping the Navy, which responded to the threatened cut of eighty percent in its budget by counter-threatening to pay off the entire "fleet" at once. But the Navy was finally salvaged by W. L.

Mackenzie King, the Liberal Party leader who in 1935 began his third protracted term as Prime Minister, a post he was to hold for a total of twenty-two years. Under him and the Chief of Naval Staff appointed in 1934, Commodore (from 1938 Rear-Admiral) Percy W. Nelles, the RCN began to revive, and by the outbreak of war had 2,000 regulars, six modern destroyers of the Canadian "River" class, all built in Britain, with a seventh due for delivery shortly, and four home-built minesweepers. The RCN shared the Royal Navy's prewar view that the submarine would be held in check by Asdic, which was hardly surprising as officers went to Britain for their training. The Canadians, ever mindful of the overshadowing neighbour to the south, also thought the Germans would not repeat their First World War error of unrestricted submarine warfare because it had been the main reason for US entry into the earlier conflict. Canadian officers were as obsessed with gunnery as their British colleagues; but the Royal Navy's hankering for battleships was translated in the Canadian context, where the main need was seen as the protection of two long coastlines, into a fixation on large destroyers. The RCN and the Ottawa Government therefore committed themselves in 1939 to the purchase of powerful British "Tribal"-class destroyers, a fact which acted as a constant drain on financial, personnel and industrial resources which might have been better used for escorts. By the time the seriousness of the submarine threat became clear on the fall of France it was too late for a complete change of policy; but the Canadian contribution to the provision of escorts was still to be prodigious.

There was little sign of this at the end of August 1939 when the Canadian Navy was mobilised in all its strength of 3,684 officers and men (including the RCN Volunteer Reserve). A week after joining the war the Navy announced that it planned to have 5,472 men in service by the end of March 1940 and 7,000 a year later. In fact the RCN mustered 10,000 by September 1940; eventually its numerical strength was to peak in 1944 at 95,705, servicing 378 warships. In all, more than 110,000 men and women served in the RCN during the war and every one of them was a volunteer. As this represents a fiftyfold increase (compared with the twentyfold increase of the US Navy, fourteenfold by the Australian and eightfold by the British) it is hardly surprising that such a phenomenal expansion brought severe growing pains and subordinated quality to quantity on too many occasions.

Mackenzie King began Canada's war with the determination to concentrate the country's effort on the RCAF and RCN, rather than the Army as in the First World War. Envisaging a limited European war, the premier believed it would be to Canada's advantage to focus on the matériel-intensive, more highly technical services rather than dissipate limited manpower in infantry units. He was also looking for important benefits to Canada's small industrial base, which could be expected to grow quickly and permanently on the strength of war-production. Mackenzie King therefore rejected a British suggestion that Canada should go to the US with its shipbuilding orders. Instead he wanted Canadian yards to build what they could (which did not at first include any kind of conventional warship) and barter this for the coveted "Tribal" destroyers. But it will be recalled that the corvette, though pressed into service as a "cheap and nasty" escort (cheap for the British, nasty for the enemy, as Churchill described it) was originally a commercial whaler, a type Canada was well placed to construct. An RCN mission had brought back the design from Britain in July 1939 and in February 1940 Canada ordered fifty-four from its own yards, adding ten to the order within weeks, together with twenty-four "Bangor"-class small minesweepers. The barter-plan, very sensible though it was on paper, fell through a month later because no "exchange rate" of corvettes for destroyers could be agreed between London and Ottawa. But Britain went on building four Canadian destroyers and Canada assigned its first ten corvettes to the Royal Navy. In August 1940 six more corvettes and ten new "Bangors" were ordered in Canada to keep the vastly expanded shipbuilding industry fully occupied. The "Tribals" did not arrive until 1943, but in the meantime three small Canadian Pacific liners, *Prince David, Prince Henry* and *Prince Robert*, were converted into armed merchant cruisers. By late 1942 the Canadians felt confident enough of their building capacity to order "Tribals" from their own yards. The first additional destroyers for the RCN were to be seven of the fifty supplied to Britain by the Americans in exchange for bases in the western Atlantic, a deal described below.

When Winston Churchill appealed for help in summer 1940 against the threat of invasion, Canada responded generously by sending all seven of her destroyers then serving to Britain. Hitherto they had been doing routine local escort work with the convoys as they set out from Halifax to Britain. These precious ships had done their prewar training with the British West Indies and America Command, and were thus better suited to the more traditional work they were about to do than to escort duty, which was something entirely new to them. They had been working closely with the British Third Battle Squadron, sent to Halifax at the beginning of the war to help cover the convoys against the large German surface raiders.

The RCN's rush to the aid of the mother-country was most cruelly rewarded. HMCS *Fraser*, after helping with the post-Dunkirk evacuations, went to the estuary of the French River Gironde to join up with other Canadian and British ships. During a manoeuvre the *Fraser* (Commander W. B. Creery, RCN) was cut in half by the bows of the cruiser HMS *Calcutta* and sank with the loss of forty-seven from her crew of 187 officers and men, on 25 June 1940. The blame for the first naval disaster in Canadian history was eventually divided evenly between the two ships' captains. The postscript to this sad story was even worse. The Canadians bought the British destroyer *Diana* and had her refitted and recommissioned as HMCS *Margaree* (Lieutenant-Commander J. W. R. Roy, RCN) to replace the *Fraser*, most of whose surviving crew transferred to the substitute. On 20 October 1940 she

left Londonderry, Northern Ireland, as the sole escort of a small convoy
which was to join a larger one bound for Halifax out at sea. Falling back on
October 22 from her position ahead of the sub-convoy in squally weather,
the *Margaree* was cut in half in her turn, this time by the freighter *Port
Fairy*. In the collision, some 300 miles west of Ireland, the captain, four
officers and 136 ratings – four-fifths of the crew, most of them survivors from
the *Fraser* – were lost. The stern remained afloat even though the *Port Fairy*
used up all the ammunition of her single gun trying to sink it, and it was
eventually abandoned. The *Margaree* was blamed for making a sudden and
unexplained turn to port which put her in the path of the merchantman. No
replacement was sought this time by the grief-stricken Canadians after one
of the most extraordinary double catastrophes on record, in which the enemy
had played no part.

The first Canadian ship to be hit by enemy action was the destroyer
Saguenay, torpedoed by the Italian submarine *Argo* (Lieutenant Alberto
Crepas) on 1 December 1940 while escorting a Gibraltar convoy. Crepas
claimed a "kill" and got a medal; Commander G. R. Miles, RCN, was however
also decorated – for saving his ship, which was towed to Barrow-in-Furness in
the north-west of England. The Canadian destroyers worked with Western
Approaches Command and then with the Home Fleet, performing all the
anti-invasion and general duties expected from this most useful (and therefore
most overworked) type of warship. For administrative purposes they came
under the command of Commodore L. W. Murray, who bore the cumber-
some title of Commodore Commanding Canadian Ships and Establishments
in the United Kingdom. By the end of 1940 he was also looking after the
first Canadian corvettes: two of them, sporting wooden guns (to be replaced
by the real thing in England), came over in December with a convoy from
Halifax. They were the first to be built and manned by Canadians, and like
their British equivalents bore the names of flowers (*Windflower* and *Trillium*).
By February 1941 all ten of the type to serve with the Royal Navy had arrived
in British waters.

Back on shore in Canada the all but unlimited expansion thrust upon
the Navy imposed matching organisational strain on the Naval Service
Headquarters (NSHQ), its commands and staff. When the British Third
Battle Squadron of, initially, two battleships and attendant vessels, arrived
at Halifax, Nova Scotia, its Flag-Officer, Rear-Admiral L. E. Holland, RN,
assumed effective local operational command. He did not hesitate to interfere
in local arrangements, which soon created a diplomatic problem with the
RCN's Commanding Officer, Atlantic Coast, Captain H. E. Reid (succeeded
by Commodore G. C. Jones). After a number of jurisdictional disputes an
uneasy *modus vivendi* was established by discussion between the NSHQ and
the Admiralty in London. The Canadians thus discovered that when a small
navy cooperates with the world's largest, there can be no parity between
unequals; the same uncomfortable truth was rubbed in when the time came

for working closely with the American Navy. Fortunately, however, the Canadians had been included in the prewar preparations for convoys made by the Admiralty: the fact that the first convoy from Halifax to Britain could sail six days after Canadian entry was mainly due to the detailed preliminary work done in advance by the Naval Control Service Officer in Halifax, Commander R. H. Oland, RCN (retired, but soon re-enlisted and promoted to captain). Another key figure in the Canadian organisational effort was Captain Eric Brand, RN, who arrived at NSHQ in Ottawa in June 1939 "on loan" from the Admiralty. He served very effectively as Canada's Director of Naval Intelligence throughout the war, and the Operational Intelligence Centre he set up soon after his arrival played an increasingly important role in support of the OIC in London, and later with US Naval Intelligence. When the Canadian Government imitated the British by putting all Canadian merchant ships under naval control on 26 August 1939, they were placed under the supervision of a Director of Mercantile Movements, whose Convoy and Routeing Section was commanded by Captain Brand.

A uniquely Canadian development was the Naval Boarding Service, set up by Lieutenant-Commander E. F. B. Watt, RCN. Its original function was to check merchant ships in Canadian ports before departure for Britain to ensure they were free of objects (and men) that might be used for sabotage on arrival. The Boarding Service was ideally placed to keep an eye on the morale and condition of merchant seamen. Canada, a demographically small country, had few shore facilities to offer the thousands of foreign mariners who suddenly found themselves far from home, their countries in many cases under Nazi occupation. There were thus many disciplinary problems which often threatened the efficiency of the convoy system when crewmen deserted, malingered, temporarily went missing or otherwise adversely affected the running of their ships. When a Canadian Privy Council order of 1940 failed to solve these problems, a more severe, even draconian, order was made in spring 1941 which imposed up to nine months' imprisonment on offenders who delayed a sailing, and tedious war-work on seamen who missed their ship deliberately. Paid pools of seamen of various nationalities were set up in Canada to provide last-minute replacements, also under the auspices of the Boarding Service. It did what it could for the welfare of the seamen and went on to train many thousands of Canadians to go to sea with their own burgeoning Merchant Navy, which was supplied with men by a Director of Merchant Seamen.

The Canadian shipyards were soon involved in a programme for the construction of ninety "off-the-peg" merchantmen of the *North Sands* type, all of which were given names beginning with the word "Fort." The Ottawa Government, which began the war with only thirty-seven merchant ships of more than 2,000 tons, set up the state-owned Park Steamship Company to operate the new vessels, of which Canada had 175 at the end of the war. The Canadians also played a part in the Defensively Equipped Merchant Ships organisation, fitting out 713 vessels with guns and other items. Halifax and a few other ports undertook ship repairs on a scale to which their limited facilities were ill-suited, with consequent delays and complaints, especially in winter, when the St Lawrence River was frozen and its harbours unavailable. The Canadians did, however, provide an effective enemy-radio monitoring service from the beginning of hostilities.

The first important contact between the Canadian and American navies took place in May 1940, when the Germans were at the French coast facing Britain and her fortunes were approaching their lowest point. A certain Major Goulet of the US Marines arrived in Ottawa from Washington to see Captain Brand. On behalf of the US Navy he expressed interest in the defences of Newfoundland, which was of concern to the Americans for three reasons. The entire island, with its suddenly important chief eastern harbour of St John's, lay to the east of 60° longitude, which was the eastern limit of the Pan-American Neutrality Zone; it was the area of land in the western Atlantic closest to Iceland and Britain, a fact of obvious significance for the convoys; and it was not then, as it is now, part of the Dominion of Canada but still had the separate status of a British self-governing colony. It was therefore not legally Canada's to defend, although Ottawa was naturally interested in it for geographical, strategic and national reasons. The only important Canadian port east of the neutrality line was Sydney, Cape Breton, at the eastern end of Nova Scotia, which was also playing a growing role as an adjunct to Halifax. Brand told Goulet that Canada was not responsible for the defence of Newfoundland. The American officer then made an announcement of startling content from a messenger of such modest rank: "I've been told to tell you unofficially that if any British ships are in trouble they would be welcome in American ports." Brand later recorded that he replied: "Well, that's an historic statement – I can't thank you enough." He could not resist adding wryly: "The only thing is this. When they get there you will only be able to provide them with food, paint, soap and brooms. You can't even give them an electric light-bulb." Brand's papers in the Canadian Defence Archives also reveal that the Canadians had given careful thought to sheltering the British Fleet in the event of a German invasion. The intelligence chief described this plan as a "spare bedroom policy" and noted that Gaspé Bay, New Brunswick, in the Gulf of St Lawrence, was considered: "the finest harbour in the world, I think, for anchoring a lot of ships: deep water, ten fathoms, easy entrance, beautiful shelter, easily boomed entrance . . ."

The already flourishing exchanges between Churchill and Roosevelt, which were to run to more than 2,000 communications in all, intensified in the days immediately following the former's promotion to Number 10 Downing Street. The Prime Minister asked on 15 May 1940 for the loan of fifty destroyers and warned that Britain was running out of the cash American neutrality

laws required her to pay before delivery. The President still felt he could
not defy the isolationists and prevaricated; he positively angered Churchill
by expressing anxiety about the possibility of the British Fleet falling into
German hands. On May 20 Churchill replied: "Our intention is . . . to fight
on to the end in this island . . . in no conceivable circumstances will we
consent to surrender." The delicacy of American domestic politics did not
however prevent Roosevelt from exploiting Britain's crisis, which had already
generated widespread alarm and pessimism in the United States, by presenting Congress with a plan unprecedented in peacetime, involving an initial
expenditure of $1,200 million to rearm América, put its industries on a
war-footing and, among other items on an awesome shopping list, build
50,000 aircraft. He went so far as to add that outstanding British orders for
aircraft should have priority (Churchill had already asked for more on the
15th). The unanimous view in the British Cabinet and among the Chiefs of
Staff was that Britain could not carry on without massive and growing
American support. Germany, by its rapid and stunning conquests of its
neighbours to the west and north, had added to its own formidable and
inventive industrial resources those of several other advanced economies,
and Hitler's totalitarian regime would have no compunction in exploiting
them by forced labour.

The first crack in the legal wall of neutrality was found by the Administration at the beginning of June. So desperate was the plight of the British
Army after Dunkirk that the British Purchasing Mission in the US, led by
the persistent and energetic Canadian businessman Arthur Purvis, added
rifles and other light weapons to the lengthy lists of wanted items which so
startled and depressed the American authorities during the June crisis. It
was discovered that the US could legally dispose of *surplus* weaponry as it
saw fit. Equipment, much of it left over from the First World War, began
to flow across the Atlantic on June 3. Although the fall of France helped to
convince Roosevelt by the end of June 1940 that he should run for an
unheard-of third term, this decision only stiffened his resistance to Churchill's
blandishments, pleas and even threats in his campaign for massive American
aid.

The area in which the President felt safest to move was the defence of the
Americas, a task on which neither the isolationists nor the interventionists,
worried by Hitler's apparent invincibility, could possibly disagree. So on 17
August 1940 Roosevelt concluded with Mackenzie King the agreement of
Ogdensburg (a small town in New York state on the bank of the St Lawrence
Seaway some fifty miles due south of Ottawa, where they met). This set up
the US–Canadian Permanent Joint Board of Defence (PJBD), whose first
task was to draw up a "Plan Black." As its name implies, this was concerned
with joint action in the event of a British defeat and the consequent likely
loss of the Royal Navy and RAF. The Americans took the view that they
should command the defences of the shared continent because the Canadians

were sending everything they could to Britain, an assumption by Roosevelt and others which naturally offended Canadian sensibilities when it became clear, even as they recognised the enormous latent power of their neighbour. Canada was in one sense the middleman between Britain and the United States, but it was also in danger of being crushed between them. The uncomfortable position was particularly well illustrated by the composition of the small Canadian Navy, with its British-trained officers and its ratings from thoroughly North American backgrounds, who had their own well-developed views on democracy and discipline.

Something else Roosevelt could do in the interest of hemispheric defence and in keeping with the Monroe Doctrine, which barred foreigners from the Americas, was suggested to him by the powerful lobby in favour of massive aid for Britain. At the very end of July Churchill had once again appealed urgently for destroyers. Roosevelt still could not *give* them; but the lobby's lawyers discovered that he was free to *barter* them. On August 13 the President offered the ships in exchange for naval and air bases in Newfoundland and the West Indies. The resulting "destroyers-for-bases" deal was announced on August 30 and confirmed in Washington on the following Monday, September 2. The Royal Navy's destroyer-strength was thereby increased, in due course but much faster than by any other available means, by one third at the stroke of a pen.

It was not only for warships that Britain looked to the United States. The already severe inroads on merchant shipping made by the German onslaught soon prompted the British to seek replacements from US yards. The Americans had built standardised cargo-ships (the *Hog Islander* type) in the First World War; mindful of this, the British approached, early in 1940, a New York firm of marine architects called Gibbs and Cox with an initial order for sixty "off-the-peg" freighters. They settled on an old design for the sake of simplicity and cheapness: the "Sunderland tramp" originally developed by Sands Ltd of Sunderland in 1879. This was a coal-burning ship with triple-expansion steam engines of equally venerable design, revamped to conform with American engineering practices by the General Machinery Corporation. The first keels were laid at the South Portland, Maine, yard of the Todd-Bath Company. These ten-knot freighters of 10,800 tons were 420 feet long and initially cost $1.8 million each, requiring a million man-hours for completion. Such was the origin of what was later to become known as the "Liberty ship," and the remarkable story of its vital contribution to victory in the Atlantic will be told in its proper place.

One of Churchill's principal headaches in the desperate days of 1940 was finance. By September 1940 British reserves had fallen below £900 million, with £600 million already owed to Canada and orders worth nearly £400 million placed in the US. American neutrality laws and suspicions of British trustworthiness in matters of money, as demonstrated by what happened after the First World War, threatened London with another crisis to add to all the rest. In December 1940 Churchill told Roosevelt that Britain would run out of cash altogether in six months. The destroyers-for-bases deal had provided one means of sidestepping both the neutrality laws and the cash crisis, but something rather more drastic was needed if Britain was to carry on the fight. Roosevelt, having won his third term in the election on November 5 (his Republican opponent, Wendell Wilkie, helpfully endorsed support for Britain in the campaign), now at last felt free to consider serious aid. In the meantime the British, in their search for cashless exchanges with the Americans, offered the US their latest radar technology.

American experts, approached in July 1940 for their reaction to an *aide-mémoire* from the British Ambassador, the Marquis of Lothian, to Roosevelt, were extremely sceptical. The director of the US Naval Research Laboratory pointed out that up to June 1939, "the British were making determined efforts to trade British submarine detection devices (underwater sound) for our radio airplane detectors." In a memorandum to the Chief of Naval Operations he went on:

> The information and equipment which we expect to get from the British in regard to radio airplane detection and submarine detection may possibly prove to be disappointing. For a nation that has been so backward in mechanical and electrical engineering as applied to naval vessels to have established outstanding progress in two other fields of engineering does not seem credible although it may be possible.

This harsh but not altogether unfair judgement reflects the result of the well-known disdain in Britain for pure and applied science among admirals and politicians. It was entirely reasonable, before the Battle of Britain showed something of what the British had made of their own invention of radar, to wonder what a nation which had come trawling for information only a year earlier had to offer in this field, where the Americans had indeed made significant progress in certain directions. The vast losses of ships to submarines in less than a year of war had also proved the prewar claims for Asdic to be overblown.

Thus the omens for the first conference in Washington between the newly arrived British Technical Mission, led by Sir Henry Tizard, and US naval experts were not propitious. The British extolled Asdic; the American record of the conference session at the end of August 1940 noted:

> A report that recently received wide circulation was to the effect that the British had a device so sensitive that they could hear German sailors in rubber-soled shoes walking around a submarine on the bottom at a distance of some miles from the listener . . . Early in the war the Germans could not understand how the British were finding them so easily. Having listening devices in mind, they began to take unusual precautions to quiet their ships, including the use of the soft-soled shoe as an article of uniform.

This is probably a testament to the effectiveness of British propaganda rather than the Admiralty's power of self-delusion over Asdic; but the Germans carried on with such precautions even after examining Asdic sets taken from French Navy ships (and finding them unimpressive).

As the sessions continued, the Americans began to discover that the British had rather more to offer than they had suspected, and that their visitors had resolutely cast aside their customary secrecy-psychosis (copper-bottomed proof, if any was needed, of how seriously they took their plight). US Navy officers went as observers to Britain to watch ships and shore-establishments at work. The American record soon began to refer to British radar work in certain areas as "well ahead of the development in this country."

Early in October the Secretary of the Navy was told that the US "Navy has received a vast amount of important information from which much benefit can be gained . . . [because it is] based, in great part, on the results of actual wartime experience." The British were keen to have American manufacturers make their equipment in large quantities for the Royal Navy and RAF. "Up to the present it is felt that the Navy has gained more than the British by the free exchange of information . . . The outstanding British developments . . . are the RDF [radar] and Asdic." A change of tune indeed.

The British also revealed to the Americans, from their unaccustomed position as suppliants, how far they had progressed with ASV radar (anti-surface-vessel, misrepresented in the US record as "anti-submarine visualiser" because that was to be its new role). ASV – "this remarkable application of RDF," said the US experts – was developed for aircraft hunting surface ships, but was now being adapted for shipboard use as a supplement to Asdic, to spot surfaced submarines at night. Asdic itself was felt to be no better than the American sonar equipment, except that it was protected by a dome affixed to the hull – and that the British maximised its performance by intensive training and constant use (the "ping" of the Asdic was routinely broadcast round the ship through the public-address system so that the entire crew could follow the hunt). By the end of October 1940, Colonel Frank Knox, one of the prominent Republicans co-opted by Roosevelt into what was now virtually a national or coalition Cabinet as Secretary of the Navy, minuted to a senior official: "It is agreed that all devices, instruments or systems in use, developed for use or under development by the War and Navy departments will be offered for release to the representatives of the British Government" with only two exceptions, a bombsight and a mine.

Enormously valuable though this promise of technical co-operation was, together with American help in the manufacture of equipment, the real breakthrough was signalled to Churchill on 17 December 1940. After reflecting for a week on the Prime Minister's forecast that Britain would effectively be bankrupt in six months, Roosevelt told him he had it in mind to help Britain with a loan and lease arrangement. The President prepared the American people for this in one of his famous "fireside chats" on the radio, on December 29. He used the homely analogy of how it was in your own interest to lend a hose to a neighbour whose house was on fire, and pictured the United States as "the great arsenal of democracy." The next day, work started at the US Treasury on the draft of the Lend–Lease Bill, which would give the President the right to "sell, transfer title to, exchange, lease, lend or otherwise dispose of" articles to any country which the President determined was vital to US security. Congress would exercise its constitutional right to appropriate the necessary funds, but the timing of repayment was to be left to presidential discretion. The Bill was tabled in the House of Representatives under the unconsciously ironic number HR 1776 (the date of the American Declaration of Independence from Britain).

Isolationism was far from dead. The great aviator Charles Lindbergh, dangerously naïve in political matters and an admirer of his fellow-flyer Hermann Göring whom he had visited before the war, spoke out against the Bill, as did the historian Charles Beard and the "America First" Committee. The Bill passed the House by 250 votes to 165 on 8 February 1941. In the Senate, Gerald P. Nye, a Republican, and Burton K. Wheeler, a Democrat, led a renewed onslaught. Wheeler warned that it would end with "every fourth American boy being ploughed under." But on 9 March the Bill passed by sixty votes to thirty-one, with virtually no amendment, and Roosevelt was able to sign it into law two days later. The President, confident that he would win his fight to give Britain "all aid short of war," had already sent Averell Harriman to London as his representative to speed up the provision of the aid. On March 24 Congress duly voted a first Lend–Lease budget of $7 billion. Roosevelt's personal assistant, Harry Hopkins, was given charge of the programme (he was succeeded in August 1941 by Edward R. Stettinius, Jr, who was given the title of Administrator of the Office of Lend–Lease Administration).

Once the United States decided to deploy its gigantic resources in the fight against Nazism, even though it was still not involved in hostilities, it did so unstintingly. It cannot be denied that American industry made enormous and permanent gains from the gearing up of the US economy for all-out war production; but there is no gainsaying that its vast material contribution was one of the main reasons for the defeat of the Axis. By the end of the war thirty-eight foreign countries had received aid under Lend–Lease, which was estimated to have amounted to $48 billion. How much Britain received is not entirely clear, but it was the lion's share – at least $13.5 and perhaps as much as $20 billion. The Soviet Union received between $9 and $10 billion. "Reverse Lend–Lease" of payments in kind from the British Commonwealth and eventually France totalled $8 billion, plus cash repayments of $650 million from Britain and $750 million from France. At the end of the war the rest of the debt was, with unprecedented magnanimity, written off. Roosevelt may have been returned with a reduced majority in November 1940, but Lend–Lease showed him at the height of his confidence in Congressional and popular support. Many Americans saw Lend–Lease as a substitute for military involvement; others saw it as leading inevitably to active participation in combat. Lend–Lease takes its place alongside the New Deal as one of Roosevelt's greatest achievements.

In parallel with the political and economic arrangements associated with the Lend–Lease Bill, the military staffs of the United States and Britain got down to detailed discussions of how they would work together if and when the US became a belligerent. The "American–British Conversations" (later known as ABC–1) took place in Washington from 29 January to 27 March 1941. Senior representatives of the three British chiefs of staff and of the American Chief of Naval Operations and Chief of Staff (army) met to determine the best strategy for the defeat of Germany, the broad co-ordination of their forces and detailed co-operation in the field. Associated with the British delegation were representatives of Canada, Australia and New Zealand; the fact that these were not present at the talks themselves naturally worried the Canadians, especially in the context of the Atlantic campaign. In response to Canada's struggle for recognition of its contribution and role in the north Atlantic, ABC–22 was annexed to ABC–1 in November 1941. ABC–22 essentially incorporated, with some adjustments, the terms of the American–Canadian co-operation agreement worked out by the two countries' Permanent Joint Board of Defence in a series of meetings from late August to early October 1940, as set down in a report of November 20.

ABC–1 took a world view, anticipating American hostilities with Italy as well as Germany and also war between the US plus the British Commonwealth and Japan. Essentially the agreement recognised Germany as the principal enemy against which the main effort would be directed. The Americans were to have strategic supremacy in the Pacific and be supported there by Commonwealth forces; in addition they would be in charge of the western Atlantic, north and south, with Canada subordinate to them except in its own territorial waters. This was to have the curious, and for the Canadians inevitably uneasy, consequence that their home-based naval forces, already at war, largely came under the command of a power that was still neutral. The Anglo-American destroyers-for-bases deal also gave the Americans naval and air bases in Newfoundland, and thereby a defence role in the colony, which was not Canadian territory but was obviously essential to the defence of Canada. Canadian protests against the bases deal were overriden. It was not until May 1941 that the one established naval base in Newfoundland, St John's, was handed over by the Royal Navy to the RCN; the Canadians always ensured that their Newfoundland presence was larger, and its commander of higher rank, than the Americans' in the island. Otherwise ABC–22 called upon Canada to place five destroyers and fifteen corvettes under US naval command in the western Atlantic, with the balance of RCN ships to go overseas (which meant operating under British command).

ABC–1 provided for an exchange of permanent military missions between London and Washington; Canada, already represented in London, made its own arrangements to send a staff mission to Washington. The Anglo-American agreement also provided for the relief by an American division of the British Commonwealth force occupying Iceland – before the US entered the war. Thus the basis was laid by spring 1941 for the co-operation of American, British and Canadian forces in the Atlantic, an arrangement which, with a number of alterations dictated by circumstances, lasted for two years. The underlying principles endured to the end of the war.

American non-belligerent involvement now stretched the definition of the word "neutrality" well beyond its semantic limits. Roosevelt correctly calculated that Hitler would be so averse to US belligerency that he had no choice but to put up with American aid for Britain. It is hardly surprising in these conditions that Nazi funds were sent to pro-German elements in the United States for use in support of the isolationists and against Roosevelt in the 1940 election campaign. The delivery of the fifty old destroyers (supplemented by ten large US Coastguard cutters) to Britain and Hitler's repeated orders not to attack US ships meant that German submarine commanders could never be sure of the nationality of such vessels, which gave them virtual immunity except in British home waters, still closed to US ships.

In July 1940 Admiral Harold R. Stark, USN, Chief of Naval Operations, sent Rear-Admiral Robert L. Ghormley, his assistant, to London for exploratory talks with the Admiralty. Baldly stated, his first task was to establish whether the British were capable of holding out. Having soon concluded that they could, Ghormley sat in almost daily on the meetings of a special committee at the Admiralty to find out how the US Navy could best help in the event of American involvement – the groundwork for the American contribution to ABC–1.

By the end of 1940 the War Plans Division of the US Navy had worked out a scheme for American transatlantic convoy-escort, to be ready to come into effect on 1 April 1941. For this purpose Stark ordered the creation of a Support Force derived from the Atlantic Fleet, as the former Atlantic Squadron was known from 1 February 1941. The new force was drawn from the Neutrality Patrol, set up to protect the Pan-American Neutrality Zone, and took a mere two weeks to organise. On March 3 Rear-Admiral Arthur LeR. Bristol, USN, raised his flag at Norfolk, Virginia, as commander of the Support Force, subordinate to the new Atlantic Fleet and its Commander-in-Chief, Admiral Ernest J. King. In March 1941 Captain Louis Denfeld, Bristol's chief of staff, went to Britain to look for naval and air bases. Gareloch and Loch Ryan in Scotland, and Londonderry and Lough Erne in Northern Ireland were chosen, the first of each pair for escorts and the second for naval aircraft; $50 million was allocated by Britain's neutral friend for building them. The American equipment and materials required for these facilities were punctiliously transported in British ships, in keeping with the neutrality regulations which still prevented US ships from entering the war-zone round Britain. The cost was insignificant compared with the $4 billion allocated by Congress in July 1940 for the construction of America's "two-ocean navy," providing for 1,325,000 tons of new warships of all types, the acquisition of 100,000 tons of auxiliary vessels and $50 million-worth of escort, patrol and other small craft. Washington was in the happy position of being able to throw money at the problem of the democracies' urgent need for more men -of-war; but even these enormous sums could not alter the fact that the United States needed two years to achieve full readiness for the anticipated maritime war on two fronts.

The swift and far-reaching development of transatlantic co-operation prompted by Hitler's staggering successes in the first nine months of the war made no noticeable difference in the short term to the perilous position of the British at sea. This period became known throughout the German submarine service as *die glückliche Zeit*, "the happy time," during which individual commanders, led by a handful of "aces," notched up huge scores of sinkings. The new strategic advantage provided by the captured bases and the virtual disappearance of enemy destroyers from the convoy-escorts and patrols provided the submarines with a plethora of targets, of which they naturally chose the easiest: independently routed ships or stragglers from convoys. Even though many convoys had just one escorting ship when British invasion fears were at their height, and despite the fact that the Germans were more prepared to attack convoys, ships sunk sailing alone outnumbered those lost in convoy by two to one during the "happy time," when the German submarines reached – and passed – the peak of their efficiency, boat for boat.

The truly startling fact about the second nine-month period of the war at sea is that there was an average of only six German boats at a time engaged in hunting ships. In the worst month so far, October 1940, submarines alone sank a total of 352,000 tons of shipping, or very nearly 60,000 tons per boat at sea, a record unmatched before or after. And during this same period, at the beginning of February 1941, the number of operational submarines available to Dönitz reached the all-time low for the Second World War of twenty-one (due mainly to the priority given to training at the time, and to delays in delivery of new boats). From August 1940 the Germans were reinforced by Italian submarines based at Bordeaux, but their crews, brought up on the calmer and warmer sailing conditions of the Mediterranean, were of little value in Atlantic weather. Their boats had impossibly tall conning-towers complete with portholes and were inferior in seakeeping quality. The Italians had twenty-six boats at Bordeaux by November 1940, but six months later their numbers were reduced to ten and they contributed almost nothing to the tally of sinkings. Early in December, Dönitz virtually excluded them from his operational planning.

The new factor of the French bases forced the British not only to divert the convoys from the south to the north of Ireland but also to send shipping destined for east coast ports north-about Scotland, which by increasing their time at sea reduced the total tonnage available. Even so, these adjustments cut losses to submarine attack by only a fifth in July, when the changes were made, compared with June (196,000 tons as against 248,000). In August losses to submarines rose again, to 268,000 tons, and in September to 295,000.

Appropriately enough the first to earn the title of ace, for which the basic qualification was sinking 50,000 tons of shipping, was Günther Prien, the "Bull of Scapa Flow," who sank eight ships in two weeks, to bring his total score to 66,600 tons. This stupendously destructive patrol of the *U47* took place before the Germans had moved into the French bases. Prien sank three freighters on June 19 from convoy HGF34 (fast, homeward–bound from Gibraltar) off the Brittany coast. He attacked on the surface in the dark, now the standard tactic of the Germans and their answer to Asdic. On the evening of the next day he sank a fourth ship, coming under the gunfire of an accompanying merchantman but escaping at top speed without being damaged. In the early hours of the 21st he attacked another convoy, HX49 (from Halifax), sinking a valuable tanker. Despite having so forcefully revealed his presence, he kept up with the same convoy for two hours and sank another of its ships. After five blank days Prien got his seventh victim and turned back for Wilhelmshaven. But he still had one torpedo left from his original stock of twelve, and on July 2, in the Western Approaches, he sighted the liner *Arandora Star*. Without compunction he hit her amidships. Tragically, the ship was transporting 1,250 enemy aliens, mostly Italian, from Britain to internment in Canada. There were also 254 army guards and 174 crew aboard. Despite the best efforts of the Canadian destroyer *St Laurent*, which rescued 857 people after they had been in the water for seven hours, 821 died. Prien was awarded the Knight's Cross with Oakleaves of the Iron Cross.

But in terms of tonnage sunk in the Second World War, the greatest ace of them all was *Fregattenkapitän* (junior captain) Otto Kretschmer, who managed to send 238,000 tons to the bottom in just under eighteen months. Born in Silesia (now in Poland) in 1912, he joined the Navy in 1930 and was in command of the coastal submarine *U23* when war broke out. He was soon given the larger, type VIIc, ocean-going boat *U99*, in which he performed most of the exploits which eventually earned him the Knight's Cross with Oakleaves and Swords of the Iron Cross. His boat carried a golden horseshoe riveted to the conning-tower, a talisman which was to bring *U99* more good fortune even than her record score of sinkings. Kretschmer was based at Lorient, like most of the other aces, from late July 1940. In the last week of that month and the first in August, Kretschmer set a record for a single patrol by sinking seven ships totalling more than 65,000 tons. When Admiral Raeder

came to offer his congratulations, he was startled to see the crew of *U99*
standing rigidly to attention in British Army uniforms. The German sailors
had got them from abandoned enemy stores when their own uniforms wore
out. Only men of the highest level of morale would have dared to do such a
thing in the service of Hitler's Germany, but the aces and their crews were
supplying Dr Goebbels's propaganda-machine with priceless material for
depressing the enemy and raising spirits on the home front. Newsreels,
radio, magazines and newspapers extolled the submariners, bands played as
they came into port after yet another triumphant patrol, captured champagne
flowed and the French bases echoed to the uproar of wild parties. No wonder
Dönitz felt at the time that if he had only possessed double the tiny number
of operational boats then at his disposal, he could have knocked Britain out
of the war.

   Shipping losses were running at two to three times the replacement
building rate; rationing in Britain, begun in earnest in January 1940, was
growing steadily more severe; imports had to be cut and every cubic inch of
cargo space in every incoming ship had to be allocated according to an ever
more stringent list of priorities. From 15 August 1940 the Luftwaffe was
fighting a war of attrition against the RAF in the skies over Britain. The pilots
Churchill immortalised as "the Few" were giving a magnificent account of
themselves, but the unrelenting attacks on the airfields and the crucial
chain of coastal radar stations, which detected the bombers and guided the
defending fighters, threatened to wear down the British air forces. But at
the beginning of September, in a display of the kind of morale the men of
U99 would have appreciated, the besieged RAF sent some of its bombers to
enrage Hitler by making a token raid on Berlin. This prompted the ineffable
Hermann Göring to make one of the greatest strategic errors of the entire war.
Instead of finishing the deadly work of destroying RAF Fighter Command, he
lost his temper and on September 7 diverted his bombers to the onslaught
on London and other cities which the British named "the Blitz." Although
British civilians were now in the front line, the change of target saved Fighter
Command, which thus narrowly retained domination of British airspace. On
September 22 "Operation Sealion" for the invasion of Britain was postponed
by Hitler (the secret of whether he ever seriously intended to proceed with
it after this, which is open to doubt, died with him). The Battle of Britain
brought the RAF one of the most important defensive victories ever and was
soon seen to have saved the country from invasion.

   At this time, however, the plight of the British at sea only got worse.
The Royal Navy had perforce become accustomed to the now routine German
submarine tactic of attacking on the surface at night, first used towards the
end of the First World War. So was the stratagem of group-attacks on
convoys, something which Dönitz had already tried once or twice by now,
with little success: he had too few boats. But the new advantage of the French
bases – Brest, Lorient, La Pallice, St Nazaire and Bordeaux – offset the

shortage sufficiently to enable him to try the *Rudel* (pack) tactic more seriously. How this functioned will become clear from the narrative.

As ever, Prien was in the van. His and two other boats were sent to support *U65* (Commander Hans-Gerrit von Stockhausen) when he reported sighting the fifty-three ships of slow convoy SC2 from Halifax. Despite the presence of seven escorts and several Coastal Command patrols the four submarines sank five ships on the night of September 7 north-west of Ireland. This modest success was enough to encourage Dönitz to try harder two weeks later. Once again it was Prien to the fore. He sighted thirty-seven ships of convoy HX72 from Halifax on September 20, before its escort joined it. Left with only one torpedo after SC2, Prien reported to Dönitz and awaited reinforcements. He shadowed the convoy from the limit of his own range of vision, which enabled him to keep the ships in sight while remaining undetectable himself thanks to his boat's tiny profile. The next day Prien, Kretschmer, *Kapitänleutnant* Heinrich Bleichrodt in *U48* and four others formed a pack, later joined by another leading ace, *Kapitänleutnant* Joachim Schepke. They sank eleven ships in seven hours, and went on inflicting their terrible punishment even after the escort of five ships – a destroyer, a sloop and three corvettes of Western Approaches Command – arrived. Schepke alone accounted for seven totalling over 50,000 tons in four hours with *U100*, which brazenly attacked from within the stricken convoy. He torpedoed the second ship in three successive columns in fifteen minutes. Kretschmer sank two in a similar attack from within. The shock and chaos induced among the victims by this unprecedented tactic led them to believe enemy agents were aboard a convoy ship equipped with concealed torpedo tubes. The escorts, except for the destroyer, were slower than a surfaced submarine and managed only one ineffectual depth-charge attack.

Bleichrodt joined the hunt four days after causing one of the most poignant tragedies of the war at sea, the sinking of the liner *City of Benares*, 11,000 tons, some 600 miles west of Ireland. She carried about 400 passengers, including ninety children being evacuated to Canada as part of the Children's Overseas Resettlement Scheme – a high-minded idea which ought surely to have been reconsidered once Hitler declared unrestricted submarine warfare round Britain on 17 August 1940. The *City of Benares* (Captain Landles Nicoll) was serving as the commodore's ship of a convoy which by the time of the attack was in the "Gap" – the mid-ocean stretch for which no escort was provided. In all over 300 passengers were lost, including seventy-seven of the children. Only a few lifeboats could be launched; there were just thirteen children among the survivors. After drifting for about a week, they were sighted by an aircraft and destroyers and rescued. Even after all the losses sustained during the war's first year, the tragedy had a greater impact on the British public than any other, not excluding the *Athenia*, because of the lost children and the epic lifeboat drama which followed for those who survived. The Resettlement Scheme was wisely abandoned (as it should have been a month earlier when the Dutch ship *Volendam* was torpedoed; happily all 321 children aboard her were saved).

In Berlin, Raeder's appeals to Hitler to broaden the naval onslaught on Britain, by building more submarines sooner and attacking British positions in the Mediterranean before the Americans could bail them out, fell on deaf ears. Hitler was now preoccupied with his plans for the invasion of the Soviet Union and with the finishing touches to the Tripartite Pact, the alliance of Germany, Italy and Japan which was signed on 27 September 1940. Meanwhile a plan by the British and General Charles de Gaulle's Free French to seize Dakar, Senegal, in French West Africa as a naval base for the protection of convoys collapsed in bungling disorder amid unexpectedly resolute Vichy French resistance.

In October 1940 the attacks on the convoys by groups of submarines, christened "wolf-packs" in the German and British press alike at this time, became an unremitting massacre. The hard-pressed British Admiralty could find no immediate tactical answer to the packs, despite the return of more and more destroyers to escort duty from anti-invasion work, a temporary reduction in the size of convoys, the use of flares to light up convoys attacked at night and experiments with the positioning of escorts around their charges.

On October 17 Bleichrodt sighted slow convoy SC7, some thirty ships escorted by two sloops and a corvette, which had left Sydney, Cape Breton, on the 5th. Instead of reporting and waiting for reinforcements as pack tactics required, the German commander attacked and sank two merchantmen. Two stragglers had already been sunk earlier by two other boats. *U48* was sighted by a patrolling Sunderland flying boat and forced under by bombing. She was then hunted for several hours by one of the sloops, which thereby became separated from the convoy. She never found it again. Dönitz was able to assemble five more submarines across the eastward path of the convoy, including Kretschmer, Schepke and *Kapitänleutnant* Engelbert Endrass, Prien's first lieutenant at Scapa Flow and now well on the way to becoming an ace himself, in *U46*. An extra sloop and corvette joined SC7 just before another ship was torpedoed. Because she did not sink, a corvette was left with her, the second escort needlessly lost to the threatened convoy.

After dark on the 18th, the Germans launched a full-scale attack. Endrass sank a Swedish ship, whereupon yet another escort fell behind to pick up survivors. Fifteen more sinkings occurred in the ensuing six hours. The escorts were completely ineffective, spending their time rescuing survivors and thus abandoning their stations, which made it all the easier for the Germans to pick off the most profitable targets. Kretschmer made a deadly diagonal thrust across the convoy, sinking five. The final account for SC7 was no less than twenty-one ships lost, including stragglers, a casualty rate of two in three. Kretschmer and two other captains had used all their torpedoes in the unequal battle and headed for home; but on the next day, the 19th, Prien sighted HX79, with forty-nine ships, to the west. No escorts were present, and Dönitz sent Schepke, Endrass and one fresh submarine to join him. But before the Germans could position themselves to attack, an exceptional escort of two destroyers, four corvettes, three trawlers, a minesweeper and a Dutch submarine arrived. After dark, however, Prien made the first pass at the convoy from the south while Endrass began an approach from the north. Prien hit six and Endrass seven ships in a series of attacks during the night. The unfortunate Dutch boat *014* was spotted, mistaken for German and attacked at least twice, which did nothing for the efforts of the defence. In all, HX79 lost a dozen ships, with a thirteenth badly damaged.

October 18 and 19 were the worst two days for shipping losses of the entire war, and the double disaster of the two convoys also marked the peak of the "happy time," which Kretschmer described as a submariner's Christmas. But the British were not to know that the crisis (neither the last nor the worst) was about to recede as the Germans paused for breath. If a convoy with no less than eleven escorts could be mangled like HX79, what on earth was to be done to avert catastrophe?

It was singularly disheartening to the British that, after all the complaints from Royal and Merchant navies about the desperate shortage of escorts, the sustained attempt to remedy this deficiency by scaling down anti-invasion precautions had been followed by a sharp increase in sinkings. It was obvious that quantity alone was no answer to the tactics now in use by the increasingly confident Germans. Dönitz was using his submarines as submersible torpedo-boats. By attacking on the surface at night they were immune to detection by Asdic at the crucial time and were also faster and more manoeuvrable than all classes of escort except the comparatively few destroyers available. They boosted their tally of sinkings by adhering to the principle they followed throughout the war – to attack the easiest targets: first the independently routed ship, then the straggler or other vessel separated from its convoy, next groups of ships without escort (a formation which does not fulfil the definition of convoy) and then weakly escorted convoys. Finally, thanks to the accumulation of experience and confidence and the much wider range of options provided by the French bases, it became possible to assemble packs of submarines capable of severely damaging convoys almost regardless of how many escorts there were in attendance.

It will be seen from the foregoing descriptions of the devastating effect of the wolf-pack that escort tactics were not just woefully inadequate against this new threat but in effect non-existent. The Senior Officer, Escort, was wont to detach a ship or ships to hunt a reported submarine which might take them hundreds of miles away from the freighters they were supposed to be protecting. Subsequent evasive changes of course by the convoy could prevent the detached ships from finding it again. The instinctive and entirely commendable attempts to rescue the crews of stricken or sunk merchantmen also weakened and disrupted the escort force. The fundamental weakness exposed by the new pack tactics was that the escorts could as yet respond only separately to a common threat. The answer was to transform a collection of individual warships into a team. The recognition of this pressing need produced the concept of the escort *group*. Dönitz's advantage in the use of pack tactics was that he could assemble a *Rudel* from the boats which happened to be within reach of an identified target in the knowledge that all the captains had been thoroughly trained in the same way to respond to instructions from the central direction in France by radio. The opposing escort, by contrast, could not count on reinforcements and had to cope with an attack as it stood and on its own. For these reasons joint training was necessary, and once given, the ships of a group needed to be kept together as far as possible.

The anti-submarine training of individual ships was transferred from Portland in the south of England to several new shore establishments in Scotland after the fall of France, which made southern English waters an unsuitable area for exercises. In July 1940 Vice-Admiral Gilbert Stephenson, who had been recalled from the retired list to serve as a convoy commodore, went to Tobermory on the island of Mull, off the west coast of Scotland, as Commodore, Western Isles. His task was to work up the smaller escorts (those below destroyers in size, mainly corvettes) in a few frantic weeks. The veteran commander of the shore base HMS *Western Isles* (it is the Royal Navy's sometimes confusing habit to name and administer such establishments as if they were ships) was nicknamed "Monkey" for his small size and frenetic energy. In his book *Convoy*, John Winton tells a delightful story of this tempestuous maritime headmaster-figure. On his first visit to a new corvette, Stephenson snatched the gold-braided cap off his head, hurled it on the deck and yelled at the party of sailors drawn up to receive him: "That's a live bomb! What are you going to do about it?" After a moment of stupefaction, a bright rating smartly kicked the cap over the side. Not to be outdone, the commodore pointed to his floating headgear and bawled: "That's a survivor! He's drowning! Jump over the side and rescue him . . ." Other anti-submarine training schools were set up at Dunoon and Campbeltown in western Scotland.

In October 1940, Admiral Sir Martin Dunbar-Nasmith, C-in-C, Western Approaches with his headquarters at Plymouth in Devon, ordered the formation of eight escort-groups, which were to train off the Clyde in south-west Scotland, the Mersey in north-west England and Londonderry, Northern Ireland. In Liverpool, principal port for the North-Western Approaches, a tactical school was set up for the training of escort officers. A group would consist of up to eight ships, including two destroyers; its composition and number would change frequently as ships were damaged, under repair or overhaul or being refitted. But every escort now acquired experience of working with other ships. Their crews were familiar with group tactics and needed little time to accustom themselves to the particular foibles of a new escort-group commander. These officers now became key figures in the convoy campaign – ace escort-leaders to put up against ace submarine commanders. The escalating losses of shipping in this period also prompted a greater sense of urgency in providing the anti-submarine forces with better equipment. Coastal Command aircraft began to acquire aerial depth-charges in increasing numbers. ASV radar sets began to be fitted to both aircraft and ships, as was the VHF (very high frequency) radio-telephone. This was the ideal means of direct voice contact between escorts and among ships and aircraft during attacks and searches, the essential means of communication which transformed the effectiveness of those responsible for protecting the convoys.

The most important administrative change in this fraught period of the war at sea was the transfer, on 7 February 1941, of Western Approaches Command from Plymouth in the south of England to Liverpool in the north. The move was a sensible 'response to the shift northward of the convoy struggle. Ten days after the new headquarters was set up at Derby House in the city, with a duplicate inland under the grounds of Lord Derby's estates, Admiral Dunbar-Nasmith was relieved as C-in-C, Western Approaches by Admiral Sir Percy Noble, the fifty-year-old former Flag Officer of the China Station. This mentally agile and highly popular admiral was renowned throughout the service for his personal fastidiousness in matters of dress and cleanliness (he had an admiral's bathroom with luxurious fittings installed at Derby House). A great deal of the credit for the eventual mastery achieved over the submarines belongs to Noble. Number 15 Group, RAF Coastal Command, led by Air Vice-Marshal J. M. Robb, was also transferred from Plymouth to the north-west of England. Derby House became the principal Area Combined Headquarters for the anti-submarine campaign, with a huge operations room linked to the Admiralty and duplicating the London Trade Plot. Its reserve operations-room inland was a precaution against the increasing bombing of Liverpool by the Luftwaffe. The new HQ was directly supplied with information from the Operational Intelligence Centre, the Submarine Tracking Room and the Air Ministry in London. OIC, Western Approaches and the Air Ministry co-ordinated their work by daily telephone conferences.

The essential inter-service co-operation between Navy and RAF was enhanced with the transfer of complete operational control of Coastal Command to the Admiralty at this same period (15 April 1941). The Cabinet's Defence Committee considered a complete bodily transfer of the Command to the Navy in November 1940 but decided this would be too radical and would create insuperable administrative strains on the already overstretched high commands of the two services. Churchill ordered an inquiry, and early in December the Defence Committee decided that the Command should remain part of the RAF for training, equipping and administration, but should come under the operational direction of the Navy. Such was the pragmatic solution of one of the greatest deficiencies in the conduct of the war on the British side. It did not overcome Coastal Command's problem of getting the right aircraft in the right numbers against the powerful competition from Bomber Command, but it put Britain's maritime air forces under those with the responsibility for protecting the seaborne supplies which underpinned the entire war-effort. Number 19 Group (Air Vice-Marshal G. R. Bromet) relieved Number 15 at Plymouth, where Admiral Dunbar-Nasmith stayed on as C-in-C of the command from which Western Approaches had been detached. All the foregoing measures were prompted by the mounting monthly shipping-losses from the fall of France to the peak for the war thus far in October 1940. There was one other: an experiment in the routeing of convoys along a relatively narrow strip of the North Atlantic, nicknamed the "tramline" system. This was an attempt to save fuel and time at sea, and to maximise the use of the still inadequate escort-forces available. At this stage, home-based escorts were taking each convoy only as far as about 19° west, where they would put about and accompany a homeward-bound convoy.

The Germans meanwhile were able to attack as far west as 25° from their French bases, well into the "Gap" between the end of the period of escort from Halifax and the beginning of that from Western Approaches. Between the two the convoys would be accompanied only by one of the forty-six armed merchant cruisers fitted out in the first six months of the war. These stopgaps were converted liners or cargo-liners, intended to deal with daylight surface attacks by submarines observing Prize Rules. Churchill had expressed his doubts about their value to Pound, the First Sea Lord, as early as January 1940. Later in the year they were shown to be of no effect at all against contemporary German submarine tactics, against conventional or disguised surface-raiders or air-attacks. No less than three AMCs were sunk by submarines in June alone, while working with the ineffectual Northern Patrol covering Germany's routes to the north Atlantic. Another was torpedoed and sunk in August in the same area, and two more in November while attached to the Western Patrol off Ireland. In December, therefore, Admiral Forbes, C-in-C of the Home Fleet, suggested withdrawing the AMCs from such lethal but almost fruitless work, at least until they had been fully equipped with the means to protect themselves against submarines.

It was the last constructive suggestion of this unfortunate commander. Sir Charles Forbes was "relieved" – innocent word, but in this context little better than a euphemism for "dismissed" – on 2 December 1940 and replaced by Admiral Sir John Tovey. Forbes, who was moved to the secondary Plymouth command, had the ill luck to be in charge of the Navy's principal formation during a period of almost unrelieved setbacks and uncertainty. He also had the moral courage to speak his mind, and most of his complaints were not only sound but also tended to be justified by subsequent events, an ability which seldom guarantees job security.

We have seen how he complained, even before the war began, of undue interference in operations by the Admiralty. He went on to protest about the deployment of his cruisers, the removal from his command of the Fleet destroyers whose primary purpose was to protect the capital ships, and against the effort devoted to laying mines against submarines (only one was destroyed by them, whereas they caused shipping congestion of considerable convenience to the enemy). During the chaos of the various Norwegian operations his tactical assessments and strategic suggestions were largely ignored or overruled, usually to the detriment of his own side. He was one of the first senior commanders to grasp the significance of the RAF victory in the Battle of Britain, which led him to say that the threat of invasion had been removed, just as Hitler, unbeknown to Forbes, began to think twice about "Operation Sealion." As early as September 28 he pressed the Admiralty to accept "that the Navy should be freed to carry out its proper function – offensively against the enemy and in defence of our trade – and not be tied down to provide passive defence to our country, which has now become a fortress." A month later he told Churchill that, "while we are predominant at sea and until Germany has defeated our fighter-force invasion by sea is not a practical operation of war." Hindsight of course proves him right, yet the British Government and the commanders who would have had to oppose an invasion cannot be blamed for being more cautious than the frustrated Forbes thought justified. The C-in-C, having learned the hard way what modern airpower could do at sea, also made a nuisance of himself by criticising the weakness of the air patrols, complaining that the Germans "always knew our dispositions and we rarely knew theirs." Forbes could not deliver an important victory during the fifteen months of his wartime command and was publicly criticised for this failure. But the Home Fleet did succeed in immobilising the bulk of the German surface-ships during the Norwegian conflict. It is impossible to escape the conclusion that he was a scapegoat for the unpreparedness in so many areas shown by the Royal Navy at the beginning of the war, when even his principal base at Scapa Flow lacked adequate protection. At least he was able to hand over to his successor a stronger fleet than the force with which he had gone to war, destroyers (now down to seventeen) excepted.

Admiral Forbes was still in command, however, when the conventional German surface-raiders began to reappear towards the end of 1940. The disguised raiders were causing considerable damage and disruption at this period but they never attacked convoys. While they were able to sink many independently routed ships, as we have noted, the convoys on the wide oceans, on the routes to Gibraltar, round the bulge of Africa and elsewhere, were able to sail almost unscathed – at least until one or two submarines were able to begin operating off the area covered by British naval forces based at Freetown, Sierra Leone. The German naval command was planning to deploy its largest warships against British trade once again, as soon as they had completed repairs after the Norwegian campaign. The first to put to sea from Germany was the heavy cruiser *Hipper*, which left for the French port of St Nazaire where the Germans now planned to base her. But, as usual, her engines let her down and she was obliged to put in to Trondheim in Norway. A sudden increase in German radio traffic in the Skagerrak area revealed to British naval intelligence that the *Hipper* was at sea on September 28. Forbes sent some of his heavy units from Rosyth and Scapa Flow to try to find her. She was not sighted.

At the end of October, the pocket-battleship *Scheer* put out to sea from the small German base at Brunsbüttel. She too evaded the attentions of RAF reconnaissance aircraft because most of them were still concentrating on detecting any sign of a German invasion of Britain. The first information that the *Scheer* was out was therefore provided by her attack on a convoy on November 5. She had already sunk an independently routed British ship, but the victim had been unable to get off a report (or at any rate no "RRR" – the signal of an attack by a surface warship – was picked up by the British). So convoy HX84, from Halifax, consisting of thirty-seven ships, had no warning. The only escort in company was the armed merchant cruiser *Jervis Bay* (Captain E. S. F. Fegen, RN), which reported that her convoy was under attack by a pocket-battleship in the very centre of the main North Atlantic route, halfway between Newfoundland and Ireland. Captain Fegen unhesitatingly decided to sacrifice his hopelessly outgunned ship, a liner considerably bulkier than her opponent but with a fraction of the firepower. In a mercilessly swift action reminiscent of the sinking of the AMC *Rawalpindi* by the two German battlecruisers, the *Jervis Bay*, like a mother-hen interposing herself between her chicks and a marauding fox, went forward with doomed gallantry to meet her fate. As the convoy scattered and put up smokescreens behind her, the *Jervis Bay* was systematically demolished by the 11-inch guns of the pocket-battleship. Captain Fegen was posthumously awarded the Victoria Cross. Considering the firepower of the enemy, the convoy suffered light damage, with the loss of only five ships, thanks not only to the bravery of the ocean escort but also to Fegen's order to scatter.

In his last messages he had given the precise position of the action, and the Admiralty and Forbes reacted by sending two battlecruisers, three cruisers and six destroyers from Scapa Flow to cover the approaches to the French ports in case the *Scheer* headed in that direction. Forbes sent two of his battleships northwards to cover the gap between Iceland and the Faroes in case the German raider decided to return by the route she had used to come out. Any chance that Forbes might have had of an interception – slender to the point of invisibility in such a vast area of sea – was reduced even further by Admiralty interference. London diverted some of his ships to the last known position of the *Scheer* – the one point on the surface of the earth where she was least likely to be – and also detached one of his battleships to cover other convoy traffic. In fact the *Scheer* (Captain Theodor Krancke) had no intention of returning to any base so soon and headed south down the middle of the Atlantic. Unable to guess his intentions, the Admiralty had no choice but to delay and divert convoys in the Atlantic with considerable disruptive effect on the flow of vital imports from North America. Three convoys were recalled, causing unparalleled congestion in the assembly-ports to which they were ordered to return. The two-week interruption on the main convoy route cost Britain rather more imports, if not shipping-losses, than the raider's guns. Since at this uniquely perilous time for Britain everything coming by ship was essential, the loss could never be made good.

The powerful Force H based at Gibraltar under Admiral Somerville was not available to hunt the *Scheer* because it was involved in operations in the Mediterranean. The pocket-battleship was in action once more on November 24, when she sank a merchantman south-east of Bermuda. But the victim, though able to get off an SOS, did not give any clue to the identity of the raider. Once again the Admiralty was forced to form ad hoc groups of ships to hunt a single raider. Force K was ordered from Britain to base itself at Freetown. It consisted of the new aircraft-carrier *Formidable* and the cruiser *Norfolk*. In fact the Royal Navy was so severely stretched that the group, one cruiser weaker than originally planned, was not ready for operations until the New Year. HMS *Hermes*, a small aircraft-carrier, and a cruiser were sent to patrol off the island of St Helena, and two cruisers were added to the strength of the South American Division which had trapped the *Graf Spee* a year before. South Atlantic convoys were diverted to pass between the Cape Verde Islands and the north-west African mainland.

The *Scheer* cruised in mid-ocean close to the equator, sinking the eighth victim of her cruise on December 1. After refuelling from a tanker on the 14th, she moved to disrupt shipping between West Africa and South America. On the 18th Captain Krancke held up the British food-freighter *Duquesa*. Uncharacteristically the Germans stood idly by while the captive sent off a detailed radio message describing her attacker. Krancke was acting on orders to provide a major diversion of British naval strength southwards, to draw attention away from a move in the far north. Her treacherous engines once more patched up, the *Hipper* was sent to sea again from Trondheim. The renewed hunt for the *Scheer* yielded no result, except to ensure that the *Hipper* (Captain Wilhelm Meisel) got into the open sea undetected via the Denmark Strait (the gap between Iceland and Greenland). Meisel was under orders to attack convoys rather than independents. Having failed to find any on the North Atlantic route, he moved south to the tropics. It was not until Christmas Eve that the *Hipper* found a target – the troop convoy WS5A, heading south some 700 miles west of Brittany and bound for the Middle East. The escort was therefore extremely strong, as was the case with all such convoys: the aircraft-carrier *Furious* and three cruisers. Attacking on Christmas Day, the Germans were taken aback by the opposing force and broke off the action after a brief exchange of fire in which minor damage was suffered by each side. The *Hipper's* engines lasted long enough to get her clear, but soon afterwards they began once more to play up. The British naval units meanwhile, having with some difficulty reassembled the scattered convoy, did not allow themselves to be diverted from their primary task of protecting the troops and let Meisel get away. The *Hipper* limped as best she could to the nearest suitable friendly harbour, the French naval base at Brest, the first major German warship to make use of the port. Although the Admiralty had guessed that the ship would make for Brest, the Coastal Command patrols sent to look for her were driven off by Luftwaffe fighters. Thus the unreliable heavy cruiser was able to make port undetected. It was not until January 4 that British air-patrols established for certain that she was there. Coastal and Bomber Commands launched a series of raids on her, but their combined total of 85 tonnes of bombs did not even scorch her paint, another illustration of the difficulty (and British lack of training) in bombing naval targets.

After six months undergoing repairs made necessary by damage sustained in Norwegian waters, the twin battlecruisers *Scharnhorst* and *Gneisenau* were the next major German surface units to try their luck on the open sea. They left Kiel on December 27, but the *Gneisenau* responded like the influenza patient who tries to go back to work too soon. She was unable to cope with the heavy weather she met off the Norwegian coast, and she and her sister-ship therefore returned to Kiel. Their abortive sortie, though brief, had been completely missed once again by British air-patrols. British helplessness at this stage against the surface-raiders is also shown by the fact that on Boxing Day the *Scheer* with her floating food-store *Duquesa* was able to meet not only the supply-tanker *Nordmark* but also the merchant raiders *Thor* and *Pinguin* in mid-Atlantic for an exchange of seasonal greetings.

Did he but know it, Captain Krancke was now engaged on the most successful cruise of the entire war by a conventional surface-raider. It is surely no coincidence that Krancke also showed the most piratical approach to his work of all the commanders of the major German warships. Although the *Scheer* was immensely powerful for her size – the British still had only three capital ships which were both better-armed and faster – Krancke had no overseas bases. He had to rely on finding German supply-ships or capturing enemy tankers for his fuel, of which he needed copious quantities. Early in the New Year, still in mid-Atlantic and the equatorial region, he met the supply-tanker *Nordmark* again in order to top up. Later in January the *Scheer* had a mid-ocean rendezvous with the disguised raider *Atlantis* and the *Tannenfels*, one of a small number of fast merchant ships in use as blockade-runners, carrying vital supplies for Germany. Two shanghaied merchantmen formed a captive audience at this extraordinary meeting of three different kinds of maritime buccaneer.

The *Scheer* now worked her way southwards, using a new deceptive tactic to lull the suspicions of potential victims. Instead of approaching them in the dark, Krancke struck in daylight, persuading them to stop by imitating British naval signalling procedures. That enabled Krancke to capture his prizes before they were able to send off an alarm signal which would have betrayed his position. This meant that the British in some cases did not know for weeks or even months precisely what had happened to the missing vessels. It was only on February 21 that a victim managed to get off the "RRR" message, revealing the German marauder's presence in the Indian Ocean, in the vicinity of the Mozambique Channel. The next day a Dutch victim was able to make a similar report. Under orders to get back to Germany by the end of March, Krancke prudently withdrew from his fruitful area of operations in the Indian Ocean and began his return to the South Atlantic. Just after his change of direction, and only some five hours after the Dutchman's signal, the *Scheer's* lookouts sighted a small aircraft. It was the spotter-seaplane from the British cruiser HMS *Glasgow*. From their various, widely dispersed positions around the region the Admiralty sent the aircraft-carrier *Hermes*, three heavy and two light cruisers to join the *Glasgow*. Still on the 22nd, however, the *Glasgow* lost contact with the *Scheer*, as daylight faded and the aircraft became useless. Two days later the Admiralty called off the hunt.

The *Scheer*, which had gone back into the Indian Ocean to evade pursuit, now put about again, passed round the Cape of Good Hope at a respectful distance and at last re-entered the South Atlantic on her way home. The pocket-battleship took part in another mid-ocean conference, with the disguised raiders *Kormoran* and *Pinguin* and the trusty tanker *Nordmark*, from which she topped up her fuel once more and carried out some urgently needed running repairs at sea. The superb efficiency of the German mid-ocean supply system was demonstrated again a couple of days later, when the *Scheer* was able to make a rendezvous with the *U124* (*Kapitänleutnant* Wilhelm Schulz). The submarine had come so far afield to provide the *Scheer* with the vital replacement parts for her radio equipment which she had requested. That it was possible for a raider, whose movements were by definition unpredictable even to her own captain, to rely on meeting the right vessel with the right material aboard in the right place at the right time was a remarkable tribute to German staff work and organisational ability. The meeting with the submarine, which had itself been refuelled at sea by the network of supply-ships, was the last friendly contact of the cruise. The *Scheer* crossed the equator on March 15, passing through the main north Atlantic convoy routes a week later – undetected. She then steamed to and fro for a couple of days, waiting for the right moment to pass through the Denmark Strait for the break back to German-controlled waters.

Her unremarked passage up the entire length of the Atlantic had been made easier by the fact that, at the time she entered the most dangerous zone in the north, the Royal Navy was preoccupied with hunting for the battlecruisers *Scharnhorst* and *Gneisenau*. London warned Admiral Sir John Tovey, the new Home Fleet C-in-C, on March 28 that wireless traffic-patterns pointed to a German attempt to send a ship or ships through the Denmark Strait. He sent the new battleship *King George V* and four cruisers out on the 29th to attempt an interception. This move was two days too late as the *Scheer* had already passed between Greenland and Iceland and was now well on her way to Norwegian waters. For the first time in more than five months, therefore, the pocket-battleship dropped anchor, at Bergen, Norway, on March 30 – Captain Krancke's forty-eighth birthday. Two days later she was back in Kiel on the German Baltic, after a most successful cruise during which she had not only sunk the *Jervis Bay* and fourteen Allied merchantmen and taken two prizes, but had also caused prolonged and serious disruption to British naval dispositions all over the Atlantic and beyond. The interruptions she imposed on the flow of supplies to Britain were much more significant for the German war effort than her total of sinkings, which fell just short of 100,000 tons.

The *Hipper*, meanwhile, had been engaged on another attempt to justify her existence. Slipping out of Brest undetected on February 1, she moved to the area between Portugal and the Azores and eventually sank a merchant ship on the 11th. The next day she sighted an unescorted "convoy" (SLS64) on its way from Freetown to Britain, and at her leisure sank seven ships, totalling 32,800 tons. Although the British were thus forcibly made aware of her presence, she was still able to return to Brest undetected on February 14, with her fuel tanks almost empty. Once again surviving several British bombing raids unscathed, Captain Meisel was ordered to take his undependable ship home to Germany for a complete refit. Setting sail unobserved on March 15 and passing round the west of the British Isles, she passed the Denmark Strait on the 23rd. She saw, but was not seen by, two patrolling British cruisers, arrived in Bergen to refuel and got to Kiel on March 28. The unseen return home of the *Hipper* and the *Scheer* within a few days of each other by broadly the same route exposed the serious inadequacy of British naval and air patrols over the vital passages between the Atlantic and German waters.

The *Scharnhorst* and the *Gneisenau* also made a lengthy sortie during this period, under the flag of Admiral Günther Lütjens, the C-in-C Fleet since spring 1940. From Kiel they went north between the Shetland Islands and Norway, and then westward to pass south of Iceland. The Admiralty had divined, once again from the pattern of wireless traffic, that another German naval breakout was about to occur, as early as January 20, and their departure three days later was discovered almost at once. Admiral Tovey himself, flying his flag in the battleship *Nelson* and accompanied by her sister-ship *Rodney*, the battlecruiser *Repulse*, eight cruisers and eleven destroyers, sailed from Scapa Flow to a position 120 miles south of Iceland, whence both passages into the north Atlantic could be watched. Extra air patrols were sent up. On January 28 the cruiser HMS *Naiad* briefly sighted the two German capital ships; but they had seen her first and put on a burst of speed, causing her to lose touch quickly. They had escaped a clash with a superior British force by a margin of a few miles. The battlecruisers continued northward to meet one of their previously dispatched refuelling tankers in the Arctic, and then turned south again, passing through the Denmark Strait on the night of February 3 to 4. It was only later that the Home Fleet discovered how narrowly they had missed their chance, despite intelligence of a rather better quality than hitherto. Lütjens had carried out his evasion with great skill and thoroughly deserved his congratulatory message from Admiral Raeder.

Refuelling again south of Greenland, the German force headed for the Halifax convoy route, and on February 8 sighted HX106. But the developing attack from north and south was broken off by the Germans when the give-away tripod-mast of the battleship *Ramillies* was spotted with the convoy. The First World War veteran spotted one of the two Germans but mistook her for a smaller type of ship (an easy mistake to make, as their silhouettes were broadly similar). The renewed threat from the surface-raiders had prompted the Admiralty to send a battleship with a convoy whenever possible. Admiral Tovey sent all available ships to the convoy route in the hope of at last bringing one of the elusive raiders to action. Despite this, and extra air-patrols, Lütjens got away once again and moved further west. He was looking for a westbound convoy this time, one which, being lightly laden, was likely to be less heavily protected. He made for the area a few hundred miles east of Newfoundland where such convoys were wont to disperse for their various destinations in North America. It was the first and only time in the war that powerful German ships risked going so close to the North American coast in search of prey. They sank five ships from a freshly dispersed convoy.

By the end of the month, having correctly assumed that at least one of the victims must have reported their presence so far north, the Germans had moved to the Sierra Leone route, refuelling on the way. On March 8 a spotter-seaplane from the battleship HMS *Malaya* sighted the battlecruisers north of the Cape Verde Islands. Shortly afterwards the British ship herself sighted them, but Lütjens had also seen her and decided not to attack the convoy SL67, which she was covering. He returned to the Halifax route, and on March 15 and 16 sank sixteen ships of 82,000 tons from dispersed convoys. The *Rodney* sighted the Germans briefly and the *King George V* steamed from Halifax at top speed to join her. Lütjens however was now under orders to return home as soon as possible. The British were once again able to guess that the battlecruisers were about to attempt the always dangerous return to port – but unfortunately were completely wrong about their destination. They assumed the Germans would return whence they had come, Germany or possibly Norway. Instead the German admiral took the shortest route to a friendly harbour and went to Brest. On being sighted by a British aircraft as he approached the French port from the south-west, Lütjens altered course to due north, as if to pass west of the British Isles, until the machine was out of sight. This ruse helped to convince the British that he was going to pass north-about Britain, since the pilot, from the carrier *Ark Royal* of Force H which had been called out from Gibraltar, omitted to report the German's original course. Bad weather then prevented the naval aircraft from keeping in touch with the enemy battlecruisers. Only on March 21 did the British divert their hunting forces to the Bay of Biscay as Bomber Command earmarked two squadrons of bombers for an attack. But by the time Coastal Command found the Germans again that evening, they were too close to the French coast to be caught by the heavy British forces which were still hundreds of miles away. Lütjens sailed triumphantly into Brest on March 22. His arrival was not confirmed to the British until six days later, thanks to bad flying weather.

As the convoys began to return to normal, the British assembled forces of capital ships, submarines and bombers in the hope of being able either to destroy the German ships in port or to bring them to action during an attempt to return to Germany. The *Scharnhorst* and the *Gneisenau* had spent two months at sea, during which they had destroyed shipping totalling 116,000 tons. They had also added to the general and very serious disruption of the convoy cycles caused by the other conventional and disguised German raiders, and provided another useful diversion of British naval strength just as the *Hipper* and the *Scheer* were returning home. All this was according to plan. The German naval staff orchestrated the movements of these four major units in such a way as to cause maximum confusion among the much superior forces of the enemy.

The deployment of the "big four" was almost a textbook example of how to use inferior naval forces in a maritime version of guerrilla hit-and-run tactics. Unlike his enemies, Admiral Lütjens was not interested in a slogging match between capital ships, which he was under orders to avoid. The skill with which he did so was such that his officers and men never had the impression that they were always running away; on the contrary, they felt they were tweaking the lion's tail, stealing his supplies and getting away with it. When Lütjens brought his ships unharmed into Brest, Raeder's second congratulatory telegram was positively fulsome. It was richly deserved. At the end of March 1941, nineteen months into a war with the world's greatest navy, the Germans had lost only one pocket-battleship and one heavy cruiser from the major ships in their small but modern and powerful surface fleet. Even if the British Admiralty had been wrong on the eve of war in identifying the surface threat as the main one, the German raiders had actually caused, thanks to their fleeting visibility, more disruption than the submarines, which got on with the main onslaught on shipping by stealth. The German Navy had every justification for complaining that it had been caught unprepared by the war now being fought, but could look back with considerable satisfaction on a year and a half in which an onslaught by mines, surface-ships and submarines had seriously affected the enemy's ability to fight on.

Before returning to the submarine operations during this second period of the Atlantic campaign, we need to consider the German air-effort, which, as has been pointed out, was very nearly as much beyond the naval command's control as the weather. It started to have a serious effect on the ocean-convoys in July 1940, when the Luftwaffe began to make use of the French airbase at Mérignac near Bordeaux. From there the Focke-Wulf 200 aircraft was soon able to fly as far out over the ocean as nine degrees west. Originally a passenger aircraft which had been adapted for long-range reconnaissance, the military version was named the *Kondor*. The first squadron was formed in April 1940. From July a total of thirty aircraft in two squadrons was based at Mérignac, flying a version fully equipped to make bombing attacks, with a range of 1,000 miles. In autumn 1940 the Luftwaffe gave them a second base at Stavanger in Norway, so that by taking off from France and landing in Norway, or vice versa, they were able to fly even further out into the Atlantic, with an endurance of 2,000 miles for the one-way trip. But the German fliers had to be confident of good weather conditions at the other end in such a risky method of operation. The Kondors were able to sink a total of fifteen ships of 53,000 tons in their first full month of operations, to add to the total of 268,000 tons sunk by submarines. The aircraft were also able to help the submarines home in on targets at this stage of the war, when the British had no aircraft capable of dealing with the German long-range bombers out at sea. The Kondors stepped up their sinking rate to 66,000 tons (eighteen ships) in November. Coastal Command's Blenheim fighters were too slow and lightly armed to deal with the new threat, which was in no way diminished by bombing raids on the German air and naval bases in France in the last two months of the year.

Much as they would have liked to, the British were not able to close their ports on the English east coast, now exposed to heavy air-attack from across the Channel and the North Sea, because the western ports were already severely congested. RAF Fighter Command was preoccupied with the Luftwaffe's bombing offensive elsewhere, and such cover as it was able to provide for shipping almost always came too late: by the time they reacted to a call for help, the raiders were well on their way back to base. Inexperienced Merchant Navy gunners, given only seconds to decide whether an approaching aircraft was friend or foe, were as wont to fire on their would-be rescuers as on the enemy. Particularly severe damage was done to shipping in the area before the opposed air forces were locked in the Battle of Britain. A "Channel Guard" of hurriedly trained seamen with machine-guns was formed to travel with ships in the danger-zone. With training the gunners improved their performance against the relatively slow but terrifying *Stuka* (Junkers 87) dive-bombers, which were eventually driven away from the ships by a special effort on the part of Fighter Command. Local surface-escorts were strengthened by diversions from the anti-invasion forces; the east-coast routes were somehow kept open until the shipping losses to short-range air attack fell away from their peak in the period from June to August 1940 (when they accounted for one casualty in three out of the total lost to all causes).

The Germans also introduced new types of mine in this fraught period, including acoustic ones, set off by a ship's noise, and delayed-action magnetic mines. British minesweepers were forced to work by night to escape air-attack, but severe shipping losses were sustained in the last quarter of 1940. It was soon discovered that convoys were as useful a defence against mines as against submarines: the safe passage of one ship entailed the safety of all that followed and there were so many eyes to keep watch. In the six months to the end of March 1941, nineteen ships in convoy but seventy independents were lost to mines. Other threats to coastwise shipping in this period included the fifteen German E-boats based in the Netherlands for hit-and-run raids and Luftwaffe heavy bombing of the ports themselves, west as well as east. In February 1941 the Germans switched to night air-raids.

The submariners' benefit represented by "the happy time" lasted roughly four months, from mid-July to mid-November 1940. During this period, when convoys as well as ships sailing alone or unescorted came under frequent attack, losses among independents still greatly exceeded those among ships in convoy (144 compared with 73, or almost exactly 2:1). German submarine losses, by contrast, were for the British depressingly small. On 1 July 1940 *U26* was sunk south-west of Ireland, the first "kill" in which a corvette (*Gladiolus*) took part, supported by aircraft of the Royal Australian Air Force based in Britain. One other boat (*U122*) was lost that month, but date, cause and precise position in the North Sea were never discovered. *U102* met a similarly mysterious fate in August, during which *U25* was lost to a mine in the North Sea and *U51* to the British submarine *Cachalot* on patrol in the Bay of Biscay. The next "kill" did not come until October 30, when convoy escorts sank *U32* – but not before the German boat had sunk the liner *Empress of Britain*, 42,348 tons – the largest ship ever destroyed by a submarine.

On November 2 *U31* (*Kapitänleutnant* Wilfried Prellberg) achieved a unique if melancholy record by becoming the only boat to be sunk twice. Originally sent to the shallow bottom off the German North Sea coast in a Bomber Command raid in March 1940, the *U31* was salvaged, overhauled and sent back to sea. She was lost for ever when depth-charged by HMS

Antelope, escorting a convoy in the north Atlantic. The last submarine to be sunk in 1940 (and until March 1941) was *U104*, destroyed by the corvette *Rhododendron*. This brought total German submarine losses for the war so far to just thirty-two. "Kills" proved very difficult for the Admiralty to confirm, a problem with which it naturally received no help from the Germans. In July Churchill succumbed to incredulous anger when told by an Admiralty staff officer that enemy losses by then amounted to only twenty-five (an educated guess which happened to be extremely accurate) – and ordered the bearer of the bad news to be sent back to sea! Throughout the war, each side heartily exaggerated its achievements against the other, with the Germans claiming mythical tonnages of merchant ships and the British unsubstantiated submarine kills. The Admiralty set up a special Assessment Committee which carefully examined all reports that a submarine had been destroyed. This damped down the wilder claims sufficiently to give a reasonably accurate, if still somewhat overblown, picture of anti-submarine successes; the German propaganda-machine however sank the entire enemy merchant fleet several times over.

In November 1940 shipping losses to submarine attack fell back sharply, to 147,000 tons, rather less than half the October figure. But losses to mines, air-attack, surface-warships and disguised raiders all rose considerably, to produce a combined total of 386,000 tons, some 57,000 fewer than in October. The temporary decline in sinkings by submarines was due to a combination of deteriorating weather, German exhaustion, evasive routeing and the slow but steady increase in quantity and quality of escorts. The lull, briefly welcomed by Churchill as the turn of the tide, was a false dawn. While overall shipping losses fell to 350,000 tons in December, those to submarine attack rose by about forty-five percent to 213,000. In January they fell again to 127,000 tons out of a total of 320,000, and in February the submarines sank 197,000 tons out of 403,000. It has to be borne in mind that throughout the nine months covered by this chapter, the Germans had fewer than thirty submarines operational (at the turn of the year twenty-one, the lowest total of the whole war). In September 1940, exactly a year after the war began, they possessed exactly the same overall number of submarines (fifty-seven); but in the quarter ending with that month fifteen new boats were commissioned as the construction rate at last began to accelerate.

In March 1941 Dönitz shifted the focus of his operations further west, to the area south of Iceland. Now that the worst of the winter weather was over, the British were using more northerly routes – a fact which was soon detected by the *B-dienst* analysts. Inevitably, the renewed offensive was inaugurated by Günther Prien, still in *U47*, which sighted the westbound convoy OB293, some 200 miles south-east of Iceland. Prien sent the customary sighting report – on March 6 – and awaited reinforcements. During the day Dönitz assembled a pack of four: Prien; Kretschmer in *U99*; *Kapitän-*

leutnant Joachim Matz in *U70*; and Commander Hans Eckermann in the experimental boat *UA*. There now developed around this convoy with its mostly unladen ships a naval action unlike any other in the war thus far. Launching the German attack in the very early hours of the 7th, Kretschmer made a pass across the front of the convoy, hitting a tanker and a huge Norwegian whaling factory-ship, the *Terje Viken* (21,000 tons). *U99* attacked on the surface as usual, and those on the conning-tower at the time were alarmed to see the upperworks of their boat bathed in St Elmo's fire. This electrical phenomenon, a spontaneous discharge of accumulated static electricity, has always been a bad omen among superstitious sailors, who believe it portends the imminent loss of the vessel. Perhaps *U99's* golden horseshoe saved her; if so, it was with some difficulty. The tanker exploded into flame; the whaling ship was crippled but stayed afloat.

Next to attack was Matz, who torpedoed a British freighter and a Dutch tanker in quick succession. His first victim sank but the second, the *Mijdrecht*, though damaged, was able to round on her attacker as the *U70* was about to finish her off and succeeded in ramming the boat before Matz completed his evasive dive. Either this or the rapidly intensifying counter-attack by the escorts caused a leak in the boat's hull.

The escort was led by Commander J. M. Rowland in HMS *Wolverine*, supported by a second destroyer, *Verity*, and two corvettes, *Arbutus* and *Camellia*, operating as a group. Reacting swiftly and in harmony to the sinkings, they subjected *U99* and *U70* to an unprecedentedly fierce attack lasting nearly five hours, during which more than 100 depth-charges were dropped. *UA* was damaged after torpedoing but failing to sink a British steamer and Eckermann withdrew to limp home. The wily ace Kretschmer dived and sat out the onslaught as his boat was rattled by near-misses which put out the lights and loosened rivets in the hull. The *U70* meanwhile was shipping water, which made it increasingly difficult to control her depth. After five hours underwater, the boat came under yet another attack from the two corvettes. *U70* went out of control, rising and sinking under the surface; as she went down, the crew rushed to the stern to try to bring her nose up; as she rose they made a bruising rush to the other end of the boat to stop her surfacing. Rivets popped, lockers emptied their contents all over the deck, the lights flickered on and off and the compressed air for controlling the depth ran out. *U70* went as deep as 650 feet (150 more than the design-depth), the crew rushed to the stern and Matz ordered full motor-power to stop the death-dive. He was all too successful: the *U70* now shot to the surface and suddenly appeared within short range of the hunting corvettes, which promptly opened fire. Matz gave the order to abandon, urged on by someone on the bridge of one of the corvettes who told him in broken German to jump overboard. The British lowered a boat, with the obvious intent of boarding; Matz bravely reboarded his stricken submarine and made sure that she was about to sink. Twenty of his crew were lost when the bow rose in the air and the *U70* sank by the stern; Matz and twenty-six others were taken prisoner. Kretschmer stole away in the battered *U99*.

Prien stayed with the convoy despite the ferocity of the escorts and even wirelessed for more reinforcements. Just before 1 a.m. on the 8th, in a rainstorm, the *U47* was sighted on the surface at close range by the *Wolverine*. Her engines could be heard, and Commander Rowland actually smelt the diesel fumes. The *Verity* lit up the scene with a star-shell and the two destroyers took turns to drop patterns of ten depth-charges each as Prien sought to escape underwater. Three hours later oil was seen on the surface. The attack was renewed with vigour. After another hour, the *Wolverine's* hydrophone operator heard "a loud clattering sound like crockery breaking" over his headphones. The *U47* then briefly surfaced within yards of the *Wolverine* and as quickly dived again. The destroyer swung round, charged over the disturbed surface and dropped one more pattern. The result was a manifestation of destruction the like of which was never seen before or after. The British sailors on the *Wolverine* saw an orange glow deep below the surface of the sea which may have burned for as much as ten seconds: some aboard swore that flames briefly flickered above the water. It was as if the mouth of hell had opened to receive the Bull of Scapa Flow. The *U47* was gone; the most famous submarine ace, who sank a battleship and 161,000 tons of shipping but failed to damage his last convoy, was dead at the age of thirty-one with all forty-six men of his crew, a hero of Nazi Germany meeting his end in a submarine *Götterdämmerung*. Even though his short but uniquely spectacular career was marked by utter ruthlessness in sinking so many ships without warning and sending so many sailors and merchant seamen to their death, the eerie destruction of Günther Prien, his crew and *U47* still seems chilling.

The loss of the *U47* evoked a unique reaction in Germany which was no less eerie in itself. Accustomed as they were to not hearing from boats for days at a time or even longer, in the light of standing orders not to transmit unless necessary, the command-staff at Kernevel took about a week to conclude that Prien was lost. But the Supreme Command of the Wehrmacht did not dare to mention in its daily public war-bulletins that he was missing in action until seventy-six days had passed. Rumours began to spread long before this among a public grown accustomed to its regular morale-boosting diet of his exploits. The *Sicherheitsdienst* or SD, the SS security-service which regularly monitored public opinion and morale for the Nazi leadership, noted in a secret report of April 28:

> The already repeatedly expressed anxieties of the population about his fate after the prolonged lack of reference to Prien in the Wehrmacht bulletin are rising again and in greater strength as it is already so long since he has been heard from.

Only on May 23 did the Supreme Command announce that "the submarine commanded by Günther Prien has not returned from its last voyage against the enemy. The loss of the boat must be assumed." Dönitz, who had opposed the long suppression of the loss of his favourite commander, thought this a miserable epitaph and personally composed a fulsome tribute in an Order of the Day to the submarine arm on May 24:

> Günther Prien, the hero of Scapa Flow, has made his last voyage. We submariners bow in proud grief and salute him and his men. Even if the broad ocean covers him, Günther Prien nonetheless still stands in our midst . . . He has become for us a symbol of our hard, unshakeable will to attack England. The struggle continues in his spirit.

Dönitz's last farewell did not still the rumours about Prien among ordinary people, who simply would not believe their hero was dead at all. A story which refused to die began to go the rounds, to the effect that Prien and his entire crew had been sent to a concentration camp. It had somehow become known that Prien had led the chorus of complaint about the defective torpedoes early in the war; whether or not his famously contemptuous remark about fighting with a wooden gun was quoted, there was widespread suspicion of a mutiny on *U47* or even politically motivated revolt. The rumour outlasted the war; "eyewitnesses" claimed to have seen Prien in the concentration camp at Torgau on the Elbe at the beginning of 1945, or to have had a sight of a file about a court martial of Prien and his crew. There was not a shred of truth in any of it.

The British were enormously cheered by their victory, which also brought the first "kills" in four months. A week later, on March 15, another bloody struggle developed around convoy HX122 from Halifax, which was about 300 miles north-west of Scotland at the time. On this occasion it was Lemp of *Athenia* fame, now in *U110*, who sighted the forty-one ships trundling along at eight knots with their precious loads and reported by wireless. Within hours four more boats joined him: the two leading aces Kretschmer (*U99*) and Schepke (*U100*), and *U37* (Commander Nicolai Clausen) with *U74* (Commander Eitel-Friedrich Kentrat). Against this formidable scratch-team was ranged the Fifth Escort Group led by Commander (later Captain) Donald Macintyre, RN, one of the best wartime group-leaders who subsequently became a distinguished naval historian. He had two destroyers, the *Walker*, of which he was also captain, and the *Vanoc* (Commander J. G. W. Deneys) with the corvettes *Bluebell* and *Hydrangea*. As the convoy was particularly important with a high proportion of laden tankers, two extra destroyers, *Sardonyx* and *Scimitar*, had been added to the escort.

Schepke took first blood in the night of the 15th to 16th by hitting a tanker, which caught fire and lit up the scene for hours yet miraculously survived to limp into port. Schepke and Clausen were driven off after hours of further vain attacks. On the evening of the 16th it was Kretschmer's turn. Infiltrating the convoy formation from the port side, he sank four tankers and a freighter inside an hour, stayed in step with the remainder in the centre row and after a quarter of an hour claimed his sixth victim, another freighter. Having fired all his twelve torpedoes he managed to withdraw his boat from the chaotic scene, bright as daylight with flames and flares. The desperate Macintyre swung out from the convoy to search for the enemy outside its perimeter, hoping to catch a submarine on the way in to attack. He did; the *U100* promptly dived, the *Walker* roared over the spot and dropped a single pattern of ten depth-charges. The *U100* was damaged but not destroyed; Schepke retained control and continued to dodge. Shortly afterwards, and for the first time in the war, the type 286 ASV radar freshly fitted to the *Vanoc* located a submarine (still the *U100*) and rammed it. The conning-tower crumpled, crushing Schepke against his periscope-tube, and the *Vanoc* rode over the boat with a terrible screeching and scraping of metal. Six German survivors were picked out of the sea as the *U100* vanished. At this moment the Asdic operator on the *Walker* got another contact, insisting against his captain's scepticism that it was a new one. Half a dozen depth-charges were dropped. Kretschmer's officer-of-the-watch had made the mistake of ordering a dive when he almost collided with one of the destroyers, and it was this which made the Asdic contact possible. *U99* was severely damaged and plunged to 700 feet (which should have caused the hull to implode), its motors and steering barely responding. Using all his compressed air to blow the main ballast-tanks, Kretschmer shot to the surface in his ruined boat and came under a hail of fire. The submarine signalled, "We are sinking" with its lamp and when the crew, except for the engineer who was caught below making sure the boat did sink, jumped into the water the firing ceased. Kretschmer and his men were taken prisoner, their captors thrilled beyond measure to have taken the greatest ace of them all in terms of tonnage sunk. He had been able to get off a last message: "Two destroyers – depth-charges – 50,000 tons sunk – imprisonment – Kretschmer." For the commander who had sunk nearly 270,000 tons of shipping and remained lucky to the last, even as the boat with the golden horseshoe sank beneath him, the war was over. His interrogators expected a slavering Nazi fiend but found a quiet, polite, educated, confident young man at the height of his powers. "I sincerely hoped that there were not too many like him," said a British staff officer after meeting him.

The British cup of joy almost ran over after March 23, when the humble anti-submarine trawler caught the *U551* unawares between the Faroes and Iceland and sank it: five boats in fifteen days and three of them commanded by top aces. Churchill was so delighted that he once again thought a turning-point had been reached. His jubilation is understandable but his optimism once again proved misplaced. The elimination of the top aces was a most welcome psychological blow against the Germans but the British had lost 3,174,000 tons of shipping to submarines alone in the war so far, out of a total loss of 5,471,000 tons, and had sunk only thirty-six submarines, or less than two per month on average. There could be no doubt that this represented an overall setback for the British of ominous proportions. March 1941 showed however that escorts trained to work together and given the right equipment were a match for the wolf-packs. The aces fell victim to their own dash in attack, which had always worked against uncoordinated escorts. The loss of U99 and U100 was announced by the Germans on April 25, five weeks after the event. The SD reported rumours among the populace that the British had developed a secret weapon against the submarines.

The true secret weapon on each side in the intensifying battle in the Atlantic, with all the faults and shaky guesswork involved, was the gathering and use of intelligence. At this stage of the war the Germans were unquestionably ahead in this concealed struggle, a fact for which three main factors helped to account. The naval *B-dienst* had almost made a science of gleaning information from British wireless traffic about the position and movement of ships, a skill which, as we have seen, they developed in the years immediately preceding the war. Naval reconnaissance aircraft and the Luftwaffe, despite the endless wrangle about maritime airpower, quickly developed regular and effective routines for keeping a watch on British ports and shipping movements. The British had not given enough attention to aerial reconnaissance before the war and lacked aircraft both for this specialised task and generally. Finally, the Germans had partly penetrated British naval codes before the war and were able to trade on this advantage for almost the whole of the first year of hostilities.

Apart from a certain complacency at the Admiralty, compounded by its rejection of mechanical codes before the war, the fault for this major security lapse on the British side lay largely with the Government Code and Cipher School at Bletchley Park. The role of this institution was not only to attack enemy ciphers, with which it was beginning to make considerable headway during this period, but also to defend those of its own side, an area which was relatively neglected as the struggling cryptanalysts demanded more and more resources. This is one clear reason for indulging a certain judicious scepticism about the importance to the British, and later the Allied, war-effort of the GC & CS. The stunning revelation, some thirty years after the war, that Bletchley Park had overcome even the naval variant of the Enigma coding machine naturally obliged historians to re-examine the course of the Atlantic campaign. The piecemeal emergence of more and more information about the extraordinary ingenuity of the many absorbingly interesting personalities at Bletchley Park led some to the often uncritical conclusion that the GC & CS had not just made an enormous contribution to ultimate victory, which it did, but had almost won the war single-handed, which is seriously exaggerated. Some of Bletchley Park's wartime work is still shrouded in secrecy and may well remain so for ever; what is more, nobody has been, or will be, able to give a comprehensive picture of what went on there even if the British Government sheds its paranoia about secrecy overnight. This is because no one had an overview of what all the various sections and the sometimes decidedly wayward eccentrics and geniuses on the staff were doing. In that most secret nerve-centre of the war there were wheels within wheels far more complicated than the inner workings of an Enigma machine. We shall be returning from time to time to the role of the intelligence services on both sides; suffice it to say at this stage that if the criterion for the success of intelligence is the use that can be made of the information it provides, then the *B-dienst* was of greater value to Dönitz than British naval intelligence was to his enemies from the beginning of the war until the Allies had enough strength to defend their shipping successfully.

But the "creative anarchy" at Bletchley Park, as the official historian of British Intelligence, Professor F. H. Hinsley, describes it, was beginning to step up its output of useful information based not only on the growing number of messages it was able to decrypt but also on a growing "feel" for the enemy traffic as a whole. At the end of 1940 the traffic analysts who had been transferred from BP to the Admiralty's Operational Intelligence Centre at the beginning of the war were returned, ending an unnecessary division of forces. In March 1941 an assistant director was appointed at the OIC to co-ordinate the work of BP's Naval Section, the OIC and Naval Intelligence exploitation of the information gained, which resulted in smooth co-operation for the rest of the war. At the beginning of 1941 an independent Central Interpretation Unit was set up to analyse all photographic reconnaissance pictures from all sources, including Coastal Command's No. 1 Photographic Reconnaissance Unit, and to distribute the results to all relevant commands. This did much to remove British weakness in this field, notably in providing accurate and current information on submarine construction. Meanwhile American naval officers were being given an ever more detailed picture of the entire naval intelligence effort in anticipation of US intervention, a valuable advance contribution to its eventual effectiveness. There was much excitement at BP in March 1941 when software relating to naval Enigma was delivered following its capture aboard the armed trawler *Krebs*: this material enabled the Naval Section to decipher the whole of the previous month's traffic and helped with cracking subsequent transmissions. The find, made during a successful raid on the Norwegian Lofoten Islands, was much more useful than anything hitherto taken from the enemy, including the cipher-settings from *VP2623* eleven months earlier and the three wheels recovered from prisoners of war from the *U33* two months before that.

PoWs were milked for all they were worth from the very beginning of the war, initially in the majestically forbidding surroundings of the Tower of

Above: HMS *Hood* (centre) photographed from the *Repulse*.

Below: HMS *Duke of York.*

Above: Tirpitz at anchor in Norway just before her destruction.

Left: Scharnhorst.

Below: Bismarck.

The Enigma Machine: The German encryption device, which, in its most sophisticated versions, provided 150,000,000,000,000,000,000 possible substitutions for each letter. The British decoded the first Enigma message in late 1939.

Alan Turing.

Roosevelt receiving from Churchill a letter from King George VI aboard the USS *Augusta*, at the Argentia Conference, August 1941.

Left: Admiral Ernest J. King, USN.

Above: "Flower" class corvette, HMS *Bluebell*.

Below: "Hunt" class destroyer, HMS *Lauderdale*.

Above: Repeated Allied bombings failed to damage the German submarine pens at Brest.

Below: Type VII taking fuel from a milch-cow.

Above: Canadian corvettes off Halifax, Nova Scotia, in 1941.

Left: The Channel Dash: the first attempt by an enemy of Britain to pass a fleet through the English Channel since the Spanish Armada in 1588: *Scharnhorst* (top right), *Gneisenau* (left) and *Prinz Eugen* (bottom).

Above: Tanks being loaded for Russia at a British port.

Below: This angry cartoon aroused fierce controversy when it appeared in the London *Daily Mirror* of 6 March 1942.

"The price of petrol has been increased by one penny."—Official.

London and later in camps outside the capital, where "stool-pigeons" (informers) were planted among them. Information from this source proved valuable in itself, and also as a cover for material gained from Sigint (signals intelligence), which could otherwise not have been exploited for fear of revealing how far the cryptanalysts had got.

During this period captured German submariners showed exceptionally high morale and usually did their utmost to deny information to their interrogators. PoWs were under particularly strict orders to conceal in the latter part of 1940 that the Germans were making heavy use of the French Atlantic ports, but this little deception was frequently exposed by the simple expedient of ordering men to turn out their pockets: a shower of occupation francs put an end to the charade. The nature of submarine warfare was such that few crewmen were captured, no matter how many submarines were sunk. Officer-prisoners were by definition much rarer still, and although they carried the most useful information in their heads they were also more aware of the dangers of letting it out. So it was only sketchily and with difficulty that the British were able to build up some kind of a picture of the command organisation just across the Channel, based as it was in a requisitioned Breton fish-merchant's villa at Kernevel, near the main submarine port of Lorient.

In its essentials the submarine arm under Karl Dönitz, its C-in-C, was remarkably small and simply organised. His deputy for the entire war was Captain (later Rear-Admiral) Eberhard Godt. There were just six other staff officers and one engineer-officer in the Operations Department, which ran the campaign, and they all had recent experience in submarines at sea. Parallel but separate was the arm's Organisation Department under Admiral Hans-Georg von Friedeburg, who had his own chief of staff and six officers as departmental heads. At Kernevel there was a "Situation Room" where huge charts showed the position at sea as collated from submarine reports, intelligence and reconnaissance material. Next door was the "Museum," its walls covered with graphs, tables and diagrams which together constituted a concurrent analysis of operations and enemy movements designed to reveal trends and changes in sinkings, submarine losses and convoy routes.

At the start of each day Dönitz, or Godt when he was away, chaired a round-table discussion with the staff officers to review the previous day's operations and consider those for the next twenty-four hours. This took place in the Situation (or Operations) Room, which was run by Godt, the operational chief of submarines under various titles throughout the campaign. His contribution to it was second only to that of Dönitz himself, a fact which has had little recognition because, unlike his chief, he stayed in the background during and after the war. It was he who actually orchestrated most of the great pack-attacks on the convoys. But Dönitz was no absentee landlord. Able to rely implicitly on such a sound operational chief, he could tour the submarine bases in France to keep in touch with the crews, and he read every returning captain's report before interviewing its author at length. No detail was too small for him, and although Dönitz came across in postwar books and interviews as a stiff and distant figure, he had all the concern for his men's welfare and morale of the great commanders. He allowed important family news to be sent to boats at sea, and his way of telling Günther Prien of the birth of a daughter was to announce the arrival of a "U-boat without periscope." Proxy marriages, especially of the "shotgun" variety, were often solemnised over the submarine radio-network.

The German submarine service, in which some 42,000 men were to serve during the war, was in many respects as close-knit as a family under its "Prussian" patriarch, whose unrelenting demand for devotion to duty at sea was offset by a certain readiness to indulge his men ashore. When they returned from the high tension and acute stress of an operational mission, pale, bearded (the custom was not to shave at sea) and stinking of diesel-oil and enforced neglect of personal hygiene, they were allowed to let off steam as fighting men have always done. Pausing only to shed their filthy uniforms, the boots and leather jackets covered in dry sea-salt, oil and green mould-stains, they would revel in a hot bath or a prolonged shower before going out on the town in fresh clothes to blow their accumulated pay, more or less doubled by the submariner's allowance, on wine, women and a great deal of raucous singing. "Living like a god in France" was a byword in the submarine service – especially, no doubt, when a crew was based in the less appealing environment of the Baltic or Norway. For those with home-leave there was the C-in-C's train, kept by the submarine command to run officers and men to Germany and bring them and vital spares and supplies back to Lorient. Crews on local leave could withdraw from the coast (and the attentions of the RAF) to one of the "submariner's meadows" (*U-bootsweiden*) – recreation camps in requisitioned high-class hotels or châteaux. Those who had to stay in the ports could unwind in bars like Les Trois Soeurs (soon restyled "Die Sechs Titten" by naval humorists) and the Hôtel Beau Séjour in Lorient, the Astoria Bar in St Nazaire and the Maritza (nicknamed "Die Giftbude" – the poison-hut) in La Baule, or the Cecilia Bar in grimy, gloomy Brest. Bordeaux was the nicest town to be stuck in, and the local French populations were mostly friendly enough to the free-spending young Germans. There was usually one last binge back in the port of departure on the eve of the next mission: when the sailors filed back aboard it was the faces rather than the seagoing uniforms which were green.

The harsh life at sea with its high risks and acutely cramped discomfort – the all-pervading dankness, the powerful stench made up of fuel, unwashed bodies and perpetually foul air – was reflected in a special, sometimes desperate hedonism ashore. These most accomplished practitioners of total war were soon having to contend with the highest death-rate in any arm of the entire Wehrmacht. It is a small wonder that they let rip so spectacularly when ashore, and a great one that they generally maintained remarkably high morale to the bitter end. "Onkel Karl's" boys had the best pay and the finest rations and were constantly hailed as heroes by the propaganda-machine, but all this is not enough to explain their morale.

Although the Nazi Party was later represented on each boat by that symbol of totalitarian militarism, the political officer (his role was the same as that of the commissar in the Soviet system), the service as a whole was not notably Nazi in its outlook but more influenced by the principle, "My country, right or wrong." The submarine arm was not a branch of the SS but an élite, a world apart. Its nearest psychological equivalent in British service was not so much the Royal Navy's submarine arm, which actually suffered an even higher percentage of fatalities but was much smaller and less central to the war effort: it was rather the frontline RAF, which in Fighter and Bomber commands also suffered exceptionally high losses, was made up of highly trained men and was also able to take the fight to the enemy throughout the war. The difference between the two specialist services was not so much the element in which they served but the fact that for the British fliers the darkest days came first, whereas for the German submariners it was the other way round.

The main technological advance on the British side during this period was the spread of radar among the escorts and maritime aircraft. The "state of the art" was still primitive because the wavelength was long (over one metre), which meant that the aerial had to be placed in as high a position as possible on a ship, a limitation which did not, of course, apply to aircraft. But shipborne radar began to remedy the main weakness of Asdic, its inability to detect a surfaced submarine, during this period. Increased use was being made of aircraft, which could already detect a surfaced submarine at fifteen miles when flying at 2,500 feet. Their new electronic eyes could also locate stragglers and their no less troublesome opposites, the "rompers" which ran ahead of convoys because they could not keep their speed down. Airborne radar enormously increased the value of air-cover, which was now much more effective in poor weather, both against enemy aircraft and for helping to keep convoys together. Shipborne radar at this early stage did not altogether inspire confidence because it was still picking up too many "back-echoes" from ships in the convoy, which could easily confuse an operator searching for submarines. But work was already in progress on more sophisticated aerials and radar-sets with much shorter wavelengths. By March 1941 a new naval set with a directional aerial was on trial, to replace the first types in general use with the Royal Navy and RAF.

Asdic's other operational drawback was its inability to give an accurate depth-reading, which was countered by widening the range of depths at which the various depth-charges in a "pattern" were set to explode. From summer 1940 the Sunderland flying-boats of Coastal Command carried adapted depth-charges: this weapon for the first time conferred on aircraft the ability to destroy a submarine, just as radar was beginning to extend their capacity to find it.

An important innovation at this time was the use of High-Frequency Direction-Finding (HF/DF, or "Huff-Duff" to sailors). Locating an enemy by getting a "fix" on his wireless transmissions from two or more listening posts – his approximate position was the point at which the various bearings obtained crossed on a chart – had its origins in the dying months of the First World War. The Germans, who used the technique themselves, knew the British were doing it but also knew that it was not very accurate when done from shore stations (the greater the distance, the less precise the bearing). They also thought that the British only used DF on medium wave at sea, so they relied increasingly on High Frequency transmissions when preparing an attack on a convoy in the hope of preserving the advantage of surprise. The British answer to this was to put HF/DF equipment on convoy escorts. This meant that DF could be exploited not only to divert convoys away from danger but also by escorts to locate submarines before they could attack.

The principal German advances during this nine-month period were tactical rather than technical. The night-attack on the surface was developed against Asdic and the pack-attack against escorted convoys (which itself began to be countered by the integrated escort-group). The occupation of the French coast enormously increased the effectiveness of the submarines as well as offering new opportunities for aircraft in reconnaissance and attacking roles. The higher monthly sinkings to be achieved later in the war tend to mask the fact that this period was the zenith of the submarine's efficiency, boat for boat. In October 1940 each boat at sea accounted for an average of ten ships totalling about 60,000 tons, for the loss of just one submarine in this heyday of the "aces."

The British responded to the escalating threat by tactical adjustments of their own. The gap between convoy columns was increased from 600 to 1,000 yards to reduce vulnerability to "browning" shots (torpedoes fired diagonally across a convoy to increase the chance of a hit); but the space had to be reduced to 600 yards again at the end of 1940 to strengthen the defence against air-attack.

The RAF's concentration on building up its strategic bomber-force did not preclude a number of air-raids on the French submarine bases but may explain why these attacks were not deadly enough to have the desired effect. In January 1941 the Germans began using forced labour to build gigantic concrete carapaces over the submarine pens which proved capable of withstanding anything to be thrown at them later (they are still used by the French Navy today). The RAF thus missed its opportunity to strike a blow against the main threat to Britain's survival by failing to concentrate enough force against it when it was still vulnerable.

*   *   *

Dönitz's strategic concerns during this period also and inevitably included the direction of German airpower against the British at sea. He was doubtless mollified by Hitler's War Directive number 23 of 6 February 1941, which opened with what sounded like a rare acknowledgment of error:

> Contrary to our former view the heaviest effect of our war-operations against the English war-economy has lain in the high losses in merchant-shipping inflicted by sea and air warfare . . . A further considerable increase is to be expected in the course of this year by the wider employment of submarines, and this can bring about the collapse of English resistance in the foreseeable future . . . It will therefore be desirable in future to concentrate air attacks more closely and to deliver them against targets whose destruction supplements our naval war . . . Special orders will be issued for co-operation between naval and air forces in reconnaissance over the sea.

In his War Diary for this period Dönitz constantly complained of the High Command's lack of appreciation of the strategic importance of the submarine campaign. This, Göring's proprietorial attitude ("Everything that flies belongs to me!") and delays in deliveries to both the Navy and the Luftwaffe were constant frustrations for the submarine chief. At the end of 1940 his only contact with Group 40 (Kondors) was unofficial and personal, but his complaints about lack of air-support appeared to bear fruit on 7 January 1941, when Hitler placed Group 40 under Dönitz's direct command. It was done behind Göring's back when the Reichsmarschall was on a shooting holiday. One month later Dönitz accepted an invitation to his first meeting with Göring aboard the latter's resplendent command-train (now owned and used by the West German Government). The Luftwaffe chief did his utmost to persuade Dönitz to hand KG40 back, but naturally to no avail. The admiral declined the offer of dinner, made his formally polite excuses and left, having gained a powerful enemy. Göring promptly reassumed control of KG40, but Dönitz's not inconsiderable consolation was that its new commander was Lieutenant-Colonel Martin Harlinghausen, a former naval officer. Naval operational command was lost, but co-operation improved enormously, and with that Dönitz had to rest content.

Precisely one month after Hitler acknowledged the effectiveness of the submarine campaign, Churchill did the same in a directive of his own, for which he coined the title, "Battle of the Atlantic."

> We must take the offensive against the U-boat and the Focke-Wulf wherever we can and whenever we can. The U-boat at sea must be hunted, the U-boat in the building-yard or the dock must be bombed. The Focke-Wulf and other bombers employed against our shipping must be attacked in the air and in their nests . . . [Among many other measures] simplification and acceleration of repairs . . . even at some risk, must be applied in order to reduce the terrible slowness of the turn-round of ships in British ports.

The directive had much more to say about congestion in the ports and diversions of labour to deal with it and it also set up the standing Battle of the Atlantic Committee with orders to meet daily and report to Churchill in person once a week to deal with shipping delays. The maintenance of imports in spite of the German onslaught by submarine, aircraft, surface-ship and mine was now at the very centre of the British Government's thinking. But Churchill's bullish prediction of victory in this most vital struggle in four months was over-optimistic in the extreme, perhaps reflecting wishful thinking on the part of a war-leader whose greatest fear, as he later admitted, was the submarine campaign against Britain's lifeline. An Emergency Port Clearance Committee was already at work under Ernest Bevin, one of the Labour Party's members of the War Cabinet, a former general secretary of the Transport and General Workers' Union, the largest in Britain, and now Minister of Labour. Bevin dragooned the British workforce into clearing the ports, running the coal-mines and generally mobilising the war-economy with hardheaded disregard of hard-won union rights, though only for the duration of the war. As such he made one of the greatest individual contributions to the war-effort, which would otherwise have been more severely hampered than it was by the long-standing bitterness of labour-relations in many industries like the docks and shipbuilding. In spring 1941, 40,000 troops were taken out of uniform and put into the ports, so serious had the congestion become, and later men were conscripted as "Bevin Boys" to work in the coal-mines. Bevin was responsible for the most sweeping mobilisation of labour in the history of democracy, made necessary by the German blockade of Britain.

In the course of the second nine-month period of the war, the stock of shipping available to Britain fell by a net total of about four million tons, to around 35 million. Roughly 5.2 million tons were lost, compared with new building of just over the million. Submarines accounted for fifty-five percent of tonnage lost and surface raiders for twenty-two. Air-attacks took fifteen percent and mines seven. The overall loss was sixty percent higher than in the first nine months. The average operational life of a German submarine had risen from three to four months, during which it sank an average of 88,000 tons. Thirteen boats were lost, but forty-five new ones were delivered, leaving Dönitz with fifty-four ocean-going boats, twice as many as he had in 1939. In all he now had 113 boats, of which eighty-one were in training and thirty-two operational. Growing British air-cover and the fact that the Royal Navy could not provide escorts beyond 20° west had made Dönitz shift the main thrust of his patrols from north-south to the west of Britain to east-west, out into the broad Atlantic. He had lost some of his finest crews with their ace commanders, and his boats had to leave and return to their bases submerged to evade detection from the air. The British were developing the art of diverting convoys away from danger, and the escorts had improved sufficiently to persuade many submarine captains to operate west of 20° west.

As in the First World War, the convoy system had mastered the threat from the individual submarine; the wolf-pack had inflicted terrible slaughter on convoys, but there were already one or two signs that an integrated escort-group of adequate strength could give the packs pause. Sinkings of ships in convoy were still heavily outweighed by the losses of vessels sailing alone (some sixty percent higher). It was therefore expedient for the attackers to move further and further west and south of Britain into the gap left by surface and air-escort – and for the defenders to look for ways of closing it. For this task they now had 375 ocean escorts, including 240 destroyers – 140 more escorts of all types than nine months before. The foregoing figures show the huge disparity between the size of the attacking force on the one hand and both the damage it could cause and the scale of the defensive effort needed to deal with it on the other. Seen purely as a means of diverting the enemy's war-effort, the submarine was far and away Germany's most cost-effective weapon.

Elsewhere, Italy, Germany's new ally which had declared war on Britain and France on 10 June 1940, soon proved more of a liability than an asset. Mussolini launched offensives on British Somaliland from Ethiopia in the Horn of Africa in June and on British-controlled Egypt from Libya in September. The United States Army started conscripting on September 16. The Italians and the British landed troops in Crete at the end of October. On November 11 the British Navy destroyed or crippled major units of the Italian Fleet in port at Taranto by air-attack from carriers, a most effective surprise-attack which inspired Japanese planning for Pearl Harbor. The Army won Britain's first victories on land against the Italians in North and East Africa in the first two months of 1941, forcing the German Afrika Korps under General Erwin Rommel to intervene to shore up their ally; yet Mussolini attacked Greece from Albania early in March, without consulting Hitler. Rommel began to drive the British back towards Egypt later in the month; but on the 28th Admiral Cunningham, RN, scored another devastating victory over the Italian Fleet in the Battle of Cape Matapan at the southern extremity of Greece. Only a massive German intervention on both sides of the eastern Mediterranean seemed likely to save the Italians from early defeat. It was not long in coming.

6

APRIL TO DECEMBER 1941

Germans move west – Greenland – USN opens fire – constant shifts in attack – British ransack U110 – Canada and end-to-end convoy – Hood and Bismarck sunk – Rodger Winn – Turing rebels – supply-ships sunk – Hitler invades USSR – Roosevelt and Churchill meet – Russian convoys – Liberator bomber – American losses – Canadian problems – German tactics – air-cover – "Johnnie" Walker – Atlantis – British home front – Japan strikes – US at war – B-dienst – losses at sea

THE Germans' move towards mid-Atlantic and away from the British air and surface-escorts at the beginning of April 1941 soon yielded a significant result. On the first day of the month, *Kapitänleutnant* Friedrich von Hippel in the *U76* sighted the slow, eastbound convoy SC26 in mid-ocean and sent the news to his headquarters. This was well clear of the Western Approaches bottleneck previously favoured by the Germans, and seven other submarines assembled across the convoy's path in time to attack two days before the escort joined it. The only protection at this stage was the armed merchant cruiser *Worcestershire*, a type which, as we have seen, was virtually impotent against any kind of attacker. The onslaught was launched on the night of April 2 to 3 under the Northern Lights, which lit up the helpless targets. Six ships out of twenty-two went down before dawn; the *Worcestershire* was crippled but stayed afloat. The surviving ships were driven out of formation by the attack and one straggler was added to the German score after daybreak. By evening on the 3rd, what was left of SC26 came together again, only to be attacked a second time during the night with the loss of four more vessels. Hippel, if not his colleagues, stayed in touch with a view to a third assault on the morning of the 5th. As the *U76* closed in on the slow-moving survivors from underwater, a single depth-charge exploded very close to the hull, causing widespread internal damage. Shortly afterwards a full pattern of ten charges crippled the submarine and forced it to the surface. The escort from Western Approaches Command, led by Commander J. M. Rowland in the destroyer *Wolverine*, had arrived. It was her Asdic that detected the *U76* and her single depth-charge, dropped after two hours of stalking, which began the destruction. The sloop *Scarborough* dropped the pattern, and as the surviving Germans scrambled out of their fume-filled boat the corvette *Arbutus* sent a boarding-party. By this time escorts were under orders to make every effort to get aboard submarines caught on the surface, but the British sailors were forced out by chlorine released when the acid of the batteries mixed with seawater, and only just got clear before the boat went down.

It had been a model attack made possible by refined use of Asdic, but the sinking of one submarine was not generous compensation for the loss of half a convoy in the period before proper escort could be provided. Just as Dönitz had changed the focus of his attacks, so the Admiralty responded with a radical change in the escort system. Work was speeded up on the provision of air bases and ship-refuelling facilities in Iceland as a direct consequence of the SC26 disaster. By the middle of the month it became possible to provide cover by one of the four Western Approaches groups as far as 35° west – more than halfway to North America. The escort-groups now sailed from Greenock in south-west Scotland or Londonderry in Northern Ireland to Iceland, which entailed a considerable northward shift of the main convoy route. The escorts would refuel there and take the convoy to 35° west, wait for an eastbound convoy and repeat the process in reverse. In addition, Coastal Command stationed a squadron of Hudson bombers and another of Sunderland flying-boats in Iceland. Both air and sea operations were supervised by a new Area Combined Headquarters in Reykjavik. The northward diversion of the convoy route also brought the advantage of longer daylight at this time of year. Whenever possible a major warship accompanied a convoy from Canada as far as 35° west as protection against surface-raiders. The pre-emptive occupation of Iceland the previous year was now revealed as one of the most important moves in the gigantic war of manoeuvre in the Atlantic.

So, of course, was the growing involvement of the neutral Americans. The creation of the US Atlantic Fleet under Admiral King in February and the enactment of the Lend–Lease Bill on March 11, followed by amendments to the neutrality laws, led to early and most welcome new assistance to the British and Canadians. Ten US Coastguard cutters, which made good ocean escorts, were earmarked for the Royal Navy for delivery by mid-June. President Roosevelt signed the relevant order on April 3, and the next day publicly announced that British warships could be repaired and refitted in American yards. On the 7th the Americans inaugurated their air and naval bases in Bermuda and also established airbases in Greenland, another important "stepping-stone" across the North Atlantic. The semi-autonomous government of Greenland, then a Danish possession, had asked for American protection nearly a year earlier, but in the meantime the Germans had established weather-stations on the long eastern coast of the vast frozen landmass to help with forecasting for naval and Luftwaffe purposes. Early in

1941 agents in Norway told the Americans of a bold German plan to base an air-squadron on the same coast, to be supplied by submarine. This was more than enough reason for another pre-emptive stroke in the far northern Atlantic, and on April 9 the Danish Minister in Washington and the Secretary of State signed an agreement transferring the defence of Greenland to the Americans until Denmark was liberated from German occupation. The construction of radio, radar, weather, air and seaplane stations in southern Greenland soon began to follow.

The Americans had already chosen sites in Scotland and Northern Ireland for air and naval bases. In the Atlantic itself, the creation by Admiral King of the Atlantic Fleet Support Group of three destroyer-flotillas and five squadrons of naval flying-boats under Rear-Admiral Bristol enabled the Americans to extend their Security Zone a long way eastward from March. In effect King redefined the western hemisphere as beginning at 26° west instead of at 60° west, the line chosen for the previous Neutrality Zone. On the day this was done (April 11, although the official announcement came a week later) the US Navy fired its first shot in a war it had not yet formally joined. While rescuing men from a torpedoed merchantman, the destroyer *Niblack* got a sonar contact and dropped a pattern of depth-charges, apparently with no effect – either on the suspected submarine or on Adolf Hitler, who was as anxious as ever not to provoke Washington. The effect of the new Zone was that warships of nations which had no territory west of the line were liable to be fired upon by American ships. Roosevelt was able to get away with this at home by pleading "Hemisphere Defence," a concept the still powerful isolationist lobby found hard to attack. The President was as yet not ready to move beyond "all aid short of war" for Britain; faced with a choice between the constant pressure of his importunate pen-friend and telephone-caller, Churchill, and strong domestic misgivings about growing American involvement, the President knew where his true interest lay. The British Prime Minister had for the time being to console himself with hopes of a major incident that would precipitate the Americans into combat. But the "arsenal of democracy" was already substantially underpinning the British war-effort, which would have collapsed long since without it.

The German move west gave the Admiralty much more searoom to route the convoys evasively, sharply reducing sightings by submarines. The northward shift of the convoys and the westward extension of the escort service after SC26 were not, however, enough to save the fast, eastbound convoy HX121, once it was spotted by *U123* on April 28. Five other boats went into the attack, despite the presence of the escort, near 23° west. For the first time since early December 1940 the submarines struck in daylight and submerged, having assembled an ambush ahead of the convoy. Three ships were sunk, including two large, fully laden tankers. As the submarines fled on the surface, the corvette *Gladiolus* sighted the *U65*, which crash-dived but blew up spectacularly when depth-charged. The four remaining boats were denied a second attack by a diversion of the convoy, but a fourth ship was caught alone and sunk.

Dönitz's spur-of-the-moment decision to revert to submerged attack by daylight had not been an unqualified success, and was therefore abandoned. During April only ten ships out of the forty-three sunk by submarines were from convoys with proper escort. The Germans' move west and the subsequent shift to the north in pursuit of the re-routed convoys had not proved fruitful, despite their new-found ability, because of the greater numbers of operational boats available, to assemble packs rapidly. The main convoy route was now much better protected by air-cover, thanks not only to Iceland but also to the long hours of daylight during which Coastal Command could usefully patrol. But there was still a large "airgap" of some 300 miles in the North Atlantic which could not be covered by shore-based aircraft. Dönitz filed this fact away for future reference.

It did not take him long to find a new opening. In May losses of ships to submarines rose by over a third to fifty-eight. More than half of these were sent to the bottom by a force of six long-range type IX boats which Dönitz detached to operate off West Africa against the largely unescorted shipping to be found there. The type IX, of which 194 were built in seven variations, began with an optimum cruising range of 10,500 miles and ended with three times this capability. Displacement varied between 1,032 and 1,616 tons on the surface. The type was second only to the VII in importance for the submarine campaign and the most comfortable ocean-going boat. It carried twenty-two torpedoes and a crew of between forty-eight and fifty-seven officers and men. Its delivery of a fresh success to the submarine arm at this stage in the war is a good illustration of the nature of the campaign against shipping and the problems of the defenders.

The central strategic consideration of the war against Germany was the supply-route from North America to Britain, the main artery of the war-effort. At this stage of the war the protection provided for it was still far from complete, though growing stronger. But the Germans retained the initiative and could direct their deadly thrusts at lesser arteries whenever they chose, thereby ensuring that the loss of lifeblood never let up. From the very beginning any vessel sunk anywhere in the world had an adverse effect on the main transatlantic lifeline because it reduced the stock of shipping available and diverted overstretched defensive resources away from it. A man with a good helmet and a stout breastplate can still bleed to death from a severed finger, to say nothing of a stab in the back. The months immediately preceding the entry of Japan and the United States into a truly global war were especially marked by changes in the focus of German submarine deployment. The Admiralty's response to the German assault on the equatorial region of the Atlantic was to reduce shipping in the area as much as possible while strengthening the Freetown, Sierra Leone, command as best it could with extra escorts and aircraft. But the submarines found rich pickings among the independently routed ships in this and other areas: four were sunk in May for every one lost by the convoys (in which the vast majority of ships were sailing for most of their passage).

The North Atlantic was not altogether quiet, as the westbound convoy OB318 was to discover soon after leaving Liverpool on May 2. By the time other ships had joined it in the North-Western Approaches, there were thirty-eight vessels and a remarkably strong escort of ten, consisting of the 7th Escort Group with extra warships. *U95* sighted it on May 7. His radio report was not penetrated by Bletchley Park but was identifiable as a sighting report from its characteristics. The Admiralty therefore diverted the convoy to the north – which put it on a collision-course with *U94* (*Kapitänleutnant* Herbert Kuppisch), who sighted it that evening. It was then that the 3rd Escort Group (Commander A. J. Baker-Cresswell in the destroyer *Bulldog*) joined the convoy to relieve the 7th, whose three destroyers were running short of fuel. They left, but the 7th's sloop and five corvettes stayed on for the time being, in addition to Baker-Cresswell's three destroyers, three corvettes, an armed merchant cruiser and an armed trawler – in all, an embarrassment of escorting riches. Undeterred, Kuppisch attacked from astern and sank two ships with two torpedoes. The sloop and two destroyers located him by Asdic and hunted him all night, damaging but not destroying *U94*. The next day the rest of the 7th was released to strengthen the escort of the eastbound convoy HX123.

Around noon on May 9, Fritz-Julius Lemp, the man who had sunk the *Athenia*, now commanding *U110*, launched a second attack from the north, hitting two ships at the front and on the starboard side of OB318. The corvette *Aubretia* got a brief contact and dropped depth-charges. The destroyers *Bulldog* and *Broadway* were about to renew the attack when the *U110* burst to the surface, its controls damaged by *Aubretia*. The *Bulldog* altered course as if to ram, but when men began to pour out of the conning-tower, she sheered off at the last moment. Then Baker-Cresswell thought the Germans were about to open fire with their single gun and machine-guns, which prompted the two destroyers to open fire with everything that could be brought to bear, including rifles. In attempting to close the submarine to prevent it diving again by dropping a warning depth-charge, the *Broadway* sideswiped *U110* and was damaged below the waterline by a slice from its hydroplane. Baker-Cresswell ordered the *Aubretia* to pick up the Germans, who were immediately taken below to an area from which they could not see out. Meanwhile the *Bulldog* had launched its whaler with a boarding-party of eight ratings under Sub-Lieutenant David Balme, RN, who had just turned twenty years old. The rescuers from the *Aubretia* were told to make sure that the Germans still in the water were all dead. Accounts of what happened next vary, but witnesses said later that Lemp had escaped from his boat and while in the water had asked some members of his crew whether the others had got out. The captain however was not among those taken aboard the corvette and was never found. According to some, he realised that his boat, though dead in the water, was not sinking but was about to be boarded. He is said to have swum back to the *U110*, whereupon he was shot dead by the boarding-party.

Be that as it may, Balme and his men found the stricken submarine completely deserted, with all its main controls out of action. The party, instructed in advance on what to look for should such an opportunity arise, began systematically to strip the submarine of anything portable and of potential interest. A telegraphist made a careful note of all the radio settings and collected the papers relating to the operation of the Germans' wireless equipment. Sailors collected documents by the armful and the whaler began to shuttle to and fro between the *U110* and the *Bulldog* with the loot. Among the material were not only the papers relating to the setting of the naval Enigma coding machine for several weeks, but, in its long, slim, hardwood box with a varnished surface, the machine itself, its wheels and plugboard in the current settings.

In volume I of his official history, *The War at Sea*, published in 1954, Captain Stephen Roskill gives the OB318 clash two lines: "In the North Atlantic convoy OB318 was intercepted early in May and lost five ships, but its escort retaliated by sinking *U110*." Between the publication of volumes II and III of his account in 1956 and 1961 respectively, Roskill found out more and decided to write a separate book on the plundering of *U110*, entitled *The Secret Capture*, to fill out the record. Describing the scene when the *Bulldog* reached Scapa Flow and handed over two packing-cases containing the material from *U110* to Naval Intelligence officers who had come from London to collect it, Roskill quotes one of them as saying: "What! This . . .? And this . . .? We've waited a long time for one of these!" That is as close as he came to revealing that "one of these" was a naval Enigma machine. That evening the First Sea Lord, Admiral Sir Dudley Pound, signalled Baker-Cresswell: "Hearty congratulations. The petals of your flower are of rare beauty." And when one of the officers of the 3rd Escort Group went to Buckingham Palace to receive the Distinguished Service Cross he had earned in the action from the King, George VI remarked, according to Roskill, that "the operation in which he had gained it was the most important single event in the whole war at sea." The consequences will be examined later, but we ought to return to OB318, whose adventures were not yet over.

After two emergency evasive turns to port, the convoy was for the moment heading south-east when it was attacked for the third time, from astern, by *Kapitänleutnant* Adalbert Schnee in *U201*. He had independently sighted and reported the ships that morning and was ordered to consult with Lemp to plan tactics. They surfaced their boats alongside each other out of sight of the convoy for a rare, face-to-face discussion in mid-ocean, leaning over the sides of their conning-towers, and agreed that Schnee would attack half an hour after Lemp. Despite being sighted by one of the escort on his approach, Schnee torpedoed two ships. He was subjected to five hours of hunting and depth-charging by three escorts; *Bulldog* and *Broadway* at one stage got a fix on *U201* with their Asdics and for a while abandoned *U110* to join in. Schnee got away despite considerable damage to his boat, a type IXb, and felt able to continue his patrol despite having left a large oil-slick at the scene.

On the next morning, May 10, *Kapitänleutnant* Herbert Wohlfarth in *U556* (the high number was disinformation) found the convoy from the sighting reports of his comrades as relayed to him from France. In what had become a pack-attack by instalments, he damaged one ship but did not sink her; but he was able to stay with the convoy and later in the day sank two merchantmen. By this time OB318 had divided into sections headed for various North American ports; since one of Schnee's victims did not sink, the convoy's formal losses are recorded as five ships sunk and one damaged. To these must be added not only Wohlfarth's two sunk and one damaged but also, later in the month, one sunk by *U38* and another by *U107*.

Meanwhile *Bulldog* had broken radio silence to report the capture of *U110* and mounted "Operation Primrose" (hence Pound's flowery message) to tow the boat to Britain. But the weather turned rough during the night of the 9th to 10th, and in mid-morning *U110* began to drag on the towline. Its stern disappeared, and as the destroyer hurriedly slipped the tow, the bow rose almost vertically into the air and sank. *Bulldog* went to Reykjavik to refuel and then sped to Scapa Flow with the booty, arriving on the afternoon of the 12th. The rest is history, although it took more than thirty years for the full story to come out.

U94 managed to complete running repairs to damage received during the successful foray against OB318 and stayed on the prowl. On May 19 Kuppisch sighted the eastbound HX126 and attacked it the next day in the vicinity of longitude 41° west – further to the west than any previous assault. In two passes he sank three ships; Wohlfarth also sank three, and the three other submarines sent to the area to make a pack sank one each, all before the escort joined at 35° west. These severe losses drove the Admiralty to take a most important step which it had been considering for some time: the institution of "end-to-end" escort by warships all the way across the North Atlantic. This seemingly obvious move had been delayed for lack of sufficient ships. The choice lay between escort groups of adequate strength, the key component being, as ever, destroyers, for part of the way or weaker escort all the way. The increase in numbers of escorts and the use of Iceland for refuelling had made it possible to cover two-thirds of the passage; the decision was now taken to provide surface-escort for the remaining third. The first move was to transfer to the Royal Canadian Air Force nine American long-range Catalina flying-boats just supplied to Britain under Lend–Lease. These could cover 600 miles of ocean from the west, while the RAF could cover 400 miles from Iceland in the north and 750 from the United Kingdom – leaving a gap of 300 miles which for the time being could not be reached by shore-based aircraft.

The surface-gap was closed by the Royal Canadian Navy. At the end of May 1941 Commodore L. W. Murray, RCN, went to St John's, Newfoundland, to fill the new post of Commodore Commanding Newfoundland Force (CCNF) under the authority of the British C-in-C, Western Approaches. The Newfoundland Escort Force started with five Canadian corvettes and two British destroyers, to which the Canadian destroyers which had been serving in British home waters since Dunkirk were soon added, followed by other Canadian and British escorts when they became available. From June, therefore, convoys bound for Britain (more important because fully laden) came under the protection of four escort-forces in succession. From Halifax (fast) or Sydney, Cape Breton (slow), the convoy was taken by a Canadian local escort to what later became known as the Western Ocean Meeting Point (WESTOMP). From there it was led by the Newfoundland Escort Force to the Mid-Ocean Meeting Point (MOMP) where (35° west) a British escort from Iceland took over as far as about 18° west. This was the eastern rendezvous (EOMP) at which an escort-group from Western Approaches took over for the final stage. As if this were not complicated enough, the incoming ships would transfer from the transatlantic to the coastal convoy network, and yet another escort, in offshore waters.

Into this intricate system, open at all times to disruption by the enemy, weather, congestion at either end (or both) and other incalculables, British and allied shipping movements round the globe had to be integrated – without the aid of computers. That this co-ordination was achieved at all despite endless hitches and complications seems miraculous even now. At the Admiralty alone it involved the Naval Control Service, the Trade Division and the Operational Intelligence Centre, the Home Fleet and Western Approaches commands and several other sections, plus Coastal Command. The Canadian and soon the American navies became increasingly involved, and in all three countries the shipyards, docks, railways, road-transport and air forces were all occupied with keeping the convoys moving on time. The movement of troops and their supplies in various theatres also had to be taken into account. Such was the uniquely complex logistical system which strove to contain the Axis powers until their enemies found the strength to attack them on land; and it was mainly the German submarine service which made this unparalleled effort necessary.

The first convoy to be escorted end to end was HX129, which left Halifax on 27 May 1941 and completed the crossing without loss or damage. The British 3rd Battle Squadron was soon withdrawn homeward from Halifax, where it had been based since the beginning of the war. With the US Atlantic Fleet now on patrol halfway across the Atlantic and the German surface threat apparently contained, the much reduced and often diverted British squadron could be brought back. But, as we have seen, even as these new arrangements for the North Atlantic were being made the German submarines shifted the focus of their attack to the area between the Azores and West Africa, where the waters were warmer and the pickings much easier.

It was in this region that Commander Günter Hessler in *U107* achieved the Second World War record for a single patrol by sinking fourteen ships totalling 86,700 tons over the end of May and the beginning of June. Dönitz could hardly have wished for a more suitable son-in-law – or staff officer (operations) to the Submarine C-in-C, as he was soon to become. End-to-end escort was introduced on the Sierra Leone route on July 14 (four days after it had begun on the Gibraltar run), and at the same time the Admiralty began to withdraw the armed merchant cruisers which had tried so valiantly, but essentially failed, to play the part of warships. Fourteen had been lost to enemy action.

The increased pressure on real escorts caused by the spread of end-to-end cover had the beneficial effect of ending by *force majeure* the old argument among the admirals, as fomented by Churchill, about hunting groups. It was now all but universally recognised on the British side that they were an unaffordable and inefficient luxury; when extra ships did become available, they were formed into support-groups – fire-brigades which could be rushed to reinforce a convoy in trouble, a concept of much greater value. Westbound convoys from Britain to Canada were also given end-to-end escort in July 1941, when each of the four components of the transatlantic relay was able to pick up a westbound convoy on handing over an eastbound one. Another important adjustment to the system was made in June, when the upper speed-limit for ships in convoy, reduced from fifteen to thirteen knots in November 1940, was raised again to fifteen. This was done after some intense lobbying by Sir Percy Noble, C-in-C Western Approaches, who was constantly concerned about the continuing high rate of losses among independently routed ships.

The German Navy did not abandon its idea of using large surface units to disrupt convoy traffic after the sorties earlier in the year. The *Scharnhorst* and *Gneisenau* (known throughout the British fleet as "Salmon and Gluckstein") were bottled up in Brest under repair, and on April 6 the *Gneisenau* was damaged again in an RAF raid. But the heavy cruiser *Prinz Eugen*, though bombed during construction in Kiel, was commissioned at about this time – only to be damaged by an RAF mine on her shakedown cruise in the Baltic on April 23. She put in to Gotenhafen in East Prussia, alongside the most formidable warship to join the worldwide hostilities so far – the freshly commissioned battleship *Bismarck*. The German fleet commander, Admiral Günther Lütjens, had transferred his flag to her and was working out the details of "Operation *Rheinübung*," imposed on him by Raeder against his advice and contrary to the misgivings of Hitler himself. Originally conceived as the hardest blow yet struck by the capital ships against the convoys and their escorting battleships, it had to be repeatedly modified and postponed thanks to the continued immobility of the battle-cruisers, the damage to *Prinz Eugen* and other difficulties. In the end the attacking force was reduced to the two new ships, which sailed in company from Gotenhafen (now Polish Gdynia) on May 18. The British naval attaché in Stockholm was able to report their passage through the Kattegat, the channel north of Denmark between the Baltic and the North Sea, on May 20. Starting with this excellent piece of intelligence, the British mounted a determined effort to locate and keep in touch with the powerful new enemy by air and by sea.

Coastal Command found the two ships in a fjord just south of Bergen on the south-west Norwegian coast. The Luftwaffe was also reconnoitring northern waters with unusual intensity. In fact it had been doing so for the past ten days, which had already prompted Admiral Tovey of the Home Fleet to prepare for a breakout by major German units. German pilots had been flying high over Scapa Flow with unusual frequency, as well as over the waters between northern Norway and Greenland, trying to locate the principal elements of the British fleet. The cruiser HMS *Suffolk* was sent to watch the Denmark Strait between Iceland and Greenland on May 18, augmented by her sister-ship, the *Norfolk*, the next day. Following the positive identification of the two German vessels near Bergen on the 21st, Tovey sent Vice-Admiral L. E. Holland from Scapa to the Icelandic naval base of Hvalfjord with the battlecruiser *Hood*, the fast modern battleship *Prince of Wales* and six destroyers. The cruisers *Birmingham* and *Manchester* were despatched to cover the gap between Iceland and the Faroe Islands, while Tovey himself remained on alert at Scapa aboard his flagship, *King George V*, with five cruisers and five destroyers, ready to sail on minimum notice. The Admiralty divested a "WS" (Winston Special) military convoy destined for the Middle East of the battlecruiser *Repulse* and the new aircraft-carrier *Victorious* and put them under Tovey's command. There was no ship in the British navy that could be safely permitted to encounter the *Bismarck* alone, which meant that Tovey had to deploy his capital ships in pairs at least.

The *Bismarck* displaced 41,700 tons (50,900 fully loaded) and had, despite her vast bulk. all the gracefulness of design which was a common feature of the German major warships of the time. Particularly noticeable was the elegant and lengthy bow section, dashingly raked back from the stem and curving smoothly inward from the upper deck to the waterline, along which she measured 242 metres (800 feet). By British standards, though not by German, she was unusually broad in the beam at thirty-six metres (118 feet). This gave her exceptional stability when firing a broadside from her eight 380mm (15-inch) guns in four turrets, two placed forward, one above and behind the other, and two similarly arranged aft. Her chief secondary armament consisted of sixteen 105mm (4.1-inch) guns. The *Bismarck* had a maximum speed of thirty-one knots, a range of 8,100 miles, the world's most effective armour of up to 12½ inches along her sides and up to 4.7 inches on her deck. Her draught was thirty-five feet and she carried six seaplanes and a crew of 2,090 officers and men, under the command of Captain Ernst Lindemann.

Her companion, the *Prinz Eugen*, was one of only three German heavy cruisers built in the Nazi era, all of the same design and in general the least successful type in Hitler's short list of major warships. She displaced 14,050 tons, carried eight 205mm (8.1-inch) guns, had a maximum speed of thirty-two knots and a range of 6,800 miles, with a crew of 1,600 men under Captain Hellmuth Brinkmann. The essence of Operation *Rheinübung* was for the *Bismarck* to distract the attention of the British capital ships while the *Prinz Eugen* attacked merchant-shipping. The other contingency Tovey had to cater for was a stroke against the increasingly important convoy-support bases in Iceland.

Bad flying weather on May 22 grounded the Luftwaffe but did not prevent Commander G. A. Rotherham of the Fleet Air Arm carrying out a perilous, low-level reconnaissance from Orkney over the Bergen coastal area and establishing beyond doubt that the Germans had sailed. Tovey therefore kept his cruisers as forward sentinels covering the Faroe–Iceland and Iceland–Greenland passages, one of which the Germans would have to use to get out into the broad Atlantic, and positioned the bulk of his force between Scapa and Iceland, whence it could move to either passage. The big ships set sail in the late evening of the 22nd, unobserved by the Germans (who knew, however, from the *B-dienst* that the British were looking for "two German battleships"). On the 23rd the weather precluded air reconnaissance, but at 7.22 p.m. the *Suffolk*, which had been searching the edge of the Greenland ice-shelf, spotted through a gap in the mist, at a distance of seven miles, the *Bismarck* and *Prinz Eugen* heading south-west off the west coast of Iceland. The British cruiser was able to exploit this remarkable piece of luck with her radar, which was of the latest type, while using the same mist as cover. Soon afterwards the *Norfolk* got a similar sighting at six miles. This time the German lookouts saw the shadower and the *Bismarck* fired her first shots in anger. The *Norfolk* managed to escape without damage behind her smokescreen and gave the first news of the Germans' whereabouts to Tovey's fleet, some 600 miles to the south-east (the *Suffolk*'s signals had not got through). Aboard *Norfolk*, Rear-Admiral W. R. Wake-Walker, Flag-Officer of the 1st Cruiser Squadron, began the dangerous game of keeping in touch, the *Suffolk* to the west of the Germans and the *Norfolk* to the east as they all headed south, while Admiral Holland came out from Iceland at high speed on a converging course. In company were the *Hood*, the *Prince of Wales* and four destroyers, and Holland expected to be in action by 2 a.m. on May 24.

Shortly after midnight, however, the Germans got away from the pair of shadowing cruisers. Holland deduced an evasive change of course by the enemy and himself altered course from westward to northerly, simultaneously reducing his speed. His strict observation of radio silence precluded his co-ordinating an attack with Wake-Walker. Having obtained no sighting by 2 a.m., Holland detached his destroyers to continue searching to the north while he turned south, which put him more or less in the wake of the Germans but well behind them. This became clear at 2.47, when the *Suffolk* regained contact with Admiral Lütjen's ships, still steaming south-west. On the basis of the cruisers' wireless reports, backed up by his own direction-finding, Admiral Holland went flat-out to catch up. He sighted the Germans to starboard (west) at 5.35 a.m.

His flagship was known to the Royal Navy's lower decks as "the mighty *Hood*," the pride of the British fleet for more than twenty years and the world's largest warship, with an unladen displacement of 48,000 tons. She had eight 15-inch guns in four double turrets, two forward and two aft, and sixteen 6-inch. Her armour did not bear comparison with that of the *Bismarck*; as with all British battlecruisers, it was totally inadequate for a capital ship with heavy guns as her main armament. The *Hood's* main weaknesses were two: her age and her design. She was in fact an almost perfect microcosm of the British Empire – ancient, glorious, biggest in the world, shrouded in ceremony and veneration – but out of date and full of defects.

This gleaming, grey symbol missed much modernisation between the wars because she was in constant use to fly the flag in distant places, maintaining the gigantic bluff which was the latter-day Empire – and the myth of her own invincibility. She had been overstretched during the war, too, by constant deployment and at this time was in much need of an overhaul. Conceived in 1914, her design radically altered after the heavy British battlecruiser losses at Jutland in 1916, the *Hood* was launched in August 1918, yet was as untried in battle as her approaching adversary. But on a good day she had a knot or two in hand over the *Bismarck*, and was just as handsome to look at. Her companion, the *Prince of Wales*, was one of the latest additions to the fleet, a 29-knot battleship of 35,000 tons with ten 14-inch guns in two quadruple turrets and one double. She carried six guns forward and four aft.

Admiral Holland had succeeded in catching up with the Germans, but on a somewhat divergent course, so that when he sighted them, still heading south-west with the *Prinz Eugen* in the lead, they were about twenty-three miles to starboard. This meant that in order to get within effective firing range he had to run at them at an angle not very far short of 90° – which in turn meant that only ten of his heavy guns (those capable of firing over the

bows) could be brought to bear in the crucial opening stage of the engagement, whereas both German ships were broadside-on.

Holland's first mistake was thus to throw away his superiority in fire-
power by opening fire too soon, eighteen minutes after sighting the enemy.
His second was to advance in close order, with only a few hundred yards
between his two ships. His third was to identify the leading enemy wrongly
as the *Bismarck* and to order both ships to concentrate their fire on the *Prinz
Eugen* (though Captain J. C. Leach on the *Prince of Wales* identified the
Germans correctly and fired at the *Bismarck* regardless). The mighty *Hood*
(Captain Ralph Kerr) and her partner, their movements personally dictated in
detail by the admiral, therefore divided their gratuitously reduced firepower.
After her first salvo the *Prince of Wales*, brought into service before being
given a proper chance to shake down, lost one of her six forward guns to a
breakdown. And by opening fire at a range of over thirteen miles, Holland
exposed the *Hood* with her old and inadequate deck-armour to plunging
shot, always a particular danger to a British battlecruiser.

The Germans concentrated both their broadsides on the *Hood* and
within minutes, with their customary and unique rangefinding skill, scored
a hit which started a fire amidships. It is not known which German ship did
the damage, but Holland was still able to order both his to turn broadside-on
to the enemy so as to be able to use all his seventeen operable main guns.
During the manoeuvre another German broadside, almost certainly from the
Bismarck, straddled the *Hood*. At 6 a.m. the pride of the Royal Navy
succumbed to a gigantic explosion in her main magazines and sank in less
than four minutes. One midshipman and two ratings survived from her crew
of 1,419 officers and men. After two inquiries the Admiralty concluded
that the superbly engineered guns of the *Bismarck*, with their excellent
high-velocity, armour-piercing shells, had sent plunging shot straight through
the deck into the *Hood's* stores of 15-inch ammunition. One week before the
twenty-fifth anniversary of the Battle of Jutland, the *Hood* blew up just as
three battlecruisers had done in rapid succession in the earlier action.

The *Prince of Wales* now came under the concentrated fire of the main
and secondary armament of both German ships, and at 6.02 took a direct hit
on the bridge. After four 15-inch hits from the *Bismarck* and three 8-inch
from the *Prinz Eugen*, and with an entire quadruple turret paralysed by
another mechanical failure, she put up a smokescreen and turned away at a
point some seven and a half miles from the Germans. But the real British
battleship's hull stood up well to the pounding, and Captain Leach scored
two hits on the *Bismarck* with his few usable 14-inch guns. One of them
damaged the German flagship's fuel-tanks, causing contamination of the
contents by seawater.

This was enough to persuade the victorious Admiral Lütjens to signal
his intention to make for France, two hours after destroying the *Hood*. As
Admiral Holland had gone down with her, Admiral Wake-Walker, whose

pair of cruisers had been too far away to join the action, thanks largely to Holland's wireless silence, took over command and with the *Prince of Wales* in company set about shadowing the Germans. Devastated by the fate of the *Hood*, which was to shock the British public as the loss of no other warship, Admiral Tovey was determined to seek immediate revenge and sailed north-west at high speed to link up with Wake-Walker, now some 300 miles away. The Admiralty scoured the Atlantic for reinforcements, ordering Admiral Somerville's Force H to sea from as far away as Gibraltar to cover a German approach to France, the battleships *Ramillies* and *Revenge* from Halifax and another, the *Rodney*, from mid-ocean. In all, nineteen major ships from cruisers upwards, together with more than a dozen destroyers, were looking for Lütjens.

On the afternoon of the 24th Tovey sent the carrier *Victorious*, escorted by the 2nd Cruiser Squadron of four ships under Rear-Admiral A. T. B. Curteis, to launch an air-attack from about 100 miles away from the Germans. The carrier, having been diverted from a run to Gibraltar with conventional fighters destined for Malta, had her hangars full of aircraft but only nine torpedo-bombers and six maritime fighters able to operate. Lieutenant-Commander Eugene Esmonde, RN, led them on a midnight attack in poor weather through a hail of anti-aircraft fire. One Swordfish hit the *Bismarck* amidships with a torpedo which bounced off the ship's massive side and caused little damage, and the British lost two Fulmar fighters.

By this time the *Bismarck* was sailing alone. Lütjens, worried about his fuel, slowed down in the early evening of May 24 for an exchange of gunfire with the shadowing British force. This was to cover the detachment of the *Prinz Eugen* to operate independently in mid-Atlantic to the south. Shortly after the British air-attack, in the very early hours of the 25th, the *Bismarck* engaged in another brief and ineffectual exchange with the contact-keepers, after which Lütjens put on a burst of speed and shook them off. At 4 a.m. the *Suffolk* reported that her radar was no longer in touch, just as Tovey was 100 miles, or less than four hours, away from his objective.

It was not until 10.30 a.m. on May 26, after more than thirty-one hours of desperate and sometimes irrational searching by British ships and aircraft, that the *Bismarck*, still pounding rapidly south-eastwards towards France, was sighted by a Coastal Command Catalina flying-boat, 700 miles west of Brest. At this moment Force H – including the battlecruiser *Renown*, the carrier *Ark Royal* and the 6-inch cruiser *Sheffield* – was, more by luck than judgement, sailing across her path about seventy miles to *Bismarck's* east. Admiral Somerville kept his distance, and at 2.50 p.m. the *Ark Royal* sent up, in atrocious weather, fourteen Swordfish, which one hour later launched an all-out torpedo attack – on His Majesty's Ship *Sheffield*. Thanks to some extremely sharp manoeuvring and faulty torpedoes, disaster was avoided by an uncomfortably small margin. The second wave of Swordfish found the *Bismarck* in just under 100 minutes shortly before 9 p.m. and launched a series of uncoordinated individual attacks. Lieutenant-Commander T. P. Coode's pilots scored two hits, one amidships which did no real damage and the other immediately under her stern. The battleship's Achilles' heel had been struck fair and square: her steering-gear was put out of action, her rudders immobilised and her propellers damaged. The *Bismarck*, fearing her doom, sent for a submarine to collect her log-books.

Next on the scene was the dashing Captain Philip Vian of *Altmark* fame, with five destroyers of the 4th Flotilla. He had blithely disregarded an Admiralty order to join Tovey as escort for his heavy ships, preferring to head straight for the enemy. In the first seven hours of May 27 the five little ships launched a series of torpedo attacks during which the Polish destroyer *Piorun* particularly distinguished herself by drawing the unimpaired fire-power of the stricken but still slowly moving giant. Two ineffectual hits were obtained and somehow the destroyers escaped unscathed, to stay in touch at a safe distance.

Now it was Admiral Tovey's turn. Approaching the meticulously plotted position of the *Bismarck* at high speed from due west, the *King George V* and the *Rodney* sighted her at 8.45 a.m. The *Rodney* opened fire with her nine 16-inch guns at 8.47, the *King George V* with her ten 14-inchers one minute later and the *Bismarck* replied at 8.49. Soon the cruisers *Norfolk* and *Dorsetshire* (from Force H) joined in from the south. The most powerful ship in German service was systematically battered to death in 109 minutes of shelling at ever-decreasing ranges. From 10.15 the Germans, having done their utmost to live up to Admiral Lütjens's farewell promise to fight to the last shell, were unable to fire back. At 2 a.m. a signal from Hitler himself had arrived, telling the crew that "the whole of Germany is with you." But the Luftwaffe had been unable to reach the *Bismarck*, and Dönitz's submarines could not impede or damage the avengers of the *Hood* (*U556* sighted *Rodney* but was out of torpedoes at the time). The *coup de grâce* was delivered by the *Dorsetshire* as Tovey turned for home on his last reserves of oil: the cruiser swept up to the flaming wreck, injected two torpedoes into the starboard and a third into the port side. The maiden voyage of the *Bismarck* ended at 10.36 a.m. on 27 May 1941 in 48° north and 16° west, when she sank with colours flying – and with the loss of all but 110 of her crew. Günther Lütjens died on the admiral's bridge. It was his fifty-second birthday. When Wohlfarth arrived in *U556* to collect the log-books, all he could do was rescue three survivors before stealing away from the scene of desolation.

The biggest naval action since Jutland pitted the bulk of the British Home Fleet, plus sizeable reinforcements, against just two German ships. Each side lost the pride of its navy and a fighting admiral, as well as the crew of a capital ship. The loss of the *Hood* and the inadequate working-up of the *Prince of Wales* thrust the problems of age and/or over-extension of British capital ships into full view at the Admiralty. The effect was redoubled by the time and effort it took to sink the *Bismarck*, a testament to the unmatched quality of German warship construction and design. The division of her hull into a honeycomb of small, watertight compartments helps to explain why she took such a long time to die. There was every reason to believe that her sister-ship, the *Tirpitz*, now approaching completion, would be even more formidable. The same cannot be said of the *Prinz Eugen*, which sailed to mid-Atlantic after parting from the *Bismarck* to refuel from one of several supply-vessels deployed in support of operation *Rheinübung*. Two days later she developed the same kind of engine problems plaguing the *Hipper*, her sister-ship, and Captain Brinkmann decided to abandon his strike at the convoys and make for Brest. The British divined his purpose from radio-traffic analysis on May 27 and tried to set a trap with submarines, but the heavy cruiser reached Brest undetected, and without anything more to show for her trouble, on June 1. Air reconnaissance found her there on the 4th.

But the war was one of brains as well as bombardments, and it is time to return to the British intelligence community, still rubbing its hands over the capture of "one of these" naval Enigma machines and its current software. Two days before the seizure of Lemp's unintended legacy from the *U110* on May 9, the British destroyer *Somali* stole up on the German weather-ship *München* in Greenland waters, forced its surrender and put a carefully briefed boarding-party on her. No Enigma machine was found (the crew had time to throw it overboard), but a large quantity of code and cipher material was taken. This was of a low order of security-grade but still valuable grist to Bletchley Park's mill in the effort to build up a broad and detailed picture of German wireless communications. Routine messages like weather-reports contained clues to the content of more important operational traffic. On June 28 a similar operation against the weather-ship *Lauenberg* provided more valuable material, such as the following month's Enigma settings, for the Bletchley Park analysts, who were now exploiting their greatest breakthrough of the war round the clock.

The great intelligence windfall came just too late for it to play more than a marginal role in the hunt for the *Bismarck*, although a brief intuitional break into the Enigma traffic from April confirmed just before the German ships were sighted at sea that a major raid on the trade route was imminent. During the week of the actions and chase it was still taking anything from three to seven days to unravel naval Enigma messages, so Bletchley Park was unable to provide information of operational value. None of the *Bismarck's* twenty-two signals home during the week was penetrated until the day after she was sunk. But Bletchley Park did discover by traffic analysis that Lütjens had been switched from Wilhelmshaven to Brest wireless transmitter for exchanges of messages with the High Command, which showed he was heading for France. The final clue to his destination, which caused the

Admiralty to support unreservedly Tovey's educated guess about Brest on the evening of the 25th, provides a good illustration of how the indirect approach helped with the penetration of naval Enigma. It will be recalled that Bletchley Park had broken into the less well-defended Luftwaffe and German Army Enigma ciphers in the previous year. It was a Luftwaffe message which finally gave the game away. At this time its chief of staff, General Hans Jeschonnek, was in Athens, directing the air force's part in the highly successful operations against Crete and Greece which were taking place amid many setbacks for the British. He abused the privilege of rank on May 25 to ask about the *Bismarck's* progress and destination – because his son was a junior officer aboard. Luftwaffe headquarters replied that she was bound for Brest and Bletchley Park passed the news to the Operational Intelligence Centre.

From the end of May, armed not only with current Enigma cipher-material but also with the German short-code books used for sending highly condensed but important weather and sighting reports – and a copy of the grid the Germans used to plot and describe positions in the Atlantic (all thanks to *U110*) – BP began to help build up a picture of German submarine operations which was virtually as clear as Dönitz's own. By the end of June 1941 the British were intercepting every message between submarines and their headquarters and deciphering them very quickly. From all this priceless new material, other more traditional intelligence sources and his own rapidly developing instinct, Commander (later Captain) Rodger Winn, RNVR (Volunteer Reserve), tuned in to the minds of Dönitz and Godt, his operational chief, from the Admiralty's Submarine Tracking Room (STR).

Winn, born in 1904, was an accomplished barrister whose boyhood ambition of joining the navy was frustrated by a severe attack of poliomyelitis in his youth, which left him with a twisted back and a limp. Standing for any length of time caused him pain. Patrick Beesly, who became his deputy, leaves no room for doubt in his book, *Very Special Intelligence*, that Winn's contribution to winning the Atlantic campaign, and therefore the war, was one of the greatest made by any individual. He volunteered at the start of hostilities to use his forensic skills in the interrogation of prisoners of war but by a happy accident was sent to OIC, originally as a civilian assistant. He was commissioned at the end of 1940 when the head of the STR, Paymaster-Captain Thring, who had done the same job in the First World War, showed signs of strain. Rear-Admiral John Godfrey, Director of Naval Intelligence and another veteran of the 1914–18 Room 40, indulged a refreshing disregard for protocol by choosing Winn to take over at the turn of the year. Since Godfrey's personal assistant was a certain Lieutenant-Commander Ian Fleming, RNVR, who was to send James Bond on so many fictional adventures as agent 007 after the war, it was clear that the DNI was more interested in talent than the irrelevances of rank and naval background. Godfrey ran Naval Intelligence in the Second World War not from Room 40 but Room 39 (Old Building). OIC, the nerve-centre, was in the underground bunker whose exceedingly ugly and indestructible overground "cap" can still be seen today, close by Admiralty Arch in London and incongruously bedecked with climbing plants.

Winn's personal charm, intelligence and skill as a raconteur belied the physical impression of a bespectacled gnome with immensely strong shoulders and arms, bent over a chart and plotting the downfall of the Third Reich. Although he now had a wealth of fresh information which transformed the struggle to outmanoeuvre the German Navy (at the cost of a staggering workload), the fight for control of the Atlantic trade routes did not suddenly become one-sided. The Germans were not only still ahead but were also constantly concerned about the security of those very communications the British had just penetrated. Separate inquiries in the first half of 1941 by Dönitz's staff and the *B-dienst* into the opportunities afforded to the enemy by unavoidable wireless traffic concluded that the British were able to obtain reasonably accurate "fixes" by direction-finding from submarine transmissions and that every wireless message must help the enemy's overall picture of events.

On June 9, therefore, Standing Order 243 was issued to all submarines, instructing boats in an attack-area to limit the use of radio to tactically important messages, responses to specific requests from the command or to occasions when the enemy already knew submarines were in the vicinity because of their attacks. The same restrictions were applied to boats on passage to and from operations unless they were in manifestly safe areas. New transmission channels were introduced, with frequent changes of wavelength – and new methods of disguising grid-square references were brought in, just as British Intelligence was familiarising itself with *U110's* charts. Instead of referring straightforwardly to the squares, messages now told captains to head for an area so many miles and degrees from one of a series of coded reference points (such as "point Franz") scattered across the chart. This code within a cipher slowed down the cryptanalysts at Bletchley Park just as they were getting into their stride and remained a handicap well into July. No sooner had they overcome this than the Germans, who were developing strong but imprecise suspicions that the British had an unknown source of information, began in September to encipher grid references twice, once before they were inserted into the original, plain-language text and again with the rest of the message when it was enciphered before transmission. The British had barely got to grips with this before another layer of security was introduced. A set of code-tables and an "address-book" were issued to the submarine fleet; which table to use for decoding grid references was given by transmitting an invented name and address in the message. The determined protection of chart-references and the change in August to calling submarines by their commanders' surnames instead of their numbers added to the burdens of Bletchley Park and OIC. They often found they could lay bare everything in a message except the most important fact in it: the submarine's position.

But it was during this period that one foundation of ultimate victory was laid, if sometimes at a rate of two steps forward and at least one back: OIC's skill in using the entire German signals output to divert convoys away from danger. This was always to be far more important than any other benefit from its work, a fact which makes it impossible to quantify the value of the British intelligence effort in the Atlantic, just as it is impossible to calculate how many crimes the existence of a police force prevents. But it is safe to assume in both cases that the number is large. In dealing with the submarine threat, as in so many other fields, prevention proved better, and a lot easier, than cure; but while it is possible to tot up submarines killed, it is not possible to count ships saved by evasive routeing.

Winston Churchill was thrilled beyond measure by the Bletchley Park breakthrough and paid the uniquely eccentric establishment a top-secret visit in high summer 1941. It was typical of the man's pugnacity that he immediately wanted to make the maximum aggressive use of the material to pinpoint and destroy German forces (an attitude which runs counter to suggestions from more than one source that he let Coventry be bombed to protect the secret of the earlier Luftwaffe decryptions). In July he expressed impatience to the Admiralty about the fact that the Mediterranean Fleet seemed unable to turn the high-grade intelligence it was then getting into a string of victories; but as was to be shown time and again, even perfect information was not enough to bring results because it was as necessary as ever to have the right forces in the right place at the right time to beat such powerful enemies. But by September he realised that "Boniface" (the original name for Ultra intelligence when it was passed off as coming from a spy, which Churchill continued to use) was far too precious to risk for the sake of a few tactical gains. As if he did not already have enough to do as Prime Minister and Minister of Defence, he began to have boxes of decrypts sent to him, which he referred to as 'my golden eggs." The people at Bletchley Park he described as the geese that laid them "but never cackled." How much he must have enjoyed having the same insight into Germany's conduct of the war as he had from 1914 to 1915 during his earlier term as First Lord of the Admiralty.

But the geese were far from happy in their overcrowded habitat in the Home Counties. Every wrestling-match with the Whitehall and military bureaucracies for more desperately needed staff – not only cryptanalysts but also "Wrens" (members of the Women's Royal Naval Service) to run the bombes and typists to transcribe material – ended in defeat. The Bletchley Park staff probably had more than their fair share of exposure to the great contemporary excuse for inertia and inefficiency: "Don't you know there's a war on?" On October 21 Alan Turing persuaded three colleagues to append their signatures to his own at the bottom of a long letter of appeal to Churchill which he composed. Giving the address "Hut 6 and Hut 8 (Bletchley Park)" – the sections which attacked Luftwaffe/army traffic and naval Enigma respectively – Turing wrote:

> Some weeks ago you paid us the honour of a visit, and we believe that you regard our work as important . . . We think, however, that you ought to know that this work is being held up, and in some cases is not being done at all, principally because we cannot get sufficient staff to deal with it. Our reason for writing to you direct is that for months we have done everything that we possibly can through the normal channels, and that we despair of an early improvement without your intervention. No doubt in the long run these particular requirements will be met, but meanwhile still more precious months will have been wasted, and as our needs are continually expanding we see little hope of ever being adequately staffed.
>
> We realise that there is a tremendous demand for labour of all kinds and that its allocation is a matter of priorities. The trouble to our mind is that as we are a very small section with numerically trivial requirements it is very difficult to bring home to the authorities finally responsible either the import-ance of what is done here or the urgent necessity of dealing promptly with our requests. At the same time we find it hard to believe that it is really impossible to produce quickly the additional staff that we need, even if this meant interfering with the normal machinery of allocations.

Turing lists the various needs of Hut 8, Hut 6 and those working with the bombes; twenty clerks here, invaluable technicians threatened with conscription there, exhaustion of undermanned staffs leading to twelve-hour delays in decrypting, not enough typists or Wrens. The letter ends:

> If we are to do our job as well as it could and should be done it is absolutely vital that our wants, small as they are, should be promptly attended to. We have felt that we should be failing in our duty if we did not draw your attention to the facts and to the effects which they are having and must continue to have on our work, unless immediate action is taken.

An appalled and angry Churchill attached a minute to his Chief of Staff, General Hastings Ismay, headed with the demand for instant gratification which has become famous: ACTION THIS DAY. "Make sure," he wrote in his cursive hand, that "they have all they want on extreme priority and report to me that this has been done." And so it was, within a month.

A reorganisation of Bletchley Park at the end of the year took Turing from Hut 8 (not surprisingly, he had proved a hopeless administrator as its unofficial leader) to long-term research as Bletchley Park's chief consultant. This took him into other realms, including the development of the first computer. He thus became the only person who might have been in a position to write a comprehensive account of the work of an essentially anarchic organisation, Official Secrets Act permitting. Had he lived.

Since he now passes out of our story, it is appropriate to add here a summary of his subsequent career. After the war he did brilliant work on computers and was elected a Fellow of the Royal Society, Britain's most august scientific body, in 1951. In 1952 he was convicted at a sordidly sensational trial of "gross indecency" – on his own typically blunt and naïve confession to the police, whom he had called after being robbed by his partner in a brief homosexual affair (then illegal in Britain). Veiled references to his war-work kept him out of prison. He was given one year's probation, on condition that he accepted "treatment" for his "disorder," including compulsory hormones. Some of the few who knew the true value of his work in defence of the British way of life thought he deserved an earldom; he had to rest content with being appointed an Officer of the Order of the British Empire (OBE), an award as often made for attainment of middling rank in government service as for genuine achievement. He was allowed to keep it after conviction. Two years later, not quite forty-two, he took his own life by eating an apple dipped in cyanide. Such was the end of the inventor of the "turing machine," a codebreaker in more senses than one.

The principle adopted for the application of Ultra intelligence (which was restricted to the highest levels of command, mainly commanders-in-chief, the head of the Secret Service – MI6 – a few ministers and the like, and from June 1941 the American and Canadian naval commands) was that an operation based on it should always be explicable as the result of some other kind of information, such as air reconnaissance, direction-finding or traffic analysis. One of the earliest such applications was on June 13, when the pocket-battleship *Lützow* (ex-*Deutschland*) was attacked by fourteen torpedo-bombers on the strength of Enigma messages about her movement from Germany to Norway. One torpedo struck home and put her out of action for seven months. The British were now well-placed to keep track of the movements of all major enemy warships. Another, rather riskier, early exploitation was the rapid elimination of fifteen tankers and supply-ships sent out in April to replenish the *Bismarck* and *Prinz Eugen*. All of them were sunk in less than ten weeks from early May; eight of them were located by penetration of Enigma, and two of these were sunk despite an Admiralty plan to let them escape in order not to arouse German suspicions!

We may mention at this stage one other direct use of deciphered Enigma: when this revealed that no less than ten submarines were gathering towards the end of June to attack the eastbound convoy HX133, the British confidently denuded two westbound convoys of much of their escort and assembled thirteen warships against the pack. Five merchantmen and two submarines (including Wohlfarth in *U556*) were sunk in the ensuing battle, a narrow victory for the defence. But it was the difficulty the Germans were having in locating convoys and the swift series of losses among supply-ships which led them to launch their inquiries into wireless security mentioned above. Even though they were not on the right track, the ensuing precautions did make life more difficult than it might otherwise have been for the eavesdroppers in Britain.

At Midsummer 1941 the war underwent one of the most violent swings of its entire duration. Once again it was Adolf Hitler who stunned the world by a stroke which he had been planning and concentrating upon all year: "Operation Barbarossa," in which 120 divisions were hurled at the Soviet Union on June 22. The effects of this gargantuan strategic blunder – a voluntary war on two fronts – made themselves felt in the Atlantic campaign even before it began, as well as immediately afterwards and in the longer term. Churchill at once adopted the attitude that "my enemy's enemy is my friend," setting aside his hearty loathing of Communism and quickly appreciating that the invasion of Russia was bound to take some of the pressure off the United Kingdom and its allies. The British Empire was no longer alone in the front line against the Axis. Before the invasion the German surface-fleet (except the *Bismarck* and *Prinz Eugen*, about whose sortie Hitler had very sensible misgivings in advance) concentrated its attention on the Baltic. As the oft-deferred invasion-date approached, German fighters, bombers and maritime aircraft were withdrawn in increasing numbers from France for the new front, to an extent not fully realised at first by the British. But as the Luftwaffe made fewer flights over the eastern Atlantic and its fighters reduced their activities against British coastal convoy traffic (and their ability to protect their own coastal shipping along the entire western European coast), the relief soon became noticeable. The Germans were also heavily committed in the Mediterranean with their operations in Greece and North Africa, which added to the burdens of the Royal Navy in the region.
     But, quite reasonably, there was a price to be paid for the easement in the west brought by the new war between Germany and Russia, only so very recently bound together by solemn treaties which made them partners in crime for the dismemberment of Poland. Marshal Josef Stalin, having kept his head down for eleven days without saying a word in public about the German onslaught, surfaced on July 3 to address the Soviet people by radio. During his speech he referred with gratitude to Churchill's BBC broadcast on the day of the invasion, offering British aid. The US Government also lost no time in promising war supplies.
     Unbeknown to Roosevelt, but all too well known to Hitler, the United States had missed being precipitated into the hostilities by the narrowest of margins only two days before Barbarossa. *U203* had sighted the US battleship *Texas* and her destroyers in the Denmark Strait, a good ten miles inside the Germans' publicly declared maritime war-zone. *Kapitänleutnant* Rolf

Mützelburg failed to get into an attacking position – but only after a deter-mined 140-mile pursuit of the zig-zagging Americans. In response to his sighting report, which Raeder mentioned to Hitler at a routine meeting on June 21, only to be subjected to one of the Führer's notorious explosions of towering rage, the German dictator issued an order to the submarines: "All incidents with the United States must be avoided in the coming weeks." Hitler firmly and correctly believed that the threat of Japan would keep the Americans out of the fighting in Europe – so long as there was no unpardon-able "incident" of the kind Churchill was praying for, which Mützelberg had come so close to providing.

Even Hitler recognised he would be overreaching himself if, having decided to take on 200 million Russians, he was to be simultaneously confronted by 150 million Americans. He had read Roosevelt's thinking correctly and believed that US domestic considerations would keep him from going to war for as long as possible. Hitler assumed that when the time came Japan would tie the Americans down, not knowing that the US and British governments had already agreed in principle on a "Germany first" strategy. The German leader seems to have underestimated America's capacity to fight a war on two fronts, which is strange since he was about to plunge voluntarily into just such a situation with rather fewer resources than the Americans had and were already mobilising.

An Anglo-Soviet mutual assistance pact was quickly negotiated and signed in Moscow on July 12. One of Stalin's first requests was for naval action against German shipping in the far north, along the Norwegian and northern Finnish coasts which were under German control. The principal Soviet strategic asset in this area was the ice-free port of Murmansk, whose importance was seen clearly by Raeder during the planning of Barbarossa, but which Hitler, with his customary incomprehension of naval strategy, began by discounting. It was through this grim harbour that Anglo-American material assistance would have to come, and when the Germans did get around to trying to capture it overland, the Russians threw everything available into a successful defence.

In an attempt to help ease the pressure in the far north, Admiral Tovey was ordered by the Admiralty to mount an air-attack on German shipping in the area with the Home Fleet's two carriers, *Furious* and *Victorious*. Rear-Admiral Wake-Walker, in the heavy cruiser *Devonshire* and supported by the *Suffolk* with six destroyers, led the raiding force out of Scapa Flow on July 23. This was against Tovey's advice because he thought German air defences in Norway were too strong (he could not know that they too had been reduced in support of the main invasion of Russia to the south). He had wanted to attack the southern Norwegian bases, whose neglect by the British because of other commitments had never ceased to surprise and comfort the Germans there. Hitler always thought the British were bound to make a serious attempt on his long and exposed north-western flank, and the vulnerability of Norway, as he saw it, was already becoming an obsession with him.

Wake-Walker's attack lost most of its point before he launched it because the force was spotted by the Luftwaffe on July 30. The Germans diverted or withdrew their shipping and the British aircraft suffered very heavy losses in their raids on the ports of Kirkenes in Norway and Petsamo in Finland, where the Germans were able to concentrate their fighter and anti-aircraft defences. No significant results were obtained in these attacks or from a raid on the Norwegian harbour of Tromsö on the way back to Scapa. But the minelayer *Adventure* which had sailed with the British force got through to Archangel with a cargo of mines – the first delivery of war-material to the Russians by sea. None of the British ships was damaged.

In London much thought was being given to the problem of what a hard-pressed Britain could send to the Soviet Union. The bulk of the material assistance would have to come from the United States, which not only implied further strain on the overstretched transatlantic convoy system but also entailed the opening of a dangerous "branch-line" from Britain to north Russia. This new strategic route lay in the operational zone of the Home Fleet, which now began to shift its attention eastward from the far northern Atlantic to the chill waters east of Iceland.

But the Germans still had strategic surface-forces immediately to the south of Britain: the two battlecruisers and *Prinz Eugen* in Brest. Tovey was reminded of this threat on July 22, when the *Scharnhorst* put to sea and he was forced to prepare for another chase. But she was only going down the coast to La Pallice for repairs. Found there on the 23rd by photo-reconnaissance aircraft, the battlecruiser was bombed by RAF Bomber Command Halifaxes on the 24th and hit five times. She limped back to Brest through a convenient fog that evening with 3,000 tonnes of water in her hull and was docked for repairs on the 25th. She was to be unserviceable for eight months. The *Gneisenau* was little better off after being hit in two separate air-raids in April, and the *Prinz Eugen* had been badly damaged by a bomb in Brest at the beginning of July. The Admiralty was extremely well informed about their condition, thanks not only to Enigma intercepts but also to hundreds of photo-reconnaissance sorties, the efforts of spies ashore and submarine patrols. Mines were constantly being laid against the currently remote possibility of a breakout. Bomber Command however resisted naval urgings to finish a job which Coastal was not adequately equipped to do: like attacking the submarine pens near by, such enterprises were regarded as a debilitating diversion from bombing Germany. The Air Staff did not grasp the significance of these two chances to concentrate on destroying two stationary targets while they were at their most vulnerable (the pens were still far from fully protected in summer 1941). It is not as if either was an easy task, but it was also a safe bet that the work would be harder to finish the longer it was delayed. The inter-service argument ended with Bomber Command agreeing to resume heavy attacks on the Brest trio if they showed signs of preparing to come out. A majority in the War Cabinet took the RAF line.

The German attack on Russia made the transatlantic route even more important than before, and the ever-cautious Roosevelt was still looking for other non-combatant means of helping. After the US cargo-ship *Robin Moor* was sunk by submarine on May 21 and the *Bismarck* had passed through the north-western Atlantic, the President declared an "unlimited national emergency" on May 27, and in the following month had Axis assets frozen and German and Italian consulates closed by executive orders. His next step towards the sound of gunfire was to "bend" the line defining the eastern limit of the western hemisphere Security Zone to take in Iceland. As constitutional commander-in-chief, Roosevelt ordered his Chief of Naval Operations, Admiral Stark, to prepare an expeditionary force of US Navy ships and US Marines to relieve the British garrison there.

There was an almighty row when the plan got out in Congress, and in Germany Raeder tried to persuade Hitler that the American move was an act of war. The Icelandic Government was pressed to ask for American protection, an idea it got at dictation speed and accepted with a great deal of reluctance. But 4,400 Marines set out on the day the Germans crossed into Russia, landing in Iceland on July 7. Shortly afterwards Harry Hopkins, Roosevelt's most intimate and important adviser, flew to Britain to confer with Churchill about joint action to help the Soviet Union. There was, the President told him, to be "no talk of war" with the British leader, who was speaking of direct American involvement in the Atlantic conflict as imminent. American hostility to the concept of empire was revealed when Hopkins tried to argue that the British were expending too much effort in the Mediterranean, where they were doing badly, at the expense of the crucial Atlantic theatre. Hopkins flew on to Moscow – a long and risky haul via Iceland – for talks with Stalin, who demanded a Second Front to take some of the German pressure off him but promised determined Russian resistance. Like Churchill, he looked to the Americans to provide the tools with which to finish the job. Hopkins flew back to London for more talks, and on August 4 he accompanied Churchill aboard the battleship *Prince of Wales*, hurriedly repaired after the *Bismarck* episode, to go to Newfoundland for the first Anglo-American summit meeting of the war.

They were bound for Argentia, the base allocated to the Americans in the British colony. In December 1940, when the US advance party arrived, the place was a ghost-town, all but abandoned when the silvermine from which it derived its name ran out. The first Marines moved in during February 1941, and a naval Catalina squadron was based there in time to make sweeps in search of the *Bismarck*. The air and naval bases were fully operational by mid-July, when Rear-Admiral Bristol arrived to command the Atlantic Fleet Support Group (eventually known as US Navy Task Force 24) from there. Its role was to protect shipping in the north-western Atlantic with authority over the Canadian ships there. Thus did part of the RCN, which was waging war in support of Britain, come under the command of an admiral from a neutral country.

Roosevelt let it be known that he was "going fishing" before secretly transferring to the cruiser USS *Augusta* for the rendezvous with Churchill. In the light of Washington's tradition of open government it was a remarkably well-kept secret which did not get out until the participants were back home. The three days of talks opened with much emotional ceremony on August 9. After rounds of general discussion involving the two leaders and their service-chiefs, the President and the Prime Minister went into private talks on grand strategy while the chiefs of staff discussed practical military matters. The Americans resolutely refused to be pinned down on joining the fighting but offered to take over the Canada–Iceland leg of transatlantic escort, which was worth at least fifty warships to the Anglo-Canadian effort. The great political result was the "Atlantic Charter," an Anglo-American declaration which was the foundation both of the subsequently agreed Allied war-aims and of the idea of the United Nations. Churchill had not got everything he wanted, but the working relationship with Roosevelt which had previously fed on teleprinted letters and telephone calls was now cemented by this lengthy and intimate personal meeting. The Anglo-American alliance was in place, and the Prime Minister thought it would not be long before it turned into a fighting partnership. American destroyers escorted the *Prince of Wales* as far as Iceland, giving Churchill a taste of the elaborate system for protecting shipping when they led him through a large convoy.

Another outcome of the Argentia meeting was a joint Anglo-American mission to Stalin to work out a programme of aid. The first small convoy to northern Russia set sail from Iceland on August 21, consisting of the First World War carrier *Argus* acting as an aircraft-ferry and a cargo-ship with more fighters in crates, escorted by an aircraft-carrier, two cruisers and six destroyers under Admiral Wake-Walker. It got through without incident and the escort made a couple of pinprick attacks on the north Norwegian coast on the way back, with little result. The daunting difficulties of operating successfully in these distant and dangerous waters had been shown once again when the newly promoted Rear-Admiral Philip Vian tried to set up an advance naval base there. Rejecting Murmansk as inadequately defended after flying there on an inspection tour, he took two cruisers and two destroyers from Iceland to the island of Spitzbergen on July 27. German air reconnaissance helped to convince him after a brief look at the frozen Norwegian possession that it too was overexposed to enemy attack. The Admiralty dropped the idea, but sent Vian back on August 19 to wreck the coal-mines, remove the Norwegians and Russians living on the island, which is still the subject of a unique international treaty allowing several European nations access to it, and to hunt German shipping in the area. He got back on September 7 after successfully raiding Spitzbergen and sinking an old German cruiser. But the British failed to establish a port of call between Iceland and Russia, which meant that convoy-escorts would have to carry enough fuel for a double journey or rely on the tanker which was to be sent with each convoy. The first to sail was given the designation QP1 and consisted of one ship – the merchantman which had delivered the crated fighters – which departed on September 28. The next day the first Russia-bound convoy, PQ1, set sail from Hvalfjord, covered by a cruiser, two destroyers and an escort-group.

Accompanying QP1 south-westward was HMS *London*, the cruiser which had taken the Anglo-American mission, led by Lord Beaverbrook, the Canadian newspaper proprietor and Minister of War Production in Churchill's Cabinet, and Averell Harriman, State Department diplomat and close confidant of Roosevelt, to negotiate with Stalin. It proved a gruelling experience. The Soviet leader pounded the table, demanding once again a Second Front, which was to be the Russian refrain until 1944, and making unrealistic requests for vast quantities of munitions, troops – and the extension of Lend–Lease to the Soviet Union on the same terms as to Britain. This was a challenge to Roosevelt's skill in handling a volatile Congress because Americans in general were more opposed to Communism than to Fascism and disliked the Russians more than the Germans; but as usual he prevailed.

The German submarines were having a comparatively lean time in summer 1941. For the first time the rate of sinking fell below one per month per boat at sea. The peak loss of shipping so far, 688,000 tons in April, fell back to 511,000 tons in May, 432,000 in June, and then plunged to 121,000 in July. These figures include losses to all causes and in all areas. The April figure was heavily inflated by huge losses in the Mediterranean (about forty-five percent). Submarine sinkings fell from 325,000 tons in May to 80,000 in August, thanks to Ultra, the reduction in Luftwaffe support and the growing strength and competence of the escorts.

Noting these figures, the ever-voracious Bomber Command tried once again to make a profit from Coastal, still the RAF's poor relation. The first eagerly-awaited delivery of American B24 Liberator long-range bombers – twenty aircraft – was made to Britain in June. It was the British rather than the Americans who first saw the value of this aircraft, designed before the war but not seriously taken up until it was realised that the Liberator could fly further than any other bomber, more than twice as far as some types in service with Coastal Command, with an unprecedented payload of twenty-four depth-charges. The first round went to Coastal Command, under its new C-in-C, Air Marshal Sir Philip Joubert, appointed in June. A few were reserved for special purposes such as the top-priority transatlantic transport-run, but the first squadron of "Consolidated" Liberators, with adaptations and extra fuel-tanks, was added to Coastal Command in September. One month later the Command was deprived of half of them for other RAF purposes, and Coastal was then put at the back of a clamorous queue for more Liberators, against powerful competition from not only Bomber Command but also the US Army Air Force, which had belatedly woken up to the capacities of an aircraft forgotten for years in its own backyard.

But it was a Coastal Command Hudson bomber, the inadequate short-range workhorse of the British maritime air forces, which scored a unique triumph over the German submarines on 27 August 1941. On patrol half an hour south of Iceland, Squadron-Leader J. Thompson saw *U570* (Commander Hans Rahmlow) sailing slowly on the surface. The type VIIc, mainstay of the Atlantic campaign, had been at sea for barely seventy-two hours on her maiden operational voyage. Thompson swooped and dropped four depth-charges, set to explode at minimum depth. Enough damage was caused for the crew to appear in life-jackets on top of the conning-tower as Thompson made his second pass at 100 feet, raking the boat with his machine-guns. Unlike the German seaplane which had clinched the capture of HMS *Seal*, the Hudson could not land on the water. Rahmlow ran up the white flag after an exchange of lamp-signals in which Thompson threatened unrelenting fire on the crew if an attempt were made to scuttle; Rahmlow said he could not do so anyway and asked to be rescued. Thompson circled overhead until relieved by a Catalina. Late that evening an armed trawler arrived from Hvalfjord to take off the crew and tow *U570* to Iceland. Although Rahmlow had the presence of mind to obey orders and dump his Enigma machine and its papers over the side, the capture was a major coup for the British, who had never managed to bring in a German submarine. The boat was repaired and refitted and joined His Majesty's Navy as HMS *Graph*, to play an invaluable role in training and the study of German submarine technique. Once again the British sailors were deeply impressed, as their comrades had been on the *U110*, with the quality of the equipment, rations and facilities aboard. Technical experts were no less impressed later on with the standards of construction, the strength of the hull and many other qualities of the boat. Ideas were freely borrowed for later British submarines.

Those in Bomber Command, Downing Street and elsewhere who thought the submarines were on the retreat after the decline in sinkings in the summer were rudely disabused in September, when they accounted for 203,000 tons sunk out of an overall total of 286,000 tons lost. The packs were back in the North Atlantic and also operating off West Africa. Dönitz now had an average of thirty-five boats on patrol and was in a position to gather more than one pack at a time. In the North Atlantic three-quarters of the sinkings occurred in the airgap. But on September 16 HX150 sailed from Halifax to Iceland with American ships in the escort – the first so protected – one day after the US announced it would escort ships of all non-enemy nations to Iceland from the American continent. As the three western navies increased their co-operation from summer 1941, it fell to the Americans to cover the fast (HX) convoys in the western Atlantic while the Canadians escorted the slow SC formations from Sydney. It was in September also that the weakness of the RCN, due mainly to its relentlessly forced growth, was cruelly exposed.

SC42 set sail on August 30 with the RCN's 24th Escort Group of one destroyer and three corvettes. The Admiralty knew of the presence somewhere south-west of Iceland of the very large *Markgraf* group of fourteen German submarines, but the previously described difficulties in discovering positions prevented British Intelligence from locating them with precision. The convoy of sixty-four ships carrying 500,000 tons of supplies was therefore diverted to the far north to pass Cape Farewell, the southern tip of Greenland, at a distance of about sixty miles. *U85's* sighting report was picked up and SC42 was diverted even further north, only to run out of room to manoeuvre because of Greenland. Three other submarines from *Markgraf* joined in an attack on the evening of September 9, from within the convoy. Eight ships were sunk during the brief night and a tanker was left damaged but still afloat. The defensive effort of the escort was diffused by rescue work (one promising Asdic contact was abandoned for this reason) and a corvette was detached to tow the stricken tanker to Iceland.

The next evening, at least seven submarines mounted a second attack and sank seven more merchantmen. The only reinforcements available to the defenders were two RCN corvettes, *Chambly* and *Moose Jaw*, which were diverted to the scene from a training exercise by the Admiralty. As they caught up with the battered convoy from astern, they got an Asdic contact and dropped depth-charges. After this admirably prompt reaction the Canadians were amazed and delighted to see *U501* (Commander Hugo Förster) rise suddenly to the surface alongside the *Moose Jaw*. Depressing her 4-inch gun as far as it would go, the corvette opened fire. The gun jammed after one round, so the Canadians tried to ram. They succeeded only in sideswiping the submarine, and for several miles the two vessels ran ahead as if locked together. The Canadian sailors were astounded to hear a voice shouting orders from their upper deck – in German. Förster had brazenly stepped over the brim of his conning-tower on to the corvette, without, as witnesses reported later, getting his boots wet. The *Moose Jaw* pulled away to try ramming again, this time more successfully, machine-gunning as she came to prevent return fire. The *Chambly* put a party aboard under Lieutenant Edward Simmons; the Germans refused even at gunpoint to go back below, having opened the seacocks and set scuttling-charges on their captain's orders. The Canadians climbed down through the conning-tower hatch but quickly came out again when they saw the hull was indeed filling with water. All save one got clear before the *U501* dived for the last time, taking eleven of the crew with her. Förster, who claimed he had boarded the *Moose Jaw* to insist on a rescue, and thirty-five other Germans were saved.

It had been a chaotic encounter, but the Canadian Navy had sunk its first submarine, thanks largely to the direction of Commander (later Captain) R. D. Prentice, the retired RCN officer who had been recalled to the colours to take charge of escort-training. The two victorious corvettes joined SC42, as did three others culled from elsewhere, and at noon on September 11 the 2nd Escort Group of five destroyers joined from Iceland. The battle continued during the next night, when the British destroyer *Leamington* sank *U207*. In all sixteen ships were lost from the convoy.

At the request of the Admiralty, the RCN increased the size of its six escort groups from four ships to six; but it was not in a position to increase the number of destroyers from one to two per group. Only corvettes were available. A Canadian staff officer was sent to Admiral King, the US Navy's CINCLANT (C-in-C, Atlantic), to ask for reinforcements since the Americans were now in charge in the north-western Atlantic. King refused, citing an acute shortage of serviceable ships suitable for escort and claiming that SC convoys were the responsibility of the Canadian and British navies. While it was true that they were providing most of the ships, this did not detract from the overall responsibility of the Atlantic Fleet. King, as will be shown, was not the easiest of men to deal with and the last person to bother himself with Canadian sensibilities. Sending a mere commander from a foreign navy to ask him for ships was a waste of the commander's time. King also insisted on doing things his way, which led him to ignore the great accumulation of knowledge about convoy operations so painfully acquired by the British, not least because it was British.

The education of the Canadians continued to be costly. SC44 lost four ships and a corvette in their sector, and SC45's escort alarmed a British commander sufficiently to prompt him to attack the Canadians in his report to the Admiralty, where a thick folder of such complaints was building up. SC48 was a blow to all three navies in the North Atlantic. During a storm in mid-October many of the fifty ships in company lost touch. So did HMCS *Shediac*, a Canadian destroyer with the escort. She was not told of an overnight change of course, which was arranged by flag-signal. Since there was no telescope aboard to read such communications it is not clear whether trying to tell her would have done much good, but the attempt should surely have been made. The convoy turned away, the *Shediac* sailed on, her wireless tuned to the wrong channel so she could not pick up general messages, and when she noticed she was alone she had no list of predetermined rendezvous points for the convoy, normally issued for just such an eventuality, to help her find it again. The destroyer spent five days searching for her own convoy and completely failed to find it.

Its escort thus reduced, SC48 ran into a German patrol-line not pinpointed by OIC and lost three ships while still trying to reassemble. On

October 16 reinforcements arrived in the shape of five US destroyers, plus one and a corvette from the Royal Navy. The submarines, under orders since August to attack escorts if they got in the way of a pack-attack on a convoy, sank the British destroyer *Broadwater* and corvette *Gladiolus* as well as six more merchant ships. The Americans, disdaining the British practice of distant cover, positioned themselves unhealthily close to their battered charges. The inexperienced escorts flooded the scene with light from Snow-flake flares and starshell (standard practice for some time to help locate surfaced submarines; but if they were outside the convoy it only lit up the targets for the Germans). This undoubtedly helped *Kapitänleutnant* Joachim Preuss in *U568* to sink *Gladiolus* in the early hours of October 17. Forty minutes before that, however, he had become the first German to inflict fatal casualties on the forces of the United States since 1918. He sent a torpedo deep into the bowels of the destroyer USS *Kearny*, killing eleven men. The crippled ship just managed to creep back to Iceland on one engine, escorted by the USS *Greer*, which had been the first US ship to depth-charge a submarine – without success – on September 4. President Roosevelt lost no time in exploiting the incident, which was both inevitable and unsurprising (but a media sensation in America, where few were aware of how much the US Navy was already doing). Condemning the attack in a broadcast, he used it to help persuade Congress to repeal some neutrality legislation. On October 30, however, the risks being taken by the US Navy were spelled out even more clearly when *U552* (Commander Erich Topp) got the USS *Reuben James* in his periscope-sight and sank the destroyer by a single torpedo amidships, with the loss of all but forty-six of the crew; 115 were killed. The German High Command braced itself for an American declaration of war; but still Roosevelt held back from urging Congress to exercise its exclusive right to make one under the Constitution.

The American ship had been escorting the fast convoy HX156, which lost no other vessel. On his way to attack it, Lieutenant Unno von Fischel in *U374* sighted SC52 in the waters off Newfoundland. British Intelligence picked up his sighting report and the German responding order to no less than three small groups of submarines to combine into one pack (named on the customary ad hoc basis as *Raubritter* – robber-knight) for an all-out attack. The Admiralty ordered a diversion to the north, but this did not prevent the Germans from sinking four ships towards the rear of the convoy; two more ships ran aground in the notorious fogs of the Newfoundland Banks. To SC52 belongs the unique record of being the only convoy in the entire war, of the hundreds which set out, to be sent back to port because of the submarine threat. In the circumstances it was probably a wise move, and the ships were able to sail again from Sydney, Cape Breton, in a few days.

The Canadian ships of the Newfoundland Escort Force were being stretched to breaking-point. The inability of the RCN to say No when requests came in for bigger escorts, and then for cover further eastward to release British ships for the South Atlantic, forced some warships to spend as many as twenty-six days in thirty at sea. Four days in harbour instead of the official twelve deprived the crews of rest and the ships of essential maintenance. Canadian corvettes were even more uncomfortable than British ones, which had been adapted through experience by such improvements as an extended bow section. This kept out the water that previously came in during rough weather and made it impossible to keep bedding dry or even to get a hot meal. Canadian zeal to expand the navy and to boost home industry helps to account for this and the fact that RCN ships often had inferior, home-made equipment.

Throughout the record of the RCN's role in the war there runs a thread of neglect by senior officers and the Ottawa Government itself, a lack of resolve to tackle the growing difficulties caused by a policy of expansion at all costs. Far too much had been asked of Naval Service Headquarters; the readiness to accept these demands by officers keen to see the navy grow inevitably had to be paid for. As always in such circumstances the strain got steadily worse as the burden passed down through the ranks to the men at sea in their inadequate little ships. Some Royal Navy officers, including Captain Donald Macintyre, the outstanding escort commander, made no secret of their view that the RCN was a liability. A British officer seconded to the Newfoundland Escort Force, Captain E. B. K. Stevens, in charge of destroyers at St John's, sent an angry memorandum to Commodore Murray, the administrative chief of the NEF (now under the operational control of Admiral Bristol, USN) in the middle of October 1941. "A grave danger exists of breakdowns in health, morale and discipline," he wrote. Murray said he did not have enough men to provide relief; the situation was so bad that men sentenced for misdemeanours had to serve their time at sea (they would undoubtedly have preferred a dry naval prison). The Americans were also worried about the morale of the Canadians and the weakness of their ships. A US escort-group commander in Iceland, Captain M. L. Deyo, reported to Admiral Bristol at about the same time that the Canadians were exhausted, with insufficient rest between voyages and no chance to relax in the harsh conditions of Iceland. "They are going to have breakdowns and ships running out of fuel at sea." Deyo did not think the Canadians could cope with the coming winter unless something drastic was done to ease their conditions of service.

By the end of November the British recognised that the Canadians were having to work twice as hard as their own crews without the experience the British themselves had, to say nothing of superior training and equipment. At the end of the year the Admiralty apologised to Murray for being overcritical out of ignorance of the true circumstances. Even Admiral King eventually succumbed to sympathy and tried to ease the load on the NEF. Captain Stevens bitterly remarked in September of Canadian ships that "at present most escorts are equipped with one weapon of approximate precision

– the ram." A contemptuous Royal Navy escort officer told a Canadian colleague: "Canadian corvettes are only useful for picking up survivors." Murray, with justice, blamed the chaotic manning and training policies at the main base in Halifax, Nova Scotia, under the Commanding Officer, Atlantic Coast, Commodore G. C. Jones, and his destroyer commander, Captain E. R. Mainguy. The leading historian of the RCN in the Second World War, Dr Marc Milner, delivers this bleak judgement in his *North Atlantic Run*:

> Bluntly put, the Naval Staff was not concerned with the operational efficiency of NEF or indeed of the corvette fleet in general . . . In light of events at sea, the navy's adherence to such a manning policy and its failure to establish firm guidelines for proper work-up of escorts seem reckless. Not only did the manning policy contribute to the legacy of incompetence which haunted the RCN's expansion from this time forward, but it had more serious consequences. Unlike inefficiency in many other forms of military or naval endeavour, inefficiency in escort forces meant destruction for the men and ships that the escorts were trying to protect, not for the warships themselves. During the Battle of the Atlantic, Allied merchant seamen paid for the RCN's inefficiency . . . Elevating this deplorable condition to the status of policy was tragic.

We shall return to the problems of the Canadian Navy, but one of the reasons for its woes was, as noted above, the increase of German submarine activity a long way to the south, which obliged the British to move escorts to cover the Gibraltar and Freetown convoys. The period under review in this chapter was marked by a series of twists and turns in Dönitz's dispositions as he looked for the weak points in the British maritime supply-system. He began by moving west of the British Isles to evade air-patrols and escorts. Then he went to the tropical region of the Atlantic to attack the lightly protected shipping there. After a lean midsummer in the eastern Atlantic he went to the far north-west of the ocean in September to probe the defences of the main trade route at their most vulnerable.

At the same time operations resumed against convoys south-west of Ireland until mid-September, an area where Kondors could help submarines to find prey by transmitting long-wave homing signals from lengthy aerials trailing behind the aircraft. British evasion leaving them few targets, the submarines were sent out in groups to try their luck simultaneously in different parts of the waters between Greenland and the Azores, Britain and Newfoundland. Dönitz was trying various combinations of packs and long patrol-lines with large gaps between boats in an effort to secure a restoration of sightings. In the ten-week period from early September to mid-November the Submarine Command tried four major movements in its efforts to get back to grips with a suddenly elusive enemy.

The boats which had been operating close together south-west of Iceland with little to show for it were redeployed on September 6 on a long patrol-line from Iceland to the east Greenland coast. The positive result from their point of view was that they caught SC42; the negative outcome was that the patrol-line was so widely spaced that only a small pack could be assembled. There were the notorious fogs in the Newfoundland-Greenland area to contend with; and when there were not, the Canadians and Americans were beginning to provide some night-time air-escort. Other boats in the line caught SC44.

The second wave began a long sweep towards Greenland five weeks later to score just one success, the attack on SC48. The Germans noted the speed with which extra escorts, however inefficient, arrived, and saw Sunderland flying-boats overhead. Several boats used up all their fuel looking for targets to no avail and had to head back to base without firing a shot.

The third deployment took place in the latter part of October, when another wave of submarines was sent hunting some 400 miles west of Ireland and north-westward from there. It was the far end of this line which sighted SC52 and drove it back into port; but from the German viewpoint this was a disappointment because a high level of atmospheric interference made it impossible to direct a larger and co-ordinated attack by wireless in the usual way.

Those boats with enough fuel were directed to join the fourth patrol-line which began a broad sweep along the 500-mile front between Ireland and the Azores by the middle of November. It achieved very little, and on November 19 Dönitz noted that "the patrol-line . . . [has] brought no success and has been dissolved." He recognised in his War Diary that a narrowly spaced line had a better chance of a successful attack because a pack could be assembled more quickly, but a broadly spaced line had a better chance of a sighting.

> . . . with one exception, no patrol-line has located the enemy without the help of a previous sighting report from a detached boat . . . It cannot depend on chance . . . It is possible that from some source or other the British obtain information on our concentrated formations and take diversionary measures which occasionally lead them into the path of detached boats. Their information might be gained:
>
> a) as the result of treachery . . .
>
> b) by decrypting our radio messages: the Naval Staff continually check up on this possibility but regard it as out of the question;
>
> c) by co-ordinating radio-traffic analysis and sighting reports . . .
>
> d) by radar . . .
>
> All these possibilities are not enough to explain the failure of our concentrated formations, and it has therefore been decided to adopt another method. The boats will be formed into several groups, not too far apart, so that if any boat sights a convoy, the others will be able to come up relatively quickly. I do not intend these groups to be stationary but to move about constantly, to make it more difficult for the enemy to escape . . .

Onkel Karl was getting warmer than he knew, and now he had enough boats available to try to have his cake and eat it. If a short, closely spaced line and a long line of individual boats did not work, he would now try a line of widely spaced groups in each of which the boats would be close together. Whether this would work in the North Atlantic proper was for the moment academic because the general course of the war had obliged Dönitz virtually to abandon the area and focus his attention on the entrance to the Mediterranean. It was one of many diversions and, from the admiral's viewpoint, secondary uses of the submarine arm about which he was constantly complaining. The Russian campaign had slowed down the rate of construction by at least a third with its demand for resources and skilled workers (some of whom had been taken out of the shipyards and put into field-grey uniform); constant repairs to the large surface-ships also drained labour resources needed by the submarines; the Luftwaffe had switched much of its attention from the war against Britain to the Eastern Front.

Dönitz never wavered from his view that the central issue was the transatlantic trade route (now supplying Russia as well) – from his first days in submarines in 1917 to his death in 1981. The only doubt he ever showed during the Second World War was over whether his campaign should be directed against tonnage (any ship sunk anywhere was a blow to the enemy's war-effort) or against supply (concentration on laden ships as a double blow to his ability to fight on). When the Germans had the choice they naturally went for ships bound for Britain and for the coastal shipping which distributed the supplies brought across the Atlantic.

By the same token the British were indifferent as to where they got the chance to sink a German submarine, if only they could assemble the necessary sea and air forces. The argument between the convoy-defenders and the hunter-killer advocates was settled as definitively as it ever would be in May 1941, when an Admiralty committee looking into the anti-submarine campaign concluded that "we cannot afford to weaken our convoy escorts to provide the ships required for searching forces until far greater strength is available than is at present in prospect."

If this policy resolved the question of ships, it did not solve the problem of air-cover, as a letter from Air Marshal Joubert of 29 September 1941 to Vice-Admiral H. R. Moore, assistant Chief of Naval Staff for trade, showed in some detail.

> I have been watching with anxious attention the results obtained against U-boats by the surface escorts . . . over the last few weeks . . . the results appear most depressing . . . I think it is fair to say that our small losses in August were due largely to good luck, successful air-cooperation (since the U-boats were mainly operating within range of our bases) and some bad guesses by the enemy. This month the luck has turned, the enemy has made some successful appreciations and has operated chiefly out of range of our aircraft . . .

> I think it is fair to say that when aircraft can be kept over a convoy, and when . . . the shadowing U-boats can be harassed and made relatively innocuous, we can hope to bring the major portion of our ships safely home. We realise . . . that to do this the convoys must be routed in sufficiently near to enable the Focke-Wulf [Kondors] to find them easily . . . unless the convoys can be routed beyond extreme Focke-Wulf range we must always expect them to be found.

How was this conundrum of keeping the merchantmen out of reach of the longest-range German aircraft while within reach of British air-cover against submarines to be solved? Joubert said one possibility was routeing the convoys west of the Kondor limit for the bulk of their voyage across the North Atlantic and on the Gibraltar route. "We should have to rely on giving aircraft-cover on the outward and inward legs . . . in such a manner as to ensure breaking contact with the U-boats about the time when the convoy passed out of Focke Wulf range." Alternatively, he suggested routeing the convoys "sufficiently close in . . . to enable aircraft from the south-west of England and from Gibraltar to maintain continuous cover. This combined with [Catapult-Aircraft Merchant] ships with the convoys would, in my opinion, give a greater measure of security." The mid-Atlantic airgap was not capable of solution by land-based aircraft, Joubert wrote, but he knew the answer: "The convoys on this part of the route should . . . be accompanied by the . . . *Audacity* class of aircraft carrier" [see below]. Since corvettes and destroyers could not provide complete security, Joubert concluded:

> The sole defence which so far appears to have hampered the enemy considerably is the air, and I feel we should go full out to exploit all its possibilities. When we get an adequate number of escort vessels, preferably destroyers, with No. 271 [radar], we can then review the position again.

After less than four months in his new job as chief of Coastal Command, Joubert had identified the final component of the solution to the submarine threat, the escort-carrier, to consolidate the gains from more and better surface-escorts (now under priority construction in the United States) and good intelligence.

Closing the air-gap was getting increasing attention, though as we have seen the attitude of Bomber Command and the general strain on limited resources both stood in the way of a solution. The CAM ship to which Joubert referred was one of the expedients in use at this time. A ramp was placed on the bow section of a merchant ship, which would still carry a full cargo. From the ramp the solitary Hurricane fighter aboard could be launched with the assistance of a rocket-propelled trolley, to tackle a Kondor. After his fuel ran out, the RAF pilot had to ditch in the sea and hope to be picked up, leaving his aircraft to sink. HMS *Audacity* started life as the large, fast and comfortably appointed German cargo-liner *Hannover*, captured by a British light cruiser and a Canadian destroyer in the West Indies in February 1940. She was converted into the first escort-carrier and went into service in June 1941. Between the CAMs and her came five fighter-catapult ships which carried several Hurricanes each. The *Audacity* was a proper carrier in that she could both launch and "land" aircraft, the latter by the use of arrester-wires as employed by the larger "fleet-carrier." Her conversion involved the same principles as had been used to produce the first aircraft-carriers of the 1914–18 war – the "scalping" of a conventional ship and the installation of a flight-deck. The aircraft – Swordfish torpedo-bombers and American Martlet fighters – had nowhere to stand aboard except on the deck, but the pilots had the luxury of single cabins with en-suite bathrooms, a legacy from the *Hannover* which the Fleet Air Arm was considerate enough to leave in place.

Her career, however, was spent entirely on the Gibraltar run and was very brief. Under Commander D. W. Mackendrick, her first convoy was OG74 (outward to Gibraltar), twenty-six ships accompanied by a sloop, five corvettes and an inspection-vessel. The convoy was sighted by a submarine whose report led to an attack by another, *U201*, which was spotted and raked by the machine-guns of one of *Audacity's* six Martlets. The boat was forced to dive: just as the main benefit of intelligence was preventive, so the principal advantage of air-cover at this stage was to forestall an attack by forcing the submarine to submerge and lose both speed and contact with the convoy. But the first boat on the scene, *U124* (Commander Johann Mohr), stayed in touch and sank two ships later that evening (September 20). *Walmer Castle*, a rescue-ship (more and more convoys now had at least one such vessel to leave escorts free for their main role) fell back to help and was sunk by a Kondor. The *Audacity* sent up two Martlets which failed to find the attacker but shot down another Kondor – the first victim of an escort-carrier. The next night *U201* (Schnee) caught and sank three stragglers from OG74.

Audacity* shot down two more Kondors for the loss of one Martlet and its pilot before setting sail with convoy HG76 from Gibraltar to England on 14 December 1941. Around this convoy of thirty-two ships, protected by Commander F. J. Walker ("Johnnie" Walker to the Navy) and his 36th Escort Group, led by the sloop *Stork*, there developed one of the hardest and most protracted battles of its kind in the war. Several submarines were known to be operating in the area; the first was sighted by a Swordfish and forced under by depth-charges on the first evening. Two hours later the same aircraft forced another submarine to dive. Early the next morning a third was similarly discouraged; no attack was made on the convoy until the 17th, soon after Walker was alerted by intelligence of the gathering of a pack of five submarines (*Seeräuber* – pirate) across his path.

Walker had been that rarest of specimens in the inter-war Navy – an anti-submarine warfare specialist. He was headed for early retirement until the war came. Even so it took him eighteen months to get a command at sea, in charge of the 36th, which at this time consisted of two sloops and six corvettes. The man who had so signally failed to impress his superiors in peacetime blossomed and became the best anti-submarine commander of them all by developing highly sophisticated group tactics. For HG76 his group was augmented not only by *Audacity* but also by three destroyers, two more sloops and three corvettes.

The first German attempt on the convoy was made by *Fregattenkapitän* (junior Captain) Arend Baumann in *U131*, on the morning of the 17th. He was spotted by a Martlet and *Stork* led four other escorts into a sweep some twenty miles to the west of the convoy. *U131* was damaged severely by depth-charges, sank to the bottom and eventually rose uncontrollably to the surface when Baumann expended his last reserves of compressed air to blow the tanks. He was again sighted by a Martlet but managed to shoot it down when it attacked. Two of Walker's destroyers saw the aircraft go down and opened fire with great accuracy at seven miles. Baumann set scuttling charges and abandoned his boat.

All this was seen from some miles away by *U434* (KL Wolfgang Heyda). On his approach twenty-four hours later, he was forced to dive when he sighted two destroyers, at which he fired a single torpedo without effect. They counter-attacked, causing such severe damage that Heyda too was forced to surface, abandon and scuttle. The two destroyers took it in turns to sweep with Asdic and attack with depth-charges; when Heyda surfaced, both opened fire on him and one scored a glancing blow in an attempt to ram. So far not one torpedo had been fired at a merchantman while two submarines had been sunk. Two destroyers were sent back to Gibraltar for other duties; two Kondors were driven off by Martlets the same morning (the 18th) without loss to either side.

At dusk a corvette got an echo from another submarine, the *U574* (Lieutenant Dietrich Gengelbach), but the German got away on the surface because corvettes were not fast enough to keep up. Gengelbach did not run away, however. He fired a salvo of torpedoes at the escort from long range without hitting anything. Then he got the destroyer *Stanley* squarely in his sights astern of the convoy in the early hours of the 19th and fired again. The *Stanley* was hit in her magazines and exploded, sending up a vast pillar of flame. But she had got off a contact report in time to bring Walker himself in the *Stork* dashing to the rear: Gengelbach fired at her as she was joining the *Stanley* but missed. After the explosion he put about and withdrew. *Stork's* pursuit forced him to dive, more than halving his speed. Walker got a contact and after two expert attacks *U574* surfaced with serious internal damage. A circular chase ensued as the submarine ran parallel with the *Stork* inside her narrowest turning circle, too close for the sloop's guns to be brought down on her. Walker's report says his gunners were reduced to swearing and shaking their fists at the enemy only yards away. Eventually

Walker, having swept the conning-tower with machine-gun fire, was reduced to the oldest maritime weapon of all, ramming. The boat turned turtle, scraped along the sloop's hull and was despatched by a last pattern of depth-charges. *Stork* picked up twenty-five British and five German survivors.

It was only now that the German attack scored its first hit on a merchant ship, which caught fire and had to be finished off by an escort when the survivors were clear. By this time two more Kondors were overhead; one was shot down and the other driven off with damage. On the afternoon of the 19th a third Kondor was shot down at such short range that the attacking Martlet actually collided with it and was very lucky to be able to land on *Audacity* afterwards.

The running battle resumed on December 20; the last submarine to attack, *U108*, had kept in touch and another five were sent to join her. A Kondor was chased off in the morning and two submarines sighted together ahead of the convoy were forced to submerge by the tireless Martlets in the afternoon. On the morning of the 21st, two more were sighted well astern of the convoy, side by side with a ladder between them. A Martlet used its machine-guns to force them both to dive. Four escorts made a search but found nothing. At this point Walker gave up evasive shifts in the convoy's course and decided that his charges, now under a permanent, mobile siege, might as well take the fastest route home.

The next attack came from astern that evening and was made by the "ace" Endrass in *U567*. Prien's former lieutenant sank one ship. Meanwhile *Kapitänleutnant* Gerhard Bigalk had worked *U751* between the starboard flank of the convoy and the *Audacity*, which was manoeuvring independently ten miles away. Because of the pressure on the convoy, Walker had been forced to turn down Mackendrick's request for an escort for the carrier, a fact the group commander (unjustly) felt guilty about: he had advised her captain to take up a position on the other side of the convoy because he knew the Germans were to starboard. Bigalk struck at about 8.30 p.m., cutting the hybrid carrier in half with three torpedo explosions. Each section sank separately with heavy casualties, including the captain. One of the escorts which came to the rescue got a contact on *U751* but Bigalk survived the ensuing attack to make a propaganda broadcast about his feat over the Christmas period. Two hours after the *Audacity* went down, Endrass made his second attack and was detected by three escorts. The sloop *Deptford* (Lieutenant-Commander H. R. White) made the final attack before the hunt was abandoned. As she was on her way back to the convoy, several minutes later, there were two loud blasts in quick succession. *U567* had exploded underwater, presumably after a fire aboard, and Endrass thus suffered a fate remarkably similar to that of his mentor, once again with the loss of the entire crew. *Deptford's* triumph (not that there was any means of knowing how exceptional it was until much later) was tarnished immediately afterwards when she ran into the stern of the *Stork*, killing two German prisoners below deck.

Still the epic passage continued, as did *Stork* at a rather reduced speed with her Asdic out of action. Walker was in pessimistic mood, blaming himself for the loss of *Audacity*. But on the morning of December 22, with some 700 miles still to go, a Coastal Command Liberator appeared over the convoy with enough endurance to circle protectively for hours until relieved by another. One more Kondor found HG76 but took no action beyond homing perhaps as many as four submarines on the convoy. But the Liberators forced two of them to dive at the same time and possibly drove off a third. An incoming destroyer contacted and depth-charged a submarine on the 23rd without result. The remaining four days of the voyage were, as it was customary to say, uneventful.

There had been larger mêlées before HG76 and there were to be some even bigger ones later, but this convoy battle stands out for its character and duration – a week of unremitting action involving submarines, escorts and a major air-effort by both sides. The British lost a carrier and a destroyer, plus just two merchantmen out of thirty-two. For the Germans the carrier was a great prize of which they naturally made the most; but the loss of four submarines, including an "ace" captain, in a battle over a single convoy was on balance a defeat.

If a British-based Liberator could come to the relief of "Johnnie" Walker and stay with him for hours while his convoy was four days from home, then Liberators based in Iceland could have closed the North Atlantic airgap for shipping using the more northerly routes, especially if supplemented with more of the same from Newfoundland. But the few Liberators left to Coastal by Bomber Command were based exclusively in the United Kingdom. In the first two years of the war aircraft destroyed one submarine, forced the surrender of a second and helped ships to sink just three others. This modest tally was largely due to inadequate armament and training, both of which had latterly been greatly improved. Radar and some radical rethinking on tactics were now making a formidable threat to submarines out of maritime aircraft. It was fully understood that the best chance of a "kill" was during the minute it took a submarine to dive from the moment it was spotted from the air, and the settings of aerial depth-charges were amended accordingly to go off at minimal depth.

It had been discovered by trial and error that aircraft were best used in the escort role for wide-ranging sweeps round a convoy rather than exclusively in close support, and better with a convoy than on general patrol. Radar enabled aircraft to provide protection at night and in reduced visibility; work was in hand on helping aircrew to see submarines spotted by radar after dark so that they could be attacked. There would always be areas out of reach of shore-based aircraft but the answer to that was already perceived to be the escort-carrier, a type which could not be built overnight but was on order in the United States, by the Americans as well as the British.

The value of airpower against the submarine and the Kondor was fully understood by those at the Admiralty and Coastal Command who increasingly depended on it and used it, so there need be no fear of hindsight in concluding that the denial of a handful of available Liberators to the anti-submarine effort was one of the outstanding examples of misplaced parsimony by government this century. It was to be eighteen months from the time operational Liberators became available in significant numbers to the RAF (in September 1941) before Coastal Command received the minimal quantity it needed. Nor need there be any doubt that the blame belongs to the War Cabinet, because it was there that all inter-service wrangles about priorities were, if necessary, ultimately resolved. When it came to allocations of aircraft, the bombing of Germany almost invariably won the day. The air lobby had the support of the majority, including Churchill, and to the regular servants of the Crown an initiative like Turing's to short-circuit the machinery of government was apparently unthinkable, no matter how many complaints were made by those confronting the threat. As the next chapter will show, it was to be only after nearly three years of mounting shipping-losses that a full-blown admiral finally drove home the message about airpower at sea as the ultimate deterrent to the submarine.

Far from the prying eyes of aircraft the Germans were wrestling with the growing difficulty of supply at sea. After the British quickly mopped up the vessels placed in out-of-the-way regions of the Atlantic to supply the *Bismarck* and *Prinz Eugen*, the German Navy still had others to support both its submarines and its disguised merchant-raiders. Much ingenuity was devoted to this problem by the Germans, whose shortage of overseas bases and ports of call was as acute in the Second World War as it had been in the First, in which the concept of the *Etappendienst* had been developed.

One comfortable little arrangement fell victim to a diplomatic torpedo in September 1941. Taking advantage of the friendly neutrality of Spain, the German submarines when they began to patrol further south into the Atlantic took to slipping into the Canary Islands, the Spanish posssession off the north-west of Africa. Two fuel-tankers were among the German merchant-shipping caught in the islands' capital, Las Palmas, by the outbreak of war: the *Charlotte Schliemann* and the *Corrientes*. The two ships were positioned at the outer extremity of the port, out of sight of shore, and never moved for two years – at least not horizontally. They did go up and down in the water as submarines refuelled at night and a supply-tanker made good the deficit during the day. It was not until the British had thoroughly penetrated the Enigma traffic that they discovered the significance of the two ships and made a formal protest to Madrid. They were moved into the harbour, but at the end of 1941, unbeknown to the British, they moved out again. The

Germans also made frequent use of the Azores for a refuelling rendezvous: the Portuguese-owned archipelago had many remote islands which were uninhabited and provided useful shelter.

For the rest such refuelling had to be done on the open sea, in the central and southern Atlantic. The first supply-ship intended for the exclusive use of submarines was sent to mid-Atlantic in May 1941. During the summer the British caught a total of seven, without, as far as can be established, much assistance from Enigma because the supply-vessels did not normally transmit messages: they took up a predetermined position in a given area and moved slowly up and down or in circles waiting for custom. The submarines were supplied with a list of their whereabouts and could be ordered by their headquarters to go to one, without the need to betray the position of the rendezvous, by the use of a simple code: "Go to point Red in area Clothing." Those caught were either spotted on the way to their posts or found by a scouting aircraft from a passing warship on patrol. In October the supply-ship *Kota Penang*, carrying oil, food, spare parts, ammunition and sailors' comforts, was found and sunk by the cruiser HMS *Kenya* between the Bay of Biscay and the Azores.

British successes against these floating commissariats had been such that the German Naval Command ordered the disguised merchant raider *Atlantis*, at sea since 31 March 1940, to supply submarines south of the equator in November. Captain Bernhard Rogge had by then taken "Ship 16" as she was codenamed (Raider C to the British) on a uniquely successful cruise, circumnavigating the globe and visiting every ocean. She was on her way home after sinking or taking in prize twenty-two ships totalling 146,000 tons, which made her the most successful surface-raider of any kind during this war, or probably any; crew leave was seriously overdue. Her change of role had to be ordered by radio and proved her undoing: British Intelligence was able to pinpoint the area to which she was diverted.

The British cruiser HMS *Devonshire* was sent from Freetown to search, and her seaplane sighted a suspicious merchant ship on November 22. Captain R. D. Oliver kept his distance while he made use of a new precautionary system brought in against the disguised raiders: the Admiralty painstakingly plotted the whereabouts of every single known ocean-going merchantman as a check on any ship sighted anywhere. No matter what disguise a raider was using, therefore, it was possible to find out quite quickly by radio whether an innocent-looking ship was what (and where) she ought to be. His suspicions thus confirmed, Oliver opened fire with his 8-inch guns at a range of 17,500 yards. The *Atlantis*, her aircraft unusable because of a defect, had just settled down to replenishing *U126*, whose commander, *Kapitänleutnant* Ernst Bauer, was tucking into breakfast in the wardroom. The submarine crash-dived without its captain as the *Atlantis*, one of her two engines also out of commission because the engineers were at work on it, went to action stations, unmasking the guns from their hiding-places in false additions to the upperworks and putting an end to the pretence of being the Dutch ship *Polyphemus*. Rogge was unable to use his outranged 5.9-inch guns and abandoned ship as the *Devonshire* hammered his vessel to destruction, helped by her own scuttling charges. Most of the crew – 308 men in all – survived, abandoned in their boats and liferafts by the *Devonshire* because of the known presence of at least one submarine.

U126 surfaced after a safe interval to allow Bauer to get back aboard from a lifeboat. He now began one of the most remarkable rescues of the war. Fifty-five *Atlantis* sailors were crammed into the hull (more than the submarine's own crew) and another fifty-two clung to the narrow upper deck. The remaining 201 survivors squeezed into four lifeboats and two *Atlantis* launches and were put under tow. The unlikely procession headed west, towards the Brazilian coast. Three days later Bauer sighted the submarine-supply ship *Python*, of whose position he had been aware, and the survivors were put aboard. Their adventures were far from over as *U126* slipped away.

The *Python*, which had been sent out from France, now proceeded eastwards across the South Atlantic, under orders to supply several submarines sent to the area by Dönitz to operate on the route round the Cape of Good Hope. On November 30 she reached a predetermined position south-west of the island of St Helena, and on December 1 she started to refuel *U68* and *UA*. To this spot also was directed the *Devonshire's* sister-ship, *Dorsetshire*, once again exploiting a radio-interception. Captain A. W. S. Agar, VC, wasted no time in opening fire from eight miles as pandemonium broke out on the *Python* and the two submarines alongside. The *UA* (Commander Hans Eckermann) was able to cast off and dive at once, but the *U68* (junior Captain Karl-Friedrich Merten), caught taking on torpedoes and badly out of trim with an uneven load, needed rather longer to submerge and could not counter-attack (*UA* fired five torpedoes at the *Dorsetshire* without effect). The *Python* gave herself away by first trying to flee and then by attempting to lay a smokescreen. As Agar fired, the Germans set scuttling charges and took to the boats. The men from *Atlantis* were now in the water for the second time in nine days. In all, 414 German sailors were left at the scene by the British, once again keen to be off because of the presence of submarines.

So it was left to *U68* and *UA* to solve the problem. Each took about 100 men aboard and five lifeboats in tow with another hundred survivors. A launch plied among the lifeboats and between them and the submarines, carrying hot food and drinks and enabling the survivors to take turns in the horrifically overcrowded submarines and the boats. Incredibly, Eckermann slipped his lifeboats on one occasion to launch a long-distance salvo of torpedoes against an independently routed tanker he had seen. He missed. Otherwise the two boats limped along on the surface at six knots or less with their charges bobbing in their wakes.

In Lorient a furious Dönitz, all thoughts of attacking enemy shipping in the South Atlantic abandoned, had to redeploy his boats, the least suitable vessels imaginable for a major rescue, in a complex effort to complete the task. *U129* (Commander Nicolai Clausen) was the first to appear, on December 3, and contributed to a modest easement of the overcrowding. Two days later Commander Johann Mohr arrived in *U124*, fresh from sinking the cruiser *Dunedin*, which had been looking for the *Atlantis*. The northward crawl continued undetected until the 14th, when the first of four Italian submarines sent to relieve the Germans was met; the last reached the burgeoning flotilla on the 18th. They ditched the lifeboats as soon as there was enough submarine space for the survivors, and the eight submarines involved in this tenacious rescue mission got into St Nazaire one by one between Christmas Day and December 29. From the time of the abandonment of the *Python* not a man was lost.

Dönitz had already decided to give up trying to supply his boats at sea in this way by the end of November because of enemy successes against the precious surface-ships sent for the purpose. The submariner's solution to this difficulty was to supply submarines by submarine – a large, new type of which the first was delivered in December 1941 (and of which more in the ensuing chapter). Two other merchant raiders had been sunk during this period while three managed to return to German-controlled ports.

At home the British were becoming accustomed to tightening their belts in the most literal sense. During 1941 "absolute" minima for imports were cut and cut again as a nation which thought it could not get by on less than 43 million tonnes learned to manage on about three-quarters of that amount. Even food-imports had to be reduced by more than ten percent to just over 13 million tonnes, which made intense import-substitution measures a matter of life and death. Thanks to these Britain proved it could survive with half the amount of imported food it bought in peacetime, and on the whole the nation's health benefited from the short commons as Lord Woolton's Ministry of Food strove for a balanced diet which was just enough to enable people to go on working. One remarkable exception was bread, which, though increasingly on the greyer side of white, was not rationed. Attempts to persuade people to eat wholemeal bread, more economical as well as healthier, were an abject failure. It was during this time of hardship that the allotment came into its own and public parks blossomed with the foliage of root vegetables. Urban Britons, constantly urged to "Dig for Victory," became amateur agriculturalists in their dwindling spare time. The Women's Land Army was created to till the fields in the absence of conscripted farmworkers amid mild ribaldry about "backs to the land."

Strange new foods and bizarre recipes made their appearance on the "Kitchen Front," like *snoek*, a large fish related to the barracuda and available in abundance in South African waters. From the United States came condensed milk, powdered egg and Spam (spiced ham), baked beans, other canned meats, vegetables and fruits supplied under Lend–Lease, which were rationed like very nearly everything else. Some items, notably meat, were rationed by price, which meant that it cost the same each week but the amount varied (usually downwards); others by quantity, such as tea; for clothing, separate coupons were issued to be "spent" in predetermined amounts which varied according to the type of garment. This led to agonising dilemmas, although quite often such difficulties were pre-empted by the fact that many items all but disappeared for the duration, like stockings and suits. Those lucky enough to have relatives in countries like the USA, Canada and Australia got the occasional gift-parcel of preserved food, clothing and tobacco.

All this ensured that the buff-covered ration book with its coarse pages of cheap, variously coloured paper was the most zealously kept document in the possession of every citizen. It was also the symbol of a unique fairness because the rationing system imposed by the German blockade was made and seen to work. The inevitable black market was a contained phenomenon which did not seriously erode the general perception of an evenly shared burden of deprivation, fostering a sense of national unity unknown before or since. The rationing programme with the accompanying propaganda against waste, full of ideas on how to make the most of what was available, stands as one of the most ingenious and successful administrative exercises in history, unmatched by any other government. It was the far from inglorious apotheosis of the oft-derided "nation of shopkeepers." But the man who coined that insult also said that an army marches on its stomach.

By following the selfsame Napoleon into Russia, Hitler had ceased to present the most serious threat of an invasion of England since the French emperor's. Although the British Government never took the risk of prompting headlines like "invasion threat over – official," fewer warships needed to be kept close to home. But the RAF's fighters were as busy as ever, not only covering coastal convoys but also trying to fend off Luftwaffe bombers from the port cities, which were under constant attack. Despite the bombing, the docks were functioning much more smoothly, although as many ocean-going freighters as possible were unloaded on the north-west coasts of Britain. Those which could not be were grouped in convoys which went north-about Scotland before being redistributed among the convoys running between the Firth of Forth in eastern Scotland, the River Tyne and the Thames.

Losses to air-dropped mines averaged 12,000 tons a month in the first half of the year, but the partial diversion of Luftwaffe strength to Russia brought noticeable relief in the second, of the order of fifty percent. But in December the Germans more than made up for it by mining 60,000 tons. To achieve this alarming total they intensified minelaying-runs by E-boats and the small but highly efficient naval air-section; they also used a new type of mine with a double detonator, activated by the ship's magnetic field and set off by its noise. This offset much of the value of "degaussing" – the installation of an electric circuit round a ship's hull to reduce its magnetic field. Nearly 1,000 vessels usually made of wood were engaged in minesweeping, which was now synchronised with the coastal convoy cycles.

The Luftwaffe sank nearly 150,000 tons by bombing in May but the air-threat fell away thereafter, although the reduced bombardment was made much more difficult for the defence by a switch to night attacks, to which Fighter Command was at first unable to respond. But shipboard and surface anti-aircraft protection was becoming much more plentiful and motor-gunboats (MGBs) were beginning to be used against the E-boats in dashing high-speed actions.

The British were unable to develop a serious air-campaign against the Germans' coastal shipping until the second half of 1941, for the all too familiar reasons of shortage of suitable aircraft in Coastal Command and lack of interest in Bomber Command. From July Fighter Command joined the fray in the Channel area with its new fighter-bomber version of the Hurricane (the "Hurribomber"), while a Bomber Command group concentrated on coastal shipping from north Germany to Normandy. Three groups from Coastal Command covered the far north, the waters off southern Norway and western Denmark, and the Bay of Biscay between Brittany and Spain respectively. British air-attacks on German shipping in the Channel caused little damage but drove the enemy to pass through only at night; from September the traffic came under attack from the new motor-torpedo-boats (MTBs) based at Dover. All in all, the British air-effort against German shipping cost more than four aircraft for every ship sunk during this period.

In the far north Coastal Command met stiff German fighter-defence; it was the air, surface and submarine raids by the Home Fleet which made a major contribution to defeating the German drive on Murmansk. In general the German onslaught on Allied shipping was far more effective than its mirror-image, the British offensive against the much smaller target of German shipping in the north-east Atlantic and the waters between the two sides. Pinprick raids late in 1941 by Royal Norwegian Navy vessels and by British combined operations using ships, aircraft and Commandos had an effect on Hitler out of all proportion to their achievements in Norway. His fear of a second British invasion of that country's long and intricate coastline now became an obsession which prompted him to commit unduly large land and air forces to its defence. He also decided to concentrate all the German Navy's big ships for the defence of Norway, including the massive *Tirpitz*, on her sea-trials in the Baltic at the end of this period. He issued orders that the battlecruisers *Scharnhorst* and *Gneisenau* and the heavy cruiser *Prinz Eugen*, bottled up in Brest, should be moved north. The British guessed that they would not just be left in such close range of their bombers, whose renewed attacks in December did little damage but were enough to keep the squadron there into the New Year.

In terms of capital ships the Royal Navy, despite the relief afforded by American cover of the north-western Atlantic against a German breakout, was plunged into an acute crisis before the end of this period. The fleet-carrier *Ark Royal* was sunk in the Mediterranean by *Kapitänleutnant* Friedrich Guggenberger in *U81* on 13 November 1941, and twelve days later in the same area KL Hans-Diedrich Baron von Tiesenhausen in *U331* sank the battleship *Barham*, the first to be lost at sea on the British side. The diversion of submarines to the Mediterranean, which annoyed Dönitz by interrupting his Atlantic campaign, at least yielded palpable results. On December 19 as the land, sea and air struggle for control of the Mediterranean and North Africa swallowed huge forces, a handful of Italian frogmen carried out a brilliant "human torpedo" attack on the British naval base of Alexandria in Egypt. The battleships *Queen Elizabeth* and *Valiant* were crippled for months by the limpet-mines stealthily attached to their hulls. Thus was the entire British Battle Squadron (the 1st) in the Mediterranean driven from the field. The three modern fleet-carriers remaining after the sinking of the *Ark Royal*, in strategic terms the worst single loss by the British navy in the war so far, were all in American shipyards under repair.

The *Hood* was long gone; and war-clouds in the Far East were turning black. The Admiralty was committed to sending a force of capital ships against the Japanese, which entailed the activation of the great naval base at Singapore – built for the purpose but denuded of major ships since before the war because of the overriding need to contain the German threat. The battleship *Prince of Wales* and the battlecruiser *Repulse* were sent out, and on December 10, devoid of air-cover, they were sunk by Japanese naval aircraft. The British imperial bluff was well and truly exposed by this stupendous error, which was only the first of many in the Far East. That campaign does not concern us directly, but its effect on the strategic situation in the principal maritime struggle in the Atlantic is made clear by the fact that, at the end of 1941, Admiral Tovey of the Home Fleet effectively had just one first-rate capital ship at his disposal, the *King George V* – and that alone was not up to the job of containing the *Tirpitz*. His other new battleship, HMS *Duke of York*, had hardly gone into commission before it was commandeered by Churchill in December for a visit to the United States. He arrived in Washington via New York on December 22.

He went to his second meeting with Roosevelt because on 7 December 1941 the strategic situation had been abruptly and brutally transformed. Even as Japanese and American negotiators were still engaged in talks in Washington, six Japanese aircraft-carriers launched 270 bombers against the main American Pacific naval base at Pearl Harbor in Hawaii. Six battleships out of eight were sunk or incapacitated, which helped to ensure that the simultaneous Japanese thrusts against British, French and Dutch territories on the other side of the ocean succeeded in the ensuing months. Fortunately three

American carriers and thirteen cruisers were absent at the time. On the day following this black Sunday, the United States declared war on Japan; three days later Germany and Italy rashly declared war on the United States, which therefore had to reciprocate.

Had Hitler stayed his hand it is not inconceivable that the Americans might, after the shock of Pearl Harbor, still not have taken on a war on two fronts immediately because Japan was the greater threat to the United States, well placed to attack its interests in the Pacific. The sinking of the two British capital ships was a useful subsidiary victory which helped the Japanese to mop up residual Allied naval strength in the Far East without difficulty. Nonetheless Churchill was hugely relieved that the military power of the Americans would now be flung into the war against the Axis with all their economic and industrial strength. But until this could be effectively deployed, the entry of Japan into the war offset the benefit to the British cause of the involvement of the Soviet Union.

Churchill could not be absolutely sure of American involvement against Germany even after Pearl Harbor; in the four days before Hitler declared war on the US Roosevelt alarmed the Prime Minister by trying to postpone their meeting. This suggests that Hitler made another of his great strategic errors in rushing to take on yet another enemy, even if Raeder and Dönitz were pleased with their new freedom to attack American forces in the Atlantic. But the second Anglo-American summit meeting of the war, code-named "Arcadia," began on time in Washington and, as at Argentia, military commanders held parallel discussions.

Two days before the talks began, Admiral King was promoted Commander-in-Chief of the United States Navy (CINCLANT became COM-INCH). As leader of the only Allied service capable of taking the fight almost immediately to the enemies in east and west in what was now a worldwide war on two fronts, he thereby became the most important officer on the Allied side. We shall look at him more closely in the next chapter, but it should be noted here that he was both a passionate Anglophobe and a convinced opponent of the "Germany first" policy formally agreed at Argentia.

Fortunately for the British, who managed to win the greater proportion of the arguments at Arcadia, King was outranked by General George C. Marshall, who had been Chief of Staff of the US Army (including the Army Air Force), since 1939 and subsequently became chairman of the Joint Chiefs of Staff. Marshall (1880–1959) took the opposite view and prevailed in the American camp.

George Catlett Marshall was born in Uniontown, Pennsylvania, and never wanted to be anything but a soldier. He studied at the Virginia Military Institute from 1897 until commissioned into the infantry in 1901 and held a variety of posts at home and in the Philippines before becoming a staff-college instructor in 1908. In the First World War he went to France and rose to be chief of staff of a corps. Later he served successively in China, as deputy commander of the Infantry School and briefly as head of the War-Plans Division before becoming deputy chief of staff in 1938.

As Chief of Staff (head of the Army under the President as Commander-in-Chief) he was responsible for transforming what was a backward force of 330,000 men in 1939 into a vast, modern army of eight million by 1945. His greatest talent was logistics, in which he had no equal. Because he held no field command in the Second World War he was not a glamorous figure; his greatest disappointment was Roosevelt's refusal to let him lead the invasion of Normandy. The President was unable to dispense with the invaluable advice of one of his shrewdest appointments.

Marshall was a distant and unfathomable leader, but always sound and courteous in argument and a man of his word. His reasonable and equable manner concealed extraordinary determination and an unerring instinct for managing and picking the right men. He may well have been the greatest officer to adorn an American uniform, and his successful insistence on "Germany first" was a crucial contribution to victory in the Atlantic. It was not to be the last time that General Marshall came to the rescue of European civilisation.

The Arcadia conference also agreed on the paramount importance of keeping open the transatlantic trade route and its increasingly important offshoot, the route to the Soviet northern ports. The Americans were to take full charge of the garrisoning of Iceland, replacing their Marines and British forces with a US Army force. Against Germany a strategy was agreed that entailed stepping up the effort in the Mediterranean, where the British position had become bogged down by naval losses which had in turn sapped the British Army's campaign in North Africa. Success there was to be followed by a build-up to an invasion of southern and then western Europe. For this the support of "Fortress Britain" was accepted as the top priority. British requests for more destroyers and flying-boats were turned down because of American needs; the Americans asked the British to lend them coastal patrol-boats and to step up the bombing of German shipyards. The most important political result of the conference was the promulgation of the "United Nations Declaration" on 1 January 1942, which twenty-two nations, including Russia, had agreed to sign. The USAAF was to join the RAF in the bombing offensive against Germany (another victory for "Bomber" Harris as C-in-C of RAF Bomber Command), and US forces were to be built up in Britain ("Operation Bolero") for land offensives against the Germans and Italians.

The Germans were still winning the "tonnage war" in this period, sinking ships much faster than they could be replaced; but the gap between losses and replacements was narrowing significantly. Here everything depended on the United States, to which British officials were resorting more and more frequently with ever longer shopping-lists, to be put on the Lend–Lease account. But with the best will in the world, and the will was there, orders could be placed from one day to the next, while delivery only followed months or even more than a year later. It was not until the middle of August 1941, for example, that the first "off-the-peg" freighter of the "Liberty" type, the SS *Ocean Vanguard*, 10,800 tons, was launched. She seemed so eager to join the fray that she began to slide down the slipway before the launching ceremony was under way.

This was the first of the sixty ordered in 1940. In April 1941 Roosevelt won approval from Congress for the finance to build another 200, together with extra yard-space to speed up production. The British also looked to America for escorts, which could be produced by the combined effort of British and Canadian yards at a rate of only eight per month. Rear-Admiral J. W. S. Dorling of the British Supply Council in the United States approached Frank Knox, the Secretary for the Navy, with a request for 100 escorts of 1,500 tons each in May 1941. Dorling had found a usable design at the US Bureau of Ships, the US Navy's marine architecture department, for what was to become a most useful new type of destroyer-escort (frigate in Royal Navy parlance). Knox agreed to supply them at the rate of ten per month, as well as twenty minesweepers and fourteen rescue vessels.

Having considered the great success of the British intelligence effort above, we may now look at the rival German operation in this intensely fought intellectual struggle. The fortunes of war, which had put so much current Enigma paperwork into British hands in spring 1941 (more important for the breakthrough than *U110's* machine itself), were not exclusively on the British side during this period. We have already seen that the *B-dienst* had been reading a great deal of British naval traffic since before the war, both codes and ciphers (in a code, a concept such as a ship or a chart-reference is represented by a letter or letters, or a word, which means that codes can be used in plain-language messages; a cipher alters every letter of a message and turns it into apparent gibberish; code and cipher can be combined as in the German grid-reference system).

In September 1941 the *B-dienst* made a deep penetration of British Naval Cipher No. 2, enabling it to read much more of the output much more quickly. And in December the German naval cryptanalysts got into Naval Cipher No. 3, which was in use for communications among the British, Canadian and American navies. Since Cipher No. 2 was the main Royal Navy internal communications medium, the Germans were now in a position to eavesdrop very effectively on both British and Allied dispositions in the Atlantic. Unlike their opponents they were never able to read virtually the entire traffic for any period, but they deciphered more than enough to give them a detailed picture of convoy and escort operations. One particular

weakness in the British system was the sailing telegram sent by the Naval
Control Service officer (the Port Director in US parlance) on the departure
of a convoy. While in port communications were by teleprinter, telephone
or on paper, none of which the Germans could hope to penetrate (although
they captured useful ship's papers from time to time). Since the final and
precise composition of a convoy was not known for certain until the last
minute, wireless had to be used to pass this essential information to those
responsible for escort. The sailing telegram also included the ships' final
destinations and overall course, which the various escorting forces had to
know. Orders for evasive diversions also had to be sent by radio. Otherwise
convoys were subject to strict radio silence (merchant-ships had their transmitters sealed) and escorts kept their traffic to an absolute minimum.

The British and Allied Merchant Ship (BAMS) code, a prewar invention
used for essential transmissions to independently routed ships, was an open
book to the *B-dienst*, whose chief, Captain Heinz Bonatz, had written an
internal monograph before the war in 1939 entitled "The System of British
Wireless Communications." It was very largely on the basis of the work of
the *xB-dienst* (the decipherment department of the *B-dienst*) that the section
of the German daily situation report at submarine headquarters headed
"intelligence on the enemy" was based. The naval intelligence service came
to employ more than 1,000 people at naval headquarters in Berlin, where
more than forty teleprinters chattered with intercepts from the listening-posts
strung out along the entire western coast of Europe from Norway to Spain.
Until the withdrawal late in 1941 of the British 3rd Battle Squadron from
Canada, the admiral in Halifax was particularly helpful to Bonatz because he
sent a daily situation report at noon his time, picked up in the European
evening by the Germans. His report invariably began with the same list of
addresses, the date and the title. No matter what variation of Cipher No. 2
he might be using, this knowledge enabled the Germans to crack it very
quickly and telex it to Dönitz's command-post.

By the end of this nine-month period an unstable stalemate had been reached
in the Atlantic. Dönitz was able to keep about twice as many submarines at
sea – an average of thirty-six – at the end as he had at the beginning. He
had been forced to change tactics and operational areas by several inhibiting
factors, including the extension and strengthening of surface and air-cover
for convoys, the need to avoid clashes with the Americans, diversions of his
boats to the Mediterranean and Norwegian waters. The Germans were
making fewer sightings but were often able to mount more powerful attacks
with packs when they found a target, especially if there was little or no
air-cover. Joint operations with the Kondors of 40 Group worked well until
British air-defence could be stiffened as on the Gibraltar route. But submarine
losses (thirty in this period, twenty of them to escorts) were mounting, from
about two a month before April to more than three after it. Replacements

were arriving at a much faster rate but the crews were not as good and many boats were lost on their first operational patrol. Training in the Baltic was not skimped but inevitably became diluted and had to be accelerated because of the expansion of the service. This was as important a factor behind the increasing use of pack tactics as the strengthening of enemy escorts.

Over the period, ships sunk by submarine fell by a quarter and the average submarine destroyed just over one ship of 5,500 tons per month, only a quarter of the score achieved in the previous period and only partly compensated for by the much higher number at sea. By the same token, fewer sightings of targets meant not only fewer losses to the enemy but also a lower proportion of submarines sunk: the average submarine now had an operational life of nine months, more than twice as long as before. The fleet was also expanding ever faster, to 200 boats at the end of 1941 compared with fifty-four in April.

From the British viewpoint, more than 1.5 million tons of shipping had been lost to submarine attack – two-thirds among independents despite the big convoy battles of the period. The net monthly loss rate after new building fell in this period by nearly half but was still ten percent higher than the replacement rate (for every 1,000 tons built, 1,100 were lost to all causes). The gap was still large but it was closing; the upward trend in net losses seemed to have gone into reverse. The number of escorts had been increased from about 375 to 500, but the struggle to improve air-cover produced as many setbacks as advances in this period.

The outstanding success of 1941 was in the preventive area, made possible by a quantum jump in the quality of intelligence. It is possible to relate the ups and downs of the struggle in this period directly to the flow of Ultra material, but there were so many other important factors in play that the case seems Not Proven. At the same time there can be no doubt that informed evasive routeing saved a large if unquantifiable number of ships, perhaps hundreds. But the escorts were getting better at their job, even if the Canadians were suffering by being torn between the very different British and American tactics, inadequate ships and second-class equipment together with the problems of forced growth. Radar and direction-finding were much better in the Royal Navy and a new weapon was rapidly coming into use: the "Hedgehog," a multiple mortar which fired a large number of miniature depth-charges 250 yards ahead of a ship. This helped to close the blind gap between loss of Asdic contact at close range and an attack (depth-charges went over the stern). But the depth-charge remained the chief anti-submarine weapon for ships and aircraft. The new ten-centimetre radar set was spreading slowly at the end of the period; with a maximum detection-range of 7,000 yards it was an invaluable aid in finding surfaced submarines, especially at night. Still equipped with the old metric radar, Coastal Command in the latter part of 1941 patrolled the Bay of Biscay, forcing submarines to cross it submerged in daylight, which reduced their operational time by increasing time in transit to and from their bases.

With three disguised raiders sunk (one, *Atlantis*, thanks to Ultra) during this period there was none at sea by the end of 1941. The German big ships achieved nothing after the loss of the *Bismarck*; in December Hitler remarked that "every ship that is not in Norway is in the wrong place." But the diminished Home Fleet had still to cover the Brest squadron, the *Tirpitz* in Norway and two pocket-battleships and one heavy cruiser in Germany. Their mere existence tied down a large British force whether they moved or not.

In the wider war the most important developments were the involvements of the Soviet Union, Japan and the United States; but Japan and Russia concluded, on April 13, a mutual neutrality pact which endured until the last weeks of the war. German interventions in North Africa and southern Europe in support of Italy put the British Army on the defensive. In May it was forced to withdraw from Greece and Crete. The Germans took Kiev in August and cut off Leningrad in September. It was not until they got within artillery range of Moscow that the Red Army halted them, on December 6. General Hideki Tojo took over as Prime Minister of Japan on 17 October 1941 and disobeyed his Emperor by pursuing a war policy which led to Pearl Harbor. Ten days after that disaster, the brilliant Admiral Chester W. Nimitz, USN, was appointed C-in-C in the Pacific. On December 19 Hitler took personal command of the German Army; on Christmas Day the British surrendered Hong Kong to the Japanese. Admiral King took up supreme US naval command on December 20, two weeks after his appointment. He was not about to be told by the British how to run his side of the Atlantic convoy struggle, which he regarded as secondary even though the protection of neutrality was gone. The education of Ernest J. King was to be hugely expensive in blood and treasure.

7

JANUARY TO JULY 1942

*Admiral King – The Second Happy Time – US naval build-up –
but no convoys in US waters – haemorrhage of shipping – the
Channel Dash humiliates the Royal Navy – Ultra fails – B-dienst
flourishes – Canada as middleman – refuelling at sea – Winn in
US – Interlocking Convoy System – Germans move south – US
shipbuilding – air-threat to submarines – Admiral Tovey's revolt
– Tirpitz – St Nazaire – Spitzbergen – PQ17 disaster – losses
at sea*

GENERAL Dwight D. Eisenhower, hardly the most vicious of men, took the considered view long before he became Supreme Allied Commander in Europe that the entire Allied war-effort would have gone rather more smoothly had Admiral King been shot. The ever-smiling general confided this uncharacteristically murderous thought to his diary.

Ernest Joseph King was born in Lorain, Ohio, in 1878 and was thus old enough to serve in the Spanish–American War of 1898 as a naval cadet. He was the son of a Scottish immigrant railroad-foreman, a fact which probably helps to explain his near-psychotic anglophobia. Commissioned in 1901, he served in a wide variety of seagoing and shore posts, accumulating experience in gunnery, engineering, torpedo-boats, mining operations, submarines, the command of ships and flotillas and teaching at the Naval Academy at Annapolis, Maryland. It was only in 1927 that he discovered the joys of flying, qualifying as a pilot at the remarkably advanced age of 48 and refreshing his career by a transfer to naval aviation. His anglophobia may also have been encouraged by his service in the First World War as a squadron engineering officer and then assistant chief of staff to the C-in-C, US Atlantic Fleet, which worked closely with the British Grand Fleet and even put substantial units under Royal Navy command.

The qualities which helped him reach the pinnacle of his profession just as he should have been gently coasting towards a pension (he was due for retirement in 1942, when he was sixty-four) included quick intelligence, ambition and ruthlessness. He was also a natural commander and teacher who exacted the highest standards from his subordinates. But he demanded the same from himself, and he was prepared to listen to those junior to him, belying his sometimes chill manner. Strong on strategy if less so on tactics, he was also a gifted administrator and a passionate and determined fighter for the Navy. Highly respected but unloved in the service, King found affection with an unending series of women and relied on copious supplies of alcohol to help him unwind, despite the US Navy's "dry" tradition. Among his other less than endearing foibles was a monumental obstinacy and a fearsome temper, as well as a sometimes stupendous rudeness. All three of these qualities were easily evoked simultaneously by what he saw as British (specifically English) affectations of manner, accent and class-superiority among the admirals with whom he now had to deal. This prejudice made it difficult (if not always impossible) for him to recognise that the Royal Navy might have something to teach the Americans at sea. A rare exception was to be Rodger Winn, as we shall discover.

King became chief of the naval Bureau of Aeronautics in 1933 in the rank of rear-admiral. He held the post for five years and thus had much to do with the US Navy's development of maritime airpower far beyond anything the British undertook. He could rightfully claim to have recognised the important potential of aircraft-carriers at sea and to have made the Navy aware of it almost single-handed. He was rewarded with the position of Aircraft Commander with the Battle Force as a vice-admiral in 1938. Two years later he took command of the US Fleet's Patrol Force, the key role in the Navy's increasing involvement in the Atlantic during the period of neutrality as uniquely defined by the Americans. In February 1941 he took charge of the Atlantic Fleet as a full admiral and only ten months later, as we have seen, became C-in-C of the US Navy. In March 1942 Roosevelt combined this post with that of Chief of Naval Operations (hitherto held by Admiral Stark, who became USN commander in Europe): King became king of everything afloat under the Stars and Stripes. Since the Senate confirmed him in the post for four years, he was to lead the Navy for the duration. His purblind insistence on doing it his way in the Atlantic stands in marked contrast with his outstanding success in the Pacific, where astutely chosen admirals were given their head and soon began to deliver unexpectedly early and heartening victories against the Japanese. His unique reward at the end of 1944 was to be named the first Fleet Admiral (five-star rank, equivalent to Admiral of the Fleet in the Royal Navy) in American history. He retired at the end of 1945, aged sixty-seven, and died in 1956.

The Japanese did not inform their German and Italian allies of their plan to knock out the American Pacific Fleet on 7 December 1941, but the German submarine service already had a strategy for exploiting the entry of the United States into the war. The naval command had found Hitler's restrictions on action in the American security zone more and more irksome as the US Navy stepped up its support for the Anglo-Canadian effort in the Atlantic,

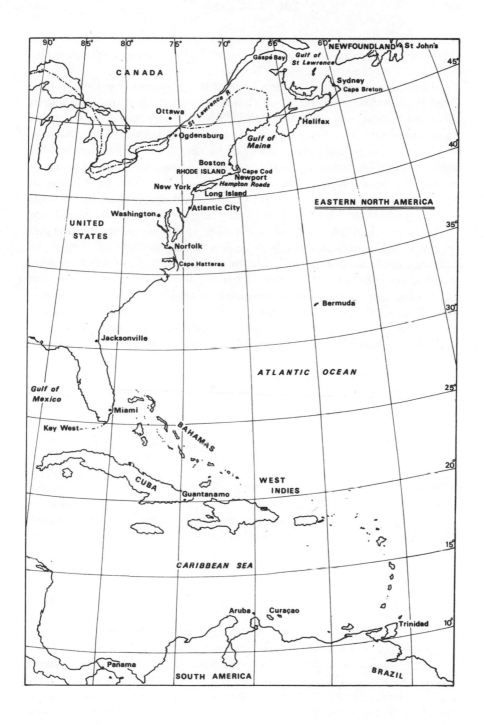

EASTERN NORTH AMERICA

even to the extent of joining in the shooting. On December 9, two days before he precipitately declared war on the United States, Hitler gave the order lifting all such restrictions.

Conditions could hardly have been more propitious for Dönitz. The Pearl Harbor disaster would force the Americans to divert warships from their east to their west coast just as the US Navy was propelled into a global war on two fronts. The forces at their disposal for the defence of their Atlantic waters were thus bound to be reduced at the very moment that they lost the protection of their neutrality. After two years of immunity they were in any case sure to be unprepared for the new requirement of coastal defence, in which they had no experience. The German submarine service, by contrast, was thoroughly battle-hardened by twenty-seven months of war. At the turn of the year it had 249 boats of which 158 were training and ninety-one operational. The exceptionally high quality of the crews which began the campaign might have been diluted by the loss of the aces and the increasing tempo of recruitment and training, but rising numbers more than compensated, especially in the light of the lack of experience of the new enemy. What is more, the sheer abundance of shipping along the east coast offered the well-practised Germans a chance to return to attacks by individual boats, of the kind which had been so successful against the British in the opening phase of the war.

This was fortunate for Dönitz because he was soon to find out that he had little choice but to adopt such tactics. On December 9 he wrote in his War Diary:

> The attempt must be made to exploit these advantages, which will disappear in the foreseeable future, and to strike a blow at the American coast with a drumbeat.

A "drumbeat" sounds feeble in English but it is the literal translation of the codeword chosen for the impending onslaught on shipping in American waters: Operation *Paukenschlag*. In German, however, the word also has the metaphorical meaning of thunderbolt, which is rather closer to what happened, if still inadequate.

Dönitz planned to deploy a dozen type IX longer-range boats from New York to the Caribbean and to send the smaller, shorter-range type VIIc to operate off Newfoundland and Nova Scotia, which were up to 1,000 miles closer to his bases. But on December 10 the Naval War Command told him he would have a maximum of six type IX for *Paukenschlag* (the type VII was to operate independently). Thus the planned blow in the far western Atlantic struck the Americans and their allies as devastating; but in the eyes of Dönitz it was a pulled punch. There were several reasons for the limited scale of the new offensive and the delay of five weeks before even that could be launched. Not only had the Japanese taken the Germans as much by surprise as the Americans; the Germans had also endured considerable submarine losses in the Mediterranean, and the High Command still insisted on keeping, in Dönitz's opinion, far too many boats there to shore up the North African campaign. An unusually severe winter in the Baltic was interfering with training schedules; and although submarine construction had accelerated in the latter part of 1941, the number of boats actually operational was still too small to meet the increasing commitments which Dönitz regarded as irritating diversions from the main campaign in the Atlantic. In the end *Paukenschlag* began with just five of type IX, operating initially along the North American seaboard from the St Lawrence in Canada to Cape Hatteras, North Carolina. Seven of type VII were sent to the chill waters off Newfoundland and Nova Scotia, and all boats were in place by the middle of January 1942.

Exactly one calendar month after Dönitz met Hitler to discuss taking the war to the Americas, *Kapitänleutnant* Reinhard Hardegen, holder of the Knight's Cross with Oakleaves and commander of *U123*, a type IXb, inaugurated *Paukenschlag* by torpedoing the British freighter SS *Cyclops*, 9,076 tons, some 300 miles off Cape Cod, Massachusetts, on 12 January 1942. Within a week he sank six more ships and damaged a tanker off the north-eastern coast of the United States. Further north, junior Captain Ernst Kals in *U130* (type IXc) sank a tanker and a freighter off Halifax on the morning of the 13th. In all, by the end of January, the Germans sank thirty-five ships totalling more than 200,000 tons between Newfoundland and Bermuda, in the 4,000 miles of North American coastal waters. In the same period the submarines sank ten ships of 63,000 tons on the North Atlantic route, of which just three were in convoy. A jubilant Hardegen reported:

> Our operation has been most successful: eight ships, including three tankers, totalling 53,860 tons within twelve hours. It is a pity there was not a couple of large minelaying submarines with me the other night off New York, or ten to twenty submarines here [off Cape Hatteras] last night, instead of one. I am sure all would have found ample targets. Altogether I saw about twenty steamships, some undarkened; also a few small tramp-steamers, all hugging the coast. Buoys and beacons in the area had dimmed lights which, however, were visible up to two or three miles.

The German submariners soon began to refer to the new front as their Second Happy Time, or "the American turkey-shoot." But conditions were not altogether blissful aboard the submarines, especially on the smaller type VII, and particularly in the north. Captain Kals wrote in his log after making a surface-attack on a ship off Cape Breton, Nova Scotia, on January 18 (showing the German taste for the historic present tense):

> By putting one engine full ahead and the other full astern I manage to evade [a US destroyer] and she misses me by about ten metres. I order "crash

dive." As I enter the conning-tower a second destroyer appears astern of the steamship. About eight tons of water enter the boat through the frozen diesel exhaust-valves, causing us to hit bottom. Here I remain bumping uncomfortably on the rocks. It is better to lie here for a while with everything stopped. There is no sign from the destroyer; presumably her depth-charge dropping gear has frozen up . . .

Kals remained unscathed in his relatively luxurious 1,100-tonner. On the VIIc of up to 750 tons, the habitual overcrowding became impossibly oppressive during western Atlantic operations. It turned out that the range of these medium-sized ocean-going boats had been underestimated: they proved capable of sufficient endurance to operate for two or sometimes three weeks, even off the US coast, which was 600 to 1,000 miles further from their bases in France than the north of Canada was from Norway. The added range was achieved at a considerable price in discomfort, made possible only by the enthusiasm and high morale of the crews.

Extra fuel was stored in the most unlikely (and dangerous) places, not excluding tanks meant for drinking-water, washing-water, trimming and ballast. When Dönitz heard about this he was horrified and banned it, apparently with scant effect. By these extreme methods it was possible to cram an extra twenty tonnes of fuel into the boat. The tanks not meant for fuel would be emptied first, but drinking-water had to be carried in cans; there was always the danger that the oil-contaminated ballast and trimming tanks would reveal the presence of the submarine underwater by sending residual traces of fuel to the surface even after it had been supplanted by seawater. Maximum fuel-economy had to be observed on the outward and return runs, such as by adhering to the shortest or "Great Circle" route (a measure soon forced on the convoys by the severe inroads into tanker-traffic), diving under bad weather and generally sailing at the most miserly speed compatible with operational requirements.

On the outward leg of three weeks there was nowhere for the crew to sit down in the bow or stern compartments (which also contained torpedoes until they could be expended); bunks and decks were stacked with cans and cases. It was all but impossible to find anywhere in the hull where a man could stand upright. And even if a sailor could find somewhere to squat and eat his rations, the quality of his sustenance deteriorated the further west his boat went. The fresh food loaded in port lasted a little over a week (one of only two "heads" – lavatories – was temporarily pressed into service as a food-store), although such famous staples of the German diet as dense rye-bread and a variety of smoked and salted sausages lasted longer. Otherwise the men ate from tins, and the food from these was somehow immediately suffused with the unique submarine miasma, made up of diesel-fumes, bad air, damp, stale sweat, unwashed clothing and bodies. Despite the best efforts of scientists ashore, nothing could be done to protect the dietary

foundations of bread and potatoes from the ubiquitous mildew. Like genera-
tions of surface-sailors before them, the German submariners were inevitably
reduced to dry biscuits ("hard tack") about halfway through a patrol, so that
by the time they returned to base they were suffering from skin ailments,
constipation and other problems associated with dietary deficiency (although
scurvy, caused by a lack of vitamin C and the curse of mariners through the
ages, was prevented by canned fruit and vegetables).

Despite these inhibitions on their performance and the fact that there
were seldom more than a dozen German boats operating off North America
at a time, they sank 1.25 million tons of shipping in the North Atlantic in
the first quarter of 1942: 216 vessels, the vast majority in waters for which
the US Navy was strategically responsible. Worldwide losses of shipping to
enemy action over the period amounted to 1.93 million tons of which
1.34 million were caused by submarines. These statistics show the hugely
disproportionate contribution which the handful of boats off North America
was able to make to the German maritime effort. Reporting these figures
from London in April, Harry Hopkins, Roosevelt's principal adviser, pointed
out that fifty-seven percent of the losses had been tankers (chosen as priority
targets by Dönitz and picked off at leisure by his new aces). Accurately
foreseeing the desperate need for this type of ship in the coming months,
Hopkins urged the President: "I doubt very much whether anything short
of convoy is going to do this job."

The implication of this advice is that there were no convoys in American
waters. Nor were there. Notwithstanding the hard-won lesson of the First
World War and more than two years of information on the course of the
Second, freely supplied by the British and appreciatively received by Admiral
Ghormley's delegation in London, the United States Navy under King set
its face against convoy in its own waters. The Americans were thereby
undoing the unremitting hard labour of the British and the Canadians in
escorting the ships across the Atlantic in comparative safety. The entire
painstakingly constructed ocean-convoy system was thus completely undermined, negating the value of American belligerency which should have been
an enormous new advantage to the Allied cause. Ships were allowed to sail
independently in their hundreds before joining or after leaving transatlantic
convoys just as they had done in the US security zone before the Americans
entered the war. This staggering omission played into the eager hands of the
newly unfettered Germans, who promptly initiated in American waters what
the official US historian, Samuel Eliot Morison, sardonically described as "a
merry massacre." The excuse given was that the US Navy had far too few
escorts; the underlying error was Admiral King's belief that "inadequately
escorted convoys are worse than none" (the absolute converse of British
anti-submarine experience).

In March 1942, faced with the new and alarming onslaught which led
the Americans to believe the Germans must have scores if not hundreds

of submarines at sea, the Royal and US navies worked out their escort requirements as, respectively, 725 and 590, counted 383 and 122 as available and deduced shortfalls of 342 and 468. Some 300 destroyer-escorts (frigates) were already under construction in American yards to British orders; it was now agreed that all escorts of all types would be allocated to the three Atlantic navies according to need, wherever they were built. Until the submarines were contained the shortage of escorts was chronic. The Americans had been as neglectful of small ships as the British between the wars and for the same reason: underestimation of the submarine. Escorts can no more be multiplied overnight than carriers or submarines, no matter how much construction is increased. A naval war can be fought only with what is available, not on promises of new vessels.

The American shortage was accentuated by the simultaneous demands of the Pacific theatre, even though Japanese ambition had long been an open secret; it had always worried people like King more than the Atlantic, which they saw as a British problem. Another disruptive factor was incorrigible American optimism. No sooner had they gone to war than they reserved huge quantities of steel, labour and construction-facilities for landing-craft for both maritime theatres. The war against Germany could indeed be won only by an invasion of Europe, but the basis of such a vast enterprise was the delivery of goods and men by sea to Britain. This entailed absolute priority for convoys. Churchill thus had to fend off not only Soviet demands but also American eagerness for an immediate Second Front in Europe. Only hindsight enabled many Americans to see he was right.

We may note here that the United States built the astounding total of 82,028 landing craft during the war. At a time when the dollar was worth between five and six times as much as today's, the US Navy spent $105 billion between 1 July 1940 and 30 June 1945. In addition to the swarms of landing-craft, the following ships were added to the fleet: ten battleships, eighteen fleet-carriers, nine escort-carriers, two large and ten heavy cruisers, 110 escort-cruisers, thirty-three light cruisers, 358 destroyers, 504 destroyer-escorts and 211 submarines. Of the money, $19 billion went on hulls, $13 billion on guns and depth-charges, $4.5 billion on other weapons and ammunition, $4 billion on radar and $8 billion on extra repair and construction facilities. Some $8 billion were spent on building more than 80,000 naval aircraft (many for Allied use) of which half were lost. Apart from miscellaneous items such as naval bases and 172 million handkerchiefs, the rest of the money went on the men and women who made the US Navy the greatest in history. Figures like these help to explain why even such a deadly combination as Germany and Japan could not hope to win the world war they had begun, even without the Soviet, British and other Allied contributions: the United States was truly the "arsenal of democracy" – and its banker.

*   *   *

But the gigantic war-machine which was eventually to be controlled by the dour Admiral King was still largely on the drawing-board and in the small print of ever-expanding war-budgets when *Paukenschlag* struck. Reporting to King at New Year 1942, Vice-Admiral Adolphus Andrews, Commander of the Eastern Sea Frontier (the US East Coast down to Florida), wrote baldly: "Should the enemy submarines operate off this coast, this command has no force available to take action against them, either offensively or defensively." He cannot be accused of concealing the appalling truth, as events were to prove within days.

Andrews was not the most gifted of admirals, but in running his command he was more sinned against than sinning. The defence of the continental United States against direct attack was not seen as a burning priority. If Great Britain, the predecessor of the USA as leading world power, could rely on a Channel barely twenty miles wide for protection against invasion for 900 years, why should Washington worry with the broad Atlantic to the east, the even wider Pacific to the west and much smaller, friendly land-powers to north and south? There had been a brief irruption by German submarines into the western Atlantic at the end of the First World War, but the Americans followed the British in believing between the wars that the submarine had been checkmated by Sonar (American Asdic). Contemporary aircraft could not reach their continent from any land-base likely to be available to any conceivable enemy. The attack on Pearl Harbor, far out in the Pacific, by carrier-based aircraft did not seriously shake this confidence despite early consequent fears of such raids on the West Coast.

Andrews' command was effectively created only in March 1941 as a direct result of the American–British Conversations on strategy (known as ABC–1) – and initially only on paper. It came under the Navy Department administratively, and variously under the Chief of Naval Operations and the Atlantic Fleet operationally. By the outbreak of America's war Andrews had established his headquarters on the fifteenth floor of the Federal Building on Church Street in downtown Manhattan. Very sensibly, the next floor down in the New York City building was later pressed into service as a joint operational office for the Navy, Army and Army Air Force in the command area.

While static defences of harbours and shore establishments were progressing well by December 1941 with the laying of protective minefields, booms and nets, the Frontier had all of twenty small vessels available to it, of which the most useful were two Coastguard cutters, and 103 naval aircraft, including three fighters, three torpedo-bombers, six patrol-aircraft, seven transports and one bomber. Three-quarters of these, as the Frontier's own War Diary confirms, were useless for anti-submarine purposes. The Army Air Force had bombers capable of flying useful distances out to sea, but its pilots were completely untrained in the delicate art of maritime patrol with its special navigational skills, ship-recognition requirements and tactics.

These USAAF aircraft were not equipped for communication with ships and completely untutored in co-operation with the rival service.

King replied bleakly to Andrews on New Year's Day, accepting his subordinate's hopeless assessment but offering no comfort or reinforcements: no ships of any kind could be detached from the US Fleet for anti-submarine work. Andrews kept up the correspondence on January 14 by asking for at least one squadron of naval patrol aircraft to add to his scratch reconnaissance force of one unarmed Coastguard plane, two bombers, a few scouts and two airships. A handful of aircraft was transferred from the Atlantic Fleet but made little difference. The Fleet itself had only thirty Catalinas, and Andrews had no aircraft capable of talking to a ship. Such Atlantic Fleet planes as were made available were provided only on an "emergency" basis, which meant irregularly, in small numbers and for short periods. Meanwhile, as the latest aircraft were being used ashore to train new pilots, experienced men such as Coastguard fliers helping the Navy were given outdated and all but useless machines. There was also an acute shortage of sonar, guns, depth-charges and machine-guns. It was Britain, 1939, all over again, and in some respects even worse.

It was soon to be 1940 again, if in reverse. Admiral Pound, the First Sea Lord, came over with Churchill in mid-December and spent five weeks looking at means of stepping up co-operation with the new ally. Mindful of the debt owed to the Americans while still neutral for both the destroyers-for-bases deal and much help with the convoys (to say nothing of Lend–Lease), Pound reflected upon the Royal Navy's overstretched resources and decided he could offer ten corvettes and twenty-four anti-submarine trawlers. King accepted and assigned the latter to the Eastern Sea Frontier. The Air Ministry could not (of course) be persuaded to provide any aircraft, even from those being built in the United States. Eventually, however, Coastal Command managed to send a squadron to fly from a base in Rhode Island in June and later, when the submarine offensive moved south, from Trinidad, then a British colony but strategically part of the North American defences.

It was not until March 19 that Pound directly told King of the "urgency" which he attached to the need for convoys in US waters. Churchill supported his First Sea Lord with a parallel plea to Roosevelt, who blandly suggested a further reduction in British imports, already cut to the bone. It was then King opined that "inadequately escorted convoys are worse than none." In the same month, Captain G. E. Creasy, RN, Director of Anti-Submarine Warfare at the Admiralty, accompanied by a senior Coastal Command officer, arrived in the United States to advise the Americans how to follow British examples. At this time Pound also called for a review of the entire British experience of anti-submarine warfare. The ensuing staff-report set down four principal lessons: hunting groups were useless; aircraft cover for convoys was invaluable; training and tactics were crucial; radar was essential. But it seemed that nothing could persuade King to deviate from a course which forced the US Navy to make all the mistakes already regretted by the British, albeit in a rather shorter period – not excluding the spectacularly ineffective deployment of Q-ships to lure hardened German submarine-commanders into a "trap" of no value in unrestricted warfare.

By the middle of February the Atlantic Fleet began to divert destroyers to the Eastern Frontier for a few days at a time. They came however from convoy duty on the North Atlantic route, which meant that they were short of supplies and ignorant of local conditions. Andrews promptly asked for fifteen to be attached permanently to his command; but King, hamstrung by lack of numbers, pointed out that "more destroyers on our coastal sealanes mean less on the trade routes to England." Unquestionably true; but the same ships that were being successfully escorted across the ocean were being abandoned, often quite literally, within sight of shore. While the British eventually went so far as to slow down the convoy cycle sufficiently to release two escort-groups for work in US waters, other remedies do not appear to have been adequately explored. Meanwhile a force of enemy submarines which in the previous phase of the campaign might have been gathered into a single pack for an attack on one convoy were wreaking terrible destruction in waters full of ships but virtually undefended.

Yet to conclude that King was opposed to convoy *as such* during this period is an oversimplification and unjust. He simply believed it to be impossible with his contemporary resources, sincerely taking the view that a weak escort was worse, not better, than nothing. Seen from the other side of the Atlantic, however, the shepherds who had been able to conduct their maritime flocks through the wolf-packs into the safe enclosure of the US security zone found after US entry into the war that their precious charges were being abandoned to the predators at the end of their journey.

The Eastern Sea Frontier Diary refutes the suggestion that King was opposed to convoy or did not understand its importance, or else had to be converted by months of enormous losses to seeing the light. It records an order from King to Andrews as early as February 12 to submit a plan for a convoy system, hardly the action of an unbeliever. Andrews consulted the commandants of the naval districts within his Frontier and found them unanimously opposed to the introduction of convoy for the same reason as King: present forces were hopelessly inadequate. They now consisted of nine vessels faster than fourteen knots and nineteen of twelve to fourteen knots capable of escort work, plus three of dubious value. Using them with convoys would mean denuding harbours and coastal sea-lanes of protection (an argument which shows a classic misconception of the value of convoy: the proper place for protective forces, *especially* when they are small, is with the ships they are supposed to protect). There were no long-range aircraft available apart from a handful of naval bombers temporarily based at Norfolk, Virginia. Andrews therefore replied to his chief with the recommendation that "no attempt be made to protect coastwise shipping by a convoy system until an adequate number of suitable escort-vessels is available." Thus when King reacted stonily to British pleas for convoy he was not a colossus standing alone against reason but was accurately reflecting opinion throughout his beloved Navy. Unfortunately he could not bring himself to accept the argument that any escort was better than none, perhaps because it came from the British Navy whose superiority in any respect, including knowledge based on experience, he was temperamentally unable to accept. In the end, as his own side began to despair, King was forced by events to take the measures the British had been pressing for.

But not before the most extraordinary expedients had been tried by US naval commanders whose policy seemed to be anything *but* convoy. As some ships' crews began to rebel in New York harbour against taking their vessels to sea because of the horrendous losses, the authorities ordered shipping to make maximum use of inland waterways, canals, rivers and passages between offshore islands and the coast. Elsewhere the ships were to sail as close to shore as possible, passing through dangerous waters by day and going into harbour by night. This system was christened "the Bucket Brigade" by Admiral Andrews on the analogy of passing buckets of water from hand to hand to fight a blaze. Coastal lanes were marked out by buoys and all shipping told to adhere to them (German submarine captains reported to Dönitz how ships would sail in straight lines from buoy to buoy, which was most convenient for aiming purposes). Such protective forces as were available were concentrated on these lanes. The response to submarine sightings (most of which were false) was to send everything on hand to the reported spot to hunt the enemy, a fundamental error so painfully unlearned by the British and now gratuitously copied by their new ally. History was repeating itself, not as farce but as tragedy.

If the Ship Lane Patrol system was ineffectual, the Coastal Picket Patrol was dangerously counter-productive. It consisted of private yachtsmen turned temporary petty officers in the Coastguard who formed a chain of floating lookouts in their own boats some fifty miles out to sea. The Coastguard tried to pass off this collection of untrained amateur submarine-hunters as the "Corsair Fleet" in its publicity material, but it was soon branded the "Hooligan Navy." One of its members was Ernest Hemingway in his yacht *Pilar* (named after a character in *For Whom the Bell Tolls*), complete with machine-gun, hunting-rifle, pistol and hand-grenades. No submarine commander was rash (or unkind) enough to ring his bell, and his dream of lobbing grenades into an open conning-tower was never realised. The Hooligans were responsible for untold numbers of false submarine sightings, which led to frenetic and exhausting diversions of Andrew's puny forces. If the Hooligan Navy was a threat to its own side the Civil Air Patrol was a rather more practical idea. Private pilots in their own aircraft could use their eyes to some effect after elementary instruction in what to look for, which included survivors as well as submarines. Eventually the CAP was made an auxiliary of the Army Air Force and some of its larger aircraft were issued with a depth-charge or bomb with simple sight. It was diverted to other work in autumn 1943, at which time the Hooligan Navy was abolished.

Among other more or less desperate ruses tried during the East Coast crisis was Project LQ, a top secret plan to send out three "mystery" or Q-ships. As mentioned above, the Germans were far too canny to be caught by this First World War ruse and a quarter of the Americans briefly engaged in it before it was abandoned lost their lives, a total of 141 men. It was in its small way the most self-destructive operation undertaken by the US Navy in the war. Observers were also put aboard hundreds of fishing vessels plying the coasts of the Eastern Sea Frontier. As professionals the fishermen were rather more reliable than the Hooligans at sea; unfortunately, they took the view that their business was fishing, not chasing Germans, and their contribution was not of measurable value. Understandably they feared that a radio report of a sighting would invite destruction by the submarine, with the result that their reports were so delayed as to be useless even if they were accurate.

That Andrews was no more opposed to the principle of convoy than King was shown by his decision in February to institute coastal convoys as soon as possible. Schedules began to be prepared for fast and slow convoys along the East Coast and it was calculated that sixty-four escorts were required for effective protection. Once again, however, it was a case of all or nothing: either no convoys at all or a complete, properly escorted convoy system (what constituted "adequate" escort was not Mosaic law but rather a matter of opinion within generous limits – a trained escort-group of four ships was worth more than an untrained one of eight). The Americans clearly set their standards too high, failing to meet a major emergency by doing the best they could as soon as they could, which is what the British did. At the same time it has to be remembered that the shipping under attack was not of vital importance to the survival of the United States in the way it was to Britain's; and that the US Navy, already deeply embroiled in the Pacific after severe losses there, had to defend a coastline which ran from Newfoundland to Brazil. But it is not at all difficult to understand British dismay at the American lack of preparedness for anti-submarine warfare after all the information which had been passed westward across the Atlantic.

British anxiety about the failure of the Americans to start convoys at once (King rejected a joint convoy-control system for the entire Atlantic, proposed by the Admiralty, on February 3) was increased by the fact that there was no attempt to impose a blackout on the East Coast. When this elementary precaution was mooted, places like Atlantic City, New Jersey, and the Florida resorts complained of the effect it would have on tourism. As a result the submarines' plethora of targets was lit up at night from behind, offering sharp silhouettes to shoot at. While merchantmen were still sailing at night, residents all along the American coast from New Jersey to Miami were likely to be presented round the clock with the spectacular but sinister sight of ships, especially tankers, the principal targets of the Germans, blazing fiercely out to sea.

Not that the Germans limited themselves to night attacks or to the easiest targets. At dawn on February 28 the destroyer *Jacob Jones* (Lieutenant-Commander Hugh Black, USN) was hit and sunk by two torpedoes from *U578* (Commander Ernst-August Rehwinkel) in sight of the coast of New Jersey. The warship had just left New York after repairs and was beginning a temporary detachment from the Atlantic Fleet to the Eastern Frontier. Despite the presence nearby of the destroyer *Dickerson*, all but eleven of the crew were lost. It was the first loss of a warship in the Frontier area and it prompted Admiral King to order more allocations of warships to Andrews but not, as yet, permanently; nor was a coastal convoy system deemed practicable at this stage. At the beginning of March a daily average of two destroyers from the Atlantic Fleet's notional stock of seventy-five was available to the Frontier on an ad hoc basis. Admiral R. E. Ingersoll, King's successor as CINCLANT, having been obliged to send so many ships to the Pacific, could do little more than this, even though the transatlantic convoy route was almost eerily quiet during this period. The sinking of the *Jacob Jones* was thus a bitter blow; even more galling however was the attack on the *Dickerson* on March 18 by the American merchantman SS *Liberator*, which identified her as a submarine. The destroyer managed to limp into Norfolk, Virginia, badly damaged by shellfire. The *Liberator* was less fortunate, being sunk by *U332* the next day.

On March 6 King once again postponed the introduction of coastal convoys until "enough" escorts were available, but at least the staff work was intensifying. Ten days later he called a conference of the commanders of the Eastern, Gulf and Caribbean Sea Frontiers to prepare for a convoy system from the Caribbean to Boston and beyond. The admirals concluded that six escort-groups would be needed – four at sea and one at each end lying over for three days. For this seventy-eight escorts were now, perhaps rather arbitrarily, held to be necessary: thirty-one destroyers and forty-seven corvettes or equivalent. A more than useful start could have been made with half these numbers, even allowing for training, repairs, reserves and crew leave. In the three Frontiers of the eastern seaboard there were present three temporarily detached destroyers, no corvettes, three patrol-craft and five "submarine-chasers." The latter were of a small type to be used by another scratch force nicknamed the "Donald Duck Navy," for which a crash building-programme was to be launched in April: "Sixty Ships in Sixty Days." The contrast between the ideal and the actual as set down in Eastern's diary could hardly be more marked, yet it is completely artificial because no one asked whether extra resources could be diverted from elsewhere. By the end of March fourteen of the promised two dozen anti-submarine trawlers had arrived from Britain, with the rest and the ten corvettes soon to follow; and at the end of March fifteen coastal patrol aircraft were added to Eastern's forces, with fifty-five to follow. It was perhaps a measure of how seriously the American crisis was taken in Britain that these aircraft had been prised from the grasp of the Air Ministry, for which they had been built in the United States.

Although the Eastern Sea Frontier bore the main burden of *Paukenschlag*, the presence of the commanders of the two Frontiers to the south at Admiral King's meeting underlines the fact that Dönitz was spreading his attack as widely as possible. The number of boats available had not risen because of conflicting demands for them elsewhere. Hitler on January 25 heartily congratulated Dönitz on the initial, spectacular success of the operation – and in the next breath ordered him both to maintain maximum pressure on the Americans and to send eight submarines to patrol the Iceland–Faroes–Scotland area. Hitler had suddenly taken it into his head that the British would soon make a second serious attempt to invade Norway, where twelve submarines were already on permanent guard-duty. Dönitz protested to Raeder in vain, but Hitler's obsession with Norway was not a fervid aberration. There had been various pinprick raids by the British in 1941, and by April 1942 Churchill himself was seriously considering a new landing in strength. He was only dissuaded by his chiefs of staff and by the Allied commitment to the Mediterranean as the necessary prelude to an assault on Europe.

In order, therefore, to disrupt the Americans and keep them off balance for as long as possible with his small forces, Dönitz switched the focus of his attack to the Caribbean a month after *Paukenschlag* was launched. Operation *Neuland* was no less devastating, opening with an attack on the oil refinery at Aruba in the Netherlands Antilles by *Kapitänleutnant* Werner Hartenstein in *U156*. He crept into the port on the island of Curaçao at dead of night and fired shells and tracer-bullets at the oil-tanks. The burning fuel spread over the water and blazed for hours, while out at sea three other submarines sank a total of seven tankers in the area on the same night (February 16 to 17). By the end of the month another ten ships, nearly all tankers, were sunk in the region.

A week later the Germans moved north again to the south-eastern US coast for more attacks on coastal traffic while one or two submarines kept up the pressure in the Caribbean with attacks on Trinidad, the Bahamas and other islands in and around the West Indies and the Gulf of Mexico. Small wonder that the Americans thought there were hundreds of submarines at work. They were now being introduced to rationing, first of rubber and petroleum products and then of other items, even coffee, made scarce by Japanese conquests and German sinkings. Any inclination by the British to strip transatlantic convoys of escorts to go to the American coast was deterred by Dönitz's occasional assembly of a wolf-pack against a convoy, notably on February 24, when four boats attacked the westbound ON67 with its American escort off Newfoundland and sank six ships. The Americans gained some consolation in March when their airmen based in Newfoundland sank a submarine on the 1st and another on the 15th, the first "kills" of the war by US forces.

Regardless of the remarkable score of sinkings in the western Atlantic, this was still a time of frustration as well as success for Dönitz because he knew better than anyone what might be achieved by a real concentration of boats in the area, before the Americans inevitably put up a proper defence. But if he could not realistically hope to get more boats in place, how could he increase the effectiveness of the few he had when they took so long to travel to and fro for such a short operational period? Dönitz, now at the height of his powers, using his gift for opportunism to cause maximum disarray among Germany's newly reinforced enemies with a minimum number of submarines, already had the answer and was on the point of putting it into effect. But before considering the second phase of the American coastal campaign, we ought to return eastward across the Atlantic. In Britain the entry of the United States into the war as a fighting ally caused only momentary cheer as a series of setbacks plunged the embattled island into new depths of gloom.

As we saw at the end of the last chapter, the Royal Navy, seriously over-stretched as it was, still had to keep in mind the German surface forces, distributed between Norway and France. We also know that Hitler thought "every ship that is not in Norway is in the wrong place." The Admiralty agreed with the Germans on this point: Brest, where the *Scharnhorst*, *Gneisenau* and *Prinz Eugen* still lay idle, was so close to Britain that they were virtually at the disposal of the RAF for bombing-practice. The British therefore fully expected the two battlecruisers and the heavy cruiser to make a run north. They also expected the Germans to take the short route, straight up the Channel; the alternative, to sail round the British Isles, would have taken so much longer that the higher intensity of the risk attached to the Channel option was well worth the huge reduction in exposure to all manner of attacks on the longer route. The British even got so far as to cater for the anticipated breakout by drawing up a counter-plan codenamed "Fuller," whereby the Navy and RAF would seek to frustrate it. British submarines kept watch on Brest; RAF reconnaissance aircraft flew over regularly; agents ashore reported any development in the French port. Light naval forces were earmarked for hit-and-run attacks while air squadrons were chosen to make torpedo raids or provide fighter-cover. The torpedo-bomber squadron kept in Scotland against a sortie by the *Tirpitz* and other major German units was to be ready to come south in reinforcement at short notice. Such heavy aircraft as RAF Bomber Command was prepared to divert to raids on Brest had done limited damage, though enough to defer a breakout more than once, which was precisely why the Germans were convinced of the need for one as soon as possible.

Their codename for the undertaking was "Operation *Cerberus*." The German Naval Command was reluctant when the idea of the breakout was first mooted in the latter part of 1941, but Hitler's preoccupation with Norway and his repeated threat to scrap the Brest squadron or at least remove its big guns for the defence of the Norwegian coast left Raeder and his admirals with no choice. By accepting the high risk of the run north, they could at least hope to keep their main surface striking-power intact if all went well. Hitler's wish to have their guns available to defend Norway could be met by delivering them still attached to the hulls. Hitler finally accepted the risks and even demanded that the breakout go ahead as soon as possible at a meeting with Raeder on 29 December 1941.

Planning was already far advanced under Admiral Alfred Saalwächter, commander of Navy Group West which covered France and adjacent waters from its headquarters in Paris. This intellectual Prussian staff officer and First World War submariner, author of an officers' manual on naval warfare, was well qualified to draw up an unimpeachable plan. He prepared an elaborate operation involving minesweepers along the route, destroyers as escorts, 250 fighters provided by Colonel Adolf Galland, the leading Luftwaffe ace, fast, small craft, and moored trawlers as marker-boats. Saalwächter's main concern was to achieve surprise, which seemed impossible given the proximity of Britain, enemy reconnaissance and the lack of searoom in the waters concerned. He achieved it by out-thinking the British. The Admiralty assumed that the Germans would want to have the cover of darkness for the most hazardous part of the journey, through the Dover Strait, little more than twenty miles wide at its narrowest point. This entailed a departure from Brest by day. Saalwächter however took the view that his only hope of catching an enemy with potential local superiority of force off guard was to use darkness to cover the departure from Brest. If he could conceal the breakout in this way, he would deprive the British of time to assemble attacking forces, especially capital ships which were the greatest threat but also the slowest. Every undetected mile of progress towards the Strait increased the chance of success. He therefore planned to move the squadron through the night so that it reached the limit of British land-based radar-cover only at sunrise, by which time the ships would be vulnerable to visual reconnaissance wherever they were. On this basis, the fact that the squadron, if it kept to time, would pass Calais at high noon made no material difference. The ships would come under the command of German Naval Group North as they moved out of Belgian waters into Dutch, passing the Netherlands naval base of Den Helder at 7 p.m. and reaching the Elbe River in north Germany at 3 a.m. the next day. In all, the run home was calculated to last thirty hours.

To cover the increasingly frantic and complex preparations for the great breakout, Commodore Friedrich Ruge, in charge of all minesweepers along the projected route, organised the most intricate pattern of sweeps to prevent anyone, including his own captains and crews, from grasping the connection between them. Galland put his three groups of aircraft through rehearsals, telling his pilots that they were going to provide cover for a convoy with a vital cargo that was to pass through the Channel "from north-east to south-west." To the British the activity looked at first like training exercises. On the battered capital ships the crews and nearly all the officers were kept in the dark for the same reasons of security. Piles of tropical equipment were ostentatiously loaded aboard. Thirty senior officers in the squadron were sent engraved invitations to a dinner with Saalwächter on February 11 (the evening chosen for the breakout) in Paris, to be followed by a shoot outside the city the next day.

In command at sea was Vice-Admiral Otto Ciliax as Flag Officer of the squadron. Tall, black-haired and unpopular for his authoritarian ways, Ciliax was nicknamed "the Black Tsar" and was notorious for perpetrating an unprecedented naval solecism. On his flagship *Scharnhorst*, of which he had once been captain, he had his admiral's bridge installed *above* Captain Kurt Hoffmann's navigational one, the reverse of the universal practice. Etiquette (and common sense) required an admiral to leave the running of his flagship to her captain but Ciliax frequently interfered. He was totally opposed to the breakout when told of it on New Year's Day but like the rest of the naval command was forced to come to terms with Hitler's demand, reiterated at a conference with the admirals concerned in the "Wolf's Lair" headquarters in Rastenburg, East Prussia. The Führer confidently predicted that the first attempt by an enemy of Britain to pass a fleet through the English Channel since the Spanish Armada in 1588 would be Germany's "most spectacular naval success of the war."

The three big ships were to be accompanied by six destroyers already in Brest, the 2nd Torpedo-boat Flotilla from Le Havre, the 3rd from Dunkirk and the 5th from Flushing in the Netherlands (five boats each), plus three flotillas of ten E-boats each (fast attack craft). These would form an inner and an outer ring of escorts. The Luftwaffe put three officers on the *Scharnhorst* to help direct the fighter-screen, which would be made up of a series of formations relieving each other and circling overhead from successive air-fields as the ships moved north-east.

By February 2 the British were convinced of the imminence of a breakout by mid-month (before the new moon on the 16th and while the tides were favourable), and they had little doubt that it would involve an attempt to force the Channel. But both Navy and RAF still believed the Straits of Dover would be passed in darkness. On February 8 Air Chief Marshal Sir Philip Joubert, head of Coastal Command, predicted a breakout two days later or very shortly thereafter. His aircraft had spotted the concentrations of destroyers and smaller vessels, the increase in minesweeping activity and movements suggestive of trials by the three large ships.

This incisive forecast remained curiously unsupported by preventive action. There was no immediate concentration of torpedo-bombers in southeast England as had been envisaged for the time when the run for home by the Germans looked imminent. Vice-Admiral Bertram Ramsay, Flag Officer at Dover, was not significantly reinforced; he had six destroyers plus light craft on hand, but these were all decisively outclassed by their German contemporaries. The Home Fleet stayed in Scapa Flow at the other end of the country, worrying about the newly commissioned *Tirpitz*, in Norwegian waters since late January. The Admiralty moved a half-squadron of Fleet Air Arm Swordfish torpedo-bombers to the Channel coast, sent six extra elderly destroyers to Harwich on the English east coast and alerted a handful of motor-torpedo-boats. Three submarines were sent to watch for a breakout.

This lacklustre response accurately reflected the condition of the Royal Navy after two and a half years of war, of which the last two months had been a catalogue of unrelieved disaster. It also reflected the exhaustion of Sir Dudley Pound, the 65-year-old First Sea Lord, who did not even have a deputy. Sceptical about the general Admiralty and RAF assessment that the Germans would try to force the Channel, he forbade a southerly countermove by the Home Fleet. Once that decision to avoid risking his few serviceable capital ships was taken, his assertion that the Navy had done all it could to prepare for the "Channel Dash" was essentially true. There were no more destroyers or submarines available because of losses and other faraway commitments. But the fast minelayer HMS *Welshman* prudently sowed 1,000 mines in the approaches to Boulogne in the Channel and the RAF dropped ninety-eight more off the Dutch Friesian Islands, which the Germans would have to pass on their way home. Joubert had three squadrons of Beaufort torpedo-bombers based in Cornwall, near Portsmouth, and at Leuchars in Scotland respectively. He ordered the latter to Norfolk in eastern England but bad weather and lax preparation on the ground delayed it by four days. Co-ordination among these scratch British forces was at best tenuous.

The first of several remarkable strokes of good fortune for the Germans was a raid by RAF Bomber Command Wellingtons on Brest on the evening of the 11th, just as the ships were getting ready to leave "on exercise," as their crews had been told. Although this routine raid damaged none of the ships, it held up their departure by nearly two hours (sixteen minutes more would automatically have aborted *Cerberus* as the operational order decreed because there would have been no safety margin left); the customary photographs taken by the bombing force however showed the German ships in port as usual when the RAF developed them during the night. But by then they had left Brest for ever, *Scharnhorst* leading, followed by *Gneisenau* and then *Prinz Eugen* with close escort in attendance.

The squadron was only one hour and twelve minutes behind schedule at midnight, when it sailed past Ushant, the island at the tip of Brittany and the designated point of no return. It was then that Ciliax told the sailors over the linked-up public-address systems of the three ships that they were going home. As the Germans pounded along at twenty-seven knots their elaborate arrangements for navigating a tricky course by radar collapsed: it was an art whose time had not quite come. This meant that the ships had to pass through the narrow channels cleared by Ruge's minesweepers by dead reckoning, a most stressful ordeal for those few in the know.

The second stroke of luck for the Germans was a series of electronic and mechanical failures on three RAF night radar-patrol aircraft which thus completely missed the squadron. By daybreak it had been at sea for some eight hours, wholly undetected, and was barely a quarter of an hour behind schedule after sailing 250 miles. The third of fortune's gifts to the Germans was a steady deterioration in the weather with rain and low cloud, fulfilling an unusually accurate weather forecast on which the decision to set sail had in part been based.

Before we stop counting these strokes of luck we may note the fourth: the daytime RAF reconnaissance patrol, flown by single Spitfires, spotted light German craft coming out of Boulogne to join the escort. As E-boats were common enough in the Channel the pilot was not suspicious; there was no clue that the battle-squadron was concealed by the bank of low cloud just a few minutes' flying-time to the south-west. Inexplicably, the patrol had not been alerted to the possibility of a German breakout or even told about "Fuller." Brilliant and carefully planned German jamming interfered with most of the British radar-chain covering the Channel, but the latest sets with the shortest wavelengths, of a type unknown to the Germans, began to pick up small swarms of aircraft flying in circles which were moving north-east at twenty-eight knots. The first alarm was therefore sounded by Squadron-Leader Bill Igoe, the controller on duty at the Biggin Hill fighter-airfield which had been in the thick of the Battle of Britain. He told headquarters of Number 11 Group, Fighter Command by telephone: "I think it's 'Fuller'!" and sent up two Spitfires from 91 Squadron at nearby Hawkinge. The Germans had been at sea for eleven hours. Two more Spitfires went up from RAF Kenley on a routine patrol at about the same time without any inkling of unusual events in the Channel. Visibility was poor.

The pair from Hawkinge sighted the three big ships at about 10.40 a.m. Even though they came under heavy anti-aircraft fire the pilots assumed the ships were British and must have been firing at some German Messerschmitt 109s which the Spitfires had just been forced to sidestep. The pair from Kenley arrived at the spot, saw the German ships and dived almost to sea-level for a closer look, unaware of the Hawkinge Spitfires which had almost attacked them by mistake. The Kenley pilots, who knew about Fuller, obeyed the standing order imposing strict radio silence "except in an emergency" and flew back to base to make their report in person later. The Hawkinge pair, having now recognised the ships as German, were not in on the Fuller secret but decided to break the silence-rule. They reported "three large German ships . . . escorted by twenty-plus craft . . . heading towards Dover" to Biggin Hill and flew home. The *B-dienst* picked up the report and relayed it to Galland at his temporary headquarters at Le Touquet; Ciliax and his crews braced themselves for a massive British attack.

For more than an hour nothing happened. Local RAF commanders wanted confirmation of the single positive sighting before launching Fuller. Nobody had the nerve to interrupt the Air Officer Commanding Number 11 Group, Air Vice-Marshal Trafford Leigh-Mallory, who was inspecting Free Belgian airmen at Northolt, west of London, despite urgent pleas to his staff. He was "on parade." His headquarters refused a request from the Navy at Dover for a confirmatory reconnaissance. On the ground, the pilots from Hawkinge at last confirmed the sighting and the information was passed to Dover – via Portsmouth because of a defective telephone line! Admiral Ramsay's air-liaison officer, though only holding the usual rank for such a post of Wing Commander, had the moral courage to order Lieutenant-Commander Eugene Esmonde to prepare an attack from Manston airfield in Kent with his six obsolete Swordfish torpedo-bombers.

As the Germans entered the narrowest part of the Channel behind a screen of ten destroyers, flanked by fifteen torpedo-boats and thirty E-boats, every man was at action stations. It was just after noon, they were on time and tension was at its height. The ships were making thirty knots. The first sign of a British response was a series of misses from the heavy guns of the coastal artillery: it was the British Army that got in the first shot, which exploded in the wake of the *Prinz Eugen*. A mist now came down to obscure the German squadron as the Wehrmacht's long guns on the other side of the water opened fire on the British emplacements. Neither side scored a hit.

The first attack by the Royal Navy was led by Lieutenant-Commander Nigel Pumphrey with five motor-torpedo-boats, briefly supported by two motor-gunboats. These tiny vessels were prevented from getting close to the capital ships by the powerful escort, causing their torpedoes to miss after a brief running battle. Next into the attack was Esmonde with his six fabric-bodied biplanes, capable of no more than ninety knots. Admiral Ramsay intervened with the Admiralty in an attempt to save them (they were meant to make a night-attack) but the First Sea Lord, Sir Dudley Pound, overruled him. Ramsay could not however bring himself to issue the order for what all concerned knew would be a suicidal mission. In leaving the decision to Esmonde, decorated by King George VI only the previous day with the Distinguished Service Order (Britain's second-highest gallantry award) for his dashing attack on the *Bismarck*, Ramsay must have known that there could be only one response. Esmonde duly led his six "stringbags" with their crews of three into the attack at 12.25 p.m. Five squadrons of Spitfires had been ordered to cover them; only one found them.

Seen from the ships of the mighty German battlefleet with its heavy air and surface escort, Esmonde's forlorn assault looked exactly like a suicide attack. The best efforts of just ten Spitfires could not fend off the swooping Luftwaffe fighters and the ships fired a hail of anti-aircraft shot, also using their big guns to send up columns of spray in the path of the lumbering Swordfish as they came in only a few feet above the surface. All six were lost without scoring a hit; five men out of eighteen miraculously survived, picked up by the MTBs which were still in the area. Esmonde was not among them.

The third and last British naval attack on the Germans was led by Captain Mark Pizey, RN, commanding the destroyers from Harwich. Ironically they had been stood down the day before from the highest state of readiness and were already at sea on their way back to Sheerness in Kent. The confusion which had lamed the British response from the very beginning, fuelled by doubt, defective equipment and almost unrelieved incompetence, left Pizey with no alternative but to head straight through Britain's own coastal mine-fields. By the time he was given an accurate appreciation of the Germans' course and speed from the Admiralty there was no time to go round them. One of his six ships fell out with engine trouble, but twelve more destroyers were ordered out of harbours further south to run north and try to join him. Having taken the dangerous but praiseworthy decision to ignore the mines on his own responsibility, Pizey was justly rewarded by passing through the fields unharmed.

As Pizey heaved a sigh of relief, the *Scharnhorst* hit a British mine off the mouth of the Scheldt near Flushing and her engines stopped. The rest of the squadron, under orders not to stop in any circumstances, raced by as Admiral Ciliax and his staff made the perilous transfer to the bucketing destroyer Z29 which had come alongside on his instructions. Four torpedo-boats stood by as the *Scharnhorst's* crew inspected the damage. Two outer compartments in the double hull were flooded and there was a large hole on the starboard side, but the inner hull held and the engines were undamaged: they had stopped only because ancillary equipment had been temporarily paralysed by the shock of the explosion. This made Ciliax look rather foolish, a fact which caused the crew of his flagship no pain. Captain Hoffmann was soon able to get his lightly wounded ship up to twenty-seven knots. The rest of the force was now half an hour ahead.

The RAF in the end sent up 675 aircraft to make countless uncoordinated attacks on the German squadron and its fighter escort. Torpedo-bombers, fighters and bombers of all the main types flying did some damage to the Luftwaffe but none to the German ships, although they mistakenly attacked Pizey's little flotilla. At 3.17 p.m. his destroyers at last sighted the *Gneisenau* and *Prinz Eugen* off the Hook of Holland. He launched a determined torpedo attack under the vastly superior gun-power of the Germans as a huge and completely chaotic air-battle built up overhead. One of the destroyers, *Worcester*, was crippled but managed to stay afloat and escape. No torpedo found its mark.

As darkness fell and the Germans passed along the Dutch west coast, the three big ships were out of sight of each other after the long series of British air and destroyer attacks. The *Scharnhorst* was catching up. Just before 8 p.m. the *Gneisenau* was damaged by a British mine off the Dutch Friesian island of Terschelling. She was able to sail on with some of her equipment out of action. Two hours later the *Scharnhorst* was hit by her second mine in the same area and once again her engines went dead. In just over half an hour she was able to muster twelve knots. Ciliax, still aboard a destroyer after the first mine, was under the impression his flagship had sunk after losing touch. Eventually he found her and the two ships headed slowly for the Elbe. The *Gneisenau* and *Prinz Eugen*, still together, got there first in the early hours of February 13 – only to find that no arrangements had been made to help them into port. This extraordinary lapse was a truly bathetic ending to one of the most spectacular escapes in naval history, the well-earned result of brilliant planning and a classic illustration of the adage that fortune favours the brave. But the luck ran out with the planning. After being made to wait until dawn for tugs, icebreakers and a pilot, the *Gneisenau* was caught by a powerful tide as she edged towards the entrance to Brunsbüttel harbour and driven onto a submerged wreck. This severely compounded the moderate damage sustained from the British mine. The *Scharnhorst* arrived in the roadstead later in the morning – to be told there were no tugs available. Hoffmann coolly took his damaged ship into the harbour unaided, without scraping the paint. Only the *Prinz Eugen* completed the Channel Dash without a scratch. The price to the Germans of the whole breathtaking enterprise amounted to seventeen aircraft lost, two torpedo-boats damaged and two men dead. Hitler was triumphant.

The Times thundered: "Vice-Admiral Ciliax had succeeded where the Duke of Medina-Sidonia failed. Nothing more mortifying to the pride of our seapower has happened since the seventeenth century" (in 1667 the Dutch Admiral M. A. de Ruyter sailed up the River Medway, attacked the English Fleet at anchor and stole its flagship). Accurately reflecting British public opinion, the London *Daily Mail* wrote: "[The escape] is symptomatic of the general feeling that there is something wrong with Britain's war-direction and this feeling is crystallised in an almost universal demand for removal from high places of the tired and the incompetent."

When Pound telephoned Churchill to tell him that the Germans had got away, the Prime Minister barked, "Why?" and slammed down the instrument. Faced with the same allegation of "bungling in high places" which forced him out of the Admiralty in the First World War, an angry but also alarmed Churchill took a unique step: he appointed a High Court judge,

Mr Justice Bucknill, to investigate a lost battle in the middle of a war. This gesture had the predictable result. With its inadequate powers the tribunal of judge, admiral and air-marshal set sail on a sea of whitewash and duly foundered. In one of the great understatements of all time it concluded that "co-ordination was not entirely successful." Several critics of the official cover-up were also posted to faraway places. A shower of medals rained down upon the many individuals who had shown remarkable personal gallantry to no avail because they were so poorly led. The highest of all, a posthumous Victoria Cross, went to the bravest, Commander Esmonde.

In Germany the escape of the Brest squadron was naturally hailed as a mighty blow against the enemy who had ruled the waves for centuries. Ciliax was awarded the Knight's Cross but was universally reviled in the Navy for abandoning his flagship without cause. Hoffmann rather more deservingly received the same award. Captain Otto Fein of the *Gneisenau* who had actually led the squadron while both its admiral and its flagship were missing, was disgracefully ignored, presumably for his misfortune in hitting the wreck after it was all over. Ten days after reaching port unscathed, the *Prinz Eugen* (Captain Hellmuth Brinkmann) was torpedoed outside Trondheim, Norway, by the British submarine *Trident* (Commander G. M. Sladen, RN). She managed to make harbour with a severely damaged stern but took no further part in the war. At the end of the month the vengeful RAF completely crippled the *Gneisenau* in three nights of bombing. She too was never seen on the open sea again. She suffered the ultimate humiliation of being sunk as a blockship in the Baltic at the end of the war. *Prinz Eugen* was used as a target and sunk in the nuclear tests at Bikini in 1948. The *Scharnhorst* needed six months to recover and later took part in the last battleship duel ever fought, an event which will be described in its place.

The British may have been humiliated at sea as never before, but the "fleet in being" which they had been forced to cover for so long had gone from France, leaving Norway as the one place from which a surface threat could now come. The only properly thought-out British measure against the breakout was the last-minute minelaying at two points, well chosen because unavoidable, along the correctly predicted route. It was only later that this was seen to have had much of the desired effect. The Germans naturally hailed the Channel Dash as an operational and psychological triumph over the Royal Navy, but Admiral Raeder, the German C-in-C, was more honest and realistic: "It was a tactical success but a strategic defeat." In that sense, if in no other, it was the Second World War's nearest approximation to the Battle of Jutland in the First.

This British victory, even though it looked remarkably like a reverse at the time, once again showed Hitler's incomprehension of naval strategy. It has been described in detail here because it also exposed the organisational weaknesses which still bedevilled the British war-effort. This chapter opened with the Americans' tragic error over convoys, but they were new to the conflict whereas the British had been at war for two and a half years. Their sailors and airmen had saved the country from a stronger enemy as the population at large endured bombing, privation and unprecedented regulation. But there were still too many in positions of authority who were so incompetent as to be "a danger to the Empire" (as Churchill himself was described by a vengeful admiral in the First World War) and to call its very survival into question. These failures contrasted starkly both with Churchill's own stature as the national symbol of defiance and with the extraordinary individual bravery of men like Esmonde and so many others.

But the Channel Dash, which laid bare some of these weaknesses, was a mere public-relations embarrassment compared with what happened four days later. On February 15 the British Army surrendered Singapore, linchpin of the Empire in the Far East, to the Japanese in one of the most ingnominious fiascos of modern military history. That episode does not belong here; suffice it to say that it did more than anything else to make this black February of 1942 the lowest point in the entire war for Great Britain. And there was no Dunkirk or Battle of Britain to relieve the despondency nor any discernible gain from American intervention – on the contrary.

Churchill had made a remarkably swift recovery from a mild stroke he suffered in Washington at the turn of the year, but no sooner was he back in London in mid-January than the bad news began to flow in from the western Atlantic, from the Channel and the Far East and from the hard-pressed British Army in North Africa.

Had Churchill, now sixty-seven years old, thrown in his hand at this point on grounds of ill health, it would have been not only understandable but also close to the truth. It would also have been precisely the kind of surrender of which Britain's pugnacious wartime leader was psychologically incapable. An uneasy British public was stuck with "Winnie" for better or for worse. And worse news for the desperate struggle in the Atlantic had already been revealed to the Prime Minister, if to few others, on the first day of the worst month.

The stream of enciphered information which sustained the German submarine effort – surely the most garrulous campaign ever fought – was intercepted by the British "Y" (interception) stations as gibberish and was passed on to Bletchley Park by the uncomprehending eavesdroppers. We have seen how the Enigma material was penetrated by using the *bombes* to attack the opening letters containing the daily settings, with help from captured material and educated guesswork. The Navy was always the most security-minded arm of the Wehrmacht and therefore made fewer revealing errors. On 1 February 1942 the submarine service was detached from the *Hydra* cipher of the Navy and given a new one called *Triton*, for use in traffic between HQ and boats in the Atlantic and the Mediterranean. For this a fourth wheel was added to the Enigma machine, making it twenty-six times harder to break into messages. The stream of priceless deciphered information, on which the Operational Intelligence Centre and Rodger Winn's Submarine Tracking Room had come to rely, dried up overnight.

For all the ensuing frustration at Bletchley Park, the setback did not come as a complete surprise. Even before the breakthrough in the assault of *Hydra* in May 1941 hints had been picked up from the occasional decrypted naval message that a fourth wheel might be added. In December it was discovered from the traffic that such a wheel was being issued to the submarines, and a four-wheel message sent on a trial run was, with superb efficiency, matched with the identical text enciphered on a three-wheel machine. This at least gave the cryptanalysts the wiring of the fourth wheel but, as detailed above, it was the setting of the wheels and not the mechanics of Enigma which was the true secret. When the blow fell, however, there were no four-wheel *bombes* with which to tackle the problem. This was not an example of the lack of foresight whose consequences have been described in the foregoing pages. For contemporary technology, despite the remarkable advances achieved in the forcing-house of war, the construction of a four-wheel *bombe* was a daunting undertaking requiring a large investment of time and expertise, both of which were in very short supply. It was not a problem of material or money. Bletchley Park was handling increasing quantities of German Army and Luftwaffe traffic from a constant proliferation of sources. The naval blackout did not affect its ability to penetrate other traffic, a fact which was one of its main consolations until four-wheel Enigma traffic could be read.

The British, though remarkably frank with the United States in many ways before it became a belligerent, had drawn the line at sharing their decipherment technique (but not the information it yielded) with a neutral power, however helpful and friendly. This meant that the British could not at first turn to American data-processing manufacturers for extra *bombes*. Britain's most expert electronics engineer in this uncharted field was put to work on the development of a four-wheel *bombe* in December 1941, when it became clear that the naval Enigma was about to be altered; but it was only when the blackout began that he was reinforced by other technicians. Given the strictly finite resources of brainpower available, Bletchley Park was probably wise to keep all of it at work on the flood of material that could be deciphered, to sustain the maximum possible output of fresh intelligence material. The Americans were let into the Ultra secret soon after they joined the fighting but there was an inevitable delay of many months before their much greater resources could be brought to bear on the problem – under British tutelage, which as noted above was not universally welcomed across the Atlantic. All this meant that Bletchley Park was to need ten and a half months to break into *Triton*, to which it had given the codename "Shark." Until then just three *Triton* messages were read by matching them with identical texts sent in other Enigma ciphers based on three wheels. One, on 14 March 1942, recorded the promotion of Karl Dönitz to full admiral, and it took six three-wheel *bombes* two weeks and three days to break into it. There was to be no early windfall in the shape of a captured German vessel to shorten the blackout.

In the circumstances, therefore, it can almost (but not quite) be seen as fortunate that the Ultra shutdown, which in any case was only partial, coincided with the diversion of the German submarine effort to the American coast. The main contribution to the ensuing heavy losses was certainly lack of intelligence, but not of the kind supplied by Bletchley Park. So long as the Americans failed to take the tried and tested defensive measures urged upon them by the British, there was little that even the highest grade of intelligence-information could have done. This is an extreme example of the principle that good intelligence is of little value unless proper use is made of it. Another illustration is provided by the Channel Dash, of which Bletchley Park picked up clear indications.

Seen from OIC the naval Enigma blackout was at worst a "dim-out" because two and a half years of getting into the minds of Dönitz and Godt enabled Naval Intelligence, particularly Rodger Winn, to carry on guessing German dispositions with considerable, if less immediate, success. By this time also, High Frequency Direction-Finding was sophisticated enough to make good a great deal of the shortfall in Enigma material. Unquantifiable though it was, the main benefit from Ultra in the Atlantic campaign was the ability to divert ships away from danger; during this black period, however, the convoys were largely left alone even though they were using the highly predictable Great Circle route to save precious fuel. Diversion of minimally protected, unconvoyed shipping along the American coast would have made no material difference.

According to Professor Hinsley, official historian of British Intelligence, GC & CS viewed the long naval Enigma blackout as its greatest failure. It is however entirely reasonable to share his view that the eventual break back into the German naval ciphers was one of its greatest feats. Indeed we may without undue rashness go further at this juncture and pose the mildly heretical question whether the importance of Ultra has not been overstated in the years since it was disclosed.

There seems to be no convincing evidence that an uninterrupted flow would have made any substantial difference to the course of the war at sea in 1942. The story of Ultra is wondrously, even quintessentially, British: a brilliant piece of sustained improvisation by a group of eccentrics achieved in the total secrecy which remains the abiding obsession of the country's rulers of this day. The revelation to an unprepared world of one of the greatest secrets of the war thirty years later was a genuine sensation which initially numbed the critical faculties of many interested parties. The leading German specialist, Professor Jürgen Rohwer, was kind enough to describe graphically to me the shattering effect which the disclosure had on Dönitz himself in his old age (he died in 1981). This was only to be expected from the most famous victim, especially when he had spent so much of the war worrying about the possibility of a major leak to the enemy; here was vindication and a new explanation for his defeat at a stroke.

The vast scale of the GC & CS effort, the secrecy, and the impact of the belated revelation all appear to lend strength to those who have even gone so far as to argue that it won the war. It certainly did not "win" the Atlantic campaign, the central struggle of the war, and there are solid grounds for believing, on the evidence from 1942 for example, that it was less of a key to ultimate victory than the closure of the mid-ocean airgap. The true significance of Ultra is something to which it will be necessary to return, but the prolonged interruption in the flow of naval Enigma material in 1942 is an important piece of evidence that the defeat of the German submarines cannot be ascribed to a single preponderant factor. The fact that the 1942 dim-out was not of itself a disaster indicates that the abruptly interrupted source was not quite as indispensable as has sometimes been suggested since its existence was disclosed. But for the hard-pressed and enfeebled Churchill the sudden reduction in his ration of "golden eggs" was undoubtedly another depressing blow just when it would hurt most.

As the Allied cause suddenly lost an aid on which it had increasingly learned to depend, the *B-dienst* presented Dönitz with another valuable gift to strengthen the advantage he held at this stage of the war. Just when it was of greatest worth, German Naval Intelligence rounded off its deep penetration of British Naval Cipher No. 3, used by the three Allied navies for Atlantic communications. This important breakthrough came in February; in March the *B-dienst* acquired a copy of the new Merchant Navy codebook from a sinking cargo-ship off northern Norway – four weeks before the new Merchant Ship Code which it contained came into use. This was a most useful supplement to the triumph over Cipher No. 3 and gained added importance when No. 3 was superseded in June 1943.

The *Paukenschlag* boats derived great benefit from American careless-ness with radio. By tuning in to the 600-metre waveband, they picked up emergency calls which helpfully gave the position, course and speed of the affected ship. Notation of these enabled the Germans to work out with ease which areas were most likely to yield targets. At the same time, early in 1942, the Germans deprived Bletchley Park of a useful fast route into Enigma traffic by issuing a new book of short signals for weather reports. The capture of its predecessor in 1941 had helped the GC & CS break into longer messages containing the stereotyped and therefore more easily recognisable brief weather summaries. The change deprived Bletchley Park of a useful means of attacking *Triton* just when it was most needed.

*   *   *

It was in intelligence and the intimately related sphere of the control of shipping movements that the Canadian Navy was able to make another unsung but important contribution during the fraught period when the US Navy insisted on learning the hard way. For once the difficult position of the smallest of the three North Atlantic navies, caught between the different requirements and approaches of the Royal and US navies, could be turned into the positive role of liaison. The Canadians became brokers of information between the British and the Americans. The US entry into the war and the concomitant submarine invasion of the western Atlantic seaboard inevitably threw enormous new strains on the RCN until the Americans were organisationally capable of asserting their agreed role of strategic responsibility for the western Atlantic.

Fortunately, Captain Eric Brand, the British naval officer on permanent loan to the RCN as Director of Naval Intelligence, was also in charge of the Trade Division which controlled the movement of ships off Canada as an adjunct of the British Admiralty system. The volume of work led to the two departments' separation in the middle of 1942, whereupon Brand became Director of the Trade Division which had been taking up eighty percent of his time. The British consular shipping agents who had been supplying Ottawa with information on movements while the US was neutral donned naval uniforms in December 1941 and seamlessly became British Routeing Liaison Officers, carrying on exactly as before but now able to work openly with the American Port Directors (equivalent to Britain's Naval Control Service officers). These men eased the Americans into the complex work of controlling individual ships and eventually organising convoys under Captain M. K. Metcalfe, USN, who laid the foundations of US co-operation with the Admiralty system on his side of the border in the months preceding American entry. An Anglo-American routeing agreement was concluded in February 1942, and US Routeing Officers oversaw movements from American ports with the BRLOs acting as their assistants for British-controlled shipping.

The Admiralty supplied Ottawa with all its trade-intelligence and Brand's staff sifted the mass of material for information to pass to Washington. The Canadians also took over the role of diverting non-American shipping in the whole of the western Atlantic north of the equator. These arrangements lasted from December 1941 to reorganisation in July 1942. The Canadian Diversion Room relied on submarine reports from London and, from February, Washington (whence information was slower in coming and often at odds with London's), as well as from Canada's own efficient chain of "Y" monitoring stations, which obtained bearings from submarine wireless transmissions. There was however much wasteful duplication of effort because the Americans retained control of their own shipping in the western Atlantic and also sent out separate submarine intelligence to ships in the area. This was often at variance with Anglo-Canadian information and therefore caused bewilderment among masters. The confusion was resolved in April 1942, when it was agreed that the Canadians should oversee the north-western Atlantic, the Americans the adjacent area to the south and south-east and the British the east. These areas were controlled by the three plotting centres in Ottawa, Washington and London, which gradually built up the efficiency of their co-operation.

The new situation in the North Atlantic, where submarines could now strike anywhere, led to a reorganisation of the trans-ocean convoy escort system. The Newfoundland Escort Force was subsumed into a new Western Local Escort Force (WLEF) and a Mid-Ocean Escort Force (MOEF). The WLEF was run by the Canadians under US operational control, taking convoys to about 45° west, while the MOEF, consisting of seven British, four Canadian and three American groups, escorted them across the central stretch, its ships using Newfoundland in the west and Londonderry, Northern Ireland, in the east as termini. The new system, tied as it was to the Great Circle route, spared the escorts the necessity of a stopover in Iceland for refuelling. The WLEF, made up of Canadian and some British ships, was based at Halifax, Nova Scotia. The British provided an Eastern Local Escort Force, mainly armed anti-submarine trawlers, in home waters as necessary until the ships joined coastal convoys.

In terms of North Atlantic ocean escorts, the British were now providing fifty percent, the Canadians forty-eight and the Americans just two percent. Immediately after Pearl Harbor the US Navy had only two destroyers in the western Atlantic; few reinforcements were available for convoy-work in the ensuing months so that the three "American" groups with MOEF (which should have been five but would soon be reduced to one) had only one or two American vessels among the six in each group. The US Navy however retained operational command of naval forces based in the western Atlantic – and in March, Admiral King, still resisting the introduction of convoy further south in the areas of greatest shipping losses, ordered WLEF to institute convoys between Boston and Halifax. This was achieved by a reduction in the size of escort-groups, but it was achieved – the first step in providing proper protection for coastal shipping south of the Canadian border.

We have seen how the Germans began their assault on North America by sending submarines to work off the Canadian and Newfoundland coasts as well as the United States, and how the focus of the attacks soon began to shift steadily southwards. It was not only the winter chill of the far northern waters that produced this result. The Canadians may have come under fire from the British for the weakness and inefficiency of their escort work in 1941, but the submarine command soon noted that its boats met more resistance sooner in Canadian waters. Here was another repudiation of King's thesis that weakly escorted convoys were worse than none. The southward shift during the first half of 1942 was entirely in keeping with Dönitz's strategy throughout the war: to go where the targets were least difficult and dangerous to obtain. Before leaving Canadian waters ourselves, we can note this wartime appreciation of the crisis by the Canadian Trade Division:

> From January to June [1942] the U-boats did pretty much as they pleased south of New York. In the Canadian area we had no escorts to spare for local escort duty, but we ran convoys all the same, escorting them with whatever warships happened to be moving about or temporarily free from ocean duties. Though these escorts would have been hopelessly inadequate in the face of a determined attack, their mere existence was enough to induce the U-boats to go further south in search of easier pickings. It was easy for the U-boats to sink ships then.

Having lost his ability to replenish and refuel his boats at sea with the elimination of surface supply-ships by the British in the latter part of 1941, Dönitz enlisted the submarine tanker to replace them. Work started on a new type XIV by the end of the year, a boat with a surface displacement of 1,688 tons which could carry 432 tonnes of oil as well as four torpedoes. The first "U-tanker" in operation was the *UA*, now converted to carry 250 extra tonnes of oil. The *UA* left Lorient on March 14 to refuel three type-VIIc boats in the Western Approaches. Following this success, the first purpose-built tanker, nicknamed a *Milchkuh* (milch-cow), to set out for the western Atlantic was the *U459*, which left on March 28. Within weeks six type XIVs were at work, doubling the operational endurance of the type VIIc which had a normal fuel capacity of slightly more than 100 tonnes. In the third week of April the *U459* was met by no less than eight clients, several of them simultaneously, which was unduly rash. Bad weather interfered with the new procedure, but by the end of the month Dönitz noted with satisfaction in his War Diary that "the supply of submarines by U-tanker has worked extremely well." The process was vividly described by Heinz Schaeffer, later commander of *U977* (in which he set a record at the end of the war by sailing sixty-six days underwater to Argentina, whereupon he was accused of giving Hitler a lift to Antarctica). His boat was down to one tonne of oil when:

> The chief engineer and some of the engine-room staff went forward and aft to open the fuelling valves and clear the way for the supply-hose. Icy-cold though it was, these men wore only bathing-trunks, the belt to which they were lashed biting into their flesh. At times one or other of them would even be washed overboard and only be hauled in again with a good deal of effort. It wasn't exactly fun for them but it was the only way.
>
> We were cruising parallel to the supply-boat, perhaps ninety yards away. A line was fired over us by pistol, and this was followed by the hose and a towing-wire. We breathed again as the precious fluid began to flow in. Altogether we took in twenty tonnes of it, not to speak of bread, potatoes, vegetables and other food in watertight sacks. The whole thing went off perfectly, though it was our first experience.
>
> Another U-boat called up, wanting to be victualled too. Short of a certain

quantity of oil, we had taken all we needed aboard, but for security reasons and also to test our manoeuvrability under water we both dived; first the supply-boat, then ourselves. The two boats proceeded one astern of the other with lines, hose and wire left in place, and so we cruised for three hours on end at a depth of twenty-five fathoms. It was a fantastic conception; we were embarking diesel oil under water for the first time in history.

But the climax of the onslaught along the coast of the United States itself (as distinct from further south) had already been reached before the milch-cows started work. Dönitz sent his type IXs into the Caribbean for the first time in February. As a diversion early in March he sent two submarines to operate in the waters off Freetown, Sierra Leone, where eleven ships of 64,000 tons were sunk in a matter of days, before the area was abandoned again in favour of the Americas. This "may well have prevented the transfer of more British anti-submarine forces to the United States Navy and thus have contributed to a prolongation of the favourable conditions in American waters," wrote Dönitz in his memoirs. In March 1942, losses to Allied shipping amounted to the stupendous total of 834,000 tons (273 ships), of which 538,000 tons (95) were sunk by submarines and 534,000 tons (also 95 ships) in the North Atlantic, the vast majority once again off the United States. The second Happy Time produced a new array of aces: Hardegen was back for his second tour in *U123* and sank eleven ships by April 20; Commander Johann Mohr in *U124* got nine and at least three others sank half a dozen each. On April 14 the USS *Roper*, a destroyer, became the first American warship to sink a submarine, *U85* (Lieutenant Eberhard Greger) off Cape Hatteras. It was not much to show for approximately 250 ships lost in North American waters since the United States entered the war.

The British, on the brink of despair at the mounting losses and the feeble response of the US Navy, had been sending a stream of advisers and experts, starting with the First Sea Lord himself, across the Atlantic to try to make the US Navy adopt convoy. Although the Americans had on British urging set up a Joint Intelligence Committee and staff in 1941, the US Navy had no equivalent to the Admiralty's Operational Intelligence Centre, which had proved itself so valuable as a central clearing-house for information. Admiral Godfrey, Director of Naval Intelligence, therefore sent Rodger Winn, head of the Submarine Tracking Room in OIC, to Washington to see if he could persuade the Americans to remedy this deficiency. And if he could also talk them into the earliest introduction of coastal convoys, so much the better, said Admiral Pound, the First Sea Lord . . . Thus was one of the most important staff missions of the war entrusted to a mere commander, a civilian in uniform for the duration who wore on his sleeves the undulating stripes of the "Wavy Navy" (the RN Volunteer Reserve).

Winn needed three days of solid argument to sell the idea of an OIC to Commander Dyer, who ran Admiral King's Information Room (concerned with strategic rather than operational intelligence). Winn persuaded him that it was possible to anticipate enemy submarine movements and to move shipping on the basis of such forecasts. The next step was to tackle Rear-Admiral Richard E. Edwards, King's deputy chief of staff. Decisively out-ranked by this anglophobe à la King, Winn nevertheless drove home his case through a wall of hostile scepticism. There was no getting round Winn's vast experience, but what probably turned the trick was a brief exchange which went to the heart of the matter and prompted Winn to a calculated display of temper. Edwards said the Americans wanted to learn their own lessons and they had plenty of ships for the purpose. Winn snapped back: "The trouble is, Admiral, it's not only your bloody ships you are losing: a lot of them are ours!" According to Winn's friend and OIC colleague, Patrick Beesly, Edwards was taken aback but grudgingly conceded the point and got Winn an appointment with King himself. To Winn's astonishment, the dreaded COMINCH proved to be a pushover (probably persuaded in advance by Edwards) and ordered the creation of a US Navy equivalent of OIC, complete with tracking-room. Once decided, the new department was estab-lished with un-British speed. As Winn went to New York to convert Admiral Andrews of the Eastern Sea Frontier, Commander Kenneth A. Knowles, USN, was ordered to set up the Atlantic Section, Operational Intelligence, reporting directly to King – "Op-20-G" for short. Knowles became the American Winn and the two men, who both finished as captains, soon established what is thought to have been the closest exercise in transatlantic co-operation of the war. Knowles too had been propelled from obscurity, as a prematurely retired officer with eye-trouble, into one of the most important backroom jobs in the Atlantic campaign.

Coastal convoys were soon to be recognised as essential, though not as a result of Rodger Winn's proselytising mission. After the meeting of the relevant Frontier commanders at the end of March, King formally accepted their proposals for a convoy system on April 3, as the losses off the US coast were at their peak. He ordered the institution of convoy in both directions between Hampton Roads (off New York) and Key West (at the southern tip of Florida) to start southbound on May 14 and northbound on the 15th. This meant that coastal shipping was now to be protected by escorts from the transatlantic terminals in Nova Scotia to the entrance of the Gulf of Mexico. Ironically, after all the bloodletting of March and April, not one ship was sunk in the Eastern Sea Frontier in the first seventeen days of May (and only fourteen in the rest of the month out of 123 lost in the Atlantic as a whole). It was almost as if Dönitz had seen the southerly extension of convoy coming, because the Germans, with up to eighteen boats operating to the west at this time, concentrated their efforts on the Gulf and the Caribbean in earnest. Tanker losses had become so desperate by April that King ordered all of them confined to port in his area for two weeks while the domestic oil reserves were used to cover the shortfall. He was obliged to release them on the 29th, when all tankers were put under the control of Admiral Andrews. This made life ever busier for his Flag Secretary, who rejoiced in the sublime name of Commander S. S. Bunting.

The new scheme was the foundation of what was soon to become the Interlocking Convoy System, a vast circulation of shipping covering the entire Atlantic Ocean. Until it was completed, however, the Germans were able with speed and determination to stay one move ahead of the game; and even then the submarine threat was far from mastered. But off the US coast, if not further south, sinkings declined dramatically. This was achieved by seven escort groups of usually seven ships each – two destroyers, a corvette, two patrol-vessels and two trawlers. The British had sent corvettes and trawlers to help and scraped together two escort groups from MOEF, at the cost of slowing down the main transatlantic convoy cycle. From May they also provided corvettes for a separate tanker-escort service, with Canadian support, between Halifax and the West Indies, largely to guarantee Canadian oil supplies on Ottawa's urging.

But if Allied shipping losses worldwide fell from the March record to 674,000 tons in April and 705,000 in May, the overall North Atlantic position deteriorated. In April 391,000 tons went down, but in May the total rose to 576,000 and in June to 624,000 tons. June 1942 proved to be the very worst month of sinkings in the entire war with a global total of 834,196 tons (thirty-two tons more than in March). Submarines accounted for 432,000 tons in April, 607,000 in May and 700,000 in June. This last was the magic figure regarded by Dönitz as the monthly total required for victory in the tonnage-war. As Dönitz wrote in his War Diary:

> . . . the enemy merchant navies are a collective factor. It is therefore immaterial where any one ship is sunk, for it must ultimately be replaced by new construction. What counts in the long run is the preponderance of sinkings over new construction. Shipbuilding and arms-production are centred in the United States, while England is the European outpost and sally-port. By attacking the supply-traffic – particularly the oil – in the US zone, I am striking at the root of the evil, for here the sinking of each ship is not only a loss to the enemy but also deals a blow at the source of his shipbuilding and war production. Without shipping the sally-port cannot be used for an attack on Europe . . . I consider that we should continue to operate the U-boats where they can sink the greatest tonnage with the smallest losses, which at present is in American waters. [15 April 1942]

General George C. Marshall, the self-effacing but determined American Chief of Staff, bore the responsibility of getting US troops and airmen with their equipment across the Atlantic to fight in the Mediterranean and Europe. On 19 June 1942 he decided that the US Navy's tardiness in introducing convoy was still potentially fatal and directly challenged Admiral King in a letter:

The losses by submarines off our Atlantic seaboard and in the Caribbean now threaten our entire war effort. The following statistics bearing on the subject have been brought to my attention.

Of the seventy-four ships allocated to the Army for July by the War Shipping Administration, seventeen have already been sunk. Twenty-two percent of the bauxite fleet [carrying aluminium-ore from Dutch Guiana (Surinam)] has already been destroyed. Twenty percent of the Puerto Rican fleet has been lost. Tanker sinkings have been 3.5 percent per month of tonnage in use.

We are all aware of the limited number of escort craft available, but has every conceivable improvised means been brought to bear on this situation? I am fearful that another month or two of this will so cripple our means of transport that we will be unable to bring sufficient men and planes to bear against the enemy in critical theatres to exercise a determining influence on the war.

King replied two days later:

I have long been aware, of course, of the implications of the submarine situation as pointed out in your memorandum . . . I have employed – and will continue to employ – not only regular forces but also such improvised means as give any promise of usefulness . . . [After listing the various stopgap measures described earlier in this chapter and the introduction of convoy as far as Key West in May, King criticises the British for not concentrating on bombing submarine bases and construction yards and coolly informs Marshall that in advocating universal convoy he was preaching to the converted.]

. . . if all shipping can be brought under escort and air-cover our losses will be reduced to an acceptable figure. I might say in this connection that escort is not just *one* way of handling the submarine menace; it is the *only* way that gives any promise of success. The so-called patrol and hunting operations have time and again proved futile . . . We must get every ship that sails the seas under constant close protection. [King's emphasis]

This answer has been presented in the past as evidence of King's belated conversion to the *idea* of convoy. That is actually unfair to a figure who has traditionally been excoriated for the huge and largely unnecessary shipping losses of the Second Happy Time. The evidence that he understood the need for convoy from the outset has been cited above; his two substantive failures lay in not recognising that any escort is better than none and in not introducing convoy, however tenuously protected, from the beginning. These errors were compounded by his failure to grasp the principle it had also taken his British contemporaries from Churchill downwards so long to learn: that in tackling commerce-raiders, whether submersible or not, the best form of attack is defence and the only defence is convoy. If British historians, starting with the scrupulously fair-minded official chronicler, Roskill, have been understandably hard on King, the verdict of Admiral Morison, the official American historian, is bleaker still:

> This writer cannot avoid the conclusion that the US Navy was woefully
> unprepared, materially and mentally, for the U-boat blitz on the Atlantic coast.
> He further believes that . . . this . . . was largely the Navy's own fault . . . it
> had no plans ready for a reasonable protection to shipping . . . and was unable
> to improvise them for several months.

As COMINCH (and CINCLANT immediately before), King cannot evade
the lion's share of the blame for the "merry massacre." By the same token
he must be given credit for the great consolations to the Allies' worldwide
cause provided in this period by the US Navy under his supreme command:
the superb victories over the Japanese Navy at the battles of the Coral Sea
(May 4 to 8) and Midway (June 3 to 6). Having gone over to the offensive in
the Pacific as early as April 18 when they bombed Tokyo, the Americans
proved there was nothing wrong with their aggressive spirit in counter-attack
(hence also the premature concentration on building landing-craft). Their
appetite for the long-haul, initially defensive slogging-match with the elusive
submarines was less keen (a failing still on view as recently as 1987–8, when
the US Navy's scornful attitude to the unglamorous task of minesweeping
brought it so much grief in the Persian Gulf). Midway was one of the most
decisive victories of the war, and it shone even more brightly at the time
against the sombre background of German victories in the Soviet Union and
North Africa (where Rommel took Tobruk on June 21). All the British could
do by way of taking the fight to the enemy at this time was to mount the first
1,000-bomber raid of the war, on Cologne (May 30). Air Chief Marshal Sir
Arthur "Bomber" Harris had been in charge of Bomber Command since
February 1942.

As Dönitz was doing his not inconsiderable best with the limited resources
at his disposal in American waters, he was still having to cope with distractions
and diversions from what he so clearly saw as his main task. In addition to
appeasing Hitler's constant concern with Norway, Dönitz was ordered on
June 21 to keep a group of submarines in reserve in case the British seized
the Atlantic islands (the Spanish Canaries and the Portuguese Azores and
Cape Verde groups). He protested in vain. Even such boats as could be
scraped together for the Americas were themselves subjected to distractions
from torpedoing ships. If the occasional minelaying missions off New York
and other major American ports, undertaken after the introduction of coastal
convoys, were obviously a sensible, if not very effective, contribution,
"Operation *Pastorius*" was rather less so.

   On May 26 *U202* and *U584* each embarked four saboteurs to be landed
on Long Island and the Florida coast at Jacksonville respectively. These
agents were to damage military targets, gather information, contact sympathisers and win converts for the German cause. The first group got as far as
New York and the second to Chicago before the FBI picked them up. They

Above: The ill-fated convoy PQ17 assembling off Iceland.

Below: German submarine on arctic patrol, winter 1942–3.

Above: Liberty ship under construction. By late 1942, the U.S. was launching three Liberty ships a day.

Above: American welder.

Below: Liberty ship fights a storm.

Right: A lighter moment
aboard the *Tirpitz* in
Norwegian waters.

Below: Admiral Fraser,
C-in-C of the Home Fleet
(with cigar) entertains the
Soviet Navy after the
sinking of the *Scharnhorst*.

Sunderland.

Catalina.

Liberator.

Focke-Wulf 200 Kondor.

Submarines: those that changed hands.
Above: HMS *Seal* after her capture by the Germans.
Below: U570 (later HMS *Graph*) under the British flag.

Above: U505, after her capture by Captain Daniel Gallery, USN, and his men.

Above: British escort-carrier stowing her Swordfish.

Below: USS *Bogue.*

Above: Admiral Sir Max Horton, the submariner in charge of Western Approaches Command, in 1944.

Above: Commander "Johnnie" Walker at Liverpool, just before his death in 1944.

Below: A Canadian party about to board a sinking German submarine early in 1944. HMCS *Chilliwack* failed to salvage it.

The German's new submarine threat at the end of the war:
Above: The ocean-going type XXI.
Below: The coastal type XXIII.

achieved nothing, and Dönitz always suspected their motives for going were less than pure. He justly saw the presence of such forlorn hopes on his boats as a security-risk because, if captured, they could reveal operational secrets; in some cases he believed that his submarines were really being used as a uniquely spectacular means of emigration. Fortunately the submarines were not expected to collect the inept agents.

A distraction of an altogether different and more fundamental nature brought a strong echo from the original Happy Time to its reprise on the other side of the Atlantic. The Germans were once again having torpedo-trouble. An analysis of submarine performance in mid-year revealed that the scoring rate was barely fifty percent: it had taken 806 torpedoes to sink 404 ships. Not without bitterness, Dönitz noted in his Diary for June 24 that, "compared with the First World War, we now have two main improvements – the bubble-free discharge and the trackless run, which, however, has reduced the speed of the torpedo to thirty knots. Yet the depth-keeping and detonation qualities have not even reached the level attained in 1918, although we have now had two and a half years of trials and strenuous efforts. The destructive effect of the warhead when used with a contact-pistol is insufficient, as is shown by the many cases of ordinary freighters needing more than one torpedo to sink them." Not quite a return to the despairing days of Prien's "wooden gun" but a cause for concern when the paucity of submarines available for the unrepeatable "turkey-shoot" opportunity made every missile count.

The Germans still had no satisfactory magnetic pistol, which would have brought the sinking rate rather closer to 100 percent. But relief was at hand in the form of the "FAT" (Feder-Apparat Torpedo), which passed its trials in mid-1942. This contained a spring-device which enabled it to run straight at first and then to veer off in a series of rightward or leftward loops, depending on the course of the victim. These "curly" torpedoes, as Allied sailors called them, were much more difficult to evade. Ultra revealed the development of the FAT in 1941 to the British, who mistakenly thought it was an acoustic homing torpedo (this had the happy consequence that, when the Germans did get around to using such a weapon, the Allies were well prepared for it).

After the introduction of US coastal convoys in mid-May the submarines concentrated their efforts on the Caribbean and the Gulf of Mexico. A few attacks were made on ocean convoys, however, and one boat entered the estuary of the St Lawrence in Canada on May 12 to sink two merchantmen. When this intrusion was less successfully repeated in mid-June, the Canadians introduced another local adjunct to the burgeoning convoy system. After the two air victories over submarines off Newfoundland in March and the USS Roper's in April, the only American submarine "kill" prior to the introduction of coastal convoys was on May 9, when a Coastguard cutter sank U352 off the East Coast. In June they sank one off Cuba and another off

Bermuda, but in July there was a marked improvement, with three sunk off the East Coast (one by a British ship) and one in the Caribbean. In addition, the Canadian Navy destroyed two boats in the North Atlantic and the RCAF one more off Nova Scotia – the latter on July 31, the first day in the war on which three submarines had been sent to the bottom, making a total of eleven for the month, also a record. But then there were so many more of them. By July Dönitz for the first time had more boats than the 300 with which he would have liked to begin the war: there were 331, of which 140 were operational and the rest on training or trials. The building rate was far in excess of the kill-rate being achieved by the Allies.

Another statistic, this time from the Allied side, was much more vital to the course of the war. For the first time since the Germans began the war by marching into Poland in September 1939, the worldwide monthly loss of shipping from all causes – still enormous at 618,000 tons but down by a quarter from the June record thanks to the spread of convoys – was marginally surpassed by the rate of new construction. Only hindsight enables us to see this moment in July 1942 as the true turning-point in the Atlantic campaign, the moment when Dönitz lost the tonnage-war. As we shall see, there were still to be many months in which the trend could have been reversed. But it never was, even if the Allies could not know for some time, during which more disasters were to occur, that they had gained the upper hand.

This astonishing shipbuilding achievement can be traced back to a conference which took place in President Roosevelt's White House bedroom on February 19. There the Director of the War Shipping Administration, Vice-Admiral Emory S. Land, was instructed to organise the building of 24 million tons in 1942, more than twenty times what had been produced in 1941. The rate was to be doubled again in 1943 to some 1,500 new ships. At the same time Land and Sir Arthur Salter of the British Ministry of War Transport set up a combined Shipping Adjustment Board to make the best possible use of existing stocks, with the newest and fastest ships earmarked for the area of highest risk and the older and slower vessels sent to ply in less dangerous areas.

The American production targets, which were more than met, contrast awesomely with the best the British could do after massive reorganisation and deals with the trade unions: 1.25 million tons of new shipping per year. The American shipbuilding programme mobilised all that was best in the free-enterprise system, complete with competition, mass production by 700,000 mostly unskilled or semi-skilled workers, media "hype" which made a national figure of "Rosie the Riveter" – symbol of female labour engaged in war-production – and cash incentives for beating deadlines. The Liberty ship which had originally taken some six months to build was taking barely three months by summer 1942. If America "won the war" – though as we have surely begun to see, attributing victory to any single factor is very misleading – the stupendous feats of her mushrooming shipbuilding industry are a prime example of how she did so. We may note that Dönitz's calculation of 700,000 tons of sinkings as the minimum monthly total needed to defeat the Allies in the Atlantic, made in May 1942, was based on an assumption of new building barely one third of what was actually achieved in 1942.

Unaware of this error, just as the Allies remained unaware of the "milch-cows" for six months because of Enigma's fourth wheel, Dönitz got on with the new war in tropical waters, managing in June and July to assemble as many as eighteen boats at a time (four Italian submarines joined in as well, taking the war on commerce as far south as the Brazilian coast from March onwards). But a wolf-pack sank seven ships in convoy ONS92 on the North Atlantic Great Circle route in mid-May and another got four ships and a corvette from ONS100 one month later. On June 14 the Gibraltar convoy HG84 lost five ships and four weeks later the Germans managed to attack two convoys on the Sierra Leone route with modest results before returning to the independently routed ships still sailing in the Trinidad region. On July 19 Dönitz withdrew his last two boats from the east coast of the United States, the formal end of *Paukenschlag* – his most successful operation of the entire campaign. The system of convoys in the western Atlantic spread steadily southward: in July they were started between Halifax and Curaçao, Trinidad and Key West, Trinidad and the eastern Atlantic and even between Panama and Guantanamo in Cuba. Despite the tanker shortage caused by the Germans, the Allies in June began to attach oilers to convoys so that escorts could refuel at sea (just as submarines had begun to do two months earlier). With rescue-ships also commonplace, the convoys were much better equipped to deal with the dangers they were formed to counter; with the simultaneous spread of HF/DF and radar among the escorts and steadily improving standards of training, so were their protectors.

Training-schools in anti-submarine warfare spread rapidly during this phase on both sides of the Atlantic. Escort commanders of the Royal Navy went to the Tactical School in Liverpool, which was set up under Captain Gilbert Roberts in January 1942. The Canadians developed a successful night-attack training system which was borrowed by the two larger navies. In March the Americans opened their Sub-Chaser Center in Miami to train escort captains and crews under Lieutenant-Commander E. F. McDaniel (it soon became known as McDaniel's Academy). In the ensuing two years nearly 50,000 officers and men passed through his none too gentle hands. Captain W. D. Baker, USN, was ordered in February 1942 to organise the Atlantic Fleet's own anti-submarine warfare school at Boston and parallel units were set up under Eastern Sea Frontier and COMINCH commands, using British methods and "attack-teachers" (simulators). Not all the Royal Navy's hard-won expertise was ignored in these early days for the United States; in these schools, at least, it was being applied where it was most readily communicable. One American who had done more to prepare the US Navy for its Atlantic war-role than any other did not live to see the lessons learned on the transatlantic run applied elsewhere after a combined loss in American waters of nearly 3.5 million tons. Rear-Admiral Bristol, head of Task Force 24 (as it was called from March 6) based at Argentia, Newfoundland, died, probably of overwork, on April 20 and was succeeded by Vice-Admiral R. M. Brainard, USN. Under Bristol's command, only eight ships were lost from more than sixty convoys. He was posthumously awarded the Distinguished Service Medal.

With the tragic scandal of the unprotected East Coast at an end and a strict blackout in force, the Americans had digested and applied the lessons of convoy: one means of losing the war against Germany had been suppressed in the nick of time. One of the tactical changes made as a result of the Allied conference on convoys in Washington late in June was the establishment of the "Chop" (change of operational control) line. This was where ships passed out of American into British care (or vice versa); although referred to as a line and at this stage roughly coinciding with the boundary between the British and American strategic zones (longitude 26° west), it was really the time at which a convoy was scheduled to cross it, whether it had done so or not. Before we cross it ourselves to consider the no less dramatic events of this period on the eastern side of the Atlantic, it is necessary to return to the vexed question of the use of maritime airpower, which was causing difficulties on both sides of the conflict and of the ocean during this period.

Having moved the bulk of the Luftwaffe's relevant forces to support the Eastern Front, the Germans found themselves acutely short of aircraft in the west. The cover so effectively provided for the Channel Dash had been a special effort in which all the night-fighters and much of the Luftwaffe's conventional fighter-strength in western Europe outside Germany were mobilised. The aircraft shortage also inhibited other movements by surface-units during this phase, including the new *Tirpitz*. On June 11 Dönitz complained in his War Diary:

> That there should be no air protection for a damaged and defenceless U-boat is deplorable, and must have a depressing effect on the crews. Even a few heavy fighters or modern bombers would suffice to keep off enemy aircraft. At least they could escort a damaged U-boat until she came under the protection of our minesweepers and patrol vessels . . . There being no defence in the Bay of Biscay against Sunderland aircraft and heavy bombers, the RAF can do what it pleases.

This unfamiliar picture of effortless RAF superiority was a local phenomenon as seen from a submariner's point of view. Coastal Command, which ran British-based maritime aircraft under naval operational control, was still the poor relation of the Royal Air Force. Sir Philip Joubert de la Ferté began his reign as its C-in-C by assessing its needs as 818 aircraft for the Atlantic and home waters. By his own reckoning in summer 1941, he was some 250 short, and he also wanted replacements for the obsolescent or inadequate types in the command. Not only were all his requests rejected, but Churchill and the Air Staff, led by Air Chief Marshal Sir Charles Portal, reserved all new bombers for raids on Germany and even wanted to divert Coastal Command's existing bombers to this purpose. The Admiralty naturally supported Joubert and the hoary issue of the organisation and use of airpower at sea came to a head again early in 1942. Two days before the Channel Dash began, the Air Ministry complained vociferously to the Cabinet about the (in their view) wasteful diversion of forty percent of British bombing capacity to ineffectual raids on Brest. The Admiralty riposted by demanding a dozen extra bomber-squadrons plus new American aircraft for anti-submarine patrols in the Bay of Biscay and the Indian Ocean.

The ensuing struggle, christened the "Battle of the Air" by Admiral Pound, the First Sea Lord, raged behind the scenes for more than six months as a constant backdrop to the rolling catastrophe in American waters. Arguing the central importance of the protection of shipping to the entire war-effort, Pound proposed doubling maritime air-strength worldwide to 1,940 planes, all controlled and trained by the Navy. The Air Ministry courteously sympathised and thought the target could be met by the end of the year with American help. The Admiralty, with reason as we have seen, feared that by then the stock of shipping would be unable to keep Britain going and pressed for immediate reinforcements from the RAF. The Air Ministry then used the shortage of radar equipment, without which diverted bombers were of little use at sea, as an excuse for its reluctance to comply, arguing that Bomber Command could best help by bombing Germany.

Joubert now found himself between the hammer of Admiralty demands and the anvil of Air Ministry resistance. The RAF, which operated Coastal Command aircraft overseas, feared that the Admiralty was trying to dismantle the junior service. In April the chiefs of staff met and agreed the transfer of four bomber-squadrons from Bomber to Coastal Command for anti-submarine operations in the North-Western Approaches (north of Ireland) and the Bay of Biscay (about which Dönitz soon began to complain). The Admiralty objected that Coastal Command still lacked strike-forces, but to no avail; the Luftwaffe was successfully flying fighters from Holland and Norway against British maritime aircraft. The row drew in more and more participants, and the Navy's case for more aircraft was most robustly expressed by Admiral Tovey, the Home Fleet C-in-C. He was at odds with the Admiralty over the direct interference in his command which had so upset his predecessor, Forbes, but when the time came to stand up and be counted, he was for the Navy (now backed by the Army with demands for more battlefield air-support). In his report of proceedings for the second quarter of 1942 Tovey scathingly summarised his letter on the issue, sent to the Admiralty on May 28:

I pointed out that the whole strategy of the war was governed by sea communication; and that disasters had resulted and would result from our failure to
protect our communications and interrupt those of the enemy. As the war
progressed air co-operation had become increasingly necessary, till now the
Navy could no longer carry out its much increased task without adequate
air-support: that support had not been forthcoming. The aircraft . . . of Coastal
Command . . . were quite inadequate . . . : Home Fleet requirements . . .
could not be met . . . The Fleet Air Arm was equipped almost entirely with
obsolete aircraft . . .

    The provision of the requisite air co-operation at sea could not but entail
a reduction in some other form of aircraft activity. [Only Bomber Command
could help.] This force had for long enjoyed absolute priority . . . Whatever
the results of the bombing of cities might be, and this was the subject of keen
controversy, it could not of itself win the war, whereas the failure of our sea
communications would assuredly lose it.

    . . . It was difficult to believe that the population of Cologne would notice
much difference between a raid of 1,000 bombers and one by 750 . . .

    I realised that Their Lordships [of the Admiralty] had for a long time been
pressing for increased air-support; but it had not materialised, and I informed
[them] that in my opinion the situation at sea was now so grave that the time
had come for a stand to be made, even if this led to Their Lordships taking the
extreme step of resignation . . .

Their Lordships, however, remained in place and continued to campaign for
more aircraft for the Fleet Air Arm as well as Coastal Command. Nearly
3,700 planes were needed for the Air Arm with thirty-one escort-carriers on
order. In May the Air Force agreed to mount a constant patrol over the Bay
of Biscay against submarines on their way to and from the French bases. At
this time Coastal Command had just one squadron of sixteen Liberators, the
American long-range bombers ideally suited for distant operations. Two more
were planned for later in the year, but the Americns also needed these
invaluable aircraft in the Pacific. The British equivalent, the Lancaster
bomber, was only just starting to be delivered and it will come as no surprise
to learn that every one was allocated to Bomber Command. Coastal Command
was once again doomed to make do and mend for the rest of 1942 – and
beyond. The fundamental dispute over air priorities was far from settled.

    The Biscay patrol had been foreshadowed late in 1941, and one submar-
ine had been sunk at the end of November by participating aircraft. Renewed
in summer 1942, the patrol contributed two "kills" to July's record total of
eleven. More important strategically was the fact that aircraft forced submarines to submerge in the Bay area, increasing their transit-time and therefore
reducing their operational time. Until Dönitz ordered all boats to cross the
Bay underwater in June, several submarines were damaged, sometimes
seriously, by the RAF, which thus further affected German operational
strength. The British by this time had more effective depth-charges in their

aircraft, but they also had an entirely new device which enormously increased their capability at night.

Squadron-Leader Humphrey de Vere Leigh, RAF, gave his name to the Leigh Light, one of those simple ideas which seem obvious in retrospect but require lateral thinking (and persistence against bureaucratic inertia) to bring to fruition. Leigh solved the problem of radar blindness in aircraft on the last 2,000 yards or so of a pass against a submarine on the surface at night. Metric radar enabled the aircraft to find the boat from many miles away, but it ceased to function reliably at close range, when there were confusing back-echoes from the sea itself just when precision was most needed for an attack. Leigh's solution was to sling a powerful searchlight under the aircraft which would come on at the decisive moment. Thus what radar did for surface-escorts when Asdic ceased to function, the Leigh Light did for aircraft when their radar went blind. This proved to be a most unpleasant surprise for submarine captains against which there was no real defence: in the short interval between the sudden dazzle of the beam and an attack they could not dive far or fast enough to evade the more efficient pattern of depth-charges now in use by the RAF. Light anti-aircraft machine-guns were issued as a stopgap, but these quickly proved inadequate. In the dark an aircraft could easily make an undetected approach until it could focus its Leigh Light on the target, which seemed helplessly transfixed like a rabbit caught in a headlight. It was a complete reversal of the usual position, when the submarine had the advantage of surprise on which it relied to operate successfully.

During their long and essentially unsuccessful wrangle with the air marshals, the admirals advanced the argument that the Germans managed air-sea co-operation much better. Raeder and Dönitz would have found this argument ironic in the extreme and would certainly have agreed with the RAF's dismissal of it. Complaints from his admirals about the lack of air-cover at sea and of co-operation from the Luftwaffe, which were inhibiting the deployment of the large surface units in the far north, led Hitler in March 1942 to order work to be restarted on Germany's sole aircraft-carrier and conversion of merchantmen into auxiliary carriers. By autumn 1941 the German Naval Air Service consisted of one coastal air-group, one under-strength reconnaissance squadron and a single squadron of ship-borne aircraft (carried piecemeal by the capital ships). So much for the promises of forty-one naval squadrons by 1942 made early in the war and before. Göring still believed that everything which flew belonged to him and achieved his ultimate victory over the Navy on 7 April 1942, when the residual Naval Air Command was absorbed into the Third Air Fleet, with one squadron going to the Fifth (the reconnaissance aircraft). In June Hitler ordered work on all carrier projects to be stopped – for ever, as it turned out, although Raeder went on believing until his dismissal that the Navy would be allowed to have a new air arm eventually.

Dönitz meanwhile, as shown by the quotation from his War Diary above, was becoming more and more angry about the lack of air-support in the Bay of Biscay. When *U71* was limping home severely damaged 120 miles west of Bordeaux on June 5, just one Kondor was found to help; when *U105* was in difficulties six days later west of Brittany not one aircraft was available. Nothing was done against the British Biscay Patrol which consisted of only a handful of flying-boats or bombers at a time. Naval requests for air-support were customarily ignored and hardly ever met. Dönitz was driven to visit Göring's Luftwaffe headquarters in East Prussia to extract from the bloated Reichsmarschall a promise to allocate a squadron of twenty-four Junkers Ju88 long-range fighter-bombers to work in the Bay area.

The United States also had jurisdictional as well as material difficulties with its maritime air forces, despite having no independent air force. The Eastern Sea Frontier began the war with a handful of planes, supplemented by occasional loans for the Atlantic Fleet. This eminently unsatisfactory arrangement led to constant wrangling among COMINCH, Andrews at Eastern and CINCLANT, other Frontier admirals and between the districts into which Frontiers were subdivided. King refused to allocate planes to the Frontiers until the Atlantic Fleet squadrons were up to strength, while the Coastguard was regularly plundered by desperate naval air-commanders. The US Navy was so overstretched that the task of flying long-range air-patrols was soon assigned to the First Bomber Command of the Army Air Force – whose pilots began without experience of maritime work. The Command initially had eighty-four bombers. An early attempt to get seventy aircraft ordered by the British for US naval use was foiled by the long arm of the Air Ministry. But in March the situation was so desperate that the British relented and the aircraft were divided between the Eastern and Gulf Frontiers; Eastern was also given a carrier-squadron. These reinforcements were provided only after Andrews had made a direct approach to Frank Knox, the Secretary of the Navy.

In July 1942 there was a radical reorganisation of the Atlantic Fleet's airpower under a new Commander, Patrol Wings (Atlantic). Of his three wings, one was based at Argentia in Newfoundland, one at Norfolk, Virginia, to cover the southern sector of the East Coast, and the third, also at Norfolk, to cover from there to the Canadian border. Squadrons were shuffled among the wings as the needs of various areas changed with the tide of battle; the aircraft were able to use airfields up and down the coast. But this did not solve the wider problems of divided control within the Navy (Fleet, Frontier and Local Defence forces) or between the Navy and Army Air Force, even when the latter's sea-patrol units temporarily came under naval operational control in 1942. The Eastern Sea Frontier Diary baldly states that the "curiously arbitrary and impractical divisions of responsibilities" were never satisfactorily resolved during the war. But this was the first general conflict in which airpower had come into its own as a major strategic factor (it had been tactical in the First World War) and as a fully-fledged third force alongside navy and army. The latter seldom had to work together; the new air forces had to work with both in a bewildering variety of roles, and neither side found a satisfactory organisational structure for this co-operation on a day-to-day basis, although specific combined operations grew steadily more successful as the war went on.

On the other side of the Atlantic, Coastal Command had to spend a strenuous and unpleasant week looking for Hitler's mightiest warship after she had completely disappeared from British ken. At 52,600 tons all up the *Tirpitz*, which completed trials in the Baltic at the turn of the year, was not the easiest target to conceal. The Germans, under the Führer's orders to deploy her in defence of Norway, used a simple ruse to get her there undetected. Instead of sailing her up the eastern side of Jutland and through the Skagerrak to its north, they brought the bristling new monster through the Kiel Canal from the Baltic to the North Sea base at Wilhelmshaven and sent her up the western side of the peninsula overnight on January 14 to 15. She crept into the sheltered anchorage of Aasfjord, fifteen miles from Trondheim, on the 16th. It was only on the next day that the Admiralty, on the basis of delayed Ultra decrypts, warned Admiral Tovey of the Home Fleet at Scapa Flow that the *Bismarck's* big sister might be on the move.

At his immediate disposal at the time were the battleships *King George V* and *Rodney*, the battlecruiser *Renown*, the carrier *Victorious*, ten cruisers and eighteen destroyers. He was for various reasons two battleships, three cruisers and many destroyers short and at this time he still had the Brest Squadron to think of. Tovey reacted to the warning by moving the bulk of his reduced forces to a covering position off Iceland, held back an imminent convoy to Russia and dropped a plan for a raid on the Norwegian coast. It was only on the 23rd that Coastal Command located the new enemy in her well-protected lair. Two days later Churchill ordered preparations for an air-attack. Sixteen aircraft set off on the night of the 29th and achieved nothing. The range was extreme for bombers and reconnaissance alike, and Coastal Command was now constantly engaged in watching the north for the *Tirpitz* and the south for the Brest Squadron, known to be coming out soon. This dissipation of the aircraft of an overstretched command inevitably led to a notably poor performance in both tasks: Joubert was unable to concentrate against either enemy force until he was absolutely certain he was not responding to a false alarm that would leave his few effective aircraft in the wrong place.

In mid-February intense air-activity along the Norwegian coast by the Germans revealed to the British, with naval Enigma now a closed book to them, that the *Tirpitz* was on exercise. Other Ultra sources revealed on the 20th that the pocket-battleship *Admiral Scheer* and the heavy cruiser *Prinz Eugen* were about to sail from Germany to Norway; they were sighted by the RAF the next day in the Heligoland Bight but seasonal poor weather helped them get away to a fjord south of Bergen on the 22nd. The next day, as Tovey hoped to make an air-attack from the *Victorious*, diverted from an attack on the Norwegian coast, the submarine *Trident* crippled the *Prinz Eugen* off Trondheim. The *Scheer* got away to Aasfjord. With destroyers and Luftwaffe cover from Norway, the Germans now had a considerable presence in the north which might make a foray into the North Atlantic or attack the convoys to Murmansk. Tovey could not with his current strength cater for both possibilities simultaneously, even though the Channel Dash had permanently removed his responsibilities further south. The Russians provided very little air and anti-submarine protection in the far north, leaving the convoys so vital to them entirely to the Anglo-Americans, despite prolonged representations.

On March 6 the British submarine *Seawolf* reported that the *Tirpitz* was at sea with three destroyers. On passage at this time were the convoys PQ12, bound for Russia, and QP8, returning to Iceland, and Tovey was already at sea to cover them, with three battleships, *Victorious*, a cruiser and twelve destroyers. On the 7th, as was discovered only later, the two convoys, the Home Fleet and the *Tirpitz* force, under Vice-Admiral Otto Ciliax, were all within seventy miles of each other; but the weather prevented air-reconnaissance. Ciliax managed to sail between the two convoys without seeing them and had no idea that Tovey was even at sea. A German destroyer sank a Soviet straggler in the afternoon. As the Germans searched for more merchantmen and Tovey sailed to and fro looking for the enemy, an aircraft from the *Victorious* saw the *Tirpitz* early on the morning of the 8th. Twelve Albacore torpedo-bombers sighted her shortly afterwards and launched an attack from astern and into the wind, which helped the battleship avoid all the torpedoes, shooting down two of the attackers. With that abortive stroke off the Lofoten Islands the Home Fleet lost its chance for a gunnery action. Both forces withdrew, the Germans to Narvik and the British to Scapa. The *Tirpitz* was back at Trondheim on the 13th, where she was found five days later by Coastal Command, which had been held up by bad weather. Ciliax complained about the high risks he had been made to take for lack of effective air-cover; Tovey complained about Admiralty interference in his operations by orders from London, and that he had been told to make the convoys and not the destruction of the new enemy "fleet-in-being" the first priority of his heavy ships. His difficulties were not eased by the unreliability of wireless in far northern latitudes. The heavy cruiser *Hipper* managed to join the *Tirpitz* undetected on March 21.

The Russian convoys are inextricable from the Atlantic campaign because the ships which so hazardously sailed in them were the same as those which sailed back and forth between Britain and America, often with the same cargoes bound for the Soviet Union. They were protected by the forces which were also detailed to prevent the German surface-ships from getting in among the transatlantic convoys, even though the Home Fleet was engaged in operations tactically different from those of Western Approaches Command.

The forces under Ciliax made no sally against the next pair of convoys, PQ13 and QP9, and the latter got to Iceland unscathed after the minesweeper *Sharpshooter* rammed and sank *U655*. PQ13 was scattered by a savage storm and came under Luftwaffe attack in the waters south of Bear Island on March 28. Three German destroyers came out of Kirkenes for an attack on the escorting cruiser *Trinidad* and the two destroyers in company. The German *Z26* was sunk in the ensuing exchanges, but the *Trinidad* suffered the uniquely bitter experience of shooting herself with her own torpedo, which had run wild in the severe cold. She managed to limp, badly damaged, to a safe haven in Russia – where the body of her rogue torpedo was found in her boiler-room. The convoy lost five ships out of twenty (two to air-attack, two to submarines and one to a destroyer) while the escort sank one submarine. Considering the effect of the storm and the fact that some ships had temporarily got caught in ice, the losses were lighter than they might have been. But it was all a graphic reminder of the terrible dangers of the Murmansk run, which was tactically, if not climatically, easier in winter than in summer, when the Luftwaffe could mount more and deadlier attacks. Tovey repeatedly complained of the appalling conditions, the Germans' advantages and the Russians' reluctance to help, but the convoys were the maritime expression of the highest political considerations: the Soviet Union had to be helped, no matter what the cost and no matter how little she felt able to contribute to her own relief. PQ14 was a fiasco; only eight ships carried on sailing out of twenty-four when the convoy ran into an ice-field, and one of those was sunk by a submarine. The southbound QP10 which set sail on the same day, April 8, lost four ships to air and submarine attack.

At the end of April PQ15 and QP11 set out. The escort of the latter was led by the cruiser HMS *Edinburgh*, which was severely damaged by two torpedoes from *U456* on April 30, some 250 miles out of Murmansk, to which she now tried slowly to return with a gaping hole in her stern. The convoy was next attacked by three German destroyers, which sank one Soviet merchantman and damaged a British escort. The Germans found the *Edinburgh* again on May 2 with four minesweepers in company, and another exchange of fire, also involving two British destroyers from the residual escort, then ensued. The *Edinburgh* managed to cripple the large German destroyer *Hermann Schoemann* before receiving her third torpedo-hit, while the Germans also immobilised the two British destroyers. The cruiser had to be finished off by a British torpedo, taking a large consignment of Russian gold to the bottom, after the Germans broke off the action to rescue the crew of her victim just before it too sank. The minesweepers managed to rescue the great majority of the cruiser's crew and went back to Murmansk with the two lamed destroyers.

The next day PQ15 was attacked by six torpedo-bombers which sank three merchantmen, but bad weather saved the rest of the twenty-five in the convoy. Since the Allied escort forces (including American ships for the first time) sank a friendly Polish submarine in error and rammed one of their own destroyers, which also sank, the cost of this exchange of convoys had been bitterly high in warships. The unfortunate *Trinidad* had to be finished off by British torpedoes on May 15 after she was caught by German aircraft while trying to limp home under temporary repair with a heavy escort. Tovey tried to stop the convoys altogether and won Admiral King's support, but the politicians were adamant: they had to continue. The next bound for Russia, PQ16, was the largest so far assembled for the perilous run, with thirty-five vessels. The pocket-battleship *Lützow* had meanwhile gone north from Germany and was with her sister-ship, the *Scheer*, in Narvik: something else for the hard-pressed Tovey to mull over aboard his flagship. PQ16 which, like QP12, had sailed on May 21, was therefore escorted by four cruisers as well as anti-aircraft and anti-submarine vessels. The air-attacks on PQ16 began on the 25th and did not let up for three days. Seven cargo-ships, including a Catapult-Aircraft Merchantman (CAM), were sunk, and one more plus a destroyer seriously damaged. There was little relief at night because already by this time there was virtually no darkness in the far north. At least there was no successful submarine attack, and the rest of the ships sailed into Russian waters in perfect convoy-formation. QP12's passage was uneventful.

Tovey was hugely relieved and delighted with the sturdy resistance so effectively put up by the escort, whose sole air-cover had been the one Hurricane aboard the CAM (which shot down one German attacker and damaged another). The relief was treacherously misleading because unless summer convoys could somehow be provided with heavyweight air-protection, preferably by escort-carriers and many more anti-aircraft guns, there was no reason to believe that the danger was past. On the contrary: even Dönitz recommended that aircraft should be the principal means of attacking the Russian convoys, and in greater numbers. But before considering the great disaster that was lying in wait for the British in the harshest naval theatre of the war, which came after a lull of several weeks, we may record how the British had driven the submarine chief out of his headquarters nearly 3,000 miles to the south. It belongs in this part of the narrative because it was all to do with the *Tirpitz*.

Her forerunner, the *Bismarck*, it will be remembered, was caught and sunk after a North Atlantic foray which, had the Germans been able to escape, was to have ended with the ship taking refuge in France. The Admiralty was determined to prevent the *Tirpitz* doing the same. Had the *Bismarck* reached France, there was only one place where such a large ship could be put in dry dock for repair: St Nazaire, the port at the south-eastern corner of the Brittany peninsula, where there was an enormous lock originally built to take the great French liner *Normandie*. By closing the huge gates at each end the lock could be made into a dry dock after pumping out the water. As Chief of Combined Operations, Vice-Admiral Lord Louis Mountbatten was given the daunting task of destroying this facility. It involved taking a raiding-force 400 miles by sea and sailing five miles up the River Loire to the lock entrance.

The force which set out on 26 March 1942 from Falmouth, Cornwall, consisted of sixteen launches, one motor-torpedo-boat, the old ex-American destroyer *Campbeltown* and, as command vessel, a motor-gunboat with Commander R. E. D. Ryder, RN, the senior naval officer, and Lieutenant-Colonel A. C. Newman, heading the Commandos (special forces), aboard. Four modern destroyers were assigned as sea-escorts. The daring mission almost went awry when *U593*, evading an attack by the destroyer-escort, sighted the convoy of small vessels and reported it on the afternoon of the 27th. By then Ryder was steering a false course, which proved enough to mislead the Germans and retain the essential advantage of surprise at St Nazaire. The submarine sighting actually assisted the British by prompting Navy Group West to send the force of five German torpedo-boats based there to sea to search to the south.

The attacking force, 353 men from the Navy and 268 Commandos, got within two miles of their goal before the alarm was sounded, at about 1.30 a.m. on the 28th. As powerful searchlights lit up the north bank of the Loire a deafening exchange of fire developed. Meanwhile the *Campbeltown* (Lieutenant-Commander S. H. Beattie) sailed on and at 1.34 (four minutes behind schedule) rammed her bow into the lock gates, where, according to plan, she was abandoned. Her bows contained three tons of explosive set to go off hours later. The troops who had travelled on her last voyage scrambled ashore and began their task of causing maximum damage to shore facilities. The crew was taken off by two of the small vessels, but one of them was soon sunk and the survivors, including Beattie, taken prisoner. Pandemonium and chaos engulfed the port as the Germans sank one launch after another and the Commandos engaged them in fierce fighting at close quarters. At 2.50 a.m. Ryder was forced to withdraw his remaining vessels from the inferno of gunfire and exploding demolition-charges, abandoning the troops still ashore. Only his MGB, number *314*, and seven launches remained, and as they were sailing down the estuary to join the two destroyers waiting for them the five German torpedo-boats returned at 6.30 a.m. to try an attack. The destroyers drove them off, but one more launch was sunk and two plus the MGB had to be scuttled after their crews were taken off. Only four of the launches survived.

Ten hours after ramming the gates, and just as a large number of German officers had unwisely gone aboard to examine her, HMS *Campbeltown* exploded and rendered the lock unusable. On the 29th, the destruction was completed when delayed-action torpedoes fired by the lost MTB *74* blew up, some thirty-six hours later than the British expected because their detonators were faulty. With few officers on hand and in a state of panic, German troops turned St Nazaire into a charnel-house, killing hundreds of local people and men on their own side. The British lost eighty-five sailors and fifty-nine Commandos (remarkably few in the circumstances); more than 100 sailors and nearly 200 soldiers were captured, many of them wounded. The whole episode was reminiscent of the raid on the Belgian port of Zeebrugge in 1918 – but much more successful, a classic if also bloody "surgical operation" against a defended target which succeeded against the odds by achieving almost total surprise. The strategic consequences extended well beyond the denial of a "garage" to the *Tirpitz*: the Germans were sufficiently alarmed to divert precious resources in men and material to defending the enormously long coastline of "Fortress Europe" because Hitler thought the St Nazaire raid presaged an early invasion. And on the 29th he ordered Dönitz to move his headquarters from Lorient to Paris that very day.

Another strategically useful British "pinprick" was the final denial of the Norwegian-administered island of Spitzbergen to the Germans in May 1942. Allied nationals living on this diplomatic curiosity had been taken off by the Royal Navy in August 1941 but it was known the Germans were operating a weather-station there and had a military presence which could have been exploited by the Luftwaffe. Free Norwegian troops were put ashore from Iceland, but their two ships with most of their stores were sunk by German bombers. The precarious situation was saved by Flight-Lieutenant D. E. Healey of 210 Squadron, RAF Coastal Command, and the crew of his Catalina flying-boat. In dreadful conditions they flew one long mission after another, ferrying supplies to the troops, bombing and strafing the Germans, rescuing wounded and incidentally spotting survivors from the Russian convoys.

On 15 June 1942 Grand-Admiral Erich Raeder unrolled a large chart on the map-table at the Wolf's Lair and with the aid of a pointer explained to Hitler the details of Operation *Rösselsprung*. The word is taken from the German chess vocabulary and means "knight's move." The knight in question was a small metaphor for the looming *Tirpitz*, which was to move out from Trondheim against the next British convoy to Russia. She was to be directly supported by the heavy cruiser *Hipper* and six destroyers, and indirectly by the pocket-battleships *Lützow* and *Scheer* with another six destroyers from Narvik, as well as by the Luftwaffe. As usual in German capital-ship operations, action against British heavy forces was to be avoided if possible, to appease Hitler's abiding concern for the big ships as guardians of Norway: the target was the shipping and its close escort.

The operation had begun five days earlier in that three submarines were already on patrol north-east of Iceland to watch for the convoy. Admiral Otto

Schniewind, the new Fleet C-in-C in succession to Ciliax, was to be in command at sea, while Admiral Rolf Carls, commander of Navy Group North in Kiel, exercised operational control. Hitler gave his consent, with one proviso: that any enemy carriers in the vicinity must be put out of action first. Since nobody could guarantee this, *Rösselsprung* would on such terms be stillborn. Raeder therefore arranged for the ships to take up their starting positions but not to move until Hitler personally gave the go-ahead on the day. Essentially the plan was to use submarines and aircraft to the west, and the surface-ships to the east, of Bear Island, which lies north of the Norwegian mainland and due south of Spitzbergen (74° north and 19° east).

Bear Island was also a key reference-point for the British as they prepared to cover the passage of PQ17 eastward to Russia and QP13 in the opposite direction, both to start on June 27. The covering force of four cruisers was ordered not to sail east of it if the *Tirpitz* was out; to the west of the island protection against German surface forces was to be provided by thirteen submarines. Distant cover was as usual to be given by the Home Fleet: HMS *Duke of York* (Tovey's flagship), the battleship USS *Washington*, the carrier *Victorious*, two more cruisers and fourteen destroyers. Eight RAF Catalinas were temporarily based in northern Russia. A bright idea on the part of the Admiralty to run a decoy convoy ahead of the real PQ17 lost its lustre when the Germans failed to notice it. The close escort was led by Commander J. E. Broome, RN, in the destroyer *Keppel*, supported by five others, four corvettes, two submarines, three rescue-ships, an oiler, two anti-aircraft ships, minesweepers and trawlers. Commodore J. C. K. Dowding, RNR, was in charge of the convoy itself, which finally consisted of thirty-three ships (two having been forced to turn back after accidents).

PQ17 was sighted by German aircraft and submarines at lunchtime on July 1. The boats were driven off by the escort after firing a couple of torpedoes, which were evaded by an emergency turn ordered by Broome and Dowding. During the afternoon Rear-Admiral L. H. K. Hamilton in HMS *London* with one other British and two American cruisers plus three destroyers sailed past the convoy to cover it from forty miles to the north. In the evening nine German Heinkel 111 torpedo-bombers attacked but were driven off without loss, and overnight the convoy was protected by a welcome fog. On the 3rd, RAF reconnaissance discovered that *Tirpitz* and *Hipper* had left Trondheim but not where they had gone (which was to their starting-point near the Lofoten Islands off north-west Norway). They were joined there by the *Scheer* and went to lie in wait in Altenfjord. The *Lützow* and three of the four destroyers which sailed with the *Tirpitz* all ran aground near Narvik and were out of commission. The RAF had been unable to reconnoitre Narvik and could offer no information on the whereabouts of any of the German surface-ships. On the night of the 3rd to 4th, PQ17 passed without incident to the north of Bear Island, the cruisers still providing cover as Admiral Hamilton exercised his discretion by sailing further east with it, as permitted in his orders. He planned to withdraw that evening. QP13 meanwhile, having passed PQ17 on the afternoon of July 2, was serenely passing south-east of Jan Mayen Island, all thirty-five ships and thirteen escorts in good order.

At 8.30 p.m. on July 4, twenty-four German torpedo-bombers made a more determined attack, damaging but not sinking a Soviet tanker and two merchantmen (the latter had to be sunk by the escort after their crews were taken off by the rescue-ships). Earlier in the day one other cargo-ship had also been similarly dispatched after a lone German aircraft launched its torpedo through a brief gap in the fog. The damaged tanker got home, and Broome and Dowding were not downcast: the convoy had kept station in exemplary fashion under air-attack and no submarines had tried to interfere.

In London, however, the complete absence of firm information about the German heavy ships made the Admiralty extremely nervous. Admiral Sir Dudley Pound, the First Sea Lord and Chief of Naval Staff, took the chair at a staff meeting on the evening of the 4th. They now knew that the German ships had joined up at Altenfjord but not whether they were still there. A surface-attack on the convoy and Hamilton's cruisers, still on roughly parallel eastward courses, could occur at any time from the early hours of July 5.

Events in the far north were of course being followed with the closest attention in the Operational Intelligence Centre, where its chief, Captain Norman Denning, was in personal charge that fateful evening. At stake were not only the ships of the convoy, the close escort and the cruisers but also 157,000 tonnes of precious aircraft, tanks and other munitions for the Red Army, and the viability of the northern supply-route itself. On this occasion OIC was not at the disadvantage which had been hampering the Submarine Tracking Room since February 1: the German surface-ships did not use the unbroken *Triton*/Shark cipher and Bletchley Park was able to penetrate both the Naval and the Luftwaffe traffic from the area, though sometimes only after delays of several hours. Thus OIC knew that the German ships had joined up but, as yet, no more.

Hamilton was told at 7.30 p.m. by the Admiralty to "remain with the convoy pending further instructions." OIC had just heard that Bletchley Park had broken into the Enigma traffic up to noon of the 4th (when the daily setting was changed). It was at this tense moment that Pound came down to OIC and asked Denning: "Can you assure me that the *Tirpitz* is still in Altenfjord?" Denning, naturally, could not prove what was really a negative proposition, that the German ships were not at sea with intent to attack the convoy and the cruisers. He could only argue that there was an absence of evidence suggesting that the enemy was out – no wireless traffic, no sightings by Allied submarines or aircraft – and therefore that he was confident the enemy was still in the fjord; he hoped to have confirmation when Bletchley Park cracked the new Enigma setting. According to Denning's own papers, this happened unexpectedly quickly and the fresh material began to flow at 8 p.m., but regrettably nothing bearing on Pound's question either way was received before the First Sea Lord opened his meeting at 8.30.

To deal with threats from aircraft and submarines the convoy needed to stay together under the protection of its flak-ships and surface-escorts. The classic response to an attack by superior surface-forces, however, was to scatter. This was Pound's dilemma: which was the greater threat to PQ17? He had told Tovey, to the latter's horror, just before the convoy set sail and the Home Fleet moved to provide distant cover well to the west, that he might feel obliged to order the merchantmen to scatter if the German ships came out, even though the Barents Sea, through which they were passing on the evening of the 4th, did not offer anything like enough searoom for an effective dispersal.

At 9.30 p.m. Admiral Pound, still without positive information on the *Tirpitz*, made up his mind and closed the meeting. Six minutes later the order was signalled to Hamilton: "Most immediate. Cruiser force to withdraw westward at high speed." This in itself caused neither surprise nor consternation, because the cruisers were already considerably further to the east than the point – 25° east – at which operational orders originally envisaged a reversal of course (because of the earlier fate of the *Trinidad* and the *Edinburgh* in the area). But almost at once another message came through: "Immediate. Owing to threat from surface ships the convoy is to disperse and proceed to Russian ports." And within minutes another: "Most immediate. Convoy is to scatter." The words "disperse" and "scatter" were (and are) not interchangeable synonyms in naval jargon. The former implies an orderly procedure whereby the convoy would gradually break up as each ship left the formation and made for its destination at its own best speed. The latter means what it says: instantaneous dispersal to all points of the compass, each ship taking a different and predetermined course away from the convoy's last position, as laid down in her sailing-orders in order to avoid collision. Less formally, the two orders could be respectively translated as, "make your own way" and "run for your lives." Hamilton, Broome and Dowding were devastated and immediately assumed a heavy surface-attack was imminent. Dowding was so astounded that he asked Broome twice for confirmation of the escort-commander's relayed order to scatter. Broome independently decided that his proper course was to join up with the cruisers to present a united defence against the anticipated attack. All three commanders regarded the actions they were ordered to take as the hardest and most distressing of their lives, even before they learned the appalling truth: the *Tirpitz* and all her consorts were still at anchor in Altenfjord at the time.

The Luftwaffe and the German submarines, however, were not idle and soon detected the abandonment and dispersal of the heavily laden convoy. In the early hours of July 5 they assembled their forces and opened what can only be described as a systematic massacre of PQ17. By noon submarines and dive-bombers had sent six merchantmen to the bottom. Shortly afterwards a submarine sank the *River Afton*, Commodore Dowding's ship. He was among the few survivors. Later in the afternoon a tanker and a minesweeper were destroyed. Altogether the Germans caught and sank twelve ships on July 5, and that was only the first day.

Braced for an immediate encounter with the invincible *Tirpitz*, Hamilton and Broome, only dimly aware of what was going on to their south but fully able to guess, were increasingly perplexed and disturbed by the fact that nothing was happening in their vicinity. Broome wanted to return to his scattered charges, but Hamilton took the view that the entire assembled force should head westward to join the Home Fleet, once again in the belief that concentration of force was the best defence against an assumed enemy of formidable strength. It was only some twenty-one hours after the fateful order to scatter that the Admiralty realised from one of Hamilton's signals that Broome was still with him, a fact for which the unfortunate Commander was subsequently criticised – by Pound himself, who bore the terrible responsibility for the consequences of his order to scatter in the face of a threat which was real but not, as he had tragically gambled, imminent.

Hitler, who liked to talk with his intimates well into the night, as usual got up at an unmilitarily late hour on the morning of July 5. Satisfied by reconnaissance reports revealing the enormous distance of the British Home Fleet with its aircraft-carrier from the last known position of the convoy, he gave Raeder his permission to go ahead with *Rösselsprung*. The *Tirpitz*, accompanied by *Scheer*, *Hipper*, seven destroyers and two torpedo-boats, at last sailed out of Altenfjord after 11 a.m., heading north and then turning east round the North Cape of Norway. As information came in during the day from the Luftwaffe, "Admiral, Norway" and Navy Group North about the dispersal of the convoy and the terrible destruction being wrought, Raeder, thankfully, decided to cancel *Rösselsprung*. Admiral Schniewind therefore put about at 9.30 p.m. and reached Narvik, down the Norwegian coast from Altenfjord, without incident of any kind. The aborted operation had already achieved as much as its execution might reasonably have been hoped to accomplish: the threat presented by the mere existence of the *Tirpitz* had been as effective as several broadsides at point-blank range, without risking the immaculate paintwork of the great battleship.

The final score against PQ17 was twelve merchantmen and a rescue-ship sunk by aircraft and ten ships by submarines. No warship was damaged. Eleven merchantmen and two rescue-ships got to Russia; one third of the total. Nearly 100,000 tonnes of munitions were lost. So were five German aircraft. "Not a successful convoy," wrote Commodore Dowding laconically in his report's closing words. He commandeered a corvette to go and look for ships which had survived. Among them were three freighters which had been led into the Arctic ice-fields by Lieutenant L. J. A. Gradwell in the trawler *Ayrshire*. They had painted themselves white to evade detection. Dowding added them to his private-enterprise convoy, which found and brought to Archangel the surviving ships that had taken refuge in various bleak hiding-places on Russia's north-west coast. This was meagre consolation for the most poignant convoy catastrophe of the war.

It was all another disaster for the Royal Navy, which was soon accused in the United States of abandoning a convoy, including many American ships, for no good reason. The British Merchant Navy took a similar view. The Admiralty instituted an internal inquiry whose results were presented to the British Cabinet on August 1. The main justification given by Admiral Pound for his order to scatter was that the whereabouts of the *Tirpitz* had been unknown and she could therefore have been in a position to attack from the early hours of July 5.

QP13 mistook a vast iceberg for the north-western corner of Iceland and therefore sailed into a British minefield. The minesweeper serving as the leader of the escort and four merchant ships were sunk and two more were damaged. The Royal Navy was short of luck.

It is suspiciously easy to condemn Admiral Pound for his fateful decision to disperse PQ17, especially after it became known that Denning, his outstanding intelligence adviser, was right about the *Tirpitz*. This is to overlook the fact that Pound was also right in anticipating a German surface-attack, which would undoubtedly have taken place had he not given the order to scatter (Schniewind did come out of Altenfjord and was stood down only when it was clear that his services were not required). The position of Admiral Tovey's heavy forces so far to the west makes it clear that the British were as unenthusiastic about a slogging-match between the big ships as the Germans. Admiralty policy was not to risk the Home Fleet in waters where the enemy had overwhelming air superiority. To have scattered the convoy too late would almost certainly have been as disastrous as doing it too soon proved to be. The real error behind the tragedy of PQ17, one of the saddest of the entire war, was the familiar bugbear of Admirals Forbes and Tovey and many more before and since: Admiralty interference in tactical decisions which should have been left to the commander on the spot, in this case Admiral Hamilton. He had been specifically ordered on setting out not to get involved in an action with the Germans if the *Tirpitz* was with them. That should have been enough.

The first seven months of 1942 took the German submarine campaign against the Anglo-American transatlantic lifeline as far to the west as geography permitted, and as far to the north. The result was the most concentrated period of high losses to shipping of the entire war – 4,765,000 tons worldwide, of which submarines sank 3,556,000 and 3,319,000 tons went down in the North Atlantic. Much of this could have been prevented by the immediate adoption of convoy in the American strategic zone (and the numerically minor losses in global terms of the Russian run could have been reduced by using the admittedly far longer route round Africa, into the Persian Gulf and overland through Iran). Even so, American and Allied shipbuilding had just begun to overtake the worst that Dönitz could do at the zenith of his career; but German yards were also turning out more and more boats with which the Allied sinking-rate was far from catching up.

Neither side produced a technological wonder during this period. On the Allied side radar and HF/DF were spreading and improving and the Hedgehog (the multiple mortar which fired small depth-charges ahead of a ship) was coming into general use. The Germans were getting better torpedoes but seriously underestimated the value and degree of use of radar on the Allied side. After the fall of France Hitler had forbidden the development of anything likely to take more than a year because he believed Germany would have triumphed by then. A device called *Bold* (originally *Kobold* – goblin) which produced a huge underwater bubble and was meant to fool Asdic proved a failure. Allied aircraft had become notably more efficient in finding, attacking and sinking submarines with the help of better radar and depth-charges and the Leigh Light.

In the Far East, meanwhile, the Japanese invaded the Netherlands East Indies (now Indonesia) and advanced into Burma, then British, in the middle of January, posing a threat to India, centrepiece of the British Empire. Before the end of the month another Axis offensive opened in North Africa. The surrender of Singapore without a real fight on February 15 was the nadir of the war for the Empire; four days later Japanese carrier-aircraft bombed Darwin, Australia, and on the 22nd General Douglas MacArthur, USA, left the Philippines, promising: "I shall return." At the end of that most dismal month for the Allies, the Japanese won the Battle of the Java Sea. Their control of the Dutch East Indies was completed by the capture of Java itself on March 3. But by the middle of April the Americans were able to counter-attack, bombing Tokyo in daylight from carrier-borne aircraft under the command of General James H. Doolittle, USAAF. On May 4 the US Navy won the Battle of the Coral Sea and one month later scored a decisive victory over the Japanese Fleet at the Battle of Midway, the turning-point in the Pacific. But in the Soviet Union the Germans still held the initiative; halted on the northern and central fronts, they overran the Crimea to the south in high summer, by which time they were also on the attack once more in North Africa, under Rommel.

At the end of July 1942 the Atlantic campaign was in the balance.

8

JULY 1942 TO MAY 1943

Dönitz warns – the airgaps – Laconia – disguised raiders beaten – Russian convoys – losses at sea – Canadian disasters – "Operation Torch" – Admiral Horton at Western Approaches – Bay Offensive – radar – Ultra returns – Dönitz succeeds Raeder – TM1 disaster – Casablanca Conference – Canada sidelined – good news from Russia – the great crisis of the campaign – four climactic convoys – the pendulum swings against Germany – airpower – Canada's first C-in-C – US Tenth Fleet – Dönitz retreats

ADMIRAL Karl Dönitz, C-in-C of the German submarine service basking in the propaganda glory of its huge success in the western Atlantic in the first half of 1942, proceeded on July 27 to make one of the most extraordinary radio broadcasts of the war. To the astonishment of the British Admiralty he went on the air to warn the German public, unaccustomed as it was to such frankness, of the inevitability of heavier losses. "The harsh realities of the submarine war" meant that "even more difficult times lie ahead of us." In his memoirs Dönitz explained that the warning was made necessary by "the exaggerated hopes that had been raised by speeches and by press and radio accounts of the tremendous submarine successes of the previous months. A correct sense of proportion had to be restored to the public mind." In London, where German public radio was as keenly monitored as military traffic, this "tip straight from the horse's mouth," as the Admiralty called it, was read as indicating a German return to the convoy routes in the mid-Atlantic airgap, south of Greenland. The submarine tide had reached the high-water mark in the west and had receded (although the Germans were in no sense on the retreat). If Dönitz himself anticipated higher losses he could only be thinking of an assault on the main convoy-artery in spite of the escorts; and he would surely choose, as he had always done, the weakest point, which was where the ships had no air-cover.

This bore out the mid-year strategic assessment of the campaign by the First Sea Lord, Admiral Pound, who had concluded that "another turning point in the U-boat war is approaching." Without the inordinately long journey to and from the furthest operational areas the Germans could concentrate three to five times the number of boats in the eastern to mid-Atlantic region, just when British escort forces had been thinned out to help close the gaps in the convoy defences to the west. With this increased commitment the escorts were so stretched that little could be done to reinforce the most threatened area. As far as surface-escorts were concerned, the Admiralty had the answer. From the approximately 170 escorts available for mercantile convoy escort in the Atlantic, ten destroyers and frigates were skimmed off to form the first support-group (known during its very brief existence as the 20th Escort Group). Its role was to go to the aid of a threatened convoy. It was formed in September – and disbanded in October for reasons described below. It was an idea whose time had come, but nothing could be done about it for six more months.

At the same time the Admiralty conceived the Merchant Aircraft Carrier (MAC) as another stopgap measure in the struggle to provide end-to-end air-cover. Six tankers of 11,000 tons and six bulk-carriers of 8,000 tons (both types having long uncluttered decks) were ordered to be converted by having their upper decks strengthened so that they could fly off and land three or four Swordfish torpedo-bombers. The ships would still carry cargoes. The idea was a considerable improvement on the Catapult-Aircraft Merchantman (CAM) with its single Hurricane which had to ditch when its fuel ran out; and the Swordfish with its low speed was very useful against submarines. But it was to be nearly nine months before the MAC made its debut. Like so many other clever improvisations, it needed time to gestate.

Meanwhile the strength of the submarine fleet had at last passed, in the second quarter of 1942, the total of 300 boats with which Dönitz would have liked to begin the war. In that quarter alone, new deliveries amounted to fifty-nine – two more than the entire German strength in 1939. On July 1 the total stood at 331, of which 140 were fully operational, as we have seen, and more than twenty were being added each month. This enabled Dönitz to shift the focus of his attack back to the main north Atlantic convoy route without abandoning operations in the Gulf of Mexico and the Caribbean. Despite the spread of convoy to those areas and the increase in air-cover, shipping in the confined waters had little searoom for evasion, and between the end of *Paukenschlag* and August 31, fifteen ships were sunk, though at the cost of three submarines.

These losses and the increasing strength of local escort drove the Germans to withdraw southward to the area between Trinidad and the Orinoco estuary. This by now secondary submarine effort surprised even the Germans by the successes it yielded them; it was allowed to continue until November, by which time they had sunk a total of 375,000 tons in the Trinidad area alone in three months. Convoy between Trinidad and points south became part of the burgeoning Interlocking Convoy System only in October. A great advantage was conferred on the Allies on August 22, when Brazil declared war on Germany after *U507* had sunk five Brazilian ships on the 16th and 17th. This German strategic blunder gave the Allies complete control by sea and air of the "waist" of the Atlantic between Brazil and West Africa where the ocean is at its narrowest. This helped not only against submarines but also against surface-raiders and blockade-runners between Germany and Japan.

The German return to the main convoy route was signalled on August 5 by a strong attack on convoy SC94, a slow, laden eastbound formation of thirty-three merchantmen with seven escorts. One ship was sunk that afternoon. On the next day the escorts had the upper hand, fending off all attacks without air-cover (because of fog). The Canadian destroyer *Assiniboine* rammed and sank *U210* but had to withdraw with serious damage to her hull. On the 8th it was the Germans' turn, with five ships sunk in the afternoon and one more abandoned, to be given the *coup de grâce* by a submarine later. But the corvette *Dianthus* destroyed *U379* by ramming, this time without serious damage to herself. The warships held their own until the afternoon of the 9th, when American Catalinas from Iceland and RAF Liberators from Aldergrove, Northern Ireland (nearly 800 miles away) appeared over SC94, while the destroyer HMS *Broke* arrived to reinforce the escort. Four more ships were sunk on the morning of the 10th, but once the air-patrols returned no further losses were suffered. The final score was eleven ships lost (one third), totalling some 53,000 tons; of the eighteen submarines sent into the attack, two were sunk and four damaged.

To match this attack in the Greenland airgap (known to the Germans as the "Devil's Gorge" and to Allied seamen as "Torpedo Junction"), Dönitz also focused on the other key area without air-cover around the Azores (known to both sides as the "Black Gap" – the Germans used the English words) to strike at the Sierra Leone traffic. SL118 lost three ships in mid-month until a Liberator from Cornwall, at the limit of its range, came to the rescue and drove the attackers under.

Although Dönitz had already chosen the main northern convoy route as his next target after the North American coastline, he had more than enough boats with which to probe and confuse the enemy elsewhere. At the beginning of this post-*Paukenschlag* period he had fifteen in the Caribbean area, five or six each off Canada and Brazil, the Azores and Sierra Leone, as well as a dozen in the Greenland gap. Another thirty boats were in transit to and from the various operational areas. In the middle of August the *Eisbär* (polar bear) group of four boats was sent from Lorient with a "milch-cow" to look for targets in mid-Atlantic south of the equator. One of them was *U156*, under Commander Werner Hartenstein, a holder of the Knight's Cross. It was he who precipitated a chain of tragic events whose effects almost culminated in the death of Dönitz himself.

On the night of September 12 while some 500 miles north of Ascension Island, Hartenstein sighted the looming grey shape of the liner *Laconia*, 19,700 tons, a former Armed Merchant Cruiser turned troopship. This British vessel had about 2,600 men aboard and, being still armed, was a legitimate target under the elastic rules of engagement in a total war. Hartenstein could not know, not even from the ship's north-westerly course which might have been evasive, that 1,800 of those aboard were Italian prisoners of war on their way from North Africa to internment in North America. He mortally wounded the ship with a torpedo and at first watched from a distance as hundreds of men poured over the sides and took to boats or liferafts. Coming closer to inspect his handiwork, Hartenstein realised what damage he might have done to the already strained German–Italian Axis. It cannot be gainsaid that what he did next, at obvious risk to his boat as would soon be made clear, was humanitarian in motive. Fortunately *U156* was a type IXc, one of the larger boats, and Hartenstein began to pick up survivors regardless of which uniform they were wearing. Apart from the Italians there were British merchant seamen, naval sailors and Polish soldiers who had been guarding the prisoners, as well as passengers including women and children. The submarine commander wirelessed his headquarters for instructions and then repeatedly transmitted this message on the international emergency wavelength (in English):

> If any ship will assist the shipwrecked *Laconia* crew I will not attack her, provided I am not attacked by ship or air force. I picked up 193 men 4°52' south 11°26' west. German submarine. [0600 hours, September 13]

Dönitz ordered the three other members of *Eisbär*, two other German boats and one Italian submarine, to join the rescue effort. He asked the Vichy French naval authorities in West Africa to send help while instructing the rescue-submarines to head for the Ivory Coast, a French colony controlled by Vichy. Hitler, on hearing of this unusual undertaking, personally ordered Dönitz not to jeopardise the submarines or the operational plans of *Eisbär*. Hartenstein meanwhile was crawling westward with some 200 survivors below and another seventy clinging to the narrow deck, with four lifeboats in tow and shepherding others as best he could. The other *Eisbär* boats and their tanker, having picked up no survivors, were ordered to sail south to operate off the Cape of Good Hope, leaving *U506* and *U507*, on their way back from patrol off north-west Africa, to help *U156*. The reinforcements reached the area on the night of the 14th to 15th and began to pick up more survivors. They were distributed as evenly as possible among lifeboats, rafts and the two rescuing boats. They and *U156* now proceeded independently, their charges scattered across a wide area of calm, warm sea, to a predetermined rendezvous with the Vichy French ships to the west. It was all highly reminiscent of the rescue of the crews of the *Atlantis* and the *Python* in late 1940. For thirty-six hours this precarious enterprise continued undisturbed at little more than walking speed. Then, according to Hartenstein's War Diary, on the morning of the 16th there came a second tragedy:

1125. Shortly before the arrival of other two boats [at the rendezvous], four-engined aircraft with American markings bearing seventy degrees. As proof of my peaceful intentions displayed large Red Cross flag four metres square on bridge facing line of aircraft's flight . . .

1232. Aircraft of similar type approached. Flew over at height of 80 metres slightly ahead of the boat and dropped two bombs at interval of about three seconds. While the tow with four lifeboats was being cast off, the aircraft dropped a bomb in the middle of the latter. One boat capsized. Aircraft cruised round in the vicinity for a while and then dropped a fourth bomb some two or 3,000 metres away. Realised that his bomb-racks were now empty. Another aircraft. Two bombs, one of which with a few seconds delayed action exploded directly under control-room. Conning-tower disappeared in a mushroom of black water. Control-room and bow compartment reported taking in water . . .

In fact a Liberator from the US Navy mid-Atlantic airbase on Ascension Island had spotted *U156* with her four lifeboats in tow and reported back by radio. He was unequivocally ordered to sink the submarine and made two separate attempts to do so. When Hartenstein reported the attack he and *U506* and *U507* were told to abandon the rescue. Hartenstein had already cleared his boat of all survivors by cramming them into the lifeboats or leaving them to hang on to the ratlines along their sides. He submerged and left the scene some seventy-five minutes after the bombing. *U506* and *U507* however carried on and Dönitz amended his orders to them early on the 17th: they were told to put all non-Italian survivors aboard into the lifeboats and to be sure to be ready to dive at any time. This was what *U506* was forced to do at lunch-time on the 17th, when a flying-boat came over and dropped a pattern of depth-charges, without inflicting any damage. Both boats reached the rendezvous with the two French ships that evening. In all, about half those who had been aboard the *Laconia* – 800 Britons and Poles but only 450 Italians – were brought to safety.

The reaction by Dönitz to this poignant brew of ruthlessness and chivalry on the part of his men and unadulterated ruthlessness by Allied airmen was harsh and immediate. At 7.24 p.m. on the 17th, just as the rescue was being completed, he issued the following order to all submarines by radio:

1) All attempts at rescuing members of ships that have sunk, including attempts to pick up persons swimming, or to place them in lifeboats, or attempts to upright capsized boats, or to supply provisions or water, are to cease. The rescue of survivors contradicts the elementary necessity of war for the destruction of enemy ships and crews.

2) The order for the seizure of commanding officers and chief engineers remains in force.

3) Survivors are only to be picked up in cases when their interrogation would be of value to the submarines.

4) Be severe. Remember that in his bombing attacks on German cities the enemy has no regard for women and children.

This order was the basis for a war-crime charge against Dönitz at the postwar Nuremberg trials of leading Nazis. With the events which provoked it fresh in our minds we may usefully complete the story here. The prosecution argued that the order was in clear breach of the London Protocol of 1936 (accepted by Germany but repudiated by Hitler in 1939), which outlawed unrestricted submarine warfare on merchant shipping. The defence claimed that the safety of the submarine took precedence over rescue and that the development of anti-submarine aircraft effectively ruled out rescue-attempts. The Tribunal found that the order did not constitute a direct instruction to kill survivors but was ambiguous and therefore merited severe censure; further it was a breach of the Protocol, which laid down that if rescue was impossible then a submarine should not attempt to sink a ship. Had the judges been convinced that the order meant that survivors should be killed, they would undoubtedly have sentenced Dönitz to death. As it was, he was convicted of waging aggressive war and of complicity in unspecified war-crimes, and was sentenced to ten years imprisonment – decidedly mild in the circumstances. Neither the German Navy in general nor the submarine service in particular was condemned at Nuremberg for its general conduct of the war at sea.

One of the most decisive elements in determining Dönitz's fate was the honesty of Admiral Chester W. Nimitz, USN, the greatest American admiral and commander in the Pacific. Nimitz told the Tribunal: "As a general rule, United States submarines did not rescue enemy survivors if by so doing the vessels were exposed to unnecessary or additional risk, or if the submarines were hindered from the execution of further tasks." The incident which probably counted most strongly against the German commander was an isolated one which took place on 13 March 1944. *Kapitänleutnant* Heinz-Wilhelm Eck in *U852* sank the Greek steamer *Peleus* in equatorial waters off West Africa. Surfacing after his torpedo-attack, Eck machine-gunned wreckage to which the survivors were clinging without regard for anything but his own desire to escape undetected. Three survived to tell the tale. He and his officers were sentenced to death by a British court martial and shot on 30 November 1945. This atrocity was unique in a submarine campaign which was always cruel, often merciless and only seldom chivalrous. On both sides. Italian survivors of the *Laconia* claimed that their guards closed watertight doors on the prisoners as the ship began to sink, which was why 1,350 Italians died compared with eleven non-Italians.

As the German submarine fleet expanded, so the ability of the German Navy to threaten Allied shipping from the surface declined. But in summer 1942 there were still three disguised raiders on the loose. In August and September the *Stier* (Raider J to the British, *Schiff 23* to the Germans) and the *Michel* (H or *28*) tried working together in the South Atlantic. Independently routed ships were now rare and the raiders found few victims. On September 27, while the pair were searching some distance apart, the *Stier* (Captain Horst Gerlach) sighted a slow-moving merchantman of what was by now a quite familiar shape – the Liberty ship *Stephen Hopkins*, 10,708 tons, flying the Stars and Stripes. The German raider, with enough armament to sink a light cruiser, and the *Hopkins* (Captain Paul Buck) with her single 4-inch gun aft, now engaged in an unequal contest which lasted for three hours. Astonishingly, with some luck and more gallantry, it was the American underdog which scored first. After about fifteen hits on the *Stier* the Americans had the satisfaction of seeing flames rising from her hull. But the *Hopkins* was taking more punishment than she could give, especially when the blockade-runner *Tannenfels*, from which the *Stier* had been resupplying herself just before the action, came up in support. The unusual action around the tropic of Capricorn in the South Atlantic ended with the sinking of both the *Stier* and the *Hopkins*. But whereas the *Tannenfels* was able to save most of the Germans, only fifteen Americans in one lifeboat reached Brazil alive – after thirty-one days at sea with no compass. They were able to tell the story of one of the finest fights ever put up by Allied merchant seamen. The *Michel* was herself picking up stores at the time from the supply-ship *Uckermark* (better known to us under her previous name of *Altmark*, partner of the *Graf Spee*) well over the horizon, and picked up but ignored the *Stier's* call for help. Captain Hellmuth von Ruckteschell, late of the *Widder*, decided to leave the area and was then ordered into the Indian Ocean. He never returned to the Atlantic (the *Michel* reached Japan in May 1943 and was sunk the following October by an American submarine when starting for home). The raider *Thor* (E or *10*) blew up in Yokohama in November 1942.

The *Michel* and *Stier* had been able to pass down the English Channel unharmed in March and May 1942 respectively despite attacks by British light forces. The *Komet* (Raider B, renumbered *Schiff 45* by the Germans) was less fortunate after she set out for her second cruise from the Dutch port of Flushing on the night of October 7. Some fifteen British destroyers and frigates with eight motor-torpedo-boats set out in pursuit, and an MTB sank the *Komet* with a torpedo after she and two of her escorts had been set ablaze by gunfire off Le Havre in the early hours of the 14th. Decrypts of the German Enigma naval coastal cipher, *Hydra* (a three-wheel cipher), alerted the British in time to the unusual activity portending her attempted breakout. But *Orion* (Raider A), in France since August 1941, managed to get back to Germany unscathed under cover of fog in November 1942. With her the considerable threat to Allied shipping once represented by German armed merchant raiders disappeared from the Atlantic.

As we have seen, the main conventional surface threat presented by the Germans was from the occupied Norwegian ports. By the late summer of 1942 the great battleship *Tirpitz*, the pocket-battleship *Scheer*, the heavy cruiser *Hipper* and the light cruiser *Köln* were ready for sea in Narvik.

Despite the PQ17 disaster in July, the British and Americans felt that an early renewal of the convoys to northern Russia was a political imperative and a strategic necessity, and it was decided to sail PQ18 eastbound and QP14 westbound in September. The Home Fleet had been preoccupied in August with helping the attempts to relieve the besieged island-fortress of Malta in the Mediterranean, and had lost one cruiser and one destroyer sunk and two cruisers damaged. Preparations for the resumption were elaborate. Four destroyers took stores and ammunition to the survivors of PQ17 in Russian ports; they would form the bulk of the returning QP14. Next twenty-four Hampden torpedo-bombers, a squadron of Catalina flying-boats and four photo-reconnaissance Spitfires were flown to operate from North Russian bases. Unaccountably the Russians refused to accept the British field hospital the RAF flew in with the Hampdens to look after the casualties from PQ17 and the medical staff were obliged to sail home with QP14 and the wounded. A temporary British Area Combined Headquarters was set up under Rear-Admiral D. B. Fisher, Senior British Naval Officer in North Russia, assisted by Group Captain F. L. Hopps, RAF. The German xB-dienst got wind of the coming convoy operation with its customary skill in the latter part of August and the Germans sent submarines, destroyers and the minelayer Ulm to sow mines in the approaches to the North Russian ports. The four destroyers returning from delivering stores caught the Ulm south of Bear Island and sank her on August 25.

The British naval preparations for covering the convoys were unprecedented. Admiral Tovey decided not to let his heavy ships provide distant cover from far to the west as hitherto, so as to be able to release sixteen fleet destroyers to work closely with the convoys themselves. Instead he placed his deputy, Vice-Admiral Sir Bruce Fraser, with the battleships Anson (flag) and Duke of York, the cruiser Jamaica and five destroyers at Akureyri on the north coast of Iceland. PQ18, which was to consist of thirty-nine cargo ships, three minesweepers bound for the Soviet fleet, three oilers and a rescue ship, was given a power ul close escort of destroyers, anti-aircraft ships and submarines (two of each), plus four corvettes, four trawlers and three minesweepers. To them was added the new escort-carrier, HMS Avenger (twelve fighters and three anti-submarine Swordfish), covered by two more destroyers.

In charge of all this, plus the sixteen Home Fleet destroyers as the first line of defence against a surface-attack, was Rear-Admiral R. L. Burnett in the cruiser Scylla. Three cruisers under Vice-Admiral S. S. Bonham-Carter were to provide intermediate cover. In addition, these enormous forces were to be accompanied for part of the way by two more cruisers, five destroyers and two oilers which were to replenish the Allied garrison on Spitzbergen Island; and seven British submarines were put on patrol off northern Norway. There can be few starker illustrations of the "fleet-in-being" theory than this formidable British deployment made necessary by the lurking presence of the *Tirpitz* and her companions. For the sake of concentration of force, QP14 was not to set out until PQ18 was quite close to its destination; there was to be no halfway crossover near Bear Island as before, and most of the escorts would have to make a complete double journey between Iceland and Russia. Admiral Tovey stayed at Scapa Flow in the *King George V* to control the operation.

The bulk of PQ18 sailed from Loch Ewe in Scotland on September 2 and its escort was duly reinforced in Icelandic waters on the 7th. It was located by German air reconnaissance the next day. On the 10th all the German ships at Narvik except the *Tirpitz* sailed north through a British submarine patrol-line (one got a sighting but failed to score) to Altenfjord on the northern coast of Norway. They made no further movement because Hitler was as worried about Norway as ever; the British were unaware of his intervention. The first attack on PQ18 was made by *U88* on the 12th, but the boat was depth-charged to destruction by the destroyer *Faulknor* ahead of the convoy. On the 13th, other German submarines sank two ships in the outer starboard column.

Once bad weather lifted, next on the scene were strong Luftwaffe forces from among the 225 bombers in northern Norway. A ferocious attack by forty torpedo-bombers on the afternoon of the 13th sank no less than eight ships in eight minutes for the loss of five aircraft. Three lighter attacks were beaten off, but the *Avenger's* old Mark I Hurricanes could not cope with the main one. Ironically, as Captain Roskill points out in his official history, the merchantmen were carrying much more modern Hurricanes in crates in their holds. Four more air-attacks were made on the 14th, none of them as severe as the principal onslaught of the previous day. Despite their concentration on the carrier *Avenger*, the Hurricanes and the escorts' anti-aircraft guns managed to shoot down twenty-two German aircraft for the loss of one ship and three Hurricanes (but not their pilots). Neither side suffered any losses in the air-attacks on the 15th, and the escorts were wholly successful in keeping some dozen submarines at bay. On the 16th, as Catalinas from North Russia began patrolling overhead, the destroyer *Impulsive* sent *U457* to the bottom. The last casualty in the convoy was sunk by an air-attack on the 18th in which the Germans lost four bombers. The last attack came on the 20th, with no result for Germans or British. The final score for this hard-fought convoy action was ten ships lost to aircraft-attack with forty-one German planes shot down, and three to submarines, of which three were also sunk. Two-thirds of the ships got through, an achievement which would have been seen as a disaster on the main convoy routes but was a moderate setback by the lethal standards of the Murmansk run, where air-attacks presented a special danger.

QP14 consisted of fifteen ships led by Commodore J. C. K. Dowding, RNR, who had flown his pennant over PQ17. He set sail from Archangel on September 13 with two flak-ships and eleven small escorts, to be picked up by Admiral Burnett on the 17th when the latter came over from PQ18 (by then out of danger of surface-attack). The first week of the homeward passage was uneventful – until a German submarine sank the British minesweeper *Leda* of the escort on the 20th, and another destroyed a merchantman. Burnett now sent the *Avenger*, the *Scylla* and three fleet destroyers home as QP14 was well out of reach of the Luftwaffe by this stage; but that left the merchantmen without anti-submarine air-cover. Shortly afterwards the destroyer *Somali* was crippled by a torpedo and had to be taken in tow. She was lost overnight in a gale. Little shore-based air-protection was available because a large battle involving the eastbound Atlantic convoy SC100 was raging to the south-west. With Captain A. K. Scott-Moncrieff, RN, now in charge of the escort in *Faulknor*, QP14 next came under submarine attack on the 22nd, when U435 (KL Siegfried Strelow), which had already sunk the *Leda*, got inside the escort screen. Strelow sank three merchantmen in as many minutes. One of them was the *Ocean Voice*, the Commodore's ship: once again the unfortunate Dowding was in the water without a ship but happily he and most of the crews of the last three casualties of QP14 were saved. Constant air-patrols shielded the eleven surviving merchantmen from the 23rd and one Catalina sank U253. The convoy arrived in Loch Ewe without further incident on September 26.

Convoys to Russia were now suspended for three months; QP15 was sailed from Russia on November 17 to bring back the survivors of PQ18 (in all twenty-eight ships took part). Terrible weather prevented attacks by both the Luftwaffe and the German surface-ships and only two cargo-vessels were sunk by submarines. That marked the end of the PQ–QP series; in the last quarter of 1942, thirteen ships were sailed independently to Russia from Iceland, of which five got through, four were sunk, three turned back and one was wrecked. In the reverse direction only one was sunk out of twenty-three. The reason for the interruption was the same as that which forced the disbandment of the first Atlantic support group: "Operation Torch."

The Allied landing in north-west Africa on 8 November 1942 under the supreme command of General Dwight D. Eisenhower was one of the great turning-points of the Second World War. It consolidated the decisive victory won by the British Eighth Army under General Bernard Montgomery at El Alamein between October 23 and November 4 by sealing the fate of the Axis in North Africa. From now on the Wehrmacht was on the retreat in the West; and with the Soviet counter-attack at Stalingrad on November 19 it was also finally checked in the East, even though it was not until 2 February 1943 that the shattered Russian city was relieved. The significance of "Torch" to our story is indirect but far-reaching. The first counter-offensive by the western Allies had been given top priority at the Arcadia Conference in Washington over the Christmas–New Year period of 1941–2, presided over by Churchill and Roosevelt. From then on the transatlantic convoy system which had begun with one task, the sustenance of Britain, and moved on to the support of Russia and the movement of American troops and war-material, would have the additional burden of supplying "Torch." At the same time, as the moment of launch of the assault itself neared, the convoys would have to be stripped of all but a minimum of escorts. The Royal Navy had to provide 125 destroyers, sloops, frigates and corvettes as well as fifty-two minesweepers for the Mediterranean. This entailed the abandonment of support-groups, of the Russian convoys (as Churchill tried to explain to Stalin in Moscow in mid-August), of the Gibraltar and the Sierra Leone mercantile convoys. It imposed the Great Circle or direct route on transatlantic convoys for reasons of economy of fuel, time and escorts, a fact which both puzzled and pleased the German submariners.

Stalin as ever proved the most curmudgeonly of allies, demanding a Second Front in Europe immediately to take the pressure off the Red Army while doing as little as possible to help the convoys to Russia which were so vital to him. Churchill, however, having won the Americans over to the "Mediterranean first" strategy on land, was not about to give it up at Stalin's behest. The effect on the Atlantic campaign was drastic as will soon be shown. Whereas the Anglo-Canadians who did almost all the work on the main route were subjected to formidable new pressure, the Germans' ability to strike was little more than marginally reduced by the diversion of some submarines to the Mediterranean in an attempt to help the Afrika Korps and the Italians. And once the mostly American expeditionary force was landed and fighting, its demands for supplies and fuel became voracious, especially when added to the similar requirements of the British Army. These new strains on the convoy system lasted a good half-year. Finally we should note that two American squadrons of VLR Liberators, the only ones in US service not working in the Pacific or bombing Germany, were based in Morocco in support of "Torch," instead of over the Atlantic, protecting the convoys which fed the operation. It was the second time that the obdurate Admiral King almost lost the war single-handed.

Worldwide Allied shipping losses to all causes rose slightly by 43,000 tons in August 1942 to 661,000, but this total was 173,000 tons lower than the blackest month of the war so far, in June. In September they fell to 567,000 tons but in October they climbed to 638,000 and again in November to 808,000 tons, the third-worst monthly total of the entire war. The most ominous aspect of the November sinkings was the record submarine contribution of 729,000 tons, the peak of their destructive achievement in the Second World War. No less portentous was the fact that in the same bleak month, despite the spread of convoy across the ocean, 509,000 tons were lost in the North Atlantic, a total exceeded only once throughout the war (in the previous May). October produced the record total of 148,000 tons of sinkings in the South Atlantic. The only consolation was that this period saw negligible losses to air-attack, mines, surface-raiders and, very noticeably, in British home waters. It was overwhelmingly clear that the submarine was the main threat to the cause of the United Nations, as the grand alliance against the Axis now styled itself, and that it was at its most deadly in the mid-ocean areas out of reach of shore-based aircraft. Another adverse effect of "Torch" was that it caused a delay of some six months in the deployment of the new escort-carriers with the transatlantic convoys, just when they were most needed.

In August and September the Germans sighted one in three of all convoys on the main route and managed to attack one in three of those they spotted, a total of seven convoys which collectively lost forty-three ships. The latter part of 1942 was marked by a series of slogging-matches in which sometimes the submarines and sometimes the escorts and on several occasions neither got the upper hand. After three solid years of struggle ranging between one polar region and the other and between the Old World and the New, each side fully understood that the climax was at hand and neither could be confident of winning. If the battle of SC94, summarised above, can be described as a draw, ON127 was a clear victory to the Germans. The westbound convoy was attacked in the Greenland gap early in September and lost seven merchantmen and the escorting Canadian destroyer *Ottawa*, with four other ships damaged, without any loss to the attackers. But when Dönitz tried to redouble the success by diverting the boats involved to the eastbound slow convoy SC100, he did less well: only three ships were sunk before long-range aircraft appeared and forced the Germans to break off. Later in the month a mass-attack against HX209, a fast eastbound formation, failed completely while two submarines were destroyed by aircraft from Iceland. But the rescue of SC100 could only be achieved at some cost to QP14 (see above).

The boats which had failed against HX209 helped to form a pack of thirteen in the comparative safety of the airgap for an attack on the forty-four ships of the eastbound SC104. Leading the escort-group was the destroyer *Fame* (Commander S. Heathcote, RN), supported by one other British destroyer and four Norwegian corvettes. When he realised from HF/DF interceptions that the Germans were massing against the convoy Heathcote sent the escorts straight down the wireless bearings in order to force the enemy under. The escorts were too few, and the weather too violent, for successful submarine-hunting. One boat got into the convoy and sank three ships on the first night. As the early October battle swung to and fro the escorts showed unusual energy in running down every possible radio or radar contact, of which there were many. At least four of them got close enough to surfaced submarines to attempt ramming. On October 14, as the weather began to calm down, Lieutenant-Commander John Waterhouse in the destroyer *Viscount* scored the first success by violently ramming *U619*, which sank almost at once. But he was forced to withdraw slowly with serious damage to his ship, reducing the escort to five. Heathcote carried on running down all the contacts he could, now able to use depth-charges in the calmer conditions, and on occasion even gunfire, against the attackers. Over five days the losses among the ships to a substantial attacking force were thus limited to seven by the time the Liberators arrived from Iceland.

The Germans now lay in wait submerged and ahead of the convoy for a last ambush. HMS *Fame* discovered the danger with her Asdic and Heathcote depth-charged the first contact, forcing *U353* to the surface. As the merchant-men came up they released the frustrations and fears of the better part of a week by blazing away at the helpless boat with their guns. *Fame* completed the work by ramming it at the cost of considerable damage to herself. The Germans poured out of the conning-tower and Heathcote had the presence of mind to send a party of sailors aboard; but they too had to abandon after five minutes as *U353* finally began to go under for the last time. The boarding party got some handfuls of papers (but not, unfortunately, "One of Those" Enigma machines as was taken from *U110*). *Fame* too had to withdraw, leaving the four Norwegian corvettes in charge of the ships. One of them scored hits with her 4-inch gun on the last attacking submarine before the Germans were driven off by the resumption of air-patrols. Given the size of the forces on each side, this arduous and energetic action can be regarded as a victory to the defenders, if an expensive one, especially as an RAF Liberator sank *U661* in the vicinity shortly after the end of the battle. It may well have been part of the pack, whose final score after the sinking of a straggler was eight.

This grim autumn was particularly hard on the Canadian Navy and, inevitably, on the ships in its care. The setback of ONS127, whose almost entirely Canadian escort had not a single working radar set, was connected to the disaster which struck SC107 at the end of October by the fact that each badly mauled convoy had the same Mid-Ocean Escort Force (C4). SC107, slow and bound for England, consisted of forty-two ships. C4 was led by its sole destroyer, HMCS *Restigouche* (Lieutenant-Commander D. W. Piers, RCN), supported by six corvettes and a rescue-ship. Only *Restigouche* had a functioning radar set, and only she and the rescue-vessel had HF/DF; only three of the escorts were regular members of C4 and accustomed to working together. The convoy was sighted on October 29 by *U522*, which, forewarned by Dönitz on the basis of sharp work by the *xB-dienst*, was looking for it in the right place. Further west, the *Veilchen* ("violet") pack of seventeen boats was positioned directly across its path and sighted SC107 on November 1, after losing *U658* to the RCAF patrol. Aided by the unremitting and accurate labours of his radio direction-finders, Piers managed to repel any serious attack until nightfall, by which time he was well into the airgap south of Greenland. But after dark the odds swung sharply in favour of the Germans, when four submarines together sank eight ships in the first night – nearly a fifth of the convoy. A ninth ship was sunk in daylight on the 2nd, when the British destroyer *Vanessa* came up in support from another convoy which was not under threat. The Germans lost contact with SC107 in squally conditions but the lull was deceptive. No attempt was made to divert the convoy out of danger in the interlude, which made it simple for the submarines to get in touch again on the 3rd, to the surprise of Dönitz who thought he had lost it altogether. The tenth victim sank at noon despite several attacks on contacts by the escorts, which may have done some damage. Four more ships went down to torpedoes that night, and the fifteenth and final victim was sunk by *U89* the next day before three American escorts and the overworked Liberators from 120 Squadron, RAF, in Iceland came to the rescue.

This disaster for the RCN was thrown into even sharper relief in the eyes of the British Admiralty by the skill with which the British B6 group (the defenders of SC104) protected the slow westbound convoy ONS144 a few days later. Five corvettes with no destroyers in support (they were still under repair after their ramming activities) limited losses to one of their number and six merchantmen, with one submarine destroyed. All the escorts had radar and HF/DF. In the two months to mid-November British mid-ocean escorts had lost thirteen merchantmen and sunk three submarines while the Canadian–American half of the MOEF system had lost twenty-eight and sunk none.

In the Admiralty and at Western Approaches concern over the markedly inferior performance of the Canadians was coming to a head. One of the few consolations for the Allies in the especially tense days of early November was decidedly backhanded. In the "black gap" to the south of the main convoy route, the Sierra Leone formation SL125 was fiercely attacked by a pack of ten and lost thirteen ships in a running battle which went on all week. But this heavy and involuntary sacrifice drew all the German submarines in the area away from the huge procession of troop and supply-convoys passing through the region on the way to "Torch" and thus helped considerably to preserve the priceless Allied advantage of surprise for the landings. An alarmed Hitler immediately ordered Dönitz to divert fifteen submarines to the western Mediterranean area, which took a little of the strain off the overstretched North Atlantic escorts.

It was at this highly nervous moment for the Allies, now heavily committed to one of the great gambles of the war – the deliberate weakening of the Atlantic defences for the sake of "Torch" – that Churchill decided to change horses in midstream. Admiral Sir Percy Noble, C-in-C Western Approaches since February 1941, was replaced on November 19 by Admiral Sir Max Horton, Flag Officer, Submarines, since 1940. Noble was to go to Washington as head of the British Naval Mission, a key liaison post which is in no sense to be seen as a "kick upstairs" or a demotion. The fact that he was succeeded by a much more flamboyant figure, the nearest equivalent the Royal Navy produced to Montgomery, should not be allowed to detract from Noble's contribution to the most important campaign of the war. He handed over Western Approaches as a going concern whose only major weakness was a shortage of the tools needed to finish the job. Noble's contribution to the eventual defeat of the German submarine campaign was second to none. He set up the integrated escort groups and the training schools and adopted the technical devices to aid the defenders, and he would have introduced the support-groups and the escort-carriers but for the overriding demands of "Torch." He also did his best to get more long-range aircraft for Coastal Command, a task beyond the wit and power of any admiral unaided, as has been made clear.

Horton was nearly sixty but looked rather younger. He joined the British submarine service at its inception in 1904 and commanded his first boat as a lieutenant a year later. He served in submarines throughout the First World War and gained the distinction of being the first British boat-commander to sink a German warship (the cruiser *Hela*) in the Heligoland Bight in 1914. To mark this victory he invented the custom in the British service of flying the Jolly Roger or skull and crossbones when returning home, to show that the submarine had claimed a victim. (This macabre badge of triumph was last seen on HMS *Conqueror* in 1982 after the sinking of the Argentine cruiser *Belgrano*.) By the outbreak of the Second World War he was vice-admiral in command of the Reserve Fleet, and for a few months until early 1940 he commanded the Northern Patrol before returning to his beloved submarine arm as its chief. Now the poacher was to turn gamekeeper, a move which proved to be one of Churchill's happier ideas: now the key Atlantic commander on each side was a submariner.

Horton was appointed because he had a reputation for decisive leadership as well as more knowledge of submarine operations than anyone else on the Allied side. As submarine chief, however, his work had been administrative rather than operational; the relatively small British submarine arm was scattered among various commands and Horton's job was concerned with training, equipment and supply, which he did very well. Western Approaches was the most important strategic command in the Navy at the time and he brought to it a thoroughly abrasive style for which the polite word is "fire-eater." More robust synonyms were used of him lower down the pecking-order, ranging from martinet to the ordinary matelot's "right bastard." He now took direct personal charge of a staff of more than 1,000 people and the effect was electric. Noble had won the respect of his command by less melodramatic methods of sound leadership – persuasion, orchestration, negotiation, conciliation; he had regularly gone to sea with the escorts and flown with Coastal Command to get a feel for anti-submarine operations. Horton favoured a much more aggressive style, ruthless, arrogant and intolerant of fools. He was one of those bullies who could be dealt with by subordinates in one of two ways: subsmission or resistance based on superior knowledge, a course by definition open to only a few bold spirits. An important early clash was with Rodger Winn, head of the Submarine Tracking Room.

Dissatisfied with perceived shortcomings in information coming from the Operational Intelligence Centre after yet another convoy had been hammered by submarines instead of being successfully diverted, Horton attacked Winn at a fortnightly meeting of the Admiralty's Anti-U-boat Warfare committee. He accused Winn of drawing the wrong conclusions from his material. After years of dealing with the autocratic idiosyncrasies of High Court judges whom it is usually fatal for a mere barrister to confront, Winn remained calm and respectful and in the most polite manner issued Horton with a brazen challenge: 'Admiral, if you give me half an hour, I will collect all the material that was available at the time as the basis for our situation-report; then you yourself can form your own picture and you can decide whether you would have drawn a different conclusion." Horton fell into the silken trap and duly appeared thirty minutes later in the Submarine Tracking Room. As the admiral began to sift through a daunting pile of decrypts, reconnaissance reports, messages of all kinds and other items and tried to relate them to the great Atlantic plot, Winn gently wielded the rapier: "The chief of staff at Western Approaches in Liverpool is waiting urgently for the situation-report." Doggedly, Horton tried to make sense of the mass of material for ninety minutes before he pushed all the paper to one side and stood up. He smiled, patted Winn on the shoulder and conceded: "Well, I think this is a bit outside my field; it's yours, Rodger." According to Patrick Beesly, Winn's deputy and the source of the anecdote, this was the foundation of an absolute mutual trust between the two men for the rest of the war. Others who found Horton hard to handle tended to discover that if they could demonstrate competence they were secure. There was now no danger that Horton would repeat Pound's mistake in not trusting OIC over PQ17.

The mounting losses to submarines of autumn 1942 had prompted Churchill to set up the Anti-U-boat Warfare Committee under his own chairmanship. It comprised relevant ministers, Navy and RAF chiefs of staff and the Government's Chief Scientific Adviser, Lord Cherwell. It was to meet weekly, starting on 4 November 1942, and almost at once became another forum for the unending tussle over the use of airpower against submarines. Once again the Navy and Coastal Command pressed the case for a few dozen extra VLR Liberators (the aircraft acquired "very long range" by the installation of extra fuel-tanks in one of their three bomb-bays).

At this time the air-effort against the submarines, apart from Coastal Command's maritime work, consisted of three main strands. Bombers with ASVII "metric" radar (which had a wavelength of 1.5 metres) and Leigh Lights patrolled the Bay of Biscay and the Northern Transit route from

Norway and Germany to the Atlantic looking for boats on their way out or home. While some successes were achieved in the "Bay Offensive," the northern exercise was seldom fruitful. Secondly, the US Army Air Force and RAF Bomber Command had taken to bombing the French submarine bases. Since these were now most effectively protected by massive concrete shelters, the only result was disruption and destruction of the port-towns: the submarines were completely protected and their crews were either in the pens, on local leave well into the country or on home-leave in Germany. Had this effort been made seriously before the pens were complete, the effect would have been rather more marked. Finally, as part of the general bombing of Germany, particular attention was paid to the yards where submarines were constructed and the towns where their engines and other equipment were known to be made. Air Chief Marshal Harris claimed without a shred of justification that this effort had put the German construction programme six months behind. In fact it achieved less than area-bombing as a whole, which was estimated at the end of the war to have had a maximum reductive effect of some four percent on German war production (its effect on the German population and its morale was rather greater but impossible to quantify).

By now Coastal Command was rather better armed in its ceaseless campaign to acquire a few dozen more VLR aircraft. For about a year Professor P. M. S. Blackett, a Nobel prize-winner, had been heading the Admiralty's Operational Research section. He and his fellow-scientists were producing a series of invaluable analyses of convoy operations and anti-submarine measures. Among their many discoveries was the principle that the bigger the convoy, the more effective its defence became: because of the mathematical relationship between the circumference of a circle and its area, an increase of one third in the number of escorts gave the same level of protection to a convoy doubled in size (a circle of six escorts two miles apart covered twenty-four ships no better than a circle of eight protected forty-eight). They also deduced that setting depth-charges to explode at a depth of twenty-five feet would magnify the effectiveness of air-attacks on submarines, as it did. In the latter half of 1942 aircraft accounted for more than half the total number of "kills," a remarkable improvement.

Blackett's team also increased Coastal Command's effectiveness by working out a streamlined maintenance system for aircraft which increased the availability of operational planes by more than half. With refined statistical analysis and using the law of probabilities the scientists showed that fewer but larger convoys would reduce the number of targets; yet if a large convoy with proper protection did come under attack, it would lose no more ships than a smaller one attacked by the same force, since the number of submarines and their torpedo-supplies were the factors which largely determined the number of sinkings. Late in 1942 Blackett concluded that larger convoys could have cut shipping losses by twenty percent: for the individual ship, a

large convoy was much safer than a small one. But none of this, not even
improving the availability of existing aircraft and their effectiveness in attack,
could close the airgaps where the submarines were scoring so highly. Only
the Mark III Liberator with extra tanks, giving it an endurance of well over
2,000 miles, or escort-carriers, could do that.

The safest place in the North Atlantic in the second half of 1942 turned
out to be aboard one of the six "monsters," the outsize liners whose speeds
of up to thirty knots gave them a charmed life without escort. Four were
British, from the Cunard–White Star Line (including the two largest ships
in the world, the *Queen Elizabeth*, 84,000 tons, and *Queen Mary*, 81,000);
one was French and one Dutch. They carried nearly 200,000 troops across
the Atlantic in six months, on occasion a division at a time, without loss. In
the South Atlantic lesser though still large liners were not so lucky. Apart
from the *Laconia*, three were lost in quick succession on the WS ("Winston
Special") run from Britain to the Middle East via the Cape of Good Hope –
the *Oronsay*, *Orcades* and *Duchess of Atholl*, all over 20,000 tons. They fell
victim to a German submarine drive southward to South African waters
which had been predicted by OIC but for which adequate escort was
unavailable. The Germans sank 161,000 tons of shipping in the region,
including the three liners, in October, but it was not until the end of the
year that a scratch-force of escorts and maritime aircraft could be gathered
at the Cape. The Germans moved on to the Indian Ocean side of South
Africa to sink another 127,000 tons in November, whereupon they returned
to their bases after a most damaging foray by half a dozen of the new type
IXd2, with a range of no less than 23,700 miles. This was almost enough to
circumnavigate the globe without refuelling but there were not many of the
type in service.

On their way back to France they were able to top up with fuel from
Dönitz's milch-cows which were now playing a crucial role in sustaining the
assault on Allied shipping. In August five were operational, in September
seven and October eight. Only two were destroyed in 1942, one in August
and one, it is thought but not confirmed, in December, when the number
operational fell to seven. For the whole of the climactic period from March
to May 1943 the submarine tanker-fleet was at its maximum strength of nine.
These supply-boats did much to increase the impact of their conventional
fellows, which were at sea not only in unprecedented numbers but also for
longer operational periods.

Dönitz was also doing his best to help his boats deal with Coastal
Command's Bay Offensive, which destroyed just three boats in July and
August but was always of nuisance value in keeping them under and thus
reducing their operational time by increasing time (and discomfort) on
passage. The Germans were well behind in the development of radar but
they were able to supply the submarines with a primitive search-receiver.
This device detected a searching aircraft by picking up its metric radar-beam

in time for the submarine to be able to dive out of harm's way before the Leigh Light could be used to pinpoint it. It took its name from the French Metox company which was pressed into service to manufacture it. The antenna was originally just a wooden cross festooned with wire, which had to be dismantled and removed from the conning-tower before the submarine submerged; the crews called it the *Biscayakreuz* (Biscay cross). Metox began to be fitted from August 1942 and was widespread by the following month. Incoming boats were told to form convoys on a submarine already equipped with Metox which would keep anti-aircraft watch for all of them (in mid-July Dönitz had ordered boats to cross Biscay surfaced by day as the risk of surprise by aircraft with radar at night was obviously greater). Boats going out carried spare Metox sets for issue to submarines already at sea, and from September the Bay Offensive lost much of its effect.

Basic radar began to be installed in German submarines only in mid-1942. It had at first a range of little more than four miles and could sweep an arc of only sixty degrees ahead of the boat; even so the pioneers in its use found it helpful. Dönitz was once more angry with Göring around this time when he accidentally discovered that the Luftwaffe had developed a smaller and better radar, *Lichtenstein*, without bothering to tell the Navy. The technology was copied from sets recovered from shot-down enemy aircraft. Although the *Lichtenstein* set was a considerable improvement, radar was never to be remotely as useful to the submarines in their search for prey as the excellent information still flowing from the *B-dienst*. Because of the Bay Offensive, Dönitz also had his boats fitted out with new and formidable anti-aircraft guns which were sited on a "bandstand" at the stern end of the conning-tower.

While still adhering to the tried and tested designs of the types VII and IX, the Germans considerably improved their survival capacity by strengthening their hulls so that they could routinely go down to 200 metres (660 feet) and in an emergency even to 300 metres. This increased the displacement of the later type VIIs by as much as fifty percent over the originals of this class, to 750 tons. The new FAT torpedo described in the previous chapter increased the rate of hits from the 50 percent achieved by its predecessors to 75 percent; but a new and much faster torpedo was still needed to cope with destroyers which at full speed could outrun the FAT's thirty knots. Work was in hand on the acoustic torpedo, but there were many technical difficulties. In its search for an effective anti-escort weapon the German Navy even turned to the experimental rocket-research centre at Peenemünde. Dönitz got the idea when he discovered, again by accident, that the Naval Command had initiated experiments with a remote-control rocket for use by surface-ships against bombers, once again without bothering to tell him (at least the Royal Navy knew of the existence of the next generation of centimetric radar even if it could not loosen Bomber Command's grip on the first sets). Peenemünde was soon working on rockets to be fired from submerged submarines, initially for use against the Russian Baltic and Black Sea coasts like some ancestor of the Polaris missile; if a sufficiently accurate guidance system could be devised, Dönitz hoped to be able to use them against destroyers.

This idea came to nothing, but in September 1942 the naval C-in-C, Grand-Admiral Raeder, called a conference of all naval branches to consider future weapon requirements. Dönitz had been arguing since June for the development of a new type of boat capable of high-speed underwater travel. The essential idea was a new power-plant invented by Professor Hellmuth Walter, a turbine powered by a mixture of diesel-oil and hydrogen peroxide. A small 1940 prototype delivered the fantastic underwater speed of twenty-three knots in short bursts, enough to evade all but the very fastest escorts. Work began that year on a 550-tonner but now Dönitz proposed a new design based on the trusty VIIc hull as well as a coastal version of 250 tons, as a preliminary to mass-production. Design speeds were to be thirty knots surfaced and nineteen submerged. Hitler's growing interest in "wonder-weapons" was more than enough to procure his agreement at a Führer naval conference on 28 September 1942.

Raeder and Dönitz fared less well on the immediately pressing problem of countering the enemy air-threat, both in the Bay of Biscay and out to sea. In summer the Luftwaffe was persuaded to provide a squadron of twenty-four heavy fighters, of the Junker Ju88C VI type, but these did not have the range to operate beyond coastal areas. As a replacement for the Kondors the Navy pressed its case for the new Heinkel He177 long-range bomber with a flying radius of 1,375 miles. Dönitz wanted to try new tactics to extend the effectiveness of the submarines inward of the airgaps. The Heinkels could be used to draw off Allied air-patrols and also to disrupt convoys by bombing, opening up gaps for the submarines to exploit. Despite promises from Göring, the aircraft were not now provided. Hitler took them for the Eastern Front. In late summer the Navy therefore tried another tack by asking the Luftwaffe to build it an entirely new long-range aircraft tailored to maritime needs. But in October Göring said flatly that he could not meet the request. Doubtless the idea would not have come to fruition in time to be relevant; but a couple of dozen He177s supporting the submarines when they were already achieving so much unsupported might well have presented the Allies with an unwelcome additional problem in the Atlantic. The German High Command proved to be even more blinkered about maritime airpower than the Allies, even as evidence mounted on the German side of its devastating effect on those occasions when enemy planes could reach a convoy under attack.

As 1942 drew to a close the longed-for defeat of the submarine in the Atlantic seemed to the British to have receded after the shattering losses of November. The fact that in December "only" 349,000 tons of shipping had been lost,

262,000 in the North Atlantic and 331,000 to submarines, cheered nobody. Some of the worst hurricanes of recent years had much to do with the apparent slackening of the German effort. Over the year the stock of shipping available to the Allies had fallen by 750,000 tons. There was no guarantee, amid all the extra demands for carrying capacity, that the last three months of 1942, which were the first quarter-year of the war when new construction clearly surpassed total losses, would set a lasting trend. Oil-reserves in Britain had reached a nadir of 300,000 tonnes, or barely enough for three months' tightly rationed non-military use. The Navy had one million tonnes but needed every ounce. Overall imports dipped below thirty-four million tonnes, only two-thirds of 1939's. Submarines had destroyed 1,160 ships of 6,266,000 tons as their share of total sinkings amounting to 7,791,000 tons. Although eighty-seven German submarines (and twenty-two Italian) had been sunk, over the year German operational strength had more than doubled to 212 at year's end, with 393 on the books compared with 249 twelve months before.

The Bay Offensive had petered out in October. The only answer to the German search-receiver was the new 9.7cm (known for convenience as "ten-centimetre" or just "centimetre") radar, a British technological break-through being manufactured in the United States. The single-minded myrmidons of Bomber Command had priority in the British queue for the limited production, rightly regarding the land-bomber H2S version as a most promising aid. The ASVIII maritime version had to wait. Worried by the collapse of the Bay Offensive, the Air Ministry made the wrong gesture in agreeing to allocate the first forty H2S sets to the Leigh-Light Wellingtons: they were not meant for use over water, and were of moderate value. But it was too late to put ASVIII production ahead of the bomber-sets. The Admiralty therefore went directly to the Americans and successfully persuaded them to fit the sea-version into each of the thin stream of Liberators coming over one by one from October. The American requisitioning authorities at least clearly perceived the need. But because of trials, modifications, training and working-up time it was not until January 1943 that the first centimetre-radar aircraft were operational. The surface-escort fleet was however making increasing use of the shipborne version, which was one of the leading technical breakthroughs of the war at sea.

With much trepidation the Russian convoys were resumed, after the Torch-imposed interlude, on 15 December 1942. The series began with the new designation JW51. It was divided into two, and JW51A took just ten days to arrive completely unruffled in Russian waters on Christmas Day. JW51B left on the 22nd but after six days ran into a gale which split both convoy and escort into two parts. Warned of the convoy's approach by a passing submarine, Vice-Admiral Kummetz put to sea from Altenfjord with the *Hipper* and the *Lützow* on the 30th, accompanied by six destroyers. The ensuing brush was marked by chaotic dispositions on both sides, some imposed by the gale, others by misjudgement. The *Hipper* sank a mine-sweeper and badly damaged two destroyers, one of which sank shortly afterwards. The *Lützow* scored one hit on a merchantman, which survived; when the covering British cruisers came up they caused some damage to the *Hipper* and sank a German destroyer. Once again Hitler's orders against risking the large ships had ensured that the Germans pulled their punches, while the British escorts defended their divided convoy with skill and determination, ensuring that no cargo-ship was lost. This "Battle of the Barents Sea" was the *Hipper*'s last bow at sea. The complementary south-bound convoy, RA51, also got through intact. "Operation Torch" had forced the Germans severely to reduce the strength of the Luftwaffe in Norway, and the shackles imposed by Hitler on the surface-ships inhibited them as a threat to the Allied traffic in the far north. As a totalitarian dictator Hitler had neither the need nor the inclination to accept responsibility for his own actions, which led to a humiliatingly ineffectual performance by a locally superior naval force. The consequences for the German Navy were to be swift and momentous.

The great consolation for British strategists in this crisis of the war at sea came on Sunday, 13 December 1942. A hugely relieved First Sea Lord sent Admiral King a signal saying that the four-wheel Enigma cipher, "Shark" to the Allies and *Triton* to the Germans, had at last been broken. It will be recalled that the Germans introduced a new short-signal book for weather reports in February, depriving Bletchley Park of its backdoor into naval traffic just as the fourth wheel came into use. On 30 October the British cornered *U559* in the Mediterranean, off Port Said on the Egyptian coast. They were able to get aboard long enough to retrieve a copy of the current short-signal book which soon found its way to Bletchley Park. On November 22 Operational Intelligence Centre became impatient and pressed Bletchley Park to give "a little more attention" to Shark. The anti-submarine campaign was the only one with which Bletchley Park was not significantly helping: "It is the only one in which the war can be lost unless BP do help." The reason for the delay was that it was taking three weeks to work through all the possible rotor-settings for one day's traffic with the "*bombes*" available (the cryptanalysts were simultaneously working through Enigma traffic from other sources and could not cut back on this profitable work). The break-through came when it was discovered that weather messages were enciphered by the Germans with the fourth wheel in "neutral" which meant that, once its setting was found, there were only three rotating wheels to deal with as in the halcyon days of 1941. Having got the setting of the first three wheels, Bletchley Park was well-placed to find the setting of the fourth when it was in full use in *Triton* messages. By Christmas OIC was once again in the happy position of having detailed information on all eighty-four submarines then in the North Atlantic.

This was doubly fortunate because Rodger Winn collapsed from overwork on the very day of the breakthrough. Like the OIC in general, the Submarine Tracking Room was chronically understaffed. Winn habitually "slept at the office" through the week and permitted himself one day off in seven. It was thus his deputy, Patrick Beesly, who took the ebullient call that Sunday announcing the triumph. When he telephoned Winn at home with the news, Beesly learned that his chief was suffering from complete physical and mental exhaustion with abnormally low blood-pressure. A long and total rest was prescribed by his doctor; even so there was no guarantee that the guiding intelligence in the anti-submarine campaign would ever return to his old form or even to his post. The work at the STR was daunting even for the fittest, and the burden on the chief that much worse; Winn was never a fit man at the best of times, and now, not surprisingly, he had broken down. Thanks largely to his own exceptional will-power and in defiance of medical advice he returned in a month. He was thus back at his post in time for the looming crisis of early 1943, as one of the few people in key positions in the conduct of the Second World War who were truly irreplaceable.

The same could not be said of the much more exalted figure of Grand Admiral Erich Raeder, Commander-in-Chief of the German Navy for fourteen years. The immediate cause of his downfall was the botched sortie by *Hipper* and *Lutzow* against the resumed Russian convoys. Summoned to the presence of the Führer on January 6, he was subjected to the humiliation of a ninety-minute tirade by Hitler, whose hysterical rage had been well primed by Göring. After vilifying the navy's record Hitler ended the interview with a peremptory order to Raeder to draw up a plan for the scrapping of all the remaining heavy ships. Never a total sycophant, the Grand Admiral retained his dignity by remaining impassive (he was given no chance to make a reasoned reply) and went off to draw up a paper in justification of keeping the surface fleet. His well-argued presentation of the role and value of seapower made the point that dismantling the *Tirpitz* and the rest would be equivalent to a huge strategic victory for the British and their maritime allies "gained without any effort on their part." When Hitler rejected his case Raeder took the only course left open to him and resigned, with effect from 30 January 1943.

Raeder, now in his sixty-seventh year, had been made to fight a war which in terms of naval planning came a good five years too soon. He opposed Hitler's march into the Rhineland in 1936 and the two-front war into which Germany was plunged on the invasion of Russia in 1941. Given the means at his disposal in 1939, he regarded unrestricted submarine warfare as Germany's only hope of defeating Britain and saw more clearly than most that this was an essential preliminary to a successful campaign in the East. On the other hand he showed no political independence or any delicate moral sense; under him the Navy was one of the few organs of the German state which Hitler did not need to suborn. It simply fell into line under the swastika ensign and carried on about its business as if nothing had happened in 1933. Few have disagreed since the war with the general assessment of Raeder as a thoroughly sound naval strategist worthy of his difficult post. Convicted of war crimes at Nuremberg in 1946, he was released from Spandau Prison in 1955 and died in 1960. His last important official act was to recommend to Hitler that his successor should be Karl Dönitz. Even Hitler was not so perverse as to refuse to recognise that there was no comparable candidate. Dönitz commanded the only branch of the Wehrmacht that was not on the defensive at this stage of the war and was still capable of achieving a strategic victory. The transfer of command took place on January 30. Raeder's parting shot to Hitler was: "Please protect the Navy and my successor against Göring." The Führer's reply, if any, is not recorded.

As naval Ultra got back into its stride after its long absence, the Torch convoys direct from the United States strategic zone to North Africa continued to enjoy virtual immunity. On 28 December 1942 a special convoy with the new designation TM1 set sail from Trinidad bound for Gibraltar. It consisted entirely of fully laden oil-tankers carrying precious fuel for the Anglo-American campaign. The escort was the British B5 group, led by the destroyer *Havelock* (Commander Boyle, RN) with just three corvettes. Although the convoy consisted of only nine ships, the value of its cargo makes the level of protection seem light. Both the corvettes' radar and the *Havelock's* HF/DF were giving trouble.

Bletchley Park located the *Delphin* group of six German submarines patrolling in the western central Atlantic between the Azores and Madeira, where it could only have been lying in wait for Torch traffic. The *B-dienst* was unable to produce the wealth of intelligence it was still providing on mercantile convoys in connection with military shipping, which generated little or no wireless traffic. It was therefore completely by accident that *U514* (KL Hans-Jürgen Auffermann), on the way to the West Indies, spotted TM1 on the afternoon of January 3, about halfway between Trinidad and the Cape Verde Islands. The same afternoon, because of *Delphin*, OIC ordered Boyle to divert sharply southward after dark; British intelligence could do no more because Ultra suffered one of the periodic interruptions characteristic of this new phase of wrestling with four-wheel Enigma. When the Germans changed the settings at noon, Bletchley Park lost touch for forty-eight hours and only caught up on the 9th. Its last tip to TM1 was a sound one, but Boyle decided to keep to his original course because he thought it would provide calmer weather for the mid-ocean refuelling of the escorts which would soon be necessary.

Ordered by Dönitz to keep in touch with this unique target at all costs, Auffermann made regular reports to help *U125* to find it (which it never did; *U514's* radio was playing up). Meanwhile, late in the evening, Auffermann made a pass at the convoy and sank the *British Vigilance*. He was sighted and fired on from other tankers in the three columns of three but escaped unscathed and was not found by the escort. During the night, however, he lost touch and was admonished by his headquarters. Still on the evening of the 3rd, *U182* sighted GUF3, a convoy returning from Gibraltar, while on passage to the South Atlantic. The escort located the boat and drove it off with depth-charges, some 400 miles west of Madeira. Dönitz now tried to divert *Delphin* against GUF3 but was too late to catch it. He placed the line of boats across the last known course of TM1 on the off-chance that it might still be heading in the same direction. If so they should sight it on or after the 7th.

It was, and they did. Had TM1 followed OIC's diversion it would have missed the waiting enemy by more than 100 miles. *U381* made contact on the afternoon of the 8th. Dönitz sent four more boats on passage in the area as reinforcements. Overnight *U436* (KL Günther Selbicke) hit *Oltenia II* and *Albert L. Ellsworth* with a single salvo, came under attack from *Havelock* and retired hurt. KL Herbert Schneider in *U522* crippled *Minister Wedel* and *Norvik* with one salvo. Some seventy minutes later Commander Hans-Joachim Hesse in *U442* torpedoed the *Empire Lytton*. *U571* also attacked but was driven off and damaged by *Havelock's* depth-charges. Not all the stricken tankers sank at once, but the Germans were able to return and finish them off on the afternoon of the 9th. On the 10th there was a lull, although *U511* got a bonus by sinking the merchantman *William Wilberforce*, an independently routed British ship which had the misfortune to be in the neighbourhood. But the enhanced *Delphin* pack, still eight strong after two boats had left to lick their wounds, kept in touch at their limit of visibility during the day and moved in on the three remaining tankers during the night. Schneider in *U522* raised his score to three with the help of *U620* by sinking the *British Dominion*, as Dönitz urged on his wolf-pack to the first 100-percent score of the war against a convoy. But it was not to be. With daylight on the 11th, an RAF Sunderland flying-boat from Gibraltar appeared from the east and forced the attackers under. They failed to regain contact and the last two tankers of TM1 reached Gibraltar unharmed on January 14. The shattering losses amounted to seventy-seven percent of the convoy, the highest proportion ever achieved in the campaign: 55,000 tons of shipping, seven tankers, over 100,000 tonnes of fuel. No wonder that General von Arnim, Rommel's successor as commander of the Afrika Korps, sent Dönitz a telegram of thanks when he heard about it. The unparalleled disaster helped to oblige the British Government to reduce the petrol ration by another ten percent.

It also helped to concentrate the minds of Winston S. Churchill and Franklin D. Roosevelt when they met again on the day the survivors of TM1 reached Gibraltar. Their rendezvous at Casablanca in Morocco had been chosen to

set the seal on the success of "Operation Torch," but the terrible incendiary
fate of TM1 was a timely reminder that the Germans were still in a position
to set a torch to all their hopes with the still unchecked submarine campaign.
It was clear to the Allies that Torch had put back their cause in the Atlantic
by several months, the price that had to be paid for success in the first major
Anglo-American offensive of the war on land. It was time to redress the
balance.

The two leaders of the West with their combined Chiefs of Staff had no
difficulty therefore in agreeing that victory over the submarines was once
again to have absolute priority ("a first charge on . . . the United Nations").
Only half understanding Professor Blackett's lesson on the relationship
between size of convoy and optimum use of escorts, the naval staffs laid
down at Casablanca that an escort should consist of three ships plus one for
every ten merchantmen where there was air-cover, and where there was
not, double. It was estimated that the number of escorts to achieve this
somewhat arbitrary ideal would be sufficient by the end of the coming
summer.

The American record of the conference notes without comment that,
"in discussing the security of sea-communications, the Prime Minister indicated that he wished German submarines to be referred to as 'U-boats' rather
than dignifying them by calling them 'submarines'." Churchill had said the
same thing in Britain in the context of coining the phrase "Battle of the
Atlantic" for the struggle over the Anglo-American lifeline. Both choices of
words have dominated all writing in English on the subject ever since. At
this distance the "Battle of the Atlantic" can more clearly be seen as a
campaign of many battles spread over nearly six years of war. "U-boat" is
merely an anglicisation of the German abbreviation *U-boot* for *Unterseeboot*,
which means no more and no less than undersea boat or, if a Latin-derived
word is preferred to one from Anglo-Saxon (in keeping with a uniquely
British form of linguistic snobbery) submarine boat, or submarine for short.
In one of his many brilliant pieces of rhetorical propaganda, Churchill as a
master of the English language single-handedly turned "U-boat" into a
pejorative term. This was very useful in wartime but need not be unthinkingly
followed nearly half a century later.

In retrospect Casablanca can be seen as a turning-point not only in the
Second World War but also in the long history of the United Kingdom. It
was the third fateful crossroad to which the British had been brought by
Germany. The first was in 1870 when the Second Reich was created by
Bismarck and ended Britain's domination of the world economy, which had
been achieved by the defeat of Napoleon and the Industrial Revolution. The
second came in 1904, when Britain abandoned the "splendid isolation" of its
imperial heyday by concluding the *Entente Cordiale* with France, largely to
counter the threat presented by the inordinate naval ambitions of Kaiser
Wilhelm II. Now Casablanca became the last occasion on which British

global interests and strategic concerns took precedence over those of the United States, the last time when Britain had as much weight to put in the scales as its main ally. The agreement to give priority to the anti-submarine campaign entailed deferment of the invasion of the European mainland, which the Americans regarded as their top priority for the eastern element of their war on two fronts, for the sake of protecting Britain's security against the German threat from the sea. It was fortunate for Churchill that the two aims coincided, in that there was not much point in pressing for an invasion which would have to be mounted from Britain unless and until the necessary troops and matériel could be assembled there. Securing the transatlantic route for them also meant that Britain's vital supplies of food and raw materials would be assured.

Casablanca was the high point of Anglo-American co-operation as equal partners. Churchill argued not only for priority for his "Battle of the Atlantic" but also for expanding the counter-attack against Germany and Italy from North Africa across the Mediterranean. General Marshall, the US Army Chief of Staff, wanted to make the invasion of France the priority; Admiral King wanted to press ahead in the Pacific, where the US Navy had been performing outstandingly well. The invasion of Europe was agreed as a goal to be achieved as soon as possible. The bombing of Germany by the USAAF by day and the RAF by night was to continue; and for the first time the ultimate war-aim of the unconditional surrender of Germany was formally declared. Although the two sides had their differences, there was little if any rancour, even if the British took away the idea that the Americans would throw everything possible into the Pacific campaign if they could, and the Americans suspected that the focus on the Mediterranean had a lot to do with its role as the main communications artery of the British Empire, whose survival was so low on the American list of priorities that it was difficult to discern without resort to a magnifying glass.

The stock of shipping, though no longer falling, was not up to the task of both feeding Britain and making possible the fulfilment of the Anglo-American promise to Stalin to open a Second Front in western Europe during 1943. The Americans therefore agreed – Admiral King's chagrin notwithstanding – to reinforce the Atlantic. They would escort the military convoys for the build-up to an invasion of Europe in 1944 and special convoys of tankers from the Caribbean. The British identified the extra requirements for overcoming the expected new submarine onslaught as sixty-five escorts, a dozen escort-carriers and as many VLR Liberators as possible, some of them to be based in Newfoundland for the first time to close the Greenland airgap. The absolute necessity of providing end-to-end air-cover was thus clearly identified, together with the measures necessary for supplying it. If a problem defined is a problem half-solved this was all very well; but as subsequent events showed, Admiral King, for one, did not leave the balmy clime of Morocco in January with the burning sense of urgency about the crisis in the Atlantic that the contemporary position inspired in most others present. The bulk of the required resources were already available; it was a question of moving them into position, and almost a quarter of a year was to be allowed to pass before the requisite action was actually taken. General Eisenhower hung on to his two squadrons of Liberators in Morocco; despite the success of Torch, which made the next step, the invasion of Sicily ("Operation Husky"), a realistic early possibility, the escort-carriers stayed in the Mediterranean.

Reinforcement was one way of tackling the Atlantic problem, even if it could not be provided overnight. The other recourse that was always available was to improve the efficiency of existing anti-submarine forces. The restoration of naval Ultra enabled the North Atlantic Allies to go back to effective diversion of convoys away from known danger. This, the record-breaking bad weather and the abandonment of the self-imposed restriction of adherence to the Great Circle route all helped to keep losses to submarines within bounds in the early part of January 1943. An intelligent evasion based on knowledge of the enemy's position was obviously worth more than the extra fuel required. Against that, the unprecedented number of submarines in the North Atlantic steeply raised the Germans' chances of fortuitous sightings and their ability to mass boats against such targets. There were leads and lags in the flow of decrypted *Triton* material which robbed much of it of immediate operational usefulness. If OIC had been blind before the December recovery by Bletchley Park, it now had one eye open, but still lacked the full perspective only both eyes can give. Yet Professor Hinsley, the historian of British Intelligence, calculates that but for Ultra the great crisis of March 1943 might well have come in February or even January. The Allied navies knew from December that the German "big push" in the Atlantic was at hand: two different wavelengths were set aside for the control of convoy action, enabling headquarters to run two major battles at the same time without the one interfering with the other. The large numbers of operational submarines were more than enough to offset the decline in individual efficiency since the days of the aces, due in part to the rising skill of the escorts and in part to the dilution of expertise caused by rapid expansion. In his account of the crisis of the Atlantic campaign, Admiral Morison, the American official historian, has this to say on the results:

By April 1943 the average kill per U-boat at sea had sunk to 2,000 tons. This might be interesting as a sort of sporting score, but the number of U-boats operating had so greatly increased that it was of little significance in solving the problem. When Daniel Boone, who shot fifty bears a year, was replaced by fifty hunters who averaged one each, the bears saw no occasion to celebrate the decline in human marksmanship.

The Royal Canadian Navy certainly had little enough to celebrate as the anticipated crunch in the North Atlantic approached. The unique scale of Canadian naval expansion in response to Britain's lonely plight in the early days of the war has already been described. The merest glance at an atlas appears to make it ridiculous to refer to "gallant little Canada" as "gallant little Belgium" was praised in the First World War. But Canada was and remains a small nation living in a very large, and largely empty, space. In quantitive terms, therefore, its contribution was astonishing. But when the British Admiralty began to look, pending the arrival of reinforcements in the Atlantic, for ways of improving the quality of the existing escort forces, its eye soon fell on the RCN as the weakest link in the defences. The Admiralty claimed that eighty percent of losses of ships in convoy late in 1942 were incurred under Canadian escort. The Canadians were providing forty-eight percent of ocean escorts in the North Atlantic compared with fifty by the British and just two by the Americans (although the two larger navies had commitments round the globe). The expansion of the RCN had proceeded at such a pace that experience gained was promptly diluted almost to vanishing point by the arrival of new ships and new crews. But the Navy's dubious and controversial manpower policy was not the only problem. Canada was also new to large-scale shipbuilding and to the manufacture of equipment such as radar. At the same time the Canadians were always at the back of the queue for the latest technical advances, whether VLR Liberators (of which they still had none) or HF/DF sets. Most of their destroyers were old and their corvettes had not been much improved from the original and highly uncomfortable basic design. All this meant that the Canadian ocean groups were the least efficient; yet they were usually assigned to slow convoys, to which the threat was greater by far than to faster ones. This showed them up even more, as did the fact that both ships and crews were even more overworked than those of their allies. The RCN compounded its problems by concealing their effects from the Government. Meanwhile the British in particular became more and more critical. So when ocean escort-groups were thinned out to meet Torch and other commitments late in 1942, Rear-Admiral Murray, RCN, Flag Officer Newfoundland, warned Naval Service Headquarters to expect disastrous results. The fate of convoy SC107, described above, unfortunately proved him right. Later in November, therefore, Vice-Admiral Nelles, the RCN Chief of Staff, made an informal but earnest approach to the Royal Navy for help.

The "new broom" at Western Approaches, Admiral Horton, and others at the Admiralty concerned to improve efficiency as the only immediately available counter to the growing crisis in the Atlantic, seized the opportunity. They planned a reshuffle of ocean escorts involving the transfer of British groups from the Gibraltar run to cover oil-convoys from the Caribbean. The four Canadian groups in the Mid-Ocean Escort Force were to replace them, which meant they would be based in Britain, where the Royal Navy could take them in hand. The Canadians would be under less pressure because the weather on the Gibraltar route was better, it was covered from the air, the intervals between convoys were greater and there were better training facilities ashore. All this would provide more time to raise standards. The British put the plan to Ottawa in the middle of December.

Not unnaturally (or inaccurately) the Canadians regarded it as a slap in the face to be invited to withdraw from what they saw as their principal contribution to the war at sea. Their resistance collapsed in the last week of 1942, when the westbound slow convoy ONS154, escorted by the RCN's C1 group, was severely mauled by the Germans. The weak and poorly-handled defence could not prevent the loss of thirteen merchantmen and a convoy-support ship. The British now decided to meet Prime Minister Mackenzie King's December request to Churchill for fourteen destroyers in their own way: instead of providing ships to be manned by a navy which in their view was already unable to cope with its existing difficulties, they began to send British destroyers with Royal Navy crews to stiffen the Canadian groups. It just so happened that the captains of three out of the four thus assigned, one to each group, were senior to any Canadian commander present and, in keeping with the custom of giving command of a group to its senior captain, took over the leadership of their escort-groups. The Canadian groups now also found themselves escorting mostly fast convoys rather than slow, which reduced their exposure to risk.

By March the four groups were based at Londonderry in Northern Ireland under Horton's Western Approaches Command, which put them through rigorous individual and group training between voyages. Then three were at last assigned to the Gibraltar route; only C3, the most competent Canadian group, was allowed to go on working the North Atlantic run. It was thus the only Canadian escort formation to take part in the climax of the Atlantic campaign in March 1943; the other three returned only at the end of that month, by which time the Greenland airgap had finally been closed. Even so, the Canadians were given the softest available assignments until the crisis was completely past, at the end of May, when all four groups were put back under RCN command. All this meant that the glory of gaining the upper hand over the Germans and forcing them to retreat from the North Atlantic went to the British. This seems in retrospect only right and proper, because to them alone the war against the submarines was a matter of life and death, which doubtless helps to explain the ruthlessness with which they moved the Canadians to the sidelines for the climactic battle. But the final victory was also partly underpinned by those convoys which the RCN brought through with little or no loss. Horton's predecessor, Admiral Sir Percy Noble, was honest and decent enough to say later: "The Canadian Navy solved the problem of the Atlantic convoys."

*   *   *

Despite the constant nagging from Stalin for more supplies from Britain, which was driving Churchill almost to distraction in January, the news from Russia was improving at this difficult period in the war at sea. JW52 arrived unscathed by the end of January, and the ensuing return-convoy, RA52, lost just one unladen ship to submarine attack. The *Tirpitz*, the *Lützow* and one light cruiser, *Nürnberg*, plus a few destroyers remained in the far north but they made no threatening move. In February, JW53 got through unharmed by enemy air-attacks even though it was scattered by storms and six merchantmen and two escorts had to turn back. RA53 was also scattered on the run south-west; one ship was lost to the terrible weather and three to submarines.

Early in March the *Scharnhorst* arrived in Altenfjord from the Baltic, making the German surface-threat from Norway the strongest it had ever been. The Americans therefore moved their Task Force 22 from the North African convoy-run to the Gulf of Maine on their own north-east coast. The group, consisting of a battleship and a fleet aircraft-carrier with cruiser and destroyer-support, was to come under British Home Fleet command in the event of a German sortie. Soviet paranoid suspicion of the British presence on their soil in support of the convoys and the North Atlantic crisis of March led the British to suspend the Russian convoys again after RA53. They were not to be resumed until the darkness of November, which meant that twenty-seven destroyers and frigates and an escort-carrier could be transferred from the Home Fleet to Western Approaches to form the five British support-groups which helped to transform the situation on the main convoy route. In terms of the war as a whole, the best news from the Anglo-Americans' prickly and difficult ally came on 2 February 1943, when the German Army surrendered at Stalingrad, a turning-point as vital to the war on land as the events in the following months were to be in the conflict at sea.

The foul weather and evasive routeing helped to reduce shipping losses worldwide to 261,000 tons in January 1943, the lowest monthly total since November 1941. Only one North Atlantic convoy – HX222 – was attacked, losing one ship. Some 173,000 tons went down in the North Atlantic, including nineteen independently routed ships, but the loss of most of TM1 was a particularly hard blow. Submarines accounted for 203,000 tons. The lull deceived nobody in the Allied commands as the Germans took their strength in the North Atlantic past the three-figure mark. The elevation of Dönitz to supreme command of the Navy made no material difference to the submarine campaign because he kept direct command of the boats, whose importance far outweighed anything else the Germans could do at sea. The Operations Room functioned just as well, and with largely the same staff under Eberhard Godt (promoted admiral) as chief of operations, in Berlin as it had done in Paris. On his appointment Dönitz, now aged fifty-one, was promoted to Grand-Admiral.

The attack by a few boats on HX224 was a relatively light skirmish, unremarkable by the standards of the time except for one fateful consequence. Two ships were sunk and one submarine destroyed from the air – and *U632* sank a straggler. KL Hans Karpf stopped to pick up a single survivor from the British tanker *Cordelia* and this individual revealed that the slow convoy SC118 was on the same route not far astern. Karpf immediately reported this by radio and Dönitz assembled a huge pack of twenty boats against it. That was SC118's first misfortune. Its second was that naval Ultra suffered one of the temporary blackouts characteristic of this period of the struggle against four-wheel Enigma. The third stroke of bad luck before action was joined came when a seaman on the Norwegian freighter *Vannik* accidentally set off a "Snowflake" flare of the kind used, with mixed results, to turn night into day round an attacked convoy. At dawn on 4 February 1943 the rocket could be seen for twenty miles in all directions. That morning boats from the earlier *Pfeil, Haudegen* and *Jaguar* packs converged on SC118.

First blood went to the escort (B2 of three destroyers and six smaller ships) when Lieutenant-Commander Richard Stannard, VC, RNR, sank *U187* from the destroyer *Vimy*, supported by the *Beverley*. *U187* had been caught by HF/DF when making a sighting report. But in the afternoon at least five submarines were in contact, including KL Klaus Rudloff in *U609* who hung on for at least three days, and Commander Siegfried Baron von Forstner in *U402*. SC118 temporarily "lost" its three port columns during an emergency evasive turn during the night, which could have proved even more disastrous for the fifty-three ships of the convoy than impending events. But by the morning of February 6 they were all in formation again, and the convoy was edging out of the Greenland airgap, as was attested by reports of planes overhead from no less than eleven different boats. Four submarines were attacked and one forced to withdraw with serious damage. So far the Germans had sunk one straggler on the 5th and another on the 6th. The B2 escort group was then a "scratch" team of vessels not accustomed to working together, but on the 6th it was comforted by the appearance of three American warships – two destroyers and a Coastguard cutter – from Iceland as reinforcements. Lieutenant-Commander Proudfoot in the destroyer HMS *Vanessa* remained Senior Officer of the escort. The attackers refused to give up despite the constant harassment from the air during daylight which forced them to lose contact. The chase continued, and during the night of the 6th to 7th the Germans struck hard. Baron von Forstner proved himself to be in the "ace" class by sinking the unusual total of six ships in two attacks, including the rescue-ship *Toward* and the American troopship *Henry R. Mallory*. Nearly 400 men were lost on these two ships alone; the total losses for the night amounted to eight ships. Before dawn on the 7th, the Free French corvette *Lobelia* detected the most persistent shadower, *U609*, and destroyed it in a single depth-charge attack.

Yet the battle continued. Forstner was still in the hunt, despite being forced to submerge seven times by air patrols. An RAF Liberator from Londonderry attacked *U624* as it transmitted a report from the surface: the message, a long account of the successful night-attack, survived; the boat did not. The indefatigable Forstner, singled out for praise by Dönitz as the chase continued, made another attack on the night of the 7th to 8th and claimed his seventh and last victim from SC118. He was awarded the Knight's Cross. Dönitz described the action as "perhaps the hardest convoy battle of the whole war"; the Germans sank thirteen vessels (including a tank landing-craft) for the loss of three submarines and two badly damaged. Before the conflict faded away on the 8th three-quarters of the submarines were attacked in a running battle which endured for four days and nights in violent weather. In all some twelve warships were involved in the defence of SC118, about twice the number of a normal escort-group of the period. The high losses despite air-cover in daylight can be attributed partly to the fact that the escorts were not an integrated group and partly to the sheer doggedness of the German attack. The battle drew attention to the fact that the VLR aircraft were not equipped with Leigh Lights, which would have enabled them to intervene effectively at night as well as by day. Since some of the escorts had run out of depth-charges it was decided to put reserve supplies of this principal anti-submarine weapon on merchant ships in future convoys.

The other great convoy battle in February centred upon the westbound ON166, escorted by the American group A3 under Captain Paul R. Heineman, USN, in the Coastguard cutter *Spencer*, with one similar US ship, four Canadian corvettes and one British. But it was an experienced group even though it defied Admiral King's oft-professed dislike for such multinational forces: they called themselves "Heineman's Harriers." Once again the *B-dienst* got wind of the sixty-three ships and their course, and Dönitz assembled seventeen submarines ahead of them; once again the defenders got in the first strike on the 21st, when *Spencer* sank *U225*. After that it was almost all the other way, with the Germans sinking fourteen ships over the next five days in the airgap, despite the best efforts of the "Harriers," reinforced by a Polish destroyer. Only one other submarine was destroyed, *U606*, whose lingering death was marked by a uniquely bizarre wake. After being depth-charged by two escorts in the moment of diving, *U606*, commanded by Lieutenant Hans Döhler, sank like a stone to 750 feet, water pouring in through the imperfectly sealed conning-tower hatch. The fifty men of the crew, who had just helped to sink three merchantmen, thought they were about to join their victims at the bottom. All the compressed air aboard was pumped into the water-tanks; the boat levelled off for a while and then suddenly shot to the surface like an express lift, only to be shelled and rammed by the cutter USS *Campbell*, which then had to be taken in tow. *U606* was still afloat, and the First Lieutenant and the Engineer emerged on deck with German sausage and champagne in their hands, which they proceeded to consume as ten other members of the crew joined them. One made his way to the First Lieutenant, a tyrannical martinet, and slapped his face, satisfying a long-nurtured ambition, as one of the escorts came to the rescue. The boat then sank with thirty-eight men aboard, including the captain, who was also one of the least popular officers in the service. ON166 gave the Germans a bigger victory at less cost than they had achieved against SC118; the battle had raged intermittently over 1,000 miles of the convoy's course, from February 21 to 25.

Losses for the month were significantly up on January's despite the continuing bad weather which hampered the Germans as much as the Allied ships. Worldwide, 403,000 tons were sunk, of which submarines took 359,000, and 289,000 tons were lost in the North Atlantic. The Germans were at a peak strength there of about 120 boats, with two milch-cows on hand to refuel them; and they seemed willing to hammer away at convoys regardless of escorts and even of air-cover. Shipping losses were mounting again in the thirtieth month of the war and there was every reason to believe the new trend would go on.

"The Germans never came so near to disrupting communication between the New World and the Old as in the first twenty days of March 1943." This was the considered assessment of an Admiralty staff review of 1943, written at the end of the year. "It appeared possible that we should not be able to continue [to regard] convoy as an effective system of defence."

The great crisis of the Atlantic campaign focused upon four consecutive eastbound (and therefore fully laden) convoys: SC121, HX228, SC122 and HX229. The first of these, consisting of fifty-two ships, left New York on February 23. The mid-ocean escort was commanded by Captain Heineman, in the *Spencer*, supported by the American destroyer *Greer* and four Canadian corvettes. This escort-group, number A3 of the Mid-Ocean Escort Force, had not fully recuperated from its considerable ordeal with the westbound ON166 which had ended only a matter of days earlier. The *xB-dienst* once again broke into the sailing-telegram and Dönitz deployed two packs across its path, *Westmark* of seventeen boats and *Ostmark* of nine. Bletchley Park picked up the wirelessed orders and OIC ordered a diversion which was initially successful. *Ostmark* was completely evaded but *Westmark* gave chase and on the morning of March 6 COMINCH told Heineman: "U-boat estimated your vicinity has made sighting report of convoy," and in the afternoon: "Wolf-pack may be preparing for an attack." Two American and two Canadian escorts were detached from the westbound ONS171 to go to the aid of the threatened convoy, which was by now in disarray because of a severe gale. The first victim was the British steamer *Egyptian*, sunk in the late evening (local time) of the 6th by *U230*. In the early hours of the 7th *Spencer* signalled that she had sighted a submarine and was attacking. "Heineman's Harriers" however failed to damage any of the submarines which harassed SC121 for five days, sinking thirteen ships of 62,000 tons, a quarter of the total. Many of them were stragglers which had lost touch in the storm. Had the lumbering convoy been able to keep formation the losses might well have been much fewer because air-cover by a succession of RAF Liberators, Catalinas, Sunderlands and Hudsons plus USAAF Fortresses was provided for hours at a time from the 9th. They too failed to damage a submarine.

Over the same period, more precisely from March 10 to 14, another fierce battle was in progress round HX228. This convoy of sixty merchantmen was escorted by the practised British escort group B3, led by Commander A. A. Tait in the destroyer *Harvester* with three others and five corvettes. British Intelligence revealed that the *Raubgraf* pack had been placed across its path and it was diverted widely to the south. But the Germans got into the diversion message and positioned the thirteen submarines of the *Neuland* pack to attack it instead. Even so it was only the most southerly boat in the line, *U536*, which sighted the convoy at noon on the 10th. The escort picked it up by HF/DF when it made its sighting-report and drove it away without hitting it. The powerful new American Sixth Support Group with the escort-carrier *Bogue* and two destroyers had meanwhile come up to help Tait. Nevertheless *U221* (KL Hans Trojer) found the ships again on the same evening and sank two, damaging a third and calling other boats to the attack. *U757* torpedoed an ammunition-ship which exploded with such force that heavy wreckage rained down on the boat, causing superficial damage. The fourth and last ship of HX228 to be sunk was the victim of *U444*, the first in a remarkable chain. As Lieutenant Albert Langfeld left his target to sink in her own time, he was sighted by *Harvester* and rammed and sunk in the act of diving. Tait's destroyer was so badly damaged as to be helpless against a lethal attack by *U432* (KL Hermann Eckhardt): Tait went down with his ship. Next on the scene was the Free French corvette *Aconit* (Lieutenant-Commander Levasseur), which first depth-charged *U432*, forcing it to the surface, then fired on it with her 4-inch gun and finally sank it by ramming. None of the subsequent submarine attacks, in which the new FAT torpedoes were used in action for the first time, were successful. Nor was the USS *Bogue*, unable to fly off her aircraft in the terrible weather and forced to take refuge in the middle of the embattled convoy. The final balance was two submarines sunk for the loss of four ships and one escort (with one of the best escort commanders).

The separate battles round SC121 and HX228 were fierce enough in themselves but were relatively mild affairs compared with the gigantic mêlée in which SC122 and HX229 both became involved less than a week later. This was the greatest convoy battle of the Second World War and marked the climax of its central struggle, the Atlantic campaign, after three and a half years of bitter fighting.

The slow convoy SC122, fifty strong, left New York on March 5, escorted by group B5, which was led by the destroyer *Havelock* (Commander R. C.

Boyle, RN), with one US destroyer, a frigate, five corvettes and a trawler. The fast convoy HX229 consisted of forty merchantmen and left three days later, escorted by group B4. This force was weakened by the absence of its regular leader with his ship because of an Asdic fault, and was temporarily led by HMS *Volunteer* (Lieutenant-Commander G. J. Luther, RNVR). The acting Senior Officer had only accompanied one convoy hitherto and was new to the group, which had three other destroyers and two corvettes. Dönitz got wind of the courses of both convoys from his intelligence staff and sent the *Raubgraf* group, still in being with eight boats after a few exchanges, to intercept SC122. Group *Stürmer* of eighteen boats was formed from some members of *Westmark* with other more recent arrivals in the operational area. It took up a position on a line behind *Raubgraf*, also to lie in wait for SC122. Eleven boats, some of them from the *Neuland* pack, were formed into *Dränger*, which was sent to intercept HX229. But a following gale drove SC122 past *Raubgraf's* allocated position before the latter got there and the pack was diverted to HX229. Even then it only briefly sighted an escort at the rear of HX229, which might thus have sailed out of danger from *Raubgraf* altogether, having also got ahead of itself because of the high winds. But the lone U653, on the way home with mechanical problems, sighted and reported HX229 on the morning of March 16. *Raubgraf* caught up in the afternoon. An extra convoy, HX229A, formed to clear the log-jam in New York, caused confusion at the *B-dienst* and was diverted out of danger.

Three ships were sunk that evening. The next morning three boats accounted for five more, a total of eight from HX229 in eight hours. "Escort weak" was the message to Dönitz as two of its ships fell out to look for survivors. *Stürmer* began to arrive during the 17th and one of its boats was damaged but not sunk by a destroyer. At the other end of the *Stürmer* line, U338 sighted SC122 early that morning and reported it. KL Manfred Kinzel then proceeded to sink four ships with five torpedoes in quick succession, and destroyed a fifth later in the day. Dönitz was understandably confused, believing that his forces were in contact with only one convoy (SC122). In fact the *Stürmer* line was engaged with one at each end while *Raubgraf* was attacking HX229 from the west and *Dränger* lurked to the south-east. Two *Stürmer* members sank two more ships of HX229 at lunchtime but the escorts, now helped by brief visits from aircraft flying at record distances of up to 1,000 miles from their bases, deterred any further attacks that day. The pilots looked down on a scene of unparalleled activity: two large convoys covering great areas of ocean, each zig-zagging in unison and only a few minutes' flying time apart. SC122 was also spared any further losses until late that night, the 17th.

Dönitz had however worked out by nightfall that his boats were in touch with both convoys at once and split his forces accordingly, dividing *Stürmer* and bringing up *Dränger* against HX229. U338 sank the destroyer *Granville* with SC122 and survived three counter-attacks by two ships and an aircraft. *U305* sank two more from SC122 before midnight. On the afternoon of the 18th, *U221* (Trojer) sank two ships of HX229, now covered by just five escorts after various ships had left with damage or because of fuel-shortage. One romper and one straggler from HX229 were sunk on the 18th, and the last vessel to be sunk while actually in convoy with HX229 was dispatched by two submarine attacks on the morning of the 19th. Shortly afterwards *U384* was sighted by an RAF Sunderland and depth-charged to destruction, the only German casualty in a double battle which had involved ninety merchantmen, twenty-two of which were sunk, thirty-eight submarines of which just one was lost, and a total of sixteen escorts (taking account of arrivals and departures), of which one was sunk and another, the sole trawler, foundered in bad weather. In this one action 146,000 tons of shipping went down, an Atlantic record, and the Germans were publicly jubilant. But their submarines had finally been called off because of the build-up of air-cover over the decimated convoys.

The Admiralty could be forgiven for thinking, as it did at the time, that the evasive routeing made possible by Ultra (which fell out for nine days from March 10 when a new German short-signal book came into use) was no longer helpful while so many submarines were at sea. What really worried the British was that no less than two-thirds of all shipping losses in the black month of March 1943 had been incurred in or near convoys (seventy-two out of 108 lost to submarines). The losses in March 1943 were also by a large margin the highest since the last peak in November 1942. But the number of independently routed ships – favourite targets of the submarines – had dwindled to twenty-eight in March; and the submarines got twenty-two of them (seventy-nine percent, compared with a loss of only four percent of ships in convoys that came under attack, which the vast majority did not). If the admirals had possessed the statistical sense of a Professor Blackett they would not have been quite so worried. OIC was more confident than the rest of the Admiralty because it thought it had detected a new note of irresolution in Dönitz's wirelessed instructions to his boats. Unbeknown to the British, submarine captains had been coming back from patrols and complaining about the strength of Allied air-cover with the convoys, a most wondrous irony in the light of the extraordinary difficulty the Admiralty in particular had experienced throughout the war in its campaign for adequate air-support.

This problem was about to be solved at last. The most important Allied convoy conference of the war took place in Washington as the crisis unfolded in the Atlantic. It started, very badly, on March 1, when Admiral King flatly told a shocked British delegation led by Admiral Noble that he intended to withdraw such few US Navy forces as were operating on the main transatlantic route altogether. Apparently the involvement of American naval and merchant ships in the PQ117 disaster eight months before still rankled and had reinforced his already powerful anglophobia, renewing his hostility to multi-national escort-groups. American ships would now work only with convoys on the central Atlantic routes and the tanker-run from Aruba to Britain. King threw the Admiralty one large crumb of comfort in the form of a sixth support-group (the *Bogue* and five destroyers), to be added to the five that the British were about to form as "fire brigades" to go to the aid of the escorts of threatened or attacked convoys. The Canadian Navy's escort-role on the northern route was correspondingly increased: it was to be responsible for convoys west of a new "Chop" line, now moved further westward to 47°, where Western Approaches took over. Canada's contribution to the Allied naval effort, unglamorous, hard and costly as it had been, was to be rewarded by the creation of the country's first independent operational command, the only one it held in either world war: Canadian North-west Atlantic, with a Canadian Commander-in-Chief (Admiral L. W. Murray, RCN). CinCCNA was to take up his new post in May.

In his remarkable statistical analysis of the value of ships and aircraft as escorts, Professor Blackett had forecast: "Very roughly, a force of 200 long-range and very long-range aircraft might be expected to save at least 400 ships (two million tons) in 1943." Only VLRs could cover the airgap south of Greenland where the submarines were sinking the majority of their victims. But at this time there were no Liberators stationed anywhere west of Iceland; Coastal Command had only three squadrons with a strength on paper of just fifty-two Liberators; the Canadians had crews but no such aircraft; all American Liberators not in the Pacific were either bombing Germany or in North Africa; and even with its sixty-six long-range aircraft added to its VLRs, Coastal Command mustered only a little more than half of Blackett's postulated strength. There was a desperate shortage of Liberator spares, forcing Coastal Command to be circumspect by confining their use to covering threatened convoys. This meant that they would often arrive late. Nothing had been done about the Casablanca Conference proposal that eighty VLRs be allocated to the Atlantic airgap; the main reason was that King was effectively subverting Casablanca and the Allied agreement on "Germany first" by giving priority to his Pacific front in vital VLR resources. His stubbornness and Bomber Command's greed had combined into a serious strategic threat to the main artery of the Allied war-effort. The huge outlay in building thousands of merchant ships and hundreds of naval vessels to escort them was in real and immediate danger of being wasted for the want of a few dozen from the tens of thousands of aircraft being flung into the war. The March convoy conference now agreed that twenty Liberators should be supplied to the RCAF; but it was only after a direct intervention by Roosevelt later in the month that the last great loophole in the Allied defence against the German submarines was closed. The US Navy would now divert sixty Liberators to the North Atlantic, the Army Air Force seventy-five and the RAF 120. The first twenty came into use in the last ten days of March.

In the first twenty days of that nerve-racking month, more than half a million tons were lost (ninety-five ships, forty-one in the first ten days, fifty-four in the second); in the closing days of March, twenty-five were sunk worldwide (about 175,000 tons) – a significant if not yet decisive drop. Submarines accounted for 108 sinkings out of 120; eighty-two were lost in the North Atlantic. The fact that two-thirds of submarine sinkings took place in and around convoys was the result of the near-disappearance in the area of independent sailings: if a submarine wanted a target it had to attack a convoy, and there were more than enough boats to form huge packs against which the ultimate deterrent was continuous air-escort. The lesson had been learned, but only just in time. Admiral Horton at Western Approaches took delivery of three new escort-carriers, the other means for plugging the airgap, before the end of the month; the first, HMS *Biter*, was assigned to the Fifth of his new support-groups which were otherwise composed of destroyers.

"Bomber" Harris was furious. Even though he was forced to concede more VLRs for the Atlantic when it mattered most, it is worth ending the narrative of the long argument with his reaction, as an insight into what the Admiralty had so long been up against. He wrote in a memorandum on March 29:

> It is obvious that a momentous decision is here involved. What is suggested is
> . . . that the bomber offensive, which is the only effective means . . . in the
> immediate future for striking directly at Germany, should be *mainly* [author's
> emphasis] employed for purely defensive purposes, which, if successful, will
> give a long-term dividend in the form of shipping to be used for offensive
> purposes. This means that practically the whole brunt of fighting Germany is
> to be thrown on to the Russians . . . [The effect on the submarine offensive
> would be "negligible" but] on the bomber offensive would certainly be
> catastrophic . . .

This reads as though Bomber Command were about to be disbanded. Everybody, he complained, expected his command to meet all requests, "real or fancy," as if it were a "residuary legatee." Such people "clearly fail to realise that my Command is fighting a battle all the time, and a battle in which relative numbers count as much as in any other battle." One is left wondering what he thought the surface-escorts and Coastal Command were engaged in. The apostle of "area bombing," a euphemism for indiscriminate, high-level bombing of cities, was as obtuse as Admiral King.

Allied worldwide shipping losses in March 1943 amounted to 693,000 tons, seventy-two percent up on February, of which 627,000 tons – second only to the record of November 1942 – were sunk by submarines. In the North Atlantic alone 476,000 tons went down, mostly in convoy. From the abandonment of *Paukenschlag* to the end of 1942, fifty-one submarines were sunk by

Allied ships and aircraft in five months, an average of just over ten or about half German new production. A few others were lost in accidents. The high point was in October, when fifteen were sunk, and the low in December – just five. The same number was destroyed in January, but in February the total jumped to eighteen, a record for the war thus far; in March twelve were sunk.

At a conference with Hitler on February 13 Dönitz presented his proposals for compliance with the Führer's decree that the big ships should be scrapped. Most of them were to be paid off and absolute priority given to the construction and maintenance of the submarine fleet and recruitment for their crews. The new C-in-C also asked for air-support, resolving from the outset not to allow himself to be bullied by Göring and to protect his back against the perpetually scheming head of the Luftwaffe. Dönitz also seemed to be able to handle Hitler himself with more skill than most, as was shown on February 26, when he persuaded the dictator to rescind his order to get rid of the capital ships. Glossing over his dutiful acceptance of this order only two weeks before, Dönitz wrote in his memoirs:

> In a brief and reasoned report I told him I was unable to give my support to his orders and requested him to cancel them. He did not expect this attitude. He was at first extremely immoderate but in the end he very grudgingly agreed and I was ungraciously dismissed. From then he treated me with exceptional civility . . . he never lost his temper . . . He did not attempt to interfere in naval affairs. He had apparently become convinced that I was doing my utmost and that he could rely on me.

By saving the capital ships he carried through Raeder's argument against presenting the enemy with a great and bloodless strategic victory. He also prevented the waste of labour and invaluable dockyard space their dismantling would have caused. He even managed to persuade Hitler to exempt 40,000 skilled workers from conscription into the insatiable Wehrmacht so that they could continue to maintain and expand the submarine construction programme. Hitler agreed without demur to Dönitz's requests for priority for this on February 13, just as he did to the appeal for air-support; but in the Third Reich it paid to have as many allies as possible. Göring never delivered the aircraft, which showed what the Führer's casual promises were worth. But Dönitz concluded what amounted to a private treaty with Albert Speer, Hitler's protégé and armaments minister, ensuring adequate supplies of steel and other raw materials for the submarine programme.

Dönitz was as aware as his enemies that the sharp decline in the effectiveness of his submarines after the peak reached in November 1942 could not be ascribed solely to the appalling weather in the North Atlantic. The *B-dienst* got the sailing details of most convoys but the patrol-lines assembled from the unprecedented number of boats available more often than not completely failed to locate them. Decrypted enemy traffic made it plain that they were being diverted away from danger. Once again the suspicion gained ground that German communications had become insecure. Had the Allies achieved a great leap forward with direction-finding, or was it their radar? Or was there a traitor in the German camp? Vice-Admiral Erhard Maertens, head of Naval Intelligence, was ordered to investigate; only Dönitz and Godt, the Chief of Staff (submarines), were spared close questioning and surveillance (when it was over, Dönitz made a rare joke to Godt: "Now it can be only me or you"). Security was tightened still further at naval headquarters, with the number of staff "in the know" on operations reduced by half to about twenty. The Allied successes in evasion were finally attributed to a sophisticated location device, probably radar, in which as we have seen the Germans knew themselves to be well behind. They had one piece of luck in February 1943, when a British bomber shot down over Rotterdam yielded a complete H2S ten-centimetre radar set. The Germans immediately and correctly assumed that a similar device might be in use at sea. The wavelength was beyond the range of the Metox radar-detector and scientists were put to work on a more sophisticated search-receiver. The new *Naxos* equipment came into service in October 1943, succeeded shortly afterwards by the *Hagenuk* which emitted no tell-tale radiations of its own.

Admiral Maertens appears to have come closest on the German side to guessing the truth about British penetration of German ciphers. During his inquiry, which involved looking through intercepted enemy traffic that might give a clue to such a compromise of Enigma, the intelligence chief examined the output of the *Atlantiksender*, the British "black propaganda" transmitter which tried to undermine morale in the German submarine service by means of extraordinarily knowing broadcasts. These revealed enormously detailed information on everything to do with submarine operations and the life of the crews ashore to be in the hands of the enemy:

> The question therefore arises whether behind this campaign is concealed a real development on the enemy side . . . This propaganda-campaign, developed almost to uproar, complaining of the danger of the submarine war, would in [certain] circumstances be a most effective means of deception . . . if on the enemy side one wishes to hide [the fact] that one is at last enjoying complete, simultaneous reading of enemy radio traffic.

This essay in psychological warfare, to which the British devoted a great deal of effort during the war, started crudely but developed more and more subtlety as it got into its stride. What Dönitz called the "Atlantic poison-kitchen" behaved as if it were a German radio station for the delectation of submariners in port or off duty. Listening to it was made a punishable offence. It derived much of its information from men taken prisoner, the lucky few who survived the destruction of a submarine to go into captivity. It undermined security by broadcasting about subjects such as armament and equipment which were supposed to be secret. The station seemed to know everything, from celebrations that got out of hand to the results of sports events among the crews ashore.

Peter Cremer, captain of *U333*, which is also the title of his war memoir, quotes the station as reporting, for example: "This afternoon Third Flotilla, La Rochelle, played Twelfth Flotilla, Bordeaux, and won 5:3" – followed by the names of the goalscorers! The whole schoolboyish but effective wheeze was the idea of Commander Ian Fleming, RNVR, of Naval Intelligence, the future author of the thrillers about Commander James Bond. Journalists such as Sefton Delmer of the *Daily Express*, for years its prewar Berlin correspondent, worked on it. What effect this extremely elaborate jape with a serious purpose had on morale is impossible to calculate. Although morale in the submarine service naturally fluctuated with the fortunes of war, it remained remarkably high to the end. The broadcasts were often illicitly heard in the boats at sea with a mixture of interest, amusement, amazement – and perhaps even a feeling that all this attention by the enemy to the submarine arm was rather flattering as a backhanded compliment to its effectiveness. The British also dropped black propaganda leaflets from bombers about the perils of the war at sea which Cremer believes did not affect the sailors anything like as much as their families. But the object of the *Atlantiksender* was not to draw attention away from Ultra: it was an end in itself.

The great German tactical victory in the battle of convoys SC122 and HX229 misled both sides. The loss of just one submarine for twenty-two merchantmen in the greatest action of its kind in the war could hardly be regarded as anything less than an outright triumph for the wolf-packs. For the escorts and those who controlled them it was a disaster so unnerving that it gave a brief new lease of life to the greatest naval heresy of the twentieth century, that convoys were an anachronism. Analysis on both sides in the immediate aftermath was not based on the full facts; only subsequent events could show that the result had been deceptive. The first escort-carrier to sail with a North Atlantic convoy, the USS *Bogue*, was of no use in the exceptional hurricane-force winds. The unintended merging of the two convoys under attack, also largely the result of the weather, helped the Germans by causing confusion and offering them a plethora of targets: half the boats in the battle scored hits whereas usually only one or two boats did most of the damage in pack-actions. Nearly all the participating boats were depth-charged, more than half were damaged, two seriously. Even the War Diary of the Submarine Command expressed reservations at the very moment of apparent triumph:

> After our successes of the first night, the enemy on the 17th used air-escorts, which allowed only five boats to make submerged attacks . . . The ever-increasing air-defence caused us to lose contact with both convoys on the night of the 17th, and the operation became increasingly difficult owing to

deterioration of weather and visibility, with the result that only one boat was successful . . . On the morning of the 20th, in increasing difficulties, due at night to near-full moon and in daytime to stronger air-defences, the operation had to be broken off . . .

At the same time the Germans believed they had sunk ten more ships than the formidable total they actually achieved, a persistent tendency which had nothing to do with propaganda. The British habitually overestimated the number of submarines sunk despite the official scepticism built into their system of evaluation of actions at sea. The Germans often scored spectacular-looking hits on ships which survived, or hit the same ship more than once, sometimes from different boats. This unavoidable and cumulative error led them to believe that they were winning the tonnage-war when they were not. Only the Allies knew for certain which of their ships had gone missing, just as only the Germans were sure which boats had been lost.

Early if not yet conclusive relief was soon provided for the Allies by the next pair of eastbound convoys at the end of March. Between them SC123 and HX230 lost just one straggler and the *Bogue* group, Admiral King's consolation prize to the escort-forces, was able to provide cover for both in turn in what had so recently been the Greenland airgap. At the same time Admiral Horton was able to fling twenty-seven Home Fleet escorts, divided among five new support groups, into the fray. Only the Fifth was built round the first of the Royal Navy's new American-built escort carriers, HMS *Biter*; her sister-ship *Dasher* tragically succumbed to a fuel explosion on exercise on March 27.

During April the struggle in the North Atlantic was evenly poised with comparatively moderate losses on each side. For the loss of fifteen submarines to enemy action, the Germans sank thirty-nine merchantmen of 235,000 tons in the North Atlantic out of a worldwide total of sixty-four (345,000 tons, 328,000 to submarines). Once again the weather concealed from both sides which way the pendulum would swing, and it was only at the very end of the month that its two heaviest encounters began; their results therefore may have been obscured by being divided among the statistics for two months.

Dönitz decided in April to revert to his old standby whenever he felt the need to catch the enemy off guard: the central Atlantic route to Sierra Leone and its offshoots. The coastal convoy TS37 from Takoradi in the Gold Coast (now Ghana) and Freetown, Sierra Leone, consisted of eighteen ships with a local escort of a corvette and three trawlers. It was sighted by U515 (KL Werner Henke, Knight's Cross with Oakleaves), whose report was detected by the escorts. Rather than break wireless-silence they asked a passing RAF patrol by signal-lamp to fetch reinforcements. By the time three destroyers arrived from Freetown, Henke had sunk seven ships, five of them in five minutes, completely on his own, on the night of April 30 to May 1.

It was an isolated success in the area, which was quickly reinforced by the British, but a remarkable one.

On the 29th, the westward-bound slow convoy ONS5 (a new designation for an old route) was sighted 500 miles east of Cape Farewell at the southern tip of Greenland. Once again exceptionally bad weather interfered with the dispositions of both sides for the coming battle. The mid-ocean escort lost its leader when the destroyer *Duncan* had to run ahead to St John's, Newfoundland, to refuel. On the day of the German sighting, intercepted and decrypted by the British, the 3rd support-group of five destroyers set off from the same port as reinforcement. It took them three days to find the all but stalled convoy in the gales. On May 4 two of the support-group's destroyers also had to withdraw for lack of fuel, and the 1st support-group was also sent from St John's – a sloop, a cutter and three frigates (the official title of these support formations was Escort Groups; they are referred to here as support-groups to avoid confusion with the escorts assigned to specific convoys). These reinforcements did not join up with ONS5 until May 6. Meanwhile Dönitz had formed the largest pack of the entire war, group *Fink* (finch), consisting of no less than forty boats in two parallel lines placed between Greenland and Newfoundland.

The convoy, of forty-three ships, lost its first merchantman on the 29th. On May 4 a Canadian Air Force Catalina sank *U630* ahead of the battered convoy, which was having the greatest difficulty keeping together. That evening ONS5 sailed into the middle of the *Fink* line and overnight seven ships were sunk. At least seven submarines were damaged by the escorts. In the morning *U192* was sunk. All attacks during the day on the 5th were beaten off and after dark *U638* was destroyed. So were three more merchantmen. In the early hours of the 6th *U531* was sunk; two hours later *U125* was rammed and sent to the bottom. Then the 1st support-group arrived and promptly dispatched *U438*. For the loss of twelve merchantmen the defenders had exacted the high price of six submarines sunk. One other, *U710*, had been sunk by Coastal Command in the early part of the convoy's passage, and *U439* and *U659* were also lost when they collided in its vicinity during the mass attacks of May 4 to 6. Even without this unearned bonus, the escorts won a resounding tactical victory with ONS5 in one of the greatest convoy battles and in atrocious conditions.

The Germans did not give up despite the large numbers of boats damaged in *Fink*. They moved south to attack the eastbound pair, HX237 and SC129 and sank three ships, but lost three submarines in what can only be seen as a most unproductive exchange. The British now had the scent of victory in their nostrils and their optimism was confirmed without the shadow of a doubt by events during the passage east of SC130. Commander Peter Gretton leading B7, one of the best mid-ocean escort-groups, told the Commodore, Captain Forsythe, RNR, that he had a pressing engagement on arrival in Britain – his wedding – and he did not want to be held up.

Forsythe replied that he had an appointment which he regarded as only slightly less important: a game of golf, on the same day. The passage of the forty-five ships, also protected by the 1st support group, became a triumphal progress as five submarines from four different packs were sunk, three by air-patrols and two by the warships. Not one merchantman was scratched. The commander and the commodore were in plenty of time to keep their respective trysts. Among the submarines destroyed was *U954*, lost with all hands: one of them was Sub-Lieutenant Peter Dönitz, aged twenty, younger son of the Commander-in-Chief. The complete reversal of fortune in the Atlantic campaign was made clear when all four of the other convoys Dönitz decided to attack in May – 161 ships in all – got through unscathed, while the attackers lost six boats.

Fifty-eight merchantmen (299,000 tons) were lost worldwide to enemy action in May. Fifty (265,000 tons) were sunk by submarines and 164,000 tons (34 ships) went down in the North Atlantic. This reversion to the relatively low sinking-rate of January made May the second month of steep decline in succession, just when the submarine fleet reached its operational peak (240 on April 1; 207 by July 1). There is one other statistic which reveals the transformation as no other can. In May 1943 Germany lost forty-three submarines, thirty-eight to enemy action – more than twice as many as in the previous worst month (eighteen in February 1943) and about twice the replacement-rate.

A significant contribution was made by a new air-offensive in the Bay of Biscay. Centimetric radar restored the initiative to the RAF, ably assisted by the Royal Australian Air Force. Intensive patrols were resumed in April, when one submarine was sunk. Another was destroyed in the less profitable transit-area north of Britain. In May six boats were sunk in the Bay, vindicating the reorganisation of local patrols made by Air Chief Marshal Sir John Slessor, who succeeded Joubert as C-in-C of Coastal Command in February. Dönitz was shaken by the unremitting harassment of his boats, made possible by ASVIII radar to which he as yet had no answer. By the end of April several boats had been damaged and all were being severely slowed down by having to stay submerged for long periods. This led him into what Roskill, the British historian, calls "perhaps his biggest mistake of the war." He ordered all boats to stay under by night and to come up in daylight only for long enough to recharge batteries. As the submarines could not detect an aircraft by the emissions from the new radar (which was good enough to render the Leigh Light almost superfluous) they were completely blind at night; at least in the daytime lookouts could see them coming. This upending of previous tactics reduced night sightings by air-patrols but increased them in daylight.

Because Cremer in *U333* had shot down an attacking Wellington in the Bay in March, Dönitz increased the anti-aircraft firepower of his boats in general, and had a few fitted with heavier weapons to serve as "flak"

(*Flugzeug-Abwehr-Kanone* – aircraft-defence cannon) submarines. Commanders were encouraged to join forces and fight it out with the aircraft on the surface, in groups of three or more. All these desperate steps were taken in April and set the stage for the unprecedented losses in the Bay in May, which were compounded by damage to many other boats. For all the terrible damage done by the Germans with their unrestricted submarine warfare, the nemesis now looming over them was awesome. The Luftwaffe which had been so miserly with help in the past, when it could have afforded support, was in no position to fight the Allied air forces for control of the airspace over the Bay of Biscay. With its inability to stay submerged for more than a few hours at a time under power, the contemporary submarine was helpless against relentless air-patrols. The aircraft involved were at a new peak of efficiency with better weapons, equipment and training.

All this was an object-lesson in the worth of the aircraft as an anti-submarine weapon. Its main value from the latter days of the First World War to the early part of the Second had been disruptive, forcing a submarine to submerge, thereby reducing its speed and its chance to catch a ship. Well before the crisis in the North Atlantic it had become an effective submarine-killer, as the navies on both sides learned before the respective air forces. Yet the naval and air commands in Germany, Britain and America alike spent so much time competing with each other that severe losses were suffered by both sides unnecessarily, for the lack of a few squadrons of aircraft. We have considered this conflict as it affected Britain and Germany; it was no less of a problem in the United States.

The US Navy had, like the British, acquired operational control of anti-submarine aircraft flown by the Army Air Force (in June 1942). The Washington convoy conference which was in session at the height of the Atlantic crisis in March agreed, on Roosevelt's prompting, on the means of reinforcing VLR strength; but the immediate need boiled down to placing a single squadron of Liberators in Newfoundland until such time as the RCAF could take delivery of those allocated to it. Admiral King controlled 112 Liberators, mostly in the Pacific with a few in the Caribbean; at this time Coastal Command had just twenty-three operational. King refused to close the Greenland gap and insisted that the Army Air Force do it; the unit which finally went to Newfoundland was No. 6 Anti-submarine Squadron, USAAF, early in April.

Among the many changes in the organisation of the war against the submarines at this climactic period was the emergence of New York as the western focus of the North Atlantic convoy organisation in place of Halifax, Nova Scotia. This took effect in September 1942, when the port's capacity was enlarged to make it the world's greatest and busiest harbour. First the "Torch" traffic and then the mounting demands of "Operation Bolero" – the transfer of troops and matériel for the invasion of Europe – kept it in a condition of permanent stress and never far from a breakdown (rather like the city as a whole today!). In February 1943 alone there were thirty-one collisions of ships within the harbour; small wonder when twelve mercantile and four military ocean-convoys had been scheduled to enter and leave New York in ten days, to say nothing of coastal and special convoys or independently routed ships.

Sixty tankers were loading each month in New York for Britain. Boston, Portland (Maine), Halifax and St John's, Newfoundland, had to be used as relief-ports. It was taking up to nine days to turn a ship round in New York, where there were no less than 114 vessels at anchor in the lower harbour on March 31. This was hardly surprising because the port was actually closed for twenty-four hours on the 29th, after a tanker blew up near the entrance of the swept channel (no evidence was found that it had been lost to a mine). Indeed it was remarkable that New York, whose harbour contained a daily average of 362 ships in February, had not seized up altogether. It very nearly came to that on April 1, when the 114 in the lower harbour – two convoys – set sail at three-minute intervals in a fog and became hopelessly intermingled. Twelve were involved in collisions; twenty in all did not sail for various reasons. An inquiry into the All Fools' Day shambles led to some streamlining of port operations at the end of the month.

The great change in the American contribution to the anti-submarine campaign at this time was the emergence of the United States Tenth Fleet. There had been desultory discussion since autumn 1942 of the idea of creating a "super C-in-C" to take charge of the entire Atlantic campaign, on land, in the air and at sea, commanding the forces of Britain, America and Canada. The latter, as we have seen, had successfully urged the creation of the first independent Canadian command with the appointment of Admiral Murray as C-in-C, Canadian North-west Atlantic. The British were not about to put their anti-submarine forces on which their very survival depended under foreign command; the importance to them of the struggle was reflected by the high-powered nature of the direct involvement of the Cabinet itself in the campaign. Operational control by the Admiralty through Western Approaches, the Home Fleet, Coastal Command and other commands as necessary had proved itself. The Americans similarly, with their growing commitment to winning the war against Germany, would not have tolerated British supreme command of the transatlantic lifeline which sustained their effort. The Casablanca Conference reflected the equipoise between the rising star of American global power and the seasoned Anglo-Canadian partnership as the backbone of the Atlantic campaign. Worldwide, the practice had developed of giving supreme command in each theatre to the nation making the greatest contribution. Thus General Douglas MacArthur, USA, was in charge in the South-west Pacific and Admiral Chester Nimitz, USN, in the Pacific; Admiral Lord Louis Mountbatten, RN, was to take charge in

South-east Asia and finally General Eisenhower, USA, in the assault on western Europe.

The follow-up to Casablanca, the Washington convoy conference in March, left each of the three Atlantic allies to its own organisational devices for the war at sea. Co-operation was to continue on the same broad lines as previously after the adjustment of responsibilities among the three described above. On April 6 Admiral King appointed Rear-Admiral Francis S. Low as his assistant chief of staff for anti-submarine warfare. Low recommended that the entire American anti-submarine apparatus be placed under CINCLANT, Admiral Royal E. Ingersoll, but on 1 May 1943 King simply took charge himself by announcing to the Joint Chiefs of Staff the creation of the Tenth Fleet. Leaving aside the pre-emptive nature of the move, it was King at his administrative best. It was a fleet with no ships, its C-in-C an absentee landlord (King wore the hat while Admiral Low as chief of staff actually ran it), but it exercised control over all Atlantic Sea-Frontiers, ships, USN aircraft and shore establishments involved in the anti-submarine campaign south of latitude 40° north. The Tenth Fleet took strategic charge of the American effort in the Atlantic while CINCLANT exercised tactical and operational control of the escort and support-groups. The one element missing from this logical exercise in unification of control, which was the US Navy's formal acknowledgment of the importance of the anti-submarine campaign, was the Anti-submarine Command of the Army Air Force. The struggle between the two services was far from resolved and will need examination in the next chapter.

In his massive history of the British war at sea, Captain Stephen Roskill, with his customary personal modesty, reached this verdict: "For what it is worth this writer's view is that in the early spring of 1943 we had a very narrow escape from defeat in the Atlantic; and that, had we suffered such a defeat, history would have judged that the main cause had been the lack of two more squadrons of very long range aircraft for convoy escort duties."

But the aircraft came and there was no defeat. The battle was not lost for the want of a nail; instead a small infusion of airpower at the critical moment proved to be the last nail in the coffin of Germany's hopes for victory in the West and therefore in the war as a whole. When the balance shifted from the submarines to the convoy-escorts it did so decisively, as the hard-won result of an immense defensive effort involving warships, aircraft, shipyards, scientific development, intelligence – and men, in the Merchant and Royal navies and the forces of their American, Canadian and free European allies. The Germans were now checked or on the retreat on all fronts; the Axis surrender in North Africa early in May reopened the Mediterranean to Allied shipping, which was equivalent to a bonus of two million tons in carrying capacity because of the time that could be saved by the renewed use of the Suez Canal.

Late in May Admiral Sir Max Horton, the submariner in charge of Western Approaches Command, sent a victory signal to all units:

> In the last two months the Battle of the Atlantic has undergone a decisive change in our favour . . . All escort-groups, support-groups, escort-carriers and their machines as well as the aircraft from the various air-commands have contributed to this great success . . . The climax of the battle has been surmounted.

In the ether over the Atlantic by means of which Grand-Admiral Karl Dönitz and his submarine commanders so lavishly communicated with each other, the dialogue was all but reduced to a monologue in the dying days of May. Messages from headquarters, no less dramatic for being enciphered and then transmitted in Morse code, were addressed to one captain after another by name: "Report position and situation." More and more often there was no reply, thirty-one times by May 22. To the survivors Dönitz sent a series of lengthy and bleak analyses of the crisis which had transformed the campaign in a matter of weeks. On May 24 he told his commanders at sea:

> The struggle for our victory, becoming ever harder and more bitter, occasions me to reveal to you in all clarity the seriousness of our situation at this moment and of our future . . . Only you can fight the enemy offensively and beat him . . . The German nation has long felt that our arm is the sharpest and most decisive and that the outcome of the war depends on the success or failure of the Battle of the Atlantic.

On the same day Dönitz ordered his boats out of the North Atlantic to the "black pit" south-west of the Azores. In his memoirs he wrote: "We had lost the Battle of the Atlantic." But a few boats stayed in the North Atlantic, generating spurious radio traffic to tie down the huge Allied escort-forces.

In other theatres, Soviet resistance in the Crimea ended with the fall of Sevastopol in July; the Wehrmacht turned towards Stalingrad. In the Pacific the US Marines began a long and bloody battle for Guadalcanal in August, overcoming the Japanese garrison in February. Montgomery's victory at El Alamein on 3 November 1942 and "Operation Torch" put the Germans on the defensive in North Africa, where all Axis resistance ended in May. The Russians counter-attacked at Stalingrad on November 19 and the German Sixth Army Group surrendered there on February 2. The month-long revolt of the Warsaw Ghetto was smashed by the Germans on May 16; on the same day the RAF "Dam-Busters" flooded the Ruhr.

Any idea that Germany could now be written off was dispelled by such ominous developments as the maiden flight of the world's first jet fighter, the Me262, in July (eight months ahead of its British rival), the first successful

launch of the V2 rocket at Peenemünde in October, and of the V1 flying
bomb at Christmas. In high summer 1943 Dönitz ordered a total mobilisation
of German technical ingenuity in a bid to regain the initiative for his
submarines in the Atlantic.

9

JUNE 1943 TO MAY 1945

*Germany down but not out – war on the milch-cows – Dönitz
fights on – submarine revolution – the Schnorchel – the struggle
against radar – rival technologies – shipbuilders' victory – the
Azores – the US air "horse-trade" – row over carriers – long death
of Tirpitz – Scharnhorst sunk – Pound dead – acoustic torpedoes
– "Johnnie" Walker rampant – the last wolf-pack – after D-day –
retreat to Norway – new boats at sea – surrender – the final
reckoning*

THE extraordinarily swift reversal of fortunes in the Atlantic Campaign proved permanent because it was the result of a convergence of the several strands in the Allied defensive effort: the closure of the airgaps by VLR aircraft and escort-carriers, the huge building programme of both naval and merchant ships, the triumph of allied intelligence and a series of advances in weaponry and equipment. The victory of spring 1943 was achieved, not in a few weeks, but after forty-five months of unremitting struggle during which the submarine offensive came close to achieving its objective – the collapse of the United Kingdom – on more than one occasion. But it was to take no less than two whole years to force Hitler's Reich to surrender; the hard-won triumph in the Atlantic needed to be constantly guarded against a formidable enemy who was full of ideas for regaining the initiative on land, in the air and at sea. Caught between the Red Army's slow but inexorable advance and the Anglo-American blockade preparatory to a second front, the severely outnumbered Germans were far from beaten in summer 1943, proving as stubborn in defence as they had been overwhelming in attack during the first years of the war. The Allies might now be confident of victory on the basis of their immense superiority in resources of manpower, material and money, over the Axis powers, but they could take nothing for granted.

The turning-point in the Atlantic came at the end of March 1943, from which moment there was no hiding-place in the entire ocean out of reach of anti-submarine aircraft. It was precisely then that airborne radar rendered the entire German operational submarine fleet obsolete at a stroke. The types VII and IX now faced the permanent risk of detection when surfaced, while their underwater endurance and performance were too weak for catching merchantmen or dealing with their increasingly strong surface-escorts. These boats were not in the strictest sense submarines at all but submersible torpedo-boats which relied for their "invisibility" on absence of air-patrols, their small profile when surfaced and their ability to submerge for short periods before, during and after mounting an attack. Although anti-submarine aircraft now had effective weapons which enabled them to destroy a boat once detected, their principal value, enormously enhanced though it was by radar, was exactly the same as it had been at the end of the First World War: prevention of attack by forcing the submarine to submerge, thereby drastically reducing its speed. They accounted for a respectable total of submarine "kills" but they never displaced the surface-escort as the principal counter to submarines (though they frequently provided it with valuable assistance). For the rest of the war, therefore, the German Navy devoted its efforts to providing submarines with real invisibility, protecting them against radar and sonar detection, enabling them to stay submerged for much longer periods and to travel faster underwater, and trying to improve their armament.

Although clashes at sea continued throughout the period and even beyond the moment of surrender, the story of the last two years of the Atlantic campaign is mainly one of technologies. It was a struggle the Germans won hands down – but six months too late. The challenge they took up and met was the instantaneous development of a third generation of submarines which were also the first true submarines, capable of staying underwater for months. To do it they had to contend with the totalitarian vagaries of the Nazi leadership; the disruption caused by untrammelled Allied bombing; huge technical problems; and the constant threat to the morale of the crews in the dark days of mounting losses against a superior enemy until the promised new era when the tables would be turned. The result was a boat to which the Allied defence had no answer, the basis of the postwar submarine fleets of all the victorious powers until the arrival of the nuclear submarine.

Just as the destruction of the *Bismarck* in summer 1941 was followed by a determined and successful sweep against German surface supply-ships, so the containment of the submarine onslaught on the Anglo-American supply-line was followed by a sustained assault on the "milch-cows" which had vastly increased the boats' endurance and effectiveness on operational cruises. In the year from May 1942 to May 1943 the submarine tankers had refuelled nearly 400 fighting boats at sea without being detected; three tankers were found and sunk while in transit during the period.

The campaign against the supply-boats, now at a brief operational maximum of ten, was an American idea. The US Navy wanted to exploit

Ultra to the limit in locating and destroying them. The British objected because they feared the compromise of the best Allied intelligence source (they had already sternly rebuked no less a figure than General Montgomery for almost giving the game away by altering his dispositions in North Africa on the basis of Ultra material). The solution was to have aircraft do the locating work so that the Germans would think they had been found by routine air-patrols rather than penetration of their cipher-communications followed by the setting of a trap.

At the end of May, when Dönitz withdrew his battered flotillas from the main North Atlantic trade-route and its newly permanent air-cover to the area round the Azores, he had all ten milch-cows in service. On June 11 a signal to the tankers *U118* and *U460* to rendezvous with the fighting boat *U758* in that region was deciphered. It was two days old but fresh enough to enable the US Tenth Fleet to plan an attack. The three boats were together on the morning of June 10; *U758* and *U460* then headed north-east while U118 went south to refuel four more fighting boats. By this time Task Force 21:12 – the escort-carrier USS *Bogue* and three American destroyers – was racing east at seventeen knots towards the latter rendezvous. The *Bogue* sent aircraft from over the horizon which found *U118* surfaced at the designated spot in the early afternoon of the 12th. Nine planes shot up and depth-charged the boat for nearly half an hour until it exploded in a massive fireball of its own cargo of fuel.

The next tanker-victim was *U119*, sighted on outward passage in the Bay of Biscay by a Coastal Command air-patrol. The pilot alerted Captain "Johnnie" Walker's support-group which was in the vicinity and raced to the area where the target had been seen to dive. The four ships, led by Walker's sloop, HMS *Starling*, soon located the boat with Asdic on June 24. The team was by now so proficient that detection by any ship of a submarine implied the latter's destruction; any boat within range of any of the group's search-equipment was nigh on certain to be found. The group forced the *U119* to the surface by depth-charges and the *Starling* rammed it. There were no survivors.

Walker's latest catch was the result of sound co-operation between air and surface-forces initiated by an alert RAF crew. The next stroke against the tanker-fleet, now down to eight, was an enormous affair instigated once again by Ultra intercepts. Bletchley Park discovered at the end of June 1943 that Dönitz was sending a group of ten type IX – the *Monsun* (monsoon) group – to operate in the Indian Ocean from the Japanese-occupied base of Penang in Malaya. The group was to refuel from *U487* south of the Azores, around 27° north and 37° west. The Tenth Fleet mobilised four support-groups, each consisting of an escort-carrier and three destroyers. The carriers were the USS *Bogue*, *Card*, *Core* and *Santee*. It was planes from the *Core* which found the tanker on the flat-calm surface early in the evening of July 13. It was promptly sunk; then there were seven.

The next milch-cow to be caught was one of the oldest, *U459* (Commander Georg von Wilamowitz-Möllendorf), sighted on July 24 by Flying-Officer W. H. T. Jennings's RAF Wellington from 172 Squadron while crossing the Bay of Biscay. As the lumbering bomber swung and dived into the attack the Germans put up a hail of anti-aircraft fire which severely damaged the aircraft. Jennings aimed his disintegrating plane at the boat and hit it broadside on, dousing the conning-tower in burning fuel and leaving two depth-charges on the deck amid the wreckage. The Germans pushed the bombs overboard, but they were armed and set to go off at shallow depth. The stricken boat was unable to move out of reach before they exploded, mortally damaging the hull. The commander set off scuttling charges and went down with the submarine; forty-one Germans and one RAF man from the Wellington were rescued by a British destroyer sent to the scene.

At the end of July two tankers, *U461* and *U462*, escorted by the fighting boat *U504*, were among eleven boats sent into the Atlantic at short intervals across the Bay of Biscay. The grouping of these three boats was in line with new anti-aircraft tactics tried by Dönitz from mid-June. Boats were to cross the dangerous Bay in company, inward usually in pairs, outward in threes, so that their combined firepower could be used to deter air-attack or at least put it off its stroke. The Allies swiftly responded by refraining from attacking such groups until they had gathered enough aircraft over the spot for multiple strikes from different directions. Dönitz also at this time tried a submarine variation on the discredited Q-ship. *U441* was crammed with all the anti-aircraft guns it could carry: two sets of quadruple, 2-centimetre, rapid-fire cannon and one 3.7-centimetre semi-automatic gun, all of which made the boat the most heavily-armed submarine of the war. The idea was that KL Götz von Hartmann should trail his coat in the Bay, inviting air-attack to which he would reply with an unprecedented hail of shot. Unfortunately for him, on July 12, he came under attack from not one but three aircraft, British Beaufighters of 248 Squadron, RAF, which repeatedly strafed *U441* and inflicted heavy casualties among the gun-crews crammed into the "bandstands" fore and aft of the conning-tower. Ten were killed and thirteen, including the captain, badly wounded. With more than half the crew out of action, the survivors abandoned the guns, piled back inside the hull through the hatches and crept back to base underwater as German Ju88s arrived overhead to tackle the gathering swarm of British aircraft. Two of the latter were shot down. Dönitz concluded that a submarine on its own was a "bad platform" for fighting aircraft, but he stuck to his idea of group-defence for the time being: "Stay up and fight," he ordered; "diving is fatal" (War Diary, July 20). Ten days later the price of staying up and shooting back was made plain.

It was on July 30 that the first aircraft sighted *U504* and its two tanker-charges in the Bay. At first no attack materialised because the aircrew misreported the location. Then two flying-boats rediscovered the group and circled overhead out of range until a total of seven aircraft were present. Meanwhile the formidable Captain Walker was on his way to the area at top speed. The first British air-attack caused some damage to *U462*, which however managed to drive off the second bomber in such condition that it was forced to make an emergency landing in Portugal. The third pass in a series of indifferently co-ordinated attacks was made by a Sunderland, which destroyed *U461* by depth-charges. The aircraft, oddly enough, came from 461 Squadron. *U462* meanwhile was still blazing away with its anti-aircraft armament in all directions – until 4-inch shells from naval guns began to throw up columns of water round the boat. Walker's group had opened fire from long range. *U462's* crew thereupon abandoned their boat after setting scuttling-charges. *U504*, which had not come under attack (sinking the tankers was the Allies' top priority), dived, laying itself open to one of Captain Walker's "creeping attacks" which he had invented himself. One ship would crawl along, tracking the submerged boat with her Asdic while directing one of her companions into a position from which the second ship could drop a pattern of depth-charges with deadly precision into the path of the victim. The chase lasted two hours, during which *U504* was hammered to destruction with the loss of all hands.

Actions elsewhere took the total of German submarines destroyed on that one day to six, four of which were sunk by aircraft. The destruction of all three in the tanker-group was a devastating blow to the Germans; now there were four. In less than eight weeks the herd of milch-cows had suffered a cull of sixty percent. In June and July the Germans lost fifty-four boats, forty-four of them to aircraft. It was the zenith of the intermittent Biscay offensive which had been heavily intensified in the period immediately following the German retreat from the North Atlantic. On August 2 Dönitz abandoned the patently disastrous "stay up and fight" policy and temporarily confined all boats to their French bases.

The next tanker to be detected was a brand-new one, *U489*. A British-based RCAF patrol-aircraft sighted it west of the Faroes on its first operational voyage and bombed it on August 4. The aircraft was forced to ditch by gunfire; five of its crew and the entire German company were saved by a destroyer. Of the ten type XIV submarine tankers built by the Germans throughout the war, only three now survived, and of these two were in dock refitting. The only recourse left to Dönitz therefore was to use the larger fighting boats of type IX as reserve-tankers to alleviate the desperate plight of other boats far from base with too little fuel to get back. One of these, the *U117*, its new role revealed by Ultra, was found and sunk by aircraft from the USS *Card* on August 7; four days later *U525* suffered the same fate at the same hand; the *Card* struck a third time on August 27 by sinking *U847*, another boat pressed into service as a substitute tanker. The Americans also sank two submarines trying to rendezvous with the temporary tankers to get fuel, and damaged a third. To complete the sorry record of the type XIVs we may add here that the *Card* sank *U460* in mid-Atlantic on 4 October 1943; *U488* was sunk in mid-Atlantic by the carrier USS *Croatan* on 26 April 1944; and *U490*, the last of a doomed line, was caught and sunk in the same area by the same ship on 9 June 1944. Of the seventeen boats built or adapted by the Germans to serve as milch-cows and launched between spring 1942 and May 1944, only one survived the war – *U219*, which went to Japanese-controlled waters in the Far East at the end of 1943 and never returned to the Atlantic.

Karl Dönitz was nothing if not a ruthless commander-in-chief. In such an exalted position he saw it as his duty to take the long view strategically. At this stage of the war this led him to send his boats to sea in the full knowledge that they were effectively obsolete. That in turn meant mounting losses among crews whose average age was now under twenty. Try as he might he could find no tactical answer to the overwhelming strength of the Allies in the air. On the other hand the German Navy in the First World War, through which he had fought, had made two fatal psychological errors, directly traceable to a major flaw in the character of the "Supreme Warlord," Kaiser Wilhelm II. After Jutland, halfway through the war, the surface-fleet had effectively been allowed to rot in port to the point where a last throw to fend off imminent defeat was rendered impossible by a total collapse in morale, leading to revolution on the lower deck. Secondly the submarine fleet had been robbed of its potential as the strategically decisive factor by being let loose, then curbed, then unleashed again as the Kaiser swung between hostile world opinion and the urgings of his commanders. Wilhelm's vacillation essentially deprived his technically superb navy of a chance to bring victory, or at least stave off defeat, in a war largely brought about by its construction.

Dönitz was therefore determined to keep his boats fighting as best they could. There were more than 400 in commission, a figure below which the submarine arm's strength was hardly to fall for the rest of the war. The admiral put his faith in German technology. He relied on it to find the answer to all his problems with new types of boat, new defences against radar, new torpedoes. Meanwhile existing forces had to do their best; at least they were still tying down an enormous enemy strength in ships and aircraft whose diversion elsewhere on the abandonment, or even a noticeable interruption, of the submarine campaign would be a new threat to Germany on other fronts. In one sense Dönitz was right: the German submarine service never succumbed to a collapse of morale, a fact which seems all the more remarkable on studying the events of the latter part of the war. The C-in-C was also right in another sense, in that German scientists and engineers had the answers to most of his needs and were hard at work translating them into reality. Dönitz lost his gamble because ideas which could have been realised a year earlier or more were fatally deferred by Hitler's faith in an early and total victory in the opening phase of the war and his incomprehension of naval strategy. Although the Führer of the Third Reich was much more ruthless and less sensitive to world opinion than the last ruler of the Second, he too vacillated, between the demands of the rival services in the Wehrmacht, promising all things to all men and going back on his undertakings shortly afterwards. Towards the end he found it ever harder to retain his waning grasp of Germany's plight, airily agreeing to conflicting requests for materials and men which Germany had long since ceased to be able to provide in the requisite quantities.

In putting his faith in the revolutionary submarine design of Professor Hellmuth Walter, mentioned earlier, Dönitz soon found that he (and Walter) had aimed too high. It will be recalled that the essential idea was to build a new, streamlined hull of the strength needed for deep diving, powered by a single propulsion-system instead of a combination of diesel-engines on the surface and battery-powered electric motors underwater. The Walter engine was a gas-turbine which ran on a mixture of refined diesel-fuel and air on the surface; underwater it was to burn a mixture of the same fuel and hydrogen peroxide. The latter was made to break down, into the oxygen needed for the engine plus water-vapour, by a catalyst (permanganate of lime). The beauty of the idea was that since the pure oxygen thus obtained gave the diesel-fuel an efficiency in burning greater than when mixed with air, higher performance would be obtained for less fuel underwater than on the surface: the boats would actually be able to travel *faster* submerged than surfaced. Against this, they would not be able to travel underwater at all once the hydrogen peroxide had run out, so time and distance underwater were strictly limited, much more so than on the surface. But the phenomenal submerged speed originally envisaged (over thirty knots) would have enabled the boat to dive deep and elude any surface-ship in existence. The Walter boats, of which several experimental models were built and tested, proved unreliable and the technology involved was never put to practical use. The first experimental boat had been completed as early as 1940, but no operational type could be produced by the end of the war. Yet not all of Walter's work was to be wasted.

On July 31 Dönitz went to see Hitler to account for the recent serious setbacks in the submarine campaign and to explain how he planned to regain the initiative with new tactics and weapons. Work would continue on overcoming the technical difficulties of the Walter boat because if this could be achieved Germany would have a true "miracle weapon" of the kind Hitler increasingly longed for as an instantaneous escape from his mounting difficulties on all fronts. In the meantime there was to be a halfway-house. So long as the Walter boat's propulsion difficulties could not be resolved, the navy could at least use his advanced hull and another idea on which the Professor had been working.

The Walter hull had markedly softer lines than previous submarines, with curves where there used to be angles. The essential idea was to borrow from nature the evolved outline of marine mammals such as whales and dolphins, fast swimmers under or on the water. This streamlining was copied for all postwar submarines in the navies of the world. These intermediate types would still be conventionally powered, with diesels for the surface and electric motors for underwater; but the Germans had done much useful work on reducing the weight of the large accumulator-batteries needed for the motors, so that considerably more battery power could be included. Two types were to be built: the XXI, an ocean-going boat displacing 1,600 tons surfaced (1,820 submerged), and the XXIII, a coastal submarine of 234 tons (258 underwater). The larger boat was designed to produce 15.6 knots on the surface (rather less than the 18-plus of the type IX and the 17 knots of the VIIc) but submerged it could travel at 17.2 knots, more than twice as fast as either of the older types which could only produce between seven and eight knots underwater. The coastal version had speeds of 9.7 knots surfaced and 12.5 submerged. Both new boats were therefore much more likely to be able to get away from a surface-ship while submerged than their predecessors. Furthermore the range of each type underwater, determined by the power and endurance of the improved batteries, was to be 285 miles for the large and 175 for the small type – three to four times as far as the older boats – before the batteries ran out and had to be recharged.

As with all previous submarines, the new types, called *Elektro-U-boote*, had to use their diesels to charge their batteries. Diesels need air, which meant that boats had to surface at frequent intervals to keep their batteries topped up – indeed they had to spend as much time as possible on the surface and as little as possible submerged, which proved to be their undoing when enemy air-cover became universal. This weakness accounted for the July 1943 massacre in the Bay of Biscay and the success of the Ultra-inspired support-groups. The "electro-boats" were much less vulnerable in this respect but would still have been exposed to high risk from the air but for the other development on which Professor Walter had been working (although this time it was not his idea).

If we regard the electro-boats as a halfway-house between the older types and the full-blown Walter submarine with its revolutionary single power-unit, the *Schnorchel* can be seen partly as a halfway-house between the old boats and the electro-boats and also as a revolution in itself. The original name for this apparatus was *snuiver*, a Dutch word meaning the same as the German – something which snorts, like a horse. It was invented by *Kaptein-luitenant* J. J. Wichers of the Royal Netherlands Navy in 1927. When the Germans overran the Netherlands in 1940 and occupied the principal Dutch naval base of Den Helder in the north-west of the country, they found two almost complete submarines fitted with a double pipe of about the same length as their periscopes. It had a cap containing a valve which closed automatically underwater; the apparatus folded down into a recess on the deck when not in use. Wicher's idea was in essence brilliantly simple (though not easy to put into reliable practice). It enabled a boat to "breathe" while submerged and, once the difficulties could be resolved, achieved the transformation from submersible craft to true submarine, removing the need to surface in order to charge batteries. The double pipe of the *snuiver* enabled the boat to inhale air and to expel exhaust from its diesel-engines while underwater. Not only could the boat stay under while recharging; it could also use its diesels for propulsion while submerged (though only slowly because of the large amount of air they needed and the ever-present risk of sudden closure of the valve whenever the cap was covered by water. This meant that the slightest error by the operator of the hydro-planes which controlled the boat's depth, or a little extra turbulence on the surface, caused the diesels to use up all the air in the hull in a few moments unless they were immediately switched off. As will be seen, the effects on the crew were quite horrible).

Considering the revolutionary potential of a device which enabled a submarine to stay submerged for days, weeks or even months, one is more than merely surprised, even with hindsight, that the Germans with their long-standing lead in submarine technology did not at once take up the idea on finding the Dutch boats in May 1940. Four Netherlands submarines fitted with *snuiver* escaped to fight alongside the British. They too failed to recognise the significance of a device which may still have been at the experimental stage in the Dutch navy but whose drawbacks were by no means insuperable, as the Germans proved when desperation inspired them to tackle the difficulties.

Not only were all the electro-boats to have the apparatus; by the beginning of 1944 it was being used to give the old types VII and IX a new lease of life. It was relatively easy technically to fit them with the folding version and its successor, which was retractable like a periscope. The cap was almost as difficult to spot with the naked eye as the tip of a periscope unless the boat was moving fast enough for the cap to create a wake; nor could ten-centimetre radar be relied upon to detect an object so small and low in the water. Only the next generation, the three-centimetre radar, was as precise as that; this was not in general use until well into 1944. When the Allies became aware of its existence, there were outbreaks of "schnorchelitis" among sailors and seamen very similar to the "periscopitis" of the early days in the First World War, causing a significant waste of effort and ammunition. Wisps of spray were enthusiastically depth-charged on suspicion of being the miniature wake of a snort or schnorkel, as the Allies called the device. Professor Walter's version of the Dutch invention was simplicity itself: two flexible hoses joined together by metal bands with the floating head at one end and fixed to and through the hull at the other. Experiments with this began in 1942, but the flexibility proved a disadvantage and the rigid, folding design was tried instead. This proved workable enough to be fitted to a number of operational boats until the third and best version, the rigid retractable tube, was developed.

Special training in the use of the schnorkel was given to minimise the considerable dangers attached to its use. The din of the diesels underwater made the submerged boat deaf as well as blind, so the engines were switched off after twenty minutes, enabling the hydrophone-operators to listen for ships. If one diesel-engine was used to propel the boat and the other to recharge batteries, eventually three hours of schnorkelling at up to four knots could provide enough accumulated power for a whole day's low-speed travel on the electric motors. Skilfully used, the schnorkel could also be made to renew the foetid air inside the submarine at frequent intervals: brief closure of the valve on the air-pipe with the diesels still running caused the engines to start swallowing up the air inside the hull, reducing the atmospheric pressure. When this happened by accident the effects were highly unpleasant, causing the crew to fight for breath and their eyes to bulge; it is believed that at least two submarines were lost through the suffocation of their crews. But deliberate manipulation of the air-valve and the engines to reduce atmospheric pressure by about twenty percent, whereupon the valve would be reopened, caused the hull to suck in fresh air without the need to surface. In daylight extreme caution was required in using the diesels underwater, to prevent the exhaust-pipe in the schnorkel from emitting clouds of smoke which would have betrayed the boat's presence.

All these developments were co-ordinated by a committee of scientists and technical experts set up by Dönitz in summer 1943, in belated imitation of the British and the Americans, who had mobilised scientific talent in this way as soon as they became involved in hostilities. This enabled the German Navy to cease to rely on the Luftwaffe for search-radar with which to look for ships and aircraft; but the Germans, thanks to Hitler's early confidence in total victory and Göring's incompetence, had fallen hopelessly far behind in a field invented and led by the British throughout the war. It was only in early 1944 that submarines got the 80cm *Gema* scanner (a poor adaptation of naval gun-ranging radar) and *Hohentwiel*, with a wavelength of 43cm. The latter proved adequate to detect aircraft at ranges of up to six nautical miles and was developed from a Luftwaffe set.

But what the German submarine service needed rather more urgently was effective defensive equipment to give warning of aircraft and to counter their growing success with radar. We have seen how the Germans, having repeatedly if also narrowly rejected the idea that their ciphers had been penetrated, came to attach a respect bordering on outright superstition to Allied detection capacity. They wasted a lot of time and effort in seeking ways to counter detection at night by infra-red light. The technical possibility was known at the time and is in general use today; unfortunately for the Germans it was not something the Allies bothered with because of their lead in radar, as well as their mastery of HF/DF – another area in which the Germans were now well behind.

The German Metox search-receiver (radar-detector) was able to register enemy radar-transmissions only of the early, long-wavelength type. Its value was thus limited and it was no use at all against ten-centimetre radar of the second generation. As submarine losses mounted in late 1943 the Germans began to suspect that the boats were being betrayed by Metox emissions so that enemy aircraft did not need to use their radar to home on to a submarine. While it was true that the Metox could be detected if left tuned into one wavelength for a long time, the risk was minimal if the set was being correctly used to scan all the wavelengths in its limited detection-spectrum. Crews were therefore told to keep the use of the set to a minimum.

German nervousness in this area was compounded by a quick-thinking RAF pilot captured when his aircraft was shot down. While being "debriefed" by German intelligence this officer concluded from the trend of the interrogation that the enemy was acutely concerned about the possibility of Allied detection of German detection-devices. Instead of limiting himself to supply his name, rank and number, which was all he was required to do under the Geneva Convention on prisoners of war, the pilot decided to plant some unsettling disinformation on his captors. He told them in mid-August 1943, by which time submarine losses had reached a peak, that the British hardly ever needed to use their airborne radar because they could rely on locating a submarine by the emissions from its radar-search receiver. He solemnly told them that this radiation could be picked up at a range of ninety miles. "Great importance must be attached to this British pilot's statement," said the War Diary of the Submarine Command. "Even if this is a deliberate attempt to mislead us, especially as the alleged range seems improbable and could only be achieved by a very sensitive receiver, the statement must be accepted as true in deciding on further measures." On August 14, therefore, the Germans banned Metox altogether.

The pilot's disingenuous "disclosure" came only weeks after German scientists had discovered that Metox did indeed emit radiation, a fact which convinced some staff officers in the Naval Command that here was the true explanation for the contemporary severe losses of submarines. The Germans still did not believe that the centimetric radar-set, recovered early in the year from the RAF bomber which crashed at Rotterdam, was of practical value, further evidence of how far behind they were. They therefore commissioned the Hagenuk company to produce a new radar-detector called (when it was not simply given the firm's own name) the *Wanze*. As it stands the word means "bug" appropriately enough, but it was an acronym for *Wellenanzeiger* (wave-indicator). This began to be supplied to submarines from mid-August 1943. It was superseded in November by the *Wanze G2*, which emitted virtually no radiation. At the same time the *Naxos* search-receiver, the first in German service capable of picking up centimetric radar-transmissions, was issued: scepticism about the practical application of ten-centimetre radar was not such that it could be ignored. This was followed early in 1944 by the *Fliege*, a much more sensitive detector in the same range, and finally by the *Mücke*, which could pick up the third-generation three-centimetre radar. Thus was the "bug" succeeded first by the "fly" and then by the "mosquito."

While the Germans were feverishly engaged in improving the defences of existing boats and developing new types, they were not neglecting their offensive capability. Work was well advanced in mid-1943 on the *Zaunkönig* ("wren") torpedo, which was to home on to the sound of a ship's propellers – the acoustic torpedo whose arrival the Allies had mistakenly but fortunately anticipated (it will be remembered that the *FAT* or "curly" torpedo, first heard of by Ultra, had been thought to be acoustic rather than one which twisted and turned with the idea of being more likely to score a hit). This new torpedo was intended principally for use against escorts and began to be supplied in August 1943. Boats thenceforward carried a cocktail of three types of torpedo: *Zaunkönig*, *FAT* and the straightforward electrically-powered weapon, the latter two for use against merchant-ships once the escort-screen had been penetrated by the former.

The mistaken deduction from Ultra decrypts that the *FAT* was an acoustic torpedo led to two developments on the Allied side. One was the Anglo-American *Fido*, itself an acoustic torpedo for dropping from the air against submarines. This began to come into use at almost exactly the same time as the German *Zaunkönig*, which the Allies codenamed the "Gnat." The other invention, by the Americans, was a defensive device called the "Foxer." Towed in the water by an escort, it was a simple noisemaker which caused the new German weapons to explode harmlessly astern of their target – essentially a bar with one tube at each end for the water to rush noisily through.

The Allies, as noted above, kept well ahead in radar throughout the war and produced the highly accurate three-centimetre set for issue during 1944. The Germans tried to decoy radar with the *Aphrodite* device, a gas-filled balloon festooned with metal foil (and later a more sophisticated version codenamed *Thetis*), but these were about as successful against the latest precision-radar as the *Bold* gas-bubble (released from a *Pillenwerfer* or pill-thrower) proved to be against the much-refined Asdic and Sonar now in use.

The British and Americans continued to develop new anti-submarine devices to ensure they remained ahead of the game. One was the "Squid," a mortar which fired three depth-charges at a time over the bow of an escort (the earlier Hedgehog fired much smaller projectiles), a British idea. The Americans produced the Magnetic Anomaly-Detector (MAD) which detected a submarine in shallow water or just below the surface by its magnetic field, from the air. The first US aircraft to be fitted with it were Catalina flying-boats which thereupon became known as "Madcats." In conjunction with this useful instrument a retro-rocket was used: the detecting aircraft was thus enabled to fire rockets backwards at a target found by MAD instead of losing time by having to circle in order to be able to make a conventional attack. Forward-firing air-to-surface rockets were also used by fighters and other aircraft against submarines from 1944. The Luftwaffe used a similar weapon against ships. Another American contribution to the electronic war was the sonar buoy, a battery-powered float dropped from the air in narrow waters which detected submarines by their noise and passed the information to aircraft. This idea came too late to make much difference, like the rubber coating (*Alberich*) the Germans applied to their submarines from late summer 1944 in an attempt to deceive Asdic.

Probably the greatest misdirection of effort by the British during the war against submarines was the huge mining campaign. The "barrier" between Britain and Iceland is known to have destroyed just one submarine for certain. Mines were most effective in constricted waters like the Channel (and for the Germans, British coastal waters); only in the last year of the war, when Allied airpower overwhelmed the Luftwaffe, could aircraft sow mines in the Baltic and German North Sea waters almost at will and in quantities sufficient to affect the submarines. We may conclude this review of the technological struggle in the latter part of the war by noting that the most important single development, the schnorkel, in large measure restored the invisibility which airborne radar had taken away for long enough to ensure the shift in the balance of power in the campaign to the Allies in the first half of 1943. The schnorkel was not efficient enough to reverse the trend but it enabled the German submarines to fight on to the end and to tie down enormous anti-submarine forces until the unconditional surrender. Developments on land and in the air saw to it that Germany collapsed before its new generation of boats could be deployed against enemies who would have been hard put to counter them.

The maximum effect that even these formidable new submarines could have had, however, would have been to make the war of attrition rather less one-sided than it was in the last two years of hostilities. The most important single fact of strategic import in 1943 was that in October Allied (overwhelmingly American) shipbuilding finally overtook the total tonnage lost to enemy action in four years of maritime warfare. In October 1942 the Liberty-ship *Joseph N. Teal* was built from start to finish in ten days and the Americans were launching three a day. One month later the *Robert E. Peary* was, thanks to prefabrication and a keen sense of publicity on the part of the Richmond, California, yard of the Kaiser Corporation, built in four days and fifteen hours – the all-time record. Stunts apart, it is impossible to see how the Germans could henceforward hope to make significant inroads on the now fully engaged industrial capacity of the United States, which built thousands of ships as if they were cars coming off an assembly-line and could have filled each one with munitions and food several times over.

The principle that no single factor was chiefly responsible for victory in the Atlantic campaign holds good under any circumstances. But the strength of the "arsenal of democracy" was surely the factor above all others that would have prevented the pendulum swinging back towards the Germans at sea, no matter what new weapons they might have deployed had the war continued beyond May 1945 in Europe. Had it done so there would in any case have been a terrible last resort which was also a product of American technical and scientific supremacy: the atomic bomb. If the German submarine service had been able to re-establish itself as the principal threat to the Allied war-effort in the European theatre, the first nuclear weapon might well have been dropped on Hamburg, a much larger city than either Hiroshima or Nagasaki. It is in this fortunately hypothetical and speculative area that the contribution of Ultra to the shortening of the time it took the Allies to gain the upper hand in the European war is of greatest significance, over and above the technical and production factors which would have come into play when they did in any case. The evasive routeing of ships made possible by Ultra saved lives and cargoes as well as the vessels themselves, while the transatlantic spread of airpower and the steady rise in quantity and quality of surface-escorts overcame the submarine itself.

Land-based aircraft were never quite capable of covering every square mile of the north Atlantic. The closure of the gap south of Greenland and the simultaneous appearance of the escort-carriers were the keystone of the Allied victory on the convoy routes which, as noted above, led Dönitz to move his boats southward to the waters south and west of the Azores. This gap could be covered only by planes from escort-carriers now continuously placed there by the Americans.

The Azores, a mid-Atlantic archipelago owned by Portugal, was much favoured by the German submarines for rendezvous with milch-cows precisely because it was out of reach of long-range air-patrols. The reason for this was diplomatic. Both sides cast their eyes on the Azores for possible occupation, but each concluded that the potential effort involved in preserving them from counter-attack was not worth it. The British, for whom Portugal was a very useful intelligence listening-post against Fascist Spain, were also conscious that the Portuguese were historically their oldest ally, an anti-Spanish arrangement which went back half a millennium. Portugal remained neutral in the war against Germany and Italy from necessity; any other position would have invited intervention from the Spanish Fascists, with their much greater military strength, on the side of the Axis. The Portuguese also lived under a right-wing dictatorship led by Dr Salazar but were cautiously friendly to the British. The latter began quietly to press Lisbon for the use of the Azores as an airbase in autumn 1941. Salazar resisted all blandishments until it became clear to him that the Allies had gained the upper hand all over the world and were likely to win.

Finally on 18 August 1943 an Anglo-Portuguese agreement, giving the British two bases on the islands of Fayal and Terceira in exchange for arms and a promise of protection against German attack, was concluded and signed. It took effect on October 8. The British, urged on by American impatience about this obvious gap in the anti-submarine defences, were in any case preparing to take the islands by force if necessary. A special convoy covered by a support-group with carrier moved in on the agreed date. Coastal Command set up a new air-group, number 247, to fly from the Azores. When the Americans wanted to use the new airfields as a staging-post and for patrols they were obliged to adopt British markings to placate Portuguese diplomatic sensitivity, after another protracted round of negotiations. Swordfish from the escort-carrier HMS *Fencer* were the first to be based on land in the Azores until the weather improved sufficiently to enable the RAF B17 (Flying Fortress) aircraft from Gibraltar to form the permanent air-garrison. The Americans were allowed in early in 1944. Land-based air-cover of the Atlantic thereupon became as complete as the ranges of contemporary aircraft permitted.

The takeover of the Azores bases and the simultaneous restoration to Coastal Command of responsibility for anti-submarine work from RAF Gibraltar left only one anomaly in the air-coverage of the eastern Atlantic region – the two VLR squadrons under American control in Morocco. There was also an administrative anomaly in the shape of the two US Army Air Force squadrons operating from Britain under Coastal Command control – and in the more general form of the USAAF's involvement in anti-submarine work in the first place. Many occasions on which the direction of maritime airpower caused problems for each of the major belligerents have already been recounted. For the United States forces the whole untidy issue finally came to a head in summer 1943.

The foresight shown by Admiral King in recognising the potential of airpower at sea with more clarity than anyone except the Japanese related to aircraft-carriers. It did not extend to land-based anti-submarine operations, to which virtually nobody in any navy or air force had given much thought before the Second World War despite the lessons of the First. We saw therefore how American shore commands like the Eastern Sea Frontier had been obliged to turn to the Army Air Force for help with maritime patrols as the only organisation with the right kind of aircraft, even though AAF pilots had no maritime training at first.

This Army Air Force involvement grew into the Army Antisubmarine Command by the middle of 1942. In March 1943 the USAAF started a campaign to win for this command a role vis à vis the US Navy analogous to the (not altogether correctly perceived) role of RAF Coastal Command with the Royal Navy: co-operation of a close but autonomous nature, as a keynote

paper by a US scientific expert in March 1943 misread it. In fact Coastal
Command was administratively under RAF control and operationally under
the Admiralty, the subject of perpetual wrangling and nearly always left
behind in the scramble for new equipment. Navies viewed aircraft as one of
a wide range of weapons they could (or would like to) use when appropriate;
air forces regarded planes as rightfully their exclusive preserve, whatever
their role. The formation of the Tenth Fleet (see the previous chapter)
inevitably raised the question of what to do with the USAAF Antisubmarine
Command, provoking a lengthy, though not unduly acrimonious, exchange
of views between King and General Marshall. The administrative modalities
were settled by an agreement to make an AAF general Tenth Fleet air-
commander, to be succeeded by an admiral, but the two services could not
agree on anti-submarine tactics. King took the hard-won view of the British
for once and insisted that aircraft belonged primarily with convoys; the Air
Force made the familiar error of seeing this as defensive and demanding
"offensive" patrols. King solidly insisted this was a luxury that could only be
afforded once the convoys were properly protected – but then by all means.

At one of the frequent Allied convoy conferences, King requested
General Arnold of Anti-submarine Command in May 1943 to send a squadron
of Liberators to Newfoundland to close the airgap. Arnold sent the planes –
with strict orders to patrol, not to escort. At an American inter-service
conference in mid-June the issue of tactics came to a head, prompting the
Air Force representatives to propose a radical solution. The Navy could have
the Army's Liberators in exchange for an equal number of unmodified naval
equivalents. The impasse was broken when King seized on the idea and put
it to Marshall, suggesting the Navy take over all airborne anti-submarine
work on 1 September 1943. Marshall and Arnold were in agreement and the
deal become known as the great "horse-trade"; it took a long time to achieve
but in the end it was a better arrangement than the one prevailing in Britain.
The two USAAF squadrons working with Coastal Command were replaced
by US Navy squadrons later in the year.

Given the inter-service rivalries experienced by each nation there need
be no surprise that the two Allies also fell out about a major aspect of maritime
airpower at this same period. The issue was the escort-carrier, specifically
its construction, which the British regarded as unsafe. The Americans not
unnaturally were upset to have made a huge effort to turn out these conversions of merchant-ship hulls at British request as fast as possible, only to find
that they were not put to operational use for six months or even longer after
delivery while the British carried out modifications.

There was reason on both sides. The British ordered their first six
carriers of this useful hybrid type under Lend–Lease at the end of April
1941; the first was ready in less than seven months, a highly creditable
performance by any standard, even if the technique derived from the First

World War. As if to admit their rudimentary nature the Americans called them "Woolworth carriers." The ships did not meet Admiralty standards on stability, which led the British to add permanent ballast of up to 2,000 tonnes; they did not allow the use of seawater in empty fuel-tanks to serve this purpose, as the Americans did. What really alarmed the Admiralty was the loss of HMS *Avenger* to a single torpedo in November 1942 with only seventeen survivors, and the fuel-explosion on HMS *Dasher* in the Clyde in March 1943, which killed 378 men and destroyed the ship. The British conclusion that the fuel supply-system was dangerous does not seem altogether unreasonable, but the consequent delay in commissioning the remaining four of the first six British escort-carriers angered the Americans to such an extent that they threatened to put US Navy crews on some of the second tranche of seven conversions ordered by the British, to ensure the ships went into action that much faster. The Allied Combined Chiefs of Staff agreed to this in September 1943, the British side not least because the Royal Navy was experiencing growing difficulty in finding naval manpower at this stage of the war against the competing demands of the Army, the RAF and the Merchant Navy. There were not enough Fleet Air Arm captains available to command the carriers or skilled shipboard crew to maintain and operate the aircraft, which were in any case often obsolete types like the trusty but slow Swordfish, vulnerable to the heavier anti-aircraft armament of German submarines of the time.

The entire dispute is an interesting illustration of the difference in approach between the Old World and the New, between British caution and conservatism and American readiness to take risks and impatience to get on with winning the war. In their different ways both sides were right, and from late 1943 the British escort-carriers steadily overcame their problems to make a sound contribution. But it should now be clear why American successes against submarines were largely achieved by carrier-groups while British "hunter-killer" successes relied on surface-escort groups like Captain Walker's.

One area in which British escort-carriers made an unquestionably important and successful contribution was the Arctic, where convoys to Russia were resumed in autumn 1943. Their reintroduction was eased by an extraordinary operation against the bugbear of the British Home Fleet which was responsible for these hazardous operations – the *Tirpitz*, shy and retiring pride of the German surface-fleet since the sinking of the *Bismarck*. The most powerful ship ever built by Germany fired her heavy guns in anger just once, on 6 September 1943, when she joined the *Scharnhorst* and ten destroyers in bombarding the Allied shore stations on Spitzbergen Island in a brief sortie from Altenfjord. This use of a sledgehammer to bruise a nut had no strategic value or consequence, but it encouraged those involved in a plan for an original stroke against the flagship of the diminished German fleet.

From May 1943 the British went ahead with the development of the X-craft, a midget submarine of just thirty-five tons measuring fifty-one feet from stem to stern. It had a crew of four and could move at a speed of 6.5 knots surfaced and five submerged. Its only weapon was a pair of detachable bombs with clockwork detonators, to be dropped on the bottom of the sea while the submarines made their escape. The X-craft were to be towed to their jumping-off point some 150 miles out of Altenfjord by conventional submarines.

On the night of September 11 to 12, six X-craft sailed under tow by six ordinary submarines from Loch Cairnbawn in the north-west of Scotland. *X5, X6* and *X7* were to attack the *Tirpitz, X9* and *X10* the *Scharnhorst*, then in Kaa Fjord by Altenfjord, and *X8* the *Lützow* in Langefjord, in northern Norway. *X9* disappeared without trace while under tow, while *X8* was forced to scuttle when its ballast-tanks failed because of air-leaks. The crew was unharmed. *X10* was overwhelmed by a series of mishaps. Between the last photo-reconnaissance and the launch of the daring mission the *Scharnhorst* had left her berth and gone on exercise down the fjord. *X10's* Australian skipper, Lieutenant K. R. Hudspeth, RANVR, was in any case forced to abort his attack when a series of collisions with the German boom and net defences put periscope and compass out of action. After lying on the bottom throughout the 22nd trying to make emergency repairs, Hudspeth crept out to sea again. It was not until six days later that he managed to rendezvous with one of the "mother" submarines, which took him in tow. *X10* was left to sink in a storm 400 miles from the Shetland Isles.

X5, X6 and *X7* slipped successfully through the German minefields on the night of September 20. *X5* thereupon lost touch with the other two and was never heard from again. The little boats were to lie on the bottom through the 21st before making their attack on the *Tirpitz* in the early hours of the 22nd. Since the Germans reported sinking a submarine in the vicinity of the Kaa Fjord on the morning of the 22nd and no other boat was in the area and unaccounted for, it is to be presumed that their gunfire sank *X5* (Lieutenant H. Henty-Creer, RNVR); there were no survivors.

X7 (Lieutenant B. C. G. Place, RN) led *X6*, commanded by Lieutenant D. Cameron, RNR, towards the heavily protected anchorage of the *Tirpitz*. It took the two boats nearly six hours to force their way through, during which both were damaged. Just after 7 a.m. *X6* bumped the bottom and involuntarily bounced to the surface, whereupon it came under a hail of small-arms fire from sailors on the main deck of the *Tirpitz*. Fortunately the great ship was incapable of depressing any of its guns sufficiently against a target so close and low in the water. Cameron dived, crept towards the looming ship without benefit of periscope, dropped his charges, surfaced so he and his three companions could abandon ship and scuttled *X6*. The four men were taken prisoner.

For at least fifteen minutes chaos reigned on the *Tirpitz*. The pandemonium was renewed when X7 was sighted at 7.40, by which time it had placed its bombs beneath the battleship, having scraped under the hull. As Place withdrew his badly damaged craft it became entangled in the German nets. It was still there when the craft yawed violently underwater to the shock of a mighty explosion which was said by eye-witnesses to have lifted the *Tirpitz* bodily several feet. The blast freed X7 which now proved uncontrollable. The battleship's secondary armament fired on it, but when X7 eventually collided with a floating gunnery-practice target, Lieutenant Place managed to jump on it as X7 sank under his feet. One of his crew was able to escape to the surface; the other two were lost. Because of the confusion it is not clear whether all four bombs went off together, separately or at all, but at least one did so directly under the keel of the *Tirpitz* (probably from X7), knocking out all three main engines and causing much secondary damage. The great ship was not dead but crippled; the Germans thought it would take them more than six months to complete repairs. Hitler was furious. Lieutenants Cameron and Place were each awarded the Victoria Cross, which they were able to collect on their release from captivity after the war.

The Home Fleet under Admiral Fraser now had only one major ship to worry about in the north – the *Scharnhorst* – and therefore had much greater freedom of action in running the resumed Russian convoys and attacking targets on the Norwegian coast. "Operation Source" was a remarkably brave stroke, matching the brilliance of the attack on Alexandria by the Italian frogmen. It did not eliminate the *Tirpitz* altogether but for more than half a year it eased the burden of thousands of sailors and seamen. And by the time the *Tirpitz* recovered from her wounds there was no other major German warship for the British to worry about. There can have been few VCs more valiantly earned.

Even as the X-craft submariners risked their all against the *Tirpitz* with the ultimate loss of all six frail boats and ten men, one of their targets, the pocket battleship *Lützow*, was under orders to return to Germany. She left Altenfjord the day after the attack on the *Tirpitz* and spent three days at Narvik. On September 26 she put to sea again, heading south, and the Admiralty cast about for a means of attacking her on passage on the 27th. The Home Fleet's borrowed American carrier, the USS *Ranger*, could not get within striking distance in time and Coastal Command was so weakened by recent losses, maintenance problems, shortage of aircraft and delays caused by re-equipment that it could not muster an appropriate strike-force. The task was given to 832 Squadron, Fleet Air Arm, from the refitting fleet carrier HMS *Victorious*, flying Tarpon torpedo-bombers. They were to fly from the Shetlands; only three Beaufighters could be scraped together as escorts from Coastal Command.

There ensued scenes of confusion, irresolution and breakdowns in communication between Navy and RAF strongly reminiscent of the botched

"Operation Fuller" which failed to halt the "Channel Dash" by the German Brest squadron in February 1942. Admiral Fraser was most keen to get in an attack; Air Vice-Marshal A. B. Ellwood, chief of Coastal Command's Number 18 Group, thought the weather too bad and the escort inadequate. Fraser overruled him but the aircraft missed the *Lützow* by forty miles, turning north to search the Norwegian coast as the Germans sailed serenely southward behind them. They entered the Baltic undisturbed on September 28 and got to Gotenhafen (Gdynia) on October 1. The subsequent inquiry by a joint Admiralty-Air Ministry committee did not even attempt to apportion blame; the main result was that the chronic weakness of Coastal Command's strike-capability was at last recognised. It was now to be built up to three strike-wings, each of twenty torpedo-bombers and twenty fighter-escorts. Once again, as after the Channel Dash, the British got an undeserved bonus with the removal of a standing threat: the *Lützow* was out of Norway, leaving the *Scharnhorst* as the sole German heavy ship in the far north capable of fighting. The *Lützow* never came back and indeed took no further significant part in the war (she was destroyed by bombing at Swinemünde in the Baltic in April 1945). Her withdrawal and the laming of the *Tirpitz* enabled the Americans to withdraw their squadron from the Home Fleet in November.

At the very beginning of that month the first Russian convoy in a new series, styled RA54A and consisting of thirteen empty merchantmen which had been stuck in Russia for more than half a year, set sail from Archangel. They all reached Scotland safely and without incident. The first new convoy in the other direction, JW54A, of eighteen ships, left Loch Ewe on November 15, followed by the fourteen ships of JW54B on the 22nd. The customary triple protection of close escort, cruisers in the middle distance and a Home Fleet battleship with another cruiser as distant cover was provided, and all the ships got through unchallenged by the Germans. The next round of double convoys in each direction starting around the middle of December was the catalyst for a chain of events which led to the last great drama of the war on the surface of the sea in the West and the last battle of its kind: a slogging-match between ships of the "line," which was already an obsolete concept in naval strategy.

Admiral Dönitz managed to sell Hitler the idea of another big-ship sortie against the British convoys to Russia in the week before Christmas, 1943. With the *Tirpitz* out of action the only force available for Operation *Ostfront* was the battlecruiser *Scharnhorst* and five Z-class destroyers, led by a new Northern Task-Force commander, Rear-Admiral Erich Bey. Nicknamed "Achmed" because his surname sounded like an Ottoman Turkish title, Bey was an imposingly large and stern figure and a natural seaman whose experience had been gained largely in destroyers (he commanded the destroyer-escort for the Channel Dash which brought the *Scharnhorst* and her companions from Brest to Germany). His appointment was in temporary replacement of Vice-Admiral Kummetz, who was ill, and his oft-quoted remark, "I have not been on a big ship since I was a cadet," did not inspire confidence. In operational control was, as usual, Admiral Otto Schniewind, Navy Group North Commander, in Kiel.

Admiral Sir Bruce Fraser, C-in-C of the Home Fleet since May 1943, was sufficiently convinced of the likelihood of a foray by the *Scharnhorst* to take his flagship, the *Duke of York*, all the way to the Kola Inlet leading to Murmansk, when he covered the safe passage of convoy JW55A from Loch Ewe in Scotland. This first visit by a British capital ship took the Russians by surprise on December 16, and inevitably made them suspicious, especially when Fraser left as abruptly as he had come two days later. Fraser, a modest man (modest enough to decline the First Sea-Lordship in favour of Sir Andrew Cunningham), was a first-class staff officer who was also capable of establishing a remarkable rapport with all ranks by the simple but neglected art of listening to what they had to say and inspiring in them the confidence to say it. No detail of equipment or comfort was too small for his attention yet he was fully able to delegate authority. He spent hours on an activity to which few other admirals would seriously admit: thinking, about strategy and tactics, the role of his command and how he would handle an action with the *Scharnhorst*. These matters would be discussed with his hand-picked staff officers and visiting commanders at an admiral's table renowned for the quality of its food and wine. He returned to Iceland because he planned to provide the distant cover for convoy JW55B, of nineteen ships, which was to leave Loch Ewe on December 20. Fraser hoped this convoy would prove a sufficient lure to draw out the Germans. It was given a close escort of ten destroyers, as was RA55A, the convoy which was to start for home from Murmansk on the 23rd. Vice-Admiral Robert Burnett in HMS *Belfast*, with two other cruisers (*Sheffield* and *Norfolk*), was to furnish the intermediate cover; the *Duke of York* was accompanied by the cruiser *Jamaica* and four destroyers. There was no air-cover.

Demands on the Luftwaffe for aircraft on other fronts had reduced German air-strength sufficiently to rule out the kind of mass-attacks mounted against earlier Russian convoys. Nonetheless Ultra revealed intense aerial reconnaissance and an order to the *Scharnhorst* group to be at three hours' notice on December 18, in the hope of being able to intercept an eastbound convoy. Only on the 21st did the ships go back to six hours' notice. All this convinced Fraser that there could well be a surface-attack on the next convoy, perhaps affording him an opportunity to catch the *Scharnhorst*.

The eastbound convoy was first found by German air-reconnaissance on December 22. On Christmas Eve, when the ships were only about 400 miles away from Altenfjord, the aerial shadowing became continuous. After the close escort reported this, Fraser took the unusual risk of breaking wireless-silence to order JW55B to put about and sail west for three hours, in his general direction, while he increased speed eastward. On the same morning the Admiralty told Fraser that the *Scharnhorst* group had been brought to short notice again on the 22nd. On the morning of Christmas Day Ultra revealed that the Luftwaffe had been ordered to look for a heavy British force, whose radio traffic indicated to the Germans that it was well to the west of the convoy. By this time the westbound, empty RA55A had not been spotted by the Germans and was virtually out of danger, so Fraser took another chance and detached four large destroyers from it to join the ten with JW55B, once again by breaking silence. He also ordered the eastbound convoy to divert north and closer to Bear Island, taking it further away from the *Scharnhorst* in Altenfjord and giving him more time to catch up. On Christmas afternoon the German signal, "*Ostfront* 1700/25/12" was intercepted, although it was not until early on the morning of Sunday the 26th that Bletchley Park deciphered it – and even then the significance of the word was not appreciated. But well within an hour OIC told Fraser, from other indications: "Emergency. *Scharnhorst* probably sailed." Shortly afterwards Fraser broke silence again to tell JW55B and Burnett's cruisers, temporarily known for this operation as Force 1, where he was and ordering them to report their positions. OIC had informed the C-in-C that his own Force 2 had not been sighted by the Germans. At 6.30 in the morning he ordered the convoy to head north and Force 1 to maintain a roughly parallel course to the east of it while Force 2 raced eastward from south-west of their positions. Assuming that the *Scharnhorst* would be heading more or less due north to intercept the convoy, now shadowed by submarines after bad weather forced the Luftwaffe to drop out, Fraser with his unusually accurate knowledge of the whereabouts of all his own forces hoped to catch the Germans between Force 1 to the north-east and Force 2 from the south-west. Even so he made his own absolute priority the safety of the convoy, a departure from the naval precept that the destruction of a major enemy force was more important if the chance presented itself.

Having gone north and found nothing, Admiral Bey turned south and sent his five destroyers to sweep to the south-west at about 7.30 a.m. Unclear orders and poor signalling in bad weather ensured that he never saw them again. *Scharnhorst* was on her own, and at 8.15 the *Belfast* picked her up on radar at just over twelve miles, heading west for the moment, only thirty miles from the convoy. In just over an hour *Belfast* sighted the German battlecruiser at about six miles and all three British cruisers gave chase. The *Norfolk* managed a couple of minor hits but the *Scharnhorst* easily pulled away to the south at thirty knots or more, before turning north again for another pass at the convoy. Burnett with his five-knot deficit soon lost touch and Fraser was reduced to anxious guesswork by shortly after ten o'clock. Burnett resisted hints from Fraser that he should split Force 1, now reinforced by four destroyers from the convoy, to search for the enemy. Burnett was by this time in touch with the convoy and covering it from ahead, with his destroyers protecting his cruisers: the *Scharnhorst* could not get at the convoy without attacking this sturdy screen. At noon the German ship once again appeared on *Belfast's* radar, one of the most modern and well-operated in the fleet. Fraser in the *Duke of York* was now only 150 miles or some six hours to the south-west.

In the ensuing exchange of fire the *Norfolk* lost a gun-turret and the *Sheffield* was lightly damaged. All three cruisers claimed hits but the Germans showed no sign of them, and a torpedo attack by the accompanying British destroyers was shaken off before it could be pressed home. The *Scharnhorst* ran south and Burnett, in giving chase, held back behind the horizon and relied on radar so as not to divert the Germans from heading conveniently towards a meeting with Admiral Fraser. Admiral Bey got a report from his detached destroyers at lunchtime saying that they had failed to find the convoy: foolishly and unaccountably he sent them back to Norway.

The *Scharnhorst* (Captain Fritz Julius Hintze) was thus alone and without hope of reinforcement when she appeared as a large blip on the radar screens of HMS *Duke of York* at 4.17 p.m. The range was twenty-two miles. Fraser reined in the four destroyers with him even though two of them were briefly well placed for a torpedo attack: he wanted to open the action with his superior 14-inch guns in their one double and two quadruple turrets. The British flagship was decidedly superior in gunpower, roughly equal (greater thickness, lower quality of steel) in armour and, at twenty-nine knots, three knots slower in maximum speed than her opponent. But Fraser had trapped her between his own guns and those of the cruisers to the north, and when he opened fire at 4.50 p.m. from six miles, supported by the cruiser *Jamaica*, the Germans were taken completely by surprise (as shown by the fact that the *Scharnhorst's* guns were aligned fore and aft at the time as if for cruising). The Germans turned away north after a creditably accurate first broadside from the *Duke of York*, a move which had the effect of giving the slower British battleship the advantage of following her enemy's movements on a shorter radius as the Germans headed towards the guns of Burnett's cruisers (reduced to two by mechanical troubles on the *Sheffield*).

The *Duke of York* was beginning to damage the *Scharnhorst* with her threequarter-tonne shells but the Germans had recovered from their surprise and were doing their best to reciprocate. An 11-inch shell was fired through each of the British flagship's hollow masts without exploding. With the cruisers out of effective range, the battle became a heavy exchange between the two capital ships lasting ninety minutes. Initially unable to use her superior speed to escape because of Fraser's dispositions, the *Scharnhorst* was sufficiently damaged to be forced visibly to slow down. Bey signalled to Hitler, echoing the *Bismarck*, "We shall fight to the last shell." The loss of speed enabled the destroyers, struggling with the heavy weather, to close in for attacks by a pair from either side, and an undetermined number of torpedoes struck home, further reducing the *Scharnhorst's* speed.

This deadly distraction, which probably set the seal on the battlecruiser's destruction, enabled the *Duke of York, Jamaica* and Burnett's cruisers to surround the solitary German ship and hammer her to pieces with their shells. The *Scharnhorst* was now limping along at a pathetic five knots but her robust construction kept her afloat beyond all reasonable expectation. Stubbornly resisting the quick and spectacular end of a magazine explosion, of the kind which had destroyed so many British capital ships, she burned until her hull seemed to the watching British to be red-hot, but still did not explode. First the British cruisers and then the destroyers were sent in on either side of the stricken battlecruiser simultaneously, to dispatch her with torpedoes. The *Scharnhorst* may have been directly hit by thirteen heavy shells from the *Duke of York*, a similar number of 6- and 8-inch from the cruisers and one in five of the fifty-five torpedoes fired at her, but she sank in her own time just before 8 a.m. Of the nearly 2,000 men aboard only thirty-six survived to be plucked out of the freezing water by the triumphant British.

Neither aircraft nor submarines took any effective part in the sinking of the *Scharnhorst*, which was therefore the last fight to the death between capital ships in which heavy guns were the main weapon on both sides. The brief reign of the naval dinosaur which began with the launch of HMS *Dreadnought* less than thirty-seven years earlier was at an end. Only the *Tirpitz* remained to the Germans, and she was still out of action after the miniature-submarine attack. For the time being, therefore, the north was free of serious surface-threat for the first time in nearly three years.

In the latter half of 1943, the Allies invaded Sicily in July as the Red Army counter-attacked in the Crimea. On the 24th Hamburg was firebombed by the RAF. Mussolini resigned on July 27; Sicily fell on August 17; on September 3 the Allies attacked the Italian mainland. On October 13 Italy declared war on Germany. The Red Army retook Kiev on November 6 and on the 28th Churchill, Roosevelt and Stalin held their first tripartite meeting at Teheran.

Although this will take us ahead of events elsewhere, the ultimate fate of the *Tirpitz* belongs here. The Russian convoys were not much troubled by the Germans from autumn 1943 to spring 1944. They resumed in autumn 1944 to the end of the war. Hardly any ships were lost in 1944, when the principal threat came from the exceptional weather; but one merchantman, one warship and five submarines were sunk in a running battle over convoys JW57 and RA57 at the end of February. At the end of March, JW58 had the biggest escort so far on the Russian run: two carriers, Johnnie Walker's five sloops, twenty destroyers, four corvettes and a light cruiser. The Germans mounted a series of air-attacks in which they lost six planes (and a submarine) to British aircraft. Three more boats were sunk by the warships; no cargo-ship was lost.

In parallel with the triumphant passage of JW58, the Home Fleet, warned by Ultra that the *Tirpitz* was expected to be ready for sea on April 1, mounted a raid from fleet-carriers against the battleship. Vice-Admiral Sir Henry Moore, Fraser's second-in-command, led the two large carriers *Victorious* and *Furious*, the battleship *Anson* (flag), four cruisers and fourteen destroyers. Four escort-carriers carried extra fighters to provide cover for the two Fleet Air Arm strike-wings, each consisting of twenty-one Barracuda bombers and based on a fleet-carrier, as well as to protect the warships themselves against the Luftwaffe. Fraser himself in the *Duke of York* came out of Scapa with a cruiser and five destroyers to provide distant cover for both the raiding force and the convoys. More operational British warships were now at sea in northern waters than at any time since the Battle of Jutland in 1916, a total of sixty-four under the overall command of a single admiral (Fraser).

The C-in-C brought the raid forward by a day in an attempt to exploit the unusually favourable weather. The first of a small swarm of carrier-aircraft took off at 4.15 a.m. on April 3: forty-two bombers accompanied by eighty fighters. Two bombers were lost on take-off. The raiders carried a mixture of armour-piercing bombs and conventional high-explosive ones. The first wave, half the force, achieved surprise and several hits in the one minute they were over their target. The second wave struck one hour later without the advantage of surprise but scored several more hits for the loss of one bomber to anti-aircraft fire. The raid, superbly executed with minimal losses, scored nine or ten hits with the first wave and perhaps five with the second. Because the pilots came in too low none of the bombs penetrated the ship's heavily armoured vitals, but widespread secondary damage was caused, 122 Germans were killed and 216 wounded, on the very day that the *Tirpitz* was due to start her final sea-trials. She was out of action once again, this time for three months. The Fleet Air Arm's bombs were not up to the job of destroying a ship so well protected, and British expectations that she would be out of action for half a year were to be disappointed. Admiral Cunningham, the First Sea Lord, ordered a follow-up attack as soon as possible in the hope of causing more damage while the target was weak, overruling Fraser's objections. But the weather frustrated the strike planned for April 21.

JW58 and RA58 having completed their passages without loss, the last convoy of the season, RA59, consisting of the unloaded ships of JW58, set out for home on April 28, covered by two escort-carriers, sixteen destroyers and four frigates. One merchantman was sunk by the twelve submarines which gathered against the convoy, but British aircraft sank three boats in return in the terrible weather – before the eyes of a Soviet admiral aboard one of the carriers. The Royal Navy may have taken its time about bringing these converted and reconverted ships into use, but there can be no doubt that once they did, they operated them to good effect. They transformed the security of the Russian convoys and gave the British complete mastery on the route.

In May two more Fleet Air Arm raids on the *Tirpitz* were planned but aborted because of the weather. No British aircraft got through to the ship until August 24, when one 1,600lb armour-piercing bomb penetrated into the bowels of the *Tirpitz* – and failed to explode. When they dismantled it, the Germans were mystified to discover that it contained only half its intended payload of explosive in any case. This can only have been due to bad workmanship at the munitions plant.

The invention of the "Tallboy" bomb finally brought RAF Bomber Command into the unending struggle to finish off the *Tirpitz*. This bomb was twenty-one feet long and weighed six tons, needing a specially adapted Lancaster long-range bomber to carry it. After several ineffectual Fleet Air Arm attacks, the British, impatient to strip the Home Fleet of heavy units for the Far East, successfully sought General Eisenhower's consent for the detachment of two squadrons of Lancasters from his supreme command. Air Chief-Marshal Sir Arthur Harris, C-in-C of Bomber Command, planned to fly the heavy planes from Scotland and to land them in Archangel, where the Russians were promising maximum co-operation, after the raid on the *Tirpitz*. Poor weather obliged the RAF to fly straight to north Russia and mount the raid from there instead; the aircraft left Scotland on September 11. Six of the thirty-nine were written off on landing at the rudimentary airfield in bad weather. Twenty-eight finally mounted the raid on 15 September 1944. One thundering direct hit and two near misses with the giant bombs tore a hole measuring thirty feet by fifty near the ship's bow. She took in 1,000 tonnes of water but did not sink. Yet she could not be repaired in Altenfjord. Even so this marine cripple, escorted by every available German destroyer and smaller vessel and covered by the Luftwaffe, was able to sail unchallenged to Tromsö 200 miles to the south, thirty-four months after she first arrived in Norwegian waters, on October 15 to 16.

What had been the mightiest ship in German service was berthed in shallow water three miles down the fjord from the Norwegian port, in the lee of a small island, reduced to the humble function of a floating coastal-defence and anti-aircraft battery. Ultra revealed that the Germans had written off the ship as no longer usable at sea and not worth the trouble of yet another protracted repair: they had rather more urgent problems to consider elsewhere. The British could therefore have left her to rot in her ignominious new anchorage. But she was now within range of the Lancasters based in Scotland, and on 29 October 1944, thirty-eight of them took off from Lossiemouth. One near-miss caused additional minor damage at the stern; low cloud and a stiff anti-aircraft barrage staved off the *coup de grâce* for the last time.

It was not until mid-November that the weather lifted sufficiently for another attempt by Bomber Command. Thirty-two Lancasters lumbered into the dark Scottish sky during the night of the 11th to 12th. Conditions over the *Tirpitz* proved to be remarkably favourable. The wind dissipated her smokescreen; the Luftwaffe was inexplicably (and inexcusably) tardy in putting up the customary fighter-screen; and the lamed battleship was left to defend herself against her tormentors. The Lancasters came on through

her ponderous broadsides and an intense barrage from her secondary armament to score at least three and probably four direct hits. The first struck
the port side and the *Tirpitz* listed sharply in that direction. Captain Robert
Weber ordered flooding on the starboard side in order to stabilise her, but
before this could take effect another Tallboy struck the main 15-inch magazine, causing an almighty explosion which blew "C" turret into the sea forty
yards away. The great hulk of the *Tirpitz* slowly rolled over to port and
turned turtle. Wing-Commander (later Group Captain) Willie Tait and the
Lancasters from 9 and 617 squadrons of Bomber Command had prevailed at
the third attempt. The *Tirpitz* was well and truly dead after three years of
less than masterly inactivity in Norway. She had, as Ludovic Kennedy wrote
in his book on the ship, "lived an invalid's life and died a cripple's death."

Some 900 men died with her while about 600 were plucked from the
sea around the wreck. A remarkable rescue operation with oxy-acetylene
cutters saved another eighty-seven men trapped in air-bubbles inside the
upturned hull. After the war Norwegians told grisly (and probably apocryphal)
stories about the unusually large mackerel caught in the Tromsö area after
the destruction of the ship. The career of the *Tirpitz* was an extraordinary
mixture of physical impotence (a few shellholes in the ice and rock of Spitzbergen were all she achieved with her great 15-inch guns) and invisible menace,
a single-ship "fleet in being" which had far-reaching effects on the conduct of
the war in the northernmost reaches of the Atlantic. The British mounted a
total of seventeen air-attacks, ten by the Fleet Air Arm and seven by the RAF,
in thirty-five months. They tried not only X-craft midget submarines but even
"Chariots" (two-man human torpedoes), although this desperate enterprise
was aborted. She became the grand obsession of the Royal Navy which hardly
ever set eyes on her; her mere existence caused the greatest convoy disaster of
the war in July 1942, even though all she did was sail a few miles and return to
port without firing a shot or sighting a ship.

Admiral Sir Dudley Pound, the First Sea Lord, was hardly the most
communicative of men but he must have carried the terrible burden of the
decision to scatter to his grave. He did not live to hear the longed-for news
of the destruction of the ship whose shadowy presence in the far north led
to his greatest misjudgement. When in Canada in August 1943 for an Allied
summit conference he had a stroke and resigned, to be succeeded by Admiral
Sir Andrew Cunningham. On his return home Pound had a second, more
severe stroke which left him paralysed. He died on October 21 – Trafalgar
Day. He was sixty-six and had never enjoyed robust health; it is entirely
possible that his crushing work-load was the real cause of his death. It was a
burden he chose to bear alone, and it was one of the heaviest of the war. At
least he lived long enough to savour the turn of the tide against his main
enemy, the German submarine, to which it cannot be denied he made an
outstanding contribution despite his greatest failing – an inability to delegate.

On the main front in the Atlantic Dönitz's boats were faring badly in their suddenly reduced circumstances. They reached the absolute nadir of their record of destruction in August 1943, when they managed to sink just four ships of less than 26,000 tons in the Atlantic, two in the north and two in the south, plus one vessel of nineteen tons in British waters. The worldwide total touched 120,000 tons thanks to somewhat better luck for the Germans in the Indian and Mediterranean oceans. At the end of the month twenty-two boats left the Biscay bases for the North Atlantic, supported by six from Norway and Germany and a milch-cow. They all had enhanced anti-aircraft firepower, the *Wanze* radar-detector and the *Aphrodite* radar-decoy. This *Leuthen* group may have been the best-equipped ever assembled and its task was to renew the onslaught on the main transatlantic route, which had been virtually abandoned since May except for a few boats whose main role was to generate artificial wireless traffic to keep the Allies on full alert. It was an attempt to turn back the clock to the triumphant days of March 1943, and this time the submarines had the *Zaunkönig* torpedo, equipped to home in on the pitch of escort-propellers. The *Leuthen* pack was in position across the path of two westbound convoys, the slow ONS18 and the fast ON202, by September 18.

When a Canadian Liberator from Newfoundland sighted and sank *U341* on the 19th, it was clear to Western Approaches command that the two convoys had been located and chosen as targets by the Germans. They were therefore ordered to combine into a single formation of sixty-six ships with a total of fifteen warships. In the early hours of the 20th the *Zaunkönig* scored its first success when *U270* (KL Paul-Friedrich Otto) blasted off the stern of the frigate HMS *Lagan*. Later in the day an RAF bomber scored the first success with the Fido, the Allied acoustic torpedo, sinking KL Manfred Kinzel's *U338*, one of the stars of the SC122/HX229 battle in March. The sinking of the *Lagan*, as intended, punched a hole in the escort-screen, enabling the Germans to sink two merchantmen. On the night of the 20th, they sank the Canadian destroyer *St Croix* and the British corvette *Polyanthus*. On the 21st the destroyer *Keppel* detected and destroyed *U229*. The climax of the battle came on September 23, when the Germans made another hole in the escort-screen by sinking the frigate HMCS *Itchen* with a *Zaunkönig* and then moved in to sink four merchantmen in rapid succession. The arrival of strong air-cover the next day after a break in the weather put an end to the running battle in which the final score was three escorts and six merchant ships sunk and one escort crippled for the loss of three submarines.

The inflated claims of the German boats, obliged to dive after firing a *Zaunkönig* in case it took an interest in their own propellers, led their command to conclude that a great rather than a modest or possibly even questionable victory had been scored. But compared with the lean pickings between June and August the result suggested to Dönitz that all was not lost. The sinking of three boats represented a fatal casualty rate of eleven percent, which was just about tolerable when so many submarines were available. The boats also claimed to have sunk not six but twelve merchant-men for sure, plus three "probables" from the double convoy. This was the result partly of wishful thinking after the dreadful setbacks in the summer months and partly of the fact that boats could not stay up to observe the effect of the *Zaunkönig*. They were thus unaware that as many as one in two either did not detonate at all or else did so prematurely in the target's wake, at a distance where no damage was done. On the other hand the Foxer swiftly introduced as a decoy by the Allies worked only at speeds up to fifteen knots, too low for submarine-hunting; and the device interfered with Asdic. A more sophisticated version allowing twenty knots and eliminating the distraction of Asdic had to be developed.

The illusory "success" which marked the return of the submarines to the North Atlantic trade route after an absence of more than three months fed false hopes among the Germans that the *Zaunkönig* and all the other new equipment would soon enable them to get back on terms. They claimed to have sunk six destroyers in the first ten days of October; the true total was just one. Because the new weapon could be fired blind from as deep as 100 feet as soon as the grinding swish of enemy propellers was heard overhead and because the Germans so desperately wanted to believe in its efficacy, they logged almost every detonation as a hit, without bothering, or in many cases even being able, to check. The British, accustomed to the exaggerated claims of enemy propaganda which was always wilder than their own, were annoyed to intercept broadcasts which seemed to be making hysterically inaccurate claims and opening up a whole new dimension of unreality. Intelligence thought of puncturing the myth of the invincible *Zaunkönig*; but then real intelligence supervened: if the Germans did not know that their wonder-weapon had already been beaten, why help them by revealing it?

Thus the first German disillusionment of the new assault in the North Atlantic was caused by the *Wanze*, which constantly broke down, leaving the boats almost as vulnerable to surprise from the air as they had been without it. This led to the loss in rapid succession of three boats of the *Rossbach* pack assembled by Dönitz south-west of Iceland early in October 1943. In the six weeks from the end of September to the beginning of November twenty-three boats were sunk by aircraft. On November 6 Dönitz confessed to his staff that it was virtually asking the impossible to send submarines into the overwhelmingly adverse conditions of this period. But he saw no choice: he told his captains that even unsuccessful missions helped the Fatherland by tying down forces that would otherwise be sent elsewhere. On November 16, however, he ordered the second German withdrawal from the broad Atlantic in less than six months. It was formal recognition that the defeat in spring had been no mere setback which tactical changes and new German ideas would soon overcome but that the strategic initiative had passed permanently to a superior enemy. Tinkering with the sturdy but obsolete types VII and IX could not solve the problem: only a technological revolution would do. As early as summer 1942, when the boats were still wreaking havoc in packs, Dönitz had taken the view that they were nearing the end of their usefulness. No more of these types were ordered from spring 1943. Some existing orders were cancelled and only boats actually under construction were to be completed. All future efforts would go into the new "total underwater boat"; existing submarines would have to manage as best they could.

To make matters worse, the *xB-dienst* was no longer able to provide the wealth of material it used to get from the British Naval Cipher No. 3 used as the Allied convoy cipher. Suspicions on the British side that the Germans had broken it finally and belatedly hardened into certainty early in 1943, thanks to close study of Ultra intercepts. The Americans blamed the British for allowing this damaging and protracted leak to develop and for not using machine-ciphers in the Royal Navy. It was true that the British had neglected the protection of their own ciphers amid the enormous effort devoted to breaking the Germans' and it was also true that Cipher No. 3 was the only one available for inter-Allied naval communication in the Atlantic. At the same time the Americans decided not to let the British in on their own machine-ciphers as used by the US Navy. But in June Naval Cipher No. 5 was introduced and from then on the Germans were unable to eavesdrop.

The boats based in France began in autumn 1943 to evade the constant air-patrols over the Bay of Biscay by sailing submerged down the French coast to neutral Spanish coastal waters. After the second retreat from mid-Atlantic in November they decided to operate west of Spain against Mediterranean convoys to and from Gibraltar, as well as in the Western Approaches, the scene of their earliest successes against British shipping. The wheel had almost turned full circle. A group of boats spent the first seventeen days of December in these waters looking for convoys but achieved nothing. Seven convoys totalling almost 400 ships passed through the area in the period. The Germans managed to sight just two but did not have the speed to organise an attack against either; and the Submarine Tracking Room routinely used Ultra and HF/DF to divert ships out of harm's way with the skill of long practice.

The Germans were now at last using long-range aircraft, notably the Heinkel He177, to overfly the latest operational area with the idea of homing submarines on to the targets which the *B-dienst* was no longer so good at providing. Dönitz had won his prolonged battle with Göring and obtained Hitler's approval. But it was very late in the day. The two arms were not used to working together, the Allies had air-superiority in the area and the German aircraft, including the new Ju290 and BV222 long-range machines, frequently lost touch with sighted convoys, which then tended to be diverted so that submarines alerted by the Luftwaffe might chase all over the ocean without effect. An attempt to use the versatile Ju88 heavy fighter against the relentless Allied anti-submarine bombers in the Bay of Biscay simply led to another escalation when the RAF sent fighters as escorts. The Bay problem was solved by sneaking in and out via Spanish waters.

When Dönitz mustered twenty-two boats west of Ireland late in January 1944 for another despairing attempt to attack a total of eight inward and outward convoys, the British quickly got wind of their presence and assembled overwhelming force against them. The four weeks from January 27, when a German aircraft reported sighting two of the convoys, to February 24, turned into a gigantic, slow-motion mêlée which showed how profoundly the situation at sea had changed in the preceding seven months. A squadron of Beaufighters was sent by Coastal Command to Northern Ireland against the German air-patrols and to reinforce the two escort-carriers in the area. The latter were protected by Captain Walker's 2nd Escort Group of five sloops; three similar groups and a third carrier were eventually sent to join the fray alongside the British, Canadian and American close escorts. Hundreds of square miles of ocean were swarming with ships, of which the Germans finally managed to sink one straggling merchantman and HMS *Woodpecker*, one of Walker's brood which fell victim to a *Zaunkönig* in the parting shot of the battle.

Two submarines were sunk by long-range aircraft on January 28; they had rashly stayed on the surface to try to catch up with a convoy. On the 31st, while still with the carriers, Walker's group detected and destroyed a third. Walker was diverted to cover a double convoy on February 7. Late the next evening the *Woodpecker* destroyed a fourth boat with a single pattern of depth-charges. "Come over here and look at the mess you have made," signalled Walker by way of congratulation. Less than eleven hours later on the morning of the 9th the *Wild Goose* and Walker's *Starling* claimed the group's third success. Its fourth came at 3 p.m. on the 9th, when these two ships helped the *Kite* and the *Magpie* to conclude an eight-hour hunt with the destruction of *U238*. It had taken 266 depth-charges and plenty of Hedgehog bombs to do it. In the early hours of the 11th the group got *U424*. Eight days later Walker's smooth teamwork brought the sixth and final success of a record cruise when *U264*, commanded by the experienced KL Hartwig Looks, was forced to the surface and then abandoned in a sinking condition after a seven-hour hunt.

The support group's last triumph was a very special one even by the standard of the most efficient anti-submarine team of the war. It was the first boat to be fitted with the schnorkel, on which Looks was supposed to send in a report. Instead he and his crew went into captivity and were assiduously milked for information about the latest technical developments. Ultra had already picked up references to the schnorkel; by February 21 Rodger Winn, now a captain, had a report on his desk about it. More valuable intelligence was gleaned from the survivors of *U406*, sunk the day before by the 10th Escort Group: they included several scientific and technical experts who were checking on the performance of the latest radar-detectors. Thus at the end of February the British probably knew as much about these novelties as the German Submarine Command, which waited vainly for reports.

The 10th sank *U386* on the afternoon of February 19, a few hours after the sinking of *U264*. By then eleven boats – fifty percent of the German force deployed west of Ireland – had been destroyed, six of them by Walker's ships. *U764* got away after blowing off the stern of the *Woodpecker* that evening; the sloop eventually sank under tow within sight of the Scilly Isles eight days later, without loss of life. The Germans also managed to shoot down two Coastal Command planes as part of their miserable return for an unprecedented loss. Altogether the immensely complex running battle marked the climax of the achievement of the surface-escorts against their doggedly persistent enemy after four and a half years of bitter struggle. When Walker returned to Liverpool with three of his four surviving sloops on February 25 the entire port turned out to cheer amid a cacophony of ships' foghorns and sirens and the whoop-whoop of destroyers. It was a fitting celebration of victory in one of the most decisive conflicts in history – not just Walker's record triumph but the entire Atlantic campaign which was the real Battle of Britain.

Still the Germans did not give up. Gritting their teeth after the shattering blows of the preceding weeks, they assembled the last wolf-pack worthy of the name from the survivors and some fresh boats. This group was given the customary temporary name. The choice was singularly poignant in the circumstances: *Preussen*, the German for Prussia. The sixteen boats once again gathered west of Ireland at the end of the month.

On patrol in the area was the 1st Escort Group, which sank a boat on the 26th. Three days later, on Leap Year day, the sloop *Garlies* with the group got an Asdic contact. She and her sisters *Affleck* and *Gore* now began a long hunt against an enemy of exceptional cunning, KL Rolf Manke in *U358*. One attack after another brought no result as Manke twisted and turned at depths down to nearly 1,000 feet. A fourth sloop, the *Gould*, joined in a creeping attack in which 104 depth-charges were used, to no avail. The British were sure the boat would surface for air when the moon went down at 2 a.m. on March 1; but it did no such thing, even though conditions inside the submarine must by then have been indescribably frightful. The hunt went on throughout the day with the weather getting worse and the Asdic operators at the end of their tether. At 4 p.m., after thirty-four fruitless hours, the *Garlies* and *Gore* withdrew under orders to go to Gibraltar. At 7.20 p.m. the *Gould* was hit by an acoustic torpedo in the stern and began to sink. Shortly afterwards *U358* was at last forced to come up for air. She was sighted at 1,500 yards by the *Affleck* which hit the boat with gunfire before finishing it off with depth-charges. The chase had lasted thirty-eight hours and was to stand as the longest continuous hunt of a submarine in the entire war. The *Affleck* rescued the crew of the *Gould* – and one German sailor.

In the ensuing days Allied escorts and aircraft continued the attrition of the pack, during which several hunts of up to thirty hours took place. In all, by March 22, seven boats from *Preussen* were destroyed for the loss of the *Gould* and a corvette. One of them was *U625*, commanded by the highly experienced KL Hans Benker who had achieved notable successes against convoys in late 1942 and early 1943. Sighted by an RCAF Sunderland on March 10, Benker stayed up and fought but the Canadians forced him to dive and then dropped depth-charges. In a uniquely romantic tribute Benker came briefly to the surface and signalled by lamp in English to the circling flying-boat, "Fine bombing," before going down for the last time. A few men were seen to escape from the stricken boat but were never found. On the 14th Walker got his thirteenth victim with the help of carrier-aircraft.

On March 22 Dönitz bitterly ordered another major withdrawal, abandoning the eastern Atlantic and with it his attempt to renew the onslaught on the convoys. In the first three months of 1944 thirty-six submarines had been sunk in the area against just three merchantmen out of 3,360 in convoy. Now only a handful of boats remained in the broad ocean; the convoys sailed serenely on, bringing endless quantities of troops, food, fuel and munitions for the invasion of Europe which the Germans now expected at any time. Submarine sinkings declined proportionally and by May there were just two left in the Atlantic to provide German forecasters with weather information needed for preparations against the coming assault by the Allies on Fortress Europe. In the North Atlantic on the main Anglo-American arterial route victory was now total and absolute as Dönitz pulled his boats back to defend the threatened Reich. Even the once hard-pressed Canadians now called the transatlantic convoy route "the milk-run."

Further south in the central ocean during this period the American support-groups with their escort-carriers and destroyers continued their sweeps. As we have seen, on April 26 they caught and sank one of the last milch-cows, *U488*, west of the Cape Verde Islands off the African "bulge." The fighting-boat *U66* which had hoped to refuel from it proved rather harder to dispatch. Lieutenant Gerhard Seehausen dived as the tanker succumbed to the USS *Croatan's* escorting destroyers and at first escaped detection. He was however forced to give himself away because he desperately needed fuel; the exchange of signals in which he was told to await assistance from *U188* was picked up by the Americans. The destroyer USS *Buckley* (Commander Abel, USN) finally found her on the surface on May 6 and exchanged shellfire with boat squarely with her bow. There ensued one of the strangest scenes in the history of submarine warfare as American and German sailors engaged in hand-to-hand fighting seldom seen since the days of sail. Captain Abel issued the ancient order, "prepare to repel boarders," as the Germans tried to scramble aboard. They were only seeking to save themselves because their boat was sinking, but the Americans did not yet realise their motive. The US sailors hurled everything they could lay their hands on at the invaders, including the empty shell-cases lying on deck and even coffee-urns. One man used a pistol and another a sub-machine-gun against the Germans. The proceedings were interrupted by a sound of tearing metal as the blazing submarine detached itself from the destroyer and slid away. As its engines were still running it sailed several hundred yards before it sank. Thirty-six Germans were rescued.

Eight days later Grand-Admiral Karl Dönitz suffered another personal tragedy when his elder son, Sub-Lieutenant Klaus Dönitz, was killed aboard *S141*, one of a flotilla of fast, light raiders sent to attack the landing-craft assembling for the invasion on the coast of the Isle of Wight. It was five days short of the first anniversary of the death of Peter Dönitz aboard *U954*.

But the losing battle pursued its relentless course. On May 28 the American escort-carrier *Block Island* with her four escorting destroyers, which had briefly joined the hunt for *U66*, headed north towards the Azores on patrol. One of the carrier's planes sighted *U549* (KL Detlev Krankenhagen) heading west towards Brazil. Hunted all night to the pinging of the American sonar, Krankenhagen decided to make a fight of it against hopeless odds. On the morning of the 29th he fired three conventional and two acoustic torpedoes. The former all struck the side of the *Block Island*, 8,600 tons, which sank shortly afterwards. One *Zaunkönig* badly damaged the destroyer USS *Barr*; the other missed. The remaining destroyers derived what satisfaction they could from sinking the *U549* in revenge. There were no German survivors. It was to be the last time in the war that a German submarine sank a major enemy warship. The Germans did not make posthumous awards; had they done so, Krankenhagen would surely have merited a Knight's Cross.

The badly battered *Block Island* group was relieved by another, led by the escort-carrier *Guadalcanal* under the command of Captain Daniel Gallery, USN. He was a curiously obsessive character who might have stepped bodily out of the pages of Herman Melville. His sole ambition was to be the first American captain since the War of 1812 against the British to capture an enemy vessel, and he trained his men to exhaustion to this end. Op–20–g, the American operational intelligence centre, told him that there was one submarine in the area towards which he was heading off the Azores, and Gallery determined to catch it. The Tenth Fleet had been plotting the movements of *U505*, a type IXc under the command of Lieutenant Harald Lange, for weeks. It had been lurking off the West African coast during that time, but the Americans were intrigued by the fact that no sinkings had been reported from the area, thanks to prudent diversions; yet the boat stayed on. Its *Naxos* radar-detector protected it from surprise air-attack.

The Americans knew, however, that it would eventually have to head northwards for home. On June 2 it did just that and Gallery's group was alerted. Constant air-patrols were sent up from the carrier to look for what Gallery's not altogether respectful crew quickly nicknamed Moby Dick. Their commander, needless to say, was restyled Captain Ahab. On the morning of June 4 the destroyer USS *Chatelain* located *U505* with her Sonar.

Gallery sent two other destroyers to join her and launched his aircraft, with orders not to bomb the Germans. The planes sighted the boat underwater and told the *Chatelain*, which forced *U505* to the surface with depth-charges. The Germans began to abandon, and the destroyer *Pillsbury* sent a boarding-party. The US sailors secured the boat against sinking by defusing the scuttling charges and closing opened valves. Captain Gallery got his heart's desire and took the *U505* home, where it is now to be seen in front of the Science and Industry Museum in Chicago. The boat's papers revealed to Allied intelligence that it was ahead of the German submarines at sea, being already in possession of orders which had not reached *U505*.

The first half of 1944 brought the liberation of Leningrad and the Allied landing at Anzio, Italy, in January. US forces fought their way from island to island across the Pacific as the Germans made a stand at Monte Cassino in southern Italy from February to May. The Japanese advanced on India through Burma in March and were only held at the Battle of Imphal at the end of June. On the 4th, the Americans entered Rome, two days before D-day in Normandy. But a week later the first V1 flying bomb, ancestor of the cruise-missile, fell on England.

The schnorkel came into general use only after D-day, against which the submarines achieved very little. The second boat to use one after *U264* was Lieutenant Wolfgang Boehmer's *U575*, which sank the corvette *Asphodel* while with the *Preussen* pack. He too never returned home but at least he was able to send a lengthy wireless report which was read with great interest by British Intelligence. He was not overly enthusiastic, reporting that the breathing device was better not used when a submarine was being hunted (he was speaking from immediate past experience). Vision was already limited to the very narrow field provided by the periscope; with the engines running underwater the boat was also deaf. Boehmer thought the boat could be betrayed by exhaust fumes and by the sound of the submerged diesels (electric motors were virtually silent). KL Heinrich Schroeteler took *U667* out for a trial run with a schnorkel in May 1944 and lived to tell the tale in person. On his return he was positively impressed, saying that he had cruised submerged for nine days without surfacing and without being detected.

Used with care after some practice, the schnorkel was the best defence available to a submarine, which needed to operate it for only three to five hours at night to recharge batteries and refresh the air in the hull in order to be able to stay submerged for the next twenty-four hours. It was as close as the Germans came to defeating radar, and when Dönitz restricted operations to the waters round Britain itself the schnorkel-boats also stood a much better chance of escaping detection by Asdic because of the shallowness of the waters and the presence of innumerable wrecks and other deceptive shapes on the bottom. Lying in total silence on the seabed for many hours enabled a boat to escape the attentions of the fleet of escorts in many instances. The boats based in Norway and Germany were fitted with schnorkels and their crews trained in its use at Horten in Norway; those in France until the evacuation had to learn the new technique by using it "from cold" once out to sea: they had to creep out along the bottom to evade detection and enemy minefields outside their bases.

One other benefit to the Germans from the widespread use of the schnorkel was that the babble of wireless traffic which had been so useful for so long to the Allies all but dried up. The boats could receive long-wave transmissions by trailing a lengthy aerial at periscope or schnorkel depth but were unable to send. Now the captains received their operational orders for lone patrols in port, and apart from emergencies and listening-in at fixed times if they could, there was no need for the command or the boat to break wireless silence. Submarines were out for weeks at a time without transmitting, which also diminished the value of Allied HF/DF. While the schnorkel was still in the experimental stage operationally, captains did wireless a long stream of complaints about the difficulties and even dangers the use of the unfamiliar device caused them. These were of course intercepted by the Allies, who were not privy· to the more considered reports made by skippers on their return; the longer schnorkel was used, the better the crews were at using it and the clearer the advantages became. It was always a tricky and sometimes a treacherous device in its infancy, but Ultra for once misled the Allies into thinking that it was not much use.

But nine days after D-day three schnorkel-boats slipped into the Channel to sink two British frigates and an American landing-ship. None of the boats was caught, despite the overwhelming Allied naval presence covering the post-invasion supply-route. On June 21 three more submarines slipped up-Channel from the French bases to Guernsey, one of the Channel Islands which were the only British territory to be occupied by the Nazis. When the British found out from Ultra, Captain Rodger Winn expressed his admiration to his colleagues for this successful run of a mighty gauntlet. On June 29 Lieutenant Heinz Sieder in U984, having damaged a frigate on the 25th, hit four American supply-ships in eight minutes off Selsey Bill, not far from Portsmouth, the holy-of-holies of the Royal Navy. None sank but only one could be used again; Sieder got away with his schnorkel despite a massive and protracted search of the area by the Allied navies. Both his attacks took place in the broad summer daylight of the early afternoon. The Allies began to realise what damage might have been done during the invasion, the most fraught moment of the war in the West, had the submarines been able to concentrate in the right area (Hitler guessed Normandy but most of his generals and admirals put their money on the Pas de Calais; the submarines were spread out with many still in Norway as usual).

The strangest submarine cruise in this period of cautious return to the most dangerous waters of all was made by U763 (KL Ernst Cordes). The boat positioned itself off Selsey Bill, where the cross-Channel traffic was very heavy, on the evening of July 5. Spotting a military convoy through his periscope, Cordes, who had already sunk a freighter in the late afternoon without being caught, fired a salvo of five torpedoes and immediately dived to the seabed. None of the missiles struck home, although three detonated, and Allied escorts, unable to get a contact, peppered the area blindly with depth-charges without success. The Germans counted the underwater explosions as the boat crept away from the scene along the bottom with countless changes of course, so many that Cordes lost his sense of direction and seriously miscalculated his position.

Coming up to periscope-depth on the morning of July 7th, by which time no depth-charges had been heard for hours, and using his schnorkel carefully to draw in some much-needed fresh air, Cordes saw land and concluded he was off Alderney, one of the Channel Islands just seven miles from the coast of Normandy. Starting to run north the boat soon touched bottom where, according to the chart, there should have been none. Cordes went back to periscope-depth and saw he was enclosed by land to starboard, to port and forward, in an area with many ships at anchor. Returning to the bottom after noting all available landmarks, Cordes worked through his navigational charts and handbooks to try to establish where on earth he could be.

His eventual conclusion was that he had arrived in Spithead, the bay close by Portsmouth where the Royal Navy has traditionally held its great naval reviews for royal occasions. Having thus taken himself by surprise, Cordes spent the rest of the day on the seabed until a chance to escape presented itself. *U763* finally crept out in the camouflaging wake of a supply-convoy which set sail that evening. He had the spirit on his agonising crawl back to base to fire a torpedo at a passing destroyer (it missed) on the 11th before reaching Brest unscathed on July 14. The British found out about this hair-raising adventure only after the war.

That life in a schnorkel boat, comparatively safe though it was, did not offer unalloyed pleasure is shown by the log of *U763* for the period of its mystery-tour:

> It is nearly thirty hours since the boat was last ventilated. The first cases of vomiting occur, and I issue each man with a potash-cartridge [as an air-filter to be used with an escape-hood]. Breathing becomes distressed. The enemy search-group is still active overhead . . . the intervals between depth-charges are getting longer, but detonations are nearly all very close . . . during the thirty hours of pursuit, 252 depth-charges were counted in the near vicinity, sixty-one at medium range and fifty-one at long range.

"Breathing" took place in the few hours of true darkness in the high summer of 1944, the only time when it was reasonably safe to use the schnorkel. The stench inside the boat, which had never been salubrious, now became truly horrifying so that even the most hardened submariner noticed it.

Condensation ran down the inside of the hull and all food tasted vile even moments after opening a tin. A serious problem of refuse-disposal developed. Inside the boat it added to the fearsome miasma; carelessness in getting rid of it could betray the boat's presence. A new type of WC began to be installed with a compressed air system which could be used to expel chopped-up waste. Refuse was crammed into used food-tins for expulsion via the Asdic-decoy firing-tube; by trial and error the best method was found to be the use of one torpedo-tube as a rubbish-chute to be "fired" when full every few days. The sacrifice in firepower was gladly made. For the rest the life of a schnorkel-submariner consisted largely of lying around doing as little as possible to conserve oxygen, sweating, coping with the din inside and outside the boat, feeling sick, trying to fend off headaches and going red in the face with incipient carbon-monoxide poisoning from the constant leaking of diesel-exhaust into the hull. It is not difficult to imagine the relief which came with the use of the schnorkel to ventilate the festering boat. Even so the maintenance-men ashore would still recoil in stupefaction when a newly returned submarine docked.

The shore-organisation behind the already severely curtailed submarine campaign was beginning to crack under the strain imposed by the fighting in France and the unfettered Allied bombing. Ultra revealed the difficulties the command was having in getting boats repaired and fitted with schnorkels. Bombing had disrupted telephone and teleprinter lines to such an extent that the German commands were forced to use wireless to talk to each other. The standard of service at the French bases declined so much that early in August 1944 Dönitz was obliged to arm himself with a special "Führer-order" to hold the German technicians to their task of fitting schnorkels regardless of the sound of heavy artillery from the front. This task had absolute priority because he was preparing another strategic withdrawal – the removal of the boats from France to Norway after more than four years. It was a 2,000-mile journey round the British Isles which they could not hope to make except submerged almost all the way.

By this time the Germans had sunk five warships, twelve merchantmen and four landing-craft since D-day and damaged seven other vessels. The price for this was twenty submarines lost, almost all of them to anti-submarine ships because use of the schnorkel nearly always frustrated the hundreds of aircraft on patrol. The support-groups ceaselessly swept the Channel and the Bay of Biscay, among them the 2nd Escort Group; but from the end of July without their redoubtable commander, Captain F. J. "Johnnie" Walker, with a record twenty "kills" to his name. He died ashore of a stroke, presumably brought on by overwork, in the last few days of July 1944, at the age of forty-eight.

No sooner had the boats departed for Norway than they refuelled and returned to concentrate on British coastal waters. The wheel of submarine warfare had now altogether turned full circle to the opening days of this war and its predecessor. KL Hartmut Count von Matuschka in *U482* shocked the British by sinking a corvette and four ships in the North-Western Approaches, the route to Liverpool via the north of Ireland. On his operational voyage of 2,729 miles he spent 2,500 or more than ninety percent underwater, and he got back to Norway unscathed after his rare success against a convoy. In September the Allies sank only two submarines and damaged two more. Successes were becoming rare at sea for both sides.

The Allies meanwhile had overrun the evacuated French bases and were stunned by the strength of the submarine pens which they had bombed so ineffectually for years. The heaviest bombs had caused only minor damage to the concrete roofs and the French postwar navy availed itself of the biggest shelter at Brest, where it now keeps its nuclear boats. A similar facility had been built at Drontheim in Norway for the last phase of the campaign. It was from there that Lieutenant R. Stollmann left for a record cruise – fifty days of continuous submerged sailing. He could not resist reporting his achievement by wireless while still at sea: "I have the feeling of the complete superiority of a schnorkel-boat. Spirit of the crew is good. They are convinced that the submarine arm is again superior to the enemy." Brave words.

And there were still some brave deeds. KL Günther Pulst in *U978* won an instant Knight's Cross for hitting three ships in a convoy in the Channel late in November. His radio report was rewarded with a reply telling him of the decoration. In the following month Dönitz urged his men to a special effort in support of the last German Army offensive in the Ardennes, when it almost broke through the American line in the "Battle of the Bulge." Losses worldwide for the month at 135,000 tons of shipping were the highest since March, with 86,000 tons sunk in British waters and 59,000 by submarine. The global total was not to reach this level again for the rest of the war, yet in its last complete month, April 1945, submarines sank a total of 73,000 tons. But the sinkings by submarines in these last bitter months were isolated events, such as the terrible destruction of the American troopship *Leopoldville* by *U486* on Christmas Eve, when 819 soldiers drowned in the Channel. In the last four months of 1944 the Germans sank fourteen ships in British waters and two in the Atlantic – but more than 12,000 ships passed through the area unharmed. Yet the Allies destroyed only six submarines at sea in December,

The last six months of 1944 saw the wounding of Rommel and his removal from France on July 17, the resignation of General Tojo as Prime Minister of Japan on the 18th and the abortive bomb-plot against Hitler on the 20th. The next day the US Marines landed on Guam, and on August 1 the citizens of Warsaw rose in revolt. Two weeks later the Allies landed in southern France and on August 25 Paris was liberated. On September 9 the first V2 rocket, ancestor of the ballistic missile, fell on England, and on the 17th the

Anglo-Americans landed paratroops in Arnhem, Netherlands, in a tragically abortive attempt to seize the Rhine bridge there: the northern Dutch were doomed by the failure to a terrible famine in the last winter of the war. At the end of October the US Navy won the Battle of Leyte Gulf in the Philippines, and on November 7 Roosevelt won a record fourth presidential election. On December 16 the Germans launched a surprise counter-offensive in the Belgian Ardennes which was contained only with the greatest difficulty. This brought the Second World War on land in the West to the same point as was reached in the First in March 1918: the last great attack of the German Army.

A. V. Alexander, as First Lord of the Admiralty the political chief of the Royal Navy, took a singularly gloomy view of the prospects at sea in the New Year of 1945. The new-found elusiveness of the German submarines was causing difficulty: "The schnorkel has given them a greater advantage than we originally supposed." He went so far as to warn of a renewed offensive by new types of boat that could lead to "losses at the level we suffered in spring 1943."

This pessimism stands out from the general optimism in the European theatre as a whole, where the Ardennes offensive had been contained and victory on land was clearly only a matter of months, if not weeks away: a gigantic pincer from east and west was closing on Germany itself, and the Allied air forces were pounding the cities to flaming rubble. But Alexander was extremely well-informed about the new German submarines which were coming off the production-lines in growing numbers and going into the Baltic for training. The Americans had been providing detailed information about their specifications from an unusual source: the interception of Japanese diplomatic traffic by wireless from Berlin to Tokyo. Since the Americans had achieved a major breakthrough into the Japanese ciphers in autumn 1940, a feat comparable with the British penetration of the German traffic, the Allies were reading the Japanese naval attaché's technical reports. A transmission on 6 March 1944 warned the Allies what to expect. They set out to cripple the building programme by bombing, knowing that the Germans were accelerating construction by prefabricating the new boats in eight sections in various parts of the country and bringing them by river and canal to three assembly-ports on their coast. The destruction of the Dortmund-Ems Canal from the Ruhr to the North Sea by heavy bombing which burst its artificial banks was a particularly serious setback to the programme, which had been intended to deliver 131 of the larger type XXI electro-boats by the end of 1944. Factories and yards making various components were also subjected to massive bombardment, as were the ports; the Baltic training areas were heavily mined from the air. Now that the bombing offensive against Germany had attained such massive proportions, it was at last able to deliver what "Bomber" Harris had prematurely promised so much earlier in the war. And now that submarines were proving so hard to catch at sea despite record numbers of escorts and air-patrols, the bombers had at last become the main instrument of destruction against the boats.

History, of a sort, was made on 25 February 1945 when Lieutenant Fridtjof Heckel in U2322 sank the SS *Egholm*, a British freighter of just 1,317 tons, off the Scottish east coast. It was the first sinking by a type XXIII, the smaller coastal electro-boat. British warships were on hand to hunt the little intruder but were amazed at the speed with which it got away underwater. Their depth-charges were hopelessly wide of the mark and Heckel had no trouble in escaping. "Ideal boat for short operations near coast, fast, manoeuvrable, simple depth-control, small surface to locate and attack. The enemy guesses that a boat is there rather than getting clear proof and the position," he reported.

Dönitz told Hitler the good news personally on February 28. "With the complete underwater vessel a transformation in the war at sea has been brought to fruition. The deadly weapon of the pure submarine is at hand." His hope now was to get enough of the new boats together to be able to wreck the Allied supply-line across the Channel and bring the advance in the West to a halt, and then to go back to the Atlantic to attack the main convoy route once again. But the Allied bombing continued and intensified.

Even so Dönitz was determined to make one last throw in the broad Atlantic. Late in March six type IXc boats with schnorkel left one by one for the open sea, and on April 9 he ordered then to join up into a small pack to which he gave the name *Seewolf*. Ultra detected the old-style radio message, and as the boats headed steadily for the coast of the United States the Americans virtually panicked. German agents managed to plant disturbing disinformation to the effect that the boats were armed with a maritime version of the V2 rocket which had been raining down on London. The "V" stood for *Vergeltung* – revenge, Hitler's last "miracle-weapon." It will be remembered that the Germans had briefly studied the idea of such Polaris-type missiles before rejecting it as impracticable. The US Navy mustered four escort-carrier groups with twenty destroyers against the six boats. The first was sunk on April 16, the second an hour later. Five days afterwards the Americans destroyed the third. On April 24 U546 crippled a destroyer with a *Zaunkönig*. Ten hours after she sank, eight American destroyers caught the boat on the surface and shot it to pieces. The other two were not found before Germany surrendered and they gave themselves up. The only success they achieved was the sinking of the destroyer *Frederick T. Davis*.

The Third Reich was at last collapsing in April 1945. Boats left the Baltic for the North Sea and were caught, often without schnorkel, trying to get to Norway despite ceaseless Allied air patrols which inflicted a last massacre on what had for so long been the most dangerous enemy of them all. Dönitz meanwhile, having been appointed Hitler's viceroy for North Germany, was concentrating his energy on rescuing two million Germans in the east from the clutches of the advancing Russians. This was one of the largest evacuations in history. On April 30 Adolf Hitler poisoned and shot himself in his Berlin bunker, having named Karl Dönitz, the military leader he came to trust and admire the most, as his successor. Dönitz had made the submarine Germany's most deadly weapon in the war and was made Commander-in-Chief of the Navy; now the *Führer der Unterseeboote* became Führer of the Reich itself in a brief apotheosis of the supreme submariner. It remained for him to seek terms for a surrender in the West that would enable him to save as many Germans as possible from the Russians.

On the very day of Dönitz's final elevation, Commander Adalbert Schnee put to sea from Bergen, Norway, in *U2511* with a crack crew. It was the first large electro-boat of type XXI, under orders to go to the Caribbean (easily within its 16,000-mile range) for a last gesture of defiance. On May 2 the boat was detected by a British patrol-group off the north of Scotland. It got away at sixteen knots underwater and subsequently evaded several other ships. The crew heard the detonation of only one depth-charge, miles away. The second and last type XXI to sail operationally was KL Helmut Manseck's *U3008*, from Wilhelmshaven on the German North Sea, with the British Army less than twenty miles away: the crew could hear the heavy artillery pounding in the distance as they hurriedly put to sea for their pointless voyage into the Atlantic on May 3. The next day General-Admiral Hans Georg von Friedeburg, as the plenipotentiary of Dönitz, met General Bernard Montgomery on Lüneberg Heath in north-west Germany and signed the surrender of all German forces in the north-west, including the Friesian Islands, the Netherlands and Denmark. That evening the submarine command repeatedly transmitted an order to all boats to cease offensive patrols and return to base.

Just as it received the message *U2511* had a British cruiser of the *Suffolk* class in its sights at a range of 600 metres, virtually point-blank. Schnee went through the motions of preparing for an attack but did not give the order to fire. Instead he dived under the ship undetected and made for his base. *U3008* found a convoy shortly after hearing the order to surrender, made a pass but did not fire, once again sailing away completely undetected.

Confusion now reigned in the residual submarine command. The code-word *Regenbogen* was transmitted at 1.34 a.m. on May 5. The German word for rainbow was the predetermined message indicating that submarines should scuttle themselves rather than surrender. At 1.42 a.m. however there came another message from headquarters, now in Flensburg in Schleswig-Holstein, which ordered that "no scuttle or destruction should be undertaken."

On the afternoon of May 5 Dönitz bade farewell to his submarines with a long wireless message:

My submariners: six years of submarine warfare lie behind us. You have fought like lions. An oppressive superiority in material has driven us into a corner. From the remaining ground a continuation of the fight is no longer possible. Submariners: unbroken and unbesmirched you lay down your arms after an heroic struggle without parallel. We recall with awe our fallen comrades, who set the seal on their loyalty to Führer and Fatherland with their death. Comrades: preserve your submarine spirit with which you have fought stoutly and unwaveringly for the future also, in the best [interest] of our Fatherland. Long live Germany.
Your Grand-Admiral.

If the English sounds stilted, the reader need only consult the German to understand why. Whatever else Dönitz may have been, he was no second Goethe.

In broad daylight on 7 May 1945 a Catalina of 210 Squadron, RAF Coastal Command, sighted *U320*, commanded by Reserve Lieutenant Emmrich, between the Shetland Isles and Norway and sank it. It was the last "kill" of the war.

The closing months of the Second World War sustained and increased the pace of Allied conquests in all theatres. The Americans under MacArthur were busy keeping his promise; back in the Philippines from October 1944 they invaded Luzon on New Year's Day 1945 and reached Manila a month later. On February 4 Churchill, Roosevelt and Stalin met for the last time at Yalta to carve up the postwar world (Roosevelt died on April 12; Churchill lost power in an election on July 26). On February 13 the RAF and on the 14th the USAAF obliterated Dresden in the last and most destructive orgy of area-bombardment of the war with conventional explosives. On March 7 the US Army crossed the Rhine at Remagen, inside Germany, while throughout the month the USAAF made incendiary raids on Japanese cities. Vice-President Harry S. Truman succeeded Roosevelt. On April 25 the US and Soviet armies joined hands (literally) at Torgau, splitting Germany in two. VE-day (Victory in Europe) was celebrated wildly, in Britain especially, on May 8. (Japan fought on, but on August 6 the first atomic bomb fell on Hiroshima; two days later the Soviet Union declared war on Japan, and on the 9th the second nuclear device incinerated Nagasaki. Hostilities in the Second World War came to an end with the Japanese surrender on August 14).

The last word in this narrative however belongs to the German submarines – three times over, because the timing of the last torpedo-attacks are not precisely clear. Lieutenant Emil Klusmeier in *U2336*, a type XXIII, sank the Norwegian steamer *Sneland I*, 1,791 tons, and the British freighter *Avondale Park*, 2,878 tons, off the Firth of Forth on the east coast of Scotland. At about the same time *U1023*, a type VIIc with schnorkel, sighted the Norwegian minesweeper NYMS 382, of 335 tons, off Lyme Bay on England's south coast. Like his colleague Emmrich, KL Heinrich Schroeteler had been submerged for days and had not heard the order to surrender. He fired what was in all probability the last torpedo of the Atlantic campaign and sank the tiny warship. It was 7.52 p.m. Greenwich Mean Time on 7 May 1945 – five years, eight months and four days after Lieutenant Lemp torpedoed the *Athenia*.

The Third Reich built 1,162 submarines. Of these 830 took part in operations, 784 were lost (696 destroyed by enemy action); 220 were scuttled by their crews rather than surrender while 156 surrendered. Two fled to Argentina. The rest were found in Germany and Norway. Of the 40,900 men who served in them, 25,870 were killed and more than 5,000 captured – a fatal casualty-rate of sixty-three percent and a loss rate of seventy-six percent.

During the Second World War the Allies lost 2,828 of their own and neutral ships, or 14,687,231 gross register-tons, to submarines. The global total of merchant shipping lost was 21,570,720 tons (5,150 vessels). Of these, 2,452 (12.8 million tons) went down in the Atlantic. How many people died in the campaign cannot be precisely computed. The British Merchant Navy lost 30,248 men and the Royal Navy 73,642 during the war; the majority of these losses took place in the Atlantic, where submarines sank 175 warships, mostly British. RAF Coastal Command lost 5,866 men and 1,777 aircraft. The Royal Canadian Navy lost 1,965 men, more than the US Navy, whose main losses were in the Pacific.

The Atlantic campaign was not an exercise in statistics but a story of waste on a numbing scale, whether of men, of ships and submarines built in haste and destroyed in moments, of food and precious cargoes sent to the bottom or of vast sums of money. A few vivid images remain: of seamen burning and choking in blazing oil, of sailors instantly freezing to death in the waters of the Arctic, of flashing magazines blowing warships to smithereens, of unspeakably gruesome remains rising from the wreckage of submarines, of aircraft crashing in flames, of the haunting death-throes of stricken ships and of endless cries for help from the water. And here and there a dash of chivalry in a total war.

Grand-Admiral Karl Dönitz, sometime author of *Die U-bootswaffe* and for ten years commander of the German submarine fleet, was arrested by the Allied Control Commission on 23 May 1945 at Flensburg, Schleswig-Holstein, the last seat of government of the German Reich. On being informed that he was now a prisoner of war, the second and last Führer replied: "Words at this moment will be superfluous."

APPENDIX

A NOTE ON SOURCES

The archive material on the German submarine campaign against British and Allied shipping in the Second World War is simply colossal. It may well be the most extensively documented campaign in all history, as befits its duration, spread and complexity. No author, even when aided by a full-time researcher, can hope to cover it all: life is too short for anything but the eclectic approach, guided by archivists with expert knowledge of what they have on file. The task is made no easier by the chaotic condition of the Admiralty material in the British Public Record Office and the American naval records at the National Archives in Washington DC.

On the other hand, the specialised collections at the Naval Library of the British Ministry of Defence in London, the Canadian Directorate of History in Ottawa and the Naval Historical Center at Washington Navy Yard are readily accessible with the necessary permission (freely given in all three cases) and proved to be goldmines. The reader may wonder why there is no reference below to the German Archives: this is because the Americans and British took possession of the German records at the end of the war and made microfilm copies before returning them to the Federal Republic of Germany some years later. Thus the Americans have copies of virtually everything and the British of all the major items such as the War Diary of the Submarine Command; the fortunate researcher can draw upon them while working at the relevant places. The Canadians also have copies of some documents difficult or impossible to find in Britain.

My wife and I should like to express our warmest thanks for assistance unstintingly given by the following: at the British Public Record Office, Dr Nicholas A. M. Rodger; at the Naval Library of the Ministry of Defence, London, Robert M. Coppock; at the Directorate of History, National Defence Headquarters, Ottawa, Commander W. A. B. Douglas, Dr Marc Milner; at the National Archives, Washington, Richard A. von Doenhoff, Barry Zerby; at the Naval Historical Center, Washington, Dr Dean C. Allard, Bernard Cavalcante, Martha Crawley; and their respective colleagues and staff. All these people provided invaluable guidance through forests of paper.

The vast documentation of the campaign has itself spawned a huge related literature. More than 100 titles consulted are listed below; once again time would defeat an attempt to absorb every book and paper touching upon or relevant to the history of the Atlantic Campaign.

Unpublished General Accounts

Allied Communication Intelligence and the Battle of the Atlantic, undated MS at US Naval Historical Center, Washington DC

Anti-Submarine Warfare in World War II, by Charles M. Sternhell and Alan M. Thorndike; Operations Evaluation Group, Office of the Chief of Naval Operations, US Navy Department, Washington, 1946

The Defeat of the Enemy Attack on Shipping 1939–1945, Admiralty Historical Section, London, 1957

Kriegstagebuch des Führers der Unterseeboote, 1939–1945, British Ministry of Defence Naval Library microfilm record

The U-Boat War in the Atlantic, by Fregattenkapitän Günter Hessler; postwar account written at Allied behest and held in file ADM 186/802, ADM 234/67 and 68, British Public Record Office

US-British Naval Cooperation 1940–1945, by Tracy B. Kittredge; undated historical monograph at US Naval Historical Center, Washington

British Records at
(a) the Public Record Office, Kew, Richmond, Surrey

ADM 1 and ADM 116 series of general files and cases on the Royal Navy in the Second World War

ADM 186 series on naval control of merchant shipping

ADM 199 series compiled for the Official History

ADM 217: residual material on Western Approaches Command

ADM 219 series on Admiralty Operations Research Branch including Professor P. M. S. Blackett's reports (No. 19)

ADM 223 series on naval intelligence including reports based on Ultra

AIR 15 series on RAF Coastal Command

AIR 24 series of command operational records

AIR 40 on air intelligence

AIR 50 on air combat reports

BT 131, 161 and 188: Board of Trade records on shipping, import allocations, oil and related matters

CAB 65–115: British Cabinet minutes and records of various Cabinet Committees

Convoy packs on various convoys

DEFE 3: series of decrypted Enigma messages (ZGTPU for submarine traffic)

Individual ship records

MT 50 and 59: records of Ministry of War Transport

PREM 1: Churchill's official correspondence

(b) Ministry of Defence Naval Library, London

Tambach Collection of records of the *Seekriegsleitung* (German Naval High Command), parts A-D; of Navy Groups North and West; and of files related to the War Diary of the Commander, Submarines.

Canadian Records at the Directorate of History, National Defence Headquarters, Ottawa

77/55 Canadian coastal convoys

77/553 ocean convoy records

77/554 Western Atlantic coastal convoy statistics

80/365 Canadian role in shipping-control

81/14 Naval Service Headquarters material on anti-submarine warfare

81/145 Papers of Captain Eric Brand on Canadian Naval Intelligence and shipping-control

81/520 series on the Battle of the Atlantic

84/123 basic narratives

United States Records

(a) at the National Archives, Washington DC

Navy Secretary's Confidential Correspondence:

A8/3–5 (American–British Conversations), A6/3, A9/3, A13/2 to A16, A14/1, A14/5 (diplomatic), A14/7 (international agreements), A16/1, A16/3 (naval intelligence), A16/4 (Lend–Lease), A17/15, A21/5

EF13, EF16, EF17 and EF73 series on Great Britain

Microfilm M975 (three rolls) of reports from the US Naval Attaché, London

SRS 548 series of captured German Naval Intelligence (*B-dienst*) reports

(b) from the Naval Historical Center, Washington Navy Yard

Eastern Sea Frontier War Diary

History of Task Force 24

Reports by Captain Paul R. Heineman, USN

SRH 006–348 selected files from Special Research Histories series on intelligence (copies of National Archives records)

Published Works

Andrew, Christopher, *Secret Service*, Heinemann, London, 1985

Bagnasco, Erminio, *Submarines of World War Two*, Arms and Armour Press, London, 1977

Beesly, Patrick, *Very Special Intelligence*, Hamish Hamilton, London, 1977
  Room 40: British Naval Intelligence 1914–18, Hamish Hamilton, London, 1982

Bennett, Geoffrey, *Naval Battles of the First World War*, Pan, London, 1983

Böddeker, Günter, *Die Boote im Netz*, Bastei-Lübbe, Bergisch Gladbach, 1983

Botting, Douglas, *The U-boats*, Time-Life Books, Amsterdam, 1979

Breyer, Siegfried, *Battleships of the World 1905–1970*, Conway Maritime Press, London, 1980

Brown, Anthony Cave, *Bodyguard of Lies*, W. H. Allen, London, 1976

Buchheim, Lothar-Günther, *Das Boot*, R. Piper, Munich, 1973

Buell, Thomas, *Master of Sea Power*, Little, Brown, Boston, Mass, 1979

Bullock, Alan, *Hitler: A Study in Tyranny*, Pelican, London, revised edition, 1962

Calvocoressi, Peter, and Wint, Guy, *Total War*, Pelican, London, 1974

Campbell, Christy, *World War II Fact Book*, Macdonald, London, 1985

Campbell, John, *Naval Weapons of World War Two*, Conway Maritime Press, London, 1985

Churchill, Winston S., *Great War Speeches*, Corgi, London, 1957
  The History of the Second World War, Cassell, London, 1948–1954

Coles, Alan and Briggs, Ted, *Flagship "Hood,"* Robert Hale, London, 1985

Conway, Robert H., *The Navy and the Industrial Mobilization in World War II*, Princeton, 1951

Cremer, Peter, and Brustat-Naval, Fritz, *"U333": The Story of a U-boat Ace*, Bodley Head, London, 1984

Deist, Wilhelm, *The German Military in the Age of Total War*, Berg, Leamington Spa, 1985

Dönitz, Grand-Admiral Karl, *10 Jahre und 20 Tage*, (memoirs), Athenäum, Bonn, 1958
  Die U-bootswaffe, Mittler, Berlin, 1939

Douglas, W. A. B., "Alliance Warfare 1939–45: Canada's Maritime Forces", *International Review of Military History*, Canadian Edition, Ottawa, No. 51

Fest, Joachim C., *Hitler*, Weidenfeld and Nicolson, London, 1974

Fitzsimons, Bernard (ed.), *Warships and Sea Battles of World War I*, Phoebus, London, 1973

Forester, C. S., *Hunting the "Bismarck,"* Panther, 1963

Frank, Wolfgang, *Die Wölfe und der Admiral*, Bastei-Lübbe, Bergisch Gladbach, 1983

Goodspeed, Lt-Col D. J. (ed), *The Armed Forces of Canada 1867–1967*, Canadian Forces Headquarters, Ottawa, 1967

Graham, Otis L., and Wander, Meghan Robinson (eds), *FDR: His Life and Times*, G. K. Hall, Boston, Mass, 1985

Gröner, Erich, *Die Schiffe der deutschen Kriegsmarine und Luftwaffe 1939–45 und ihr Verbleib*, J. F. Lehmanns, Munich, 8th revised edition, 1976

Hennessy, Peter, and Hague, Sir Douglas, "How Adolf Hitler Reformed Whitehall," *Strathclyde University Papers on Government and Politics*, No. 41, Glasgow, 1985

Herlin, Hans, *Verdammter Atlantik*, Heyne, Munich, 1983

Hinsley, F. H., *British Intelligence in the Second World War*, three vols, HMSO, London, 1979–1983

Hodges, Andrew, *Alan Turing: The Enigma*, Burnett Books/Hutchinson, London, 1983

Hough, Richard, *Former Naval Person*, Weidenfeld and Nicolson, London, 1985
The Longest Battle: the War at Sea 1939–45, Weidenfeld and Nicolson, London, 1986
The Great War at Sea, Oxford, New York, 1983

Hughes, Terry, and Costello, John, *The Battle of the Atlantic*, Collins, London, 1977

Humble, Richard, *Aircraft Carriers*, Michael Joseph, London, 1982
The Rise and Fall of the British Navy, Queen Anne Press, London, 1986
Undersea Warfare, Chartwell Books, Secaucus, New Jersey, 1981

King, Ernest J., with Whitehill, M., *Fleet Admiral King: A Naval Record*, Eyre and Spottiswoode, London, 1953

Jones, Geoffrey, *Autumn of the U-boats*, William Kimber, London, 1984

Jones, Tristan, *Heart of Oak*, Triad Grafton, London, 1986

Kahn, David, *Hitler's Spies*, Arrow, London, 1980

Kemp, Peter, *The Oxford Companion to Ships and the Sea*, Oxford, 1976

Kennedy, Ludovic, *The Life and Death of the "Tirpitz,"* Sidgwick and Jackson, London, 1979

Kerr, J. Lennox (ed), *Touching the Adventures of Merchantmen in the Second World War*, Harrap, London, 1953

Kieser, Egbert: *Unternehmen "Seelöwe"* (Bechtle, Munich, 1987)

Lenton, H. T., and Colledge, J. J., *Warships of World War II*, Ian Allan, London, second edition, 1973

Lewin, Ronald, *Ultra Goes to War*, Hutchinson, London, 1978

Liddell Hart, B. H., *History of the Second World War*, Cassell, London, 1970
History of the First World War, Cassell, London, 1970

Macintyre, Captain Donald, *The Battle of the Atlantic*, Pan, London, 1983
U-boat Killer, Weidenfeld and Nicolson, London, 1956

Mann, Golo, *The History of Germany since 1789*, Pelican, London, 1974

Mason, David, *U-boat: The Secret Menace*, Ballantine, New York, 1968
Who's Who in World War II, Weidenfeld and Nicolson, London, 1978

Middlebrook, Martin, *Convoy: The Battle for Convoys SC122 and HX229*, Penguin, London, 1978

Middlebrook, Martin, with Everitt, Chris, *The Bomber Command War Diaries*, Viking, London, 1985

Milner, Marc, *North Atlantic Run*, University of Toronto, 1985

RCN Participation in the Crisis of 1943, paper to "The RCN in Retrospect" conference, Victoria, BC, 1980

RCN-USN 1939–1943: Some Reflections on the Origins of a New Alliance, paper to the 7th Naval History Symposium, Annapolis, Maryland, 1985

Monsarrat, Nicholas, *The Cruel Sea*, Penguin, 1956

Three Corvettes, Cassell, London, 1945

Moore, John E. (ed), *Jane's Pocket Book of Submarine Development*, Macdonald and Jane's, London, 1976

Morgan, Ted, *FDR: a Biography*, Grafton, London, 1986

Morison, Rear-Admiral Samuel Eliot, *History of the US Naval Operations in World War II*, Little, Brown, Boston, Mass: Vol. I, 1947, and Vol. X, 1956

Muggenthaler, Karl August, *German Raiders of World War II*, Pan, London, 1980

Mullenheim-Rechberg, Baron Burkard, *Battleship "Bismarck": a Survivor's Story*, Triad Granada, London, 1982

Padfield, Peter, *Dönitz: The Last Führer*, Gollancz, London, 1984

Peillard, Léonce, *Sink the "Tirpitz,"* Granada, London, 1975

Philpott, Bryan, *History of the German Air Force*, Bison, London, 1986

Poolman, Kenneth, *Escort Carrier*, Secker and Warburg, London, 1983

Potter, John Deane, *Fiasco: The Breakout of the German Battleships*, Heinemann, London, 1970

Price, Alfred, *Luftwaffe Handbook 1939–1945*, Ian Allan, London, 1977

Prien, Günther, *Mein Weg nach Scapa Flow*, Libreria Goethe, Buenos Aires, 1941

Rayner, Commander D. A., *Escort: The Battle of the Atlantic*, William Kimber, London, 1955

Robertson, Terence, *Night Raider of the Atlantic*, Evans Brothers, London, 1981

Rössler, Eberhard, *The U-boat*, Arms and Armour, London, 1981

Rohwer, Jürgen, *Axis Submarine Successes 1939–1945*, Patrick Stephens, Cambridge, 1983

The Critical Convoy Battles of March 1943, Ian Allan, London, 1977

Rohwer, Jürgen with Jäckel, Eberhard (eds), *Die Funkaufklärung und ihre Rolle im Zweiten Weltkrieg*, Motorbuch, Stuttgart, 1979

Roskill, Captain S. W., *The War at Sea 1939–1945*, three vols., HMSO, London, 1954 to 1961

Naval Policy between the Wars, two vols., Collins, London, 1968

The Secret Capture, Collins, 1959

Ryder, A. J., *Twentieth Century Germany: From Bismarck to Brandt*, Macmillan, London, 1973

Schaeffer, Heinz, *U-boat 977*, William Kimber, London, 1953

Schofield, Vice-Admiral B. B., *The Russian Convoys*, Pan, London, 1984

Schull, Joseph, *The Far Distant Ships*, King's Printer, Ottawa, 1950

Shirer, William L., *The Rise and Fall of the Third Reich*, Secker and Warburg, London, 1960

Showell, Jak P. Mallmann, *The German Navy in World War II*, Arms and Armour Press, London, 1979

Speer, Albert, *Inside the Third Reich*, Weidenfeld and Nicolson, London, 1970

Taylor, A. J. P., *The Origins of the Second World War*, Penguin, London, 1964

Terraine, John, *The Right of the Line: The RAF in the European War*, Hodder and Stoughton, London, 1985

Trevor-Roper, H. R. (ed), *Hitler's War Directives 1939–1945*, Pan, London, 1976

Van der Vat, Dan, *The Grand Scuttle*, Hodder and Stoughton, London, 1982

  The Ship that Changed the World, Hodder and Stoughton, London, 1985

Walton, Francis, *Miracle of World War II: How American Industry Made Victory Possible*, Macmillan, New York, 1956

Waters, Captain John M., Jr., *Bloody Winter*, revised edition, US Naval Institute Press, Annapolis, Md, 1984

Werner, Herbert A. *Die eisernen Särge*, Heyne, Munich, 1984

Williams, Mark, *Captain Gilbert Roberts, RN, and the Anti-U-Boat School*, Cassell, London, 1979

Wilson, David, *Rutherford*, Hodder and Stoughton, London, 1983

Winton, John, *Convoy*, Michael Joseph, London, 1983

  The Death of the "Scharnhorst", Panther, London, 1984

  Ultra at Sea, Leo Cooper, London, 1988

Wistrich, Robert, *Wer war Wer im Dritten Reich*, Harnack, Munich, 1983

INDEX

INDEX

Ranks and titles are generally the highest attained during the period covered by the book.